KEVLAR LEGIONS

The Transformation of the U.S. Army, 1989–2005

BY
JOHN SLOAN BROWN

MILITARY INSTRVCTION

Center of Military History
United States Army
Washington, D.C., 2011

Library of Congress Cataloging-in-Publication Data

Brown, John Sloan
  Kevlar legions : the transformation of the U.S. Army, 1989–2005 / by John Sloan Brown.
      p. cm.
  Includes bibliographical references and index.
1. United States. Army—Reorganization—History—20th century. 2. United States. Army—Reorganization—History—21st century. 3. United States. Army—History—20th century. 4. United States. Army—History—21st century. 5. Military doctrine—United States—History—20th century. 6. Military doctrine—United States—History—21st century. I. Title.
  UA25.B78 2011
  355.00973'09049—dc23

                                                        2011025096

CMH Pub 70–118–1

First Printing

For sale by the Superintendent of Documents, U.S. Government Printing Office
Internet: bookstore.gpo.gov   Phone: toll free (866) 512-1800;   DC area (202) 512-1800
Fax: (202) 512-2104 Mail: Stop IDCC, Washington, DC 20402-0001

ISBN 978-0-16-089190-8

CONTENTS

Illustrations

All illustrations are from the files of the Department of Defense.

FOREWORD

The U.S. Army is such a vast institution that change appears to occur slowly, if at all. Yet when looking back only a few decades, an intelligent observer can only marvel at how much the Army has changed, indeed transformed, in the period since the end of the Cold War. This reconfiguration has been due less to any posited "Revolution in Military Affairs" than to the careful and methodical investment of Army leadership in thoughtful doctrinal refinement, innovative experiments, and the intelligent adoption of specific technologies. Evolution is harder to see and track than revolution, but the result of those decades of thoughtful and gradual change is that the U.S. Army—flexible, adaptable, and deadly—stands as the most capable ground force in the world today.

Kevlar Legions: The Transformation of the U.S. Army, 1989–2005, argues that from 1989 through 2005 the United States Army attempted, and largely achieved, a centrally directed and institutionally driven transformation relevant to ground warfare that exploited Information Age technology, adapted to post–Cold War strategic circumstances, and integrated into parallel Department of Defense efforts. The process not only modernized equipment, it also substantially altered doctrine, organization, training, administrative and logistical practices, and the service culture. The resultant digitized expeditionary Army was as different from the late Cold War Army as the late Cold War Army was from that of the early Cold War or from the mobilization-based Armies of World Wars I and II. *Kevlar Legions* further contends that the digitized expeditionary Army has withstood the test of combat, performing superbly with respect to deployment and high-end conventional combat and capably with respect to low-intensity conflict.

Whatever one believes about the author's conclusions, his discussion of the history and processes of transformation should prove invaluable to students of the period and to all who might wish to change the Army in the future. Brigadier General (Retired) John Sloan Brown served as the Executive Officer for the Deputy Chief of Staff for Operations and Plans in 1995–1997, Chief of Programs and Requirements for the Supreme Headquarters Allied Powers Europe in 1997–1998, and Chief of Military History in 1998–2005. In these positions he was privy to many of the deliberations in this volume. Collateral and subsequent research broadened his grasp. He has exploited a robust mix of documents, briefings, meeting notes, oral and e-mail testimony, studies, publications, and comments from veterans. In addition, General Brown consulted dozens of key players who commented on portions of the manuscript relevant to their experiences and responsibilities. *Kevlar Legions* thus combines participant observation with solid scholarship. It goes a long way in telling us what happened in the transformation of the Army over the past twenty years, why it happened, and who was involved. It also describes hard choices, accepted risks, processes of decision making, and institutional results.

The U.S. Army Center of Military History is pleased to add *Kevlar Legions: The Transformation of the U.S. Army, 1989–2005,* to its inventory of published titles. The book joins a growing number of publications dealing with the post–Cold War era and with events subsequent to 11 September 2001. It perpetuates the Center's tradition of commenting thoughtfully on today's issues while continuing its principal work of interpreting the entire scope of the Army's past. Histories written proximate to the events they describe are, of course, necessarily early drafts. More will certainly follow. And, as always, the true heroes of this account are American soldiers, tirelessly serving their country at home and abroad and transforming their Army for the future by their actions while serving the needs of today.

Washington, D.C.
1 August 2011

RICHARD W. STEWART
Chief Historian

THE AUTHOR

John Sloan Brown was commissioned as a second lieutenant in the Armor branch after graduating from the United States Military Academy in 1971 and retired in October 2005 as a brigadier general after more than thirty-four years of service to the United States Army.

General Brown's most recent active-duty assignment (1998–2005) was as Chief of Military History for the U.S. Army. In that capacity, among other duties, he formulated and executed the Army Historical Program; supervised historical studies supporting the development of plans, policies, doctrine, force structure, and equipment; provided historical services and publications in support of Congress, the Department of Defense, headquarters, staffs, and schools; edited and managed a publications account supporting over six hundred active titles; coordinated history education in the Army school system; managed the honors and lineages for Army units, active and reserve; maintained contact with foreign counterparts and coordinated conferences with them; coordinated the training and deployment of military history detachments and individual historians in support of ongoing operations overseas; supervised the Army Museum System and Army Art Collection; and coordinated support for the National Museum of the United States Army.

Earlier in his career, Brown served as Chief of Programs and Requirements for the Supreme Headquarters Allied Powers Europe; Executive Officer to the Deputy Chief of Staff for Operations and Plans; Commander of the 2d Brigade, 1st Cavalry Division, in Texas and Kuwait; G–3 Operations Officer of III Corps; G–3 Operations Officer of the 24th Infantry Division; and Commander of the 2d Battalion, 66th Armor, in Germany, DESERT SHIELD, and DESERT STORM. General Brown has commanded armor units at every level from platoon through brigade and has served on staffs at every level from battalion through theater.

Brown received M.A. and Ph.D. degrees from Indiana University and has taught at the United States Military Academy. He is also a graduate of the U.S. Army Command and General Staff College and the U.S. Naval War College. He is the author of published works that include *Draftee Division: The 88th Infantry Division in World War II*; chapters on the Army in the 1990s and in the Global War on Terrorism, in *American Military History*, vol. 2, *The United States in a Global Era, 1917–2008*; "The Battle for Norfolk," in *Leaders in War: West Point Remembers the 1991 Gulf War*; and "No Gun Ri Revisited: Historical Lessons for Today's Army," in *Today's Best Military Writing: The Finest Articles on the Past, Present, and Future of the U.S. Military.*

Since retirement, General Brown has been actively engaged as a historical consultant for the American Battle Monuments Commission (ABMC), in which he participated in designing the Normandy American Cemetery Visitor Center, the Pointe du Hoc Visitor Center, the ABMC Comprehensive Interpretive Plan, digitized campaign interactive displays concerning the Normandy campaign and the battle of Pointe du Hoc, and a digitized interactive timeline of World War II. He also writes the monthly column "Historically Speaking" for *Army* magazine and is completing "Barbarossa: The Invasion of the Soviet Union" for the Center of Military History.

ACKNOWLEDGMENTS

I am extraordinarily indebted to many people for the valuable assistance rendered advancing this project. Their numbers and contributions are so great I will undoubtedly fail to acknowledge some. For that, I apologize in advance. Where titles and military ranks are indicated, they represent the titles and ranks at the time of the correspondence to which I refer.

As an intellectual process, this project began as Chapters 13 and 14 of *American Military History,* Volume 2, published by the Center of Military History in 2005. I authored these chapters, the first of which was "Beyond the Wall: Operations in a Post–Cold War World, 1990–2001," and the second "The Global War on Terrorism." *American Military History* was ably shepherded by its General Editor, Dr. Richard W. Stewart, who in turn justly recognized the involvement of his Department of the Army Historical Advisory Committee: Dr. Eric Bergerud, Mark Bowden, Lieutenant General Franklin L. Hagenbeck, Brigadier General James T. Hirai, Lieutenant General Anthony R. Jones, Brigadier General Daniel J. Kaufman, Dr. Adrian R. Lewis, Dr. Brian M. Linn, Howard Lowell, Colonel Craig Madden, Dr. John H. Morrow Jr., Dr. Reina Pennington, Dr. Ronald H. Spector, and Dr. Jon T. Sumida. In addition to the thoughtful counsel of these and others cited below, my chapters benefited particularly from the attentions of the Center of Military History's Editor in Chief, John W. Elsberg, and the remarkably thorough editing of Ms. Diane M. Donovan.

When the time came to expand subchapter-length discussions of Army transformation during 1989–2005 into a book-length study, I was fortunate to receive the mission. I was also grateful to again gain the oversight, counsel, and mentorship of Dr. Stewart, at that time newly the Army's Chief Historian. He has labored through every word of my prose, masterfully improving upon it in things great and small. In this he was joined by my predecessor once removed as Chief of Military History, Brigadier General Harold W. Nelson. General Nelson not only made the manuscript better, he also vetted it to Army senior leaders most familiar with the full breadth of the story. General Gordon R. Sullivan, an ardent supporter of military history, read every chapter, commented thoughtfully, and further assisted in engaging key players as discussed below. General Dennis J. Reimer read and commented on most chapters, forthrightly but graciously refining my grasp on a number of critical topics, especially resourcing. General Eric K. Shinseki read the material pertaining to his tenure when *American Military History* was aborning and provided commentary that has become a source in itself. General Peter J.

Schoomaker read several chapters, cleared his busy schedule for a number of invaluable exchanges and particularly sharpened the linkages between Army transformation and the Global War on Terrorism. Chiefs of Staff do not work alone, of course, and the manuscript was further aided by soldiers who served within the inner circles of their staff groups. In addition to General Nelson, cases in point include Colonel Raoul H. Alcala, Lieutenant Colonel James J. Carafano, Colonel John R. Gingrich, and Brigadier General Christopher C. Shoemaker. Mrs. Gay Sullivan, Mrs. Mary Jo Reimer, and Mrs. Patty Shinseki graciously read, commented on, and immeasurably improved the chapter on the Army family.

Our story extends almost a score of years, and it was critical to hear from key players in many positions. In addition to those I encountered personally in my own dealings as Executive Officer to the Deputy Chief of Staff for Operations and Plans (DCSOPS) and then as Chief of Military History, I am deeply grateful to Lieutenant General Ted G. Stroup for his contacts. From his twin perches in the Association of the United States Army and the United States Military Academy Association of Graduates, it seems unlikely that there is a living officer with whom he is not connected. Association of the United States Army Executive Assistants Ann Belyea, Ruth Flanagan, and Connie Williams ably assisted in the hunt. Greater specifics appear in the endnotes, but those active participants who took the time to discuss aspects of this project, submit to an interview, review portions of the manuscript, or exchange e-mails include Lieutenant General John P. Abizaid, Lieutenant General Michael W. Ackerman, Major General Lawrence R. Adair, Lieutenant General Keith B. Alexander, Major General John D. Altenburg Jr., Major General Max Baratz, Lieutenant General David W. Barno, Lieutenant General Paul E. Blackwell, Lieutenant General Ronald R. Blanck, Major General Buford C. Blount III, Major Stephen A. Bourque, Lieutenant General Steven W. Boutelle, Assistant Secretary of the Army Reginald J. Brown, Acting Secretary of the Army Romie L. Brownlee, Colonel Terry Bullington, Lieutenant General Kevin P. Byrnes, Lieutenant General James L. Campbell, General George W. Casey, Major General Peter W. Chiarelli, Lieutenant General Claude V. Christianson, General Wesley K. Clark, General Richard A. Cody, Lieutenant General Joseph M. Cosumano Jr., Lieutenant Colonel Deborah R. Cox, Lieutenant General Peter M. Cuviello, Under Secretary of the Army Gregory R. Dahlberg, Brigadier General Robert L. Decker, Colonel Robert A. Doughty, Lieutenant General John A. Dubia, Lieutenant General Larry R. Ellis, Lieutenant Colonel Marcus R. Erlandson, Brigadier General David A. Fastabend, General Frederick M. Franks Jr., Brigadier General Robert E. Gaylord, General Benjamin S. Griffin, Major General Gaylord T. Gunhus, Lieutenant General Franklin L. Hagenbeck, General William W. Hartzog, Lieutenant General James R. Helmly, Colonel James P. Herson, Mr. Walter W. Hollis, Mr. Joel B. Hudson, Major General David H. Huntoon Jr., Lieutenant General Anthony R. Jones, General John M. Keane, Lieutenant General Claudia J. Kennedy, General Paul J. Kern, Mrs. Sylvia Kidd, Major General Kevin C. Kiley, Major A. J. Koenig, Lieutenant General John M. Le Moyne, Major General William J. Lennox Jr., Brigadier General William J. Lesczcynski Jr., Mrs. Gigi G. Linder, Lieutenant

General James J. Lovelace Jr., Major General Larry J. Lust, Lieutenant General Rick Lynch, Colonel Douglas A. Macgregor, Lieutenant General Charles S. Mahan, Colonel Stephen J. Marshman, Mr. Michael D. Martin, Mr. John W. McDonald, Brigadier General H. R. McMaster, General Dan K. McNeill, Lieutenant General Thomas F. Metz, Major General John G. Meyer Jr., Lieutenant General Paul T. Mikolashek, Lieutenant General Thomas M. Montgomery, Colonel Anthony A. Moreno, Lieutenant Colonel Terry R. Moss, Colonel Matthew Moten, Brigadier General John W. Mountcastle, Colonel James L. Mowery, Mr. Tim Muchmore, Major General William A. Navas Jr., Lieutenant General David H. Ohle, Major General Eric T. Olson, Brigadier General Mark E. O'Neill, Lieutenant General James B. Peake, Brigadier General Paul D. Phillips, Lieutenant General John M. Pickler, Major General Thomas J. Plewes, Colonel Roy E. Porter III, Senator John F. Reed, Lieutenant General Thomas G. Rhame, Colonel Mark A. Riccio, Major General Joe W. Rigby, Lieutenant General John M. Riggs, Under Secretary of the Army Bernard D. Rostker, General Crosbie E. Saint, Major General Robert J. St. Onge Jr., Major General Robert H. Scales Jr., Lieutenant Colonel Quentin W. Schillare, Major General Roger C. Schultz, Major General Bruce K. Scott, Lieutenant General Jerry L. Sinn, Colonel Richard H. Sinnreich, Dr. Roger J. Spiller, Lieutenant General Carl A. Strock, Brigadier General Guy C. Swan III, Major General Antonio M. Taguba, Sergeant Major of the Army Jack L. Tilley, Lieutenant Colonel John A. Tokar, Lieutenant Colonel Lee Torres, Lieutenant General Robert L. Van Antwerp Jr., Major General Hans A. Van Winkle, Major Donald E. Vandergriff, Mr. E. B. Vandiver III, Lieutenant General Michael A. Vane, Major General Howard J. von Kaenel, Dr. James A. Walker, General William S. Wallace, Brigadier General Lloyd T. Waterman, Mrs. Peggy Waterman, Secretary of the Army Thomas E. White, General Johnnie E. Wilson, and Mr. Gary A. Wright.

Historians feed on each other, and profit immensely when their projects overlap. Hopefully, my endnotes and bibliographical note will do justice to the actual publications I have relied on, but I would also like to recognize the valuable conversations I have had with others pursuing research at the same time. By generously sharing thoughts on their ongoing projects and commenting on mine, they have greatly enriched the material with which I have worked. I am particularly indebted in this regard to Dr. Bianka Adams, Mr. Charles R. Anderson, Mr. Dale Andrade, Mr. Rick Atkinson, Mr. Edward N. Bedessem, Dr. Andrew J. Birtle, Colonel John Bonin, Lieutenant Colonel Keith E. Bonn, Dr. Charles H. Briscoe, Dr. Shannon A. Brown, Dr. John M. Carland, Dr. Stephen A. Carney, Dr. Donald A. Carter, Dr. Jeffery A. Charlston, Lieutenant Colonel Roger Cirillo, Dr. Mary Ellen Condon-Rall, Dr. Elliott V. Converse III; Dr. Graham A. Cosmas, Ms. Romana M. Danysh, Dr. William A. Dobak, Dr. William M. Donnelly, Colonel Michael D. Doubler, Mr. William W. Epley, Mr. Stephen E. Everett, Colonel Gregory Fontenot, General Frederick M. Franks Jr., Mr. Stephen L. Y. Gammons, Dr. Stephen P. Gehring, Dr. Terrence J. Gough, Dr. William M. Hammond, Dr. W. Blair Haworth, Dr. Charles D. Hendricks, Colonel Jon T. Hoffman, Dr. David W. Hogan Jr.,

Mr. Robert D. Hormats, Dr. Lawrence M. Kaplan, Dr. Peter S. Kindsvatter, Dr. Charles E. Kirkpatrick, Dr. Brian M. Linn, Dr. John A. Lynn, Colonel Douglas A. Macgregor, Colonel Mike Matheny, Mr. John J. McGrath, Ms. Janice E. McKenney, Mr. John E. McLaughlin, Major Edward G. Miller, Dr. Allan R. Millett, Dr. Walton S. Moody, Colonel Bettie J. Morden, Dr. Williamson Murray, Colonel Clayton R. Newell, Ms. Jennifer A. Nichols, Colonel George F. Oliver III, Mr. R. Cody Phillips, Dr. Walter S. Poole, Dr. Edgar F. Raines Jr., Mrs. Rebecca C. Raines, Lieutenant Colonel Mark J. Reardon, Colonel Timothy R. Reese, Dr. Bernard D. Rostker, Dr. Gordon W. Rudd, Command Sergeant Major Robert S. Rush, Lieutenant Colonel Nathan Sassaman, Major General Robert H. Scales Jr., Dr. Mark D. Sherry, Colonel Lewis S. Sorley III, Colonel Richard W. Stewart, Major William S. Story, Lieutenant Colonel Adrian G. Traas, Dr. Gary A. Trogdon, Dr. Erik B. Villard, Dr. James L. Yarrison, and Dr. Lawrence A. Yates.

Projects of this nature are enhanced greatly by occasional "trial balloons": articles, briefings, presentations, and the like that test component facts, ideas, or interpretations in the face of a critical audience. In the text and notes, I refer to briefings I gave as Chief of Military History that served such a purpose. Since retirement from active service, I have been fortunate to author "Historically Speaking," a monthly column in *Army* magazine. Aspects of *Kevlar Legions* have appeared from time to time to draw either praise or fire—or both. The extraordinarily capable staff of *Army,* headed up by Editor in Chief Ms. Mary B. French and including Mr. Jeremy P. Dow, Ms. Tenley Wadsworth, and Ms. Fran Wright, have been instrumental in this regard. They also have been extremely generous and forthcoming with the impressive array of publications, sources, and graphics in the Association of the United States Army archives. I am proud to be a Burdeshaw Associate, and involvement in the "Long War Project" under the company's auspices provided another opportunity to vet aspects of *Kevlar Legions.* For this I am particularly grateful to General William W. Hartzog, Lieutenant General Larry R. Jordan, Colonel Milton S. Newberry, and Lieutenant General Leonard P. Wishart III. The Training and Doctrine Command recurrently assesses the direction of the Army, and I was invited to present a paper at and participate in the Unified Quest 2010 "Army in 2025 Seminar." The paper proved a valuable test run for much of Chapter 10, and I am indebted to Mr. James N. Anderson, Mr. George R. Conrad, Ms. Rachel R. Fowler, and Brigadier General H. R. McMaster for all they did to help me air it. Similarly, the Combat Studies Institute 2010 Symposium "Cultivating Army Leaders: Historical Perspectives" allowed me to air much of Chapter 1. I appreciate Mr. Kendall D. Gott, Major John C. Mountcastle, and Dr. William G. Robertson for all that they did to facilitate this participation. While on the subject of opening up oneself for comment and evaluation, I might flag up the United States Military Academy Class of 1971 Web site, ably shepherded by Colonel Robert D. Weiss. Not all that is discussed is serious, but enough is to subject historical interpretations to useful criticism and few are less inclined to let you hide behind your credentials than your classmates. Students provide another great chance for resonance, and teaching at Regis University in Denver as an adjunct professor considerably enhanced my ability to fit this story into a larger historical whole. I am grateful to Father James Guyer S. J. and Mr. Michael D. Martin for their roles in affording me this opportunity.

Just as it takes a village to raise a child, it takes the entire Army Historical Program to produce an Army history. In addition to those cited above, I would also like to thank the many others who assisted with the gritty business of locating sources and coping with matters of detail. At the pinnacle, Chief of Military History Dr. Jeffrey J. Clarke, Chief Historian Dr. Richard W. Stewart, Chief of the Histories Division Dr. Joel D. Meyerson, and Chief of the Field Programs and Historical Services Division Dr. Richard G. Davis provided cheerful and unrelenting support to my frequent forays within their domains, as well as beneficial personal insights. Within the Center of Military History, Mr. Stephen J. Lofgren seconded by Dr. Brian T. Crumley and Dr. Christopher N. Koontz provided excellent assistance with respect to oral testimony; Mr. William W. Epley seconded by Command Sergeant Scott Garrett with respect to the products of Military History Detachments; Mr. Frank R. Shirer seconded by Ms. Patricia A. Ames, Mr. Joseph R. Frechette, and Ms. Dena Everett with respect to archival holdings; and Mr. Keith R. Tidman seconded by Mr. Bryan J. Hockensmith with respect to publications. Force Structure complexities can be particularly perplexing, and with respect to these I was guided from sources through manuscript revisions to final editing by the tireless teamwork of Mrs. Rebecca C. Raines, Mr. Edward N. Bedessem, Mr. Stephen E. Everett, and Ms. Jennifer A. Nichols. I relied heavily upon electronic versions of the Center of Military History's holdings, particularly with respect to *Department of the Army Historical Summaries* (*DAHSUMs*). I owe the ready availability of these cyber-versions to the head of the Center's Website Operations Activity, Mrs. Donna C. Everett. My expansive use of Center of Military History resources would not have been possible without the cheerful and effective coordination provided by Executive Secretary Ms. Cherrie Johnson. Outside the Center of Military History, I am similarly indebted to Ms. Renee Hylton, Major Les A. Melnyk, and Captain Jeffrey C. Larrabee of the National Guard Bureau; Colonel Robert J. Dalessandro, Dr. Conrad C. Crane, Dr. Richard Sommers, and Mr. Thomas L. Hendrix of the Army Heritage and Education Center; Dr. Stephen B. Grove of the United States Military Academy; Mr. Michael P. Bellafaire of the Military Surface Deployment and Distribution Command; Mr. Bruce H. Siemon, Mr. Kevin E. McKedy, and Dr. Andrew N. Morris of the United States Army, Europe; Dr. Charles E. White, Dr. Mason R. Schaefer, Major Doug Hendy, and Mrs. Tammy Cheely-Howle of Army Forces Command; Dr. Lee S. Harford and Dr. Kathryn Roe Coker of Army Reserve Command; Dr. Robert G. Darius, Dr. William T. Moye, and Ms. Wilma Fields of the Army Materiel Command; Dr. John T. Greenwood of the Army Medical Command; Dr. James A. Walker of the Army Space and Missile Defense Command; Dr. James T. Stensvaag, Dr. J. Britt McCarley, and Mr. Steven McGeorge of the Training and Doctrine Command; Colonel Clay Edwards and Colonel Timothy R. Reese of the Combat Studies Institute; Dr. Alfred Goldberg and Dr. Stuart Rochester of the Office of the Secretary of Defense Historical Office; Brigadier General

David A. Armstrong of the Joint History Office; Mr. C. Richard Anderegg and Mr. William C. Heimdahl of the Air Force History Office; Colonel John W. Ripley and Mr. Charles D. Melson of the Marine Corps Historical Center; Dr. Edward J. Marolda of the Naval Historical Center; Dr. Gregory Pedlow of the North Atlantic Treaty Organization Historical Office; Dr. Robert M. Browning Jr. and Dr. Scott T. Price of the Coast Guard Historical Office; and Dr. Maria Christina C. Mairena of the Army Family and Morale, Welfare, and Recreation Command. When the time came to turn a draft manuscript into an actual book, the Acting Chief of the Center of Military History's Publishing Division, Ms. Beth F. MacKenzie, ably assumed the lead. In this she was capably seconded by Mrs. Diane Sedore Arms, Mr. Gene Snyder, and Ms. S. L. Dowdy.

Family inevitably bears a great burden in projects of this type. My wife Mary Beth cheerfully soldiered through this "ten-year pregnancy," immeasurably assisting in great things large and small. Daughter Amy, son-in-law Brendan, daughter-in-law Kris, and even grandsons John, Michael, Brian, and Joey have served capably as sounding boards and put up patiently with project-related distractions time and again as we shared our lives. My father Colonel Horace M. Brown and mother Lucia "Chick" Sloan Brown have been ever-generous with their time and provided an invaluable personal link to Army transformations that precede the one of which I write. Son Todd (Major Robert Sloan Brown) was a teenager when this story began, a lieutenant when I commenced writing it, and a field grade veteran of Iraq and Afghanistan as I wrap it up. He has tirelessly and generously kept me aware of the practicalities of twenty-first-century warfare as it has existed on the ground because my own experience of war was in the twentieth century.

Finally, I would like to particularly acknowledge two individuals essential to the success of this project who are not with us as it comes to fruition. Mrs. Donna C. Everett headed the Center's Website Operations Activity as it grew from a nascent idea into a mature instrument for scholarship, education, and research. It would have been impossible to gather materials as I did had not so many primary and secondary resources been readily available through her efforts. Colonel Donald W. Warner was Deputy Commander while I was Chief of Military History, keeping the Center of Military History humming with flawless efficiency while I was out and about in the Army Staff and the Army at large. I could not have enjoyed the personal connections I had with Army transformation as a process had I not been so confident that all was well at the Center. Donna and Don left us far too soon. Their legacies are far grander than this study, but this study certainly folds within their legacies.

KEVLAR LEGIONS

THE TRANSFORMATION OF THE U.S. ARMY, 1989–2005

CHAPTER 1

Introduction

The OH–58D helicopter went down hard in the urban sprawl of Tall' Afar. The pilots, injured but mobile, escaped the wreckage and made it to the relative safety of a nearby rock wall. Within minutes a race developed between American soldiers trying to rescue them and Iraqi insurgents trying to kill or capture them. Parallels to the book *Black Hawk Down,* about the infamous October 1993 incident in Mogadishu that took many lives including those of Master Sergeant Gary I. Gordon and Sergeant First Class Randall D. Shughart (both posthumously awarded the Medal of Honor), were immediately apparent to any who had been there, read the account, or seen the movie. The earlier incident provided ample testimony to the courage, tenacity, and initiative of the American soldier. It also furnished examples of columns lost in a rabbit warren of streets, unknown friendly locations, unknowable enemy locations, huge difficulties bringing firepower to bear, soft-skinned vehicles overmatched by ubiquitous enemy arms, and confusion. However, the Tall' Afar helicopter crash was on 4 September 2004, and things would be different.[1]

The first to the scene was the Scout Platoon of the Stryker-borne 5-20 Infantry. The OH–58D's icon had remained visible on the screens of the platoon's Force XXI Battle Commands, Brigade and Below (FBCB2s), so the Scouts knew where the helicopter was. Scalable electronic downloadable maps gave platoon members an exact appreciation of the geography, global positioning systems gave precise knowledge of their own positions, and blue force tracking showed the locations of friendly vehicles. They knew where they were going and how to get there, and they got there first. The Scouts won the race but not by much. Increasing volumes of fire attested to the arrival of the enemy. Unmanned aerial vehicles (UAVs) flying overhead detected even more hostiles on the way, many arriving by automobile and unloading machine guns and rocket-propelled grenades (RPGs) from their civilian vehicles. Fortunately a relief column, Company B of the 5-20 Infantry, was already churning its way toward the Scouts through the dusty streets of Tall' Afar. Ever more numerous insurgents divided their attention between attempts to overwhelm the Scout Platoon and blocking positions to delay the Stryker Company. The blocking positions did not last long. They disappeared in dirt plumes raised by precisely laid GBU31 bombs dropped from F–16s hastily summoned by the 5-20 Infantry's Joint Tactical Air Controller. Company B members rolled on, ignoring residual small arms that pinged harmlessly off the Kevlar armor of their Strykers. When

Stryker-borne infantry on patrol in Mosul, Iraq

Company B arrived at the crash site, the half-score soldiers clattering out of the back of each vehicle bore a formidable panoply: Kevlar body armor, laser designators, Single Channel Ground and Airborne Radio System (SINCGARS) radios, Rapid Fielding Initiative (RFI) accoutrements, a mix of automatic weapons, and lots of ammunition. The insurgents tried to overwhelm the now reinforced position. This was a mistake. Hurricanes of well-aimed fire swept them off the rooftops, out of the streets, and then out of surrounding buildings room by room. Americans were hit, but Kevlar body armor minimized the damage done. With the coolness of troops who completely dominate their battlefield, the Americans now brought forward a heavy expanded mobility tactical truck (HEMTT) wrecker and a Palletized Load System (PLS) flatbed truck. The recovery team sawed off the helicopter blades and loaded the wreckage onto the flatbed, and then the entire contingent disengaged by stages and drove away. There would be no bodies dragged through the streets, no hostages, no captured materials, and no pictures of jubilant insurgents dancing on a downed helicopter. There also would be no book and no movie.[2]

As capable as the leaders and soldiers of the 5-20 Infantry certainly were, success did not originate with them alone. Revolutionary technologies they so ably employed had been a generation in the making and had been progressively fielded in the last dozen years. Exploiting these technologies—and adapting to the new circumstances of the post–Cold War world—required changes in doctrine, organization, training, administrative practices, infrastructure, and even Army culture. The process came to be known as Army transformation. Army transformation dominated deliberations on the Army Staff and throughout the Army from 1989 through 2005. It competed for attention with and was mutually influenced by other hot topics: wrapping up the Cold War, force downsizing, Somalia, the Balkans, 9-11, Afghanistan, Iraq, and the Global War on Terrorism. It existed before it firmed up a name. The term *Army transformation* evolved over time and retroactively applied to developments as early as 1989. The term continued in use after 2005 but with a significantly different meaning. A history of Army transformation from 1989 through 2005 should start by establishing a working definition. It could then canvass history for earlier examples of such Army transformations and ascertain how these worked and how they worked out. Armed with this background, one could then attempt the actual history of Army transformation from 1989 through 2005.

Defining Transformation

Funk and Wagnalls *Standard College Dictionary* tersely identifies "any change" as its lead definition for the word *transformation*. Its second definition is "the act of transforming . . ." and its third, "a wig worn by a woman." It is difficult to argue with Funk and Wagnalls, yet these usages hardly seem likely to have inspired passionate debate throughout a generation of Army officers or to have attracted billions of dollars in investment from Congress. Surely *transformation* when coupled with *Army* must mean something more. By 2000 it did, although in 1989 not so much so. Building on work inspired by his predecessor, Army Chief of Staff General Gordon R. Sullivan, as we shall see, did more than any other single person to get Army transformation as it came to be defined under way. At his June 1991 arrival ceremony he variously stated that the Army must "change" or "reshape" to face its future. He used the word *transformation* once, to describe what was happening to the environment wherein the Army operated at home and abroad, not to describe what was happening in the Army. His subsequent addresses and correspondence similarly advanced such imperatives as *adapt, transition, change*, and *reshape* and did not much employ *transform* or *transformation*. Sullivan's immediate priority was maintaining Army effectiveness amid plummeting budgets and force structure and accelerating deployments, so a little vagueness with respect to long-term plans can be understood. By 1994 Sullivan's modern Louisiana Maneuvers, to be discussed in Chapter 3, were well under way. An umbrella term was desirable to communicate their essence. In a 1994 Chief of Staff message Sullivan pointed out that the Army had undertaken "an enormous and very important transformation," and then went on to identify key constituents of that transformation: shifting intellectually beyond the Cold War and the Industrial Age, broadening training from traditional missions, rescoping modernization, redesigning doctrine, refurbishing force generation, enhancing strategic mobility, adopting Information Age management techniques, and more. Transformation in this context meant more than change alone. It implied breadth, heft, and vision. Sullivan's successor, General Dennis J. Reimer, similarly noted the progress of an Army "transformation" under way and identified a similar broad mix of progressive measures to describe that term. Initiatives such as Division XXI, Force XXI, and Strike Force emerged to advance the Army's transformation in a systematic manner. Not everyone picked up on transformation's maturing definition, however. More than one pundit commented that the Army had been transforming for two hundred years and more and would continue to do so. Air Force planners helpfully advised their Army counterparts to transform a little bit with each procurement cycle. That way transformation would never become too big of a challenge. To the first group, the words *transformation* and *change* remained interchangeable, and to the second *transformation* and *modernization* did.[3]

Chief of Staff General Eric K. Shinseki solidified Army transformation into a comprehensive Army-wide program, called Army Transformation. It linked into Defense transformation efforts also under way, figured in Planning, Programming, Budgeting, and Execution System (PPBES) deliberations, dominated such institutional documents as the Army Strategic Planning Guidance, and inspired its own hefty Transformation Campaign Plan. The supervisory Army Transformation Office advanced a definition of sorts. Army Transformation was "the process of converting the Army's focus and structure from a Cold War construct to a full spectrum combat force that is strategically responsive and dominant at every point on the spectrum of conflict. . . ." The Army Transformation Office went on to insist that transformation was about more than technology alone and encompassed doctrine, training, leadership, organizations, material readiness, installations, and soldiers. The definition fit in well with ongoing adaptations to circumstances following the fall of the Berlin Wall in 1989 and the collapse of the Soviet Union in 1991. It also tracked with efforts to enhance Army deployability and strategic mobility under way since the same period. Shinseki's intent statement, promulgated on his first day as Chief of Staff, listed increasing strategic responsiveness, improving operational jointness, and fully integrating the active and reserve components as three of six stated objectives. Each would allow the Army to do more with less anywhere in the world at any time. Adaptations to post–Cold War circumstances had also figured prominently in lists Sullivan and Reimer had used to explain Army transformation as they employed the term. Adaptation was intrinsic to Army transformation. Shinseki and others spoke of the Army's need to remain "relevant" in changing circumstances. In due course broad ranges of adaptation were characterized as transformative: redeploying from Europe to the continental United States (CONUS), acquiring additional airlift and sealift, improving railheads and airfields on stateside posts, reengineering medical facilities, relocating Army and Air Force Exchange Service (AAFES) and commissaries, reducing unit weight, redesigning military assistance programs, courting new allies, rewriting doctrine for the low end of the combat spectrum, and so on. The world had changed, and transformation would enable the Army to change with it.[4]

As important as adaptation to post–Cold War circumstances undoubtedly was, adaptation alone does not quite explain the fire in the belly of Sullivan, Reimer, Shinseki, and others as they envisioned the future. The Army Transformation Office briefing slide that somewhat limply defined Army Transformation as "the process of converting . . ." had the teasing preface "It's about changing the way we fight, deploy, sustain and use information . . ." and a follow-on bullet promising "fundamental change in capabilities to better support joint warfighting and operational objectives." Sullivan, an enthusiast for history, opined that the Industrial Age was being superseded by the Information Age and that "Third Wave warfare" was imminent. Reimer distinguished between advances that "creep ahead" and those that "leap ahead," and clearly favored the latter. Shinseki sought a transformation that was "major" and anticipated "dramatic and dynamic" changes. Sullivan, Reimer, Shinseki, and, perhaps even more important, their subordinates and staffs were well aware of a rising tide of interest in so-called "revolutions in military affairs" (RMAs). Depending upon whom one consulted, bronze weapons, iron weapons, pike phalanxes, manipular legions, the longbow as employed at Crecy, drilled musketry, the national *levee en masse*, Railroad Age warfare, battleships, combined-arms *Blitzkrieg*, and aircraft carriers—among others—all represented revolutions in military affairs. A workable definition described a revolution in military affairs as "a major change in the nature of warfare brought about by the innovative application of new technologies which, combined with dramatic changes in military doctrine and operational and organizational concepts, fundamentally alters the character and conduct of military operations." Just as drilled musketry had been revolutionary in its day, contemporary advances with respect to microelectronics, sensors, precision-guided munitions, and information technologies promised yet another watershed in the conduct of war. The degree of change associated with a revolution in military affairs was often characterized as exponential. Technically, this implied something increased by a factor of ten. The transformed force would be ten times as lethal, survivable, or effective as its former self. Perhaps when war gamed against a standing adversary, it would come away with one-tenth the casualties to achieve the same results. Army Transformation, and the Army transformation that preceded it, clearly sought such dramatic results. Army transformers were not entirely agreed upon what a revolution in military affairs was, but all seemed to want one.[5]

Why did the term *revolution in military affairs* not figure more prominently in Army definitions of Army transformation? One consideration is that it might have sounded pretentious in gritty budget battles before Congress or even when "selling" transformation within the Army itself. In the relatively benign defense circumstances of the 1990s, it was better to mollify the parsimonious or conservative by speaking in less grandiose terms. Another consideration is that the term *revolution in military affairs* rapidly acquired baggage the Army did not want to embrace. Within the Department of Defense (DoD) a leading proponent for a possible revolution in military affairs was Andrew W. Marshall of the Office of Net Assessment. Despite protestations to the contrary, DoD ruminations took a technologically centric bent, as we shall see. A popular example of "network centric warfare," for example, featured F–15C fighters networked with Joint Tactical Information Distribution System (JTIDS) terminals in mock air-to-air combat, with other fighters not so equipped. The JTIDS-equipped fighters had near-perfect friendly and enemy information and understandably outperformed their opponents. Army officers doubted that a few planes flying at altitude represented the intricacy and confusion of ground combat, and they said so. They also spoke of the low end of the combat spectrum, where such technical sophistication might count for less. Some regarded them as troglodytes. In due course Air Force commentators declared their service the leader in "the" revolution in military affairs and opined on whether they could win future wars without, or without much, assistance from other services. The Navy was divided as to whether or not it needed a revolution in military affairs but was comfortable with a techno-centric vision of its future. Both Air Force and Navy planners tended to perceive a revolution in military affairs as already embedded in existing modernization plans—they had already thought of it. Army planners did want to advance technology but had reservations concerning how far it could take them. They balanced images of future technologies with icons of the timeless infantrymen using them: heroic, "on point," and at risk. Within DoD talk often turned to reducing personnel to free up funds for research and development and procurement. To the Army, this was scary. Army transformers may have wanted a revolution in military affairs, but not one that shredded Army force structure or questioned the Army's reason for existence.[6]

At this point the groundwork has been laid to propose the definition of Army transformation to be used in this study. From 1989 through 2005 Army

Army leaders and the Army Staff had yet another caveat with respect to transformation as a revolution in military affairs. They wanted to control it. Clearly Army efforts should nest within a national security strategy and a national military strategy. In this context Department of Defense and Joint oversight were tolerable, but the service nevertheless sought to substantially control its own destiny while transforming. The point was philosophical as well as parochial. MacGregor Knox and Williamson Murray, distinguished scholars with Army connections, joined others in distinguishing between military revolutions and revolutions in military affairs. Military revolutions, as they described them, are dramatic paradigm shifts embedded in even grander socioeconomic and political revolutions of which they are part. Examples include the rise of the modern nation-state, the French Revolution, the Industrial Revolution, and the generation-long cataclysm that began with World War I. Military institutions find themselves swept along by the tide and at best can hope to adapt capably to changing circumstances. Revolutions in military affairs are generally constituent within military revolutions and are more amenable to design and direction. The rise of the modern nation-state, for example, generated resources that enabled innovators to field standing units of drilled musketry. The Industrial Revolution allowed the Prussian general staff to design campaigns based upon railroads and mass-produced rifles. The bloody stalemate on the Western Front inspired the eventual development of *Blitzkrieg* to unlock it. The Information Age and related technologies were on hand and irreversible. How these manifested themselves in ground combat was yet subject to design. Army planners did believe that there would be continuities in war on the ground and that usages appropriate in the air or at sea might not fully translate into their medium. They, veterans of Vietnam, JUST CAUSE, DESERT STORM, and innumerable lesser contingencies, had seen ground warfare as it actually was. Who could be better prepared to apply new technologies and develop new solutions for old problems than they were?[7]

At this point the groundwork has been laid to propose the definition of Army transformation to be used in this study. From 1989 through 2005 Army transformation was a centrally directed and institutionally driven attempt to achieve a revolution in military affairs relevant to ground warfare that exploited Information Age technology, adapted to post–Cold War strategic circumstances, and integrated into parallel Joint and Department of Defense efforts. This definition is not, to our knowledge, elsewhere agreed upon. It seems, however, to capture what Army leaders intended. It also seems to have been tacitly accepted. For six years running and through the administrations of three Chiefs of Staff, the Army's Chief of Military History presented a standard briefing labeled "Army Transformations Past." The colorful slides provided a brief but popular introduction to numerous Army Staff deliberations, transformation off-sites, Quadrennial Defense Review sessions, multi-star conferences, and so on. At times the Director of the Army Staff had the briefing trotted out simply because someone important needed to be entertained. Each of the historical transformations, discussed in the briefing and below, were centrally directed and institutionally driven, and all were revolutions in military affairs. Several were pre-Joint and pre–Department of Defense, but all incorporated significant technological advances. An organizing principle of the briefing was that Army transformation simultaneously represented adaptation to new strategic circumstances, socioeconomic change, and technological advance. This principle was never disputed, although virtually all of the Army's most senior leadership and most of the Army Staff heard the briefing at one time or another. These men and women, collectively pursuing Army transformation, clearly sought to achieve something on the order of that accomplished under the leadership of Elihu Root or George C. Marshall. Whatever the words chosen, the vision was grand.[8]

Army Transformations Past

To find historical Army transformations as defined above, one would probably begin with the so-called "Root Reforms" of the early twentieth century. Americans had participated in nineteenth-century revolutions in military affairs, but not in a manner that was centrally directed or institutionally driven. The mammoth American Civil War was arguably the first true example of Industrial Age warfare, and it wedded mass production with the mass social mobilization inaugurated by the French Revolution. Huge armies deployed across the breadth of the continent, linked together by telegraph and supported by rail communications and steamships. Factories and depots churned out tens of thousands of rifles, thousands of artillery pieces, and uniforms, supplies, and accoutrements for hundreds of thousands of soldiers. At the beginning of the war armies marched out in Napoleonic array, by its end they contested trench lines not unlike those of World War I. By and large the Army, War Department, and federal government itself were swept along by the tide of military revolution rather than actually controlling it. At the war's onset the War Department consisted of a handful of clerks, the Army numbered 16,000 widely scattered along the nation's frontiers, and the defense organization was a curious patchwork of geographical departments and functional bureaus. The Regular Army did not much expand, nor did it provide cadre for newly raised units. Instead individual states and even cities raised scores of regiments, hastily equipped them, and officered them with elected leaders, political appointees, and a sprinkling of former military men then in civilian life. Regiments from all over the continent, north and south, sped by rail to the baptismal battle of Bull Run. This was not because the military as an institution (as opposed to individual engineers with military backgrounds) had pioneered with respect to such transportation, but because in the last dozen years railroads had become integral to American life. Steamships and telegraphs similarly were commercial phenomena that rapidly demonstrated practical military utility. Indeed, in some respects traditional military leadership seemed to impede innovation. Cases in point included the desultory fielding of breech-loading rifles, the persistence of Napoleonic tactics (to maintain control) in the face of horrific casualties, and initial resistance to such higher-level organizing principles as corps headquarters. It is not entirely coincidental that officers like George B. McClellan and Henry W. Halleck were considered paragons of the profession before the war and came up short within it, whereas those such as Ulysses S. Grant and William T. Sherman were embarrassments before the war and rose to prominence within it. In time—by 1864—President Abraham Lincoln, his War Department, and his chosen generals did get a grip. Mobilization, training, and logistics increasingly came under federal supervision. The strategic leadership team of President Lincoln, Commanding General of the Army Grant, Secretary of War Edwin M. Stanton, Chief of Staff Halleck, and Quartermaster General Montgomery C. Meigs provided superb direction and mobilized extraordinary support. At the operational level generals like Sherman and Philip H. Sheridan fought brilliant campaigns and were well supported by the innovative Railroad Construction Corps. Tactics, largely driven by grassroots adaptation, evolved to accommodate modern weapons. All this took time, however, at a huge cost in casualties and with considerable risks to ultimate success. By the time Lincoln and his generals were in control of events, the military revolution had already occurred. The Civil War was testimony to courage, sacrifice, determination, and improvisation, but not to the artful management of a revolution in military affairs. Postwar critics mined its record for examples of how not to implement change and came up with better ideas of their own.[9]

In the aftermath of the well-fought but poorly managed Spanish-American War, the Army did transform itself. Strategic circumstances had radically altered. The Indian fighting frontier had closed upon itself, and the nation had assumed quasi-imperial responsibilities overseas. Socioeconomic changes were equally profound. Industry had eclipsed agriculture as the nation's principal money maker, the nation was the world's foremost producer of steel and other indexes of industrial might, and overseas trade and investment soared. Far-flung bases secured maritime access to the Caribbean and Far East. Breech-loading repeating rifles, metallic cartridges, smokeless powder, artillery hydraulics, and nascent machine guns were altering the technology of war. Secretary of War Elihu Root initiated an effort to overhaul the Army, starting at the top. Rather than the creaking stove-piped department and bureau system that had muddled through the Indian Wars, Root proposed a general staff under a Chief of Staff

U.S. infantry fighting the Moros in the Philippines

responsible through him to the President. His new Army War College would capstone a hierarchy of post-commissioning education, and directly support operational and long-term planning. The 1903 Springfield rifle, a three-inch gun with an advanced recoil mechanism, and improved smokeless powder—each exploited contemporary technology. The Army more than doubled in size from its prewar precedents and by 1907 took to individual replacements rather than unit rotations to sustain its strength overseas. The Dick Act of 1903 regularized relationships between the Army and the "Organized Militia," now the National Guard. Guardsmen would be federally equipped, committed to a standardized program of training, and subject to inspection. In 1908 the establishment of the Army Medical Reserve proved the first step in developing an expansive federal Army Reserve. Meanwhile sustained security requirements in the Philippines encouraged the organization of native soldiers into the Philippine Scouts, who soon became capable and potent auxiliaries. A reorganized and reenergized Medical Department took on the potentially catastrophic diseases of the new areas of operation. In the Spanish-American War the Army lost 932 to combat and 5,238 to disease. Fear of yellow fever was so palpable in Cuba it almost aborted operations. Armed with advances in germ theory and preventative medicine reinforced by their own practical research on-site, Army doctors counterattacked. In a few years they virtually eliminated yellow fever as a threat and brought malaria well under control—in both cases by declaring war on the relevant mosquito. Nowhere was this success more consequential than during the prolonged construction of the Panama Canal. Interpolating from previous experiences, one source reasonably assumed Army medicine saved seventy thousand lives—a figure exceeding the entire strength of the Army at the time—on this project alone. This is not to mention preventative medicine applied elsewhere, or results from the general introduction of clinical thermometers, hypodermic syringes, ophthalmoscopes, vaccines, and special purpose drugs. If one were looking for advances with respect to this Army transformation that could be considered exponential, one would certainly include the radically enhanced medical capability to keep troops alive in the tropics—or anywhere else, for that matter. As the reforms envisioned by Elihu Root came to fruition, the United States had a respectable "Army for Empire" and hemispheric defense. A Chief of Staff supervised a capable Army Staff and an increasingly professionalized Army school system. The Army had more than doubled in size, acquired modern weapons, and become expansible both within its units and by the virtue of an orderly system of reserves. It sustained continuing operations overseas, drawing upon native troops, individual replacements, and modern medicine to keep its strength up. It had capably assumed a global role.[10]

By 1910 the Army was well postured to police its overseas responsibilities as they then existed and to undertake colonial wars on the scale of the Philippine-American War or security requirements on the Mexican border. It was not particularly postured for mass mobilization. Root was considerably impressed with the writings of Emory Upton and others suspicious of growth beyond the robust professional framework of established units. Manageable numbers of untrained privates could be whipped into shape by seasoned officers and noncommissioned officers (NCOs) in such units while routine security progressed by virtue of those already trained. A proper *expansible Army*, a term popularized in the early nineteenth century by John C. Calhoun when he was Secretary of War, could perhaps double in size during a training cycle and still retain its quality. The duration of such a cycle was variously estimated as between six months and two years. Commitment to the concept of an expansible Army was commitment to amoeba-like growth, with the Army doubling in size with each mitosis. This seemed adequate in 1910, even with a Regular Army of fewer than one hundred thousand. Given the breadth of the Atlantic, the relative weaknesses of Canada and Mexico, and the insular nature of America's overseas possessions, who would the Army fight and on what scale? Only the European powers were capable of mass mobilization in the near term, and the United States had long avoided "entangling alliances" with any of them. Upton and others studied and even admired European mobilization mechanisms, built upon peacetime conscription, massive reserves, and large standing armies, but their application to the United States seemed speculative and fanciful. Then strategic circumstances changed. World War I ground on for years, consumed enormous quantities of blood and treasure, and sucked the non-European world into its vortex. The United States, as we have seen, had a large and ever-expanding interest in international trade. It also grew to be a principal supplier to the Allied powers, who in turn owed American businessmen a lot of money. The Germans came across as ruthless, capable, imperialistic, and insatiable, heightening a national sense of alarm. The Germans resorted to, relented, and then resorted again to unrestricted submarine warfare, taking American lives and sending American ships to the bottom of the sea. They conspired to offer United States territory to the Mexicans, or seemed to. President Woodrow Wilson, long committed to keeping the United States out of the conflict, ultimately asked Congress for a declaration of war on 2 April 1917.[11]

It is reasonable to characterize the mobilization for World War I, the post-war retrenchment, and the mobilization for World War II as three separate Army transformations. It may be more accurate, however, to envision a single transformation into a mobilization-based Army. In that light World War I was an imperfect rehearsal for World War II, with a reversion to the Army for Empire in between. As the vast scope of the European bloodbath became apparent, the National Defense Act of 1916 expanded both the Regular Army and the National Guard and rendered both further expansible along Uptonian lines. It also introduced measures for industrial and economic mobilization. Most important to our point, it recognized the universal military obligation of the "unorganized Militia" under federal auspices. This laid the groundwork for mass conscription, followed by the organization and training of new divisions under the supervision of small cadres of professional soldiers. Veterans of Civil War volunteer regiments and advocates of such preparedness programs as the Plattsburg Idea had long campaigned for this more egalitarian approach. Given that it expanded the pace of mobilization more than tenfold, it was the only feasible way to field forces large enough and quickly enough to matter on the Western Front. Eighteen of the new "National Army" divisions joined eight constructed from the Regular Army and seventeen from the National Guard to tip the scales in Europe. Their battlefield worth remained incompletely proven, however. General John J. Pershing, commander of the American Expeditionary Forces, was Uptonian in his thinking. He insisted on lengthy in-theater retraining even for his Regular Army divisions and summarily broke up six of the National Army divisions to provide individual replacements to units in combat. He designated three others as replacement training centers rather than combat units, and turned one over piecemeal to the French. Two never saw serious combat. Of the six that did, the first was not into action until 11 August 1918, three months before the Armistice. The third-rate status accorded National Army divisions notwithstanding, the individual draftees and draftee divisions of World War I performed capably enough to inspire favorable commentary—even from Pershing himself. Egalitarian theorists such as John McAuley Palmer seized upon this to advocate a rethinking of roles and missions. Rather than merely serving as an expansible core, the Regular Army was of value because it could deploy on short notice. The National Guard would take longer to prepare but was a readily accessible reserve. Behind this glacis of early deploying units, a great mass of new divisions under tiny cadres of experienced officers and NCOs could organize, train, and deploy. This approach solidified in the National Defense Act of 1920, although inter-war frugality much diminished the preparedness of the Regular Army and National Guard. In World War II new Army of the United States (AUS) divisions, supervised by perhaps one professional soldier for forty in the ranks, drilled through a methodical one-year training program and then competed to deploy. The first into combat performed well, cracking the Gustav Line in Italy after fierce fighting. Subsequent arrivals swelled the accolades for draftees and draftee divisions. By the end of the war the performance and manning of Regular Army, National Guard, and veteran Army of the United States divisions were virtually indistinguishable, with draftees dominating the rank and file throughout. Over two-thirds of the divisions fighting had been activated after Pearl Harbor, and all had been kept up to strength by drafted individual replacements. The great American defense gamble had paid off. Even in the face of modern weaponry, Americans did not need a large Army in time of peace to have a large and effective Army in time of war.[12]

Hotly debated, the transformation to a mobilization-based Army was institutionally driven throughout. In addition to addressing the strategic shift to major warfare in Europe and Asia, it also harnessed dramatic socioeconomic changes. Industrial growth had churned ahead, and scientific advances fielded such technologies as the internal combustion engine, radio, and general electrification. Meanwhile bouts of economic depression and political movements such as Progressivism and the New Deal led Americans to expect much more of their government and to cede it much more authority in return. The Sixteenth Amendment authorized a national income tax beginning in 1913. The federal government heavily supervised the economy during World War I, the New Deal, and World War II. Conscription, a fierce issue during the Civil War, aroused modest opposition during World War I and barely a whimper during World War II. Taken together, these advances and mind-sets enabled industrial mobilization of mind-boggling proportions. During World War II the United States superbly equipped and supported its own massive armed forces while contributing heavily to the logistics of its allies as well. Much of the discussion of a revolution in military affairs beginning in World War I centers on technological advances harnessing tanks, airplanes, artillery, radios, storm troopers, and motorized transportation into combined-arms tactics eventually characterized as *Blitzkrieg*. The United States Army did not particularly lead in this regard until late in its transformation. By the time it arrived in France in World War I, nascent combinations of tanks, artillery, infantry, and planes were already contesting the battlefield dominance of trench line, barbed wire, and machine gun. The United States participated, but with tanks, artillery, and planes largely provided by the British and French. American soldiers did some experimentation and a lot of reading and writing concerning combined-arms warfare in the interwar years. Congress took little note until the Germans overran Poland and France in lightning campaigns, however. As money flowed Army transformers designed robust panoplies of modern equipment to fit out redesigned divisions, borrowing heavily from European experiences and practices. Training programs and logistical procedures adapted as well. The results were breathtaking with respect to lavishness, scale, and standardization. Whereas the Germans had mechanized or motorized but a fraction of their forces, the Americans put virtually everything except infantry in contact on wheels or tracks during their battle for France. The 1945 American campaigns in Germany and the Po Valley were the most thoroughgoing examples of *Blitzkrieg* yet. They looked easy but would not have been had the Army not transformed.[13]

World War II witnesses mass mobilization.

The transformation to a mobilization-based Army prioritized organization and then applied technology to it. Transformation to the early Cold War Army, extant from 1949 through 1973, was driven largely by atomic weapons and the new world order that they had created. Atomic weapons rendered the strategic bombardment visions of Italian General Giulio Douhet and other airpower enthusiasts feasible and hastened the departure of the Air Force to become a separate service. This in turn fueled the National Defense Act of 1947 and the organization of the Department of Defense as the overseer of three services. Meanwhile the construction of a network of alliances overseas to contain communist expansion, most famously the North Atlantic Treaty Organization (NATO), embedded American forces within larger security arrangements. For a period the United States offset emerging Soviet hostility and intransigence with its atomic monopoly and calculated military assistance. The Army shrank into a constabulary overseas, with a robust mobilization base at home should it be called upon to refight World War II. Instead it was called on to fight a limited war in Korea, shortly after the Soviet Union had acquired atomic bombs of its own. The fall of China to Mao Zedong radically expanded the perimeter within which communism was to be contained. The Regular Army enlarged to fight the Korean War and then remained large to man the "frontiers of freedom" in Europe and Asia. Renewed conscription and individual replacement kept up its strength. A tiered mobilization system stretched down through established National Guard and Army Reserve units to training divisions and related assets capable of raising altogether new units.

13

Cold War "tactical" nuclear weapons included the Davy Crockett.

This allowed for another World War II type of mobilization complete with draftee divisions. Nuclear weapons proliferated and miniaturized, to include atomic munitions for tube artillery and intermediate-range ballistic missiles such as the Jupiter and Pershing. The Army briefly introduced the five-battle-group Pentomic Division with a much-reduced division overhead, a philosophy of dispersed mobile combat, and integrated nuclear weapons. The design exceeded the technology of the time, particularly with respect to command and control, logistics, and sustained mobility. By 1964 the Pentomic Division had been replaced by the Reorganization Objective Army Division (ROAD), consisting of an enlarged division base and three maneuver brigade headquarters to which varying mixes of standing battalions could be assigned. ROAD gave up some nuclear survivability as compared with the Pentomic Division, but it was far more capable of sustaining conventional and low-intensity conflict. This fit in with a progression from nearly complete reliance on nuclear deterrence prior to 1949 through heavy reliance on nuclear deterrence with Eisenhower's "New Look" to the more balanced capabilities of "Flexible Response" in the 1960s. An enlarged peacetime force structure dictated continuous industrial mobilization, with generations of equipment cascading from the Regular Army through the National Guard and Army Reserve into "mothballs" and obsolescence as technology progressed. President Eisenhower groused about the emerging power of a "military-industrial complex," but such

The Vietnam War saw the widespread tactical use of helicopters.

a phenomenon proved necessary to keep large forces continuously supplied and consistently modernized. Within North America early warning systems and matrices of antiaircraft and later antiballistic missile sites ringed key cities and facilities. Many of these were manned by National Guardsmen, defending their country from their "own backyard." Nuclear war implied horrific casualties. This was all the more reason for the Army to maintain a depth of reserves and an expansible mobilization base. The early Cold War Army was relatively large, dependent on conscription, backed by robust industrial and mobilization bases, nuclear armed, embedded in alliances, partnered to other services under Department of Defense auspices, and committed to be the ground component of a flexible response.[14]

In keeping with notions of flexible response, the Army undertook an expanding counterinsurgency to hold the line in Vietnam while maintaining nuclear armed deterrence elsewhere. While in Vietnam the Army radically expanded its use of helicopters, first for mobility in rough terrain and then as multipurpose platforms for a variety of tactical uses. It also evolved considerable sophistication in operations at the lower end of the combat spectrum. As the United States Army withdrew from Vietnam in the early 1970s, however, it by and large walked away from this experience—as we shall see. It also transformed from the draftee Army of the early Cold War to the all-volunteer force of the late Cold War. Political leaders determined that the American people would no longer support a "peacetime" draft and that the draft as it existed aggravated socioeconomic tensions within the United States. Peacetime conscription ended in 1973. The strategic situation also changed. The People's Republic of China and the Soviet Union had visibly fallen out, clashing along their borders while the Vietnam War was under way. President Nixon courted China with an unprecedented visit in 1972, and the Soviets committed to a series of strategic arms limitations treaties at about the same time. The threat of nuclear war seemed much reduced, as did the specter of monolithic communist expansion. The Arab-Israeli War of 1973 demonstrated the lethality of antitank and antiaircraft-guided missiles which, with other technological advances, tilted conventional warfare in favor of the tactical defense. It now seemed feasible to hold back a Soviet or North Korean conventional attack without resorting to nuclear weapons, buying time to address whatever miscalculation had initiated hostilities. A doctrine labeled the "Active Defense" envisioned highly trained professional soldiers maneuvering quickly in the face of a mechanized advance, wearing down their adversaries with incredibly accurate fires. Beginning in 1982 the Active Defense morphed into "AirLand Battle," achieving more balance between defensive and offensive operations and articulating notions of "deep battle." Equipment was to be thoroughly upgraded and modernized, complementing the higher professional caliber of the soldiers. Cases in point included but were by no means limited to the so-called "big five": the M1 Abrams tank, the M2/3 Bradley fighting vehicle, the AH–64 Apache attack helicopter, the UH–60 Black Hawk utility helicopter, and the Patriot air defense missile. Training technology leaped ahead as well, incorporating such advances as the unit conduct-of-fire trainer (UCOFT), the Multiple Integrated Laser Engagement System (MILES), and distributed tactical simulations. Skillful, highly trained volunteers were necessarily more expensive than draftees and required considerable investment in recruitment and retention. The Army became smaller, with the active Army numbering 785,000 in 1974—still large by historical standards—as opposed to 1,570,000 in 1968. These reductions were partially offset by increased reliance upon the reserve component. In accordance with the new Total Force policy over two-thirds of the Army's combat support and combat service support ended up in the reserve component, rendering it unfeasible to sustain significant operations without them. Focus on high-end mechanized conventional combat in Central Europe, or a similar setting, dominated tactical thinking. The basic mobilization structure of the early Cold War remained, albeit thinned, as did a military-industrial complex cascading generations of ever-more modern equipment. The draft was programmed for resurrection, should circumstances require. The active units of the late Cold War Army were fewer in number, all volunteer, and more professional. They were designed to preclude a quick or easy Soviet conventional victory and thus to deter miscalculation. Should circumstances get out of control, the nation was reasonably prepared to revert to the conscription, mass mobilization, and heavy reliance upon nuclear weapons of the early Cold War.[15]

How Transformation Works

The transformations discussed above were at different times and led to different armies. However, they shared features in common that may allow general comments on Army transformation as a process. Each occurred proximate to a strategic, socioeconomic, and technological watershed. At some point the leadership of the Army committed itself to centrally directed and institutionally driven transformation. To succeed, they had to decide on a way ahead, wrap up debate, and market the transformation inside the Army and out. Transformation will not occur if Congress has not approved and funded it. A vision without funding is a hallucination. Thus transformation took time up front just to get under way. Once under way, a host of secondary and tertiary effects had to be identified and worked through. Technology may have advanced the ball, but exploiting it required changes to doctrine, organization, training, administrative practices, and even military culture. Experimentation, feedback, and trial and error proved necessary. All this took time, perhaps as much as a generation, because true transformations overlapped, with one superseding the other across messy temporal boundaries. It can be easier for historians to identify an Army transformation than it was for the participants. Let us reexamine Army transformations past in the light of these common features.

Army transformations have occurred at strategic, socioeconomic, and technological watersheds. By 1898 the United States had acquired significant overseas possessions in the Pacific and Caribbean, while the Indian frontier that had been the Army's principal area of operations for three hundred years ceased to exist. Industry surpassed agriculture as the engine driving the national economy, railroads linked the United States into a socioeconomic whole, and overseas markets and investments were increasingly essential to the national well-being. Breech-loading smokeless repeating rifles, breech-loading smokeless artillery with recoil mechanisms, and machine guns emerged to dominate the land battlefield, and armored battleships were dominant at sea. In 1917 the United States Army departed for the first of two colossal wars in Europe alongside allies and against adversaries primed for massive national mobilizations. It had to raise huge forces, dispatch them overseas, and sustain them in combat once there. Meanwhile an industrial revolution based on electrification and the internal combustion engine raced ahead, and the American people accepted unprecedented socioeconomic discipline and paid unprecedented taxes as the role of the government with respect to the economy evolved. Military technology harnessed the internal combustion engine that appeared in tanks and airplanes and in swarms of combat support and combat service support vehicles to complement both. By 1949 the United States accepted the strategic military leadership of a "Free World" attempting to contain communist expansion along vast frontiers in Europe and Asia. The Free World represented liberal capitalism and socioeconomic integration as well as political compatibility. Institutions such as the World Bank and International Monetary Fund, along with a host of agreements, policies, and usages, emerged from the Bretton Woods Conference of 1944

New technology, in this case an antitank missile, required doctrine, training, and appropriate organization to be useful.

and its successors. Socioeconomic integration merged with military necessity to embed the United States Army in standing alliances of long duration, most notably NATO. The preeminent military technology of the era was the nuclear weapon and systems associated with it, although sustained mobilization also led to cascades of ever-more modern conventional equipment replacing itself a generation at a time. By 1973 it was clear that communism was no longer monolithic, if it ever had been, and the threat of nuclear war had somewhat receded. The Cold War and containment were still there, but the prolonged Vietnam War had exposed socioeconomic cleavages within the United States and exhausted its tolerance for conscription short of a major war. At the same time radically improved guided antitank and antiaircraft missiles made it feasible to withstand a major conventional attack with a smaller Army without resorting to nuclear weapons. Each of these complex watersheds had a banner year—1898, 1917, 1949, and 1973—with a much broader temporal footprint. What of 1989? Without getting too far ahead of our story, one might suggest that the end of the Cold War profoundly altered strategic circumstances, the Information Age marks a socioeconomic revolution, and the military potential of the microchip is only on the cusp of being realized.[16]

Historical watersheds are easier to see in hindsight than they are at the time, rendering the need for an Army transformation less visible as well. Debate within the Army family concerning transformation can be fierce and resistance to change substantial. When Elihu Root perceived the need to remake the Army for its new world role, he was immediately opposed by Commanding General Nelson A. Miles and the Army's bureau chiefs entrenched in Washington. To Miles the transition to a Chief of Staff supervising a general staff implied a loss of grandeur, whereas to the bureau chiefs it implied a loss of influence. They could not accept that worldwide responsibilities required forward-deployed leadership and improved integrated management rather than the stovepipe system that had been adequate for the Indian Wars. Debate and resistance dragged on for at least a dozen years. The mass mobilization for World War I was grudgingly accepted by some Army senior leaders and followed prolonged debate between disciples of Emory Upton and more egalitarian theorists such as Leonard Wood concerning how big a role citizen-soldiers could play—and how quickly. The conduct of operations during World War I indicated an enduring professional bias against conscripts, and musings continued postwar concerning how much of a "Sad Sack" a draftee would inevitably be. Only with the Victory Program authored in 1941 did the Army accept the draftee and the draftee division as full partners, a faith that demonstrated itself as well placed by mid-1944. With the advent of atomic weapons theorists within the Army fell into at least three camps. One saw the huge strategic potential of ballistic missiles, with the Army in control of them. For these the future of war was Douhet-style strategic bombardment sans the manned aircraft, with other ground forces playing a distinctly subordinate role. This group was largely excised when President Eisenhower transferred strategic nuclear missiles to the Air Force in the late 1950s. A second group argued for designing an Army optimized for a tactical nuclear battlefield while a third group, with limited wars like Korea in mind, considered nuclear weapons best left to the Air Force and Navy and sought an Army dominant in conventional ground combat. Transformation landed somewhere between the second and third groups, with the first ascendant during the Eisenhower administration with the Pentomic Division and the second ascendant with ROAD after 1960. The Volunteer Army was forced on the Army before it was embraced by the Army. After initial foot dragging with respect to implementing it at all, several lines of contention emerged within the context of implementation. Efforts to improve living conditions, relax disciplinary requirements, and raise pay in order to recruit and retain high-quality soldiers brought resistance from those who thought the troops were being "coddled." The Total Army concept demolished precepts that had been intact for years, threatening vested interests in the active component and the reserve component alike. The recruitment of women multiplied several fold and women were admitted to West Point, bringing on a whole new debate with respect to the essence of soldiering. Transformation has never occurred without resistance within the Army itself.[17]

Army transformations inevitably required funding and thus congressional support. Ideally debate within the Army would wrap up before Congress became involved, but this has not happened. Discord complicates the procurement of funds Congress is often loath to give, particularly when the interests of constituents are at stake. Elihu Root, for example, did not have much trouble convincing Congress to expand the standing Army from its pre–Spanish-American War strength of 28,000 to its post–Philippine War strength of 70,000, adding five regiments each of infantry and cavalry in the process. The greater security requirements and greater national means were both obvious. His desire to consolidate units at fewer locations and close down tiny "hitching post" forts scattered across the former frontier met much greater resistance. These figured in local economies and were also destination points for resources generated by the Army's antiquated bureau system. So great was the leverage of the bureaus in Congress that Root's promulgation of a thoroughly empowered general staff was only partly achieved. Similarly the landmark Dick Act of 1903 represented compromises between the Uptonian direction Root was trying to go and the political influence of the National Guard. The transformation to a mobilization-based Army pitted Uptonian notions of professionalism against more egalitarian views held by Generals John A. Logan, Leonard Wood, and others. Congress came down on the side of the egalitarians by default; it was so unwilling to consider a peacetime expansible Army of the scale a great war would have required that Army planners inevitably fell back on a cadre system when great war was thrust upon them. Ironically, congressional parsimony totally reversed itself when war arrived. This prompted Chief of Staff General George C. Marshall's famous remark that before Pearl Harbor the Army had unlimited time and no money and after it unlimited money and no time. Following the war congressional parsimony returned, complicated by the reorganization of military forces into three services and a department of defense. The so-called "Key West Agreement" (actually the policy paper *Functions of the Armed Forces and the Joint Chiefs of Staff*) defined roles and missions for the services and particularly apportioned air assets. The Navy and Air Force received far more planes and strategic nuclear weapons and inevitably were dependent on more costly platforms and technologies. As the Cold War continued, this reverberated in the budget, year after year. Business allies of the Navy and Air Force seemed more potent in Congress than those of the Army, given that the Navy and Air Force budgets were dominated by costly procurements whereas that of the Army was dominated by personnel costs. The Army's sense of being a budgetary third priority became particularly acute during the period of Eisenhower's "New Look." With the all-volunteer Army of the late Cold War, congressional deliberations over personnel costs took a new twist. Now recruitment and retention were high priorities, and cash incentives were mobilized to facilitate both. Military pay competed with civilian pay to maintain end strength. Arguments over force structure became even more acute, with ever more powerful financial incentives for trimming it. Each Army transformation evolved through the wickets of congressional funding processes, with setbacks and compromises along the way.[18]

Army transformations drive and are driven by changes in doctrine. At the dawn of the twentieth century breech-loading repeating rifles, breech-loading artillery with recoil mechanisms, and machine guns partnered with battlefield experience to require greater dispersion, even at the risk of degrading command and control. Soldiers shed traditional "Army Blue" uniforms for drabber shades of brown. During the world wars the mobilization-based Army raced to catch up with doctrine that was already being applied by allies and adversaries, transitioning to the new equipment necessary on the fly. Pershing aspired to restore maneuver warfare to the Western Front, but instead got better at hammering away with massive artillery fires, fierce infantry assaults, and a sprinkling of tanks and planes. Much of his heavy equipment was British and French. American military leaders were as shocked as anybody else by the early World War II effectiveness of *Blitzkrieg* in Poland and France and rushed to make their own Army capable of such tactics. After some hard knocks and lessons learned they succeeded, liberally borrowing combined-arms tactics from ally and adversary alike. This doctrinal ecumenism inspired the iconic scene in the motion picture *Patton* where the triumphant hero shouts across the battlefield to the defeated Rommel ". . . you magnificent bastard, I read your book!" The early Cold War Army strove mightily to weave tactical nuclear weapons into the combined-arms doctrine it inherited from World War II. Subject matter experts down to the company level, generally nuclear, biological, and chemical (NBC) officers and NCOs, shepherded detection kits, dosimeters, and gas masks and balanced downwind safety diagrams against vehicle protective factors to determine defensive positions and schemes of maneuver. At higher levels appropriately trained officers plotted targets for the introduction of friendly nuclear weapons and anticipated targets the enemy would select. With the late Cold War this preoccupation with nuclear weapons faded, and attention shifted to the battlefield effectiveness of conventional guided missiles and computer-assisted gunnery. Admonished that "What can be seen can be hit, and what can be hit can be killed," company commanders designed layers of kill zones wherein each of their weapon systems came together at optimal ranges. At higher levels commanders were to shuffle units in such a manner that kill zones and engagement areas stretched across a continuous front. In accordance with "AirLand Battle" they capitalized on aircraft, guided missile–bearing helicopters, and intermediate-range ballistic missiles to plan "deep battles" well within ground controlled by the enemy, and protected their own forces from interdiction with an equally thoughtful "rear battle." Each Army transformation featured its unique doctrine adapted to anticipated tactical circumstances and the technology of the time.[19]

Changing doctrine drives changes in organization. Root aspired to gather a scattered frontier constabulary into larger units, and his successors designed nominal division organizations to tie them together. In 1913, for example, the 2d Division efficiently mustered on the Mexican border after having received a message of only five lines, reflecting a degree of coordination that would have been impossible ten years earlier. Overseas security was considerably enhanced by newly organized native units such as the Philippine Scouts and the Puerto Rico Regiment. The mobilization-based Army radically enlarged command hierarchy to control much increased size. Divisions solidified in World War I and corps and armies were added to them. To these higher headquarters World War II added army groups. Division composition changed with doctrine. In World War I the massive two-brigade, four-regiment quadrangular division was organized into four division corps supported by masses of artillery and provided a relentless battering ram for the Western Front. Leading regiments were replaced by fresh regiments and leading divisions by fresh divisions as offensives ground on. World War II placed more emphasis upon maneuver, and armored divisions and separate battalions were added. A stripped-down three-regiment infantry division with artillery served as a base to which separate battalions of other arms could be added. Armored divisions featured combat commands that were even more readily tailored, and the war introduced the all new airborne division. The early Cold War Army, as we have seen, flailed to adapt to the nuclear battlefield. The Pentomic Division optimized a capacity to disperse units and mass fires, although its success depended on technology that did not yet exist. It was replaced by the ROAD, which had tailorable brigades and a division overhead better able to sustain conventional combat. With the late Cold War Army the proliferation and miniaturization of guided missiles morphed organization. Mechanized infantry and armored task forces became more interchangeable as every vehicle sported long-range tank-killing weapons. Rocket batteries proliferated, dispersed to the rear, and added new dimensions to division and corps battle spaces. Swarms of missile-armed attack helicopters came into their own as maneuver task forces and brigade combat teams, controlling ground rather than merely serving as occasionally useful auxiliaries. Each Army transformation featured new patterns of organization unique to the circumstances and technology of its time.[20]

New organizations must be trained. The Army War College was the most tangible product of the Root reforms. It drove the training and education of the general staff while also serving as the capstone to a refurbished hierarchical Army school system. Perhaps the most important feature of the Root-era Dick Act was the training relationship it established between the active Army and the National Guard. Newly envisioned as a tiered reserve, the National Guard was to be routinely drilled against federal standards in peacetime to improve its efficiency should war occur. The mobilization-based Army was predicated on the notion that small cadres could train large units to appropriate standards within reasonable periods of time. This approach worked satisfactorily in World War I and well in World War II. The rigorous year-long Army Training Program of World War II systematically drilled draftees through basic, individual, unit, combined-arms, and large-unit maneuver phases. The new units by and large performed capably in their first combats, and got better from there. World War II infantry divisions particularly drilled artillery-infantry teamwork, and their battlefield performance demonstrated that strength. The integration of air and armor with infantry was less well rehearsed in the Army Training Program, which led to embarrassments and then adaptations overseas. The early Cold War Army was forward deployed and evolved a robust capability to conduct basic and individual training in stateside institutions in order to dispatch trained soldiers as individual replacements overseas. Units reinforced individual training and assumed full responsibility for collective training. Tank battalions were by now organic to infantry divisions, so combined-arms unit training received appropriate emphasis from the outset. The training of the early Cold War drove skills necessary to survive on the nuclear battlefield down to the individual and crew level. The largely drafted early Cold War Army featured high turnovers, and the volume of its training programs took this into account. The all-volunteer late Cold War Army heavily emphasized reenlistment and featured generally longer tours and less turnover. It refined and standardized the Noncommissioned Officer Education System (NCOES) to get the most out of retained soldiers at all levels. Increasingly sophisticated equipment and smaller units argued for the increasing percentages of noncommissioned officers the late Cold War Army deployed. Each Army transformation evolved a training paradigm of its own to accommodate its unique circumstances.[21]

Transformation implies changes in administrative practices. We have discussed the prolonged contention beginning with the Root reforms between the general staff system and the traditional bureaus of the nineteenth century. During this period the Army also shifted to an individual replacement system to maintain the strengths of units overseas. With the mobilization-based Army elaborate civil and military mechanisms to control the draft and direct the flow of draftees evolved. Huge masses of manpower were to be efficiently accessed, sorted through, distributed, and ultimately released. Standardized testing came into its own, with profound effects on both individuals and institutions. Terms such as *Category III* or *4F* acquired social as well as administrative importance. Units and agencies competed to get their fair share of individuals with purportedly desirable characteristics. Adjutants and personnel officers at every level codified, managed, and tracked human capital with unprecedented levels of detail. The early Cold War Army creditably supervised the reconstruction and reintegration of Germany and Japan and settled in with major units forward deployed to defend these and other allies. Even when combat operations were not ongoing, this forward-deployed posture and reliance on an individual replacement system implied massive personnel movements. Recruits and draftees were inducted, trained, deployed, and released or reenlisted. Career soldiers cycled through assignments in the United States and overseas, each being expected to take his or her fair share of "hardship" tours, accompanied overseas tours, stateside tours, and professional school assignments. An elaborate bureaucracy emerged to supervise all this traffic, as did personal relationships between professional soldiers and their career managers (also affectionately known as career manglers) in the National Capital Region. With the late Cold War Army new bureaucracies emerged to better manage recruiting and retention. District Recruiting Commands (later battalions) scattered recruiters and recruiting stations across the United States in ubiquitous bids to "make contact." Mass media were mobilized, most famously with the long-standing slogan "Be All That You Can Be, in the Army." To manage retention full-time Retention NCOs were assigned down to the battalion level. These scheduled reiterative interviews with eligible soldiers and then vectored in with the reenlistment options that seemed most likely to appeal to each. Commanders and staffs monitored reenlistment closely, and relevant comments almost inevitably appeared in officers' efficiency ratings. Each Army transformation evolved administrative practices to keep pace with the newly morphing Army.[22]

Some aspects of Army transformations are best described as cultural. During the Army for Empire perhaps the profoundest cultural shift was new-found deference to preventative medicine and medical advice. As late as the Spanish-American War commanders often ignored doctors and characterized the smell of excrement around their camps as the "patriotic odor." In a few short years Army doctors bested historically debilitating tropical diseases, catapulted in prestige and influence, and controlled major aspects of soldiers' lives with prescribed health and welfare routines. A rare commander ignored medical advice, whether with respect to his unit or his person. The mobilization-based Army swept away much of the isolation that had traditionally separated the American Army and its people. Enlisted men and officers alike were far more representative of the American people as a whole. With this greater openness came greater exposure of service practices to outside scrutiny. The theretofore somewhat arbitrary disciplinary system evolved toward the far more circumscribed Uniformed Code of Military Justice (UCMJ). Citizen-soldiers expected to retain their rights as citizens, and an energetic media was on hand to assist. Patton's infamous slapping incident in Sicily illustrates this cultural evolution. What other army—or what previous American Army—would have relieved a military superstar because he had slapped a soldier? The early Cold War Army remained mobilization-based and egalitarian, albeit with a more cosmopolitan tone. Soldiers of all ranks routinely served overseas amid diverse cultures, and most could expect a tour in Germany, Japan, or Korea. Intermarriage with locals became common enough that virtually every company had a few wives born overseas in its family. Local languages were similarly familiar to at least a few of the NCOs. It is true that soldiers spent most of their time in isolated enclaves, but few escaped the notion that they were somehow ambassadors for their country and for democracy in general. In this context racial discrimination became awkward at first, and then positively embarrassing. Social mores were already progressing toward integration when President Truman's executive order integrated the Army. The Army that invaded Germany and occupied Japan was ferociously segregated. By the late 1960s officers and NCOs were canvassing local bars, retailers, apartments, and the like, identifying which refused to provide service regardless of race, and placing offenders off-limits to all soldiers. If racial and ethnic discrimination was the greatest social challenge for the early Cold War Army, gender discrimination was the greatest social challenge for its successor. As we have seen, percentages of women in the Army multiplied several fold when the draft ended and the shift to an all-volunteer force began. The separate Women's Army Corps (WAC), venerated by many who served in it, was disestablished in 1974 to allow for a broader and more egalitarian distribution of women throughout the force. Restrictions on women's service disappeared one by one, until only a relative few remained. Each Army transformation proved to be in part cultural.[23]

It should perhaps be noted that each of the historical transformations discussed above involved a slightly different cast of institutional players. Root seems to have been virtually alone when launching his principal reforms. Those bureau chiefs who were not actively hostile were preoccupied with day-to-day responsibilities, and the Commanding General of the Army was actively hostile. An improvised War College Board served as a surreptitious staff, and Root got valuable help before Congress from such distinguished retirees as Generals John M. Schofield, Wesley Merritt, and Grenville M. Dodge. The transformation to a mobilization-based Army was largely authored by the general staff Root had envisioned. Secretaries of the Army and Chiefs of Staff worked Congress in concert for funding and legislation, and staff officers coordinated details. Remnants of the bureau system remained to work the routine within

24

Army transformations include administrative and cultural change.

their purviews, but long-range planning increasingly fell to the general staff, and it grew more specialized and refined over time. The War College retained an active role, largely to shepherd and sort through good ideas. The early Cold War Army inherited this refined general staff. One particularly notable addition was the Vice Chief of Staff in 1947. This critical officer generally took charge of the day-to-day running of the Army, freeing the Chief of Staff to deal with external players and longer-term visions. With the National Security Act of 1947 critical external players had been added, namely the Departments of Defense and of the Air Force. The Department of the Navy had long been there, but acquired a new and different relationship with the Army now that both received funding and supervision through the Department of Defense. Given that technology muddied once clean boundaries between land and sea, and that air was everywhere, there was much to sort out. The late Cold War Army added the Training and Doctrine Command (TRADOC), the Army Materiel Command (AMC), and a number of other agencies to deliberations envisioning the future course of the Army. These cooperated with and occasionally competed with such Army Staff components as the Deputy Chief of Staff for Operations and Plans (DCSOPS) or the Deputy Chief of Staff for Logistics (DCSLOG). The increasing elaboration of staffs and commands was paralleled by increasing structure and sophistication in agencies given over to analysis, testing, and "consumer" evaluation. Army transformations became ever more multiorganizational, influencing the precept that they would be centrally directed and institutionally driven.[24]

Army transformations take time to mature, and the resulting forces overlap considerably. The Army for Empire arguably lasted from 1898 through 1941. The constituent shift to a general staff did not tip the balance with respect to the control of the bureaus until 1912, with the dramatic resolution of the so-called "muster-roll controversy." Overseas units settled into a steady rhythm of forward deployment supported by individual replacements and trained units of Philippine Constabulary at about the same time. The mobilization-based Army rehearsed in 1917–1918 and lasted from 1940 through 1973. As we have seen, the status of draftees and draftee divisions was not fully settled until 1944. The appliqué revolution in military affairs applied to the mobilization-based Army went considerably faster, but this was largely because of time gained by drawing upon European experimentation and experience. The early Cold War Army lasted from 1945 through 1973. It was sufficiently dependent on conscription and mobilization plans to end about the same time as the mobilization-based Army, although it was, as we have seen, conscientiously atomic. The late Cold War Army began with the commitment to end conscription in 1969. It is a matter of debate whether this Army remains with us today. One purpose of this study is to define the extent to which the Army of 2005 had changed from its late Cold War predecessor, and to ascertain whether the differences were enough to characterize as a transformation—and as a revolution in military affairs. Lest the timelines described seem too lengthy and the overlaps too extensive to qualify as transformative or revolutionary, one might consider other historical examples. Many historians consider the European introduction of drilled musketry as revolutionary. The proportion of French musketeers/fusiliers to pikemen evolved from two to three in 1622 through one to one in 1630, two to one in 1650, three to one in 1680, and four to one in 1695. Pure fusilier battalions did not appear until about 1705, and even these did not make the logical leap to deploying as integral companies until about 1750. Similarly, the Prussian revolution in military affairs that so benefited Chancellor Otto von Bismarck arguably extended from 1836 through 1871, the dreadnaught revolution from 1837 through 1917, and the harnessing of the internal combustion engine to military purposes from 1909 through 1944. To employ a nonmilitary analogy, the American Revolution was not conceptually complete until an elected government first superseded an opposing incumbent in 1800—twenty-four years after the Declaration of Independence. Timelines characterized as transformative or revolutionary are necessarily relative.[25]

Given the discussion to this point, what might one expect to find if an Army transformation indeed occurred between 1989 and 2005? First, the front end of that period would mark a broad strategic, socioeconomic, and technological watershed forcing the Army into major changes, if only to adapt. Second, this watershed would not be unarguably apparent or uniformly agreed upon, provoking debates within the Army and the Department of Defense concerning appropriate responses. Unresolved debate would complicate overtures to Congress for funding, once decisions internal to the Army had ostensibly been made. Third, transformation would not be modernization alone, nor would the harnessing of new technologies alone complete it. Instead doctrine, organization, training, administrative practices, and service culture would change substantially as well. Fourth, transformation would involve multiple actors, inside the Army and out. If the pattern established over previous transformations continued, even more individuals and institutions would be players this time than had ever been the case before. Finally, temporal boundaries would be indistinct and the institutional overlap with legacy forces considerable. The very existence of a transformation might be debatable—and thus worthy of a study.

Conclusions

From 1989 through 2005 Army senior leaders attempted a centrally directed and institutionally driven revolution in military affairs relevant to ground warfare that exploited Information Age technology, adapted to post–Cold War strategic circumstances, and integrated into parallel Joint and Department of Defense efforts. Were this transformation to succeed, it would be as dramatic and consequential as the shifts to an Army for Empire around the turn of the last century, to a mobilization-based Army to fight World Wars I and II, to the atomic-armed early Cold War Army, and to the all-volunteer late Cold War Army. As had been the case in these earlier transformations, they would have adapted to radically altered strategic, socioeconomic, and technological circumstances. They also would have driven the Army to dramatic doctrinal, organizational, training, administrative, and cultural changes relevant to the Army's new circumstances. The purpose of this study is to ascertain the origins, nature, and relative success of the Army transformation attempted between 1989 and 2005. Hopefully the results will enlighten and inform and also will be of use to those called upon to author yet another Army transformation at some future point in time.

Notes

[1] Mark J. Reardon and Jeffery A. Charlston, *From Transformation to Combat: The Initial Stryker Brigade Deployment to Iraq* (Washington DC: Center of Military History, 2007), 49–57; Mark Bowden, *Black Hawk Down: A Story of Modern War* (New York: Penguin Books, 1999); *United States Forces, Somalia After Action Report and Historical Overview of the United States Army in Somalia, 1992–1994* (Washington DC: Center of Military History, 2003).

[2] Reardon and Charlston, 49–57.

[3] Funk and Wagnalls *Standard College Dictionary* (New York: Harcourt, Brace and World, 1966), 1422; General Gordon R. Sullivan, Arrival Ceremony Speech, 25 June 1991, in *The Collected Works of the Thirty-second Chief of Staff, United States Army* (Washington DC: Center of Military History, 1995), 3–4; General Gordon R. Sullivan, "Maintaining Momentum While Accommodating Change," *Army 1991–1992 Green Book*, October 1991, 23–28; General Gordon R. Sullivan, Speech to the Association of the United States Army Louisiana Maneuvers Symposium, in *The Collected Works of the Thirty-Second Chief of Staff United States Army*, 142–48; General Gordon R. Sullivan, Chief of Staff Msg, "Building the Force for the 21st Century—Force XXI," 7 March 1994, in *The Collected Works of the Thirty-second Chief of Staff, United States Army*, 318–21; General Dennis J. Reimer, "Where We've Been . . . Where We're Headed: Maintaining a Solid Framework While Building for the Future," *Army 1995–1996 Green Book*, October 1995, 21–26; Remarks of General Dennis J. Reimer to the 1999 Division Commanders/Training and Doctrine Command (TRADOC) Commandants Conference, Fort Leavenworth, Kansas, 19–21 April 1999, Historians Files, U.S. Army Center of Military History (CMH); General Frederick J. Kroesen, "Transformation," *Army* (August 2003): 9–12; Army General Staff Council Offsite Meeting notes, 30–31 January 2004, Historians Files, CMH.

[4] Department of the Army Memo, 8 October 2002, sub: Transformation Campaign Plan (TCP)—Final Draft, Historians Files, CMH; *The Army Strategic Planning Guidance 2005–2020* (Washington DC: Department of the Army, 2002); *Key Issues Relevant to the U.S. Army's Transformation to the Objective Force* (Arlington, Virginia: Association of the United States Army, 2002); Briefing, Army Transformation Office, "US Army Transformation," 20 May 2003, Historians Files, CMH; Intent of the Chief of Staff, 23 June 1999, Historians Files, CMH; Richard Hart Sinnreich, "The Army Should Quit Agonizing About Relevance," *Army* (February 2002): 10–11; Major General Wolfgang H. Korte, "The German Army: Operations and Transformation," *Army* (August 2006): 50–56; Colonel Robert B. Killebrew, "The Army and Changing American Strategy," *Army* (August 2007): 25–34; Colonel Gregory Fontenot and Colonel Kevin Benson, "Transformation? Or Reclamation?—Organizing to Win the War We Have and Those We May Have Yet to Fight," *Army* (March 2009): 39–44; Colonel Robert B. Killebrew, "Toward an Adaptive Army," *Army* (January 2002), 21–26; Brigadier General John S. Brown, "Thoughts on Our New Strategic Environment: A Review Essay," *Army* (December 2005): 17–22; Lieutenant Colonel Mitchell Brew and Dana Baker, "The Transformation of Medical Logistics Since Operation DESERT STORM," *Army* (June 2003): 28–29; Colonel David A. Fastabend, "That Elusive Operational Concept," *Army* (June 2001): 37–44.

[5] Briefing, Army Transformation Office, "US Army Transformation," 20 May 2003; General Gordon R. Sullivan, Letter to the Army's General Officers, "Force XXI," 5 March 1994, in *The Collected Works of the Thirty-second Chief of Staff, United States*

Army, 316–17; General Dennis J. Reimer, "Remarks to Armed Forces Communications and Electronics Association—TECHNET 97" in *Soldiers Are Our Credentials: The Collected Works and Selected Papers of the Thirty-third Chief of Staff, United States Army* (Washington DC: Center of Military History, 2000), 124–28; General Eric K. Shinseki, "America's Army, Ready Today, Tomorrow and Into the Next Millennium: CSA Thoughts on the Line of Departure," Historians Files, CMH; Dr. James Blackwell, Briefing, SAIC Strategic Assessment Center, "Transforming the Army: Learning from the Past," Historians Files, CMH; Barry Watts, Northrop Grumman Analysis Center Assessment, "Revolutions in Military Affairs (RMAs): A Pre-Quadrennial Defense Review (QDR) Update on Transformation in the Department of Defense (DoD)," 7 February 2001, Historians Files, CMH; MacGregor Knox and Williamson Murray, *The Dynamics of Military Revolution, 1300–2050* (Cambridge, United Kingdom: Cambridge University Press, 2001); Michael Roberts, *The Military Revolution, 1560–1660* (Belfast, Ireland: M. Boyd, 1956); Geoffrey Parker, *The Military Revolution: Military Innovation and the Rise of the West, 1500–1800* (Cambridge, United Kingdom: Cambridge University Press, 2001); George and Meredith Friedman, *The Future of War: Power, Technology and American World Dominance in the 21st Century* (New York: Crown Publishers, 1996); Martin Van Creveld, *The Transformation of War* (New York: Free Press, 1991); Major General Robert H. Scales, Jr., *Yellow Smoke: The Future of Land Warfare for America's Military* (New York: Rowman and Littlefield, 2003); D. Robert Worley, *Shaping U.S. Military Forces: Revolution or Relevance in a Post–Cold War World* (Westport, Connecticut: Praeger Security International, 2006); Mark D. Mandeles, *Military Transformation Past and Present: Historic Lessons for the 21st Century* (Westport, Connecticut: Praeger Security International, 2007); Max Boot, *War Made New: Technology, Warfare and the Course of History, 1500 to Today* (New York: Gotham Books, 2006); 1999 Division Commanders/TRADOC Commandants Conference notes, Fort Leavenworth, Kansas, 19–21 April 1999; Army General Staff Council Offsite Meeting notes, 30–31 January 2004, Historians Files, CMH.

[6] Army General Staff Council Meeting notes, 20 November 2000, Historians Files, CMH; Vice Chief of Staff of the Army Council Meeting notes, 7 June 2001, Historians Files, CMH; Watts; Andrew W. Marshall, "Revolutions in Military Affairs," Statement Prepared for the Subcommittee on Acquisition and Technology, Senate Armed Services Committee, 5 May 1995; Defense Science Board 1998 Summer Study, *Joint Operations Superiority in the 21st Century: Integrating Capabilities Underwriting Joint Vision 2010 and Beyond* (Washington DC: Office of the Under Secretary of Defense for Acquisition and Technology, 1998); Admiral William Owens and Ed Offley, *Lifting the Fog of War* (New York: Farrar, Straus and Giroux, 2000); John Garstka, "Network Centric Warfare: An Overview of Emerging Theory," *Phalanx*, December 2000; Vice Admiral Arthur K. Cebrowski and John J. Garstka, "Network Centric Warfare: Its Origin and Future," *Proceedings* (January 1998); Brad C. Hayes et al., *Transforming the Navy* (Newport, Rhode Island: United States Naval War College, 2000); Army General Staff Council Meeting notes, 3 September 2002, Historians Files, CMH.

[7] Mark Sherry, *The Army Command Post and Defense Reshaping, 1987–1997* (Washington DC: Center of Military History, 2008); Briefing, DAMO-SS Strategy Task Force, 1 November 1996, Historians Files, CMH; Briefing, "Quadrennial Review (QDR): Army Plans and Preparations," October 1996, Historians Files, CMH; DAMO-SS Slide Series, "Army Units Have Contributed Over 60% of the Engaged Forces on 25% of the Budget," Historians Files, CMH; DAMO-SS Fact Sheet, Army Lessons Learned from DAWMS, Historians Files, CMH; General Dennis J. Reimer,

"Address at the Annual Meeting of the Association of the United States Army, Washington D.C.," in *Soldiers Are Our Credentials*, 124–28; General Eric K. Shinseki, "America's Army, Ready Today, Tomorrow and Into the Next Millennium: CSA Thoughts on the Line of Departure," Historians Files, CMH; Knox and Murray, 1–14; 1999 Division Commanders/TRADOC Commandants Conference notes, Fort Leavenworth, Kansas, 19–21 April 1999; Army General Staff Council Offsite Meeting notes, 30–31 January 2004.

[8] Briefing, Center of Military History, "Army Transformations Past," Historians Files, CMH.

[9] Richard W. Stewart, ed., *American Military History*, vol. 1, *The United States Army and the Forging of a Nation, 1775–1917* (Washington DC: Center of Military History, 2005), 197–300; Russell F. Weigley, *History of the United States Army* (New York: Macmillan, 1967), 197–264; James M. McPherson, *The Battle Cry of Freedom* (New York: Oxford University Press, 2003); Richard E. Beringer et al., *Why the South Lost the Civil War* (Athens, Georgia: University of Georgia Press, 1986); David H. Donald et al, *Why the North Won the Civil War* (New York: Simon & Schuster, 1996); Edward Hagerman, *The American Civil War and the Origins of Modern Warfare: Ideas, Organizations and Field Command* (Bloomington, Indiana: Indiana University Press, 1988).

[10] Stewart, *American Military History*, vol. 1, 341–85; Weigley, 313–41; James L. Abrahamson, *America Arms for a New Century: The Making of a Great Military Power* (New York: Free Press, 1981); James E. Hewes, *From Root to McNamara: Army Organization and Administration, 1900–1963* (Washington DC: Center of Military History, 1983); Graham A. Cosmas, *An Army for Empire: The U.S. Army in the Spanish-American War* (College Station, Texas: Texas A&M University Press, 1998); Brian Linn, *Guardians of Empire: The U.S. Army and the Pacific* (Chapel Hill: University of North Carolina Press, 1997); David McCullough, *The Path Between the Seas: The Creation of the Panama Canal, 1870–1914* (New York: Simon & Schuster, 1977); "Early Military Medicine," in Office of Military History, U.S. Army Medical Department, http://www.armymedicine.army.mil, accessed 3 June 2010.

[11] Weigley, 313–41; Stewart, *American Military History*, vol. 1, 365–86; Richard D. Challener, *Admirals, Generals and American Foreign Policy* (Princeton: Princeton University Press, 1973); Richard W. Leopold, *Elihu Root and the Conservative Tradition* (Boston: Little Brown, 1954); Stephen E. Ambrose, *Upton and the Army* (Baton Rouge: Louisiana University Press, 1964); Emory Upton, *Military Policy of the United States* (Washington DC: Government Printing Office, 1912); Howard K. Beale, *Theodore Roosevelt and the Rise of America to World Power* (Baltimore: Johns Hopkins University Press, 1984); David Pletcher, *The Diplomacy of Trade and Investment: American Economic Expansion in the Hemisphere, 1865–1900* (Springfield, Missouri: University of Missouri Press, 1998); Harvey A. DeWeerd, *President Wilson Fights His War: World War I and the American Intervention* (New York: Macmillan, 1968).

[12] John S. Brown, *Draftee Division: The 88th Infantry Division in World War II* (Lexington: University Press of Kentucky, 1986); Marvin A. Kreidberg and Merton G. Henry, *History of Military Mobilization in the United States Army, 1775–1945* (Washington DC: Department of the Army, 1955); Richard W. Stewart, ed., *American Military History*, vol. 2, *The United States in a Global Era, 1917*–2003 (Washington DC: Center of Military History, 2005), 7–75, 105–28; Weigley, 342–450; Leonard Wood, *The Military Obligation of Citizenship* (Princeton: Princeton University Press, 1915); Edward M. Coffman, *The War to End All Wars: The American Military Experience in World War I* (Lexington: University Press of Kentucky, 1998); Paul F. Braim, *The Test of Battle: The American Expeditionary Forces in the Meuse-Argonne Campaign* (Shippensburg, Pennsylvania: White Mane Books, 1998); Robert R. Palmer,

Bell I. Wiley, and William R. Keast, *The Procurement and Training of Ground Combat Troops* (Washington DC: Department of the Army Historical Division, 1948).

[13] Brown, *Draftee Division*; Kreidberg and Henry; Stewart, *American Military History*, vol. 2, 7–75, 105–28; Weigley, 342–450; Coffman; Mary Beth Norton et al., *A People and a Nation: A History of the United States* (New York: Houghton Mifflin, 2005), 567–765; Allan R. Millett and Williamson Murray, eds., *Military Effectiveness: The Interwar Period* (Boston: Allen and Unwin, 1988); Boot, 205–304; Knox and Murray, 132–74.; Ernest F. Fisher, Jr., *Cassino to the Alps* (Washington DC: Center of Military History, 1977); Charles B. MacDonald, *The Last Offensive* (Washington DC: Center of Military History, 1973).

[14] Weigley, 485–556; Stewart, *American Military History*, vol. 2, 199–215, 251–83; Robert A. Doughty, *The Evolution of U.S. Army Tactical Doctrine, 1946–1976* (Washington DC: Center of Military History, 2001); Norman Friedman, *The Fifty Year War: Conflict and Strategy in the Cold War* (Annapolis: Naval Institute Press, 2001); Daniel J. Nelson, *A History of U.S. Military Forces in Germany* (Boulder, Colorado: Westview Press, 1987); James M. Gavin, *War and Peace in the Space Age* (New York: Harper, 1958); Robert E. Osgood, *Limited War: The Challenge to American Strategy* (Chicago: University of Chicago Press, 1957); John B. Wilson, *Maneuver and Firepower: The Evolution of Divisions and Separate Brigades* (Washington DC: Center of Military History, 1998); John L. Gaddis, *We Now Know: Rethinking Cold War History* (New York: Oxford University Press, 1997).

[15] Stewart, *American Military History*, vol. 2, 369–406; Robert M. Citino, *Blitzkrieg to DESERT STORM: The Evolution of Operational Warfare* (Lawrence, Kansas: University Press of Kansas, 2004), 153–266; Robert K. Griffith, *The U.S. Army's Transition to the All-Volunteer Force, 1968–1974* (Washington DC: Center of Military History, 1997); Romie L. Brownlee and William J. Mullen, *Changing an Army: An Oral History of General William E. Depuy, USA Retired* (Washington DC: Center of Military History, 1987); Daniel P. Bolger, *Americans at War: An Era of Violent Peace* (Novato, California: Presidio Press, 1988); Anne W. Chapman, *The Origins and Development of the National Training Center, 1976–1984* (Fort Monroe, Virginia: U.S. Army Training and Doctrine Command, 1992); John L. Romjue, *The Army of Excellence: The Development of the 1980s Army* (Fort Monroe, Virginia: U.S. Army Training and Doctrine Command, 1993); Michael D. Doubler, *I Am the Guard: A History of the Army National Guard, 1636–2000* (Washington DC: Department of the Army, 2001), 217–400; James T. Currie, *Twice the Citizen: A History of the United States Army Reserve, 1908–1995* (Washington DC: Office of the Chief, Army Reserve, 1997), 115–316.

[16] Weigley, 295–556; Stewart, *American Military History*, vol. 1, 365–84; Norton et al., 479–508, 567–710, 739–826; Beale; Abrahamson; Stewart, *American Military History*, vol. 2, 7–23, 53–97, 105–30, 199–216, 251–84, 369–408; Kreidberg and Henry; Brown, *Draftee Division*, 1–69; Melvyn P. Leffler, *A Preponderance of Power: National Security, the Truman Administration and the Cold War* (Stanford, California: Stanford University Press, 1992); John L. Gaddis, *Strategies of Containment: A Critical Appraisal of Postwar American National Security Policy* (New York: Oxford University Press, 1982); Lawrence Kaplan, *The Long Entanglement: NATO's First Fifty Years* (Westport, Connecticut: Praeger, 1999); Griffith; Romjue, *The Army of Excellence.*

[17] Weigley, 295–556; Hewes; Leopold; Mabel E. Deutrich, *Struggle for Supremacy: The Career of Fred C. Ainsworth* (Washington DC: Public Affairs Press, 1962); Brown, *Draftee Division*, 1–11, 140–63; John A. Logan, *The Volunteer Soldier of America* (Chicago: R. J. Peale, 1887); Upton; Wood; John McAuley Palmer, *America in Arms: The Experience of the United States with Military Organization* (New Haven,

Connecticut: Yale University Press, 1941); Charles E. Kirkpatrick, *An Unknown Future and a Doubtful Present: Writing the Victory Plan of 1941* (Washington DC: Center of Military History, 1990; Palmer, Wiley, and Keast; James Walker, Lewis Bernstein, and Sharon Lang, *Seize the High Ground: The Army in Space and Missile Defense* (Washington DC: Center of Military History, 2004); Wilson, *Maneuver and Firepower*; Griffith; Bettie J. Morden, *The Women's Army Corps, 1945–1978* (Washington DC: Center of Military History, 1990).

[18] Weigley, 295–556; Stewart, *American Military History*, vol. 1, 365–84; Hewes; Martha Detrick, *The National Guard in Politics* (Cambridge, Massachusetts: Harvard University Press, 1965); DeWeerd; Palmer, Wiley, and Keast; Kent Roberts Greenfield, Robert R. Palmer and Bell I. Wiley, *The Organization of Ground Combat Troops* (Washington DC: Center of Military History, 1947); Stewart, *American Military History*, vol. 2, 7–24, 53–76, 105–30, 199–216, 251–84, 369–408; Samuel P. Huntington, *The Soldier and the State: The Theory and Politics of Civil-Military Relations* (Cambridge, Massachusetts: Harvard University Press, 1957); Leffler; Douglas Kinnard, *President Eisenhower and Strategy Management, A Study in Defense Politics* (New York: Pergamom-Brassey's, 1989); Griffith; Romjue, *The Army of Excellence*; Edgar F. Raines Jr. and David R. Campbell, *The Army and the Joint Chiefs of Staff: Evolution of Army Ideas on the Command, Control and Coordination of the U.S. Armed Forces, 1942–1985* (Washington DC: Center of Military History, 1986).

[19] Weigley, 295–556; Brian M. Linn, *The Echo of Battle: The Army's Way of War* (Cambridge, Massachusetts: Harvard University Press, 2007), 40–243; Stewart, *American Military History*, vol. 1, 365–84; Brian M. Linn, *The Philippine War, 1899–1902* (Lawrence, Kansas: University Press of Kansas, 2000); Frederick Funston, *Memories of Two Wars: Cuban and Philippine Experiences* (New York: Scribner, 1914); Coffman; William O. Odom, *After the Trenches: The Transformation of U.S. Army Doctrine, 1918–1939* (College Station, Texas: Texas A&M University Press, 1999); Citino; Ltr, Army Ground Forces to Commanding Generals, 19 October 1942, sub: Training Directive Effective November 1, 1942, Historians Files, CMH; Doughty; Field Manual 100–5, *Operations* (Washington DC: Department of the Army, 1976); Brian Alexander and Alistair Millar, *Tactical Nuclear Weapons: Emergent Threats in an Evolving Security Environment* (Washington DC: Brassey's, 2003); Field Manual 100–5, *Operations*, 1986; John L. Romjue, *From Active Defense to AirLand Battle: The Development of Army Doctrine 1973–1982* (Fort Monroe, Virginia: Historical Office, U.S. Army Training and Doctrine Command, 1984).

[20] Weigley, 295–556; Stewart, *American Military History*, vol. 1, 365–84; Hewes; Elting E. Morison, *Turmoil and Tradition: A Study of the Life and Times of Henry L. Stimson* (Boston: Houghton Mifflin, 1960), 150–69; Linn, *The Philippine War*; Stewart, *American Military History*, vol. 2, 7–23, 53–97, 105–30, 199–216, 251–84, 369–408; Kriedberg and Henry; Wilson, *Maneuver and Firepower*; John J. McGrath, *The Brigade: A History, Its Organization and Employment in the US Army* (Fort Leavenworth, Kansas: Combat Studies Institute Press, 2004); *Tables of Organization of Infantry Units* (Washington DC: Infantry Journal, 1941); Romjue, *The Army of Excellence*.

[21] Weigley, 295–556; Harry P. Ball, *Of Responsible Command: A History of the U.S. Army War College* (Carlisle Barracks, Pennsylvania: Alumni Association of the U.S. Army War College); Timothy K. Nenninger, *The Leavenworth Schools and the Old Army: Education, Professionalism and the Officer Corps of the United States Army, 1881–1918* (Westport, Connecticut: Greenwood Press, 1978); Brown, *Draftee Division*, 33–48, 140–63; Ltr, Army Ground Forces to Commanding Generals, 19 October 1942, sub: Training Directive Effective November 1, 1942; Palmer, Wiley, and Keast; Jean R.

Moenk, *A History of Large-Scale Maneuvers in the United States 1935–1964* (Fort Monroe, Virginia: U.S. Army Continental Army Command, 1969); *Army Training and Evaluation Program 71–2* (Washington DC: Department of the Army, 1980); Presentation, Howard C. Crowell Jr. (DC TNG TRADOC) to the U.S. Army Armor Conference, "The Army Training System," Fort Knox, Kentucky, 14 May 1981; Anne W. Chapman, *The Army's Training Revolution, 1973–1990: An Overview* (Washington DC: Center of Military History, 1994); Chapman, *The Origins and Development of the National Training Center*; David W. Hogan Jr., Arnold G. Fisch Jr. and Robert K. Wright Jr., *The Story of the Noncommissioned Officer Corps: The Backbone of the Army* (Washington DC: Center of Military History, 2003), 12–40, 185–99.

²² Hewes, 3–56; CMH Information Paper, Robert S, Rush, The Individual Replacement System: Good, Bad or Indifferent? Army Replacement Policy, Cold War and Before (Washington DC: Center of Military History, undated); The Replacement System in the United States Army: An Analytical Study of the World War II Experience (Washington DC: Office of the Chief of Military History, 1950); Brown, *Draftee Division*, 12–32, 140–63; C. M. Virtue, *Company Administration and the Personnel Section* (Harrisburg, Pennsylvania: Military Service Publication Company, 1957); Presentation, Major General John M. Elton (Commanding General, U.S. Army Military Personnel Center [MILPERCEN]) to the U.S. Army Armor Conference, "Personnel Operations for Tomorrow's Force," Fort Knox, Kentucky, 13 May 1981; Bernard Rostker, *I Want You! The Evolution of the All-Volunteer Force* (Santa Monica, California: RAND, 2006).

²³ Weigley, 295–556; Cosmas; *The Path Between the Seas: The Creation of the Panama Canal, 1870–1914* (New York: Simon & Schuster, 1977); "Early Military Medicine," in Office of Military History, U.S. Army Medical Department, http://www.armymedicine.army.mil, accessed 3 June 2010; Vincent J. Cirillo, "'The Patriotic Odor': Sanitation and Typhoid Fever in the National Encampment During the Spanish-American War," *Army History* (Spring 2000): 17–31; Lee Kennett, *G.I. The American Soldier in World War II* (New York: Scribner's Sons, 1987); Edward F. Sherman, "The Civilianization of Military Law," *Maine Law Review* 22 (Spring 1970); Edmund M. Morgan, "The Background of the Uniform Code of Military Justice," *Military Law Review* 28 (April 1965); Richard Dalfiume, *Desegregation of the U.S. Armed Forces: Fighting on Two Fronts* (Columbia, Missouri: University of Missouri Press, 1972); Army Regulation 600–21, *Race Relations and Equal Opportunity* (Washington DC: Department of the Army, 1973); Larry H. Ingraham, *The Boys in the Barracks: Observations on American Military Life* (Philadelphia: Institute for the Study of Human Issues, 1984); Major General Jeanne Holm, *Women in the Military: An Unfinished Revolution* (Novato, California: Presidio Press, 1982); Morden.

²⁴ Weigley, 295–556; Hewes; Leopold; Stephen Skowronek, *Building a New American State: The Expansion of National Administrative Capacities, 1877–1920* (Cambridge: Cambridge University Press, 1982); Edgar F. Raines Jr., *Evolution of the Office of the Deputy Chief of Staff for Operations and Plans, 1903–1991* (Washington DC: Center of Military History, 1992); Francis T. Julia, *Army Staff Reorganization 1903–1985* (Washington DC: Center of Military History, 1987); Mark Skinner Watson, *Chief of Staff: Prewar Plans and Preparations* (Washington DC: Center of Military History, 1950); Maurice Matloff and Edwin M. Snell, *Strategic Planning for Coalition Warfare: 1941–1942* (Washington DC: Center of Military History, 1953); Maurice Matloff, *Strategic Planning for Coalition Warfare:1943–1944* (Washington DC: Center of Military History, 1959); Raines and Campbell; Brownlee and Mullen; George C. Wilson, *This War Really Matters: Inside the Fight for Defense Dollars* (Washington DC: CQ Press, 2000); Mandeles, 1–13, 71–101.

[25] Weigley, 295–556; Stewart, *American Military History*, vol. 1, 365–84; Cosmas; Rush; Deutrich; Stewart, *American Military History*, vol. 2; Brown, *Draftee Division*; Maxwell D. Taylor, *The Uncertain Trumpet* (Westport, Connecticut: Greenwood Press, 1974); Knox and Murray, 1–56; Parker; John A. Lynn, *Giant of the Grand Siecle: The French Army, 1610–1715* (Cambridge: Cambridge University Press, 1997); Dennis E. Showalter, *Railroads and Rifles: Soldiers, Technology, and the Unification of Germany* (Hamden, Connecticut: Archon Books, 1975); Jon T. Sumida, *In Defense of Naval Supremacy: Financial Limitation, Technological Innovation, and British Naval Policy, 1889–1914* (Boston: Routledge,1993); Jonathan M. House, *Combined Arms Warfare in the Twentieth Century* (Lawrence, Kansas: University Press of Kansas, 2001); Don Higgenbotham, ed., *Reconsiderations on the Revolutionary War: Selected Essays* (Westport, Connecticut: Greenwood Press, 1978); Bernard A. Weisberger, *America Afire: Jefferson, Adams and the Revolutionary Election of 1800* (New York: Morrow, 2000).

CHAPTER 2

The Tectonic Shift, 1989–1991

We have characterized historical Army transformations as redesigns in response to radically altered strategic, socioeconomic, and technological circumstances. The United States Army has not changed for the sake of change alone but has proven creditably adaptive when pressed. It would again find itself pressed by dramatic developments during the period 1989 through 1991. Within these few years strategic, socioeconomic, and technological changes occurred or became apparent whose cumulative effect would be tectonic. Army leaders recognized the imminence of a paradigm shift, even though its direction and ultimate dimensions remained unclear. They solidified a framework for change, initiated relevant planning, and undertook some changes that had immediate effects. Let us examine the Army as it existed in 1989, discuss the dramatic events of 1989–1991, and describe the Army's initial efforts to adapt to its newly emerging circumstances.

The United States Army in 1989

Going into 1989, the United States Army had focus. Chief of Staff General Carl E. Vuono unequivocally stated "the Soviets continue to present the most dangerous threat to our interests and allies throughout the world."[1] Not only that, the Soviet threat continued "to grow and become more sophisticated."[2] Only the Soviet Union had the capability to destroy the United States and deployed forces requisite to do so. In Europe, confrontation between the superpowers had been visible and direct for forty years. In the Middle East, American war plans envisioned a Soviet drive south for oil and saltwater access. Cuba and North Korea remained afloat by the virtue of Soviet largesse. Perturbations in the Third World were generally painted in some shade of red. Only Communist China posed a significant threat external to the Soviet umbrella. China's threat boiled down to the Taiwan Straits, however, and that was a Navy problem.[3]

The Army's disposition reflected the threat. The Commander in Chief, United States Army, Europe (USAREUR), and Seventh Army, General Crosbie E. Saint, began his annual report in the Association of the United States Army's *Green Book* with the words "general defense plan," thus giving the "GDP" pride of place in the priorities of his command.[4] More than 200,000 of the Army's 770,000 active-component personnel were assigned to

Heavy forces deploy from the United States to Europe
for REFORGER exercises.

Europe: two corps, four heavy divisions, three separate brigades, two armored cavalry regiments, and numerous supporting units. These served alongside six corps of similarly heavily equipped allied units. In case of crisis, the Americans were to be reinforced in accordance with a national commitment to provide the North Atlantic Treaty Organization (NATO) ten divisions within ten days. Units rapidly flown in from the United States would draw Pre-positioning of Materiel Configured to Unit Sets (POMCUS) equipment from sites in Belgium, Germany, Luxembourg, and the Netherlands, and then race to their deployment areas. Procedures were rehearsed in massive annual Return of Forces to Germany (REFORGER) exercises, wherein thousands of combat vehicles streamed along the *Autobahnen* and into the German countryside. Beyond these early arrivals, the remainder of the Army's twelve active-component and ten reserve-component divisions stationed in the United States—and many smaller units besides—figured somewhere in the war plans for Europe, as did further divisions to be activated and trained by the reserve component's twelve training divisions in accordance with mobilization plans. The European allies were similarly committed to national mobilization on a gigantic scale. Beyond Europe, war plans existed based upon the Army's two remaining active-component divisions—an infantry division each in Korea and Hawaii—and upon contingencies in the Middle East. These were, by comparison with those pertaining to Europe, modest.[5]

The GDP was not just stacks of papers locked in the safes of obscure staff officers. They were organizing principles for a way of life. From them units at every level derived mission essential task lists (METLs) defining what they were to prepare for. USAREUR platoon sergeants and leaders in the chain above them sported "battle books" with maps, diagrams, photographs, and checklists detailing where they would go and what they would do "when the balloon went up." Monthly readiness tests spilled soldiers out of homes and barracks in races through the darkness. Woe be to the unit that did not "bust the gate" of its motor pool on time or could not readily achieve the cherished status of "REDCON One." Training was a continuous rehearsal for the envisioned future battle. Home station training stressed requisite individual skills and drills at the small-unit level. Once or, more happily, twice a year USAREUR combat battalions trekked to major training areas at Hohenfels and Grafenwohr. At Hohenfels they maneuvered through tough terrain against an experienced opposing force and engaged their adversaries with Multiple Integrated Laser Engagement System (MILES) gear under the watchful eyes of seasoned Observer Controllers (OCs). At Grafenwohr they tested their marksmanship, time after time, target after target. A tank commander's sense of self-worth, for example, was largely associated with how quickly and with how few rounds his crew dispatched two moving targets from beyond twelve hundred meters, along with the nine other specific engagements prescribed by Tank Table VIII. Soldiers in other branches had similarly well-defined tasks, conditions, and standards to govern their training. Heavy units stationed in the United States mirrored this studied preparation for a Soviet-style opponent, capping their training year with gunnery and maneuvers against Soviet surrogates in the expansive and thoroughly modernized National Training Center (NTC) at Fort Irwin, California. "Stateside" commanders sported their own "battle books," elaborating on their POMCUS sites and anticipated races down the *Autobahnen* into GDP positions. There was also a Joint Readiness Training Center (JRTC), then at Fort Chaffee, Arkansas, designed for the Army's more lightly equipped units. Even here the diminished threat had Soviet-inspired adversaries in mind.[6]

The Army of 1989 had as much reason to be proud of the quality of its personnel as it did the rigor of its training. Over 98 percent of its soldiers were high school graduates, and fewer than 5 percent tested as the less desirable Category IV. A decade of stressing personal and vocational development—"Be All You Can Be"—in recruiting for the all-volunteer Army had attracted young people intending to make something of themselves. In the preceding ten years the percentage of active-component accessions with high school diplomas had almost doubled, and the percentage of Category IV accessions plummeted tenfold. The notion of developing socioeconomic opportunities through military service appealed most to those whose opportunities outside of the Army seemed circumscribed. Thirty-three percent of the enlisted strength was black, for example, up from 14 percent in the draftee Army of 1971. The percentage of women had leaped from 1.5 percent to 10.5 percent during the same period. Soldiers may have joined the Army intending to serve a single tour, learn a vocation, and take advantage of the Montgomery GI Bill's educational opportunities thereafter, but many stayed. Of 87,232 first-term soldiers eligible to reenlist in Fiscal Year (FY) 1989, for example, 42,911 reenlisted—almost half.

Reenlistment rates for more senior soldiers exceeded 90 percent. Such robust retention provided an ample supply of noncommissioned officers (NCOs), and a thoughtfully layered Noncommissioned Officer Educational System (NCOES) guaranteed that these officers received appropriate training as they advanced into each level of rank. Each military occupational specialty (MOS) featured a hierarchy of skill qualification tests (SQTs) that further defined the expectations of every soldier. For some time active- and reserve-component soldiers had been enabled to focus on soldiering proper, since Department of the Army (DA) civilians carried the lion's share of the weight for depot, logistical, communications, and training support functions. At the end of FY1989, 487,852 DA civilians were on the books, of whom 71,431 were foreign nationals. Of the foreign nationals, about 48,000 served in Germany.[7]

The 594,000 soldiers of the United States Army Reserve (USAR) and 467,000 soldiers of the Army National Guard (ARNG) reflected the superb qualitative potential of their 770,000 brethren in the active component, but enjoyed far less training and preparation. Their 38 or 39 days a year for unit training was perhaps a sixth of the time active units spent, and geographical dispersion proved problematic as well. National Guard battalions averaged a geographical footprint 150 miles in radius, with constituent units averaging 130 miles to their major equipment storage sites. "Late deploying" units were equipped to a standard of 65 percent or less, further complicating training. Since the advent of the Total Army concept in the 1970s reserve-component units had been integral to the war plans of active-component units, however, and many combat support and combat service support specialties disproportionately resided in the reserve component. For example, 97 percent of the Army's civil affairs and 87 percent of its psychological operations capability was in the Army Reserve. Tens of thousands of Guardsmen and Reservists participated as individuals or small units in overseas deployment training (ODT) to sharpen skills and enhance coordination with active-component counterparts with whom war plans associated them. There nevertheless was a broad understanding that the "citizen-soldiers" of the reserve component were a mobilization asset more so than an immediate capability and were to be committed "in time of war or national emergency." The Army Reserve sustained 24 percent of the Total Army force structure with 4 percent of its budget, and the National Guard contributed 46 percent of the Total Army's combat strength even more parsimoniously. This had profound implications for training, sustainment, and—perhaps most topical at the time—modernization.[8]

Modernization was on the mind of the United States Army in 1989. To soldiers in the field the term was more often associated with something they were wrapping up rather than with something yet to come. A post-Vietnam "renaissance" with respect to training and doctrine, and radically increased defense spending during the 1980s, led to the development and fielding of the so-called "big five": the M1 Abrams tank, the Bradley infantry fighting vehicle, the AH–64 Apache attack helicopter, the UH–60 Black Hawk utility helicopter, and the Patriot Missile System. Advanced munitions such as the Hellfire missile, the Copperhead artillery round, and the Multiple Launch Rocket System (MLRS) promising quantum leaps in accuracy and firepower were also being

In the 1980s the so-called "big five" modernized U.S. Army equipment. Top to bottom, *Abrams tank, Apache helicopter, Patriot Missile System, Black Hawk helicopter, and Bradley infantry fighting vehicle*

fielded. Major "end items" such as tanks or helicopters required a panoply of auxiliary and constituent equipment: radios, sights, machine guns, diagnostic equipment, and so on. This had to be replaced as well. A "modernized" battalion was one that rolled or flew with this latest hardware. Each division had a force modernization office, generally under the supervision of its operations and training officer (G–3), overseeing the "rollover" of constituent units from antiquated to new equipment.[9]

"Rollover" was an elaborate and carefully coordinated process. A battalion "stood down" from an active training status for ninety days and prepared its legacy equipment for turn-in. The legacy equipment, destined for units the GDP characterized as "late arriving" or for war reserves, was inspected and its shortcomings identified by specialist teams external to the battalion. The battalion corrected the shortcomings, brought the equipment to a fully operational status, serviced it, submitted it for reinspection, and shipped it out for disposition if it passed. The process was neither easy nor cheap. The first USAREUR battalion to roll over from the M1 to the M1A1 tank, for example, complied with ninety-five "turn-in standards" on each tank and submitted over $1,200,000 in requisitions. Once shorn of its heavy equipment, the battalion "covered down" on a "unit set" of the new equipment intended to replace it. The unit set was an intimidating array of end items and auxiliary and constituent equipment, all of which had to be inspected, inventoried, serviced, and signed for. The battalion next took to the field to familiarize itself with its new equipment. Rigorous training progressed from individual skills such as licensing drivers or safety-proofing loaders through challenging fire and maneuver at the company level. Leaps had to be made with respect to doctrine, organization, and logistics as well as mechanical technique. A Bradley infantry battalion performed altogether differently than one borne by M113 personnel carriers, for example, and thermal sights totally altered the nature of night combat for those equipped with them. The M1A1 tank guzzled diesel to the tune of two gallons per mile, and logisticians had to reorganize and reequip to accommodate such consumption. High-tech repair components were often "black boxes," items organizational mechanics simply replaced rather than attempted to repair. This in turn increased the technical complexity of diagnostic equipment and the volume of repair parts shuttling forward and back.[10]

Some in the Army worked toward technologies beyond those embedded in the "big five" and other systems already being fielded. Soldiers and scientists under the auspices of the Army Materiel Command (AMC) envisioned future conflicts featuring robotics, directed energy, advanced materials and materials processing, advanced power generation and storage, biotechnology, microelectronics, photonics, acoustics, signal processing, artificial intelligence, low observables, and space technology. The AMC Commander, General Louis C. Wagner Jr., postulated a 2010 scenario wherein American soldiers armed with such capabilities defeated a Warsaw Pact invasion of Central Europe. Interestingly, neither the deliberations nor the vision particularly anticipated the Information Age as we now define it. The dramatic breakthroughs of hypertext markup language (HTML), hypertext transfer protocols (HTTP), and practical browsers remained in the future. Concerning these, more later.

It should also be noted that the Army was already doing a great deal digitally, even if the term "digital" was not yet in its lexicon as such. Trainers drilled with such computer-driven simulations as the Battle Command Training Program's (BCTP's) Corps Battle Simulation System (CBS), Army Training Battle Simulation System (ARTBASS), and unit conduct-of-fire trainer (UCOFT). Logisticians retailed through the Tactical Army Combat Service Support Computer System (TACCS), accounted through the Standard Property Book System–Redesignated (SPBS-R), and maintained through the Standard Army Maintenance System (SAMS). Personnel managers relied upon the Standard Installation/Division Personnel Reporting System (SIDPERS) and were developing a computerized Company/Battalion Administrative System (CBAS) and an Optical Digital Image Military Personnel Records System. Network-centric warfare was a phenomenon of the future, but the soldiers of 1989 were already gaining experience with bits and pieces that would be relevant to it.[11]

The United States Army of 1989 was a muscular, well-organized machine poised to take on its Soviet adversary around the world. Robust forward-deployed forces were trained to the highest standard and supported by war and mobilization plans directing rapid and sustained reinforcement. Soldiers, whether active or reserve, were of unprecedented quality and thoughtfully prepared for roles they were to play. Long-term modernization plans were coming to fruition, depositing cascades of advanced equipment working from the Army's front line back. The Army was committed to the Cold War for the long haul, envisioning mammoth conflict with the Soviets at least as far as twenty years out. It was comfortably on an azimuth it had been on for forty years.

Defense Reorganization

The Army's senior leadership could take comfort that it had both near-term modernization programs running on their own momentum and long-term visionaries contemplating potential new technologies. The issues dominating its immediate attention that most likely might be characterized as transformational were not technological, however. The Department of Defense Reorganization Act of 1986 (Goldwater-Nichols Act), the FY1987 National Defense Authorization Act (establishing the United States Special Operations Command, among other provisions), and the Intermediate-Range Nuclear Forces (INF) Treaty ratified on 27 May 1988, substantially altered the role of the Department of the Army.

Defense reformers had long aspired to reduce the autonomy of and improve coordination among the Army, Navy, Marine Corps, and Air Force. The Goldwater-Nichols Act was a dramatic demonstration of congressional authority directed toward that purpose. It reinforced the authority of the Chairman of the Joint Chiefs of Staff over the Joint Staff and singularly identified him as the voice of the uniformed services. It enhanced the control joint theater commanders overseas had over forces assigned to them, focusing their chain of command through the Secretary of Defense rather than the Joint Chiefs as a body. It expanded the Joint Staff from 1,400 to 1,627 and from five to eight directorates. Headquarters, Department of the Army, was to be reduced from 3,653 to 3,105, and the other services similarly trimmed. The act established the four-star position of Vice Chairman of the Joint Chiefs of Staff, assuming additional seasoned leadership would be necessary to drive the enlarging Joint Staff, to coordinate with the newly more autonomous theater commanders, and to bring recalcitrant services to heel. Future generations of officers would be inoculated against service parochialism by prescribing joint training and experience from an early age. In due course promotion to flag rank would require at least one extended joint assignment as a field-grade officer, and blocks of joint instruction would enter the curriculum of all service schools. Goldwater-Nichols did not change existing war plans, however, and sharp lines separating service responsibilities for training, sustainment, and readiness from theater responsibilities for operational control were not always easy to draw. The Army in the field continued on its Cold War azimuth; the effects of Goldwater-Nichols outside the "Beltway" were yet to be seen.[12]

Somewhat less visible than Goldwater-Nichols' emphasis upon joint integration was its emphasis upon civilian control. Functions that had previously resided wholly within the uniformed Army Staff migrated to the Army Secretariat or the Office of the Secretary of Defense. These included acquisition, auditing, budget, comptroller, information management, inspector general, legislative affairs, public affairs, and research and development. This was to tighten the Secretary of Defense's grip on processes whereby services might slink back into parochial nonconformity. As the Department of the Army reorganized, political appointees newly in charge of such functions found themselves teamed up with nominally subordinate career civil servants who had been at their jobs for years and with senior officers enjoying a breadth of uniformed experience. The resultant teams generally worked out, and a three-star Director of the Army Staff (DAS) assumed the mission of coordinating the activities of the uniformed Army Staff with those of the increasingly empowered civilian Secretariat. The Chief of Staff's control over procurement and sustainment had been diffused, however, and he now had to consult with the Secretary or Secretariat rather than commit on his own authority with respect to them. It remained to be seen whether the parochialism precluded trumped the delay and inefficiencies introduced. It may be worth noting that the ongoing "modernization" functions of getting such items as the M1A1 Abrams tank or AH–64 Apache helicopter to units in the field remained largely under uniformed control, whereas more distantly focused research and development migrated to the Secretariat.[13]

A provision of the FY1987 National Defense Authorization Act established the Assistant Secretary of Defense for Special Operations and Low Intensity Conflict (ASD SO/LIC). Another provision split off the United States Special Operations Command (USSOCOM), envisioning it as a joint command in its own right, with a budget independent of the services. Ultimately such "special operators" as Army Green Berets, Navy SEALs, and aviators in various classified programs would migrate here. The idea was to achieve more effective coordination of such special operations forces across service lines, especially when operating at the low end of the combat spectrum. The failed 1980 hostage rescue mission in Iran offered an example of the price paid absent such coordination, as did some features of the Grenada intervention in 1983. The Special Operations Command would be analogous to a theater with respect to command and control—and relatively autonomous once forces had been committed to it. Unlike a theater command, however, its area of operations would be worldwide. The overwhelming majority of Special Operations Command manpower would come from the Army. The redesign removed the Army—and to a lesser extent the Marine Corps—from primacy with respect to envisioning and executing low-intensity conflict. Now another headquarters would be responsible for operations, resource planning, and, increasingly, training. This threatened the Army's standing argument for multipurpose forces—forces prepared for the high end of the combat spectrum that could adapt when necessary to the low end—in favor of forces tailored for the low end.[14]

The Pershing missile gave the U.S. Army a nuclear punch.

The Army's role was diminishing at the top end of the combat spectrum as well. The INF Treaty ratified on 27 May 1988 eliminated all ground-launched and cruise ballistic missiles with ranges between 500 and 5,500 kilometers. This struck the Pershing II missile from the Army's inventory and took long strides toward eliminating the Army as a nuclear player. Since the 1950s the Army had fielded somewhat euphemistically labeled "non-strategic nuclear weapons" in the expectation they might prove necessary to offset numerically superior Soviet forces. One 1987 Department of Defense study credited the Soviets with 211 divisions.[15] In the thawing atmosphere of the late 1980s American diplomats eagerly embraced a mutual destruction of nuclear weapons and were negotiating treaties restricting conventional forces as well. The numerical disadvantages that had been the original logic for "tactical" nuclear weapons had not yet actually disappeared, however. In late FY1988 the Army secured Department of Defense approval for a new 270-mile-range nuclear missile. This would extend the deterrence still provided by artillery-fired atomic projectiles and the venerable seventy-mile-range Lance missile out to the limits permitted by the INF Treaty. Like the GDP, tactical nuclear weapons drove a culture and a way of life. Generations of artillerymen had grown up in the zero defects mind-set of the nuclear surety program. An excruciating regime of exercise and inspection assured soldiers were up to their tasks and that nuclear materials were never in the wrong hands. The Army remained a nuclear player for the moment, but its nuclear capabilities had been considerably reduced.[16]

The uniformed Army's sense of prerogative and autonomy was eroded by the Goldwater-Nichols Act. The near simultaneous establishment of USSOCOM and ratification of the INF Treaty, reducing responsibilities at both the high end and the low end of the combat spectrum, seemed likely to focus the Army on conventional warfare even more so than it was already. As long as adversaries and war plans remained unchanged, however, what difference would these perturbations make?

The Collapse of the Warsaw Pact . . .

On 9 November 1989, crowds of elated Berliners poured through holes battered into the walls that had for so long divided their city. The youthful and nimble among them danced along the top of the wall, celebrating their newly arrived freedom to move between east and west in a miles-long street party that lasted late into the night. That same day the foreign minister of Bulgaria, Petar Mladenov, led reform-minded colleagues to promise free elections and summarily replace the repressive leadership of Todor Zhivkov. Eight days later Czech police truncheoned student demonstrators in Prague and provoked massive strikes by Czech citizens. For ten days huge crowds paraded "Down With Communism" banners through Wenceslas Square, and on 24 November the Czech Communist Party leader and his entire Politburo resigned. Poland and Hungary had already passed tipping points several months before. In Poland decades of generally surreptitious Roman Catholic, nationalist, and independent trade union resistance to communist rule burst into the open, and the trade union turned political party Solidarity swept up 80 percent of the vote in parliamentary elections on 4 June. The ballot had been rigged for communists to sustain a majority, but voters scratched out the names of communist candidates—giving them a negative vote even if effectively unopposed. In Hungary change came from the top, with communist party officials authoring reform plans of their own, establishing a stock exchange, encouraging foreign investment and entrepreneurial initiative, allowing freedom of expression, and resigning themselves to an eventual multiparty system. If there was a singular galvanizing moment in Hungary, it was the massive 15 June funeral service in honor of former Prime Minister Imre Nagy and other martyrs of the 1956 Hungarian uprising. Their memory had long been proscribed by communist authorities. By and large the collapse went bloodlessly; in Romania it did not. A secret police raid on the Inner City Reform Church in Timisoara provoked protests followed by street fighting. Army units changed sides, leading to further savage conflicts with the dreaded security police. Dictator Nicolae Ceausescu—in power since 1965—provided a rallying point for diehards until he and his wife Elena were gunned down by a firing squad on Christmas Day.[17]

The United States Army's initial reaction to the populist *tsunami* sweeping Eastern Europe was cautious and operational more so than grandly strategic. What needed to change in the war plans? Uprisings against communist rule had occurred before: East Germany in 1953, Hungary in 1956, Czechoslovakia in 1968, Poland in 1956, 1970, 1976, and 1980. Some of these episodes were prolonged; the "Prague Spring" of 1968 lasted eight months. Time and again the Soviets had crushed popular movements with overwhelming force. They invented the so-called "Brezhnev Doctrine" to legitimate themselves:

> When forces that are hostile to socialism try to turn the development of some socialist country towards capitalism, it becomes not only a problem of the country concerned, but a common problem and concern of all socialist countries.[18]

Thus the Soviets asserted a right to intervene to protect "socialism" within socialist countries. At least as far back as its refusal to assist Hungarian revolutionaries in 1956, the United States had tacitly accepted the separate spheres of influence implied by the Brezhnev Doctrine. It was not likely to risk nuclear war now on the behalf of dissidents in what many still viewed as Soviet "territory." As recently as June 1989 the United States and other democracies had done nothing but complain when the Communist Chinese brutally suppressed pro-democracy demonstrators in Tiananmen Square. It was true that the democratization of Eastern Europe was a long-term goal. An underlying premise of the decades old Containment Policy was that the contrast between liberal capitalist regimes defended by the United States and communist regimes imposed by the Soviet Union would become so stark that oppressed peoples would take a hand in liberating themselves. Whether this moment had actually arrived remained to be seen, however.[19]

General Vuono celebrated developments in Eastern Europe but cautioned that "the struggle is not yet over" and went on to point out "History teaches us that the collapse of great empires seldom takes place without great upheaval . . . revolutionary changes in regimes, however benignly they may begin, often quickly dissolve into massive conflict."[20] Secretary of the Army Michael P. W. Stone was even more wary, pointing out "Another area of major concern is the increasing instability in Eastern Europe and within the Soviet Union."[21] The Soviets had sacrificed twenty million lives to secure hegemony over Eastern Europe in World War II; would they give it up now without a fight? General Saint counseled "the need to consider the capabilities of potential adversaries, not just their announced policies. The world still is unpredictable. . . ."[22] If hard-liners determined to reassert Soviet authority once again seized the reins of power in the Kremlin, was it not possible they would blame the West for their troubles and overreact? A book popular at the time, *The Third World War* by General Sir John Hackett and other prominent NATO senior officers, had posited such a scenario, as did a number of USAREUR training exercises.[23] The fate of Eastern Europe was not yet settled and the success of its popular revolts not yet irreversible. The immediate responsibility of the United States Army remained the defense of the United States and its allies.

If the grand strategic vision of a democratized and peaceable Europe had not yet been reliably achieved, unrest in Eastern Europe certainly tipped the operational balance in NATO's favor. About a third of the ground forces

45

available to the Warsaw Pact were from non-Soviet allies, and these were increasingly recognized as unreliable. Front-line East German, Czech, and Hungarian units would undoubtedly have to be replaced. Disaffected satellite units securing Soviet lines of communications would have to be replaced as well. The 10th Special Forces Group had long focused on Eastern Europe. Among other missions, in the event of hostilities they were to operate against Soviet lines of communications. This would be by direct action in the short run and in concert with increasingly organized and well-supported indigenous forces in the long run. USSOCOM's highest procurement priority was long-range aircraft to surreptitiously carry troops into and out of "unfriendly" territory. Prospects for success—both with respect to clandestine operations and with respect to the overall conventional defense of NATO—immeasurably improved with the alienation of former satellites from their Soviet masters. The dark side of this otherwise bright picture was that unfavorable circumstances might encourage the Soviets to "go ugly early"—to rely upon nuclear weapons from the outset. Was NATO ready? Planners throughout USAREUR and NATO understandably tinkered with existing general deployment plans as events developed.[24]

Opinion concerning the permanence of change in Eastern Europe pivoted upon an appraisal of the character and grip on power of the General Secretary of the Communist Party of the Soviet Union, Mikhail Gorbachev. Gorbachev enjoyed rock-star appeal throughout much of the West. His domestic policies of *glasnost* (openness, liberalization), *perestroika* (restructuring), and *demokratizatsiya* (democratization) challenged the corruption, secretiveness, and over-centralization of the Soviet economy and the Soviet state. Abroad he ardently pursued improved relations, trade, and disarmament. By 1988 four sets of arms reduction talks—the Strategic Arms Reduction Treaty, the Intermediate-Range Ballistic Missile Treaty, weapons-in-space negotiations, and the mutual balanced force reduction talks—were ongoing. The highest-ranking Soviet military officer, Marshall Sergei Akhromeyev, visited the Pentagon twice. In 1989 Gorbachev replaced the Brezhnev Doctrine with a policy his foreign ministry spokesmen playfully renamed the "Sinatra Doctrine." The term referred to Frank Sinatra's famous song "My Way," and committed to allowing satellite nations to determine their own destinies in their own way without Soviet intervention. Gorbachev began withdrawing troops from Mongolia and Afghanistan and committed to withdrawing them from Eastern Europe as well.[25]

As welcome as the direction set by Gorbachev might be, American reaction was equivocal. Gorbachev could be making a virtue out of necessity. The costs of the arms race, the war in Afghanistan, and the suppression of dissidents throughout the Warsaw Pact had become more than the moribund Soviet economy could bear. Retrenchment was inevitable. The communist parties of Eastern Europe were directed to work out their own national solutions—in the hopes they would somehow land on their feet. Gorbachev's reforms in the Soviet Union were not intended to destroy the Communist Party, but rather to strengthen it and make it more efficient. Could not Eastern European communist parties reform themselves in their own way? If former satellites assumed a posture akin to that of Finland Soviet influence would be weakened, but this would be offset if Germany were "Finlandized" as well. The prospect of reunification conjured up powerful emotions within the German people. If neutrality were the price of reunification, NATO's military posture in Central Europe would collapse. Given that there already was no NATO infrastructure in France, withdrawal from Germany would confine NATO's military forces north of the Alps to the tiny triangle formed by Belgium, Luxembourg, and the Netherlands. In some future scenario, Soviet forces pouring across the Polish border would enjoy huge advantages over allies trying to wedge themselves into Central Europe through a few North Sea ports. Were nuclear weapons to be introduced, the vulnerability of the compressed NATO footprint would be even more acute. Thinking deep, General Vuono cautioned, "The Soviet armed forces may well emerge from their own *perestroika* both leaner and more capable than they are now and with a force structure that will be several times larger than our own."[26]

Fortunately for the United States and NATO, the German people were at this critical moment well served by the chancellor of the Federal Republic of Germany (West Germany), Helmut Kohl. Kohl would be the longest serving chancellor since Otto von Bismarck. Like Bismarck he would steer German reunification through complex international challenges—albeit without Bismarck's heavy-handed use of "blood and iron." Kohl participated in lengthy talks with the new leaders of the German Democratic Republic (East Germany), which had overwhelmingly committed by plebiscite to a unified democratic German nation. He monitored negotiations among the former occupying powers: France, the Soviet Union, the United Kingdom, and the United States. Most significantly, he flew to Moscow several times to conduct intense personal diplomacy with Mikhail Gorbachev, inching him toward a favorable resolution. There were concessions: Germany would give up all claims to lands beyond the Oder-Neisse and in the Sudetenland; Germany would never acquire nuclear, chemical, or biological weapons; German armed forces would not exceed 370,000; non-German armed forces (in particular nuclear weapons and their carriers) would not be permitted in the former East Germany; Germany, assisted by its allies, would foot the bill for an impressive array of grants, trade arrangements, and economic aid to assist the ailing Soviet economy; Germany would particularly assist in financing the relocation of Soviet forces, due out of their country by 1994. Gorbachev and Kohl ultimately struck a deal. The Treaty on the Final Settlement with Respect to Germany was signed in Moscow on 12 September 1990. It was also called the "Two Plus Four Agreement"—two being the Federal Republic of Germany and the German Democratic Republic, and four being France, the Soviet Union, the United Kingdom, and the United States. On 3 October 1990, Brandenburg, Mecklenburg-Vorpommern, Saxony, Saxony-Anhalt, Thuringia, and Berlin officially joined the Federal Republic of Germany as constituent states. Notably, Germany remained a member of NATO and the European Union, and the disposition of American forces within Germany remained unchanged.[27]

Elated citizens celebrated the fall of the Berlin Wall in November 1989.

This was a great time to be an American soldier serving in Germany. German neighbors, and Germans they had never met, stopped soldiers in uniform on the street to thank them and their countrymen for having protected them through the long night of the Cold War. East Germans exploring the West in sputtering Trabants pulled into American military convoys momentarily halted at *Autobahn Rast Platzen* to add their thanks in halting English or incomprehensibly accented German. American soldiers standing in lines at filling stations reached the cashier, only to find that their bill had already been paid by the German in line in front of them or was spoken for by the German in line behind them. Patrons in *Gasthausen* were eager to share their tables, make complimentary conversation, and buy the brew. Partnership battalions feted the success of the alliance in celebratory rounds of beer, bratwurst, dining, and dancing. Euphoria was in the air. The Cold War was over. Democracy had triumphed.[28]

Gorbachev did remain true to his word and allowed the former satellites to go their own way without Soviet military intervention. Street demonstrations receded, and nations got down to the gritty business of establishing workable multiparty democracies. Gorbachev was awarded the Nobel Peace Prize in 1990. However, fears of a coup by Soviet hard-liners were not unfounded. On 18 August 1991, conspirators isolated Gorbachev in his Crimean *dacha*. On the following day they declared a state of emergency and rolled tanks and troops to Russia's parliament building. The timing was intended to preempt the signing of a "New Union Treaty" creating a less centralized and more democratic "Union of Soviet Sovereign Republics"—a concession to both nationalists and reformers. Fighting broke out, and a number of civilians protesting the intruding armored vehicles were killed. The president of the Russian Soviet Federal Socialist Republic, Boris Yeltsin—ironically a long-term rival of Gorbachev's—galvanized mass protests to face down the invading troops. In a trickle, and then a flood, soldiers joined the mobilized citizenry. Other soldiers redeployed from the area of the parliament building, and the conspiracy collapsed. Boris Yeltsin was a Russian nationalist who had declared the primacy of Russian laws over those of the Soviet Union within Russia. In this he was not unlike nationalists in each of the other Soviet republics. On 8 December Yeltsin met with his counterparts from Belarus and Ukraine in Belovezhskaya Pushcha, and together they announced the dissolution of the Soviet Union and its replacement by a Commonwealth of Independent States (CIS). Russia took the seat of the former Soviet Union in the United Nations on 24 December, and President Gorbachev resigned the following day. The Soviet Union had in fact ceased to exist.[29]

Critics fault the United States Army for not shedding its Cold War paradigm more quickly than it did. It was not clear that the changes were irreversible until Christmas Day of 1991, however. Even with the Soviet Union gone, a resurgent Russia would be the most dangerous of NATO's planning scenarios for at least another decade[30]—concerning which, more later. Even as this book is written, only Russia realistically has the capability to destroy the United States, and only Russia and China realistically have the capability to inflict a strategic military defeat upon its deployed forces. Whatever their relative likelihood, should not these most dangerous scenarios be taken into account? As the Army emerged from the Cold War, it could not completely abandon the *genre* of battle the Cold War had come to represent.

. . . and Other Significant Developments

The collapses of the Warsaw Pact and the Soviet Union radically altered the strategic circumstances of the United States. Even as these dramatic events unfolded, other developments—strategic, socioeconomic, and technological—broadened the paradigm shift. The dissolution of the Soviet Union had ripple effects on relations with other nations and non-state actors elsewhere in the world. Demographics at home and abroad crossed watersheds in 1990 that reverberated as well. The term "globalization" took on a new meaning as economic relationships shifted and breakthrough technologies made their presence felt. The United States Army would find no lack of threats and challenges in this dynamically altering world.

During the Cold War the United States had indulged, or even made common cause with, a number of Third World tyrants and dictators to better focus on the Soviet Union—then the greatest danger. Of these strongmen, none proved more embarrassing than General Manuel Antonio Noriega of Panama. His rise to absolute power had been facilitated by corruption, fraud, blackmail, extortion, intimidation, drug dealing, and murder. It also had purportedly been facilitated by a liaison with the Central Intelligence Agency wherein he assisted covert operations against Central American leftists and in spying on Fidel Castro's Cuba, allegedly for cash. As the Cold War wound down, it became harder to overlook Noriega's misconduct. A Florida court indicted him for drug smuggling. He was suspected of smuggling contraband to Cuba and of providing illicit arms to Colombian rebels. In May 1989 his handpicked candidate for president was defeated in national elections, and he declared them invalid. A few days later thugs from Noriega's "Dignity Battalions" savagely beat opposition candidates in a public setting. American complaints aroused his ire, and American citizens in Panama came to be victims of harassment, intimidation, and assault. On 15 December 1989, Noriega declared Panama to be "in a state of war" with the United States. The following day his soldiers killed a United States Marine officer at a roadblock and assaulted a Navy officer and his wife. President George H. W. Bush determined to intervene.[31]

The 20 December 1989 American intervention into Panama, Operation JUST CAUSE, was an operational masterpiece (*Map 1*). Despite unfavorable weather in several staging areas, 13,000 soldiers from multiple posts in the United States flew in to join 13,000 soldiers and marines already in Panama in near-simultaneous assaults on almost two dozen objectives. To preclude the Panama Defense Forces and Dignity Battalions from taking to the jungle for a prolonged campaign, every enemy unit of company size or larger was isolated and attacked on the same night through some combination of clandestine, ground, airborne, and air assault. Planning had been meticulous; in many cases American

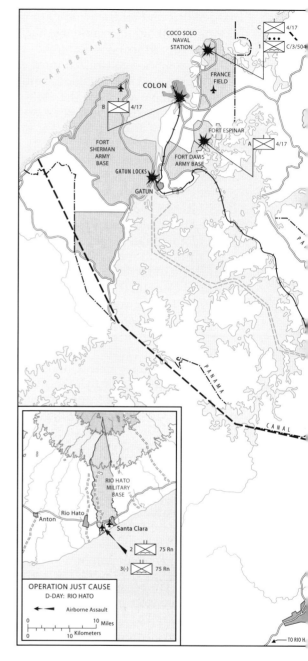

Map 1

units had already been on the ground they were to seize or secure in the course of artfully designed "training exercises." An H-Hour of 0100 allowed optimal exploitation of night-vision devices and night training. The newly introduced AH–64 attack helicopter and UH–60 utility helicopter performed superbly, as

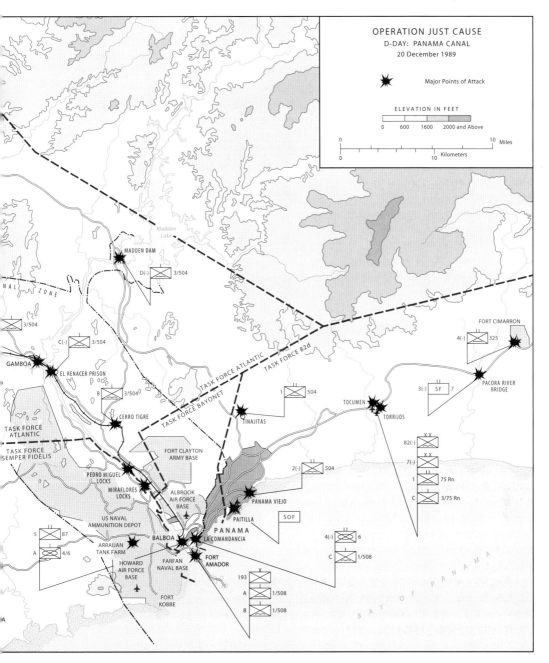

OPERATION JUST CAUSE
D-DAY: PANAMA CANAL
20 December 1989

Major Points of Attack

ELEVATION IN FEET

0   600   1600   2000 and Above

did such aging stalwarts as the M551 Sheridan armored reconnaissance airborne assault vehicle and the M113 armored personnel carrier. Snafus occurred, but initiative, daring, and competence at the tactical unit level quickly overcame them. Significant combat terminated within seventy-two hours, all geographical objectives were secured, and Noriega surrendered after a brief siege of his

51

hiding place in the Vatican Embassy. American losses were 23 killed and 322 wounded, as compared with 314 killed and 5,300 captured among their adversaries. Post-combat operations proved to be somewhat improvised. Fortuitously, Panamanians by and large welcomed the Americans as liberators, legitimately elected Panamanian leadership existed to expediently turn civil affairs over to, relatively little physical damage to civilian communities and infrastructure had occurred, and the Americans enjoyed extensive cultural familiarity—to include the ubiquity of Spanish speakers within their ranks.[32]

Operation JUST CAUSE is worthy of examination in its own right. For the purposes of this study it is even more valuable for flagging issues with which Army transformation would ultimately have to deal. One, as mentioned, was the embarrassment some erstwhile allies would cause when examined in the light of their character rather than of their posture toward communism. Another was drug-enriched international organized crime having become so powerful as to be a national defense issue rather than a police and judicial matter. A third was the fluidity with which soldiers found themselves shifting from combat to post-combat roles. Perhaps most sobering was the extent to which the pervasive presence of casual and civilian Americans overseas increased vulnerability to those willing to consciously target noncombatants.

One of the most perplexing aspects of JUST CAUSE was the task of protecting noncombatant American civilians. About forty thousand were in Panama. Military dependents clustered in housing areas and securing these was an early priority as the intervention commenced. This left several thousand American citizens without a military connection scattered throughout the country. Most of these made it to secure areas or were protected by their neighbors. A number of hostage crises did occur: passengers seized at the Torrijos Airport, tourists and businessmen seized at the Marriott Hotel south of Panama Viejo, scientists and technicians seized from a Smithsonian Institution research team, and a college professor abducted from his home. These were happily resolved except in the case of the college professor, who was killed by his captors. Although Panama was an extreme case, the presence of American civilians would have complicated operations anywhere in the world. A mid-1990s Bureau of Consular Affairs compilation identified 3,142,849 private American citizens residing abroad—not including military and United States government employees and their dependents, or tourists and businessmen temporarily traveling. This demographic footprint manifested itself in some theretofore unlikely places: 9,677 in La Paz, Bolivia; 8,150 in Mumbai, India; 7,000 in Beijing, China; 6,116 in Kuala Lumpur, Malaysia; 3,600 in Almaty, Kazakhstan; 1,182 in Bratislava, Slovakia; 1,250 in Kampala, Uganda, and so on.[33]

The expanding presence of American citizens abroad in part resulted from the increasing globalization of the American economy, concerning which, more later. It also reflected changing national demographics. With the 1990 census, the foreign-born of Asian descent and the foreign-born of Latin American descent in the United States both surpassed the foreign-born of European descent for the first time.[34] This was a generation-delayed result of the landmark Immigration Act of 1965, which removed quotas heavily favoring European immigration. Family ties and possibilities of dual citizenship connected Americans to the world more broadly than ever, as opposed to the largely Eurocentric character of such connections a half century earlier. The 1990 census also established that Hispanic and Asian American populations in the United States were younger and more fertile than native white and black counterparts, promising even more diversity in the future. Almost 60 percent of the nation's population growth at the time could be attributed to immigration, more necessary than ever to provide an expanding labor force in an expanding economy.[35] America's European allies were graying even more quickly than whites and blacks in the United States and thus would be even more dependent on immigration as a source of labor. Millions from North Africa and the Middle East flooded into Europe. Unfortunately, most European nations were far less rehearsed than the United States with respect to assimilation, and many featured blood-related impediments to citizenship. Under these circumstances the children of immigrants too often perceived themselves as an underclass and proved prone to alienation. Islamic extremists would find fertile soil among these disaffected youth. Even as the United States was becoming more global in its demography and in the distribution of its citizens abroad, immigration and demographics emerged as polarizing security issues among a number of its allies.[36]

The rediscovery of ethnicity as a European security issue related to immigration in part. It also related to the collapse of the discipline the heavy-handed communist system had imposed. In January 1990, two months after the Berlin Wall came down, the 14th Congress of the League of Communists of Yugoslavia dissolved in a row concerning the relative autonomy of constituent nationalities. In June 1991 Slovenia and Croatia declared their independence, precipitating armed conflict with the Serbian-dominated Yugoslav National Army. In September Macedonia declared its independence as well, securing the protection of a United Nations observer force that included five hundred American soldiers. Serbs within Croatia and Bosnia-Herzegovina declared their independence of those polities, while Albanian Kosovars pursued autonomy from Serbia. Hungarian hotheads bemoaned the minority status of their countrymen across the border in Transylvania (Romania) and Vojvodina (Serbia). Czechoslovakia gracefully disassociated itself into independent Czech and Slovak republics. The defections of Estonia, Latvia, Lithuania, Moldova, Georgia, Armenia, and Azerbaijan from the Soviet Union were largely ethnic in origin. The Armenians and Azeris immediately took to fighting with each other over Nagorno-Karabakh, provoking a bloody war of some years' duration. Within Russia, disaffected ethnicities such as the Chechnyans contemplated independence, as did Ossetians and Abkhazians in Georgia. Islamic extremists in Central Asia and the Middle East, triumphant after forcing Soviet withdrawal from Afghanistan in 1989, fomented religious and ethnic differences to advance their own purposes.[37]

When ethnic rivalries resulted in open conflict, ample arms were found to fight them. The post–Cold War world was awash in weapons. Huge Soviet stockpiles passed to successor regimes with little attention and few controls. Manufacturers and arms dealers competed fiercely in a market that was shrinking overall, although locally profitable. Weapons the West had provided to resistance movements in Afghanistan and elsewhere found their way into other hands. Through much of Africa and South Asia warfare and illicit arms traffic were already endemic. Between 1956 and 1995 Angola was at war a total of thirty-eight years, Ethiopia and Sudan thirty years, and Mozambique twenty-nine years, for example. By one count fifty-four wars—sustained armed conflicts over power or territory between organized opponents—were ongoing in 1990, and that number rose to sixty-five in 1991. The worldwide refugee population rose as well, up to an estimated 41.5 million in 1990 from 23 million in 1985. Taking advantage of the turmoil, non-state actors such as criminal gangs, drug lords, and terrorists expanded their grip and armed themselves heavily, threatening the welfare and stability of the states wherein they resided. Through all of this the most frightening specter was the fear that nuclear, biological, or chemical weapons might fall into irresponsible hands. For all their flaws, the Soviets had kept a firm grip on such weapons of mass destruction.[38]

Ironically, even as ethnic strife rent societies through much of the world, processes of "globalization" increasingly integrated the world's most prosperous economies representing the majority of its people. Globalization as a phenomenon arguably extends back through Magellan, Columbus, and Marco Polo. It accelerated markedly with such post–World War II initiatives as the Bretton Woods Conference, the General Agreement on Tariffs and Trade (GATT), the International Bank for Reconstruction and Development, and the International Monetary Fund. Relatively steady growth with respect to economic integration through the Cold War years spiked again as the Cold War ended. One reason was the energy with which newly liberated Eastern European and former Soviet nations sought to shed their communist pasts and become full players in the liberal capitalist system. Another reason was the culmination of some twenty years of economic restructuring by the United States and other top-tier economies. These transitioned the majority of their workforces from industrial to service sectors. Automation rendered the production they retained increasingly energy and labor efficient, and their labor-intensive production steadily migrated overseas—capitalized by international corporations as they moved. This created a new international division of labor and doubled the volume of the world export trade within two decades. Americans would buy inexpensive textiles from China rather than North Carolina, for example. A third reason for the circa 1990 spike in globalization lay in the so-called Uruguay Round of GATT negotiations, which progressed from 1986 through 1994. By 1990 the major players were substantially agreed on initiatives to extend international regulation into such services as banking and insurance and onto such tricky ground as intellectual property rights. This cemented the emerging international division of labor and was a considerable leap beyond merely regulating currency exchange rates and tariffs for the seventy member nations that accounted for 80 percent of the world's trade. More so than ever, the health of the American economy and the welfare of its citizens depended on an expansive worldwide network of commercial relationships.[39]

A fourth reason for radically accelerated globalization during this period was the "invention" of the Internet. Computers had existed for some time, evolving from the room-sized Electronic Numerical Integrator and Computer (ENIAC) developed during World War II under an Army Ordnance Department contract to facilitate ballistic computations. Computers downsized with the successive developments of the transistor, the integrated circuit, and the microprocessor. Computers had been linked together in relatively small networks, largely hard-wired. Broader networking required conceptual breakthroughs. Between 1989 and 1991 Tim Berners-Lee, a researcher working in Switzerland, developed HTML and HTTP. These allowed anyone with an appropriate connection to gain access to information stored on a computer server by typing in a specific uniform resource locator (URL). Artfully distributed computer servers would add up to a worldwide net. Shortly thereafter Marc Andreessen and Eric Bina, researchers at the University of Illinois, developed the first practical browser. This was eventually commercialized as Netscape Navigator. Taken together, HTML, HTTP, and the browser were to digital communications what the alphabet was to writing or movable type was to printing. The Internet and the Information Age as we now define them were born. Within a dozen years 665 million users would surf 40 million Web sites worldwide, up from zero in 1991. The economic effects, including computer-assisted design, inventory management, wholesaling and retailing, niche marketing, practical international credit cards, and trillions traded on world currency markets weekly, were revolutionary.[40]

Electronic communications were not the only venue wherein microprocessors and microchips were making their presence felt. Military uses beyond communications had been under development for some time. When wedding sensors with computers, microchips promised ever more timely and ever more comprehensive target acquisition. When wedding advanced ballistics controls and guidance systems with computers, they promised ever more precise target destruction. The term *precision-guided munition*, or PGM, gained currency. Prototypes arguably existed as early as World War II and certainly had been used in Vietnam. These earlier variants had not been particularly consequential, limited in their use and isolated in their effects. Even so, the sky was no longer the limit insofar as technical ambitions were concerned. What if accurate space-based photography or signals intelligence could be dispatched to ground forces in a timely manner? What if triangulation from satellites could be exploited to reliably establish ground locations—or to guide munitions to such locations? While such prospects for a "revolution in military affairs" were debated, the evolution of proven technologies—plastics, lighter metals, improved automotives and fire controls, night-vision devices, lasers, better medicines, and others—continued as well. In 1989 these concepts and possibilities bubbled along in the research and development community and had resulted in a fistful of fielded weapons. None of these systems and weapons had been tested in combat, however, and their consequences for warfare remained theoretical. This would soon change.[41]

Within months of the Berlin Wall's demise, the contours of a significantly altered defense paradigm were beginning to emerge. On the negative side, ethnic violence erupted in a number of formerly communist countries, and these threatened international stability. Freed from preoccupation with the Soviets, the United States had less excuse for indulging tyrannies or ignoring conflicts in the Third World, increasing the likelihood of interventions. On a more positive note, aspirations for global community had leaped forward. A newly affirmed global division of labor inextricably intertwined the seventy nations that accounted for 80 percent of the world's trade. The Internet would substantially reinforce that interdependence. For Americans, increasingly global in their composition and patterns of investment, such an agreeably regulated world order boded well. It suited most of their Cold War allies too, although these varied in their ability to absorb the immigration that greater openness implied. Globalization did present a security dilemma, however. There would be no Iron Curtain—no clearly defined "limes" separating civilization from barbarism—to police. Rather, a threat to the welfare of any of seventy geographically dispersed nations would threaten the welfare of them all. Even before the Soviet Union finally disintegrated, Americans would fight their first war on behalf of the emerging global community. In so doing, they would collaterally unmask revolutionary, albeit theretofore untested, technologies.

DESERT STORM

Saddam Hussein of Iraq bested Iran in an eight-year war that ended in 1988 but accrued huge debts as a consequence. The costly victory left him with a war machine capable of fielding up to a million men and of reliably sustaining half of that number. Soviet largesse and international arms bazaars enabled him to equip his forces with a formidable panoply, including 5,500 tanks and 700 fighter aircraft. Kuwait was a small, weak, oil-rich neighbor. Many in Iraq viewed Kuwait as a nineteenth province purloined by the British, and many in the Arab world viewed it as a colonial contrivance. Iraq and Kuwait had squabbled about boundaries and oil rights before, to include allegations of "slant-drilling" to access a neighbor's oil. Nevertheless, it came as a shock when Iraq's Republican Guards overran Kuwait within a few days beginning 2 August 1990.[42]

The disruption of Kuwaiti oil supplies had immediate consequences for the interdependent world economy. The disruption of Saudi oil supplies, should Saddam Hussein continue his aggression into Saudi Arabia, would have been catastrophic. Although Japan and several European nations were more dependent on Saudi oil than the United States was, only the United States was capable of quickly reinforcing the desert kingdom. Setting aside traditional antipathy to foreign troops in lands sacred to Mohammed, King Fahd bin Abdul Azziz approved American intervention, and a brigade of the 82d Airborne Division arrived on the ground on 8 August. Over the next two months XVIII Airborne Corps—an airborne division, an air assault division, two heavy divisions, and an armored cavalry regiment, plus supporting troops and aircraft—arrived in Saudi Arabia. The defense of the peninsula, codenamed DESERT SHIELD, ultimately mustered 120,000 American troops with 700 tanks, 1,400 armored fighting vehicles, and 600 artillery pieces. These were joined by some 32,000 troops with 400 tanks from local Arab allies. When complete, DESERT SHIELD presented a formidable defense in depth, command of the seaward flank along Saudi Arabia's Persian Gulf, and air supremacy. It also featured a growing coalition, as nations rallied to defend the international system of which they were a part. Wealthy nations like Saudi Arabia, the Arab emirates, and Japan shouldered much of the expense.[43]

World order would not be convincingly defended if Saddam Hussein retained the fruits of his aggression. When United Nations mandates and diplomacy failed to dislodge him, President George H. W. Bush resolved to evict him from Kuwait by force. The campaign to do so would be labeled DESERT STORM (*Map 2*). To this purpose the VII Corps—three American heavy divisions and an armored cavalry regiment reinforced by a British armored division—deployed from Europe following an announcement on 9 November. Two United States Marine Corps divisions reinforced with a United States Army armored brigade deployed to theater as well, as did a French light armored division and further Arab forces. In addition to the United States, Egypt, France, Saudi Arabia, Syria, and the United Kingdom provided a division equivalent or more to the fight. Kuwait provided two brigades and Qatar the framework for a brigade more. The Gulf emirates, Saudi Arabia, Jordan, and Turkey provided critical basing for coalition air, naval, and special operations forces. Disparate coalition membership affected strategic and operational options. The Arabs, with the possible exception of Kuwait, did not want to invade or operate in Iraq. In concert with Turkey, they did not want to destabilize Iraq, encourage Kurdish separatism, or lose Iraq as a bulwark against Iran. European allies were cool about ambitions greater than liberating Kuwait, although they were willing to temporarily operate in Iraq to do so. The ultimately agreed-upon coalition objectives were fairly modest: liberating Kuwait, restoring the Kuwaiti government, freeing prisoners, and defanging Iraq to the point that it was not a threat to its neighbors—particularly with respect to chemical and nuclear weapons. Regime change was not specified as an objective, although many hoped someone would assassinate Saddam Hussein, take over his regime intact, and restore the status quo ante—perhaps with reparations and apologies.[44]

Saddam Hussein had confidence he could survive the onslaught. With months to prepare, his forces dug themselves in depth behind formidable protective barriers: embankments, barbed wire, minefields, and booby traps. Infantry defended well forward, backed up by capable artillery and local mobile armored reserves. These were backed up in turn by formidable divisions of the heavily mechanized Republican Guard, acting as an operational reserve. Stockpiles of munitions and supplies were built up throughout the theater to support the many units along the line or reinforcing it. In the open desert Saddam's forces were exposed to air attack, but the country was ringed by radar stations integrated into a sophisticated air defense system bristling with over 7,000 antiaircraft guns and 16,000 surface-to-air missiles. His forces in Kuwait and nearby southern Iraq totaled 550,000, and these could draw upon substantial reserves and replacements not yet in theater. For all of this panoply, Saddam's greatest source of confidence was psychological. He had famously opined of Americans, "Yours is a nation that cannot afford to take 10,000 casualties in a single day." He did not have to win in the conventional sense; he only had to make victory so costly that Americans would cease to pursue it—leaving him in possession of his ill-gotten gains.[45]

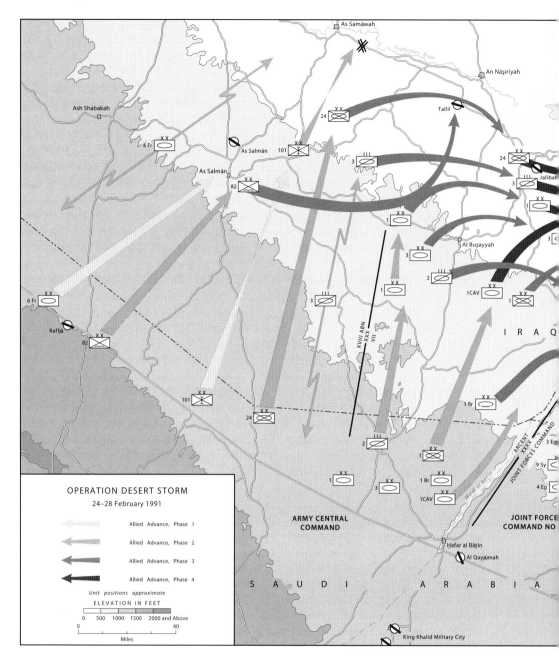

Map 2

Fighting began on 17 January 1991, with American strikes on critical radar stations by laser-guided Hellfire missiles. These were fired from AH–64 Apache attack helicopters speeding undetected through the darkness seventy-five feet above the desert floor. The helicopter pilots' daring feat was made possible by terrain-following radar, satellite navigation, night-vision goggles,

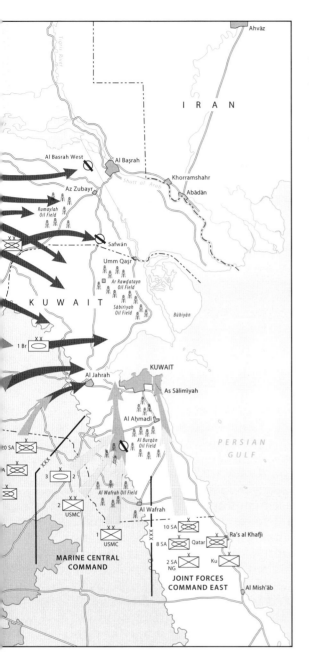

and precision-guided munitions—a package theretofore untested in combat. Further technological wizardry poured into the fray: F–117A Nighthawk stealth bombers with hull designs virtually invisible to radar, EF–111A Ravens with jamming equipment to spoof or disrupt enemy electronics, laser-guided GBU27 bombs delivering two thousand pounds of explosives with extraordinary precision, BGM109 Tomahawk and AGM86C cruise missiles skimming along at undetectably low levels, AGM88 high-speed anti-radiation missiles homing in on radar emissions, E–3 Airborne Warning and Control System (AWACS) aircraft coordinating hundreds of aircraft speeding through the air at the same time, and Patriot air defense missiles streaking upwards to intercept incoming Soviet-designed "Scud" missiles—to cite a few examples. In a thirty-eight-day campaign Coalition air forces systematically smashed Iraqi air defenses, secured air supremacy, smothered Iraqi command and control, isolated the Kuwaiti Theater of Operations (KTO), attrited Iraqi ground forces, and cut off supplies to forward units. Meanwhile Coalition ground forces engaged in technologically assisted siege craft of their own. Dominating hours of darkness with night-vision devices, they forced back enemy outposts, corroborated satellite imagery of enemy defenses, and thinned out Iraqi artillery with effective counter-battery fire. Most notably, once the enemy was effectively blinded by the air campaign they moved the XVIII Airborne Corps and VII Corps deep into the desert, positioned to outflank direct approaches into Kuwait that ran along the Persian Gulf or up the Wadi al Batin.[46]

The ground war began in earnest on 24 February. The XVIII Airborne Corps rushed to seal off Kuwait from Iraq proper. Its French 6th Light Armored Division seized As Salman and faced west, while the 101st

*Vehicles of the 24th Infantry Division (Mechanized) loading
in the port of Savannah*

Airborne Division (Air Assault) helicoptered past it to establish a forward operating base 176 kilometers into Iraq. From these and subsequently established positions swarms of Gazelle, Cobra, and Apache helicopters fanned out to interdict Iraqi movements. The 24th Infantry Division (Mechanized) backstopped these units until they were set, then raced to the Euphrates River and turned east to join the main attack. Far to the east the Marines, flanked by a corps-sized contingent of Arab allies on either side, methodically breached Iraqi defenses along the Kuwait-Saudi border. Breach teams led by M60A1 tanks with dozer blades and mine plows bored through minefields and obstacles while sniper tanks and tube-launched, optically tracked, wire-guided (TOW) missiles picked off tanks, and artillery suppressed infantry and destroyed artillery. Between the XVIII Airborne Corps and the Marines the five heavy divisions of the 50,000-vehicle VII Corps launched the main attack, oriented on the eight divisions of the elite Republican Guard. Crushing Iraqi forward infantry divisions in the wake of massive bombardments and methodical breaches, VII Corps divisions rolled deep into Iraq, hooked east, and came on line. M1A1 tanks extended from horizon to horizon the forward edge of armored phalanxes tens of kilometers in depth. Night and day they drove forward, main guns booming when they encountered worthy targets and machine guns chattering for targets of lesser import. The attack swept all before it from the Saudi border to the Euphrates and from the depths of Iraq to the Persian Gulf. In one hundred hours it was over. Rather than the

10,000 battle deaths suggested by Saddam Hussein the Americans suffered 146 and their allies 99 more. This compared with perhaps 20,000 Iraqis killed and 50,000 captured in one of the most lopsided victories on the historical record.[47]

The striking victory in the Persian Gulf inspired understandable self-congratulation. American equipment, in particular the "big five" that had been the focus of Army modernization efforts, had performed superbly. The effectiveness of precision-guided munitions had been breathtaking, auguring a revolution in military affairs. Traditional virtues had proven their worth as well. The professionalism, rigorous training, and technical competence of American soldiers, sailors, airmen, and marines were clearly manifest. A generation of studied attention to officer and noncommissioned officer professional development, part of a broader post-Vietnam renaissance, had paid off. American officers were consistently and demonstrably competent, and American noncommissioned officers were in a class by themselves. There had been warts, however. The pace of deployment left the earliest arriving forces vulnerable for an uncomfortably long period. Battlefield management and awareness had been imperfect, as evidenced by episodes of confusion and fratricide. Indeed, fratricide seems to have caused the deaths of 35 of 146 service personnel killed and accounted for 72 of 467 wounded. Logistics reached a troubling culminating point near the hundredth hour of the ground war. Imperfect battlefield awareness and constrained logistics limited the net worth of precision-guided munitions. The Army was clearly and immediately dependent upon the reserve component, without having adequately resourced it in many cases. Operations after combat ceased were improvised and of uneven quality. Let us address these warts—soon to be the subject of Army transformation initiatives—in turn.

Wags amid the first brigade of American paratroopers to arrive in Iraq stoically referred to themselves as "speed bumps," acknowledging how overmatched they initially were by Iraqi armor and firepower. Further airborne forces and combat aircraft flowed into Persian Gulf airfields quickly, but only the seaborne arrival of the 24th Infantry Division (Mechanized) several weeks later stabilized prospects for a successful forward defense. Pentagon planners and soldiers in the field breathed palpable sighs of relief when the mighty M1 tanks of the heavy division rolled across the Saudi docks. Compared to precedent, the buildup for DESERT SHIELD progressed quickly and efficiently. Never before had the United States moved so much so speedily from a cold start. This historical detail was not entirely comforting. The window of vulnerability early on afforded Saddam Hussein significant advantages, had he dared to exploit them. Forces arriving by air were too light to contend with a capable adversary on open ground, and forces arriving by sea took too long. This is not to mention the huge amount of shipping a heavy division and its supporting slice required, and sealift shortfalls within the Navy and United States Merchant Marine that had to be made good from other sources. During the world wars and Vietnam, allied forces carried the fight long enough for United States forces to deploy. During the Cold War, heavily armored forward-deployed forces were to bear the brunt of Soviet attack until reinforced. In the case of DESERT SHIELD, forward-deployed forces did not exist, and allied forces were hopelessly overmatched. Within American historical experience, only the opening months of the Korean War seemed to parallel what might have been, had Saddam Hussein attacked early on.[48]

Battlefield management and awareness advanced during DESERT STORM, but not quickly enough to accommodate the pace at which forces moved and the ranges at which weapons engaged. Strategic intelligence was the product of agencies external to the Army such as the Central Intelligence Agency (CIA), Defense Intelligence Agency (DIA), and National Security Agency (NSA), and coordination among them and with the services was imperfect. Division headquarters and above were reliably served by digital mobile subscriber equipment (MSE) and satellite-based communications when stationary. From the division level down, communications relied on a venerable mix of radios vulnerable to topographical interference and range limitations. When moving at a modest pace, the leapfrogging of requisite MSE and satellite nodes worked reasonably well and kept headquarters dependent on radio communications under a reliable umbrella. As the pace of the advance accelerated, times required to take down, move, and set up MSE and satellite nodes stretched effective communications to the breaking point as radio relays insufficiently bridged ever-expanding gaps. A last-minute infusion of largely commercial satellite-based global positioning systems (GPSs) dramatically enhanced the ability of units to locate themselves and navigate the featureless desert. The reporting of unit positions was still by radio, however, and the tracking of unit positions within the operations centers of higher headquarters featured grease pencils, unit tokens and maps—as it had since World War I. GPSs were seldom distributed beneath the platoon level, so there was no immediate way to validate the locations of individual vehicles. Logistical vehicles were particularly likely to have neither radios nor GPSs. Hampered by eroding communications and increasingly dispersed vehicles, the generally shared picture of the battlefield became fuzzy. Pursuit and exploitation became particularly fluid in the aftermath of overrunning the Republican Guard. Advanced sensors, sights, and munitions allowed crews to engage targets at ranges considerably in excess of being able to reliably identify them. Virtually all brigades involved in serious intermingled combat encountered fratricide, or "blue on blue" engagements, and fratricides accounted for a significant proportion of American and accompanying British casualties. At higher levels, whole units disappeared into the fog of war. Perhaps the most celebrated piece of battlefield misinformation was General H. Norman Schwarzkopf's assumption that Safwan Airfield was occupied by American ground forces. He designated it as the site whereupon he would dictate cease-fire terms to the Iraqis with all the world watching, only to find that the Iraqis still occupied it. Near-comedic bullying by the nearest American brigade—in the aftermath of the cease-fire—nudged the Iraqis off the airfield in time for the media event.[49]

By the hundredth hour of the ground war, concern for fratricide rendered American maneuvers cautious and methodical. The ground offensive reached a culminating point for logistical purposes as well. The M1 tank was enormously fuel consumptive, perhaps a mile for two gallons, and tens of thousands of other vehicles required fuel as well. To ensure that fuel tanks sustained optimal levels of fill, heavy battalions and brigades refueled about every seventy kilometers. Combat battalions were accompanied by organic modern heavy expanded mobility tactical trucks (HEMTTs) bearing fuel, ammunition, and supplies of other sorts. These kept up reasonably well with advancing armored vehicles, but the fuelers among them had to cycle back to refueling points when empty. Mobile refueling points that were pushed forward to service the HEMTTs depended on antiquated fleets of trucks from brigade, division, and corps trains to be supplied themselves. Alternatively, there were stationary refueling points south of the Saudi border—at ever increasing distances from the leading battalions of VII and XVIII Airborne Corps. Fuel resupply did not keep pace with the race across the desert, and M1s crossing the Basrah Highway on the last days of the war were "running on fumes." Ammunition presented an opposite problem. Anticipating historical levels of expenditure, battalions kicked off with a "basic load" of ammunition in their vehicles, and another one—and sometimes two—following along in heavily loaded cargo HEMTTs. Phenomenal American gunnery, often characterized by one shot per vehicle kills, and the collapse of Iraqi resistance rendered the huge mass of ammunition excess, yet it took up precious cargo space that could have gone to other things. Most notably, units brought fewer Class IX (repair parts) items with them than they might have wanted. The Army's shift to modular line replaceable units (LRUs)—for example, swapping out and evacuating engines to higher maintenance rather than repairing them on the spot—radically increased the volume required by prescribed load lists (PLLs). Although units sustained high vehicle availability rates throughout the ground war, by the hundredth hour their cupboards were bare with respect to repair parts. Part of the overall logistical problem stemmed from the simple mathematics of projecting so much consumption so quickly through so much distance in a hostile environment. Another part of the problem was information lag. Units had no practical way to quickly anticipate and reliably communicate detailed consumption rates, logistical bases maintained a fuzzy accountability of rapidly moving commodities, and few had confidence newly identified needs could be quickly filled. The tendency at all levels was to horde supplies of all types "just in case," and to carry them along behind in vast vehicle fleets. At the theater level the tendency manifested itself in the so-called "iron mountains" of the logistical bases. Indeed, the Army's ranking logistician in theater appropriately entitled his memoir *Moving Mountains.*[50]

Precision-guided munitions had their limits. At the time they were pricey, running from fifty thousand dollars for the cheapest through multimillions of dollars for the more expensive. It did not make economic sense to fire million-dollar missiles at a ten thousand–dollar truck. It also did not make tactical sense when combat consumption drove down limited theater inventories and threatened strategic reserves. Precision-guided munitions were best reserved for high-value targets. Laser designators, television guidance, and terrain-tracking radar were vulnerable to atmospheric conditions and could be degraded by vegetation. Fortuitously, the open desert within which most combat occurred limited such degradation. Precision-guided munitions did require precisely identified targets, and procedures for identifying, tracking, and handing off such targets remained immature. This immaturity manifested itself most notably in cat-and-mouse operations in the western desert, wherefrom Saddam Hussein lobbed Scud missiles into Israel while the Coalition, desperate to keep Israel out of the war, hastened to destroy the launch vehicles. The launch vehicles proved fleeting targets, and detection by satellites, the Joint Surveillance and Target Attack Radar System (J-STARS), or overflight seldom resulted in identified positions retained long enough to bring in a lethal strike. At times 40 percent of the theater air effort was dedicated to neutralizing the missiles, with minimal effect. Ground commanders, mindful of fratricide, preferred to keep air strikes well clear of their own formations. Inside of the umbrella served by tank and observed artillery fire, such strikes seemed superfluous in any case.[51]

During the DESERT STORM buildup the active Army achieved a total mass of 871,948, of which 60,427 were activated members of the National Guard and 79,118 activated members of the Army Reserve. Of the 227,800 soldiers deployed to Southwest Asia, 37,692 were members of the National Guard and 35,158 members of the Reserve. In earlier wars, the reserve component had generally added like type mass to a steadily growing mobilization. In DESERT STORM the contribution was more often complementary, deploying individuals and units with skill sets not on hand in the active component in sufficient quantity. Significantly, more Reservists and National Guardsmen served in activated units than were individually called up. The performance of the National Guard and Army Reserve overall was a success that strikingly affirmed the validity of the Total Force policy that had been in effect and improved upon since the 1970s. However, given that this was the largest mobilization of the reserve component since the Korean War, miscarriages with respect to notification, disposition, medical screening, and deployment understandably occurred. Differences with respect to post privileges and the processing of pay inquiries grated on activated soldiers. Family support proved problematic, since the families of the reserve component were scattered over wide geographic areas rather than concentrated in the vicinity of capable installations. Roundout brigades filling out active-component divisions were not ready to deploy as quickly as their active-component counterparts would have liked, although they were prepared as quickly as existing mobilization plans envisioned. A number of "CAPSTONE" units designated in advance for specific missions or active-component headquarters also demonstrated readiness shortfalls. With the reserve component now so central to the success of even the earliest deploying units, a candid postwar reassessment of resourcing and readiness would be called for.[52]

When fighting ceased, Coalition forces had liberated Kuwait and occupied a significant fraction of Iraq. Postwar operations were largely improvised. In Kuwait they went well enough, buoyed by a friendly population, helpful allies, host-nation support from wealthy neighbors, and international goodwill. Significant challenges included putting out fires in oil fields retreating Iraqis had set aflame, clearing minefields and munitions, reconstructing infrastructure, and processing refugees. Refugees proved to be an issue in Saudi Arabia as well, most notably at a camp an American infantry battalion constructed virtually overnight near Rafha. In Iraq the situation was trickier. American, British, and French forces remained present for coercive diplomacy, garrisoning the oil fields until the Iraqis agreed to and complied with cease-fire terms. Interaction with the local population was minimal, and units generally remained clear of the settled areas. Although regime change was not a Coalition war aim, it seemed sufficiently agreeable to the Americans to inspire, if not directly encourage, Shi'as in the south and Kurds in the north to revolt. America's Sunni Arab allies argued for nonintervention on the behalf of the Shi'a, thought to be agents of Iran, and the sensitivities of the Turks limited options in Kurdistan. The Coalition stood by while resurgent Saddamists slaughtered the Shi'a, and it provided belated and circumscribed succor to the Kurds—concerning which, more later. Saddam Hussein accepted the cease-fire conditions, negotiated the withdrawal of Coalition forces, and survived.[53]

A Framework for Change

In two short years the comfortably defining strategic focus of the Cold War had dissipated. Going into 1991, Army Chief of Staff General Carl E. Vuono acknowledged that "the conditions that have undergirded our nation's security strategy for more than four decades are being rendered obsolete . . .,"[54] and flagged up alternatives to resurgent Soviets as security concerns: instability in the Middle East; upheavals in the former Warsaw Pact, North Korea, and Iraq; interstate rivalries in the developing world; ethnic and religious strife; arms traffic; insurgencies; terrorism; drug traffic; natural disasters; and others. Neither he nor anyone else knew what the future would bring, but it seemed obvious that the United States would need a rather different Army than it then had. The lessons of DESERT STORM, in the process of being digested, would suggest further change. With the tectonic shifts of 1989–1991 not yet complete, the Army developed a framework for changes that would inevitably occur.

Vuono was a good choice to position the Army for change. An artilleryman, he had commanded at every level from battery through division—to include two tours in Vietnam. He also had commanded at several levels in the Training and Doctrine Command (TRADOC), to include commanding the Combined Arms Center and Fort Leavenworth and commanding TRADOC itself. These educationally oriented positions immersed him in theories of warfare, modernization, and change as discussion progressed with respect to them at the time. Earlier in his career he had earned a master's degree in public administration, served as an operations research systems analyst, assisted the project manager for the reorganization of the Army, and was chief of the budget division in the plans, programs, and budget directorate of the Army Deputy Chief of Staff for Personnel. These complex staff positions gave him a fuller appreciation of the defense bureaucracy and what it takes to move it. As a colonel he served as the executive officer to the Chief of Staff of the Army, perhaps the best single position from which an officer of that rank can gain an appreciation of the Army as a whole. The sum of his experiences suggested to him that thoughtful change entailed the complex interplay of multiple variables. In particular, Vuono was

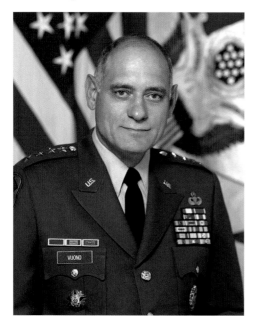

General Vuono

wary of overly emphasizing technology as the driving force. He also believed transformational deliberations could not be confined to small groups if the organization as a whole was to progress. An educator, he distilled his thinking into six "imperatives," promulgated these widely in his own writing and speaking, and had them taught throughout the Army school system. The imperatives provided a framework within which conceptualization of change progressed. Veterans of the era may remember a wallet-size card with the imperatives listed and defined on it, available lest junior leaders forget the direction in which the Army needed to be going. Vuono's six imperatives were doctrine, force mix, modernization, training, leader development, and quality people.[55]

Doctrine is the body of agreed-upon principles and common language that governs the use of forces in war and operations other than war. It provides a vision of how units at every level will employ weapons and other assets. At the time Army doctrine was labeled AirLand Battle, taught throughout the Army school system, rehearsed time and again by units training in the field, and promulgated through dozens of field manuals and other publications. Anticipating geo-strategic and technological change, deliberations concerning an AirLand Battle Future were already under way on the Army Staff and within TRADOC. Doctrine could drive technology as well as be driven by it. The vision of how future battles were to be fought governed the distribution of research and development funds, and these in turn governed the pace at which technologies of military provenance were developed and fielded. In similarly reciprocal relationships, doctrine governed the development of force mixes best designed to employ it, leadership development necessary to apply it, training programs necessary to rehearse it, and the recruitment of quality soldiers capable of implementing it.[56]

Force mix defines the organization and composition of the forces that will implement the doctrine. One criterion is the weight and lethality of their armament. Heavier forces will be best able to slug it out with a like type opponent, but they lack strategic mobility. Lighter forces are more strategically mobile but lack staying power. Special operating forces deploy unique skills against unique challenges. For any given scenario some mix of the three will be optimal, complementing one another's strengths and offsetting each other's weaknesses. For the Army as a whole, the mix should match up with the most probable and the most dangerous scenarios. Another criterion with respect to force mix is balance among combat, combat support, and combat service support forces. Operations will collapse if logistical support is inadequate. Attacks may fail if fire support is insufficient to suppress the enemy. Movement will stop if obstacles remain unbreached—and so on. A final criterion with respect to force mix is the relative inventory of active and reserve units. At the time, active-component units were more immediately available but were so at the cost of sustaining high standards of training and readiness. Reserve-component units were cheaper to sustain over time but took longer to prepare, invoked political costs to mobilize, and could be less frequently used. DESERT STORM–vintage concerns with respect to the CAPSTONE and Roundout programs have already been mentioned. Force mix decisions accrue at every level, from the weapons mix in a rifle squad through the numbers and types of divisions in an army. The force mix of 1989 was designed for Cold War scenarios; the force mix beyond 1991 would be designed for others.[57]

Modernization preserves technological advantages and defers obsolescence. Falling a generation behind in technology can lead to horrific battlefield results, as Saddam Hussein's army amply demonstrated during DESERT STORM. Some technological developments emerge outside of the Army's purview and must be recognized and exploited. Other technologies are driven by research and development resourced or encouraged by the Army. Modernization is more than developing and fielding new equipment. Total package fielding envisioned updating doctrine, refining organization, training operators, and guaranteeing sustainment to ensure that the new equipment was employed to best effect. An M1A1 tank, for example, was more than just a new tank. It was the capstone in a system of systems revolutionizing armored warfare. Doctrine had to be updated to accommodate its radically improved engagement ranges and night-vision devices. Maintenance organizations had to be redesigned to accommodate their potpourri of diagnostic equipment and "black box" LRUs. Recruits to the armor force had to be capable of handling its computerized technology and checklist operator's maintenance procedures. Their leaders had to govern engagement and maneuver boxes that had quadrupled in area. Training had to refine all of this disparate activity into rehearsed and routine procedures. Fortuitously, veterans of the "big five" fielding were familiar with the expansive nature of modernization efforts. This did not mean that they would ever become easy.[58]

Training converts the theoretical into the practical. There is a huge gulf between knowing what an organization should achieve and causing the organization to actually achieve it. Training progresses at every level. Individuals must learn skills all soldiers should have and also skills unique to their MOS and grade. Small units learn and rehearse their battlefield responsibilities. Training progresses through units of increasing size as the organization as a whole becomes better prepared and more proficient. The rigors of combat and the fog of war should be introduced into training insofar as practical. Changes in equipment, organization, or doctrine force training revisions at every level. This in turn forces a cascade of republished manuals, memorandums, and training aids. Training technology advances as well, offering better ways to simulate the challenges of combat. The Army of 1989 was the beneficiary of a recent revolution in training technology. Tank and Bradley crews rehearsed individual and crew gunnery skills in computerized UCOFTs. Units of larger size maneuvered against each other and registered hits with multiple integrated laser engagement systems (MILES). Battalions and brigades deployed to such capstone training centers as the National Training Center in California, the Joint Readiness Training Center (JRTC) in Arkansas, and the Combat Maneuver Training Center (CMTC) in Germany. Here trained opposing forces engaged them in MILES battles, while a hierarchy of observer controllers mirroring their chain of command monitored their actions. Excruciating after-action reviews (AARs) featured observer controller testimony, participant self-examination, taped conversations, and vehicle dispositions captured electronically. Brigade, division, and corps staffs with leadership running two levels down exercised in the virtual environment of the Battle Command Training Program. Here after-action reviews mixed comments from seasoned "grey beard" observer controller mentors with participant self-examination and recoverable electronic files. Fortuitously, these virtual environments could be modified to anticipate—or test—battlefield circumstances that did not yet exist. As we shall see, this characteristic would soon be brought into play.[59]

The integration of new equipment, force structure, and doctrine into an effective training program requires capable leadership. The Army acts on the premise that leaders are made more so than born, and Vuono consciously involved himself in leader development throughout his career. His recent priority had been to bring NCO professional development (NCOPD) on line with the structure and expectations of officer professional development (OPD). The three "pillars" of leader development were institutional training, operational assignments, and self-development. Beginning with basic training or the officer basic course, NCOs and officers periodically cycled back through schools preparing them for positions of increasing responsibility. For officers this institutional training hierarchy had for some time been solidified as the officer basic course, the officer advanced course, the Command and General Staff College, and the Army War College. In 1982 a nine-week Combined Arms Service Staff School (CAS3) was added to hone staff skills at the captain and junior field-grade level. A constellation of specialized schools supported the basic hierarchy with more narrowly focused educational and preparatory offerings, and a number of assignments or career transitions included attending civilian institutions as well. The School of Advanced Military Studies at Leavenworth, for example, was particularly noteworthy from the mid-1980s on in developing selected officers into broadly educated operational planners with an accredited Master of Military Arts and Sciences (MMAS) degree. School of Advanced Military Studies graduates, playfully called "Jedi knights," were instrumental in the planning for Desert Storm. In 1990 Vuono approved an NCO leader development action plan that brought NCOPD more on line with the formal training and educational progression expected of officers. Operational assignments gave officers and NCOs the opportunity to put theory into practice. A mix of line and staff positions of increasing responsibility was preferred, to ensure a requisite breadth of preparation as a leader advanced. Branch career managers—affectionately renamed "career manglers"—shepherded officer assignments from the Total Army Personnel Command in Arlington, Virginia. Much of the time they assigned officers into specific positions; at other times—particularly in the case of junior officers—they assigned them to commands or agencies that in turn were responsible for determining appropriate billets. NCOs received similarly centralized treatment when senior, but through the rank of E-6 were effectively in the hands of battalion command sergeant majors with respect to career management. A third pillar of leader development was self-development. Schools and commands promulgated professional reading lists, professional organizations encouraged the exchange of ideas among colleagues, and during some assignments civilian schooling facilitated by Veterans Affairs (VA) benefits was practical. Senior officers and NCOs were expected to mentor those junior to them—in particular their own subordinates—to ensure career development remained on track.[60]

Quality leaders come from quality soldiers. We have already described the impressive quality of the Army's human material in 1989 and the considerable success the Army enjoyed retaining it through reenlistment. Here we might add the Army's growing realization that it had to recruit and retain families to sustain a quality force. Over 50 percent of the Army's active-duty soldiers were married in 1989—a percentage that rose markedly at higher ranks and in the reserve component. Family members outnumbered their active-duty sponsors by a factor of three to one. Over half of the career soldiers' spouses worked outside of the home, and these brought in a third of the family income. The leading reason soldiers who chose to leave left the Army was that their spouses, generally wives, were not happy. Recognition of these consequences of the shift to a volunteer army during the 1970s crystallized in Chief of Staff General John A. Wickham's *The Army Family White Paper* of 1983. From that point family issues became a priority, with worldwide spousal representation at annual conferences in accordance with the newly institutionalized Army Family Action Plan (AFAP) providing a mechanism to smoke them out. Beginning with the XVIII Airborne Corps in 1984, commanders directed units subject to deployment to organize family support groups for mutual support. This process was largely complete by DESERT STORM. During General Vuono's watch the Army and its sister services pressed for and secured the Military Child Care Act of 1989. This landmark legislation cleared away a thicket of resourcing and policy issues concerning the Army's hottest family issue. Broad mandates to recruit and retain quality soldiers had expanded to include their families as well.[61]

The Army is a large organization. Concepts as complex as General Vuono's imperatives could not survive without proponents—individuals and agencies driven by their mandates to advance them. Vuono recognized this and fixed responsibilities in such a manner that each of his imperatives had bureaucratic champions. For these champions, career success would be in part defined by the insight and energy with which they advanced their imperatives in the face of necessary change. In most cases proponency was the logical extension of traditional responsibilities. In a number of cases several agencies shared proponency, generating a hopefully creative interplay among them. Doctrine was clearly in the purview of the four-star TRADOC commander. He presided over a constellation of two-star branch schools, each of which generated doctrine within its area of expertise. The TRADOC commander integrated branch efforts, developed service-wide doctrine, and coordinated joint doctrine, leaning heavily on the three-star Combined Arms Center and the two-star Combined Arms Combat Developments Activity at Fort Leavenworth, Kansas, and on the three-star Combined Arms Support Command at Fort Lee, Virginia, as he did so. TRADOC also had much to do with force mix, since units ideally should be designed to match the doctrine that applied to them. Senior commanders in the field had their own strong ideas concerning the force mix they needed, however, and were authorized to modify tables of organization and equipment (TOEs) into MTOEs. The distribution of forces among the active Army, the National Guard, and the Army Reserve had a significant political dimension. Reconciling the force mix views of TRADOC, commanders in the field, and the major components fell to the Army Staff, and in particular the three-star Deputy Chief of Staff for Operations and Plans (DCSOPS). He supervised a robust two-star staff division specifically addressing this responsibility and enjoyed immediate access to the Chief of Staff. Modernization fell to the four-star Army Materiel Command insofar as it was a matter of providing new equipment and sustaining it in the field. The AMC commander was a primary player with respect to developing new equipment and led a dozen systems-oriented commands and a Test and Evaluation Command to do so. TRADOC had the important responsibility of envisioning the future and defining requirements, and the Department of the Army retained a significant role with respect to weapons development, concerning which, more later. Training split between institutional training, individual training, and unit training. TRADOC governed institutional training and commanded most of the institutions wherein it occurred. TRADOC also promulgated guidance for individual and unit training and commanded such capstone institutions as the National Training Center. Commanders in the field determined the actual content of individual training in units and unit training, consistently reviewed through quarterly training briefs (QTBs) at each level of command. The four-star United States Army Forces Command (FORSCOM) was particularly significant in this regard, since it commanded virtually all stateside deployable units. Leader development split between institutional training, operational assignments, and self-development. TRADOC again governed institutional training. As we have seen, operational assignments were the result of give-and-take between the Total Army Personnel Center, a two-star field operating agency of the Army Staff, and commanders in the field. The mission of recruiting quality people remained under Department of the Army purview, with the three-star United States Military Academy, the two-star Army Recruiting Command, and the one-star Army National Guard Personnel Center and one-star Army Reserve Personnel Center serving as Army Staff field operating agencies. The Reserve Officers' Training Corps (ROTC) Cadet Command aligned under TRADOC, however. The retention of quality people through reenlistment was expected of commanders in the field, and unit performance in that regard was reported monthly.[62]

The above discussion is incomplete, but it does identify the most significant players and illustrates the institutional proponency sustaining Vuono's imperatives. In addition to traditional relationships, the recently passed Goldwater-Nichols Act introduced the Joint Staff and the Army Secretariat into the working mechanics of Army processes to an unprecedented extent. Reinforced primacy of the Chairman of the Joint Chiefs of Staff over the service chiefs extended beyond operations alone. The new position of Vice Chairman of the Joint Chiefs of Staff provided an ideal chair for the service vice chiefs, who traditionally administered service staffs day-to-day. It also provided a focal point through which Defense Department agencies with responsibilities for administration, acquisition, or budgeting could more directly influence the services. Given emphasis on streamlining administration and reducing redundancy, the forum of vice chiefs chaired by the Vice Chairman, and the expanded Joint Staff, soon became significant factors in Army deliberations with respect to doctrine, force mix, and modernization. Stipulations within the Goldwater-Nichols Act, previously discussed, mandated joint education and experience and bore heavily upon training and leader development.[63]

The Army Secretariat became more involved in change as well. Secretary of the Army Michael P. W. Stone had a strong business background and had served as Assistant Secretary of the Army for Financial Management from 1986 through 1988 and as Under Secretary of the Army after that. In these positions and as Secretary he played a leading role implementing the Goldwater-Nichols Act within Department of the Army headquarters. As previously discussed, Goldwater-Nichols migrated the Secretariat into more direct control over acquisition, auditing, budget, comptroller, information management, inspector general, legislative affairs, public affairs, and research and development. Implementing recommendations of the so-called Packard Commission, Stone and his colleagues streamlined acquisition management and inaugurated a centrally administered Army Acquisition Corps of military and civilian specialists. Project managers would report through program executive officers to the Army Acquisition Executive. They would be funded directly from the Department of the Army rather than through their traditional commands. The Army Acquisition Executive was to be the Assistant Secretary of the Army for Research, Development, and Acquisition, a political appointee. Other members of the Army Secretariat experienced similarly expanded authority into similarly deeper levels within the organization. Collectively considered, these realignments considerably increased the voice of the Secretariat with respect to Vuono's imperatives of modernization, force mix, and the acquisition of quality people.[64]

One of the primary objectives of the Goldwater-Nichols Act was to reduce friction and redundancy among the services. Streamlined leadership exerted by the Chairman and streamlined administration chaired by the Vice Chairman of the Joint Chiefs of Staff would bring unruly services in line, whereas functions that migrated to the Secretariat would enhance the grip of the political administration upon Pentagon policy. Arguments would be internal and firmly resolved; Congress and the public would no longer be exposed to the cacophony of service rivalry. As attractive as such centralization can be with respect to efficiency, it can stifle the broad debates that have contributed much to American military effectiveness. It is hard, for example, to imagine the revolutionary leap to carrier-borne warfare had there not been a creative tension between the Navy and the Army over airpower, the American lead in amphibious warfare had the Marine Corps not been determined to preserve its autonomy, or America's simultaneous lead in both tactical and strategic air-power absent strident dispute between the World War II Army Ground Forces and Army Air Forces.[65] With the services potentially muzzled, privately funded professional organizations heavily populated by retirees preserved the prerogative of open debate. In the case of the Army, the most notable such organization was the Association of the United States Army (AUSA). Founded in 1950 to provide a voice for Army interests broadly defined, by 1990 it sported a capable staff, prestigious trustees, a dozen interlocking advisory committees, and respectable access to both the administration and Congress. Its Institute of Land Warfare facilitated and encouraged education, dialogue, and debate. Corporate membership wove representatives of the defense industrial base into its deliberations. AUSA's resolutions committee carried advice and counsel to members of Congress and the administration alike.[66] Periodic conventions, most notably an annual convention in the National Capital Region in October, drew active Army, National Guardsmen, Reservists, retirees, representatives of industry, and political figures into days of demonstration, discussion, and deliberation. Here debate was freewheeling and the sensitivities of other services not particularly protected; naval personnel continued to be affectionately referred to as "squids," marines as "jarheads," and pilots as "fly-boys." On a parallel course, Congress also preserved its access to potential debate by asking candidates at confirmation hearings if, when asked a question by a member of Congress, they would answer with what they truthfully believed rather than parrot the position of the administration. The answer had to be "yes" to be confirmed, and virtually every position three-star or above required confirmation. Given the ferocity with which the uniformed services inculcated personal integrity into their service culture, this simple measure of holding officers to their word gave Congress ample access to contrary views, should they exist.[67] Parochial service interests retained a voice of their own while complying with Goldwater-Nichols and taking advantage of its better features.

Secretary Stone and General Vuono saw change coming and positioned the Army to deal with it even though the future was far from clear. The Army headquarters was redesigned into compliance with the Goldwater-Nichols Act and prepared to accommodate a greater role for the Joint Staff and the Secretariat in its internal deliberations. Interservice acrimony would be muted, but service interests would nevertheless find a public voice. A theory of change existed that recognized the interplay among doctrine, force mix, training, modernization, leadership, and soldier quality. Each of these imperatives would be addressed simultaneously, and each had one or more institutional proponents committed to advance its assigned imperatives to the best effect. Of particular note, the Army would not allow its transformation to a post–Cold War force to be dominated by technology alone. There was not yet an overwhelming sense of urgency, since the final Soviet collapse did not occur until the waning days of 1991, but change was clearly in the wind. Three items did have to be prepared for immediately: declining budgets, downsizing, and denuclearization.

Declining Budgets, Downsizing, and Denuclearization

The Department of Defense and the Army had been tightening their belts with respect to budgets since the peak of the so-called "Reagan Buildup" in the mid-1980s. The $77.7 billion allotted to the Army in FY1990 marked the fifth straight year of modest declines in real purchasing power. Congressional disgruntlement with rising deficits had led to the passage of the Gramm-Rudman-Hollings Balanced Budget and Emergency Deficit Control Act of 1985, imposing spending caps on the federal government and threatening automatic across-the-board cuts ("sequesters") should they be violated. This led to bruising confrontations between the administration and Congress with the approach of each fiscal year. The most notable of these occurred in October of 1990, when time and money ran out and the federal government actually closed down over the Columbus Day weekend. The Army emerged from subsequent negotiations with $73 billion for FY1991, an effective 7 percent cut from the previous year. Fortuitously DESERT STORM was not compromised by this parsimony, since its costs to the Army were funded by a supplemental appropriation outside of the normal budget cycle. Prosperous allies offset many of DESERT STORM's actual costs with cash or through goods and services provided. Indeed, some wags argued that the Department of Defense had actually turned a profit on the war. The direction that would be taken by future budgets was clear, however. The imminent end of the Cold War sent a desire for a "peace dividend" rippling through Congress. The belt-tightening of the past few years would soon accelerate into dramatic cuts.[68] (*See Chart 1.*)

Vuono sought to conceive a way ahead for the Army in the face of inevitable cuts and then to convince his superiors of the merits of his proposed approach. He was mindful that the Joint Staff and Office of the Secretary of Defense were undertaking their own studies and galvanized the Army Staff to stay far enough ahead to influence events. Beginning in 1989 Project QUICKSILVER examined the TOE units within the Army, and Project VANGUARD examined the Army's table of distribution and allowances (TDA) structure. TOE units broadly encompass deployable units, whereas TDA defines the institutional structure of schools, depots, supporting agencies, and the like. More secretively Project ANTAEUS, named for the mythical titan who remained powerful as long as he touched the ground, had already examined specific reductions that included the hypothetical loss of two divisions, a corps, and other units in Europe. It seemed to Vuono and his staff that the Army's viable options boiled down to two basic alternatives. One was to maintain something like the present force structure of five corps, twenty-eight divisions (twenty active component and eight reserve component), twenty-eight separate combat brigades (five active component and twenty-three reserve component), and supporting units intact. Budget reductions could be accommodated by reducing the manning and training of units, prolonging the modernization of equipment within them, and diminishing research and development expenditures. Within units, rank structure would end up top-heavy as the lower ranks thinned out. In times of recognized crisis, increased budgets would allow the Army to infuse manpower, training, and equipment into this retained force structure. Such a proposal would be yet another version of the "expansible army" concept familiar to the Army since the days of Secretary of War John C. Calhoun and would mesh well with renewed conscription and national mobilization. A second alternative was to slash force structure and maintain appreciably fewer units at high levels of manning, training, and readiness. Savings on manpower would allow research and development to remain robustly funded. Units would be recurrently modernized with infusions of new equipment. The residual force would be small, ever ready, and deployable. Vuono had previously articulated the merits of deployability, versatility, and lethality in a modern army. Vuono's second alternative would maintain such character in a smaller force.[69]

Sobered by the abruptness with which JUST CAUSE and DESERT STORM had come upon them, and mindful that there was no longer a global peer opponent in the short term, Army planners ultimately favored the second alternative, as did General Vuono. This signaled an important step away from long-established tenets of mass mobilization in favor of an immediately available expeditionary army. For the first time in almost a century, deployable readiness would trump mobilization potential as the highest priority for the Army. The last time the United States had had a small but ever ready Army, it was intended to fight Indians. Vuono's chosen second alternative would get a half dozen divisions into an overseas theater much faster than his first, but would get two dozen there much more slowly. Forces beyond that would be generated even more slowly still. This shift from a big war to a small war paradigm was seminal. Secretary Stone and Secretary of Defense Richard Cheney concurred with Vuono. Cheney submitted a plan to Congress envisioning manpower cuts of 25 percent across the Department of Defense over a five-year period, with the active Army plunging from 770,000 to 520,000. In accordance with this plan active-component divisions would drop from eighteen to fourteen by the end of 1995, a planning figure that further dropped to twelve in FY1991. If the United States was between wars, downsizing reflected a familiar historical pattern. What was new was the determination to retain the residual force at the highest possible standards of readiness and modernization (*Chart 2*).[70]

Downsizing the Army was still a vision in 1991, delayed by DESERT STORM and phased well into the approaching decade. The dramatic shift from being to not being a nuclear player progressed more quickly. The implications of the INF Treaty of May 1988 have already been discussed. The effort to wedge a 270-mile-range nuclear missile under the treaty's limits proved short-lived. This initiative, the venerable seventy-mile-range Lance surface-to-surface missile, and artillery-fired atomic projectiles for 8-inch and 155-mm. howitzers were all swept away by a series of "presidential nuclear initiatives." Eliminating the Army's tactical nuclear weapons made sense at the time. Mammoth Warsaw Pact forces that had been their original logic were dissipating. Nonnuclear precision-guided munitions (PGMs) seemed capable of many roles envisioned for tactical nuclear weapons, offsetting lesser yields through greater accuracy. European allies, striving to put Cold War dangers behind them, were eager to be rid of weaponry that might make them an

Chart 1—The Army Budget, 1985–2005
(In five-year increments in billions—constant 2009 dollars)

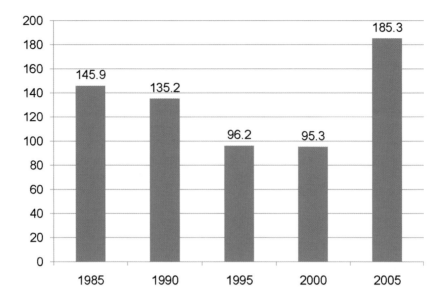

Chart 2—Army Active-Duty Strength, 1985–2005
(In five-year increments in thousands)

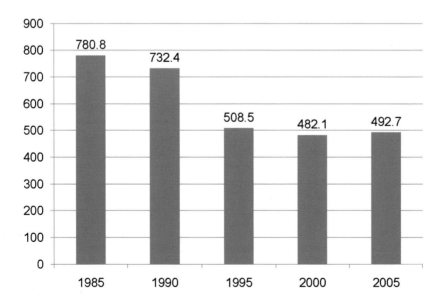

attractive nuclear target. The Goldwater-Nichols Act, emphasizing jointness and hostile to redundancy, reinforced a notion that nuclear munitions could best be left to the Air Force and Navy. An expeditionary army would be nimbler if unencumbered by nuclear weapons and their attendant support and security apparatus. Most important, the elimination of American tactical nuclear weapons was associated with a corresponding elimination of Soviet tactical nuclear weapons and facilitated further diplomatic engagement. As the Soviet Union crumbled, defense analysts feared nuclear weapons might fall into the wrong hands. Tactical nuclear weapons seemed the most vulnerable to such displacement. The mutual destruction of tactical nuclear weapons made such risks far less likely. Propelled by these incentives, the presidential nuclear initiatives moved swiftly. In 1989 the Army had 141 nuclear weapons–certified units. In 1992 it had none. Nuclear weapons had been redefined as strategic, and the Army had been redefined as nonnuclear.[71]

Conclusions

The world looked very different to the Army in 1991 than it had in 1989. The strategic focus on the Cold War and the Soviet Union had dissipated, leaving a diffuse multitude of less dangerous but more likely threats in its wake. Military technologies that had been untested proved their worth in DESERT STORM. After initial self-congratulation, however, reflections on DESERT STORM flagged up worrisome issues with which the Army had yet to deal. It seemed a harbinger of future capabilities more so than a demonstration of capabilities that had already arrived. Socioeconomic change crossed important watersheds during this brief period as well. The United States was demonstrably more global, and the globe was demonstrably more integrated. The Internet was just emerging to push this process along. This new world order required security, and the United States was the only truly global power capable of providing it.

To their credit, the leaders of the United States Army recognized change was coming and prepared themselves and the institution to achieve it. Direction and details were not yet clear, but a framework for change was articulated and proponency for aspects of that framework established. With respect to downsizing and denuclearization, planning had advanced to the point that execution could commence. Some now characterize the events of 2001 as the pivot point that launched the Army in new directions. As we shall see, the pivot point was actually 1989, and the Army since 2001 has been following through and capitalizing on changes that started because of the end of the Cold War.

Notes

[1] General Carl E. Vuono, "Our 'Clearest, Most Valued Symbol of Resolve,'" *Army 1988–1999 Green Book: The Year of Training,* October 1988, 34.

[2] Ibid., 33.

[3] International Institute for Strategic Studies, *The Military Balance, 1989/1990* (London: Oxford University Press, 1989).

[4] General Crosbie E. Saint and Major (P) Michael L. Hammack, "Changes Pose Challenge for Army Forces, Europe," *Army 1988–1999 Green Book: The Year of Training,* October 1988, 56–70.

[5] Ibid.; Vincent H. Demma, *Department of the Army Historical Summary, Fiscal Year 1989* (Washington DC: Center of Military History, 1998), 11–28, 63–75; Charles E. Kirkpatrick, *"Ruck It Up!" The Post–Cold War Transformation of V Corps, 1990–2001* (Washington DC: Center of Military History, 2006), 3–20, 34–39. Here, the author might also cite his own personal experience, having served a total of ten years in Germany as an Armor officer and participated in many REFORGERs.

[6] Demma, 247–66; Kirkpatrick, 3–45; *Army Training and Evaluation Program 71–2* (Washington DC: Department of the Army, 1987); Army Field Manual 17–12–1, *Tank Combat Tables* (Washington DC: Department of the Army, 1987); Secretary of the Army John O. Marsh Jr., "Army Training: Ancient Roots, Future Benefits," *Army 1988–1989 Green Book: The Year of Training,* October 1988, 12–18; Anne W. Chapman, *The Army's Training Revolution, 1973–1990, An Overview* (Fort Monroe, Virginia: Office of the Command Historian, U.S. Army Training and Doctrine Command, 1994). Again, the author might cite twenty-six years of personal experience as an Armor officer, thus serving in ranks from second lieutenant through full colonel.

[7] Lieutenant General Allen K. Ono and Raymond J. Sumser, "Personnel: An Army Tightens Up Its Belt," *Army 1988–1989 Green Book: The Year of Training*, October 1988, 158–65; "Distribution of Active Duty Forces by Service, Rank, Sex and Ethnic Group," Office of the Deputy Assistant Secretary of Defense (Equal Opportunity), 22 June 1994; Robert K. Griffith Jr., *The U.S. Army's Transition to the All-Volunteer Force, 1968–1974* (Washington DC: Center of Military History, 1997); Department of the Army Pamphlet 623–205, *The Noncommissioned Officer Evaluation Reporting System "In Brief"* (Washington DC: Department of the Army, 1988); David W. Hogan Jr., Arnold Fisch Jr., and Robert K. Wright Jr., *The Story of the Noncommissioned Officer Corps* (Washington DC: Center of Military History, 2003); Demma, 109–32.

[8] Ono and Sumser; Major General Don Burdick, "The Guard: America's Army 'On Call,'" *Army 1988–1989 Green Book: The Year of Training*, October 1988, 125–32; Major General William F. Ward Jr., "Buildup Over; Reserve's Focus Is on Fine-Tuning, *Army1988–1989 Green Book: The Year of Training*, October 1988, 112–21; James T. Currie and Richard B. Crossland, *Twice the Citizen: A History of the United States Army Reserve, 1908–1995* (Washington DC: Office of the Chief, Army Reserve, 1997), 287–368; Michael D. Doubler, *I Am the Guard: A History of the Army National Guard, 1636–2000* (Washington DC: Government Printing Office, 2001), 269–300.

[9] Demma, 3–11, 201–46; Department of the Army, *Weapons Systems: United States Army, 1991* (Washington DC: Government Printing Office, 1991); Frank N. Schubert and Theresa L. Kraus, gen. eds., *The Whirlwind War: The United States Army in Operations DESERT SHIELD and DESERT STORM* (Washington DC: Center of Military

History, 1995), 28–33; General Fred Franks Jr. with Tom Clancy, *Into the Storm: A Study in Command* (New York: Berkley Books, 1997), 103–57.

[10] Letter of Instruction, 3d Infantry Division, 13 May 1986, with chg 1 dated 18 July 1986, sub: M1A1 Rollover; Memorandum for Record (MFR), 4th Battalion, 66th Armor, 7 January 1987, sub: M1 Turn-In. Both Historians Files, CMH. In the case of this paragraph, the author might also cite his personal experience as the Executive Officer of the first United States Army, Europe (USAREUR), battalion to roll over from the M1 to the M1A1 tank.

[11] General Maxwell R. Thurman, "TRADOC Prepares for the Future: Training to Fight and Win Now and Beyond the Year 2000," *Army 1988–1989 Green Book: The Year of Training,* October 1988, 82–97; General Louis C. Wagner Jr., "AMC's Full-Throttle Effort to Capture Technology: Today's Concepts, Tomorrow's Edge," *Army 1988–1989 Green Book: The Year of Training*, October 1988, 100–109; Lieutenant General Jimmy D. Ross, "Army Logistics: Top Priority Is Support of War-Fighting CINCs," *Army 1988–1989 Green Book: The Year of Training*, October 1988, 170–86; Demma, 132.

[12] *Department of Defense Reorganization Act of 1986* (Public Law 99–143); James R. Lochner III, *Victory on the Potomac: The Goldwater-Nichols Act Unifies the Pentagon* (College Station: Texas A&M University Press, 2002); Mark D. Sherry, *The Army Command Post and Defense Reshaping, 1987–1997* (Washington DC: Center of Military History, 2009).

[13] Ibid.; Demma, 201–46.

[14] S. 2453, *A Bill to Enhance the Capability of the United States to Combat Terrorism and Other Forms of Unconventional Warfare;* H.R. 5109, *A Bill to Establish a National Special Operations Agency Within the Department of Defense to Have Unified Responsibility for All Special Operations Forces and Activities Within the Department*; *National Defense Authorization Act for Fiscal Year 1987*; Demma, 35, 76–78; Sherry, 36.

[15] United Stated Department of Defense, *Soviet Military Power, 1987* (Washington DC: Government Printing Office, 1987).

[16] *Treaty Between the United States and the Union of Soviet Socialist Republics on the Elimination of Their Intermediate Range and Shorter Range Missiles*, entered into force 1 June 1988, U.S. Department of State (http://www.state.gov); Brian Alexander and Alistair Millar, *Tactical Nuclear Weapons in an Evolving Security Environment* (Washington DC: Brassey's, 2003), 1–41; Demma, 74–76, 232.

[17] William Echikson, *Lighting the Night: Revolution in Eastern Europe* (New York: William Morrow, 1990); George Bush and Brent Scowcroft, *A World Transformed* (New York: Knopf, 1998); John Lewis Gaddis, *The United States and the End of the Cold War: Implications, Reconsiderations, Provocations* (New York: Oxford University Press, 1992).

[18] Speech of Leonid Brezhnev to the Fifth Congress of the Polish Workers Party, 13 November 1968; Matthew Ouimet, *The Rise and Fall of the Brezhnev Doctrine in Soviet Foreign Policy* (Chapel Hill: University of North Carolina Press, 2003).

[19] Dennis G. Heapy, "NATO Mobilization and Reinforcement: Can We Get There from Here?" (Fort Leavenworth, Kansas: School of Advanced Military Studies, 1990); James L. Moody, "Awaiting an Enemy: The Operational Significance of Politically Induced Force Reductions to Parity in Central Europe" (Fort Leavenworth, Kansas: School of Advanced Military Studies, 1990); Charles Gati, *Failed Illusions: Moscow, Washington, Budapest and the 1956 Hungarian Revolt* (Palo Alto, California: Stanford University Press, 2006); Amnesty International, "Preliminary Findings on Killings of Unarmed Civilians, Arbitrary Arrests and Summary Executions Since June 1989," 30 August 1989, at http://www.amnestyusa.org; Bush and Scowcroft; Gaddis.

[20] General Carl E. Vuono, "Guided by Six Imperatives: The U.S. Army in the 1990s," *Army 1990–1991 Green Book*, October 1990, 20.

[21] Secretary of the Army Michael P. W. Stone, "The Army's Challenges: First Echelon of Strategic Deterrence in a Turbulent World of Diverse Threats," *Army 1990–1991 Green Book*, October 1990, 11.

[22] General Crosbie E. Saint, "USAREUR Maintains Readiness: Commitment to Europe's Security Has Deep Roots," *Army 1990–1991 Green Book*, October 1990, 87.

[23] General Sir John Hackett et al., *The Third World War: August 1985* (New York: Macmillan, 1978).

[24] General Carl W. Stiner, "U.S. Special Operations Command: Prime-Time Players in the Third World Network of Conflict," *Army 1990–1991 Green Book*, October 1990, 191–97; Gordon C. Bonham, *Special Operations Forces: The Combination Tool in the CINC's Operational Toolbox* (Fort Leavenworth, Kansas: School of Advanced Military Studies, 1991); Mark R. French, *Shield of Blows or Rubber Dagger: An Analysis for an Operational Concept for NATO After Forward Defense* (Fort Leavenworth, Kansas: School of Advanced Military Studies, 1990); Paul A. Lovelace, *Science and Art of Operational Maneuver in Post CFE Europe* (Fort Leavenworth, Kansas: School of Advanced Military Studies, 1990); William H. Parry III, *Search for an Operational Warfighting Doctrine: What Are NATO's Options After CFE?* (Fort Leavenworth, Kansas: School of Advanced Military Studies, 1990).

[25] Michael R. Beshloss and Strobe Talbot, *At the Highest Levels: The Inside Story of the End of the Cold War* (Boston, Massachusetts: Little Brown, 1993); John F. Matlock Jr., *Reagan and Gorbachev: How the Cold War Ended* (New York: Random House, 2004); Gaddis.

[26] Ibid.; Vuono, "Guided by Six Imperatives," 23.

[27] Beshloss and Talbot; Matlock; Gaddis; Bush and Scowcroft; Archie Brown, *The Gorbachev Factor* (New York: Oxford University Press, 1997); *The Unification of Germany in 1990* (Bonn, Germany: Press and Information Office of the Federal Government, 1991); *Treaty on the Final Settlement with Respect to Germany, September 12, 1990* (Washington DC: German Embassy, 2004).

[28] Author's personal experience serving as a tank battalion commander in Germany.

[29] Bush and Scowcroft; Beshloss and Talbot; Gaddis; David Pryce-Jones, *The Strange Death of the Soviet Union* (New York: Metropolitan, 1995).

[30] Secretary of Defense William S. Cohen, *Report of the Quadrennial Defense Review* (Pentagon: Department of Defense, 1997); Briefing, General Wesley K. Clark, Supreme Allied Commander Europe, to the NATO Norfolk Conference, "The 21st Century Force, Defining Requirements," 12 November 1998, in Historians Files, CMH.

[31] R. Cody Philips, *Operation JUST CAUSE: The American Incursion into Panama* (*Washington* DC: Center of Military History, 2004); Thomas M. Donnelly et al., *Operation JUST CAUSE: The Storming of Panama* (New York: Maxwell Macmillan International, 1991).

[32] Ibid.; Ronald H. Cole, *Operation JUST CAUSE: The Planning and Execution of Joint Operations in Panama, February 1988–January 1990* (Washington DC: Joint History Office, 1995).

[33] Philips, 21, 38; U.S. Bureau of Consular Affairs, *Private American Citizens Residing Abroad* (http://travel.state.gov/amcit_numbers.html).

[34] U.S. Census Bureau, *Historical Census Statistics on the Foreign-born Population of the United States* (http://www.census.gov/population/www/censusdata/hiscendata.html).

[35] David M. Reimers, *Still the Golden Door: The Third World Comes to America* (New York: Columbia University Press, 1985); Sanford J. Ungar, *Fresh Blood: The New*

Immigrants (New York: Simon & Schuster, 1995); U.S. Census Bureau, *Demographic Trends in the 20th Century* (http://www.census.gov/population/www/censusdata/hiscendata.html).

[36] Thomas P. M. Barnett, *The Pentagon's New Map: War and Peace in the Twenty-First Century* (New York: Barnes and Noble, 2004); Shireen Hunter, ed., *Islam, Europe's Second Religion: The New Social, Cultural and Political Landscape* (Washington DC: Center for Strategic and International Studies, 2002); A. Labor, *A Heart Turned East; Muslims in Europe and America* (London: Little Brown and Company, 1997).

[37] Christopher Bennett, *Yugoslavia's Bloody Collapse: Causes, Course and Consequences* (New York: New York University Press, 1995); Laura Silber and Allan Little, *Yugoslavia: Death of a Nation* (New York: Penguin Books, 1997); Trevor N. Dupuy, *Future Wars: The World's Most Dangerous Flashpoints* (New York: Warner Books, 1993); Pryce-Jones.

[38] Dan Smith, Kristan Ingstad Sandberg, Pavel Baev, and Wenche Hauge, *The State of War and Peace Atlas* (Oslo, Norway: International Peace Research Institute and Penguin Books, 1997).

[39] Jagdish Bhagwal, *In Defense of Globalization* (Oxford, Oxford University Press, 2007); Thomas L. Friedman, *The World Is Flat* (New York: Farrar, Straus and Giroux, 2005); Manfred Steger, *Globalization: A Very Brief History* (Oxford: Oxford University Press, 2003); Mary Beth Norton et al., *A People and a Nation: A History of the United States* (New York: Houghton Mifflin, 2005), 771, 924–25; World Trade Organization Web site (http://www.wto.org).

[40] Janet Abbate, *Inventing the Internet* (Cambridge, Massachusetts: MIT Press, 1999); Max Boot, *War Made New: Technology, Warfare, and the Course of History, 1500 to Today* (New York: Gotham Books, 2006), 307–17; Katie Hafner and Matthew Lyon, *Where Wizards Stay Up Late: The Origins of the Internet* (New York: Touchstone, 1998).

[41] Demma; Boot, 307–17; James F. Dunnigan, *Digital Soldiers: The Evolution of High-Tech Weaponry and Tomorrow's Brave New Battlefields* (New York: St. Martin's Press, 1996); George and Meredith Friedman, *The Future of War: Power, Technology and American World Dominance in the 21st Century* (New York: Crown Publishers, 1996).

[42] Dilip Hiro, *The Longest War: The Iran-Iraq Military Conflict* (New York: Routledge, 1991); *Conduct of the Persian Gulf War: Final Report to Congress* (Washington DC: Department of Defense, 1992), 2–29; U.S. News and World Report, *Triumph Without Victory: The Unreported History of the Persian Gulf War* (New York: Time Books, 1992), 3–39.

[43] *Conduct of the Persian Gulf War,* 30–47; Schubert and Kraus, 49–99; Robert H. Scales Jr., *Certain Victory: The US Army in the Gulf War* (Washington DC: Office of the Chief of Staff, United States Army, 1993), 39–102; H. Norman Schwarzkopf with Peter Petre, *It Doesn't Take a Hero: The Autobiography* (New York: Bantam Books, 1992), 295–406.

[44] *Conduct of the Persian Gulf War*, 64–87; Stephen P. Gehring, *From the Fulda Gap to Kuwait: U.S. Army, Europe, and the Gulf War* (Washington DC: Department of the Army, 1998); *Triumph Without Victory*, 90–109, 150–83; Harry G. Summers Jr., *On Strategy II: A Critical Analysis of the Gulf War* (New York: Dell, 1992).

[45] *Conduct of the Persian Gulf War*, 252–54; Schubert and Kraus, 133–36; Scales, 112–21; John S Brown, "Beyond the Wall: Operations in a Post–Cold War World, 1990–2001," in *American Military History*, vol. 2, *The United States Army in a Global Era 1917–2003*, ed. Richard W. Stewart (Washington DC: Center of Military History, 2004), 412–15.

[46] *Conduct of the Persian Gulf War,* 88–181, 661–731, 755–56, 773–78; Boot, 318–22; Schubert and Kraus, 153–72; Scales, 157–212; Rick Atkinson, *Crusade: The Untold Story of the Persian Gulf War* (New York: Houghton Mifflin, 1993), 165–356; Thomas A. Keaney and Eliot A. Cohen, *Gulf War Air Power Survey: Summary Report* (Washington DC: United States Air Force, 1993); Task Force Iron Debrief for Troop Information, 2d Armored Division Forward, TAA [Tactical Assembly Area] Manhattan, Saudi Arabia, 19 February 1991, Historians Files, CMH; Intervs with Major General Thomas Rhame, 26 Jul 1991, and Colonel Terry Bullington, 24 Jul 1991, Center of Military History (DESERT STORM) Interview Collection, Washington DC.

[47] *Conduct of the Persian Gulf War,* 226–97, Schubert and Kraus, 173–206; Scales, 213–320; Atkinson, 375–487; Brown, 417–23; James Blackwell, *Thunder in the Desert: The Strategy and Tactics of the Persian Gulf War* (New York: Bantam Books, 1991), 183–238; Franks with Clancy, 362–561; John S. Brown, "The Battle for Norfolk," in *Leaders in War: West Point Remembers the 1991 Gulf War,* ed. Frederick W. Kagan and Chris Kubik (New York: Frank Cass, 2005); Eric T. Olson, "Attacking the Republican Guard," in *Leaders in War,* ed. Kagan and Kubik.

[48] Schwarzkopf, 295–374; Scales, 49–79; Charles Lane Toomey, *XVIII Airborne Corps in DESERT STORM: From Planning to Victory* (Central Point, Oregon: Hellgate Press, 2004), 75–128; Katherine McIntire, "Speed Bumps: 82nd Airborne's Shaky Line in the Sand," *Army Times,* 21 October 1991; John S. Brown, "DESERT STORM as History—and Prologue," *Army* (February 2001): 50–51.

[49] *Conduct of the Persian Gulf War,* 236–37, 543–76, 589–98; Schwarzkopf, 272–78; Franks, 544–68; Interv with Colonel Anthony Morreno, 26 Jul 1991, Center of Military History (DESERT STORM) Interview Collection; Sean D. Naylor, "Friendly Fire: The Reckoning," *Army Times,* 21 August 1991.

[50] *Conduct of the Persian Gulf War,* 393–450; Peter C. Langemus, "Moving an Army: Movement Control for DESERT STORM," *Military Review* (September 1991); William G. Pagonis with Jeffrey L. Cruickshank, *Moving Mountains: Lessons in Leadership and Logistics from the Gulf War* (Cambridge, Massachusetts: Harvard Business School University Press, 1992); Interv with Lieutenant Colonel Steve Marshman, Commander, 498th Support Battalion, 2d Armored Division Forward, May 1989 to May 1991, 11 October 1991; Kent Laudeman, "Theater Support," in *Leaders in War,* ed. Kagan and Kubik; Sandra L. Vann-Olejasz, "Tactical Logistics Support" in *Leaders in War,* ed. Kagan and Kubik; Chris Kubik, "Platoon Leader Challenges," in *Leaders in War,* ed. Kagan and Kubik; Author's personal experience as commander of 2-66 Armor.

[51] *Conduct of the Persian Gulf War,* 773–90; Boot, 339–41, 347–49; Atkinson, 272–96, 345–46; Keaney and Cohen.

[52] *Conduct of the Persian Gulf War,* 471–85; James T. Currie and Richard B. Crossland, *Twice the Citizen: A History of the United States Army Reserve, 1908–1995* (Washington DC: Office of the Chief, Army Reserve, 1997), 369–548; Michael D. Doubler, *I Am the Guard: A History of the Army National Guard, 1636–2000* (Washington DC: Department of the Army, 2001), 301–32.

[53] Scales, 321–54; *Triumph Without Victory,* 399–415; Toomey, 399–418; Stephen A. Bourque and John W. Burdan III, *The Road to Safwan: The 1st Squadron, 4th Cavalry in the 1991 Persian Gulf War* (Denton, Texas: University of North Texas Press, 2007), 213–26; Janet A. McDonnell, *After DESERT STORM: The U.S. Army and the Reconstruction of Kuwait* (Washington DC: Center of Military History, 1999); Gordon W. Rudd, *Humanitarian Intervention: Assisting the Iraqi Kurds in Operation PROVIDE COMFORT* (Washington DC: Center of Military History, 2004).

[54] Vuono, "Guided by Six Imperatives," 23.

[55] Ibid.; William G. Bell, *Commanding Generals and Chiefs of Staff, 1775–2005: Portraits and Biographical Sketches of the Army's Senior Officers* (Washington DC: Center of Military History, 2005).

[56] Vuono, "Guided by Six Imperatives"; Field Manual 100–5, *Operations* (Washington DC: United States Army, 1986); Robert A. Doughty, *The Evolution of U.S. Army Tactical Doctrine, 1946–1976* (Washington DC: Center of Military History, 2001); John L. Romjue, *American Army Doctrine for the Post–Cold War World* (Washington DC: Center of Military History, 2001).

[57] Vuono, "Guided by Six Imperatives"; Dennis J. Reimer, "Focus on Global Mission Puts Emphasis on Power Projection," *Army 1990–1991 Green Book,* October 1990, 124–28; John B. Wilson, *Maneuver and Firepower: The Evolution of Divisions and Separate Brigades* (Washington DC: Center of Military History, 1998); William M. Donnelly, *Transforming an Army at War: Designing the Modular Force, 1991–2005* (Washington DC: Center of Military History, 2007), 3–18; Field Manual 1, *The Army* (Washington DC: Department of the Army, 2005), 2-8 to 2-12.

[58] Vuono, "Guided by Six Imperatives"; William G. T. Tuttle, "Seven Missions Power the AMC Contribution," *Army 1990–1991 Green Book,* October 1990, 74–83; Demma, 3–11, 201–46; Department of the Army, *Weapons Systems: United States Army, 1991* (Washington DC: Government Printing Office, 1991); Boot, 7–18.

[59] Vuono, "Guided by Six Imperatives"; John W. Foss "Superb Quality While Using Fewer Forces," *Army 1990–1991 Green Book,* October 1990, 56–64; Chapman; Demma, 247–66; Kirkpatrick, 3–45; *Army Training and Evaluation Program 71–2* (Washington DC: Department of the Army, 1987); Field Manual 1, *The Army*, 1–19.

[60] Vuono, "Guided by Six Imperatives"; Julius W. Gates, "Bootprints That Will Never Fade," *Army 1990–1991 Green Book,* October 1990, 33–36; Lieutenant General William H. Reno and Raymond J. Sumser, "Maintain Momentum, Minimize Turbulence, Maximize Strength," *Army 1990–1991 Green Book,* October 1990, 130–35; Field Manual 1, *The Army*, 1–18.

[61] Vuono, "Guided by Six Imperatives"; Reno and Sumser, 130–35; "Distribution of Active Duty Forces by Service, Rank, Sex and Ethnic Group," Office of the Deputy Assistant Secretary of Defense (Equal Opportunity) , 22 June 1994; Department of the Army Pamphlet 623–205, *The Noncommissioned Officer Evaluation Reporting System "In Brief"* (Washington DC: Department of the Army, 1988); Hogan, Fisch, and Wright; Demma, 109–32.

[62] Field Manual 1, *The Army*, 2–8; Vuono, "Guided by Six Imperatives"; Reimer, "Focus on Global Mission Puts Emphasis on Power Projection"; Foss; Tuttle; Demma, 29–37; "Command and Staff Directory," *Army 1990–1991 Green Book*, October 1990, 217–36; Edgar F. Raines Jr., *Evolution of the Office of the Deputy Chief of Staff for Operations and Plans, 1903–1991* (Washington DC: Center of Military History, 1991).

[63] *Department of Defense Reorganization Act of 1986* (Public Law 99–143); Lochner; Sherry.

[64] Ibid.; Demma, 201–46; Michael P. W. Stone, "First Echelon of Strategic Deterrence in a Turbulent World of Diverse Threats," *Army 1990–1991 Green Book*, 11–14; Stephen K. Conver, "RDA Budget Reflects Requirements, Reductions and Political Realities," *Army 1990–1991 Green Book*, 66–71.

[65] Mark D. Mandeles, *Military Transformation Past and Present: Historic Lessons for the 21st Century* (London: Praeger Security International, 2007), 28–71.

[66] "Association of the United States Army, Officers and Council of Trustees," *Army 1990–1991 Green Book,* October 1990.

[67] Colonel Matthew Moten, "'The Stuff of Tragedy' Shinseki's Reply to Levin," *Armed Forces and Society* (April 2008): 509–16.

[68] Demma, 29–32, 38–44.

[69] Vuono, "Guided by Six Imperatives"; Sherry; Demma, 63–74; E-mail, General Gordon L. Sullivan to Brigadier General John S. Brown, 4 May 2008, sub: John Brown's First Substantive Chapter, in Historian's Files, CMH.

[70] Vuono, "Guided by Six Imperatives"; Sherry; Demma; John S. Brown, *Draftee Division: The 88th Infantry Division in World War II* (Lexington, Kentucky: University of Kentucky Press, 1986).

[71] *Treaty Between the United States and the Union of Soviet Socialist Republics on the Elimination of Their Intermediate Range and Shorter Range Missiles*, entered into force 1 June 1988; Alexander and Millar, 1–41; Demma, 74–76, 232.

CHAPTER 3

The Sullivan Years, 1991–1995

General Gordon R. Sullivan was sworn in as Chief of Staff of the Army on 23 June 1991. He was thoroughly familiar with retiring Chief of Staff General Carl E. Vuono's vision of the way ahead for the Army and was well prepared to carry it forward. He had served for a year as Vice Chief of Staff of the Army when selected to be Chief of Staff and had served as Vuono's Deputy Chief of Staff for Operations and Plans (DCSOPS) before that. Such Vuono-era studies as QUICKSILVER and VANGUARD bore his fingerprints, as did the discussions and deliberations that matured Vuono's six "Army Imperatives." Sullivan adopted these imperatives as his own, featuring them prominently in speeches and correspondence and in such promotional literature as the Association of the United States Army's annual *Army Green Book.* Vuono and Sullivan had served together off and on for over a dozen years, and the two men remained close after Vuono retired. Sullivan included Vuono within the circle of intimates with whom he sounded out concepts and plans as they emerged.[1]

This kindredness of vision and spirit assisted in sustaining an azimuth, but the devil remained in the details—in the formulation of practical measures to carry the work forward. For Sullivan budget cuts, manpower drawdowns, and congressional pursuit of a "peace dividend" were not forecasts; they were crippling contemporary realities. Even as resources drained away, he led the struggle to maintain quality, sustain morale, and fulfill current mission requirements. These immediate priorities could easily have trumped shaping the Army of the future. Sullivan was determined that they would not. A 1959 graduate of Norwich University, he had served as an Armor officer before, during, and after the Vietnam War. In Vietnam he was wounded while serving as an adviser to the Civil Guard and Self Defense Corps, and he served two additional tours in Vietnam as well. He commanded at every level from company through division and served several assignments each as a personnel officer, operations officer, and in Training and Doctrine Command (TRADOC)—each time in positions of increasing responsibility. His broad experience included the Vietnam buildup, the rigors of the war itself, the postwar downward spiral into a "hollow army," and the renaissance leading into JUST CAUSE and DESERT STORM. Throughout his tenure as Chief of Staff he kept two books on his desk: *The Seeds of Disaster: The Development of French Army Doctrine, 1919–1939,* by Colonel Robert A. Doughty, then Professor and Head of the Department of History at West Point, and *America's First Battles, 1776–1965,*

General Sullivan

edited by Lieutenant Colonel Charles E. Heller and Brigadier General William A. Stofft—Stofft being a former Chief of Military History. Sullivan was determined to prepare the Army for the next war, not to lose its way amid the challenges of the present.[2]

The Modern Louisiana Maneuvers and Processes of Change

Speaking at his arrival ceremony as Chief of Staff on 25 June 1991, General Gordon R. Sullivan touched upon a perennial dilemma of global power. Contemporary responsibilities and missions are ever present and prone to trump long-term vision or preparation. In the aftermath of World War I, for example, British, French, and German officers alike had been exposed to prototypes of the awesome combinations that would prove decisive in World War II. The British and French had empires to police, however, and ongoing missions to absorb overseas territories wrested from the Germans and Ottomans. Given peacetime funding, they found it difficult to give much attention to the more distant future. Indeed, British political leaders went so far as to impose a "Ten-Year Rule," forbidding military planners from contemplating great power wars for at least that period. The German military had no such distractions. Beginning with postwar seminars shepherded by General Hans von Seekt, they prepared themselves for future war in a deliberate manner.[3] Sullivan, at the head of yet another army with global responsibilities in the aftermath of a successfully concluded worldwide contest, commented in his speech that there would be no "time-out from readiness," and that "the American people expect us to be a strategic force for our nation's land battles—today, next week, and years from now." His comments proved prescient; during his tenure the tempo of deployments from home stations increased threefold and continued unabated thereafter. Amid this steadily increasing busyness Sullivan nevertheless resolved to prepare for a more distant future. To further quote his speech, "at home and abroad the environment in which the Army operates is undergoing fundamental transformation . . . the Army too must change." In a time of plummeting budgets, it would be a Herculean task to "reshape the Army while maintaining readiness."[4]

The Cold War Army and the Cold War Department of Defense had designed themselves to evolve: continuously, thoughtfully, and incrementally. Generations of tanks, aircraft, ships, vehicles, and equipment of other types replaced their predecessors in frontline units, cascading older equipment through units lower down in deployment plans and in the reserve component before washing it out of the inventory altogether. One motor pool in Aschaffenburg, Germany, for example, witnessed the M47, M48, M60, M60A1, M60A3, M1, and M1A1 tanks during the career-span of a single soldier. During this same period, prospective opponents across the Inter-German border similarly progressed through the T55, T62, T72, and T80 tanks. The pattern was much the same for other services and equipment. At the highest level the process tied into congressional budget cycles and annual budget submissions by the administration to Congress. Since the tenure of Secretary of Defense Robert S. McNamara military input to proposed administration budgets had emerged from a relatively orderly Planning, Programming, and Budgeting System (PPBS). PPBS involved the services and defense analysts in an annual round of threat assessments, discussions of requirements to counter the threats, comparisons of cost-effectiveness, and determinations of the priority in which requirements would be resourced and filled. The Army labeled its own version the Planning, Programming, Budgeting, and Execution System (PPBES), acknowledgment that the services also had to "execute," to actually spend the money once they had obtained it. An important contributor to PPBES was the Army's parallel Concepts-Based Requirements System (CBRS), analysis working down from the agreed national military strategy to determine the forces necessary to achieve it. CBRS offered a deliberate, albeit cumbersome, methodology for determining future weapons and force structure that was familiar to sizable numbers of staff officers who had been trained in its use. It had been informed and enriched by the incorporation of General Vuono's six imperatives. Thus Army modernization reached beyond technical developments alone to address doctrine, training, force mix, leader development, and the retention of quality people as well. The services, increasingly disciplined by the Joint Staff and the Defense Secretariat in the aftermath of Goldwater-Nichols, jockeyed with each other as each annual PPBS submission came due. Prospective submissions also were of great interest to Congress, an interest further kindled by those of their constituents who represented industries identified to provide goods and services to the Department of Defense.[5]

In addition to top-down change, the Army had institutionalized methods for improving itself from within. The pre–DESERT STORM "training revolution" that fielded Multiple Integrated Laser Engagement System (MILES) gunnery and sprawling Observer Controller (OC)–shepherded exercises through the National Training Center (NTC) was predicated on the gritty after-action review (AAR). AARs were facilitated by mentors and trainers, but their essence was confessional. Participants reviewed their performances, acknowledged their flaws, and identified ways to do better next time—and there always was a next time. Assessments were generally candid and blunt, soldiers of all ranks were encouraged to opine in the presence of superiors and subordinates alike, and defects were inevitably paired with proposed resolutions. The AAR process pervaded training at every level throughout the Army—from individual skills through crew gunnery to battalion maneuvers and corps exercises—and dominated operational postmortems as well. Indeed, the guns were

Participative after-action reviews sharpen the focus of training.

hardly silent after DESERT STORM when American units, reflecting on their battlefield performances, took to the desert to polish up aspects of gunnery and maneuver. Astonished allies and bemused local civilians wondered at the restlessness of this triumphant army that never quite seemed satisfied with itself. In 1985 the Center for Army Lessons Learned (CALL) stood up at Fort Leavenworth to collect, analyze, and disseminate lessons learned, tactics, techniques, procedures, research materials, and security assessments. Originally focused on making better use of data being generated at the National Training Center, CALL quickly expanded its portfolio. It solicited information from the field during and after DESERT STORM and dispatched teams of experts to drill in on specific topics. During this same period Inspectors General assigned from division levels through the Department of the Army began to focus less on enforcing unit and agency compliance with specific policies and more on assessing Army-wide systems for potential improvement. Personnel policies reinforced the potentially transformative effect of all this reflection and analysis. Key leaders generally rotated in from eighteen months to two years, thus exposing their organizations to fresh views and new departures as their successors arrived.[6]

Sullivan initially expressed confidence in the Army's inherent mechanisms for change, but he soon had misgivings on at least four counts. First, the evolutionary adaptiveness of CBRS seemed better suited to deal with a known adversary and specific threats than with the new unknowns. Sometimes derided as "bean counting," the process featured recurrent intelligence assessments of Soviet and Warsaw Pact force structures and capabilities, against which Allied force structures and capabilities could be matched up and improved upon. Research and development endeavored to keep fielded American technology at least one step ahead of that of the Soviets, but procurement was an intricate multi-participant process. Sullivan frequently commented that it took fifteen years to field the redoubtable M1 tank, for example. Insofar as adversaries other than the Soviets were concerned, Cold War forces and capabilities were considered so mammoth that they could readily handle contingencies in the Third World that would require fewer resources than those needed to face the Soviets. Now the Army's radically reduced force structure faced diverse and imprecisely calculable threats. With the paradigm so different, would incremental adjustments prove adequate?[7] Second, commanders and agencies tended to focus on immediate priorities, "pissing on the flames" that would burn them first rather than on the ones that might burn them worst. Field commanders were scrambling to inactivate units, process facilities and equipment, sustain training, and support such contingencies as those in Northern Iraq and Somalia. Within the logistical arena, sustainment and research and development fell under the same commander for any given commodity. Harried logistical chiefs were being taken to task for present shortfalls, not for the future character of their products. TRADOC, the institutional repository for future thinking, was itself in the throes of downsizing. As schools cut staff, preserving the quality of classroom instruction took precedence over furthering doctrine. For TRADOC as a whole, redesigning institutional training and resourcing the maneuver training centers to sustain high standards in the face of significant cuts became priorities.[8]

Third, the newly assertive Joint Staff and Office of the Secretary of Defense threatened to get ahead of the Army in envisioning the Army's future. As early as 1989 the Joint Staff had undertaken its so-called Base Force Study and the Office of the Secretary of Defense a Defense Management Review. Both envisioned substantial cuts for the Army. The effects of these initiatives had been suspended during DESERT STORM, but in the aftermath of that war they regained their momentum. The Army risked losing its voice in Defense reshaping deliberations if it did not promulgate a cogent and coherent way ahead for itself.[9] Finally, Sullivan sensed that too many in the Army were feeling sorry for themselves, nonplussed by downsizing, turbulence, and a public that still envisioned them as Willie and Joe or Beetle Bailey—as juxtaposed to the Air Force's Steve Canyon (a long-running hero of the Sunday comics) or the romantic naval pilots of the movies *Top Gun* or *An Officer and a Gentleman*. Certainly the Air Force and Navy stole a march in taking credit for DESERT STORM, benefiting from audiovisuals creating an impression the Army and Marines merely cleaned up the battlefield after they won the war. The Army needed an inspiring vision that advanced both its traditional values and its place on the high-tech battlefields of the future.[10]

Sullivan was not alone in his desire to fast-track change or in his angst that customary means might not evolve it fast enough. The new TRADOC commander, General Frederick M. Franks Jr., did not believe the Army was properly positioned to experiment with the changing nature of warfare. Twice wounded in Vietnam and commander of VII Corps in DESERT STORM, Franks

General Franks

also had considerable experience in force development, training analysis, and the development of combat doctrine. Through a succession of TRADOC assignments over the years, Franks had witnessed dramatic advances with respect to electronic simulation. He believed they offered a virtual means to experiment with circumstances that theretofore had only been theoretical. Franks and Sullivan had served together before, shared penchants for brainstorming and historical musings, and enjoyed each other's company. When opportunity permitted, they shared cigars, fishing, and wide-ranging conversations aboard Frank's boat on the lower Chesapeake. The Army's Chief of Military History, Brigadier General Harold W. Nelson, was another confidant of Sullivan's, and an ardent promulgator of his specialty. Historical grist he provided included the Center of Military History's recently published *The U.S. Army GHQ Maneuvers of 1941* by Dr. Christopher R. Gabel of Fort Leavenworth's Combat Studies Institute. The book described the gigantic exercises wherein the Army tested and improved upon doctrine, organizations, and equipment prior to America's entry into World War II. Sullivan and Franks seized upon the metaphor, confident that the Army now needed a similarly expansive shakeout to redesign itself for the post–Cold War era. After further deliberation and give-and-take among staff, confidants, and subject matter experts, Sullivan described his vision of "modern Louisiana Maneuvers" to the Association of the United States Army (AUSA) Winter Symposium in Orlando, Florida, on 19 February 1992. This forum allowed him to simultaneously engage serving Army leaders, thoughtful and connected retirees, soldiers at large, and captains of the defense industries. A few weeks later Sullivan detailed "Louisiana Maneuvers 1994" in a "personal for" message to his senior commanders. Sullivan personally would lead the initiative. His deputy exercise director would be General "Fred" Franks.[11]

The modern Louisiana Maneuvers and the Louisiana Maneuvers (LAM) Task Force, their institutional embodiment, evolved over time. Several key features relevant to long-term change stand out. First, they mobilized computer simulations on a wide scale to test doctrine, organization, and equipment. TRADOC organized an expansive system of "Battle Labs": "Battle Command" was at Fort Leavenworth; "Dismounted Battle Space" at Fort Benning; "Mounted Battle Space" at Fort Knox; "Depth and Simultaneous Attack" at Fort Sill; "Early Entry, Lethality, and Survivability" at Fort

Monroe; and "Combat Service Support" at Fort Lee. These labs drilled issues within their own specialties and linked together through "distributed interactive simulations" (DIS) to explore concepts broader in scope. Distributed interactive simulations enabled the labs to play in theater and major Army command (MACOM) exercises and even to interplay with tactical units on real exercises "in the dirt." Soldiers of the time were amazed to find themselves competing with adversaries hundreds—or even thousands—of miles away in real time. Periodic "General Headquarters Exercises" (GHQx—from the acronym that designated the Army's headquarters in 1941) mimicked the historical Louisiana Maneuvers in their Army-wide scope and implications. Second, LAM short-circuited customary bureaucracy to quickly surface critical concepts and issues. Some of these announced themselves in the course of exercises. Others were introduced into exercises because Sullivan routinely assembled a "General Officer Working Group" (GOWG) representing all the major commands to debate among themselves and forward critical concerns to his "Board of Directors"—the Army's four-star generals and selected three-stars. Initiatives such as "total asset visibility," "owning the night," "digitization," "common battlefield picture," and rapidly fielding "off-the-shelf" technology came under scrutiny more quickly than they otherwise would have because the most powerful men in the Army routinely came "out of their lanes" to deliberate collectively on transformational subjects. Third, the exercises increasingly linked theory with practice as concepts that showed well in simulation were fielded as hardware and tested "in the dirt." "Advanced Technology Demonstrations" (ATDs) provided proof of principle for technologies jointly defined by Army systems managers, Army users, and representatives of industry. "Advanced Concept Technology Demonstrations" (ACTDs) further involved Army users in assessments of emerging technology. The "Advanced Warfighting Demonstration" (AWD) and the "Advanced Warfighting Experiment" (AWE) were mechanisms to experiment with capabilities over even broader ranges of branch and service interaction. Processes of "spiral development" emerged, wherein technical advances were conceived in simulation, experimented with "in the dirt," and returned with comments to the manufacturer—who participated in the field exercises—for yet another round of development, experimentation, and critique. Fourth, the momentum of LAM experimentation propelled the Army irreversibly into the "Information Age." In July 1994 the Army Digitization Office stood up to provide further focus to the development and acquisition of digital communications hardware and software. This was but a precursor of further institutional commitment to digital technology. Finally, the modern Louisiana Maneuvers and the LAM Task Force provided General Sullivan a transformational mechanism under his personal control whereby he could shepherd—and accelerate—developments directly. Geographically, the LAM Task Force resided first at Fort Monroe, Virginia (where it could exploit TRADOC assets to fullest advantage), and later in Washington, D.C. (where it could most directly influence the Army Staff, other MACOMs and services, and the Department of Defense). Change of location reflected a change of focus, as it transitioned from primarily coordinating brainstorming exercises to primarily synchronizing a campaign to achieve the vision that had emerged. It was led by a brigadier general and totaled forty-nine officers and civilians organized into a half dozen functional directorates when at its prime. It reported directly to the Chief of Staff, who personally chaired the "Board of Directors" mapping the way ahead for the Army.[12]

Sullivan set no particular time frame for the termination of the modern Louisiana Maneuvers or for the LAM Task Force, but he did not envision them as permanent institutions. The solution for the inertia of a bureaucracy is seldom the construction of a parallel bureaucracy. LAM was a means to galvanize and accelerate processes of change in his time and hopefully to change the manner in which the Army went about change. Within a few years the relatively freewheeling brainstorming of LAM crystallized into a more focused vision of the way ahead for the Army labeled "Force XXI." On 8 March 1994, General Sullivan announced the inauguration of a Force XXI "campaign." Concerning Force XXI, more later. The LAM Task Force evolved into an agency synchronizing the milestones and delivery of Force XXI. Traditional means for developing and executing policy reasserted themselves. PPBS and PPBES were still omnipresent, as were the Joint Staff, the Department of Defense, Congress, and the administration. The give-and-take of "making things happen" "inside the Beltway" required robust bureaucracies led by powerful men. These powerful men and their staffs were now armed with a rather different vision of what the Army should look like, and they could work toward this new vision with their customary determination and energy. Some features of the modern Louisiana Maneuvers became irreversible aspects of Army change mechanisms. Sprawling distributive interactive simulation exercises were embedded forever as a means to test concepts, exercise staffs, and ensure the dynamic interplay of organizations affected by prospective decisions. Digitization had been institutionalized as the way ahead into the Information Age. Spiral development linked simulators, industrial representatives, and field soldiers together in reiterative cycles of experimentation and improvement. A cohort of colonels and young generals had been encouraged to "get out of their lanes" and "think outside the box," and would bring broadened perspectives to future initiatives. Some of the changes they envisioned—and convinced their bosses to endorse—were immediate in effect and others were longer term. Collectively considered, the changes shook the Cold War paradigm and set the Army on a very different course than it had been on for forty years.[13]

In Pursuit of Strategic Mobility

A recurrent theme of LAM deliberations—and of broader Department of Defense ruminations—was the Army's need for greater strategic mobility. The early days of DESERT SHIELD, wherein lonely undergunned paratroopers held a "line in the sand" against vastly superior Iraqi armored forces, haunted Army planners. A comparable period during the Korean War emerged as a metaphor for what might have happened had Saddam attacked—or what might yet happen if a future adversary proved less complacent. Sullivan, ever fond of historical analogy to reinforce important points, vowed that there should be "No more Task Force Smiths," referring to the Army's mismatched first combat in 1950. The pursuit of strategic mobility would work several avenues in parallel: expanding sealift and airlift, pre-positioning equipment and supplies overseas, and trimming the weight of units to be deployed. It would require reeducation and retraining, overcoming cultural impediments built up during two generations of Cold War service. It would also require negotiations with the Marine Corps, as operational aspirations for the two services appeared to converge. Within four years the Army's capabilities with respect to strategic mobility would be considerably improved, and it would demonstrate this improvement under operational circumstances.[14]

The primary incentive for pursuing greater mobility was grand strategic. JUST CAUSE and DESERT STORM illustrated the likelihood that distant contingencies would emerge with little notice, and subsequent deployments to Northern Iraq, Somalia, Haiti, the Balkans, and elsewhere reinforced this insight. Globalization increased American national security interests everywhere, whereas the collapses of the Warsaw Pact and the Soviet Union radically diminished the likelihood of a major confrontation in Europe. The United States Army could no longer concentrate on a few key regions where it could readily reinforce robust forward-deployed forces. Instead it would have to be capable of rapidly inserting itself into far more numerous trouble spots scattered around the world—where it might have little or no prior presence. Spurred along by Louisiana Maneuver deliberations, contemporary events, and its own internal staffing, TRADOC revised and republished Field Manual 100–5, *Operations*, in 1993. The new version gave a great deal more attention to "power projection," as well as to such "operations other than war" (OOTW) as peacekeeping and humanitarian relief.[15]

The notion that bases in the continental United States would serve as sustainable, centrally located "power projection platforms" for worldwide contingencies had strategic roots, but also happily coincided with congressional interests and internal Army developments. Most congressmen looked forward to a post–Cold War "peace dividend," but few welcomed the idea of shutting down military facilities in their own districts or states. United States Army, Europe (USAREUR), commanders did make the case that Europe was closer to many of the world's most likely trouble spots than the United States, and therefore its American infrastructure should be preferentially preserved to support future contingencies. This argument made little headway in Congress, other than perhaps preserving the most critical nodes and bases amid USAREUR's plummeting force structure. During Fiscal Year (FY) 1993 alone the Army shed almost two hundred installations, and its plant replacement value, a measure of the relative worth of land and facilities, declined by $7.4 billion. The lion's share of these cuts occurred in Europe. By the end of 1995 only 65,000 soldiers were assigned to USAREUR, down from more than 200,000 in 1989. Major troop installations in the United States suffered far less; indeed, several grew as units from Europe and elsewhere collapsed into them. The Army's emphasis on what installations were supposed to do changed as well. Installations were not only to support resident military populations but also were to launch units overseas through state-of-the-art airfields, railheads, and connections with prospective ports of embarkation. In 1992 the Corps of Engineers solidified this more comprehensive expectation in a newly rewritten Army Regulation 210–20, *Master Planning for Army Installations*. Two years later the Office of the Assistant Chief of Staff for Installation Management (ACSIM) stood up as a major Army Staff agency and promulgated its own visionary Installation Management Action Plan (IMAP). Perhaps most notably, beginning in December 1993 the Army centrally selected O-5 and O-6 garrison commanders through the Department of the Army Command Selection Boards. This meant that garrison commanders would be drawn from the same professional "gene pool" as table of organization and equipment (TOE) battalion and brigade commanders—and presumably would demonstrate similar talent, energy, and ambition. Newly selected garrison commanders disappointed by a diversion from troop duty were reassured that their commands would bear the prestige and general officer attention of those of their TOE comrades and that their careers would remain competitive. These several trends converged. In a few years' time a number of major posts sported much improved deployment infrastructure, the results of installation initiatives and a congressional infusion of $506 million into railheads, airfields, and ports. Premier early deployment posts such as Fort Bragg, Fort Stewart, and Fort Hood benefited particularly in this regard. Congressional delegations from North Carolina, Georgia, and Texas, respectively, proved capable, diligent, and artful in steering construction funds into such projects—and into Corps of Engineer upgrades for such nearby ports as Wilmington, Savannah, and Beaumont. By concentrating its troop and infrastructure losses in Europe, redefining its approach to installations, and proving attractive to congressional allies, the Army did improve upon its stateside "power projection platforms" despite weathering huge budget cuts overall.[16]

An obvious first step in the pursuit of greater strategic mobility was to increase sealift and the pace at which it moved. During DESERT SHIELD and DESERT STORM, sealift delivered 95 percent of all cargo—and 99 percent of all petroleum products. Sealift was a Joint rather than an Army phenomenon, of course, coming under the auspices of the United States Transportation Command (USTRANSCOM). Prior to DESERT STORM, USTRANSCOM had effective control over service-component transportation assets only in wartime. In peacetime the services controlled funding, procurement, and maintenance. Sustaining sealift for the Army does not seem to have been at the pinnacle of the maritime services' priorities, and the system had not been challenged on short notice since the Korean War. During DESERT SHIELD and preparations for DESERT STORM only twelve of the forty-four Ready Reserve Force ships initially activated were ready according to the timeline, and only six of twenty-seven in a second wave. Ships scheduled for a five-day breakout averaged eleven days to prepare, and those scheduled for eleven days averaged sixteen. In one particularly embarrassing episode the USNS *Antares* broke down in the Atlantic with a major fraction of the 24th Infantry Division (Mechanized)'s equipment aboard. The *Antares* was towed to Spain; its cargo was trans-loaded onto

A roll-on/roll-off (RO/RO) ship sped maritime transportation of vehicles.

other ships and arrived in Saudi Arabia three weeks late. After such initial fumbling the sealift gained its stride, moving more farther and faster than ever before: over three million tons of dry cargo and six million tons of petroleum products. In part this success resulted from rapidly chartering 213 commercial ships of various nationalities and from adding containerized freight onto ships—including tankers—routinely en route to the Middle East. A disadvantage of this additional shipping was that virtually all was break-bulk or containerized, and such cargo requires considerable heavy equipment and time to offload—unlike the roll-on/roll-off (RO/RO) ships in which units ideally would have deployed. Fortunately the Saudis had the port-servicing heavy equipment, and Saddam Hussein allowed the time. Another bright spot was the impressive performance of the modern RO/RO Fast Sealift Ships (FSSs) that did come into play. They sped along at twenty-seven knots and carried brigade sets of more than seven hundred vehicles each, a load equivalent to scores of World War II Liberty Ships. Postwar postmortems determined that strategic lift was too important to be left to the individual services. On 14 February 1992, the Secretary of Defense gave USTRANSCOM a greatly expanded charter, including control over its service components in both peace and war. In addition, the Ready Reserve Force expanded from seventeen RO/ROs in 1990 through twenty-nine in 1994 to thirty-six in 1996. The Department of the Navy did explore the possibility of deferring this significant investment of resources. The Secretary of the Navy and his General Counsel sought a private session with General Sullivan, then the Acting Secretary of the Army, and sounded out the origins of the requirement, the option of leasing ships rather than building them, and the prospects for delay. Sullivan, unable to resist historical drama, responded that the requirement had originated in the Spanish-American War, leased ships were inevitably "out of pocket" when needed, and any delay procuring reliable sealift would be dangerous to deployed or deploying soldiers. To his credit, the Secretary of the Navy scrupulously supported the endeavor from that point. His support, the undistracted institutional focus of USTRANSCOM, and the nearly doubling of the most capable sealift ships promised more impressive maritime performances in future deployments.[17]

Airlift proved less problematic than sealift during DESERT SHIELD and DESERT STORM, although it did carry only 5 percent of the total cargo. The Air Force Reserve and Air National Guard speedily mobilized to man 118 of 126 C–5 and 195 of 265 C–141 cargo planes flying. Four Navy Reserve transportation squadrons with C–9 aircraft joined the effort. Beginning 17 August the Civilian Reserve Air Fleet (CRAF) was activated, ultimately providing seventy-seven long-range international passenger aircraft and thirty-eight long-range international cargo aircraft of civilian design. Heavy demands on Saudi ramp space and refueling capability led the Air Force to refuel many of its strategic lift aircraft from KC–10 tankers in flight. Airlift was crucial to the earliest deliveries of equipment and also during such emergencies as the hasty deployments of Patriot missile batteries to Israel and Turkey. Even more significant, airlift accounted for more than 500,000 passengers—about 99 percent of the total. Ready access to passenger aircraft changed the manner in which deployment progressed, especially during its later stages. Troops remained at their home station, training and preparing, while equipment moved by sea to Saudi Arabia. At the right moment the troops flew out to intercept the arriving ships, radically reducing the time they were exposed without their equipment in congested ports. Some USAREUR armor units arrived in Saudi Arabia and offloaded their tanks within days of having fired qualification gunnery off tanks borrowed from other units in Grafenwohr, Germany. One senior staff officer from Third Army headquarters, concerned about training readiness, inquired of tank crewmen arriving on the tarmac how long it had been since they had fully qualified with the weapons and equipment appropriate to their military occupational specialty (MOS). Referring to wristwatches and interpolating for time zones, their answer was, "Four days, sir." This peak of training readiness upon arrival was a far cry from the weeks or months of idleness in transit associated with earlier wars. In the aftermath of DESERT STORM, USTRANSCOM assumed peacetime control over its wartime air component and endeavored to sustain and further improve capabilities. Most notable in this regard was the procurement of the new C–17 aircraft. The C–17 was robust enough to carry the heaviest armored vehicles, but it could take off and land on much shorter runways than the C–5 or cargo aircraft of civilian design. Defense planners also noted that 84 percent of all strategic airlift missions had passed through Torrejon Air Base in Spain and Rhein-Main Airport in Germany, underscoring the USAREUR commander's point that at least some European bases needed to be retained and secured.[18]

Prospects for early deploying units could be much improved by prepositioning supplies and equipment close to likely contingencies. Army planners noted with interest, and perhaps some chagrin, that the first substantial

The C–17 Globemaster III delivered large cargoes to austere airfields.

American mechanized contingent—beyond the 82d Airborne Division's lightly armored M551 Sheridan armored assault vehicles—into DESERT SHIELD rolled with the 7th Marine Expeditionary Brigade (MEB). The 7th MEB flew from California to marry up in Saudi Arabia with a brigade set of equipment and thirty days of supplies aboard Maritime Pre-positioning Squadron (MPS) ships that steamed in from Diego Garcia. The marines' armor was somewhat antiquated and their amphibious vehicles awkward on shore, but they provided a potent tactically mobile force early in the crisis. In due course further MEBs married up with equipment steaming in from Guam, Saipan, and the western Atlantic. The Army had appreciable experience with pre-positioning under the auspices of Pre-positioning of Materiel Configured to Unit Sets (POMCUS) during the Cold War. Several divisions' worth of equipment and supplies were pre-positioned in Germany and the Benelux countries to support reinforcements arriving from the United States. Annual Return of Forces to Germany (REFORGER) training deployments exercised these stockpiles and the units intended to draw from them. This mass of equipment, stockpiled in Western Europe, was out of place for the more likely contingencies in a post–Cold War world. As the Army downsized, further fleets of modern equipment became available for stockpiles as well. Army logisticians redistributed these supplies and equipment to achieve greater flexibility with fewer forces. By 1995 five reconfigured Army War Reserve (AWR) stockpiles were in progress: AWR-1 in the United States, AWR-2 in Europe, AWR-3 afloat, AWR-4 in Korea, and AWR-5 in Southwest Asia. Of these, AWR-3 was the most flexible and

AWR-5 the most dramatically positioned. AWR-3 grew to be a brigade set of equipment for two mechanized battalions and two tank battalions with thirty days of sustainment aboard a small fleet of roll-on/roll-off ships. Several ships in the flotilla were loaded and configured to collaterally support disaster relief, humanitarian assistance, and operations other than war. AWR-3 could have been pre-positioned anywhere, but it stood up and by and large remained in the Indian Ocean. AWR-5 deposited a brigade set of equipment and supplies in Camp Doha, a fortified compound just outside of Kuwait City. Should Iraq or Iran begin moving forces to threaten American allies in the Persian Gulf, the country would almost immediately find an American heavy brigade athwart its prospective line of departure—this in addition to much improved forces now fielded by Gulf allies.[19]

A third approach to enhanced strategic mobility would be to diminish the overall weight to be transported. Perhaps heavy units could become lighter, or light units could become more potent—and thus less in need of augmentation from heavy forces. In the short run, replacing the redoubtable M1A1 Abrams tank or M2/M3 Bradley fighting vehicles with lighter vehicles of equivalent capability seemed unlikely. The technological breakthroughs necessary to push these top-of-the-line vehicles into obsolescence were not on the near horizon. The general use of on-board auxiliary generators, particularly in the case of the fuel guzzling M1A1, could reduce fuel consumption, however, and traditional formulas for ammunition consumption had proven far too lavish during DESERT STORM. Prospective automated "total asset visibility"—concerning which, more later—also held some promise of thinning out the logistical footprint of heavy units. It seemed the M1A1 would not get lighter anytime soon, but the infrastructure supporting it might. Rendering light units more potent seemed more likely in the short run. The man-portable Javelin antitank missile went into initial production in 1994. It boasted a 2,000-meter range, a top attack capability (armored vehicles are most vulnerable from above), fire-and-forget technology, and a soft launch feature that allowed the missile to be fired safely from cover. The Javelin markedly improved the staying power of light infantrymen in the face of mechanized attack. Other strategically mobile systems improved in their capabilities to readily support infantrymen. The AH–64 Apache attack helicopter continued to upgrade with respect to avionics, sights, and sensors. Its formidable Hellfire missiles became even more lethal and flexible, to include achieving a fire-and-forget capability through millimeter-wave radar technology. The Army Tactical Missile System (ATACMS) upgraded to a 250-kilometer range with Brilliant Anti-armor Technology (BAT). The submunitions of BAT were small gliders that, when released, could autonomously acquire, track, and hit vehicles and other targets. When added to Joint assets and prospective Allied capabilities, these enhancements promised to make such light units as the 82d Airborne Division far more formidable "speed bumps" in the case of future DESERT SHIELDS.[20]

During General Sullivan's tenure, a revised, refined, and rehearsed program for Army strategic deployment emerged. More capably armed and equipped light forces would deploy quickly and, if necessary, enter forcibly. At the same time contingents from heavy divisions would deploy equally quickly by air to marry up with pre-positioned equipment, man it, and roll on to join their airborne comrades. If logisticians guessed right with respect to pre-positioning, these heavy contingents could be on hand about as quickly as their light counterparts. Meanwhile, further heavy forces would roll or rail to nearby ports and ship out to join the embattled vanguard. The mathematics describing improvements to railheads, seaports, and sealifts suggested—theoretically at least—that these reinforcing heavy divisions would deploy twice as quickly as comparable forces had deployed to DESERT SHIELD and in preparation for DESERT STORM. It was not enough to change only infrastructure, doctrine, and equipment to achieve this result, however. Training and culture were at issue as well. The Army had to overcome its heavy-light divide, entrenched philosophies with respect to combat service support, and a bias toward the upper echelons with respect to combined and joint operations if it was to make the new paradigm work.[21]

The prolonged Cold War advanced and hardened a polarization between the Army's Eurocentric heavy forces and light forces that seemed optimal for a fight anywhere except Europe. Tankers epitomized the heavy forces, with vehicle-borne fellow travelers from other branches riding alongside them and armored cavalrymen as a somewhat more ecumenical version of themselves. Paratroopers epitomized the light forces, with fellow travelers from other branches jumping out of planes alongside them and Rangers as a somewhat extreme tribal version of themselves. The two camps had their prejudices. Paratrooper banter stereotyped tankers as corpulent dwarves, strong enough in the shoulders to sling ammunition and break track, short enough to get around in the confines of their turrets, and fattened by their aversion to running—or even walking—and by a diet dominated by *Bier* and *Bratwurst*. Tanker banter envisioned paratroopers as equivalent to the *Eloi* of H. G. Wells' *The Time Machine,* prancing around in the great outdoors but never doing the real work of logistics, maintenance, and motor pools. Short-notice strategic mobility was something paratroopers did to get to the difficult out-of-the-way places where they were likely to fight. Tankers would roll out of their German motor pools to fight on the great plains of Central Europe or would join the European battle from the United States in accordance with well-choreographed war plans. Nowhere was the heavy-light divide more pronounced than with respect to attitudes toward vehicles. Paratroopers, according to tankers, did not love their vehicles—what few that they had. To them one truck was as good as another to ride around in, and they happily accepted horrific attrition as they parachuted vehicles out of planes in flight or shoved them off the ramps of planes rolling down a runway. Tankers lavished two hours of maintenance on their tank for every hour that they operated it, knowing that if they took care of it, it would take care of them. This wedding of man and machine was particularly pronounced with respect to gunnery. By virtue of both faith and science, tankers understood that each weapon on each tank had a unique signature with respect to the strike of its rounds on target. These signatures were unlocked by elaborate and arcane processes of bore sighting and zeroing, after which tank commanders and gunners bore the dial settings for each weapon and type of ammunition in a small notebook in their breast pockets—close to their hearts. Once a year tankers measured their worth in qualification gunnery, Tank Table VIII. A good tank (a term that included the crew) could put a round through a windowpane at two thousand meters or have two targets down before observers realized the first had been engaged. Tank Table VIII surpassed all other indicators as a measure of merit. By tradition, tank company commanders were the first crews down range on qualification day, leading from the front and by example. Battalion operations officers, battalion commanders, and brigade commanders of armor provenance invested heavily from their personal time to be members of a qualifying crew—not so much because of combat requirements but to maintain the respect of the men they commanded. Extraordinary expectations of men and machines fostered emotional attachments. Tankers would fight or shoot from a tank other than their own about as readily as they would wear another tanker's underwear. If a tank were evacuated to higher levels of maintenance, at least one crew member went with it. Sometimes crewmen actually assisted in the maintenance; often they merely waited around like family members outside an operating room. Tankers were an extreme case of the man-machine interface, but all who rode with them—armored artillerymen, mechanized infantrymen, combat engineers, mechanics, truckers, and other combat support and combat service support troops of many types and specialties—were measured by the performances of the machines they manned. Each specialty had its version of crew qualification that enhanced competence and confidence with respect to the equipment they were on, and correspondingly diminished confidence with respect to equipment they had not themselves maintained. It is true that REFORGER and other training deployments set crews onto unfamiliar vehicles, but these had generally been demonstrations for show or tactical maneuvers, seldom involved serious gunnery, and never featured qualification gunnery. If a rapid deployment paradigm was to include putting heavy forces onto unfamiliar vehicles, better means needed to be devised to render crews competent and confident with respect to vehicles they hastily manned.[22]

Philosophies with respect to combat service support also reflected an accumulated mix of the practical and the theological. The Army had long enshrined "Unity of Command" as a principle of war. A single commander or, in some cases, agency should be in charge of each important endeavor. Command relations were reciprocal. Subordinates obeyed the lawful orders of a single commander, and in turn expected to singularly derive combat and combat service support from that commander. Units deploying from one theater to another shed their support relationships with the theater they departed and became dependent on the support of the theater in which they arrived. Each theater had its own hierarchy of upper-echelon support commands and stockpiled "iron mountains" of supplies and equipment for the contingencies it envisioned. Time-phased force and deployment lists (TPFDLs) programmed units to deploy with a "slice" of combat and combat support forces sufficient to sustain them in theater. These became subordinate to the hierarchy of support in theater, generally through the agency of a service component command. Individual replacements, equipment, and supplies of all types flowed through the theater into the unit. One of the most remarkable aspects of

DESERT SHIELD had been the monumental effort whereby it stood up Third Army and the support architecture for DESERT STORM. DESERT STORM was not, however, the ideal logistical model for most contingencies that planners had envisioned as likely in the early 1990s, and it was not ideal for contingencies units actually found themselves in either. These contingencies were smaller in scale than those envisioned during the Cold War, and the participation of a given unit might well be conditional or fleeting. For example, and as we shall see, Northern Iraq featured a uniquely cobbled together potpourri of small units, Somalia featured a rotation of units in and out of theater, and for Haiti there were two contingency forces en route at the same time, one anticipating forcible entry and the other a welcoming reception. In this fluid—perhaps a better description would be kaleidoscopic—environment, consolidating iron mountains to support long-anticipated TPFDLs made little sense. Logistical footprints in overseas contingencies needed to be as malleable as the mix of units actually operating in them. "Split basing" or "split-based logistics" emerged as an acceptable dilution with respect to unity of command. Home stations remained responsible for such hard-to-conjure-up items as trained individual replacements of appropriate rank, major end items of equipment, or relatively exotic repair parts and other maintenance items. Theater assets provided such routine consumables as food, water, and fuel. The theater also coordinated the transportation that enabled the flow of support from home stations. Munitions would probably be provided by the theater, but they might also be drawn from home stations—depending on inventories. Casualties would be evacuated into a theater asset first and then flown to a stateside hospital like Walter Reed Army Medical Center or to the home station—if not returned to duty. Light forces had been involved in enough small Cold War–era contingencies to already have a feel for split basing and had adopted the notion of an out-of-the-conflict-zone intermediate staging base (ISB) that rendered logistical support triangular. Support was at least an order of magnitude simpler with light forces than heavy, since they had so little unique or specialized equipment with them and deployed with relatively little equipment overall. Aviation generally accompanied light forces and generated support requirements akin to those of heavy forces but had a much greater capacity to self-deploy. Transitioning heavy forces to a split-based paradigm would be hard. A major fraction of the challenge would be managing extraordinary amounts of information: inventories and the movements of people, equipment, parts, and other supplies. In an earlier era materiel had been piled up in iron mountains and management rendered easier by excesses of supply.[23]

Another practice appropriate to a post–Cold War world of lesser contingencies would be that of driving combined and joint operations to lower echelons of command. A general defense plan (GDP) in Germany had featured a "layer cake" of autonomous national corps sectors stacked from south to north. The United States V Corps was responsible for a sector facing the "Fulda Gap," and the VII Corps for a sector facing the "Hof Gap" and the Czech border. Support assets within each of the sectors were by and large American, although local nationals were employed on most installations, and host-nation support of various types was planned in the case of hostilities. Each of the two American corps coordinated with a German corps on one flank. Direct coordination between specific American and Allied divisions was envisioned for some contingencies, and most brigades and battalions had "partnership" counterparts with whom they shared occasional social and training outings. Combined training did occur, largely with units training alongside each other rather than being truly dependent on one another to achieve tactical success. The North Atlantic Treaty Organization (NATO) did publish and enforce a body of standardization agreements (STANAGs) governing processes, terms, and conditions relevant to common procedures and equipment. Allied officers in NATO by and large spoke English, making interoperability feasible when pressed. Nevertheless, American soldiers of all ranks spent very little time interacting with Germans in a professional capacity, lived much or most of their overseas tours in American barracks or housing areas, and theoretically could have gotten by without ever having spoken a word of German. Contact with other services when in Germany was similarly biased toward the upper echelons. The Navy and Marine Corps were virtually invisible to soldiers in Europe. The Air Force had self-contained enclaves of its own. Since World War II the Air Force fiercely defended the notion that Air Force assets in a theater should be centrally controlled, an idea that made sense given the range, mobility, and relatively brief "loiter time" of their aircraft. This led the daily theater-level Air Tasking Order (ATO) to become the premier device controlling missions assigned to aircraft. As a practical matter, the Army corps was the lowest echelon that could significantly influence the theater ATO. Air liaison cells were routinely manned at division level, unevenly manned at the brigade level, and generally present in battalions only when deployed to higher-level maneuvers in the field. These lower-level cells had little influence on the ATO process, but they did coordinate the direct support the ATO distributed to their commands. Often even this potential interaction was resolved by virtue of a fire support coordination line (FSCL), beyond which anybody could bomb or shell at will without detailed coordination. Pilots were directed to the far side of the FSCL, and soldiers happily went about fighting the battle closer to them without thinking too hard about what airpower could or should do. Units in the United States had little exposure to combined operations and joint experiences parallel to that of their colleagues in Germany. Korea was a special case with respect to combined and joint operations, concerning which, more later. The relevant operational "chip on the board" was the corps. How much would change when operations devolved to smaller units?[24]

The Army values the notion that it should train as it would fight. The modern Louisiana Maneuvers, LAM Task Force deliberations, and developing contingencies all underscored the need to better prepare for joint expeditionary combat. The Army would have to train toward this altered focus, and heavy forces would have to train the hardest. Heavy divisions in the United States designated task force–size division ready forces (DRFs), prepared to deploy by air on short notice. These trained and prepared for the task, to include working through theretofore unfamiliar air load planning processes to develop load plans for each type of plane they might lift out on. NTC rotations took on the character of Emergency Deployment Readiness Exercises (EDREs), with heavy units falling in on and drawing equipment under tactical circumstances. They rolled to the field for exercises that included serious gunnery. For tankers this gunnery included Tank Tables VII and XI and a combined-arms live-fire exercise (CALFEX). Tank Table VII was as complex and demanding as Tank Table VIII, although not characterized as crew qualification. Tank Table XI similarly mimicked the platoon qualifications of Tank Table XII. CALFEX was live fire conducted at team or task force level and increasingly included live air strikes as part of the training package. Motivated by challenging gunnery that would be observed and scored, tankers found ways to accelerate their nesting behavior—their settling in—on unfamiliar tanks. Commanders hustled their units to impromptu ranges for bore sighting and zeroing. The general introduction of optically improved muzzle bore sight devices greatly facilitated this process. The computerized M1A1 rendered tankers independent of mechanical dial settings, since settings could be reliably "punched up" on their consoles. In the aftermath of DESERT STORM, active-component units acquired expanded roles in the training of reserve-component units, concerning which, more later. In a fine example of educational reflux, active-component soldiers assigned to such duties picked up on the manner in which long-serving National Guard tank crews deprocessed tanks from maintenance sites for annual summer training, brought them to a fully operational status, and qualified with them on Tank Table VIII. Actual deployments—some for training and some for deterrence—required tankers to man, operate, and shoot from equipment pre-positioned overseas. Tankers never acquired the promiscuous attitude toward vehicles that paratroopers had, but they did become capable of a species of serial monogamy with respect to tanks, rapidly achieving competence and confidence in the one they were with. They brought unfamiliar vehicles into play within a few days' time, and then treated them as if they were their own. This proved true for the other branches who rode with them as well. The heavy force as a whole acquired the practical and psychological attributes necessary to efficiently man and field pre-positioned unit sets of equipment. Rigorous training also enhanced the capability of heavy forces to move by sea. In FY1994, for example, $26 million went to Sea Emergency Deployment Readiness Exercises (SEDREs). Heavy units raced to ports on short notice, loaded their vehicles and equipment on ships, and deployed to training events that featured some combination of amphibious, over-the-shore, and through-port entry. SEDREs were inevitably joint, featuring maritime transportation and air support during the tactical phases. Preparations for SEDREs took on aspects of the old European GDP, with units reconnoitering railheads, routes to port, and the ports themselves and compiling "battle books" full of maps, diagrams, and pictures to focus their efforts—and to enable them to better initiate newly arrived soldiers.[25]

The fact that Army heavy forces were increasingly capable of roles that had been the province of the Marine Corps did not go unnoticed. Marines envisioned themselves as the nation's rapid response force of middle weight, more capable and more joint than Army light forces of equivalent or greater strategic mobility. With Army light forces becoming more capable and Army heavy forces more deployable, distinctions between the services muddied.

Naval advocacy of "operational maneuver from the sea" depended in part on the physical location of Marines afloat—or of pre-positioned equipment—to achieve timeliness. Once the Army pre-positioned equipment afloat and dispersed caches of pre-positioned equipment ashore, it might end up deploying heavy forces to an unexpected contest in a distant theater as or more quickly than the Marines did. Marines for some time had considered the preservation of their operational uniqueness as a matter of institutional survival. The Joint Staff, refusing to believe that there could be too much of a good thing, took a more sanguine view. The 1993 *Report on the Roles, Missions and Functions of the Armed Forces of the United States* blandly observed, "The similarity of Army and Marine Corps capabilities provides alternatives to the President and the Secretary of Defense during a crisis." Increasingly enforced joint collegiality muted debate, but competition to be the nation's "911 force" remained.[26]

The combination of institutional emphasis, training, and operational deployments had its intended effect. By 1995 heavy units in the United States were appreciably more deployable and flexible than they had been five years earlier. An illustrative example may make the point. On 8 August 1995, Lieutenant General Hussein Kamel Hassan, a powerful son-in-law of Iraqi dictator Saddam Hussein, and his brother Colonel Saddam Kamel Hassan defected through Jordan with their families and aides. Hussein Kamel made contact with the Saudis and called for regime change in Iraq. Saddam Hussein was understandably paranoid about defections from his inner circle—Hussein Kamel had been in charge of "military industrialization"—and for a time it seemed he might lash out against the Kuwaitis, Jordanians, and Saudis he viewed as in league with his treacherous son-in-law. Fortuitously, 2,000 United States Marines were already conducting a major combined exercise with the Jordanians, providing a readily reinforcible deterrent force. The Joint Staff determined to put a like-size force into Kuwait. The Division Ready Force 1 (DRF1) for the 1st Cavalry Division was Task Force 1-5 Cavalry, consisting of two tank and two mechanized infantry companies with supporting units. This was a start, but joint force planners decided they wanted another tank company, a complex artillery battalion equivalent that included a Multiple Launch Rocket System (MLRS) battery, a full engineer company, enough of a forward support battalion to accommodate the potential deployment of the rest of the parent brigade, and the brigade headquarters (in this case the 2d Brigade of the 1st Cavalry Division) to coordinate the enlarged force structure and to interface with the theater and the Kuwaitis. Despite these and other last-minute changes, the 1,500 troops chosen flowed smoothly through the recently revamped airfield at Fort Hood, Texas, at a pace such that they were waiting on planes and planes were not waiting on them. Equipment to accompany troops loaded speedily, facilitated by the airfield's newly arrived load-handling equipment. The MLRS battery and target acquisition battery loaded quickly aboard aircraft with all of their equipment in accordance with predesigned load plans. The rest of the deploying force drew vehicles and heavy equipment from AWR-5 at Camp Doha in Kuwait. The equipment draw in Kuwait progressed efficiently, with company-size units averaging less than six hours to inventory, inspect, upload, and roll out. The units averaged less than twelve hours between touching down in Kuwait and achieving readiness condition 1 (REDCON 1) in their assigned positions in the desert. Meanwhile, the rest of the 2d Brigade Combat Team at Fort Hood prepared to follow these lead elements onto AWR-5 if called, planners from the 1st Cavalry Division, 2d Armored Division, and 24th Infantry Division (Mechanized) postured their commands for flows through the ports of Beaumont and Savannah if necessary, and AWR-3 prepared to steam into the Persian Gulf. The Kuwaitis had four heavy brigades of their own, and the calculus of the potential buildup suggested the Americans would never be outnumbered by more than three to one in a defense of Mutla Ridge, north of Kuwait City. Given qualitative advantages, these were favorable odds.[27]

The no-notice deployment to Kuwait was tucked into a Kuwaiti-American exercise program labeled INTRINSIC ACTION. It somewhat resembled REFORGER, but much had changed. The climate was different, of course, with horrific daytime temperatures well above a hundred degrees and a merciless sun. The troops had been drilled with respect to hydration, diurnal cycles in the desert, getting camouflage nets up quickly for shade, local flora and fauna, and field sanitation. They kept their daily sick call rate to well under 2 percent throughout, and dropped it to under 1 percent over time. The threat of hostile action was real, and force protection was the highest assigned priority. Deployment was not in accordance with a long-familiar GDP; instead leaders absorbed a skeletal Central Command (CENTCOM) contingency plan en route. Once on the ground they conducted reconnaissance and maneuvered their units through the ground they were to defend, refining the contingency plan into an operational plan that had many of the features of the old GDP. Emerging battle books included positions for and guidance to potential reinforcing units. Upon arrival crews "screened" their vehicles. In the case of the tankers this meant bore sighting and zeroing with live ammunition. Portable pop-up targets had been imported into Kuwait from Germany, and tank and Bradley crews undertook challenging gunnery exercises early on, quickly settling into their new vehicles. Support was split-based. Vehicles drawn from Camp Doha were supported through Camp Doha, which was also the source for consumable supplies. Unique vehicles, such as those of the MLRS and target acquisition battery (TAB), were supported from Fort Hood, which also remained the source for personnel support. Thoroughly acclimatized after a few days, the task force had the enormous satisfaction of hosting a Marine Battalion Landing Team that arrived considerably after them in a live-fire exercise on Udairi Range. Even more important than this joint training was combined training with the Kuwaiti Army. The American 2d Brigade paired off with the Kuwaiti 6th Mechanized Brigade, and American Task Force 1-5 Cavalry with Kuwaiti Task Force 154 Armor. Combined training progressed from the individual level, with significant interpersonal contact at every rank. The Kuwaitis were equipped with Yugoslavian-provided XM84 tanks and had adopted the former East Bloc practice of firing from bore sight. This was anathema to the American tankers, who demonstrated the merits of zeroing as well. The culmination of the combined training was an expansive CALFEX through miles of open desert under the watchful eyes of senior American and Kuwaiti observers. The fire and maneuver was tightly integrated, with Kuwaiti

105

companies dependent on American overwatch, and vice versa. This interplay was a far cry from national corps operating independently of each other in their own sectors. The theater Air Tasking Order for these several days was designed at the brigade and battalion levels as well, since there was no higher tactical level with which to coordinate the CALFEX.[28]

INTRINSIC ACTION 95–3 demonstrated the new paradigm for Army heavy forces that had emerged over the past four years. Doctrine and training had shifted from the expectation of forward deployment to an expectation of expeditionary combat. Units as small as companies and detachments nimbly swapped out with each other as the design of the deploying force package matured. The hardware of much-improved installation infrastructure and equipment and the software of standing load plans combined to facilitate the smoothness of the launch. Experience falling in on pre-positioned equipment during training ensured efficiency falling in on pre-positioned equipment during this actual contingency. A grander strategic scheme envisioning reinforcing airlift and sealift was positioned for speedy execution, had it proved necessary. Once in Kuwait, the soldiers acclimatized quickly and performed capably in a theretofore unfamiliar environment. Split-basing effectively supported the force package on the ground, despite the unusualness of its design. Joint and combined operations had been pushed to the task force level and below, with a degree of service and international interface that would not have existed a few years prior. Three months into the mission the 2d Brigade contingent conducted a relief in place with the 3d Brigade, 4th Infantry Division, flying in from Fort Carson, Colorado. Perhaps the greatest compliment was unintended, when the Battalion Landing Team commander training on Udairi Range casually commented that the heavy soldiers had hastily deployed "as good as Marines."[29]

Escalating Contingencies

INTRINSIC ACTION 95–3 was but the latest in a series of troop deployments to Kuwait, several of which had occurred on short notice in the face of crisis. These deployments in turn numbered among an escalating mix of contingencies. Such operations increased threefold between the end of the Cold War and 1995. On an average day, FY1995 saw more than 20,000 soldiers deployed into about eighty different countries. This did not include troops assigned overseas at permanent stations. Globalization, and the now-altered strategic role of the United States in the emerging global community, underlay the increase. DESERT STORM reflected, as we have seen, the determination of a broad American-led coalition sanctioned and blessed by the United Nations to reverse aggression and preserve world order—economic and otherwise. Incoming President William J. Clinton articulated and eventually published a *National Security Strategy of Engagement and Enlargement*. "Engagement" implied making new friends around the world, particularly where Americans had been unwelcome or inattentive during the Cold War. "Enlargement" spoke to the peaceful advance of liberal capitalism and democracy into lands where they theretofore had been alien. The armed forces necessarily would carry much of the weight.

Military participation in escalating contingencies bunched under several headings: consolidating the results of the Cold War and DESERT STORM, accommodating expanded public and United Nations appetites for humanitarian intervention, and filling in when civilian policy makers did not have appropriate tools. With respect to Army transformation, increasing deployments had a reciprocal effect. The move to an expeditionary paradigm rendered the service more available for deployment; deployments increased the incentive to become more expeditionary. This give-and-take affected the nature of transformation as it progressed. It is also worth noting that this escalation in deployments occurred while the Department of the Army adjusted to ever less operational involvement in how the forces were used once deployed. Goldwater-Nichols left operational planning to the theater commanders in chief (CINCs). Some theaters proved more prepared to carry the load than others.[30]

The Warsaw Pact, and then the Soviet Union, collapsed quickly, and transfers of power to successor regimes were uneven and fragile. Suspended ethnic tensions reemerged, disintegrating Yugoslavia and Czechoslovakia and provoking strife in a dozen other newly independent nations. The situation had unhappy historical precedents. After World War I most of Central and much of Eastern Europe attempted democratic governance. Instability, insecurity, economic collapse, political inexperience, and politicized militaries led virtually all of them into authoritarian rule even before Nazi Germany and the Soviet Union—themselves the products of failed democracies—overwhelmed them. In the immediate aftermath of World War II, prospective democratic institutions in Central and Eastern Europe offered feeble resistance to communist takeovers. The nations of NATO resolved to do better in the aftermath of the Cold War. Beginning in December 1991 NATO hosted the North Atlantic Cooperation Council to facilitate dialogue and cooperation with the newly independent states. The long-term vision was to encourage and materially assist evolution toward democracy, open market economies, and ultimate integration into the liberal Euro-Atlantic family of nations. Immediate military priorities were to head off destabilizing humanitarian disasters, preclude nuclear proliferation, and nurture Western *mores* in former East Bloc armed forces.[31]

Humanitarian issues surfaced quickly. Going into the winter of 1991–1992, secession and political turmoil led to some scarcities and more maldistribution of food and medical supplies in the former Soviet Union. NATO planners feared that desperation might lead to destabilizing strife in major cities. Fortuitously, enormous stockpiles horded for a Soviet invasion of Western Europe were now in excess. The American Assistant Secretary of Defense for Humanitarian and Refugee Affairs took the lead in PROVIDE HOPE, an operation that delivered over 27,000 tons of food and supplies supported by teams of medical personnel to the former Soviet Union between February and August 1992. The 7th Medical Command (7th MEDCOM) was particularly instrumental in this joint operation, delivering supplies, installing medical equipment, and training local medical personnel in the uses of both. PROVIDE HOPE continued through September 1994, increasingly civilianized and internationalized after August 1992. Interestingly enough, coordination on the ground was provided by the On Site Inspection Agency, U.S. military

107

personnel with appropriate language skills serving in the former Soviet Union as inspectors facilitating various arms control agreements. This connection between carrot and stick was not entirely accidental, as the United States encouraged successor states to remain treaty-compliant and wanted to ensure that nuclear weapons and materials remained in the hands of Russia alone. PROVIDE HOPE confidence building seems to have contributed to this happy result. The potential humanitarian crisis in the former Soviet Union was soon eclipsed by actual humanitarian crisis in former Yugoslavia. In support of the United Nations Protection Force (UNPROFOR), Operation PROVIDE PROMISE provided humanitarian relief and medical support to civilians and United Nations troops. The 212th Surgical Hospital (Mobile Army) deployed to Zagreb in November 1992 and treated more than 5,000 patients from thirty-five nations in six months. From that point, mobile surgical hospitals rotated to relieve each other in Zagreb. For a time the United States was spared the lead in Yugoslavia, as largely European contingents under United Nations auspices strove to contain conflict and restore security. By the summer of 1993 UNPROFOR was stretched too thin, however, and USAREUR contributed a three-hundred-plus contingent from 6th Battalion, 502d Infantry Regiment, for observer duties in Macedonia. This mission oriented on threats from Serbia and evolved into the rotational ABLE SENTRY.[32]

Humanitarian relief, peacekeeping, and nuclear nonproliferation were immediate and visible post–Cold War imperatives. A longer-term but even more consequential imperative was to nurture habits appropriate to democracies in the newly independent nations. Civil governments of the United States and European community could provide economic safety nets, materially assist democratic processes, and negotiate security issues. It fell to the uniformed officers of NATO to facilitate the transformation of Soviet-designed armed forces into institutions appropriate for liberal democracies. There was no guarantee of a happy result, with the possible exception of Germany. With stereotypical efficiency the *Bundeswehr* had taken over its eastern counterpart, retired all officers above the rank of lieutenant colonel on sensible pensions, liquidated huge masses of Soviet-designed equipment, and diverted residual and incoming manpower into its own units. Germany's status had been settled by treaty, and Helmut Kohl's government had the domestic and international prestige to design and enforce grand solutions. Circumstances were more uncertain elsewhere. Romania's army had been kingmaker in a violent overthrow. Poland's army remained respected by many as a counterweight to the potential volatility of *Solidarity*. In Hungary and Bulgaria change had been largely top driven, with modest displacement of traditional elites. The Czech armed forces were buoyed by Czech military-industrial expectations. Soviet armies had disintegrated into ethnic militia. The Yugoslav army was running amok. Senior leaders of Warsaw Pact vintage armies headed powerful bureaucracies, habituated to the control of their nation's young men. Fear of a resurgent Russia and social values concerning the virtue of service translated into continuing conscription in most cases, further empowering military elites. Ironically, the former Warsaw Pact middle-grade and senior-grade officers most capable of dealing with NATO, wherein the international language of command was English, were often active or former intelligence and counterintelligence operatives. These highly vetted positions required English proficiency, whereas most operational positions did not. Cold War success could not be consolidated without military reform, and this would be no easy thing. NATO's approach to the challenge was prolonged engagement. Over time senior officers in the former Warsaw Pact could be nudged or lured into retirement, perhaps in association with industrial contracts that allowed some to pursue wealth rather than power. Democratic regimes, once their grip was sure, could be encouraged to abandon conscription. Necessarily slimmed down militaries could then be redesigned along Western lines, junking huge masses of Soviet-era equipment for inventories of a more modern design. Operational emphasis would shift from Kursk-like tank battles to peacekeeping, search and rescue, and humanitarian relief. These operations other than war seemed more appropriate to the new era, and training toward them would seem less threatening to their neighbors—particularly Russia. Schooling and assignments in the West would be offered, and training regimes would heavily emphasize international operations. NATO officers and officers from the former Warsaw Pact and the Commonwealth of Independent States (CIS) would intermingle extensively in school, on assignment, when training, and on operations. Hopefully such values as deference to democratically elected governments, transparency in defense budgeting, and respect for international protocols would be nurtured in the course of this interface. A new generation of military leaders would emerge, gaining personal prestige through successes in challenging multinational assignments and being rendered more cosmopolitan by complex multilingual requirements. In January 1994 this package of initiatives acquired a name, Partnership for Peace. Moving quickly, USAREUR and its NATO allies hosted a potpourri of exercises and exchanges intermingling officers and soldiers from both sides of the former Iron Curtain. These were more focused in scope but concurrent with operational intermingling that was already occurring in expanded United Nations peacekeeping. For example, the 212th Surgical Hospital (Mobile Army) and its successors in Zagreb were already routinely treating UNPROFOR Russian, Ukrainian, Polish, and other former East Bloc soldiers. Partnership for Peace exercises escalated in scope and ambition. In late 1995 COOPERATIVE CHALLENGE brought together thirteen battalions—including Americans, Austrians, Belgians, Czechs, Dutch, Estonians, French, Lithuanians, Poles, Slovaks, and Swedes—in a sprawling exercise through 140 square kilometers of the Czech Republic. The scenario was multinational peacekeeping under the supervision of a combined international staff. The immediate intent was to train to a standard at each echelon involved and to work out practical standard operating procedures for forces of such size and complexity in the future. The long-term intent was, of course, engagement. A great deal remained to be done, but the process was beginning.[33]

Engagement had replaced containment as the priority in Europe, but in East Asia containment remained a priority, as did demonstrations of cooperative resolve to reassure regional allies. TEAM SPIRIT and ULCHI FOCUS LENS continued as major joint and combined exercises involving deployments from the United States to Korea, as did ORIENT SHIELD in Japan. COBRA GOLD reinforced cooperation with Thailand, as did TIGER BALM with Singapore. BALIKATAN demonstrated an American capability to quickly reinforce the Philippines. To these and dozens of smaller exercises in the Pacific and Indian Oceans, the Army added requirements to contain and deter Iraq in the aftermath of DESERT STORM. As we have seen, INTRINSIC ACTION periodically deployed heavy task forces to draw pre-positioned equipment and deploy in support of the Kuwaitis. Sometimes these deployments occurred with little or no notice in times of crisis; more often they were routine. The United States and the Coalition had enforced "no fly zones" on Iraq to better secure their neighbors and restrain their operations against Kurds in the north and Shi'a in the south. SOUTHERN WATCH, and later NORTHERN WATCH, enforced these sanctions and secured Saudi, Kuwaiti, and Turkish airspaces. The Army rotated Air Defense battalions and logistical contingents in support of SOUTHERN WATCH and NORTHERN WATCH. IRIS GOLD similarly rotated special operating forces through Kuwait, and BRIGHT STAR provided a repeatable major combined exercise with the Egyptians. There were others, some oriented on Iran more than on Iraq. Throughout Asia in general and the Arab Middle East in particular, recurrent deployments proved far more acceptable to national sensibilities than forces permanently deployed. Koreans and Japanese were generally agreeable to a permanent American presence; few others were. Sensitive allies wanted American troops present in moments of crisis or when they needed them, but otherwise preferred them out of sight—deep in the desert or over the horizon. Frequent combined exercises and deployments separated by gaps preserved an American presence while avoiding an impression of permanence. Wags characterized the constant movements to and fro as "commuter containment." The new modus operandi radically increased the pressure on the Army to generate deployable contingents, even if for relatively brief periods of time.[34]

In the aftermath of the Cold War, and given the triumph of the United Nations–sanctioned DESERT STORM coalition, further advances resolving the quarrels of the world seemed possible. The United Nations in particular scaled up its ambitions. It seemed to be a brave new era of international cooperation. Between 1945 and 1989 the United Nations Security Council was paralyzed by veto 279 times. Between 1990 and 1994, it never was. In 1987 perhaps 10,000 troops had been deployed under United Nations auspices to seven contingencies at a cost of $230 million. In 1995 more than 80,000 were deployed to twenty contingencies at a cost of $3.5 billion. Traditional United Nations peacekeeping before 1989 had interposed lightly armed observers between forces, generally national armies, which had agreed to a cease-fire and needed neutral observers to help them police it. Observation forces were small, fragmented into representation among many nations, and altogether dependent on moral authority to succeed. Such forces had reasonably successfully separated Indians from Pakistanis, Israelis from Egyptians, Israelis from Syrians, and Greek Cypriots from Turkish Cypriots, to cite a few examples. Their success depended largely upon the discipline and goodwill of the former belligerents and upon there being "a peace to keep." United Nations forces had had less success in such chaotic environments as Lebanon or the Congo, wherein multiple adversaries and heavily armed desperadoes fought in the absence of military discipline or national control and demonstrated little interest in the peaceful resolution of ongoing violence. Peacemaking was far more difficult than peacekeeping and required forces more robust and better organized than the loose military patchworks of the past. Beginning in 1989 the United Nations coordinated the dispatch of 4,500 troops to Namibia, 15,500 troops to Cambodia, 6,500 troops to Mozambique, 7,500 troops to Angola, and observer missions to El Salvador, Costa Rica, Guatemala, Honduras, and Nicaragua. These had been surrogate Cold War battlefields, but now the great powers had a much diminished interest in them. Within a few years violence subsided, and these missions withdrew from all except Angola. The United Nations had considerably less luck in the former Yugoslavia, despite dispatching 40,000 troops to UNPROFOR. We will discuss this in the next chapter. Traditionally the United States Army had been little involved in United Nations peacekeeping, tacit recognition of how unlikely the United States was to be regarded as a disinterested party during the Cold War years. The Sinai mission was an exception, committing the United States to position the equivalent of a reinforced battalion between the newly friendly Egyptians and the ever friendly Israelis from 1982 on. In particularly difficult situations the United Nations had endorsed the United States as its lead agent for peace enforcement. This allowed the robust military and command and control capabilities of the United States to come directly into play, legitimated by an international coalition. The Korean War and DESERT STORM were examples of such peace enforcement. Within a few years this basic model would appear three more times: in Northern Iraq, Somalia, and Haiti.[35]

In the aftermath of Saddam Hussein's eviction from Kuwait during DESERT STORM, restive Shi'a in the south of Iraq and Kurds in the north revolted against his rule. Unfortunately for them, Saddam had extricated or withheld from combat forces sufficient to crush both uprisings. Coalition forces did not perceive support of these revolts as within their mandate, deferring to Sunni Arab suspicion of Iran and the Shi'a and to Turkish concerns about Kurdish autonomy. Lopsided fighting soon generated hundreds of thousands of refugees. The Shi'a by and large fled into xenophobic Iran and remained invisible to the West and the rest of the world. A half million Kurds fled into the mountains separating Iraq from Turkey. Their desperate plight, dying by the hundreds in the wintry mountains without adequate food, water, clothing, or shelter, provoked international furor when televised around the world. On 5 April 1991, the United Nations passed Resolution 688 condemning the ruthless Iraqi repression and justifying international action. The United States took the lead in operations to halt the dying and suffering, resettle the refugees in temporary camps, and return them to their original homes as soon as possible. In Operation PROVIDE COMFORT more than 12,000 American military personnel would be joined by 11,000 coalition partners and supported by tens of thousands of Turks, dozens of nongovernmental agencies and private volunteer organizations, and cadres and work crews drawn from the Kurds themselves. Relief progressed from frantic airdrops through sprawling heliborne deliveries to routine truck-borne resupply as coalition forces lured the Kurds off of the peaks into steadily expanding encampments. Once their medical

Kurdish refugees flee fighting in northern Iraq.

conditions stabilized, the allies resolved to return the refugees to their homes. This in effect required a second invasion of Iraq, since the Kurds would not return without coalition forces to protect them. The Iraqis melted away in the face of the allied advance, and civilian relief agencies accompanied the returning tide of refugees. The Kurds resettled, protected by international observers, air patrols, U.S. forces on the ground initially and in an expeditionary posture thereafter, and by their own rearmed *Peshmerga.* Humanitarian disaster had been averted.[36]

Somalia was an arid land racked by sectarian and clan violence after the overthrow of strongman Mohammed Siad Barre in January 1991. Drought hugely complicated the political chaos. Famine ravaged the land as factions fought over dwindling supplies and food became a weapon. International relief efforts proved ineffectual when rival warlords looted supplies and robbed convoys. A hastily deployed United Nations Operations in Somalia (UNOSOM) force had no better luck, and its small contingent of five hundred Pakistani soldiers ended up virtual hostages at the Mogadishu Airport. Meanwhile international television broadcast footage of starving children covered with flies and dying in filth, night after night. Hundreds of thousands, perhaps millions, were at risk. On 3 December 1992, the United Nations Security Council passed Resolution 794, endorsing a robust relief expedition led by the United States. Operation RESTORE HOPE arrived with overwhelming force beginning 8 December, cowing the warlords and securing their cooperation. A Unified Task Force (UNITAF) of about 10,000 soldiers from the 10th Mountain Division, a like number of U.S. Marines, 5,000 U.S. personnel of other types, and 13,000 coalition partners from twenty-two nations secured Mogadishu, organized the

U.S. troops patrolling in Somalia

hard-hit southern half of Somalia into nine Humanitarian Relief Sectors, and fanned out through the countryside to guarantee humanitarian relief. Within a month 40,000 tons of grain had been effectively delivered, relief agencies and military medical personnel were working the interior without interference, and the worst of the crisis had passed. As the drought relented, local agriculture began to revive. Somalia was primitive enough that its rural areas generally survived by subsistence whether or not there was an effective central government—and often there was not. With mass starvation averted and nightly television no longer haunted by horrific imagery from Somalia, international public attention moved on. The United States government wanted to move on as well and to turn Somalia over to a more traditionally organized United Nations force. On 4 May 1993, control passed to United Nations Operations in Somalia II (UNOSOM II) commanded by Turkish General Cevik Bir. By October UNOSOM II had dwindled to 16,000 peacekeepers from twenty-one nations, of whom about 4,000 were from the United States—primarily in support roles. UNITAF had focused on humanitarian relief and regarded serious efforts at nation building and disarming the warlords as beyond its mandate. Unfortunately, the much less capable UNOSOM II became drawn into renewed clan rivalry for the port of Mogadishu. Coordination among the United Nations contingents, between the United Nations and the United States, and between United States forces

113

working under United Nations auspices and those outside of them was seriously fragmented. Taking advantage of the confusion, warlord Muhammed Aideed of the Habr Gidr subclan forcibly advanced his own interests, attacking rival clans and United Nations troops as he did so. The American contingent, reinforced by a Joint Special Operations Task Force (JSOTF), responded with raids on Aideed's facilities and henchmen. Six of these raids went well. A seventh precipitated a sprawling all-night battle through the streets of Mogadishu wherein eighteen Americans and perhaps five hundred Somalis died. The casualties were lopsided, but American viewers were shocked and revulsed by televised imagery of Somalis desecrating American bodies and dragging them through the streets. The nation was in no mood to sustain casualties in a humanitarian mission among people who could so turn on their benefactors, particularly since the starvation that had brought American forces into the country had subsided. American units were out of Somalia by 25 March 1994, and the United Nations mission terminated within a year later. The Somali experience had a chilling effect on further American intervention in sub-Saharan Africa. During the horrific bloodbaths in Rwanda and Burundi, the United States Army deployed 2,400 soldiers to purify water, facilitate humanitarian relief, and secure transportation nodes but did not play a leading role. Subsequent responses to violence in the Congo, Ethiopia, Eritrea, Zimbabwe, Sierra Leone, and the Ivory Coast were similarly muted.[37]

Haiti had a long history of repressive dictatorship, but in 1991 it was governed by its first elected President, Jean-Bertrand Aristide. This changed on 30 September 1991, when a military coup led by Lieutenant General Raoul Cedras swept him into exile. Political backsliding was bad enough; economic and political repression soon caused thousands of Haitians to flee on rickety boats, threatening an even more damaging humanitarian crisis. Economic sanctions and diplomatic efforts proved futile. Thugs in Cedras' employ prevented United Nations personnel intended to retrain the Haitian Army and police from landing with small-arms fire and attacked the car of the United States Charge d'Affaires with clubs. United Nations Security Council Resolution 940 authorized the application of the means necessary to restore democracy in Haiti. The United States took the lead with Operation UPHOLD DEMOCRACY and prepared for two distinct contingencies. The 82d Airborne Division and selected Special Operations Forces prepared for forcible entry and the battlefield destruction of the Haitian Army. Meanwhile the 10th Mountain Division and other Special Operations Forces prepared for a permissive entry should diplomacy work in the eleventh hour. It did. With invasion imminent, a last-minute delegation headed by former President Jimmy Carter secured a nonviolent capitulation. The forcible entry air armada returned to its bases, and the permissive entry force landed on 19 September 1994. The newly arriving American soldiers and marines found themselves in an ambiguous situation, policing the streets alongside soldiers of the previously hostile regime while Cedras and his cronies prepared to depart and Aristide and his colleagues prepared to return. United States forces were to preserve civil order, protect the interests of American citizens and third-country nationals, restore the legitimately elected government, and provide technical assistance. They were not tasked to disarm Haitian forces or to undertake significant "nation building." In Port-au-Prince they initially deferred to Haitian counterparts in maintaining public order and soon were embarrassed by egregious incidents of Haitian-on-Haitian violence. The Joint Chiefs of Staff sped an additional 1,000 military policemen to the streets of Port-au-Prince, United States forces firmed up their grip there and in other cities, and Special Forces' A Teams worked through community leaders to establish order in the rural interior. Criminals and pro-Cedras attachés were rounded up, Haitian police rotated through courses taught by international monitors, and the bloated Haitian Army downsized into a border patrol of 1,500. International forces arrived in increasing numbers, most notably the multinational Caribbean Command drawn from nations in the region. On 31 March 1995, the United States handed over its responsibilities to the newly formed United Nations Mission in Haiti (UNMIH). Despite some warts, Haiti offered a respectable model of great-power-led peace enforcement followed up by United Nations peacekeeping.[38]

In many cases the Army and its sister services assumed missions because they offered readily available pools of organized manpower with useful equipment rather than because the task at hand was particularly military. Cases in point include humanitarian relief expeditions in the aftermath of a cyclone in Bangladesh (Operation SEA ANGEL) or the eruption of the Pinatubo volcano in the Philippines (Operation FIERY VIGIL), both in 1991. These were not unlike domestic humanitarian relief in the aftermaths of Hurricane Andrew in Florida and Hurricane Iniki in Hawaii in 1992. Contingents committed to humanitarian relief could add up. Going into October 1992, for example, the Army had about 16,500 active component, 6,000 reserve component, 1,000 Department of the Army civilians, and 3,500 civilians under contract so employed. When coup and turmoil in Haiti provoked thousands to flee, the United States Coast Guard and Navy intercepted—in many cases rescued—huge numbers and deposited them safely at Guantanamo Bay for processing. By February 1992 more than 12,000 Haitian refugees were living there in hastily established camps, about half of them under the auspices of the 96th Civil Affairs Battalion. The Haitian refugee situation worsened until Operation UPHOLD DEMOCRACY and the United Nations mission in Haiti resolved the most pressing political issues. Cuban refugees fleeing a post–Cold War crackdown and economic malaise in Castro's Cuba added to the challenge. Refugees in Guantanamo peaked at about 22,000 Haitians and 33,000 Cubans in 1995. Joint Operation SEA SIGNAL stood up with an Army brigade headquarters and 3,900 soldiers, including twenty-three security companies and a robust mix of combat service support, to support the refugees in Guantanamo. This effort spun off Operation DISTANT HAVEN in Surinam and Operation SAFE PASSAGE in Panama to accommodate refugees overflowing from Guantanamo. The Caribbean was also a transit route for illicit drugs, and the Army became increasingly involved in staunching the flow. In 1989 Congress made the Department of Defense the federal lead agency for detecting the aerial and maritime transit of illegal drugs and for integrating relevant command, control, communications, and intelligence. Joint Task Force 6 (JTF-6), commanded by an Army brigadier general, stood up at Fort Bliss,

Texas, to provide and coordinate reconnaissance, augment law enforcement agencies with military-specific capabilities, support intelligence analysis, and provide engineer support to civil authorities. By 1995 more than 4,000 soldiers and 46,000 flying hours were committed to counterdrug operations.[39]

The threefold increase in deployments during the period 1991–1995 had transformative effects on the Army. We have already discussed the manner in which installations such as Fort Bragg, Fort Hood, and Fort Stewart evolved into force projection platforms, routinely launching contingents of wildly varying sizes overseas, and continuing to support them once deployed through split-based logistics. Procedures became routines. Within less than a year in Haiti, for example, troops from the 10th Mountain Division from Fort Drum, New York, were replaced by troops from the 25th Infantry Division from Fort Shafter, Hawaii, who were replaced by troops from the 82d Airborne Division from Fort Bragg, North Carolina, who were replaced by troops from the 101st Airborne Division from Fort Campbell, Kentucky. Deployments became an expectation and a way of life. Since the early 1980s over half of all soldiers had been married, and soldiers were considerably outnumbered by family members—this resulting from the shift to an all-volunteer Army. Leaders clearly understood that satisfying the family needs of deployed soldiers was central to retaining their services over the long haul. By the period of DESERT STORM family support groups were required in deployable units and on most installations. These featured routine meetings for social or informational purposes, mechanisms to maintain contact with deployed soldiers, provisions for mutual support, access to counseling, recreational activities, and "telephone trees" or some other means to maintain communication. Quality varied, however, and little existed to define expectations. Well-intentioned volunteer group leaders too often devoted an overwhelming amount of their time to a tiny fraction of spouses who were overly demanding, excessively dependent, determined to secure the early return of their spouses, or beset with problems too deep for an amateur's expertise. Failure with such hard cases was discouraging, and detracted from coping with the more modest emotional and practical needs of the vast majority of the families involved. Community resources too often went underutilized or untapped. Coordination among relevant supporting agencies too often fell short. Homecomings were too often imagined as to be unambiguously joyous, lulling family members to be unaware of potential problems associated with them. The Army Community and Family Support Center (CFSC), established in 1984, recognized a need for training and standardization. In 1994 it fielded a comprehensive package of instructional materials under the auspices of Operation READY (Resources for Educating About Deployment and You). The associated "Family Support Group Leader's Manual" became the equivalent of doctrine and was incorporated into leadership training at every level. In the same year, a program labeled Army Family Team Building introduced a multilevel train the trainer program that encouraged volunteers and family members to progress through levels of preparation and responsibility. English as a Second Language (ESL) programs, originally targeted at soldiers, were now made available to spouses as well. Family support groups became miniature power projection platforms, capable of sustaining their members through the hardships of separation.[40]

The Army's shift to an expeditionary posture and a radically increased operational tempo of deployments particularly affected the reserve component. Through the end of the Vietnam War and the advent of the all-volunteer Army, the National Guard and Army Reserve had provided strategic depth, forces available for mobilization at a pace somewhere between that of the active component and new units raised from scratch. After Vietnam a disproportional allocation of combat support and combat service support units to the reserve component guaranteed that they would be integral to major deployments and deployment plans of the active component. However, the relative absence of such deployments generally confined the new relationships to planning and some training. DESERT STORM saw the first real test of the post-Vietnam system; Guardsmen and Reservists deployed in large numbers and were integral to the effort. Soon we will discuss post–DESERT STORM efforts to enhance the readiness of reserve-component units. Here we want to discuss the transformative effects of recurrent deployments on the National Guard and Army Reserve. First, overseas deployment became more of an expectation and a routine. Although during General Sullivan's tenure the deployment of individuals was by and large voluntary—"worked out" by official and unofficial means—every major deployment featured reserve-component soldiers. A bureaucratic manifestation of this increased usage was the extension of presidential call-up authority from 90 to 270 days (Section 673b of Public Law 103–337). Once Guardsmen and Reservists were routinely deployed in appreciable numbers, ninety days offered far too little time for preparation, train-up, significant service overseas, and redeployment. Another innovation related to usage was the "derivative unit identification code" (UIC). "Derivatives" were a subset that allowed one to characterize a unit as "mobilized"—with all of the policy, procedure, and support that implied—when only selected personnel from the unit were actually on active duty. Second, like the active component, reserve-component units shifted focus from a single theater (generally Europe) to multiple contingencies overseas. The CAPSTONE program had given units direct wartime assignments to specific active-component units or headquarters and had associated them with specific war plans. Beginning in 1992 CAPSTONE morphed into the WARTRACE program, envisioning standing training relationships but anticipating a breadth of possible missions. Finally, the reserve component would be called on to assume the lion's share of selected complex missions from the active component, rather than merely supplementing active-component units with respect to skills and numbers. A case in point was the composite 4-505th Parachute Infantry Battalion, activated on 4 November 1994, to serve in the Multinational Force and Observers (MFO) Sinai. Over 80 percent of this battalion consisted of volunteers from the reserve component. As the Army became increasingly challenged by overseas deployments, the reserve component would assume an increasing share of the weight. In due course this would change the nature of duty as a Guardsman or Reservist.[41]

Deployments following DESERT STORM pushed American soldiers to lower levels of resolution with respect to alien cultures and peoples. This reflected more assertive United Nations and United States concepts of humanitarian relief, as well as the underlying philosophies governing "engagement." During the Cold War and prior, it was generally considered inappropriate for nations to meddle in the internal affairs of others. This did not mean that it was not done, but to do so risked international opprobrium. The sentiment stretched back at least as far as the Treaty of Westphalia in 1648, which in a series of treaties enshrined legal concepts that eventually contributed to the modern nation-state. The Cold War era was also the era of decolonization, and newly independent nations were acutely sensitive to any breaches of national sovereignty, regardless of justification. A number of America's Cold War allies had dissident or potentially dissident minorities—Basques in Spain, Kurds in Turkey, Irish Catholics in the United Kingdom's Northern Ireland, to name a few—and preferred no precedents for international involvement. This reticence receded in the early 1990s. In quick succession the United Nations sanctioned American-led interventions into Northern Iraq, Somalia, and Haiti, while promulgating a dozen other interventions as well. The concept of a "failed state" gained currency as former colonies and dependencies triaged into the more, less, and least successful. Governments guilty of unconscionable abuse, neglect, or even genocide against their minorities could and should be acted against. This sensitivity eventually evolved into doctrine espousing an international "responsibility to protect." During the period 1991–1995 this pushed American soldiers out of conventional war paradigms and into the streets for operations "amongst the people." Squads went on joint patrols with Kurds, Somalis, Macedonians, Haitians, and United Nations troops from dozens of nations. The metaphor of the "strategic corporal," the relatively low-ranking soldier whose actions in a media age could have international implications, became popular. In this environment, linguistic skills were at a premium, concerning which more later. For many American soldiers, the nature of overseas service itself was changing.[42]

Digitization

It is popular, and justifiable, to speak of the years surrounding the end of the twentieth century as marking the transition from the "Industrial" to the "Information" Age. As we have seen, the nearly simultaneous developments of HTML (hypertext markup language), HTTP (hypertext transfer protocols), practical browsers, and much improved personal computers made the Internet possible. Within a dozen years of 1991, 665 million users surfed forty million Web sites—up from zero when the period began. Digital technology heavily influenced or dominated broad ranges of human endeavor. Generals Sullivan, Franks, and others saw no reason to evade this trend but instead saw positive advantages to the Army in embracing it. The Army had appreciable experience with computers extending back through World War II, albeit not in a rigorously coherent fashion. The Army annually enlisted tens of thousands from the age cohorts most likely to be computer savvy. DESERT STORM had flagged up specific Army shortcomings that digitization seemed to offer solutions for, and the shortcomings were compelling enough to attract congressional funding and support. If there was to be a revolution in military affairs, digitization would have something to do with it, and the United States armed forces were in a better position to lead the way than those of any other nation.[43]

The Army pioneered in the development of digital computers at least as early as its sponsorship of the Electronic Numerical Integrator and Computer (ENIAC) during World War II. This thirty-ton behemoth sported 18,000 vacuum tubes and was the marvel of its age, conducting calculations five hundred times faster than any previous device and sucking down 175 kilowatts— enough to dim the lights across the entire University of Pennsylvania—when turned on. The successive inventions of the transistor, the integrated circuit, and the microprocessor enabled equivalent calculating power with far less mass. ENIAC and its immediate successors were intended to speed calculations associated with artillery ballistics and cryptography. During this same period card readers of various designs facilitated the management of personnel and logistical data. As technology advanced, computers and card readers converged with respect to design and capabilities, but the Army continued to envision their use in discrete, vertically integrated functional areas. Artillerymen, for example, progressed through a series of automated assistants to ballistics computations and fire support coordination, culminating in the Tactical Fire Direction System (Army) (TACFIRE) with which they fought DESERT STORM. Similarly, air defenders, air traffic management controllers, personnel managers, logisticians, and the Army Security Agency (responsible for signals intelligence and electronic warfare) developed generations of hardware and software uniquely appropriate to their needs. The Army, in particular its Signal Corps, did attempt horizontal integration through such initiatives as Army Tactical Data Systems (ARTADSs) beginning in 1971 or Sigma Star beginning in 1978. These initiatives did not integrate the various "stovepipes" in a manner that was effective in the field. Even more troubling, commercial development and utilization of digital equipment began outstripping the Army's ponderous development and acquisition cycle. Systems developed by and for the Army were too often obsolescent upon delivery. In 1984, to catch up with the digital revolution in progress, the Army approved procedures whereby units and agencies could directly acquire and use "nondevelopment items" of commercial design. Proponents of the existing stovepipes, and of some new ones as well, rushed to modernize themselves. The notion of Army-wide digital interoperability was temporarily abandoned.[44]

In the aftermath of DESERT STORM, powerful incentives for horizontal integration and digital reform asserted themselves. The most harrowing and immediately visible was fratricide. Americans were shocked to find that almost one in five of their killed and wounded were victims of their own comrades. A major fraction of the British killed and wounded were also the victims of American firepower. It was true that less than 1 percent of the firing engagements executed during DESERT STORM proved to be fratricidal and that performance with respect to fratricide was arguably better than that at the instrumented combat training centers or in earlier wars. These data points proved of little consolation to bereaved families, and the general public was baffled that its technologically sophisticated armed forces could be so deadly to themselves. In fact, the technologically sophisticated armed forces were "hoist with their own petard." The night-vision sights and redoubtable gunnery of the M1A1 tank, the Apache helicopter, and other modern direct-fire systems enabled them to reliably engage at ranges and under conditions that would have been inconceivable a few years earlier. Unfortunately, this capability promoted engagements at ranges beyond which gunners could reliably identify their target visually. Targets were indistinct blotches. Troop carriers such as Bradleys and M113s were particularly prone to be nondescript through thermal sights. Not wanting to surrender the advantages of superior range, Americans fought most of the ground war, making determinations whether or not to fire based on where the enemy was believed to be. About 1 percent of the time friendlies were where the enemy was believed to be, and superb American gunnery picked them off as well. Since the outranged and outclassed Iraqis were not inflicting significant casualties with return fire, these fratricides became disproportional to the total casualties. In the last twenty-four hours of the ground war commanders at various levels, mindful of recurring incidents of fratricide, imposed a potpourri of restrictions and clearance procedures on their forces engaged. Collectively considered, these impositions significantly impeded fire and maneuver and introduced a hesitation and timidity that could have proven lethal against a more capable foe. This is not to mention the shame and grief perpetrators bore with them through the rest of the battle and thereafter.[45]

In May 1991 the Army Chief of Staff established a task force to investigate the incidence of fratricide and recommend a way ahead. The associated Senior Officer Review Group, consisting of distinguished retirees, was adamant that restrictions imposed during the waning hours of DESERT STORM were dysfunctional and dangerous, dismissing them as "defensive control measures for offensive operations." Measures that would increase engagement times surrendered critical advantages to the enemy. Acknowledging the roles of fatigue, darkness—virtually all of the vehicle-on-vehicle fratricides occurred at night— dust, smoke, rain, fog, featureless terrain, pace of operations, and the turmoil of combat as contributing factors, the task force boiled the root causes down to two: failures with respect to target identification and failures with respect to situational awareness. With creditable dispatch, the task force raced to design a live test scenario reflecting the circumstances of DESERT STORM combat and invited major corporations to demonstrate proposed technological fixes during it. Corporate America responded with equal dispatch, and record trials were set for technology demonstrations beginning in April 1992. Given precedent, this demonstration of proposed fixes within less than a year of problem identification was breathtaking. Virtually all of the proposed fixes focused on target identification, with some equivalent of "identification friend or foe" (IFF) devices already on combat aircraft in mind. Hughes presented a laser interrogation by the potential shooter followed up by radio-linked reply by the potential target, all occurring automatically within milliseconds. AIL envisioned a laser detector on the potential shooter picking up on multispectral beacons from the potential target. Litton tested a laser on the potential shooter identifying an electronically shuttered corner reflector array in a retro-responder on the potential target. Raytheon envisioned the potential shooter making a range finder interrogation to which the potential target would automatically respond with global positioning system (GPS) derived coordinates. Magnavox also proposed GPS feedback from the potential target to the potential shooter, but via a unique power-managed UHF wave-form radio. McDonnell Douglas competed with low probability of detection millimeter wave transmitters on potential targets and directional receivers on potential shooters. C2NVEO proposed laser-activated thermal identification devices on potential target vehicles. The effect of encountering all these potential solutions in the same place was awesome. Wags compared the experimental range to the bar scene in the movie *Star Wars*; one encountered yet another alien thing with each step or turn. Interestingly, the only system seriously under consideration that focused on situational awareness rather than target identification was a variant of the Enhanced Position Location Reporting System (EPLRS), first fielded to the Army in 1987 and shepherded by Unisys. Available in man-portable or vehicle-borne versions, it automatically reported transmitter locations in coordination with an EPLRS Grid Reference Unit (EGRU). Initially EPLRS did not seem like much of a contender with respect to fratricide prevention; briefing officers did not even accord its slide the dignity of the boxed title and developmental timeline accorded the other systems in their briefing to the Senior Officer Review Group.[46]

EPLRS may not have seemed the likely winner at the vehicle identification technology demonstration, but its emphasis on situational awareness fit in well with efforts to resolve another dilemma exposed by DESERT STORM, that of battle command and battle-space management. General Frederick M. Franks Jr., the TRADOC commander, had been the commander of VII Corps during DESERT STORM. During the fast-paced maneuver war, he was struck by how primitive commanders' means for tracking the battle were. Amid constellations of computers for various purposes with satellite telephones and precision-guided munitions on call, Tactical Operations Center (TOC) officers were still posting locations on acetate-covered maps with grease pencils, pins, and little sticky pieces of paper—techniques extending back at least as far as World War I. Reporting from combat units was generally by voice, relayed through several echelons by radio before other means became available. A favorite prewar training technique had been to visit battalion, brigade, and division TOCs at the same time during exercises and to ascertain the extent to which the maps in each TOC reflected a common picture shared by others. Generally there were significant discrepancies. It also could be unnerving to approach a map and find pins and sticky pieces of paper that had popped off it onto the floor. How long would it take to set that lost information right? EPLRS envisioned vehicles automatically self-reporting their locations at frequent intervals. Icons representing all of the reporting vehicles showed up on a map generated on a computer screen and could be interpolated visually into units on the same screen. If EPLRS or something like it could be horizontally integrated with other digital systems, even more could be achieved through automatic self-reporting. What if, for example, vehicles reported their fuel and ammunition status along with their locations? This would eliminate elaborate chains of logistical reports that progressed from radio to radio in parallel with the tactical reporting—with just as many possibilities for discrepancies. During the last day of DESERT STORM forward units were low on fuel, patchily supplied with respect to repair parts, and towing around far more ammunition than they needed. Theater logistics had generated awesome "iron mountains," but too often difficulties in distribution overshadowed excesses of supply. The term *total asset visibility* emerged to describe the happy—albeit theretofore unachievable—state of knowing where everything was and who needed what. Some form of digitized self-reporting analogous to EPLRS might offer a way to achieve it.[47]

Deliberations with respect to fratricide, battle command, battle-space management, total asset visibility, and digitization were all grist for the modern Louisiana Maneuvers and the LAM Task Force. For his first several years General Sullivan "let a thousand flowers bloom" in the interest of maximum brainstorming. Hardware change recommendations for the M1A1 tank, for example, included both IFF and situational awareness/land navigation devices, along with two dozen other genres of technical improvement. It was in this freewheeling atmosphere that the combat identification technology demonstration transpired. Unfortunately, none of the IFF-inspired target identification devices particularly worked out. Technologies capable of keeping a few planes separated by miles of air space from shooting each other worked far less well in intermingled masses of dozens of vehicles. Those dependent on laser interrogation or response could be hugely degraded by omnipresent swirling dust. Even if vehicles were protected, nothing seemed suitable for protecting the dismounts. Meanwhile General Franks had an epiphany in another location. In September 1992 he observed the first National Training Center rotation of an M1A2 tank platoon, equipped with a situational awareness successor to EPLRS called the Inter-Vehicular Information System (IVIS). This featured small screens at the driver's and commander's stations that assisted navigation in a manner analogous to the commercial global positioning systems that had been hastily distributed prior to DESERT STORM. The screens also depicted the locations of the other IVIS-equipped vehicles in the platoon. Conversations with crew members established that they quickly adapted to monitoring the screens and consistently had a refined appreciation of the locations of their fellow vehicles. To Franks, the solution to DESERT STORM fratricide and the solution to DESERT STORM battle command had run together. Target identification continued to be a training priority and tank tables and field exercises now included friendly targets down range, but technological solutions for target identification faded from view. Improved situational awareness would be the technological way ahead for preventing fratricide, and that improved situational awareness would be the product of digitization.[48]

Franks' IVIS epiphany somewhat preceded General Sullivan's determination that the Army was approaching a "good idea cutoff line" with respect to the modern Louisiana Maneuvers and LAM Task Force deliberations. At some point the bureaucracy had to be given tangible goals toward which it could progress. Ambitions had to come on line with funding and resources. Deep thinkers and near-term operators had to resume responsibilities for their respective lanes—albeit hopefully with more fluidity between them than

A Joint Forces Command digitized exercise

before. We have already discussed the way ahead as it emerged with respect to expeditionary posture. With respect to modernization, the way ahead would be dominated by digitization. At the time the term *digitization* evoked the metaphor of the old cavalryman who, when asked about logistics, remarked that he did not know what logistics was, but he wanted some. Few senior leaders—indeed, few Army leaders of any rank—had much practical experience with the hardware and software that digitization implied. Nevertheless, the intellectual give-and-take of the last several years had hammered out broad parameters within which digitization would progress. First, digitization would be comprehensive, coherent, and centralized, progressing under the newly introduced label "Force XXI." Force XXI featured axes for both the institutional and the deployable Army and synchronization matrices extending out a dozen years. Second, digitization would be by and large by appliqué with off-the-shelf technology onto existing weapons and systems over the near term. This approach would economize on funds, envisioned as limited for the foreseeable future. Third, the term *off-the-shelf technology* would no longer imply a grab bag of systems collected by independent agents. The Army Digitization Office (ADO), established on 8 July 1994, would discipline procurement, policy, and use. The ADO represented both the Army Acquisition Executive (AAE) and the Vice Chief of Staff. This meant it was empowered by both the Secretariat and the Army Staff, an important consideration in the aftermath of the Goldwater-Nichols Act. Fourth, digitization would be incremental and methodical. ATDs and AWEs would progress through units and headquarters of increasing size and complexity. Finally, digitization would progress in

123

the light of all six imperatives—doctrine, force mix, modernization, training, leader development, and quality people—inherited from General Vuono. In July 1994 Sullivan pulled the LAM Task Force out of the cerebral atmosphere of the TRADOC headquarters and brought it to the Pentagon, to more directly facilitate the emerging Force XXI Campaign Plan. In April Task Force 1-70th Armor conducted an Advanced Warfighter Experiment at the task force level at the National Training Center. In December the 2d Armored Division from Fort Hood, Texas, was designated as the Experimental Force (EXFOR) for digital experimentation. In March 1995 Mr. Gilbert Decker, the Assistant Secretary of the Army for Research, Development, and Acquisition (ASA [RDA]) and thus the Army acquisition executive, approved the "technical information architecture" for execution. This fleshed out details with respect to organization and appliqué. By the time of General Sullivan's departure the use of digital equipment within the institutional Army was well advanced. Use in the deployable Army was modest, experimental, and prototypical. A way ahead, however, was clear.[49]

The United States Army in 1995

The most immediately visible difference between the Army of 1989 and the Army of 1995 was size. The active component numbered 510,000 en route to a target end strength of 495,000, down from 770,000 in 1989. Within the reserve component, the Army National Guard had dropped from 467,000 to 375,000, and the Army Reserve from 594,000 to 241,000 during the same period. The Army's civilian workforce had declined from 488,000 to 324,000. Historically, downsizing is not something that the United States Army has done well. The collapse after World War II was qualitative as well as quantitative, resulting in the embarrassments of Task Force Smith and other early losses when the Korean War broke out. After the Korean War the downsized Army fell under the specter of the nuclear-centric "New Look," which barely morphed into the more broadly capable "Flexible Response" in time to prepare for the Vietnam War. After Vietnam the downsized Army deteriorated so rapidly its own Chief of Staff characterized it as "hollow." Vuono, Sullivan, and their colleagues were, as we have seen, determined to avoid repeating these unhappy experiences. They brought down force structure along with manpower. Eighteen active-component divisions shrank to ten. Some major headquarters such as Second Army and Sixth Army disappeared, whereas most others downsized or streamlined. Cuts in active-component force structure proportionally exceeded the 38 percent cut in the Army budget and the 35 percent cut in Army manpower between 1989 and 1995. This allowed the Army to keep the units that remained at full strength and to sustain the customary training operational tempo of eight hundred miles per vehicle crew per year. Seventy-seven battalions rotated through the combat training centers during FY1995 alone, for example.[50]

Carving out time and resources for training was a considerable achievement, given the demands downsizing placed on units and soldiers. Huge masses of vehicles and equipment from inactivating units had to be stood down, maintained, reprocessed and stored, redistributed, or disposed of. Much of the equipment was destined for the POMCUS sites of the Army War Reserve and thus had to be altogether battleworthy when stored. As had been the case with earlier "rollovers" from one fleet of vehicles to another, equipment turn-ins were elaborate multiweek processes incorporating detailed turn-in standards, inspections, scrambles to achieve compliance with inspection results, and reinspections. Even before their motor pools were emptied of departing vehicles, soldiers and family members from inactivating units began separating from the service or trickling into subsequent assignments. Tens of thousands more than usual were in motion at any given time. When the troops and equipment were gone, barracks and installations had to be cleaned up for turnover to whatever organization or agency was to inherit them. This process was bedeviled by the fact the installations had been occupied during eras when practices with respect to oil spills, pollution, and environmental damage were far more permissive than the era wherein they were being turned over. In FY1995 alone, the Army spent more than $1.6 billion on environmental cleanup. This is not to mention the fact that environmental cleanups can be extraordinarily manpower intensive.[51]

As proud as the Army might have been for sustaining a respectable training tempo amid the turbulence of downsizing, it had even more reason to be proud of the quality of the people it had retained. Sullivan, his colleagues, and allies in the Association of the United States Army (AUSA) and other organizations had taken great pains to convince the Joint Staff, Secretariat, and Congress that if downsizing had to occur, it should be gradual enough to avoid temporary eviscerations of units and uncontrolled hemorrhages of talent. Their arguments were assisted by ongoing operations and international challenges. Cuts came to an average of fewer than 50,000 a year, and were largely attritional, voluntary, and accompanied by incentives. For example, of 2,478 officers separated under various programs during FY1995, 258 went to the Voluntary Early Release/Retirement Program (VERRP), 1,079 to the Voluntary Selective Incentive Program (VSIP), 732 to the Early Retirement Program (ERP), and only 409 were involuntarily separated by a Selective Early Retirement Board (SERB). A dreaded involuntary "pink slip" reduction in force (RIF) had been contemplated for captains that year but proved unnecessary when enough applied for VSIP to cover the planned reductions. Enlisted downsizing that year progressed even more satisfactorily; no one involuntarily separated other than for cause. Reliance on voluntary means of separation and the continuing presence of visibly capable units favorably affected Army morale. Army lore holds that there is no place worse to be than in "a theater closing out." This stems from World War II memories of shiftless hordes of men, masses of rusting equipment, unfathomable separation or redeployment policies, and general ennui in theaters that seemed to have lost their purpose. In the early 1990s gradualist separation policies worked out in such a manner that the truly qualified generally stayed if they wanted to, and if they did they belonged to capable, dynamic, and busy organizations. In this atmosphere retention proved relatively easy. During FY1995 the Army reenlisted 104 percent (19,960) of the first-termers and 100 percent (23,358) of the mid-termers

By the 1990s recruits were better educated than ever but still in need of a drill sergeant's careful attention.

personnel managers sought to retain. It also inspired 105 percent (13,737) of the separating soldiers it sought to join the National Guard and Army Reserve. Perhaps even more important, it continued to attract and recruit young men and women of the highest caliber. Of 62,931 new accessions to the active Army during FY1995, over 95 percent were high school graduates and almost 70 percent scored test results in the highest categories of the Armed Services Vocational Aptitude Battery.[52]

The demonstrably talented manpower of the 1995 Army served in an organization that had, as we have seen, shifted to an expeditionary posture. In Korea the lines and missions associated with the Cold War remained the same. Elsewhere units were acquiring the training, habits, infrastructure, and experiences appropriate to the full-spectrum expeditionary doctrine espoused by the 1993 version of Field Manual 100–5, *Operations*. At the time, the Army had set itself the long-term goal of deploying a corps headquarters and one light and two heavy divisions to a distant contingency within thirty days and of bringing that force up to a full corps with five divisions within seventy-five days. In 1994 an independent study chose Mozambique as a scenario and determined that the means then available could approximate the goal, albeit with the divisions deployed at thirty days being two light and one heavy rather than one light and two heavy. Enhancements envisioned through FY2000 would fully achieve the goal and considerably brought forward the first of the heavy brigades to arrive. Such a performance would double the pace of Desert Shield/Desert Storm, then the frame of reference for expeditionary combat. The frame of reference for the field training of the heavy force also remained Desert Storm, albeit with more guerrillas, unconventional operations, and operations other than war thrown into the mix than had been the case prior to 1993. The frame of reference for the field training of the light force shifted to an ever heavier emphasis on operations other than war. By and large forces actually deployed to Kurdistan, Haiti, and Somalia had been light, and those deployed to deter Saddam Hussein heavy. The tactical equipment, organization, roles, and missions of the heavy forces had not appreciably changed since Desert Storm; what had changed was the pace at which they could make their presence felt in distant theaters.[53]

The reserve component was increasingly critical to plans for rapid deployment and operations other than war. They too had been hard hit by downsizing, and the downsizing had forced somewhat more specialization upon them. After extensive negotiation the Army Reserve committed to focus even more heavily on combat service support, whereas the National Guard committed to orient more on combat units. To this purpose the National Guard planned to turn over 128 units with 11,062 authorizations to the Army Reserve, whereas the Army Reserve would turn over 44 units with 14,049 authorizations to the National Guard. The National Guard would particularly focus resources and preparatory efforts on fifteen "enhanced" combat maneuver brigades. National Guard brigades would no longer "round out" or "round up" specific active-component divisions, but instead would serve as a readily accessible strategic reserve for the Army as a whole. The enhanced brigades benefited from cascades of modern equipment as active-component units inactivated and as contemporary procurement specifically targeted them. In one respect they were to lead the Army. Geographical dispersal, limited training time, and infrequent opportunities to field units as a whole on premier training facilities had long plagued the reserve component. These challenges seemed particularly appropriate for the use of simulations and distributed learning. Simulation in Training for Advanced Readiness (SIMITAR) originated in 1992 as an Advanced Research Projects Agency (ARPA) effort to apply the latest training technologies to reserve-component training issues. At about the same time, the National Defense Authorization Act for FY1993 directed that the active component expand its support to the reserve component from 2,000 to 5,000 advisers. These men and women would work full time to enhance the training posture of the National Guard units to which they were assigned.[54]

Working definitions of modernization evolved. In 1989 modernization for units had meant wrapping up the fielding of the "big five" and related equipment. Ruminations concerning the more distant future were largely confined to TRADOC and the Army Materiel Command (AMC). The 1988 AMC commander, General Louis C. Wagner Jr., described a 2010 scenario in the *Army 1988–1989 Green Book* wherein highly trained American troops turned back a Warsaw Pact invasion with a Buck Rogers array of directed energy weapons, robots, advanced power generation (to power the directed energy weapons and robots, one presumes), biotechnology, microelectronics, low observables, and space-based systems. Interestingly enough, the 1994 AMC commander, General Leon E. Salomon, also chose to describe a 2010 scenario in the *Army 1994–1995 Green Book*. In Salomon's scenario the highly trained American troops were rescuing American citizens in the dark of night from a civil war ravaged land rather than hammering Soviet tank columns. The robots and ray guns were gone, replaced by decidedly digital assemblages of computers, sensors, visual displays, navigation devices, fire controls, and communications. The future had changed and with it approaches to modernization. The "big five" and related equipment were still being fielded, albeit increasingly in updated or product-improved forms. The distant future was still being tended to. Salomon's article dutifully displayed a prototypical hypervelocity electronic rail gun, for example, and experimentation with respect to cruise and high-altitude missile interception had been particularly intense. In addition to immediate modernization and long-term developments, however, a third venue of intermediate-term modernizations had emerged. These were envisioned as initially experimental, incremental, largely digital, and often off-the-shelf. Given the pace of commercial digital developments, procurement philosophies had to change. The Assistant Secretary of the Army for Research, Development, and Acquisition, Gilbert F. Decker, noted that the traditional military specifications (MILSPECs) process would have produced a 17-pound single-channel global positioning system that cost $34,000 each. Instead the Army bought acceptably durable olive drab colored 3-pound multichannel commercial global positioning systems for $1,300 each—and the price dropped to $800 over the next several years. Cascades of digitized equipment swept into the Army, albeit more comprehensively and effectively in the institutional Army than in the turrets of tanks. The worldwide Secure Internet Protocol Router Network (SIPRNET) was an instant success, revolutionizing traffic in classified information. Intelligence operators leaped into whole new paradigms with respect to the volume, flow, synthesis, and distribution of information. Desktops throughout the Army sprouted with personal computers (PCs), and officers and noncommissioned officers (NCOs) who had never learned to type were expected to use them. In due course civilian secretaries and company clerks would disappear, displaced by the expansive memories of the electronic devices now manned by their erstwhile bosses. Digitization in the field was more tentative, as systems generated to support AWEs competed with personal laptops brought along for the ride to be useful amid the turmoil, vibration, and dust of active operations. Someday tankers accompanied by robotic wingmen would streak across the battlefield armed with phased energy weapons and hypervelocity rail guns. Well before that time M1 tanks and M2/M3 Bradleys sporting an appliqué of digital equipment would conduct operations with old weapons and unprecedented information advantages. This intermediate future was Force XXI, and it was a work already in progress.[55]

Conclusions

On his first day as Chief of Staff, General Gordon R. Sullivan set himself and the Army the tasks of maintaining readiness while downsizing in accordance with congressional mandates, accomplishing contemporary missions, and preparing for wars the future might bring. The most measurable of these accomplishments was the superb caliber—with respect to manning, training, equipment, personnel quality, and much else—of the ten divisions and other units that remained when the downsizing was complete. The reserve component mirrored the accomplishments of the active component, with their enhanced brigades, for example, being even more battleworthy than those that had gone before. The mission accomplishment of the Army was also of a demonstrably high caliber. What embarrassments there were had little to do with the quality of the Army and its soldiers. Success with respect to future wars was immeasurable, of course, since no one knew what the future would bring. There was reason for optimism, however. Processes for envisioning the future had been intelligently revamped, harnessing the latest in simulations technology to do so. Shortcomings identified during DESERT STORM seemed well on their way to resolution. Most notably, the Army as a whole had made unprecedented advances toward achieving the expeditionary posture the new era demanded. Digitization—progressing at an uneven pace but in a sure direction—seemed to promise the resolution of battle management, fratricide, and logistical intervisibility issues. Concepts appropriate to the Information Age had progressed from the general brainstorming of the Louisiana Maneuvers to the comparative rigor of Force XXI. The reserve component was more capable and integrated than ever before, and the Army was accumulating experiences with respect to operations other than war that corresponded well with a renewed doctrinal emphasis on them. Deliberations had addressed doctrine, force mix, training, leader development, and quality people as well as modernization per se. The future Army was not to be a mere collection of gadgets. No American Army had ever demonstrated so much capability across such a broad spectrum of potential combat five years after a war. This was no mean achievement.

Notes

[1] General Gordon R. Sullivan, "Maintaining Momentum While Accommodating Change," *Army 1991 Green Book: The Year of DESERT STORM*, October 1991, 24–32; "General Gordon R. Sullivan," in William G. Bell, *Commanding Generals and Chiefs of Staff, 1775–2005: Portraits and Biographical Sketches of the Army's Senior Officers* (Washington DC: Center of Military History, 2005); Speech to the 113th General Conference of the National Guard Association of the United States, in *The Collected Works of the Thirty-second Chief of Staff, United States Army* (Washington DC: Center of Military History, 1995), 4–9; James L. Yarrison, *The Modern Louisiana Maneuvers* (Washington DC: Center of Military History, 1999), 1–8; Memorandum for Record (MFR) of Telephone Conversation, Brigadier General (USA, Ret.) John S. Brown with General (USA, Ret.) Gordon R. Sullivan, 091300 May 2008, in Historians Files, CMH.

[2] Ibid.; "Resume of Service Career, General Gordon Russell Sullivan," in *The Collected Works of the Thirty-second Chief of Staff, United States Army*, xvi–xix. See also John L. Romjue, *The Army of Excellence: The Development of the 1980s Army* (Washington DC: Center of Military History, 1997).

[3] Robert A. Doughty, "The French Armed Forces, 1918–40," in *Military Effectiveness: The Interwar Period*, ed. Allen R. Millett and Williamson Murray (London: Allen and Unwin, 1988), 39–69; Brian Bond and Williamson Murray, "The British Armed Forces, 1918–1939," in *Military Effectiveness: The Interwar Period*, 98–130; Manfred Messerschmidt, "German Military Effectiveness between 1919 and 1939," in *Military Effectiveness: The Interwar Period*, 218–55.

[4] General Gordon R. Sullivan's Arrival Ceremony, in *The Collected Works of the Thirty-second Chief of Staff, United States Army*, 3–4.

[5] *Army Command, Leadership and Management: Theory and Practice, A Reference Text, 1992–1993* (Carlisle Barracks, Pennsylvania: U.S. Army War College, 1992); Interv with Dr. Jacques S. Gansler, 12 September 2002, sub: Acquisition Policy: Research and Development—OSD, Defense Acquisition History Project, Center of Military History; Yarrison, 9–10; George C. Wilson, *This War Really Matters: Inside the Fight for Defense Dollars* (Washington DC: CQ Press, 2000). With respect to the motor pool in Aschaffenburg, the author was executive officer for the tank battalion stationed there, and when preparing for the arrival of the M1A1 found class IX repair parts, photos, and records relating to the earlier generations of tanks amid the debris being removed. The experience was akin to dating layers at an archaeological site by the shards of pottery discovered therein.

[6] Anne W. Chapman, *The Army's Training Revolution, 1973–1990: An Overview* (Washington DC: Center of Military History, 1994); Briefing, Center for Army Lessons Learned for the Chief of Military History, 20 January 2000, in Historians Files, CMH; General Frederick M. Franks, "After the OPFOR, the Medina Ain't Nothin'!" *Army 1991 Green Book: The Year of DESERT STORM,* October 1991, 72–77; Lieutenant General Ronald Houston Griffith, "In Their Most Proactive Role: The IGs and DESERT STORM," *Army 1991 Green Book: The Year of DESERT STORM*, 175–76.

[7] Yarrison, 7–25; *Army Command, Leadership and Management;* Interv with Dr. Jacques S. Gansler, 12 September 2002, sub: Acquisition Policy: Research and Development—OSD.

[8] Mark D. Sherry, *The Army Command Post and Defense Reshaping, 1987–1997* (Washington DC: Center of Military History, 2009), 67–121; General Edwin H. Burba Jr., "The Mission and the Base Force," in *Army 1992–1993 Green Book,* October 1992;

General Frederick M. Franks Jr., "TRADOC: Seeding Future Victories," *Army 1992–1993 Green Book*, October 1992; General Jimmie D. Ross, "Enlightened Balance Is AMC's Watchword," *Army 1992–1993 Green Book*, October,1992; Interv with General Donald R. Keith, in *Reflections of Former AMC Commanders* (Alexandria, Virginia: U. S. Army Materiel Command Oral History Program, 1989), 195–216.

[9] Sherry, 67–121.

[10] Ltr, General Gordon R. Sullivan to the author, in response to the author's inquiries, 19 April, 1999, Historians Files, CMH.

[11] Yarrison, 7–25; General Fred Franks Jr. with Tom Clancy, *Into the Storm: A Study in Command* (New York: G. P. Putnam's Sons, 1997), 488–511; General Gordon R. Sullivan, "The Army in the Post-Industrial World," speech to the Land Warfare Forum of the Association of the United States Army, 9 January 1992, in *The Collected Works of the Thirty-second Chief of Staff, United States Army*, 23–27; Chief of Staff Message, "Louisiana Maneuvers 1994," 9 March 1994, in *The Collected Works of the Thirty-second Chief of Staff, United States Army*, 103–05.

[12] Yarrison, 20–75; General Frederick M. Franks Jr., "TRADOC at 20: Where Tomorrow's Victories Begin," *Army 1993–1994 Green Book*, October 1993; General Gordon R. Sullivan's Speech to the Association of the United States Army Louisiana Maneuvers Symposium, 25 May 1993, in *The Collected Works of the Thirty-second Chief of Staff, United States Army*, 142–48; Memo, LAM Exercise Directorate 24 February 1993, sub: Initial Planning Conference, GHQ-X 93, LAM TF Files, CMH; John C. Dilbert, "General Headquarters Exercise Insights," *Military Review* (March-April 1997); Army Information Paper, 1 February 1994, sub: Special Digitization Task Force; Charter for the Army Digitization Office, 9 June 1994, signed by Vice Chief of Staff of the Army J.H. Binford Peay III and Assistant Secretary of the Army (Research, Development and Acquisition) Gilbert F. Decker, Historians Files, CMH; Major General Joe W. Rigby, "Digitizing Force XXI: A Team Effort," *Army* (May 1995): 36–44.

[13] Yarrison, 56–71; Sherry, 163–74.

[14] *National Military Strategy* (Washington DC: Government Printing Office, 1992); General Colin L. Powell, *Report on the Roles, Missions, and Functions of the Armed Forces* (Washington DC: Government Printing Office, 1993); "Speed Bumps: 82nd Airborne's Shaky Line in the Sand," *Army Times*, 21 October 1991; General Gordon R. Sullivan, Address to the United States Military Academy Department of History Faculty Dining-In, 22 February 1992, in *The Collected Works of the Thirty-second Chief of Staff, United States Army*, 33–38; General Gordon R. Sullivan, "The Chief on Army Readiness: 'No More Task Force Smiths,'" *Army* (January 1992); Roy K. Flint, "Task Force Smith and the 24th Division: Delay and Withdrawal, 5–19 July 1950," in *America's First Battles, 1776–1965*, ed. Charles E. Heller and William A. Stofft (Lawrence, Kansas: University Press of Kansas, 1986), 266–99; Birger Bergesen and John McDonald, *Assessment of Contingency and Expeditionary Force Capabilities* (McLean, Virginia: Science Applications International Corporation, 1994).

[15] Sherry, 102–10; *National Military Strategy*, 1992; Field Manual 100–5, *Operations* (Washington DC: Department of the Army, 1993); Franks with Clancy, 488–511.

[16] General David M. Maddox, "Breakout at D+50: Projecting America's Power in Europe into the Future," *Army 1994–1995 Green Book*, October 1994, 77–84; Charles E. Kirkpatrick, *"Ruck it Up!": The Post–Cold War Transformation of V Corps, 1990–2001* (Washington DC: Center of Military History, 2006), vii–xv, 89–124; Army Regulation 210–20, *Master Planning for Army Installations* (Washington DC: Department of the Army, 1992); Dwight D. Oland and David W. Hogan Jr., *Department of the Army Historical Summary, Fiscal Year 1992* (Washington DC:

Center of Military History, 2001), 165–69, 178–84; Steven E. Everett and L. Martin Kaplan, *Department of the Army Historical Summary, Fiscal Year 1993* (Washington DC: Center of Military History, 2002), 112–16; L. Martin Kaplan, *Department of the Army Historical Summary, Fiscal Year 1994* (Washington DC: Center of Military History, 2000), 124–29. The author served as G–3, 24th Infantry Division, from June 1992 through June 1993 and as G–3, Operations, III Corps, from June 1993 through November 1993. These positions intimately associated him with installation planning for Fort Stewart, Georgia, and Fort Hood, Texas, respectively.

[17] Department of Defense Final Report to Congress, *Conduct of the Persian Gulf War: Pursuant to Title V of the Persian Gulf Conflict Supplemental Authorization and Personnel Benefits Act of 1991 (Public Law102–25)* (Washington DC: Department of Defense, 1992), 377–90; Bergesen and McDonald; Lieutenant General Johnnie E. Wilson, "Power Projection Logistics Now . . . and in the 21st Century, *Army 1994–1995 Green Book,* October 1994, 137–43; U.S. Transportation Command: A Short History (Scott Air Force Base, Illinois: U.S. Transportation Command Office of Public Affairs, 2005); MFR of Telephone Conversation, Brigadier General (USA, Ret.) John S. Brown with General (USA, Ret.) Gordon R. Sullivan, 091300 May 2008.

[18] Ibid.

[19] *Conduct of the Persian Gulf War: Pursuant to Title V of the Persian Gulf Conflict Supplemental Authorization and Personnel Benefits Act of 1991 (Public Law 102–25),* 379–91; Kirkpatrick, 3–20, 34–39; Sherry, 106–12; JCS 1454/161, "Service Recommendations for Prepositioned Sealift Package in the Persian Gulf," 8 February 1980, cited in Sherry, 112; Wilson, "Power Projection Logistics Now . . . and in the 21st Century, 137–43; Lieutenant General James R. Ellis, "Third . . . Always First!" *Army 1994–1995 Green Book,* October 1994, 113–19.

[20] General Leon E. Salomon, "At AMC the Future Begins Today," *Army 1994–1995 Green Book,* October 1994, 69–75; Lieutenant General Paul E. Blackwell, "Winning the Wars of the 21st Century," *Army 1994–1995 Green Book,* October 1994, 121–34; "Army Weaponry and Equipment," *Army 1994–1995 Green Book,* October 1994, 233–319.

[21] Bergesen and McDonald; Wilson, "Power Projection Logistics Now . . . and in the 21st Century, 137–43; Blackwell, 121–34.

[22] Bergesen and McDonald; Field Manual 100–5, *Operations*; Army Training and Evaluation Program 71–2 (Washington DC: Department of the Army, 1987); Army Field Manual 17–12–1, *Tank Combat Tables* (Washington DC: Department of the Army, 1987). The author's description of tanker beliefs and prejudices comes from twenty-five years of serving as a tanker. The source of paratrooper beliefs and prejudices is Brigadier General (USA, Ret.) William Leszczynski, a lifelong friend, airborne Ranger, and former commander of the ranger regiment (MFR documenting this exchange appears in the Historians Files, CMH). Banter between the branches begins early, in the case of West Point graduates, during branch selection senior year—when branch representatives make the strongest possible cases to gain branch commitments. It lasts a lifetime.

[23] Bergesen and McDonald; Field Manual 100–5, *Operations; Conduct of the Persian Gulf War: Pursuant to Title V of the Persian Gulf Conflict Supplemental Authorization and Personnel Benefits Act of 1991 (Public Law 102–25),* 240–43, 393–450; William G. Pagonis with Jeffrey L. Cruickshank, *Moving Mountains: Lessons in Leadership and Logistics from the Gulf War* (Cambridge, Massachusetts: Harvard Business School University Press, 1992); Wilson, "Power Projection Logistics Now . . . and in the 21st Century, 137–43; Kirkpatrick, 99–107; Gordon W. Rudd, *Humanitarian Intervention: Assisting the Iraqi Kurds in Operation PROVIDE COMFORT, 1991* (Washington DC: Center of Military History, 2004); Walter E. Kretchick,

Robert F. Bauman, and John T. Fishel, *Invasion, Intervention, "Intervasion": A Concise History of the U.S. Army in Operation* UPHOLD DEMOCRACY (Fort Leavenworth, Kansas: U.S. Army Command and General Staff College Press, 1998); Lieutenant General Thomas M. Montgomery, "United States Forces, Somalia, After Action Report," in *United States Forces, Somalia, After Action Report and Historical Overview: The United States Army in Somalia, 1992–1994* (Washington DC: Center of Military History, 2003).

[24] Field Manual 100–5, *Operations*; *Conduct of the Persian Gulf War: Pursuant to Title V of the Persian Gulf Conflict Supplemental Authorization and Personnel Benefits Act of 1991 (Public Law 102–25)*, 237–40, 589–98; Kirkpatrick, 3–32, 82–88; *Army Training and Evaluation Program 71–2*; Author's personal experience as a battalion commander in Germany (1989–1991), division G–3 in Fort Stewart, Georgia (1992–1993), and corps G–3 operations in Fort Hood, Texas (1993).

[25] General Dennis J. Reimer, "The Tempo Increases for FORSCOM Units," *Army 1992–1993 Green Book,* October 1993, 36–45; Franks, "TRADOC at 20: Where Tomorrow's Victories Begin," 46–55; Lieutenant General Leon E. Salomon, "Power-Projection Logistics," *Army 1992–1993 Green Book,* October 1993, 162–71; General Dennis J. Reimer, "Freedom's Guardian: U.S. Army Forces Command Focuses on Readiness," *Army 1994–1995 Green Book,* 47–56; General Frederick M. Franks Jr., "Preparing the Army for the 21st Century, *Army 1994–1995 Green Book,* 59–66; Wilson, "Power Projection Logistics Now . . . and in the 21st Century, 137–43.

[26] Bergesen and McDonald; Powell; Mark D. Mandeles, *Military Transformation Past and Present: Historic Lessons for the 21st Century* (Westport, Connecticut: Praeger Security International, 2007), 48–70.

[27] "Kuwait on Guard; US Beefs Up Forces; Iraq Air Force on Alert," *Arab Times,* 17–18 August 1995, 1; ARCENT-K Public Affairs Office, Current Public Affairs Summary, Camp Doha, Kuwait, 15 October 1995; "We're Back: First Team Returns to Kuwait for INTRINSIC ACTION," *Desert Voice,* Camp Doha, Kuwait, 4 September 1995, 1; *Desert Voice Special Edition*, Camp Doha, Kuwait, 17 October, 1995; 2d Brigade, 1st Cavalry Division, INTRINSIC ACTION 95–3 After Action Review, 17 October 1995, Historians Files, CMH.

[28] Ibid.; Memo, General J. H. Binford Peay III, Commander in Chief, U.S. Central Command, for Major General James B. Taylor, Deputy Commander, Third U.S. Army, 12 October 1995, Historians Files, CMH; 2d Brigade, 1st Cavalry Division, Operation Plan (OPLAN) Brief, "If We Fight Tonight . . .," Historians Files, CMH; 2d Brigade, 1st Cavalry Division, OPLAN Brief, "If We Fight Next Week . . .," Historians Files, CMH; "Devil Dogs: Destination Desert," *Desert Voice,* Camp Doha, Kuwait, 2 October 1995, 1; "Combined Live Fire Exercise, 11 October 1995, INTRINSIC ACTION 95–3," Historians Files, CMH; Briefing, "ARG/MEU (SOC) Capabilities Brief," 29 September 1995, Historians Files, CMH.

[29] "Kuwait on Guard; US Beefs Up Forces; Iraq Air Force on Alert," 1; ARCENT-K Public Affairs Office, Current Public Affairs Summary, Camp Doha, Kuwait, 15 October 1995; "We're Back: First Team Returns to Kuwait for INTRINSIC ACTION," 1; *Desert Voice Special Edition*, Camp Doha, Kuwait, 17 October, 1995; 2d Brigade, 1st Cavalry Division, INTRINSIC ACTION 95–3 After Action Review, 17 October 1995; "Mission Accomplished," *Desert Voice*, Camp Doha, Kuwait, 16 October 1995, 1; Briefing, "INTRINSIC ACTION 95–3 Relief in Place Concept," Historians Files, CMH.

[30] William J. Webb, *Department of the Army Historical Summary, Fiscal Year 1990–1991* (Washington DC: Center of Military History, 1997), 3–14; Oland and Hogan, 3–10, 37–43; Everett and Kaplan, 3–6, 55–62; Kaplan, 3–7, 63–66; Stephen L. Y.

Gammons and William M. Donnelly, *Department of the Army Historical Summary, Fiscal Year 1995* (Washington DC: Center of Military History, 2004), 3–7, 46–48; William J. Clinton, *National Security Strategy of Engagement and Enlargement* (Washington DC: White House, 1995).

[31] William Echikson, *Lighting the Night: Revolution in Eastern Europe* (New York: William Morrow, 1990); John Keegan, *The Second World War* (London: Hutchinson, 1989), 10–44; *NATO Handbook* (Brussels: NATO Office of Information and Press, 1995), 43–58.

[32] Oland and Hogan, 37–43; Everett and Kaplan, 55–62; Kaplan, 63–66; Graeme P. Auton, *Arms Control and European Security* (New York: Praeger, 1989); General Crosbie E. Saint, "Aftershocks and Challenges in the Cold War's Wake," *Army 1992–1993 Green Book*, October 1992, 78–88; General David M. Maddox, "USAREUR: 'A Highly Deployable Force,'" *Army 1993–1994 Green Book*, October 1993, 66–78; General David M. Maddox, "Projecting America's Power in Europe into the Future," *Army 1994–1995 Green Book*, October 1994, 77–83; Kirkpatrick, 193–320.

[33] Echikson; *NATO Handbook*, 43–58; General William W. Crouch, "U.S. Army Europe: A Security Mission Redefined," *Army 1995–1996 Green Book*, October 1995, 69–76; Kirkpatrick, 110–16; Major A. J. Koenig, "Partnership for Peace Exercise Summary," V Corps History Office, July 1997; *Partnership for Peace Framework Document* (Brussels: North Atlantic Council/North Atlantic Cooperation Council, 1994); Author's personal experience and observations while serving as the Chief of Programs and Requirements, Supreme Headquarters Allied Powers Europe, Mons, Belgium, 1997–1998.

[34] Oland and Hogan, 37–43; Everett and Kaplan, 55–62; Kaplan, 63–66; General Robert W. RisCassi, "No Letting Down Guard at Cold War's Last Wall," *Army 1992–1993 Green Book*, October 1992, 104–10; Lieutenant General Johnnie H. Corns, "U.S. Power Is Vital to Asia-Pacific Peace," *Army 1992–1993 Green Book*, October 1992, 132–38; General Robert W. RisCassi, "Still Keeping Peace on Cold War Lines," *Army 1993–1994 Green Book*, October 1993, 80–91; Lieutenant General Johnnie H. Corns, "A Tradition of Hard-Won Battles and Cooperative Engagements," *Army 1993–1994 Green Book*, October 1993, 92–100; General Gary E. Luck, "Last Outpost of the Cold War," *Army 1994–1995 Green Book*, October 1994, 85–89; Lieutenant General Robert L. Ord III, "America's Army in the Pacific," *Army 1994–1995 Green Book*, October 1994, 103–10; Lieutenant General James R. Ellis, "Third . . . Always First!" *Army 1994–1995 Green Book*, October 1994, 113–19.

[35] John Hillen, *Blue Helmets: The Strategy of UN Military Operations* (Washington DC: Brassey's, 2000); Boutros Boutros-Ghali, *An Agenda for Peace: Preventive Diplomacy, Peacemaking and Peacekeeping* (New York: United Nations, 1992); Field Manual 100–23, *Peace Operations* (Washington DC: United States Army, 1994); *Peace Operations: Information on U.S. and U.N. Activities* (Washington DC: U.S. Government Printing Office, 1995); John P. Abizaid, "Lessons for Peacekeepers," *Military Review* (March 1993): 11–19.

[36] Rudd; Donald G. Goff, "Building Coalitions for Humanitarian Operations: Operation PROVIDE COMFORT" (Carlisle Barracks, Pennsylvania: U.S. Army War College, 1992); *Kurdish Relief and Repatriation: DOD-AID/OFDA Partnership, The Kurdish Response After-Action Report* (Washington DC: U.S. Agency for International Development and Office of U.S. Foreign Disaster Assistance, 1991).

[37] Richard W. Stewart, *The United States Army in Somalia, 1992–1994* (Washington DC: Center of Military History, 2004); Everett and Kaplan, 55–62; Kaplan, 63–66; Kenneth Allard, *Somalia Operations: Lessons Learned* (Washington DC; National

Defense University Press, 1995); Mark Bowden, *Black Hawk Down: A Story of Modern War* (New York: Penguin Books 1999); Montgomery.

[38] Kretchick, Bauman, and Fishel; Kevin M. Benson and Christopher B. Thrash, "Declaring Victory: Planning Exit Strategies for Peace Operations," *Parameters* (Autumn 1996): 69–80; Lester H. Brune, *The United States and Post–Cold War Interventions: Bush and Clinton in Somalia, Haiti and Bosnia, 1992–1998* (Claremont, California: Regina Books, 1998).

[39] Webb, 3–25, 134–39; Oland and Hogan, 37–43; Everett and Kaplan, 55–62; Kaplan, 63–66; Gammons and Donnelly, 46–49; Information Paper, Lieutenant Thomas J. Cleary, 27 October 1999, sub: Army Counterdrug Program, DCSOPS Security, Force Protection and Law Enforcement Division-Counter Drug; Newsletter Number 93–6, *Operations Other than War* (Fort Leavenworth, Kansas: U.S. Army Center for Lessons Learned, October 1993); William G. Bell et al., *Two Centuries of Service: The Army's Civil Contributions to American Society* (Washington DC: Center of Military History, 1975).

[40] Gammons and Donnelly, 46–49; Eric K. Shinseki, *The Army Family: A White Paper* (Washington DC: Center of Military History, 2003); *Army Families and Soldier Readiness* (Santa Monica, California: Rand Arroyo Center, 1992); *What We Know About Army Families* (Arlington, Virginia: Army Research Institute for the Behavioral and Social Sciences, 1993); *The Reciprocal Nature of Work and Family: Spouse's Perception of the Army/Family Interface and Its Impact on Soldier Retention* (Washington DC: Walter Reed Army Institute of Research, 1989).

[41] *Conduct of the Persian Gulf War: Final Report to Congress Pursuant to Title V of the Persian Gulf Conflict Supplemental Authorization and Personal Benefits Act of 1991 (Public Law 102–25)*, 471–86; James T. Currie and Richard B. Crossland, *Twice the Citizen: A History of the Army Reserve, 1908–1995* (Washington DC: Office of the Chief, Army Reserve, 1997), 521–80; Michael D. Doubler, *I Am the Guard: A History of the Army National Guard, 1636–2000* (Washington DC: Department of the Army, 2001); Major John R. D'Araujo Jr., "Army National Guard: The Nation's Strategic Insurance," *Army 1994–1995 Green Book,* October 1994, 91–95; Major General Max Baratz, "Army Reserve: Committed Force of Citizen Soldiers," *Army 1994–1995 Green Book,* October 1994, 97–99.

[42] Hillen, 1–33, 139–82; Rudd; Stewart; Kretchick, Bauman, and Fishel; *NATO Handbook,* 31–92; *The Responsibility to Protect: Report of the International Commission on Intervention and State Sovereignty* (New York: United Nations, 2001); General Rupert Smith, *The Utility of Force: The Art of War in the Modern World* (New York: Alfred A. Knopf, 2005).

[43] Max Boot, *War Made New: Technology, Warfare and the Course of History, 1500 to Today* (New York: Gotham Books, 2006), 307–474; Franks with Clancy, 488–511; James E. Dunnigan, *The Evolution of High-Tech Weaponry and Tomorrow's Brave New Battlefield* (New York: St. Martin's, 1996); James R. Blaker, *Transforming Military Force: The Legacy of Arthur Cebrowski and Network Centric Warfare* (Westport, Connecticut: Praeger Security International, 2007), 1–200; Thomas K. Adams, *The Army After Next: The First Postindustrial Army* (Stanford, California: Stanford Security Studies, 2008).

[44] Ms, Clayton R. Newell, Digitizing the Army (Arlington, Virginia: Association of the United States Army); John D. Bergen, *Military Communications: A Test for Technology* (Washington DC: Center of Military History, 1986); Rebecca R. Raines, *Getting the Message Through: A Branch History of the U.S. Army Signal Corps* (Washington DC: Center of Military History, 1996), 352–74.

[45] *Fratricide: Reducing Self-Inflicted Losses* (Fort Leavenworth, Kansas: Center for Army Lessons Learned, April 1992); *Fratricide Risk Assessment for Company Leadership* (Fort Leavenworth, Kansas: Center for Army Lessons Learned, March 1992); Memo, 3d Brigade, 2d Armored Division (Forward), 10 March 1991, sub: Informal Investigation of the Night Attack Conducted by 3d Brigade on 26–27 February, 1991, in Historians Files, CMH; Briefing, Department of the Army, "Friendly Fire Determination," 9 August 1991, in Historians Files, CMH; Patrick E. Tyler, "Pentagon Reassesses the Vulnerability of Its Tanks," *New York Times International*, 15 August 1991, A10; "Thermal Sights of Tanks Linked to Worst Case of Friendly Fire Deaths in Gulf," *Providence Journal*, 18 September 1991, B6.

[46] *Fratricide: Reducing Self-Inflicted Losses; Fratricide Risk Assessment for Company Leadership*; Briefing, Combat Identification Task Force, 22 November 1991, sub: Combat Identification, in Historians Files, CMH; Ltr, Lieutenant Colonel John S. Brown to Colonel David O. Bird, Director, Combat Identification Systems Program Office, 20 January 1992, sub: Combat Vehicle Identification, in Historians Files, CMH; Ltr, Mr. Frank Fox, COLSA Inc., to Lieutenant Colonel John S. Brown, 6 February 1992, sub: Tactical Scenario Concept, in Historians Files, CMH; Briefing, Combat Identifications Systems Program Office to Senior Officer Review Group, 14 February 1992, sub: Combat Identification Technology Demonstration Presentation, in Historians Files, CMH; Combat Identification Program Second Draft, 17 October1991, in Historians Files, CMH.

[47] Franks with Clancy, 488–511; Franks, "TRADOC at 20: Where Tomorrow's Victories Begin," 46–55; *Conduct of the Persian Gulf War: Final Report to Congress Pursuant to Title V of the Persian Gulf Conflict Supplemental Authorization and Personal Benefits Act of 1991 (Public Law 102–25)*, 236–37, 393–450, 543–76, 589–98; Pagonis with Cruickshank; Kent Laudeman, "Theater Support," in *Leaders in War: West Point Remembers the 1991 Gulf War*, ed. Frederick W. Kagan and Chris Kubik (New York: Frank Cass, 2005).

[48] Yarrison, v–ix, 33–56; Memo, Department of the Army, Program Executive Office, Armored Systems Modernization, 20 November 1991, sub: Abrams Tank ODS Lessons Learned—Hardware Change Recommendation, in Historians Files, CMH; Memo, Headquarters, VII (US) Corps, 22 March 1991, sub: VII Corps Master Gunners Conference, in Historians Files, CMH; Briefing, Combat Identifications Systems Program Office to Senior Officer Review Group, 14 February 1992, sub: Combat Identification Technology Demonstration Presentation; Combat Identification Program Second Draft, 17 October 1991; Franks with Clancy, 509–11.

[49] Yarrison, 49–71; Ltr, General Gordon R. Sullivan to the Army's General Officers, 5 March 1994, sub: Force XXI, in *The Collected Works of the Thirty-second Chief of Staff, United States Army*, 316–17; Msg, General Gordon R. Sullivan, Chief of Staff, 7 March 1994, sub: Building the Force for the 21st Century—Force XXI, in *The Collected Works of the Thirty-second Chief of Staff, United States Army*, 318–21; Headquarters Department of the Army, Charter for the Army Digitization Office, 9 June 1994; Information Paper, DACS-AD, 27 September 1994, sub: Army Digitization Office Status and Future Strategy; Army Digitization Office, *Report to the Congress on Army Digitization*, February 1995.

[50] Webb, 3–14; Gammons and Donnelly, 3–7, 46–48; *America's First Battles, 1776–1965*, 266–353, Franks with Clancy, 84–127.

[51] Gammons and Donnelly; Kirkpatrick, 20–28; Maddox, "Breakout at D+50: Projecting America's Power in Europe into the Future," 77–83.

[52] Gammons and Donnelly; Sergeant Major of the Army Richard A. Kidd, "NCOs Make It Happen," *Army 1994–1995 Green Book*, 31–36; Major General Wallace C.

Arnold, "The Army's Most Valuable Resource: People," *Army 1994–1995 Green Book,* 151–57.

[53] Bergesen and McDonald; Wilson, "Power Projection Logistics Now . . . and in the 21st Century," 137–43; Blackwell, 121–34; Field Manual 100–5, *Operations*, 1993.

[54] Gammons and Donnelly; Currie and Crossland, 521–80; Doubler; D'Araujo, 91–95; Baratz, 97–99; Kidd, 31–36; Arnold, 151–57

[55] Gammons and Donnelly; Yarrison, 49–72; Adams, 25–45; General Louis C. Wagner Jr., "AMC's Full-Throttle Effort to Capture Technology: Today's Concepts, Tomorrow's Edge," *Army 1988–1989 Green Book: The Year of Training*, October 1988, 100–109; Salomon, "At AMC the Future Begins Today," 69–75.

CHAPTER 4

The Reimer Years, 1995–1999

General Dennis J. Reimer was sworn in as Army Chief of Staff on 20 June 1995. He was thoroughly familiar with retiring Chief of Staff General Gordon R. Sullivan's vision of the way ahead for the Army and was well prepared to carry it forward. He had served as the Army's Deputy Chief of Staff for Operations and Plans (DCSOPS) during Desert Shield and Desert Storm and had served as Vice Chief of Staff through the first two years of General Sullivan's tenure. Promoted to four stars, he commanded the United States Army Forces Command (FORSCOM) from April 1993 through his selection to be Chief of Staff. Thus he was a long-term member of General Sullivan's four-star Board of Directors, experienced the initial brainstorming of the Louisiana Maneuvers from the vantage point of Vice Chief of Staff, and then followed concepts thus developed into the field as units under his command participated in the exercises, Advanced Technology Demonstrations (ATDs), and Advanced Warfighting Experiments (AWEs) that matured them. Reimer's challenges continued those of Sullivan, albeit with new nuances in some cases and significant changes in others. Diverse and extensive obligations and operations overseas guaranteed a high operational tempo. Current missions inevitably were more time-sensitive than modernization, and they distracted attention from it. Downsizing was by and large complete, but austere budgets, slender manning, and tough fiscal decisions remained. With the Quadrennial Defense Review and its associated National Defense Panel, Congress, the Secretariat, and the Joint Staff involved themselves in Army deliberations with unprecedented organization, energy, and rigor. If there had been a grace period during downsizing it was over, and the Army's long-term visioning had to be ever more visibly agreeable to others. Force XXI as it then existed became threatened both by those who preferred the Army as a low technology constabulary and by those advocating immediate leaps to technologies and organizations not yet proven. Soft-spoken, yet compelling as a speaker, Reimer persevered as an advocate of a middle course, evolutionary in the short run in order to be more efficiently revolutionary in the long. He particularly sought to keep the soldier visible in deliberations too often dominated by technology and simulation. A 1962 United States Military Academy graduate from Oklahoma, Reimer had served two tours in Vietnam and commanded at every level from battery through division. He consciously promulgated General Vuono's six imperatives and echoed Sullivan's holistic approach to transformation. His slogan was "Soldiers Are Our Credentials," and one of his favorite

General Reimer

stories was the World War II incident in Brittany during which Brigadier General Charles Canham of the 8th Infantry Division coined the phrase. During his tenure, soldiers of all ranks would be challenged by the competing demands placed upon them.[1]

Force XXI

As General Reimer assumed responsibilities as Chief of Staff, Force XXI offered a broad template for leading the Army into the Information Age and a calendar for experiments of increasing size and complexity. The Army was to continue its shift from a "threat-based" force oriented on the Soviet Union to become a "capabilities-based" force designed for the full combat spectrum. Much hardware and software had been proposed, but little as yet had actually been developed and decided upon. Success in the Information Age implied a mastery of "C4ISR." This horrific acronym stood for "command, control, communications, computers, intelligence, surveillance, and reconnaissance," a laundry list inviting huge variations in interpretation or emphasis. Fortuitously Reimer's Training and Doctrine Command (TRADOC) commander, General William W. Hartzog, had a knack for reducing complexity into essentials. In his view, reflecting insights developed during the course of the modern Louisiana Maneuvers, the "dominant knowledge" required of Information Age armies boiled down to achieving relative advantage with respect to three basic questions: "Where am I?" "Where are my buddies?" and "Where is the enemy?" If one knew the answers to these, effective command and control and modernized weaponry would enable one to destroy an adversary with fire and maneuver. Why would achieving advantage with respect to these three basic questions be revolutionary?[2]

Where am I? (The Problem)

Troops and units lost on the battlefield are a leitmotiv running through military history. West Point cadets marching several hundred feet from their barracks sally ports to occupy designated positions on the parade ground, send out unit guides to find and stand on markers placed in the grass, and thus ensure that units end up in the right place. Off the parade ground and onto the battlefield, everything becomes harder by at least an order of magnitude. One would be hard put to identify a major maneuver battle without significant contingents lost or disoriented at some point. United States military history begins with a battle named after the wrong hill, since the Battle of Bunker Hill was actually fought over Breed's Hill, several hundred yards away. Brigadier General Irwin McDowell began the first battle of our greatest nineteenth-century war by dispatching a main attack that collided with friendly forces moving in a different direction and then, after sorting that out, inched along poorly reconnoitered routes through the Virginia countryside. This main attack finally got across Bull Run hours late, with predictable consequences. Twentieth-century developments dispersed soldiers in tiny groups across vast battlefields, rendering land navigation even more problematic. The lethality of

General Hartzog

modern weapons encouraged attackers to kick off in hours of darkness or limited visibility, further complicating the process of finding their way. One World War II technique for maintaining direction was to continuously fire machine guns with uniquely identifiable tracers along the boundaries between units. This worked when the soldiers were confident enough to look around, fires were not so prolific as to mask the tracers, and the machine guns did not get knocked out. World War II also surfaced navigational disconnects between infantrymen progressing at a mile or so an hour, tankers and other mounted troops aspiring to thirty miles an hour, and pilots cruising along at several multiples of that speed. The embattled Rangers holding out at Normandy's Pointe du Hoc witnessed relieving American tanks racing back and forth past them several times before the tanks figured out where they actually were and made contact. Tankers had a special problem: their mammoth vehicles threw off commonly issued magnetic compasses. Indeed, the infantryman's approved solution for using a magnetic compass was to ground his steel helmet several yards away. For tankers, the equivalent was to separate from one's vehicle by half a football field. This was not often practical when under fire. Evidence concerning how much time troops spent disoriented or lost was anecdotal rather than empirical until the National Training Center (NTC) began accumulating a continuous record on instrumented exercises. Virtually every NTC after-action review featured a discussion of land navigation errors or unit disorientations, brief or prolonged. Qualification programs such as the Expert Infantryman's Badge (EIB) or Expert Field Medical Badge (EFMB) emphasized land navigation but nevertheless lost a major fraction of their candidates to it. Theorists estimated that even in the best units as many as a third of the soldiers and weapons never came into play in combat. If improved land navigation could halve that figure, this alone would mark a revolution in military affairs.[3]

Where are my buddies? (The Problem)

In previous chapters we discussed the horrors of fratricide and difficulties with respect to battle command and battle-space management during DESERT STORM. These issues were hardly new, of course. Fratricide, or "blue on blue" engagement, has been ever-present in war, and ever more vexing as the ranges and lethalities of weapons increased. Effective coordination of units and allocation of battle space is essential to the art of war. Knowledge of friendly locations is essential both to prevent fratricide and to enable command and control. As the twentieth century progressed, elaborate doctrinal protocols developed to ensure that commanders knew where subordinate units were—and that units each knew where the other was. Leadership down through the platoon level carried 1:50,000-scale maps covered with acetate and marked with proliferations of boundaries, phase lines, battle positions, checkpoints, target reference points, and routes or axes of multiple genres. These in turn became grist for battlefield reporting, first by wire strung along behind advancing columns, and then by radio. When moving, subordinates dutifully called in whenever their units crossed phase lines or passed checkpoints and advised their bosses when they had or lacked intervisibility with other friendly forces. When stationary, units submitted reports not less than daily detailing battle positions, contingent locations, activities, and logistical status. Responding to reports, officers and noncommissioned officers (NCOs) manning command posts updated maps with penned icons, pins, or sticky pieces of paper. Often they called back for clarification when they had not heard all that was transmitted or something did not look right when posted. Communications nets were alive with traffic of this sort, given that every headquarters commanded by a field-grade officer customarily had a half dozen to a dozen subordinate headquarters reporting to it. The cacophony was formidable even when things were going well and could become overwhelming when the acetate on someone's map slipped, it became apparent people were working off of different overlays, or some other mishap required elaborate descriptions rather than terse commentary. The acting supply sergeant lost making a night logistical run, and not particularly good at reading a map, was a cultural icon for maneuver training. Hours could be spent talking him in, guessing what intersection he was at by his description of it, and drawing upon such landmarks as a dead tree leaning on a telephone pole, an open space with a herd of cows in it, or where the First Sergeant ran his jeep off the road last summer. An additional level of complexity could be achieved when trying to bring two small map-challenged contingents together in the dark of night—perhaps, for example, the wingman's tank that had thrown track and mired deep in the woods and the M88 recovery vehicle commanded by a Specialist 4 that was riding to the rescue. Huge amounts of radio traffic and supervisory time were given over to keeping buddies apprised of each other's location and activities. Commanders got in the habit of driving all of this chatter off of their command

142

net, which they preserved for orderly conversations of which they approved, and onto one or more "admin-log" nets. This preserved the equanimity of a few key individuals without altering the volume of communications involved. This is not to mention the fact that admin-log nets were already busy with reports itemizing arrivals, departures, sick calls, maintenance status, resupply plans, and inventories of beans, bullets, repair parts, and the like. One estimate held that operators spent 70 percent of their time and effort collecting information and 30 percent planning what to do with it. Halving the time given over to collecting information would again in itself mark a revolution in military affairs. It would also be helpful if the buddy intervisibility built up on one radio net could be readily transferred to another. Historically, it has been challenging for maneuver units to keep supporting artillery apprised of their positions, and even more difficult to keep the Air Force informed. This accounted for disproportionate amounts of fratricide attributed to artillery and air support. It also accounted for the tendency of many ground commanders to forgo actual close air support and to direct pilots to the opposite sides of a fire support coordination line (FSCL), so far away it would be virtually impossible for the pilots to accidentally bomb them.[4]

Where is the enemy? (The Problem)

This, of course, has been the core intelligence requirement since antiquity. Ancient armies sent spies and scouts ranging well beyond the mass of their troops and fought for information closer in with light troops and cavalry. Every era has adapted the technology of its time to provide arrays of alarms, signals, and other communications speeding information on the enemy to the leaders who would act upon it. The dispersed and camouflaged battlefield of the twentieth century made information harder to find, and the advent of mechanized warfare reduced the time available to react. To be useful, intelligence had to be timely, accurate, and understandable. Timeliness could be compromised by the number of layers through which information had to travel. In ancient times, fleet scouts might ride directly to the supreme commander and report their findings. In the twentieth century scouts or outposts with eyes on the enemy reported through multiple layers of command. Each such transmission of information took time, and each presented a unique opportunity for the message to become garbled. What was true of information going up was also true of information going down. Frontline troops could remain blissfully unaware of alarming news that was already available to their senior headquarters. Garbled communications degraded the accuracy of intelligence as well as its timeliness. Accuracy could be degraded by multiple communications as well. Dispersed outposts reporting the same enemy element could create the impression of multiple elements. This was particularly likely if the outposts were not altogether sure where they were and lacked means to confidently determine the location of the enemy. This is not to mention sensory limits to seeing, hearing, smelling, or otherwise detecting the enemy in the first place. As information on the enemy accumulated, someone had to sort it out and make sense of it. Ideally, pieces of a puzzle could be brought together to reveal a coherent picture of enemy size, organization,

143

equipment, and capabilities—and perhaps even intentions. Familiarity with the enemy's modus operandi facilitated this gathering of clues. Prisoners from different units captured in the same area could indicate the enemy was concentrating for an attack. Recurrent reports of vehicles moving about in the dark could indicate the same thing. Conversely, an unexplained drop in radio traffic could indicate the enemy was trying too hard to keep his preparations a secret, relying on alternate means of communications to mask his preparations. Commanders and their intelligence officers knew they needed to manage the clutter of information coming in and to focus assets on gathering the most noteworthy clues. By the 1980s this imperative had developed into the concept of commander's critical intelligence requirements (CCIR). These valuable bits of information were to be sought, fought for, and speeded through the reporting system above all others. What could the Information Age bring to the timeless cat-and-mouse game of intelligence and counterintelligence? That was the intent of General Hartzog's third question.[5]

The Army's approach to developing and proofing Information Age technologies in the field was incremental. As we have seen, the modern Louisiana Maneuvers harnessed simulations to propose technological developments and first experimented with their implications in cyberspace. Results were informative, but not a substitute for testing actual equipment "in the dirt." In September 1992 an Inter-Vehicular Information System (IVIS)–equipped M1A2 tank platoon accompanied the 1st Cavalry Division to a National Training Center rotation. In December 1992 and March 1993 the Mounted Battlespace Battle Lab conducted Battlefield Synchronization Demonstrations at the company team level at Fort Knox and followed up by deploying an M1A2-equipped company team to a National Training Center rotation in July. Operations at the company level exposed significant difficulties sustaining communications across a mix of vehicles, some of which had the modernized equipment and some of which did not. Hastily assembled working groups addressed the phenomena of "Horizontal Technical Integration" (HTI) to ensure interoperability. By April 1994 field experimentation progressed to the task force level. The digitally equipped Task Force 1-70 Armor of the 194th Separate Armored Brigade (Fort Knox, Kentucky) participated in DESERT HAMMER VI, a 24th Infantry Division (Mechanized) rotation at the National Training Center. By this time it had become apparent that practical, in-the-dirt testing was progressing to a level beyond that wherein TRADOC could provide a realistic command and control overhead. In December 1994 the 2d Armored Division (later redesignated as the 4th Infantry Division [Mechanized]) at Fort Hood, Texas, was announced as the Army's Experimental Force (EXFOR) for further digitization. It would eventually become the Army's first digitized division, and its parent III Corps the Army's first digitized corps. The next, and greatest, leap was to fully digitize a brigade combat team. A heavy brigade combat team features all branches and includes field-grade commands of armor, infantry, artillery, combat service support, and often engineers. Digitization required the installation and proofing of almost 5,000 pieces of equipment on over 900 vehicles. Of these pieces of equipment, 1,200 items were appliqué computers—appliqué because Force XXI by and large relied on traditional platforms and vehicles. Training and preparations drove toward two AWEs: a digitized brigade combat team NTC rotation in March 1997 and a follow-on division exercise integrating the digitized brigade at Fort Hood in November 1997. The scope of the experimentation would be huge. The brigade task force would test almost a hundred discrete innovative concepts, fielding eighty-seven different systems to do so. More than 1,200 additional contractors and data collectors accompanied the brigade—about one for every four soldiers. Wags had it that the Army now deployed with as many contractors as the Marine Corps did with photographers. Be that as it may, the configuration represented a determined commitment to spiral development and to the integrated efforts of soldiers and industrial representatives in the field. For all these additional layers of complexity, however, the principal fruits of NTC Rotation 97–06 were still assessed in terms of General Hartzog's three basic questions.[6]

Digitization became an important component of training in the field.

Where am I? (The Solution)

Land navigation was being revolutionized by the general introduction of satellite-based global positioning system (GPS) technology. The Army hastily distributed commercial variants of GPS during DESERT STORM, with impressive results. American formations raced across the trackless Iraqi desert with elegant precision, falling upon hapless Iraqis who were far more likely to be lost in their own country than the invading Americans. The experience was so satisfactory that Army procurement officers dropped the notion of "developmental" GPS receivers in favor of "nondevelopmental"—which is to say commercial—receivers instead. They also increased their appetite for such equipment. Original plans called for about 8,000 units, largely for aircraft and selected ground users. By the time of NTC Rotation 97–06 procurement plans called for 94,000 units distributed ubiquitously. During DESERT STORM GPS was available to but a few vehicles in a company, and satellite coverage was dangerously spotty. Virtually every vehicle in NTC 97–06 had a variant of GPS, and satellite coverage was worldwide and full time. The AN/PSN–11 precision lightweight GPS receiver (PLGR) could be used mounted or dismounted, and technological development was moving in the direction of achieving the same results with an embedded module and then a chip. Maintenance was simple; the direct support unit issued the operator a new PLGR and mailed the malfunctioning PLGR to the manufacturer. For all its virtues, GPS alone was not an immediate fix for all land navigation problems. Operator training was required, and soldiers acquired finesse with the equipment as they used it. Ironically, finesse seemed to be inversely proportional to age and rank, with the most effective users being disproportionately the youngest soldiers. Absent a map, it was not uncommon to become disoriented even when one knew one's location, particularly when moving in the dark. This could occur because directions for further movement (e.g., "left twenty degrees" or "right thirty degrees") became more radical as one closed on one's destination. During DESERT STORM, for example, one unit determined that it was in the right place but did not know what direction it was facing. It remedied this situation by calling on its supporting artillery to fire an illumination round over a stipulated point—a technique dating from World War I. When more GPS receivers were available and with more practice, a formation could avoid such disorientation if operators cross-talked and used sister vehicles as well as their own GPS as a frame of reference. By the time of NTC Rotation 97–06 even better methods were available. Appliqué computers featured downloadable digital maps that appeared on the screen and could be "zoomed in" or "zoomed out" to achieve different levels of resolution. Icons representing one's own vehicle or PLGR and those of one's comrades appeared on the screen as well. Armed with such information, a capable operator could orient on the terrain and his comrades to maintain his orientation at all times. In his 1997 update for the *Army Green Book,* General Hartzog chose to feature the proverbial acting supply sergeant speeding along on his resupply mission. The soldier was pictured intently perusing the appliqué computer mounted in the cab of his 2½-ton truck. The screen of the computer prominently displayed his present location and depicted his vehicle and his destination superimposed on a topographical map of the terrain that surrounded and separated them. Soldiers were creative enough to find new ways of getting lost, but in the presence of GPS-derived technology the probability of doing so had become an order of magnitude less.[7]

Where are my buddies? (The Solution)

As we have seen, satellite-based GPS technology enabled each vehicle and PLGR to automatically and precisely identify its location at all times. Vehicles and PLGRs participating in NTC Rotation 97–06 featured transponders that forwarded this information into a shared tactical intranet. Appliqué computers translated this information into a visual representation on an electronic topographical map depicting the locations of all similarly equipped platforms. Information was updated automatically; transponders self-reported frequently enough that depictions remained current. Because of this automatic self-reporting, huge volumes of radio traffic altogether disappeared. The prolonged give-and-take of units reporting locations, headquarters confirming locations, travelers asking for directions to facilities, and contingents coordinating rendezvous points disappeared from the ether. All that information moved along quietly, effortlessly, and seamlessly on bandwidth other than that being used by the radios. We earlier mentioned the rule of the thumb that operators spent 70 percent of their time collecting information and 30 percent of their time figuring out what to do with it. Operations officers committed to NTC Rotation 97–06 asserted that they had reversed that statistic. The friendly tactical information they needed was readily at their disposal, with a minimum of effort. The capacity of the system to self-report logistical information was not yet so mature, concerning which, more later. Tactical Operations Centers (TOCs) were now quieter places and more in the way of planning was getting done. Issues remained. Information developed within one electronic network was not yet automatically available within another one. Air Force systems could not automatically depict Army positions, for example, and horizontal information across Army elements was incomplete. The several different batches of data could be packaged, however, and energetic TOC officers improvised ways to share relevant information with counterparts. They also rediscovered that not everyone had to know everything to the same level of detail. Their lessons learned would fuel further progress with respect to horizontal integration. Perhaps most significantly, easy intervisibility reduced the risk of fratricide. Operators knew where units and vehicles were with elegant precision. It was harder to keep track of dispersed dismounts, since man-packed PLGRs were more difficult to carry about and use than the vehicle-borne variety. Proportionately there were fewer PLGRs per dismount than there were PLGRs per vehicle, of course. Whatever the residual limits, knowledge of friendly locations had made a revolutionary leap forward.[8]

Where is the enemy? (The Solution)

Some believed that the technology of the Information Age would dissipate the proverbial "fog of war" forever. "Unblinking eyes" aloft in satellites would detect enemy movements and set in train a cycle of monitoring, assessment, and destruction that would incapacitate the enemy with little risk to friendly forces. Understandably, this line of argument was more widely believed in the Air Force than in the Army. Historical experience suggested that determined and adaptive adversaries would find ways to render themselves imperfect victims of American technology. Reimer, Hartzog, and their colleagues aspired to something less than absolute knowledge and pursued "dominant knowledge" instead. If you knew more that mattered about your enemies than they knew about you, had a capacity to build up useful intelligence more quickly than they did, and could act decisively in cycles that outpaced theirs, you could accrue huge—perhaps even revolutionary—advantages. Information can be overwhelming, and Information Age technologies had the capacity to serve up streams of data so vast they could become incomprehensible. Intelligence is about winnowing as much as it is about harvesting. Doctrine calls for overlapping and not entirely sequential cycles to plan, prepare, collect, process, and produce intelligence. Planning determines what one most wants to know. If you are conducting a tank attack, for example, you want to know where the enemy's antitank weapons are. Preparation is positioning assets to gather the information you most want, and collecting is gathering it. Processing is winnowing and establishing relationships, and producing is putting information in a usable format in the hands of the commander. In our example of a tank attack, a 1:50,000 topographical map depicting enemy antitank weapons would be such a product. Although imperfect at the time of NTC Rotation 97–06, the networks of computers committed to intelligence that deployed there seemed most promising with respect to processing and producing. Digitization significantly increased the pace at which data could be assessed and analyzed, and it radically increased the pace at which it could be disseminated. Once determined, a common picture of the enemy—generally an electronic map of some kind, but often text—arrived at all echelons of command simultaneously with the speed of thought. Means of collection registered advances during NTC Rotation 97–06 as well. The Air Defense Artillery matrices of sensors, radars, communications links, and automated slew-to-cue Avengers showed particularly well. In its first three "battles" the task force shot down 12 of 16, 17 of 18, and 21 of 28 incoming enemy aircraft. The networked integration of sensors aboard Joint Surveillance and Target Attack Radar System (J-STARS) aircraft, helicopters such as the Apache Longbow, and ground scouts artfully distributed about the battlefield also collected useful data at an unprecedented rate—particularly when enemy vehicles were moving in mass. The Hunter unmanned aerial vehicle (UAV) showed considerable promise, although maintenance and operator proficiency were as yet uneven. Information gained by these advanced means came in alongside that gathered by such traditional means as visual observation followed up by radioed spot reports. In short, revolutionary advances with respect to collecting, processing, and producing intelligence seemed within the grasp of NTC Rotation 97–06. Planning and preparing for intelligence remained more art than science, still leaning most heavily upon the skill and experience of intelligence operators.[9]

The Information Age technologies that tied together the players on the battlefield and radically improved the answers to Hartzog's three questions were to be wedded to precise and effective fires to achieve optimal results. Thermal sights and other long-term initiatives to "own the night" considerably advanced this prospect, as did the precision-guided munitions then available. However, the breakthrough that truly redefined the paradigm in this regard was not yet apparent at the time of NTC Rotation 97–06. It would be shortly thereafter. In March 1997, precision-guided munitions still presented dilemmas with respect to cost-effectiveness. Costs affected inventories available, and the depletion of inventories reintroduced reliance on more primitive and less accurate munitions. In Desert Storm less than 8 percent of the ordnance expended was precision-guided, yet this accounted for 84 percent of the cost of ordnance expended. At close ranges such direct-fire systems as the M1A1 tank, benefiting from superb computer-facilitated fire controls, fired "dumb" munitions with such accuracy that cost-effectiveness was not a problem. During Desert Storm one representative tank battalion fired 168 main gun rounds and destroyed 103 armored vehicles, translating into several hundred dollars per vehicle destroyed. At greater ranges precision became more expensive. The Joint Air to Surface Standoff Missile (JASSM) cost $400,000 each. The Tactical Tomahawk cruise missile cost $730,000. The term *high-value target* emerged to describe aim points worthy of such pricey munitions. Generally such high-value targets were not of much immediate interest to the embattled infantryman. In DESERT STORM, for example, of about 120,000 air sorties close to 20,000 were strikes against ground order of battle targets. These resulted in about a thousand tanks, personnel carriers, or artillery pieces destroyed. Clearly the ground order-of-battle targets were not the priority for air sorties and not a priority for the use of precision-guided munitions either. Even as NTC Rotation 97–06 progressed, the Air Force and Navy were taking delivery on prototype Joint Direct Attack Munition (JDAM) kits for operational testing. These kits added aerodynamic controls, inertial guidance, and GPS navigation to "dumb" bombs in such a manner as to convert them into precision-guided munitions. The original incentive had been to use GPS to overcome the limits imposed by smoke, fog, dust, and rain on munitions dependent on infrared, lasers, and other weather-degradable means for terminal guidance. The JDAMs achieved a 95 percent circular error probable (CEP) of ten meters or less in the worst of such conditions. Even more remarkably, they were cheap. Originally estimated at $40,000 a kit, they were driven under $20,000 by the volume of sales and competitive bidding. Within a few years, and after further experimentation and training, these precision-guided munitions became practical components of the maneuver battle as it was fought at the battalion and brigade level.[10]

National Training Center Rotation 97–06 was a seminal event in advancing Force XXI and was, as we have discussed, part of a larger continuum of experimentation and spiral development "in the dirt." By the time it occurred, General Reimer had declared mission complete for the LAM Task Force and reabsorbed its functions back into such traditional agencies as TRADOC and the Office of the Deputy Chief of Staff for Operations and Plans (ODCSOPS). The Army adopted the convention of characterizing Force XXI as the current process of transformation and Army XXI as the product that would emerge from that process. Army XXI could not emerge all at once; units would phase in as time and resources permitted. TRADOC began speaking of "Legacy," "Interim," and "Objective" forces. Legacy forces were those that then existed, less the instrumented Experimental Force. Interim forces would be capable of digital command and control and in the process of acquiring a full suite of digital equipment but would not yet be complete in that regard. The Objective Force would have altogether adopted the Force XXI design. The brigade task force of NTC Rotation 97–06 featured prototypes of the appliqué systems that were to characterize the Objective Force. The Army aspired to field an Interim Division by Fiscal Year (FY) 2000, an Objective Division by FY2003, and an Objective Corps slice by FY2006. Success would depend on funding. The Assistant Secretary of the Army for Research, Development, and Acquisition, Gilbert F. Decker, cautioned of a reduction of the budget within his purview from $29 billion in FY1986 to under $11 billion in FY1996. General Reimer directed a careful scrub of the funding projected through FY2003 to ascertain how realistic the Force XXI goals were. Answers to this question depended on the battlefield operating system involved. Intelligence had long been a player with respect to digitization and was on track to equip a digitized division even prior to FY2000. Its linchpin All Source Analysis System (ASAS) had been robustly funded since 1984, was well along, and seemed capable of quickly integrating such new technologies as the Remote Battlefield Sensor System (REMBASS), tactical unmanned aerial vehicle (TUAV), and the integrated meteorological system (IMETS). Air Defense was not far behind. The sophisticated Patriot and Avenger air defense systems had been fielded in the 1980s and improved since, and the Forward Area Air Defense Command and Control (FAADC2) system had successfully weathered considerable testing. The air defenders did have their hearts set on getting their Stinger antiaircraft missile teams into the technologically advanced Bradley Stinger Fighting Vehicle–Enhanced (BSFV-E), and success in this regard depended on the supply of and priorities for Bradleys. Artillerymen similarly were in a competition for Bradleys for their fire support teams (FISTs) and had tied modernization plans to the not yet developed and fielded Crusader 155-mm. self-propelled howitzer. On the plus side, the Advanced Field Artillery Tactical Data System (AFATDS) was well advanced and robustly funded. It would field a division equivalent prior to FY2000 and benefited from predecessor systems in automatically managing data and providing fire support solutions. Command and control and logistics were patchy, dependent on fielding over a dozen systems each at the division level to achieve Force XXI objectives. Of these, some, such as the frequency-jumping (and thus more difficult to jam) Single Channel Ground and Airborne Radio System–System Improvement Program (SINCGARS-SIP), were already in the field and demonstrably successful. Others, such as a wireless local area network (LAN), were yet to be perfected. Some command and control and logistics systems were projected as available in division equivalent sets beyond FY2006, if then. Predictably, the greatest gap between Force XXI objectives and projected resources was with respect to the maneuver arms of armor and infantry and their supporting engineers. M1A2 tanks and appliquéd M2/M3A3 Bradleys were to be numerous and expensive in the Objective Force, as were swarms of vehicles that would directly support them. The Battlefield Combat Identification System (BCIS) was experiencing significant developmental problems, as previously discussed, and the Future Scout and Cavalry System (FSCS) depended on advanced technologies and accompanying robotics that seemed appreciably beyond the FY2006 horizon. Upgraded AH64–D Apache attack and OH58–D Kiowa Warrior armed reconnaissance helicopters were on hand, funded, and performing well, but the RAH–66 Comanche intended for the next generation was slipping to the right with respect to development. As is so often the case, the prospects for Force XXI generating Army XXI boiled down to money. NTC Rotation 97–06 demonstrated potentially revolutionary technologies in the hands of an organization well on the way to mastering them. The brigade involved was but a tiny fragment of the Army, however, and even a division would be but one in ten in the active Army. Were there to be a revolution in military affairs, it would ultimately require mass. The architects of Army transformation continued to wrestle with two distinct but related questions.

How quickly could a consequential inventory of "Objective Force" units be fielded? How quickly could technologies and techniques developed in the EXFOR migrate into the "Legacy Force," and would they be affordable and helpful if they did?[11]

Contingencies

Deployments overseas continued to escalate during General Reimer's tenure, in accordance with the shape-prepare-respond grand strategy of the Clinton administration and for about the same reasons that underlay the escalation during General Sullivan's tenure. In FY1996 an average of 21,500 soldiers were operationally deployed away from home station on any given day. By FY1999 this figure rose to 31,000. The elaborately executed "commuter containment" of Saddam Hussein continued, as did more traditional engagement and deterrence throughout the remainder of the Middle East, Asia, and the Pacific. Army capabilities continued to be tapped for military support to civilian authority, particularly in circumstances wherein nonmilitary assets could not come into play quickly or cheaply. Peacekeeping in the aftermath of wars in the Balkans drove the Army's deployed manpower to new highs. Ironically, these very peacekeeping missions proved to be part of a larger framework that enabled the United States and its allies to consolidate success in the Cold War. Commitments overseas furthered evolutionary processes in venues as different as service lifestyle, expectations of the reserve component, and prospective force structure.[12]

INTRINSIC ACTION 95–3, discussed in the previous chapter, was but one in a sequence of deployments intended to contain Saddam Hussein. Indeed, INTRINSIC ACTION 95–3 tucked into the more expansive Joint Operation VIGILANT SENTINEL (August–December 1995), which itself was a successor to Joint Operation VIGILANT WARRIOR (October–December 1994). In both cases political perturbations provoked Saddam to rail against his neighbors, and deployments of American ground forces provided precautionary deterrence. Saudi Arabia, Kuwait, Jordan, and neighboring friendly states were loathe to host permanent American presences of significant size, so tiny American cadres in country coordinated the comings and goings of larger contingents and units. In August 1996 Saddam Hussein intervened in internal Kurdish fighting and seized the city of Irbil, allegedly on the behalf of the Kurdistan Democratic Party (KDP). This was an alarming intrusion into territories north of the 36th Parallel that had been protected by Operation PROVIDE COMFORT II since 1991. Within a few days the United States Navy and Air Force rained cruise missiles on Iraqi high-value targets in Joint Operation DESERT STRIKE, prompting an Iraqi withdrawal. Concerned that the Iraqis might retaliate against facilities in Kuwait, particularly since some aircraft involved in the strike had been based there, the Joint Staff hurriedly deployed yet another brigade combat team onto the pre-positioned equipment at Doha. About this time Kuwait agreed to a near-continuous presence of American brigade combat teams, as long as each stayed for only a few months and participated in clearly distinct, albeit rotational, training exercises. The Saudis agreed to the continuous presence of

Patriot air defense battalions on about the same terms. A devastating terrorist attack on troops housed in the Khobar Towers in Saudi Arabia killed nineteen U.S. airmen. This prompted redeployment to more isolated sites and the rotational presence of an infantry battalion, labeled DESERT FOCUS, to secure U.S. forces in Saudi Arabia. The Iraqis became increasingly restive, firing at planes enforcing the no-fly zones of Operation SOUTHERN WATCH and the newly instituted Operation NORTHERN WATCH (initiated on 1 January 1997 as the follow-on to PROVIDE COMFORT II), refusing to cooperate with United Nations inspectors enforcing Gulf War sanctions against weapons of mass destruction, and threatening further havoc. Allied planes retaliated when fired upon, methodically debilitating Iraqi air defenses. One crisis followed another. Throughout most of 1998 Operation DESERT THUNDER provided a readily reinforcible shield to Kuwait and Saudi Arabia in the face of continuous saber rattling. In August 1998 terrorist bombings of the American embassies in Kenya and Tanzania provoked Operation INFINITE REACH, missile strikes into Afghanistan and the Sudan. Shortly thereafter the United States and United Kingdom conducted Operation DESERT FOX, a four-day bombing campaign to degrade potential Iraqi weapons of mass destruction facilities Saddam had rendered inaccessible to United Nations inspectors. Although these retaliatory and preemptive strikes were conducted by naval and air forces, Iraqi counterstrikes were likely to be on the ground. The visible presence of American troops preempted that threat. Army pre-positioned capabilities expanded from a heavy brigade to a heavy division in or proximate to the Persian Gulf during this period. In addition to the brigade set already in Kuwait, another brigade set went into Qatar, and Army War Reserve–3 (AWR-3) (afloat) was configured as a brigade set as well. Containing Iraq had matured into continuous rounds of operational deployments.[13]

The containment of Saddam Hussein was dynamic, altering to accommodate his bizarre yet threatening behavior. Elsewhere in the Middle East, Asia, and the Pacific, somewhat more routine, but no less important, deployments added to the operational tempo. North Korea seemed a particularly dangerous Cold War relic. The collapse of the Soviet Union and progressive economic developments in China degraded the enthusiasm of traditional props for the repressive and parasitic regime. The North Korean economy shrank to the point that malnutrition was significant, defections to South Korea rose, flight into China soared, and medicine was in perilously short supply. The North Korean economy shrank to one-twentieth the size of the prosperous South's, yet the North Koreans continued to maintain a huge army, train it rigorously, and gave evidence of nuclear ambitions. The death of Kim Il Sung and the succession of his son Kim Jong Il improved nothing, and the possibility existed that a desperate North Korean military bureaucracy might lash out before it collapsed altogether. The American response was steady and visible support to its South Korean ally, including recurrent annual deployments from outside the theater. Exercise ULCHI FOCUS LENS annually exercised command and control, rehearsed campaign plans, and conducted selected operations from the theater through the tactical level. Exercise FOAL EAGLE annually exercised mobilization, special operations, and rear area security. In FY1999

FOAL EAGLE involved 500,000 personnel, of whom 5 percent were Americans. Annual reception, staging, onward movement, and integration (RSO&I) exercises tested the ability of units to quickly fall in upon equipment pre-positioned in Korea. Exercises BALIKATAN in the Philippines, COBRA GOLD in Thailand, and BRIGHT STAR in Egypt similarly demonstrated commitment to regional allies on a recurrent basis, as did a fistful of other bilateral and multilateral exercises scheduled less frequently. United States Army, Pacific (USARPAC), pursued an "expanded relations program" providing an umbrella for a wide variety of essentially bilateral exercises tailored to the interests and sensitivities of individual friendly armies. In some cases these were training for conventional operations, in other cases for demining, medical assistance, seminars, personnel exchanges, and so on. Although generally small, these investments did add up. In FY1995, for example, the expanded relations program deployed over 8,000 soldiers to twenty-six countries throughout the Asia-Pacific region. Another figure adding to overall totals was the thousand soldiers sustained in the Multinational Force and Observers (MFO) Sinai, discussed earlier.[14]

Military support to civilian authority remained a significant incentive for deployments overseas and within the United States. Ten thousand soldiers were deployed to support the 1996 Olympics in Atlanta, Georgia. Operation SAFE HAVEN in support of Cuban refugees, discussed in the previous chapter, continued into this period, as did humanitarian relief efforts associated with operation UPHOLD DEMOCRACY in Haiti. In April 1996 soldiers from the Southern European Task Force (SETAF) deployed in Joint Operation ASSURED RESPONSE to rescue Americans and third-country nationals from factional fighting in Liberia. During FY1997 Operation PACIFIC HAVEN facilitated the evacuation and relocation of 6,000 Kurdish refugees particularly at risk in their own country. During this same period the Army supported the somewhat bizarre Task Force MARATHON PACIFIC, whereby illegal immigrants from China were intercepted in the Atlantic Ocean, cared for and processed at Wake Island in the Pacific, and then repatriated. Throughout General Reimer's tenure joint exercises such as TRADE WINDS and NEW HORIZONS provided a framework through which to engage Latin American armies and funnel humanitarian assistance into their region. The National Guard and Army Reserve proved particularly active, visible, and suitable in these Latin American exercises. Engineer, medical, civil affairs, and other combat service support units rotated past each other in active-duty training that left behind a legacy of new schools, paved roads, medical services, and community support. U.S. Army, South's tiny contingent of three thousand soldiers and two thousand civilians was thus reinforced annually by 25,000 from the reserve component. This effort spiked in commitment and effectiveness after Hurricane Mitch, one of the most powerful storms on record, savaged the Caribbean and Central America during the fall of 1998. Over ten thousand were killed, over two million left homeless, and half the paved roads in the path of the hurricane ruined. NEW HORIZONS participation surged to sustain two thousand soldiers committed at a time for months. Fifty-four separate medical exercises tended to 248,000 people and 30,000 animals. This excitement and effort incidentally eclipsed preparations for a historical watershed within the region, the transfer of properties associated with the Panama Canal to the Panamanian government by 31 December 1999. Latin America was the principal setting for another genre of support to civilian authority, the "war" on drugs. Army aviators provided surveillance along the Mexican border and in the Caribbean. Within the United States Reconnaissance and Interdiction Detachments (RAIDs) based in thirty-one states supported law enforcement officers with state-of-the-art OH–58 reconnaissance helicopters. The National Guard averaged three thousand soldiers a week committed to counterdrug efforts as varied as surveillance, barrier construction, intelligence analysis, and canine support. This was in addition to the two hundred thousand man-days Guardsmen averaged in support of their own governors and states, generally in the course of disaster relief. Out of this broad portfolio of operations and commitments, few were particularly military in their genesis or in their essence. All made use of the Army as an organized reservoir of trained manpower. Collectively considered, they significantly drove up the operational tempo of troops deployed.[15]

Operations in the Balkans dominated as a source of escalating deployments during General Reimer's tenure. We discussed the breakup of Yugoslavia in earlier chapters and the ineffectiveness of the United Nations Protection Force (UNPROFOR) in bringing peace to war-torn Bosnia-Herzegovina. The North Atlantic Treaty Organization (NATO), and its member the United States, found itself increasingly drawn into efforts to curb violence and arrest aggressive "ethnic cleansing," perpetrated most visibly by the Serbs. In August 1995 a particularly egregious mortar round lobbed into a Sarajevo market place provoked a 3,500-sortie NATO air campaign that broke the Serbian siege of that city. About the same time Croatians and Bosnian Muslims, evidently benefiting from outside assistance, began driving back the theretofore successful Bosnian Serbs on the ground. These reversals brought Serbian strongman Slobodan Milosevic to the conference table. Military provisions of the resultant Dayton Accords stipulated a NATO-led Implementation Force (IFOR) that would ensure compliance with the cease-fire, separation of forces, collection of heavy weapons into agreed cantonments, the safe withdrawal (or transfer to NATO control) of United Nations forces, and NATO control of Bosnian airspace. Mindful of how quickly the underarmed UNPROFOR had been cowed by the Serbs, NATO dispatched a heavily armed and armored force of sixty thousand, of whom about a third were Americans. Built up around the German-based 1st Armored Division, the American contingent deployed overland through an intermediate staging base in Taszar, Hungary, to assume responsibility for the northern third of Bosnia-Herzegovina, headquartered at Tuzla. En route the Americans conducted a challenging late December pontoon bridging operation to get across the unseasonably swollen Sava River. Once deployed, IFOR accomplished its immediate military objectives fairly readily. The belligerents were war weary, and the military capabilities of the deployed NATO forces impressive. Energetic mounted and dismounted patrolling generated around-the-clock surveillance, zones of separation were emptied of opposing forces, and the cease-fire held. The former warring factions attempted to cheat with respect to accounting for heavy weapons, but NATO persistence

U.S. soldiers patrolling in Donja Dubrava, Bosnia-Herzegovina, April 1997

brought them under inspection and under control. Profligate wartime use of land mines—perhaps more than 750,000 throughout Bosnia-Herzegovina—had created huge hazards for soldiers and civilians alike. IFOR, contractors, and the former belligerents pecked away at clearing these as years-long projects. The routine of patrols, collateral training, and camp life was occasionally punctuated by spikes of violence, particularly when members of one ethnic group attempted to assert their freedom of movement through the territory of another, or to reclaim property lost in the fighting. Demonstrators could be media savvy, busing in "rent-a-mobs" when they particularly wanted to underscore a point. The American soldiers worked through all of this with patience, discipline, and imagination. Houses were rebuilt some, refugees resettled, elections held, and economic initiatives launched. Progress did not include much actual cooperation among the former warring parties, however. The results of ethnic cleansing by and large held, and the ethnic groups lived separated from each other by zones policed by NATO-led soldiers. Interplay between the groups was generally brokered by outsiders. This fragmented peace was infinitely preferable to what had gone before. In December 1996 IFOR transitioned to become the Stabilization Force (SFOR). Conditions had improved sufficiently that the force structure halved to about thirty thousand. The mission continued through 2004, when responsibility transferred from NATO to the European Union (EU). The forces deployed steadily diminished, but a respectable international presence remained necessary. From December 1995 through December 1996 the project in Bosnia-Herzegovina was labeled JOINT ENDEAVOR, from December 1996 through June 1998 JOINT GUARD, and from June 1998 through November 2004 JOINT FORGE.[16]

Even as circumstances settled into an acceptable routine in Bosnia-Herzegovina, they spiraled out of control in nearby Kosovo. The root causes were Serbian determination to maintain control over a province that was now demographically 90 percent Albanian, and violent Albanian resistance to that domination. A shadowy Kosovo Liberation Army (KLA) waged sporadic guerrilla warfare within the province, and the Serbs responded with occasionally stunning brutality. NATO-brokered peace talks at Rambouillet, France, broke down on 19 March 1999, when the Serbs refused to accept NATO peacekeeping troops in Kosovo. On 20 March heavily armed and armored Serbian forces launched a massive terror campaign that clearly had been under preparation for some time. They systematically ravaged towns and villages in an orgy of arson, mayhem, murder, and rape. Their intention was ethnic cleansing on a scale that would dwarf that of Bosnia-Herzegovina, reversing Kosovo's demographic profile into an overwhelming Serbian majority. Soon thousands of Albanian Kosovars were dead and tens of thousands fleeing into the mountains or nearby Albania and Macedonia. The United Nations mounted a gigantic humanitarian relief effort, while NATO resolved to punish the defiant Serbs from the air. The Kosovo Air Campaign lasted seventy-eight days and launched 38,000 sorties, of which 60 percent were American. It featured the first general use of JDAMs, and these now cheaper precision-guided munitions accounted for 35 percent of the overall NATO strikes. An ineffectual asymmetry dominated the first half of the fighting, with NATO planes demolishing strategic targets in Serbia while artfully camouflaged Serbs terrorized Albanian Kosovars without much impediment. NATO had forgone a ground option other than the controversial Task Force Hawk, concerning which, more later. Eventually the KLA became effective enough to fill this empty space, forcing the Serbs to concentrate and facilitating air and missile strikes upon them with timely intelligence. NATO effectiveness shot up from sixty armored vehicles destroyed in the first sixty days of the air campaign to 350 destroyed in the two weeks after effective synergy with the KLA had been achieved. The Serbs capitulated and withdrew their forces from Kosovo, closely followed by NATO peacekeepers coming in behind them. The United States contingent numbered about seven thousand and assumed responsibility for one of five national sectors into which the province had been divided. Ironically, the lion's share of that effort went to protecting remnant Serbian civilians from vengeful returning Albanian refugees—who generally regarded the Americans as liberators. The situation was complicated by rampant smuggling and lawlessness—unless clan mores qualify as law—and by the ambitions of some Albanian militants concerning immediate independence and expansion into ethnic Albanian holdings in Macedonia. Unlike Bosnia-Herzegovina, there were no effective zones of separation, and the demographics were so lopsided the resident Serbs had little capacity for self-defense except in the far north.

Resettlement of the Albanian refugees progressed tolerably well, inversely mirrored by the migration of embittered Serbs from much of the province. Violence, horrific at first, did decline over time, in part because of NATO's surer grip and in part because of the gradual removal of ethnic Serbs as a target. NATO soldiers undoubtedly saved thousands of lives that otherwise would have been lost in factional fighting, while softening the de facto ethnic cantonization that did occur.[17]

Operations in Bosnia-Herzegovina and Kosovo were creditable peacemaking and peacekeeping efforts in their own right. They also offered unprecedented opportunities for constructive engagement with soldiers of the former Warsaw Pact. The thirty-two nations represented in IFOR, for example, included Albanians, Austrians, Czechs, Estonians, Finns, Hungarians, Latvians, Lithuanians, Poles, Romanians, Russians, Swedes, and Ukrainians. Whatever the fate of several million Bosnians and Kosovars, the paths followed by the hundreds of millions of citizens these soldiers represented would be far more consequential to the interests of the United States. The Cold War could not be considered successfully resolved unless democratic governance, civil rights, respect for private property, military deference to civilian authority, and the peaceful resolution of disputes were habitual throughout most or all of the former Warsaw Pact. As we have mentioned before, this was no sure thing. In the euphoria of 1989 a number of Eastern European nationalists assumed power politics alone would catapult them into alliances with a NATO eager to press its advantage and secure its frontiers. NATO took a different view, stipulating that aspirants would have to prove themselves worthy of membership. Within the military realm this included dismantling conscription-driven state-dominating military machines, deference to civilian authority, transparency in planning and expenditure, interoperability with NATO forces, and forswearing force to resolve border and other disputes. NATO did not want to alarm Russia by moving too quickly and certainly did not want to inherit such ancient border quarrels as Hungarian claims to Vojvodina or in the Carpathians. Partnership for Peace (PfP) offered a robust menu of training, education, and exchange opportunities that intermingled soldiers from NATO and NATO aspirant nations. The training became even more energetic and relevant as peacekeeping exercises prepared soldiers for actual peacekeeping operations. At higher echelons the PfP Planning and Review Process (PARP) grounded aspirants in transparent defense planning while helping them redesign forces compatible with those of NATO and the new security environment. Reluctantly at first, and then with more confidence and enthusiasm, senior delegations from NATO aspirants detailed force structure plans to NATO counterparts and to representatives from other aspirants. Preconditions for these talks included parliamentary oversight, public accountability, and the rejection of territorial claims beyond one's borders. Wags had it that PfP stood for "policy for postponement" or "partnership for procrastination," but sometimes ponderous processes of engagement did move in the right direction. Force structure came down, conscription relaxed, parliamentary leaders acquired a grip, and younger Western-oriented military leaders rose to the top. Forces actively training or operating with NATO were particularly likely to be professionalized, volunteer, and be upgraded with respect to equipment and organization. They constituted an elite that served as an example to others and provided cadres from which future leaders could be drawn. Overwhelmingly their interface with the West was through the American soldier and his NATO counterparts. The non-Soviet Warsaw Pact militaries had been heavily ground centric, and the practical demands of peacekeeping were ground centric as well. It was no exaggeration for the United States Army, Europe (USAREUR), commander to refer to his soldiers as "our ambassadors for democracy," a notion that fit in well with Reimer's "soldiers are our credentials." On 12 March 1999, Poland, Hungary, and the Czech Republic were admitted into NATO, an opportunity they had earned. They were different nations than they had been ten years before, served by even more different military establishments. A dozen other nations demonstrated similar interest and were somewhere along the path behind them. The Cold War only seemed to have been over in an instant. Turning apparent triumph into long-term success was an arduous process.[18]

Accelerating operational tempo continued to have a transformative effect on the Army as it further adapted to an expeditionary posture. Initiatives with respect to deployment infrastructure, pre-positioned equipment, sealift, and airlift that had begun during Sullivan's tenure continued into Reimer's. Notions of "home stationing" began to take root as well. Throughout the Cold War personnel managers had avoided "homesteading," the sending of career soldiers to recurrent assignments in the same place. They needed to spread overseas and hardship assignments equally across the force and further argued that variety in jobs and geographical locations provided a breadth of professional experience. This was unlike practice in the Navy, which concentrated job opportunities in a relatively few mega-bases and tended to leave families in one place while their sponsors deployed and moved through various career positions. The difference can be illustrated by a 1991 conversation between an Army wife and a Navy wife when their husbands were attending the Naval War College. The Army wife said she felt sorry for the Navy wife, since her husband had spent so much of his career deployed at sea. The Navy wife replied that she felt sorry for the Army wife because her Army husband had dragged her all over the world to set up house in a variety of isolated "dumps," whereas wherever her own Navy husband was ashore or afloat, at least she and her children were comfortably settled in San Diego. She might also have added that stability was ever more important to spouses as an increasing percentage worked outside the home. The Army was subtly shifting toward the Navy paradigm. Downsizing, base realignment and closures (BRAC), and withdrawal of forces from Europe closed well over a hundred bases and facilities. The precipitous drop in overseas tours (as opposed to overseas deployments) eliminated one of the principal arguments against homesteading. Expeditionary contingents flowed out of such growing mega-bases as Fort Bragg or Fort Hood, rightly recognized as where career opportunities increasingly resided. Conscious that the Army needed to recruit and retain families as well as soldiers, in 1996 Congress passed the Military Housing Privatization Initiative (MHPI), intended to eliminate inadequate housing. It featured an aggressive privatization program to attract private-sector capital to build, manage, and maintain on-post housing. Soldiers would be allowed to use their Basic Allowance for Housing to rent such housing. Significant advances also continued with respect to child care, vital if two spouses were working. By 2000 95 percent of all military child-care centers were accredited by the National Association for the Education of Young Children, as compared to 8 percent nationwide. This was in sharp contrast to the 70 percent that did not even meet fire and safety codes two decades before and in part underscored the advantages of consolidating facilities. About this time a survey established that whereas 62 percent of spouses were satisfied with their housing, this included 51 percent of those renting, about 55 percent of those in government housing, and a whopping 92 percent of those who had bought their own homes off post—most of whom had used their housing allowances to make payments. Clearly this was yet another argument for sufficient stability to plant roots in local communities. TRICARE, a program of medical coverage subsidizing access to civilian health-care facilities enacted in 1994 and implemented by 1997, further supported the notion of living off post. Home stationing was not yet official policy, but Army families were informally positioning themselves for stability amid recurrent deployments.[19]

The Army Staff and staffs of subordinate headquarters attempted to track and control deployment tempo (DEPTEMPO) in order to spread the load across the force, sustain morale, and encourage retention. In 1997 General Reimer established a DEPTEMPO goal of not more than 120 days per unit per year, with the days at issue being those wherein a soldier did not sleep at his home station in his "own bunk." In this he was staunchly supported by Secretary of the Army Togo D. West Jr., whose mantra was "doing right by soldiers" throughout his tenure. West went on to serve as the Secretary of Veterans Affairs. DEPTEMPO included local training, training off the installation, joint exercises, and operational deployments. A factor driving up DEPTEMPO was specialized training in anticipation of a specific operation or deployment, followed by more general "warfighting" training on a unit's return to regain combat skills that might have atrophied. Units deploying to Bosnia, for example, spent weeks on and off post training extensively with respect to patrolling, crowd control, manning checkpoints, mine detection and clearance, civil military operations, and related subjects. This time was generally well spent; many soldiers commented on the extent to which the training paralleled their actual Balkan experiences. Upon their return, however, they would inevitably be less prepared for conventional wartime missions. This precipitated a spate of gunnery and maneuver training to refurbish eroded skills. Reimer understood these mechanics and that it would be impossible to stay beneath his goal in all cases, but he did stipulate that DEPTEMPO transcending 180 days would require his personal approval, unit by unit. Of 1,462 reporting units, 126 (8.6 percent) exceeded the 120-day limit and 54 (3.7 percent) exceeded the 180-day limit. The DEPTEMPO tracking system proved imperfect, but it did mark a dramatic advance in the Army's capability to manage the personal consequences of escalating contingencies. Attention to these statistics did expose an aspect of DEPTEMPO that had previously gone under-noticed, the disproportionate share borne by officers and senior NCOs. The issue was illustrated by a staff snit between Supreme Headquarters Allied Powers Europe (SHAPE) and USAREUR. Evoking Reimer's guidance, USAREUR proposed to reduce its annual commitment to NATO exercises from 57,744 man-days to 24,575, its commitment to bilateral exercises from 15,544 to 12,399, and its commitment to Partnership for Peace from 10,633 to 10,068. For the same period, it proposed to leave its internal Army programs of exercises and training unchanged at 1,031,028 man-days, and anticipated no change in its mission to commit approximately 978,925 man-days to operational deployments. SHAPE protested that the National Military Strategy was shape (i.e., engage allies and potential allies), prepare (e.g., train), and respond (i.e., deploy on actual operations). USAREUR's proposal would commit a mere 2.2 percent of its effort to shaping, whereas 50.5 percent would go to preparing and 47 percent to responding. USAREUR responded that the man-days committed to operational deployments were beyond its control, the man-days committed to Army exercises and training were overwhelmingly those of soldiers of junior rank, and the man-days committed to NATO, bilaterals, and Partnership for Peace disproportionately required officers and senior NCOs by a wide margin. Since these same officers and NCOs had to lead their units in training and, when deployed, some relief was necessary to keep the DEPTEMPO of these particular individuals within acceptable limits. A negotiated solution resolved the immediate priorities of the two headquarters, but the exchange underscored a phenomenon of the new era. Officers still serving could remember the damage done when recurrent tours to Vietnam coupled with training demands elsewhere and inadequate family support discouraged the reenlistment of mid-term NCOs and the retention of junior officers. This caused units to be under-led at the most basic level. No one wanted to repeat that experience.[20]

Fortuitously, the continuing transformation of the reserve component enabled it to offset an increasing fraction of the active component's commitments, to include those that were leadership-intensive. We have already mentioned the extent to which the reserve component carried the weight with respect to deployments in Latin America, supported such regional initiatives as the war on drugs, and was heavily represented in deployments from DESERT SHIELD on. With statistics such as 97 percent of the Total Army's civil affairs and 86 percent of its psychological operations capabilities being Army Reserve, or 70 percent of its field artillery being National Guard, such a heavy representation was inevitable. Overall 52 percent of the Army was in the reserve component during this period, a statistic that accorded with funding available. With respect to leadership-intensive exercises such as Partnership for Peace or NATO bilaterals, one reason they were leadership-intensive is that they were often command post exercises (CPXs) wherein headquarters participated full up but maneuver units were simulated by computer. They might also be exchange visits involving key personnel for limited periods. Such exercises were of limited duration and could be worked into the annual rhythm of the reserve component. Indeed, an initiative pairing American states with nations newly independent of the Warsaw Pact seemed ideal for the low-key junior leader engagement Partnership for Peace envisioned. Some pairings evoked historical patterns of immigration, others reflected geographical similarities, some were matters of choice, and a few were near comical marriages of opposites—but all took pressure off of the active component while allowing America's citizen-soldiers to represent democracy abroad. Alabama paired with Romania, Arizona with Kazakhstan, California with the Ukraine, Colorado with Slovenia, Georgia with Georgia, Illinois with Poland, Indiana with Slovakia, Louisiana with Uzbekistan, Maryland with Estonia, Michigan with Latvia, Minnesota with Croatia, Montana with Kyrgyzstan, Nevada with Turkmenistan, North Carolina with Moldova, Ohio with Hungary, Pennsylvania with Lithuania, South Carolina with Albania, Tennessee with Bulgaria, Texas with the Czech Republic, Utah with Belarus, and Vermont with Macedonia. Adding together participation in such exercises, training and operational deployments led to impressive totals. In 1987 the National Guard logged 143,000 man-days of federal service, whereas in 1997 it logged in 3.6 million. This is not to mention its own internal training or support to state governors. The Army Reserve offset 5.8 million active-component man-days in 1996 alone. As a frame of reference, the previously discussed row between SHAPE and USAREUR had been over an exercise and deployment regime that totaled about two million man-days. Offsetting active-component man-days drew the reserve component ever more closely into the daily workings of the Army. Garrison Support Units (GSUs), for example, backfilled deploying active-component units by providing the installations they had departed from such support as transportation, supply, or medical services. An associate transportation company (ATC) was a "truckless truck company" whose soldiers fell in on the vehicles left behind when active-duty counterparts deployed to fall in on pre-positioned equipment overseas. The option existed to deploy this company as well, perhaps accompanied by newly acquired equipment, at some later point. In 1995 the National Guard activated the Operational Support Airlift Command (OSACOM), which took responsibility for all Army airlift support missions within the continental United States, whether active or reserve. Further examples abound. Downsizing and multiplying deployments forced the Army into greater reliance on the reserve component, both as troops and units deploying for full tours, and through imaginative uses of their skills and services for periods that better fit customary annual cycles. The reserve component in turn sharpened its ability to provide such support and evolved ever more effective integration with the active component.[21]

The continuing escalation of contingencies overseas drew the Army into diverse geographical and operational environments. It contained Iraq, engaged allies and potential allies, kept the peace, consolidated the aftermath of the Cold War, and served the country in other ways. The Army continued its transformation toward a more expeditionary posture. Units, installations, and families further adapted to rhythms of deployment and developed coping mechanisms that would see them through. The Army experimented with various means of controlling its deployment tempo in order to sustain morale and reenlistment and collaterally identified the internal segments of its population most roughly used. The National Guard and Army Reserve came forward to relieve pressure, employing techniques both traditional and innovative. In the process the active component and reserve component became more integrated and interdependent, one seldom deploying in the absence of the other. These adaptive processes were valuable at the time and would prove even more critical in days that were to come.

The Quadrennial Defense Review . . . and Related Subjects

Although the Goldwater-Nichols Act was signed into law in 1986, it took ten years to evolve processes to synchronize service and defense efforts in the pursuit of a post–Cold War force structure. As we have seen, the first initiative anticipating post–Cold War downsizing, Project ANTAEUS, was a secretive Army effort to stay conceptually ahead of budget cuts. General Colin L. Powell, Chairman of the Joint Chiefs of Staff, followed shortly with his own "Base Force" study. Base Force deliberations were largely confined to the Joint Staff, relied upon somewhat simplistic analysis, and came to recommend proportional budget cuts without much in the way of restructuring, redesign, or fiscal reapportionment. The results went in the direction ANTAEUS had anticipated but at an accelerated pace. The Army paralleled the Base Force with QUICKSILVER (applying to deployable units) and VANGUARD (applying to the institutional Army), efforts to keep in front of cuts mandated by the Joint Staff and Congress with an orderly program of downsizing. About this time the Office of the Secretary of Defense (OSD) conducted studies of its own, including a detailed Defense Management Review (DMR). The DMR focused on overlaps and inefficiencies among major headquarters and agencies and resulted in little that directly applied to the deployable Army. All of these initiatives were effectively suspended by DESERT SHIELD and DESERT STORM and had not regained much traction before the political campaigning season that led to a change of administrations. Incoming President William J. Clinton's new Secretary of Defense, Les Aspin, undertook a "Bottom-Up Review" (BUR). This creditably integrated Secretariat, Joint Staff, and service representatives into standing committees addressing major topic areas. It proposed a two major regional contingency (MRC) grand strategy—Iraq and Korea, for example—as its premise. That strategy provoked debate with respect to credibility as deliberations progressed. More damaging, analytic underpinnings were spotty, with each service pressing its own metrics without appropriate referees or agreed joint doctrine. Results seemed to reflect the leverage of various defense programs in Congress more so than military thinking per se. This seemed understandable, given the large overlap between the BUR studies and those done by congressional staffers to support Aspin in his previous role as chairman of the House Armed Services Committee. Finally, results were in part compromised when Secretary Aspin assumed responsibility for failing to send armor when needed to Somalia and departed ingloriously. Shortly thereafter a congressionally mandated Commission on Roles and Missions (CORM) conducted a review of efficiencies, overlaps, and effectiveness within the defense establishment and made a number of recommendations. The services and Joint Staff were only marginally involved and noted the commission's recommendations more so than embraced them. Decisions made by OSD and the Joint Staff during this period provided a framework within which the Army downsized, reduced its forward presence, and shifted to an expeditionary posture. These did not originate from a systematic defense establishment or Department of Defense decision-making process, however.[22]

Congress had taken note of these various efforts but was dissatisfied with post–Cold War defense transformation to that point. It directed a "comprehensive examination of the defense strategy, force structure, force modernization plans, infrastructure, budget plan and other elements of the defense programs and policies . . ." to be completed in 1997.[23] The initiative was envisioned as the first in a series of such reexaminations timed to each national change of administration and thus came to be called the Quadrennial Defense Review (QDR). This legislation included a National Defense Panel of distinguished outside experts to review and comment on the Pentagon's product. Profiting from lessons learned in previous efforts, the Office of the Secretary of Defense attempted to construct an integrated analytic structure. A Senior Steering Group (SSG), cochaired by the Deputy Secretary of Defense and Vice Chairman of the Joint Chiefs of Staff, with membership including the service Vice Chiefs of Staff, directed the effort. The Vice Chief of Staff of the Army at the time was General Ronald H. Griffith. In addition to this QDR responsibility and the day-to-day running of the Army, he also supervised a redesign of the institutional (TDA) Army—concerning which, more later. Six QDR functional panels—strategy, force structure, modernization, readiness, infrastructure, and human resources—were cochaired by relevant deputy under secretaries or assistant secretaries from OSD and one- or two-star officers from the Joint Staff and included one- or two-star representatives from the services as well. At lower levels subpanels, ultimately numbering over fifty, were similarly balanced among the Secretariat, Joint Staff, and services. An Integration Panel, upon which the Army was represented by its newly created Assistant Vice Chief of Staff, coordinated results and distilled them into findings "briefable" to the SSG and other parties. The Clinton administration's newly minted *National Security Strategy of Engagement and Enlargement,* and the National Military Strategy ("shape, prepare, respond") derived from it, drove deliberations. Published joint doctrine existed in the newly published Joint Publication 3.0, *Joint Vision 2010,* and several dozen subordinate manuals. This happy confluence of articulated strategy and published doctrine offered an overarching conceptual framework that had not previously existed. The Quadrennial Defense Review would avoid the phenomenon of each service hiring its own defense contractors and developing its own metrics by stipulating methods and models to be used and by directing multiservice analytic drills of its own. Of these, the most consequential for the Army would be the DYNAMIC COMMITMENT exercise series and the Deep Attack Weapons Mix Study (DAWMS), concerning both of which, more later.[24]

The Army Staff had reason for both confidence and anxiety going into the Quadrennial Defense Review. On the plus side, the Army had worked extensively with simulations-based analyses during the modern Louisiana Maneuvers and before. It had thus acquired depth and polish with respect to the genre of analyses and models OSD envisioned using; indeed, it had pioneered in the development of several of them. An influential contemporary congressman, Newt Gingrich, delighted in describing congressional stereotypes of service overtures for funding. The Air Force solicitor would present himself as a "fighter jock": affable, engaging, and, incidentally, God's gift to women. He would share a few platitudes about the clean efficiency of airpower but in the end deserved the money because he was so eminently likeable. The Navy request would be carried in by a leathery "old salt," imbued with the aura of years at sea. There would be a few comments on the timelessness of sea power, but in the end you just had to trust him because he had seen and done so much that his understanding was beyond anything you (the congressman) could ever hope to comprehend. The Army representative would deploy with a phalanx of book carriers, chart tenders, and technical experts of all types. He had a prepared briefing with layers of detail and dozens of backup slides and was determined to take you (the congressman) as far through them as your bladder would allow. Insofar as these stereotypes were valid, they indicated an Army prepared for the excruciating analyses the Quadrennial Defense Review legislation described. Of concern to the Army, a difficult balance had to be struck with respect to technology, and a lot was at stake. The Army had committed to digital communications, advanced sensors, precision-guided munitions, networked computers, and other harbingers of the Information Age, but it could suffer if too much came to be expected of technology. If infallible sensors could invariably detect all relevant targets, digital command and control could perfectly match them up with appropriate "shooters," and precision-guided munitions could flawlessly dispatch them on a one-for-one basis, why not let the Air Force do the job? A sizable defense lobby argued that ground forces were overbuilt for the new era dawning, since their battlefield role was merely going to be to detect targets for omnipresent aircraft and provide local security for air bases. Manpower was expensive. Dramatic cuts in Army manpower would free up funds for modernization, particularly the further modernization of the already highly technical Air Force and Navy. The Army manpower that remained could shed its heaviest equipment and reorganize itself, in all or in part, into standing constabularies to clean up battlefields after wars had been won or to assist in local security. The Army Staff believed such sentiments had already been responsible for disproportional losses the Army suffered in the aftermath of the Base Force Study and the Bottom Up Review. Two further divisions now seemed to be on the chopping block; the Army would be hard put to protect ten in its active structure. To succeed in the Quadrennial Defense Review, the Army would have to protect modernization efforts it already had under way while also diminishing arguments that technological advance alone would soon render maneuver warfare, "boots on the ground" or the "fog of war," obsolete.[25]

Dynamic Commitment was a tiered series of seminars internal to the Quadrennial Defense Review that involved representatives from OSD, the Joint Staff, the services, and the major overseas commands. Ultimately participants worked their way through forty-six vignettes—scenarios—ranging from humanitarian relief through major regional wars. Historical precedents over the last dozen years were taken into account and served as models for over half the vignettes. This was good news for the Army, since it could easily establish that more than 60 percent of the force structure required over the broad mix of contingencies during that period had been Army. When one added in the Marines, the requirement for ground forces came to be over 80 percent of the totals required. The overseas commands became heavily involved in the deliberations, drawing on recent experience and their own contingency plans to frame requirements. Readiness issues, particularly those resulting from other contingencies (i.e., vignettes) played as going on or being recovered from, were taken into account. This discussion was considerably enriched by two collateral studies. The Baseline Engagement Force Study forecast the fraction of the force structure that would be routinely committed at any given time and thus not immediately available. The Multiple Lesser Regional Contingency/Small-Scale Contingency Assessment distilled twenty years of actual experience into projections of forces likely to be deployed to such contingencies in the future. Predictably, the services jockeyed to get their favorite vignettes into play, with the Navy favoring maritime security and interdiction and the Air Force proposing a mosaic of no-fly zones to enforce. The Army and Marines competed to be the boots first put on the ground, and too often vignettes ended up with a mix of Army and Marines that made more sense with respect to service politics than with respect to the working mechanics of combat service support. Readiness became a matter of debate, with the Army's fixed tiering based on anticipated deployment dates contrasting with the cyclical readiness favored by the Marines and Navy. Depending on the sequencing of the vignettes, readiness status could determine which service was most readily able to field a contingent. These interservice perturbations within DYNAMIC COMMITMENT were minor when compared with its overall result, a heightened awareness of the probable demands and complexities of prospective deployments extending through 2004. This in turn established different points of departure for separate studies addressing major theater contingencies. The Bottom Up Review had proposed two major regional conflicts, loosely Iraq and Korea, and then ground through simulations to identify the forces necessary to fight them. The Quadrennial Defense Review's Two Major Theater Warfight Analysis ran multiple excursions of these scenarios varying timing, sequence, and the possible involvement of weapons of mass destruction. More important, it also took into account the insight from DYNAMIC COMMITMENT and related studies that not all forces would start combat ready and at the home station. If seven divisions was an approved solution for bringing a major regional contingency to a successful conclusion, appreciably more than seven divisions would have to be in the force structure to account for all of the other commitments under way. At the top end of the requirements envisioned by the Quadrennial Defense Review, a Peer Competitor Analysis proposed war with an equivalent adversary in fifteen years' time. This drill investigated modernization more so than force structure, but it did take force structure into account. On balance, the interplay among these various Quadrennial Defense Review analyses favored the Army, underscoring a sustained and undiminishing demand for ground combat troops.[26]

DYNAMIC COMMITMENT and the more specific studies clustered around it made the case that the quantitative Army force structure was, if anything, too small. Another study initiated before the Quadrennial Defense Review that rolled into it, the DAWMS, made a case favoring certain Army qualitative objectives as well. DAWMS proposed a mix of enemy targets worthy of engagement beyond direct-fire range and then simulated various weapons systems against each other to determine their cost-effectiveness in dealing with the targets. Modeling relied on the somewhat venerable but familiar simulation-driven Tactical Warfare Model (TACWAR) system, in addition to a new Weapon Optimization and Resource Requirements Model (WORRM) developed for the study by the Institute for Defense Analyses (IDA). DAWMS sought technology and force structure that could carry the fight deep into enemy territory, allowing one to shape the battlefield and perhaps even inflict defeat while minimizing the costly attrition of front-line combat. Deep battle had traditionally been a purview dominated by the Air Force, and some Air Force advocates believed DAWMS would make a case for redirecting funding the Army spent on manpower into Air Force procurement and modernization. Such a redirection would prove particularly welcome to air enthusiasts, given escalating costs predicted for the F–22 and the Joint Strike Fighter. DAWMS deliberations yielded a different result. Army attack helicopters launching Hellfire missiles showed well in DAWMS, as did the surface-to-surface Army Tactical Missile System (ATACMS). Even venerable tube artillery firing "dumb" munitions continued to show promise as a cheap way to suppress imprecisely located enemy air defenses. Army systems were generally cheaper, deployed farther forward, more tactically flexible, and more weather-proof. Air Force systems had greater range and destructiveness. In one "excursion" after another, balanced mixes of Army and Air Force systems performed more capably than those dominated by a single genre of weapons systems. If DAWMS had led to a redistribution of funding among the services, it would have led to a greater investment in Hellfire and ATACMS II. After eighteen months of joint work, the Army Staff's greatest concern with respect to DAWMS was that the so-called "fixed-wing advocates" might discover a way to discount, discredit, or "walk away" from its results.[27]

In the end, the Quadrennial Defense Review came to modest recommendations. Results proposed that the Army would keep its ten divisions and merely shave 15,000 from its active-component and 45,000 from its reserve-component force structures. The Air Force would lose 27,000 from its active component and cut F–22 fighter purchases from 438 to 339 for the period projected. The Navy would keep twelve aircraft carrier groups but reduce its attack submarines from 73 to 50 and cut its purchase of new F/A–18 fighter bombers from 1,000 to 548. The Marines would remain unaffected with respect to the boots they could put on the ground but would see purchases of the controversial and as yet unproven V–22 Osprey aircraft reduced from 425 to 360. Excess infrastructure from all services would be divested, should Congress permit. All factors considered, the platoons of Army analysts reflected in Gingrich's stereotype had done their work well. In one working group after another they made a persuasive case for ground combat power, and they deflected cuts

A Multiple Launch Rocket System (MLRS), capable of hitting targets at three hundred kilometers if firing the ATACMS missile

F–16 jet fighters

many thought would be far worse. Monies to be saved would come from fixed-wing aircraft and submarines—genres wherein the United States was already supreme—more so than from soldiers and marines. The National Defense Panel, distinguished outside experts empowered to review and enlarge upon the Quadrennial Defense Review, were generally supportive of its results. They did suggest that the 1998–2003 focus of the analysis had not been deep enough and that the two major regional contingency "strategy" would not long survive as a paradigm defining future defense needs. Debate did not end with Secretary of Defense William S. Cohen's "final" report to Congress, however. The Quadrennial Defense Review results were greeted with derisive rants, both from those advocating more sweeping and dramatic changes and from those taking issue with particular cuts and shortcomings. The particularists struck first. Congressional champions of attack submarines and various aircraft heard out their similarly interested constituents and jawboned their colleagues. Well-connected National Guardsmen reiterated that they had state as well as federal responsibilities, provoked hard negotiations with the Army Staff at an intra-Army off-site, and hunted down their senators and representatives state-by-state. Most of the cuts envisioned for these several parties soon evaporated from congressional consideration. The recommendations for further infrastructure cuts, on the other hand, fell on deaf ears. Within a few months' time the somewhat baffled Joint Chiefs found themselves publicly scolded by Congress for not having asked for enough money in the first place and for having conducted the Quadrennial Defense Review in the context of budget caps Congress no longer supported—now that they saw where they would lead. Each Chief was required to submit a wish list for further funding and by and large focused on readiness. Congress responded with plus-ups of its own and by and large focused on construction and procurement. The economy was booming, and an additional $112 billion for defense during FY2000 through FY2005 was agreed upon—and did not seem to either Congress or the administration as too much to pay. Critics lamented that the "pork machine" had undercut the Quadrennial Defense Review. Army participants had a more nuanced view. To this point the politically expedient approach to reduce defense spending had been to slash Army force structure, with lesser cuts for the programs of other services. During the Quadrennial Defense Review agreed processes of analysis reversed this trend, determined that the downsizing of ground forces had gone far enough, and recommended savings elsewhere. The fact that politics ultimately watered down the results as they played out in budgets did not diminish this underlying conceptual victory.[28]

Having built a case during the Quadrennial Defense Review that underscored the limits of technology, the Army exposed itself to critics who believed a "revolution in military affairs" was overdue, that the Quadrennial Defense Review results were unimaginative, and that the Defense Department once again demonstrated a sauropodian inability to reform itself. General Reimer and the Army Staff had anticipated such feedback. Even as the Quadrennial Defense Review was getting under way, Reimer took advantage of the annual meeting of the Association of the United States Army (AUSA) to promote the Army's approach to this issue. Describing recent or ongoing operations in

Haiti, Bosnia, Liberia, Kuwait, Iraq, Ecuador, Peru, and elsewhere, he established that there would be no "time-outs" from immediate responsibilities. He also spoke to the limits of technology, remarking that it "takes soldiers . . . to separate warring parties, to reassure fearful civilians, to restore public order, to keep criminals from taking advantage of the vacuum in civil order, to deliver humanitarian assistance, to prevent and win the nation's wars"—all of which required "boots on the ground." He discussed Army XXI, the emerging result of methodical spiral development embedding Information Age technologies into contemporary platforms and organizations. Existing platforms and organizations would experience a rapid expansion in their capabilities without visibly changing all that much. Finally, he introduced the "Army After Next," the radically different Army as it would be in 2025. Army XXI would be an intermediate step in the direction of the Army After Next. Army XXI would field technologies that proved reliable in the near term. The Army After Next would envision a more distant future, nominate technologies that did not yet exist for experimental development, and deliver a redesigned force wherein transformation was comprehensive rather than via appliqué. The approach to the Army After Next would begin with brainstorming seminars not unlike those of the modern Louisiana Maneuvers, but this process would be disciplined by the fact that Army XXI—tangible, programmed, and dependent on proven technology—would be achieved first. This framed the Army's position for the Quadrennial Defense Review, which focused on the period through 2003. Within this time horizon the Army would emphasize the tested, the proven, and the technologically reliable. Soldiers' lives were immediately at stake; there would be no gambling. Army planners would unleash their more imaginative energies when queuing up prospective technologies for the Army After Next. Here they would cast their nets broadly. Indeed, as a prelude to a meeting of the Army's most senior leaders, Reimer required a review of the controversial book *Breaking the Phalanx* by Colonel Doug Macgregor, one of the Army's more creative thinkers and severest critics. Concerning this, more later. Whatever ideas emerged from this ferment, one presumes they would ultimately be tested and developed with the same rigor as the systems going into Army XXI. The pace of development and fielding would be heavily dependent on budgets, as was the case with Army XXI. The vision was thoughtful, deep, methodical, and evolutionary. The cumulative result might be a revolution in military affairs, but it would take a generation to mature. In support of this systematic approach, Army historians described the generation that separated the Battle of Cambrai from truly mechanized warfare as General George S. Patton practiced it, and similarly pointed out the evolutionary aspects of other so-called revolutions in military affairs. Conversely, they also described the hazards of such hasty redesigns as the Pentomic Division, wherein ambitions exceeded technological capabilities.[29]

The Army soon came under pressure to abandon this calculated approach. Task Force Hawk, the introduction of a ground component into the Kosovo war, encountered enough of Murphy's Law to create operational hiccups and public relations disaster. On 4 April 1999, a Pentagon spokesperson announced that an AH–64A Apache attack helicopter task force would be on the ground in the Balkans within eight days. The air war was not going well at the time, the formidable Apache had gotten rave reviews in the Gulf War for its effectiveness against ground targets, and the press anticipated it bringing an end to the asymmetry between high-flying planes and low-lying concealed targets. The eight-day goal captured media attention, but it never was particularly a mark on the wall for the Army. Indeed, the operations order defining the mission was actually issued on 22 April. Prior to that time the Macedonians balked at plans admitting such a force onto the airfield at Skopje, so basing shifted to the significantly less capable airfield at Tirana-Rinas, Albania. Albania was a much less secure environment than Macedonia would have been, so the manning of the overall task force ballooned from less than 2,000 to more than 5,000 to accommodate additional security and increased expectations for artillery—to include incorporating twenty-seven long-range rocket launchers. Tirana-Rinas airfield was already overwhelmed with aircraft and agencies supporting humanitarian relief for refugees flooding into Albania, and unremitting spring rains turned the ground surrounding it into a morass. Task Force Hawk ultimately required 475 C–17 sorties to deploy and sustain itself, but weather conditions and the priority accorded humanitarian relief limited it to but a handful of sorties a day into Tirana-Rinas for appreciable periods. The mud was so bad and apron space so limited that engineers had to construct several dozen pads for the Apaches lest they sink upon landing. The AH–64As self-deployed from Germany but were delayed because the Austrians denied them overflight and the Italians took seven days to approve uploaded munitions. Commanders in the field and commanders in major headquarters worked through these perturbations in daily video-conferences, without becoming unduly exercised by them. Not so the press, who kept the originally announced eight days in mind. As it was, Task Force Hawk was mission-capable with fifty-one aircraft on 26 April, eighteen days after it kicked off and four days after it received an actual operations order. It did not attack the Serbs, however. Reimer visited the task force and assessed the battlefield and shared his operational concerns with General Wesley K. Clark, the Supreme Allied Commander. Routes into Kosovo were constrained by mountainous terrain, and the Serbs had considerably thickened their air defenses in this area in anticipation of an attack. Heavy artillery suppressive fires would be necessary to get the aviators through. Such fires would risk substantial and publicly visible collateral damage; flying without them would risk unacceptable casualties. Sentiment was again veering away from direct NATO ground force involvement. Better weather was improving fixed-wing bombing results, cooperation with the KLA was generating improved target information, and target-detection assets deployed with Task Force Hawk itself were generating targets more quickly than the airmen could engage them. The Serbs were cracking, and ground combat, with all its attendant risks of casualties, did not prove necessary.[30]

The non-use of the Apaches in Kosovo emboldened the Army's critics. In their minds the Army had proven itself too slow, too cautious, and too evolutionary. They advanced this case by misunderstanding or misrepresenting much that had gone on in Albania, particularly the priorities and timelines the operators themselves had actually envisioned. Negative impressions fed into a larger critique characterizing the Quadrennial Defense Review results as too modest in scope, and all that had gone into Force XXI as too deliberate. It seemed the critics did not want the Army After Next after next, or even next; they wanted it now. The "weight" of the Army was particularly subject to vilification. The term *weight* is slippery when overall assessments of force structure and logistical means come into play, but recurrent metaphors evoked at the time were the Army's continuing reliance on the seventy-ton Abrams tank and its aspirations for a nearly as hefty Crusader advanced self-propelled artillery system. To this point, significant advances with respect to strategic mobility had been made by virtue of Pre-positioning of Materiel Configured to Unit Sets (POMCUS) and improved sealift and airlift, without much altering of the "look" of the forces that would fight on the ground—although their capabilities had certainly improved. Indeed, the innovative Armored Gun System, intended to replace the antiquated M551 Sheridan as a lightweight, strategically mobile fighting platform, had recently fallen victim to budget cuts. The Army's near-term approach to strategic mobility had been to move heavy forces faster and render light forces more capable with the Javelin antitank missile and other improved weapons. It would make the heavy force's platforms lighter at some future time, probably with the Army After Next. General Reimer had experimented with a "Strike Force" based on the 2d Armored Cavalry Regiment, intended to capitalize on advanced information technologies and to more flexibly integrate diverse assets from the heavy, light, and sustainment forces. He envisioned the regimental headquarters as a "receptacle" into which one would "plug in" organizational mosaics of capabilities needed. This experimental design did not particularly address the avoirdupois of vehicles on the ground, but rather the mix and match of units depending on them. Pressure would soon mount on the Army to speedily field lighter vehicles as a third way to strategic mobility. It remained unclear how such lighter vehicles would have played out in the mud of Tirana-Rinas airfield, where a donkey cart on pneumatic tires would have sunk into the morass, much less a multi-ton vehicle of any size.[31]

The Revolution in Military Contracting

Contractors have had a long and colorful history in the United States Army. They were critical participants in military affairs even before the American Revolution and have remained so through today. During the Civil War contractors dominated the top and the bottom of the logistical spectrum, providing tens of thousands of laborers, stevedores, and teamsters and also providing skilled professionals and technicians who kept trains running, manned telegraph services, and provided medical support. This was in addition to their military-industrial dominance with respect to manufacturing, procurement, and supply. The battlefield visibility of contractors faded with the massive draftee armies of World Wars I and II and the early Cold War. General mobilization permitted the Army to draft tens of thousands of laborers, stevedores, teamsters, skilled professionals, and technicians; organize them into combat service support units under military discipline; and deploy them overseas as circumstances required. Extensive reliance on what we now call "host-nation support" also made contracting less visible within the Army, although much of this support was in fact provided by contractors serving the host nation. Whether direct or indirect, contracting continued to imply risks with respect to reliability and quality control. During both world wars pilferage and damage attributed to contracted personnel was problematic in port operations and along lines of transportation in every theater. In the World War II Persian Gulf Command, for example, native truck drivers managed to drive the vehicular accident rate up an astonishing 900 percent—a feat they later approximated during DESERT SHIELD/DESERT STORM. Nevertheless, sustaining operations without contracting for local support was never realistic. During the Korean War, for example, the 393,000 soldiers of the Far East Command were supported by 100,000 Koreans, 42,000 Japanese, and 14,000 American civilians—the latter by and large Department of the Army civilians. Even with such robust reliance as a background, during the 1990s military contracting became dramatically more visible, pervasive, and consequential within the Department of Defense and the United States Army. This resulted from government policy, downsizing, the flexibility demanded by diverse operations on short notice, increasingly complex weapons systems and equipment, and worldwide expansion with respect to the sophistication, availability, and market savvy of military contractors.[32]

United States government policy has long espoused that the government should not compete with its citizens in venues best controlled by market forces. Commitment to a competitive free enterprise system is manifest in the Constitution and was formally reinforced by Bureau of the Budget bulletins beginning in 1955. Office of Management and Budget Circular A–76 was promulgated in 1967 and has been repeatedly updated and reissued since. It holds that, excepting discrete "inherently governmental" functions, those goods and services that can be most economically provided by commercial sources should be. The interest of business leaders, lobbyists, and congressmen in such provisions is obvious. Through the long years of the Cold War most Department of Defense activities escaped scrutiny with respect to Circular A–76, exceptions being military-industrial activities with respect to manufacturing, procurement, and supply and Corps of Engineers projects within the United States. Indeed, "activities performed by military personnel who are subject to deployment in a combat, combat support, and combat service support role" were specifically identified by A–76 as inherently governmental. The Department of Defense could be as deferential to A–76 as it chose to be. As the Cold War evaporated, this insulation waned. The pursuit of the "peace dividend" manifested itself as a "bogey drill" to slash set percentages off of military budgets. Comparing projected with actual Defense budgets from 1990 through 1999, Congress cut back $750 billion. Desperate service chieftains pursued efficiencies in management as an alternative to losing "muscle." General Reimer, for example, negotiated a drop in active-component end strength to 480,000 rather than 475,000 by promising fiscal efficiencies to pay for the 5,000 he saved. In such efforts service chiefs were abetted by administration advocates for "reengineering government" and by advisory bodies with the ears of Congress. The National Defense Panel, for example, flagged up insufficient and insufficiently imaginative use of contracting in its critique of the Quadrennial Defense Review. Expert opinion held that an organization under fiscal pressure should focus on its "core functions," and divest "non-core" functions to other agencies or to contractors. The Office of the Secretary of Defense took up the refrain. In 1998 Defense Reform Initiative Directive 20 (DRID 20) made virtually every element of the Defense establishment subject to study with respect to the relative advantages of contracting. In its pursuit of efficiencies and budget reductions, the Department of Defense clearly endorsed much increased contracting as a feasible way ahead.[33]

Downsizing greatly reinforced incentives to rely upon contracting. Most visibly, combat service support units and personnel dropped in number. Within the active component these dropped even more sharply than in the reserve component, given a desire to maximize the number of "trigger pullers" within organizations most ready to deploy. The drop in Department of the Army civilian manpower was even more dramatic than the drop in uniformed manpower. Their numbers went from 487,852 in 1989 to 224,900 in 1999. This civilian workforce dominated base operations, depot operations, and most aspects of communications and logistics within the United States. Their workload did not decrease at the same pace as their numbers. Congress was loath to approve stateside base closures, and the Army was called upon to maintain infrastructure the Department of Defense might otherwise have divested itself of. Base and depot operations cannot necessarily be scaled back in the same proportions as the personnel or items of equipment they support. A certain overhead of skills and capabilities is necessary to service a population of M1A1 tanks, for example, regardless of their number. The inverse of achieving economies of scale as numbers go up is experiencing ineconomies of scale as numbers go down. Similarly, the sustainment of communications and logistics within the United States also implied a numerical floor with respect to manpower regardless of the overall population being served. To the advocates of DRID 20 and its predecessors, stateside functions that had already been civilianized seemed particularly amenable to contracting. Definitions of "inherently governmental" functions migrated up the supervisory chain. In 1989 the average Department of the Army civilian was forty-three years old with thirteen years of government service. In 1999 he or she was forty-seven years old with over seventeen years of government service. Increasingly policy and management decisions were made by Department of the Army civilians and executed by contractors. Where the work was repetitive and steady, habitual relationships developed. Contractors became a shadow workforce, backfilling government employees they had replaced and often demonstrating considerable job stability. Indeed, an iconic figure of the time was the civilian, soldier, or noncommissioned officer who terminated his government employment one day and came back to the same position as a contractor the next. In several functional areas contractors rose to elevated positions in the supervisory chain. In 1996 Congress passed the Military Housing Privatization Initiatives Act, encouraging the services to draw upon private-sector expertise and capital to refurbish their housing. Agencies like DynCorps were contracted to take over the maintenance and management of post housing from Department of the Army civilian housing offices that had formerly done the job. In 1999 a pilot program at Fort Carson, Colorado, went even further. Contractors built or refurbished more than 2,600 housing units, managed and maintained them, and collected rent directly from their military tenants. These tenants in turn received a housing allowance equivalent to what they would have been paid had they lived off post. In an earlier era uniformed community and agency leaders, routinely rotating in and out of jobs, had relied on Department of the Army civilians to provide stability, continuity, and depth of knowledge. Now repeat contractors would share this load.[34]

Insofar as operations overseas were concerned, both raw numbers and a need for flexibility provided incentives to contract. Cuts in force structure drove even larger proportions of the Army's combat service support structure into the reserve component, and even in the reserve component these assets would have been too thin for many contingencies. Capabilities as diverse as heavy equipment transport, water supply, petroleum transport, linguists, and regionally savvy civil affairs units—along with much else—were less available than operational circumstances were likely to require. Even if such assets could have been mobilized and brought to a deployable status in a timely manner, they would tie up precious airlift and sealift at awkward times. Cold War Germany and Korea were mature theaters with ample logistical capabilities already deployed forward. Post–Cold War contingencies seemed likely to send troops where combat service support did not yet exist. In 1992 the Army initiated the Logistics Civil Augmentation Program (LOGCAP) with the Corps of Engineers as executing agent. Under its auspices Brown and Root Services Corporation provided extensive infrastructure and combat service support in Somalia, Haiti, Croatia, Hungary, Bosnia, and elsewhere. In 1997 responsibility for LOGCAP migrated to the Army Materiel Command (AMC), and DynCorps assumed responsibility as the primary contractor. The contract signed with DynCorps was the commercial equivalent of a contingency plan. DynCorps would plan for and be prepared to initiate specified support for a force of up to 20,000 for 180 days in one of five geographic regions. It would anticipate one rear area base and four forward operational areas and operate beyond 180 days and in support of up to 50,000 personnel if required. The contract envisioned DynCorps as a fallback source for whatever the Army did not have enough of or forgot to bring, in addition to providing specified support up front. DynCorps would provide its own commercial transportation into theater, thus eliminating competition for strategic airlift and sealift. The business model assumed DynCorps would import supervision and critical equipment from the United States but hire labor and procure other equipment and supplies locally insofar as possible. It was not long before contractors were embedded amid the key leadership planning or executing operations, taking over many functions that had previously gone to uniformed contracting officers. As early as 1992 V Corps Exercise DRAGON HAMMER, an "out of sector" deployment to Sardinia, concluded that LOGCAP and "those guys

Aviation repair in Bosnia: Even though staged far forward, maintenance of advanced technology remained heavily dependent on defense contractor support.

with the briefcases full of money" would be critical to future deployments. When Task Force Hawk hastily dispatched its reconnaissance party to Tirana-Rinas Airport, a contracting officer, a representative of Brown and Root Services Corporation, and a civilian real estate expert were among the first on the ground.[35]

Contractors had long provided specialized technical skills to the Army. The railroad and telegraph personnel of the Civil War have already been mentioned. Bell Telephone dispatched two hundred female switchboard operators to the American Expeditionary Forces (AEF) in World War I. In 1969 over two thousand contract maintenance personnel or field service representatives served in Vietnam, primarily because of the proliferation of helicopters and communications systems of civilian design. Within the Department of Defense, the equipment categories most likely to require contracted maintenance support or contractor field service representatives have traditionally been aircraft, missiles, communications and electronics, and items in the process of research and development. The transforming Army was making significant investments in each of these areas. Attack helicopters experienced nearly continuous upgrades, with the Apache Longbow pushing the state of the art and the Comanche envisioned as the wave of the future. Missiles were proliferating in numbers and roles, ranging from strategic weapons for high-altitude air and missile defense through surface-to-surface ATACMS, air-to-ground Hellfires, and such close-in tactical systems as the Javelin or Dragon.

Communications and electronics of civilian design were a particularly energetic growth area within the Army. The shift to "off-the-shelf" technology
and decisions to appliqué Force XXI onto legacy platforms accelerated the
process. The Information Technology Management Reform Act (ITMRA)
and the Federal Acquisition Reform Act (FARA) of 1996, together referred
to as the Clinger-Cohen Act, streamlined the acquisition of off-the-shelf
communications and electronics and raised the thresholds at which purchases
were subject to review. Information technologies flooded both the deployable
and the institutional Army, and hastily cobbled together systems electronically linked networks into ever larger wholes. Each of these networks had its
own contingent of contracted information technology specialists, affectionately referred to as "geeks," to ensure that systems performed as designed.
During this period virtually every material program within the Army, from
several-ounce meals ready to eat (MREs) through seventy-ton M1A2 tanks,
was in the process of research and development. Product improvements (PIPs)
superseded each other in continuous flows of modernization. This advance
almost inevitably came accompanied by contract maintenance personnel or
field service representatives of some sort. We have already mentioned National
Training Center Rotation 97–06, wherein 5,000 soldiers were accompanied by
1,200 contracted technicians and data collectors. This was an extreme case,
but it underscored the critical role contractors had assumed when sustaining
newly developed or acquired equipment.[36]

Military contractors were more sophisticated, available, and broadly capable than they had been before. This was a worldwide phenomenon. The end
of the Cold War led to a dramatic downsizing of armies on both sides of the
former Iron Curtain, releasing considerable military talent and experience into
the civilian sector. This was in addition to that already available by virtue of
routine retirement. During the same period, former Warsaw Pact countries were
eager to redesign their armies along Western lines, a flush of post–Cold War
idealism propelled United Nations agencies and nongovernmental organizations (NGOs) into troubled regions in unprecedented numbers, and a number
of Third World countries lost their Cold War patrons. Pursuing stability, the
Department of Defense quadrupled its budget for International Military
Education and Training (IMET) between 1994 and 2002. For practical and
political purposes, much of this training was executed by or in cooperation
with private firms. Military Professional Resources International (MPRI),
Science Applications International Corporation (SAIC), Vinnell, DynCorps,
and other contractors hired veterans from many nations and trained tens of
thousands of military personnel in the Balkans, former Warsaw Pact countries, Africa, Latin America, and elsewhere. Their ability to field seasoned
instructors was drawn on within the United States as well. Downsizing slashed
uniformed manpower within the institutional Army at least as dramatically as
within the deployable Army. During the 1980s TRADOC schools were well
populated with faculties of intermediate rank responsible for course development, doctrine writing, and instruction. An easy fluidity existed between those
who wrote doctrine and those who taught it, and the vast majority of those
who wrote and taught doctrine cycled back into the deployable Army to apply

their acquired knowledge in the field. During the 1990s TRADOC experienced huge cuts. Course development and doctrine writing by and large migrated to contractors, as did an appreciable amount of the instruction. Contractors were pervasive at all levels. Even such highly sophisticated training programs as the Battle Command Training Program (BCTP) benefited from the return of retired senior general officers, "gray beards," under contract. The intellectual footprint of contractors was not confined to training and education; we have already mentioned the influence of "think tanks" for hire such as IDA, RAND, and SAIC upon the Quadrennial Defense Review. In the former Third World contractors were pervasive and at times pernicious. NGOs pushing into post–Cold War vacuums for humanitarian reasons often encountered high-risk security situations. If locally hired security proved unreliable, such international firms as Erinys, Executive Outcomes, or Stabilico might provide better services. These international firms often hired locals but superimposed seasoned supervision. In 1994 the U.S. State Department took to contracting with private security contractors in countries where it felt exposed or at risk. Many governments, corporations, and even citizens in the former Third World had come to rely on private security contractors, at times characterized as mercenaries.[37]

In 1999 Blackwater, Halliburton, and Southern Cross Security were not yet household words, but the Department of Defense and the United States Army had crossed important watersheds with respect to reliance on military contractors. In addition to traditional external interfaces with respect to manufacturing, procurement, acquisition, and supply, they were now heavily dependent on contractors for internal functions as well. Most base and depot operations, broad genres of logistical support at home and abroad, an increasing menu of technical and maintenance services, and a substantial fraction of institutional intellectual capital were in the hands of private contractors. The firms providing such services were heavily populated by military veterans and retirees, most of whom welcomed this opportunity to continue to serve. Nevertheless, the shift to reliance on contracting was not problem-free. In the short run contracting often proved to be more expensive than reliance on civil servants. Savings were downstream in the form of reduced commitments to pensions, medical benefits, and the like. Contracts gave one flexibility if one got them right on the first iteration, but they could be difficult and expensive to change if not. The relative ease of redirecting the energies of soldiers and civil servants was no longer there. Contractors could be patriots, but inevitably they were businessmen. To succeed they had to turn a profit, and this imperative could trump commitment to a mission per se. Contractors were not under military discipline in a legal sense, although a number of mechanisms served to control the behavior of United States citizens on the battlefield—and some governments similarly influenced the behavior of their nationals contracted to the United States. Contractors demonstrating the courage of soldiers when under duress did so because of personal character, not legal commitments. Contractors tended to be secretive with respect to knowledge that affected their profits. Lack of transparency virtually guaranteed disconnects when transforming a body of work from one contractor to another. Knowledge acquired by contractors did not necessarily migrate to uniformed counterparts either. In an earlier era young uniformed instructors and doctrine writers rotated to and from the "schoolhouse" and the "line," to the mutual benefit of both, and reinforced the professional development of the soldiers involved. Contracted instructors and doctrine writers did not rotate in such a manner. This litany of complications provoked more than one survey respondent to exhort "reclaim the Army from the contractors!" That horse was already out of the barn. Multiple causes of a greater reliance on contracting were irreversible, and soldiers, civil servants, and contractors were just going to have to work things out.[38]

The United States Army in 1999

The United States Army of 1999 was smaller than that of 1995, but not by large numbers. The active component had dropped from 510,000 to 480,000. Within the reserve component the Army National Guard had dropped from 375,000 to 357,000 and the Army Reserve from 241,000 to 208,000. The most dramatic post–Cold War downsizing was complete by 1995, and cuts beyond that point were on a gentler scale. As we have seen, the Army and its advocates arrested the risk of substantial further cuts during the course of the Quadrennial Defense Review. The Army's civilian workforce fared less well during this period, dropping from 324,000 to 225,000. Much of this related to privatization and outsourcing more so than downsizing per se, as previously discussed. Relative stability in the uniformed ranks allowed the Army to regain its footing with respect to assignment cycles, progressive assignments, and career development. The Army once again met Defense Officer Personnel Management Act (DOPMA) time-of-service guidelines for promotions, for example, and soldiers could once again generally anticipate three-year tours at most accompanied stations. In the case of junior officers and noncommissioned officers, this allowed time for the mix of jobs most likely to be developmental. During the downsizing evaluative ratings had understandably inflated, largely because officers and noncommissioned officers performing less well had left in huge numbers. More than 85 percent of officers had received a "top block" from senior raters on their most recent officer evaluation report (OER), for example. This prompted General Reimer into a dramatic overhaul of the OER system, accompanied by a year-long Army-wide draconian tutorial directed at senior raters to recover something looking like a bell curve. In its first year the new OER system drove top blocks under 30 percent, restoring the OER's apparent value as a basis for comparison. This initiative was embedded in Officer Personnel Management System XXI (OPMS XXI), a larger effort to revamp the personnel system to best support Force XXI. OPMS XXI sought to place middle-grade officers inclined to information operations, operational support, and institutional support on a more equal footing with those in the traditionally more successful operations (deploying, employing, and sustaining land combat forces) career field with respect to assignments and promotion. Revisions included solidifying assignment progressions within the alternative career fields, deemphasizing such prestige assignments as battalion command in specialties wherein they were less relevant, and heavily emphasizing counseling and mentorship in selecting and developing officers within all career fields. With respect to the enlisted ranks, prolonged downsizing had created a bit of a holiday with respect to emphasis on recruitment. As downsizing bottomed out, the necessity of continuous refurbishment via recruitment returned. In 1999 the United States economy was booming, and the Army faced stiff competition for the thirteen out of a hundred young Americans who were at that time fully qualified to join it. Recruiting fell short. The active component recruited 68,209 new soldiers (down 8 percent from its target), and the Army Reserve recruited 57,090 (down 20 percent). The National Guard did recruit 52,084 to squeak by at two-tenths of a percent over its target. Fortuitously these shortfalls were offset by abundant retention. The active component reenlisted 20,803 first-termers (103 percent of its target), 24,174 mid-careerists (105 percent), and 26,130 career soldiers (120 percent). Manning remained robust, although soldiers were older.[39]

Gentler downsizing and renewed stability in units allowed the Army to improve on its training posture as well as its professional development. In FY1995 seventy-seven combat battalions rotated through the major combat training centers at Fort Irwin, Fort Polk, and Hohenfels. In 1999 181 did. The perturbations caused by increased operational tempo (OPTEMPO) were more than offset by the end of unit inactivations, relocations, and base closures and the prolonged preparations associated with each. Active-component commanders reasonably anticipated at least one combat training center rotation during their tour of duty, and their tours of duty generally lasted two years. The combat training centers were employed to reinforce preparations for deployments—particularly those to the Balkans—as well as to prepare for the more traditional combat envisioned in unit mission-essential task lists. This preparation came in two formats. All units cycling through the combat training centers experienced an infusion of "operations other than war" type missions in addition to their customary mechanized bashes with Soviet-style opponents. In addition, units on the verge of deployment rotated through "mission-rehearsal exercises" or "mission-readiness exercises" adapting combat training center equipment and usages to scenarios inspired by the circumstances into which they expected to deploy. These exercises could be surprisingly prescient. An informal 1996 survey of soldiers in Bosnia, for example, determined that virtually all of their experiences once deployed had been anticipated by training they had received in Hohenfels. The combat training centers provided capstone events of several weeks' duration for unit training cycles. Since the 1980s units had organized annual training in accordance with the principles of Field Manuals 25–100 (*Training the Force*) and 25–101 (*Battle-Focused Training*). These prescribed an orderly structure that included determining a mission essential task list (METL), echeloned quarterly training briefs (QTBs) committing to specifics in pursuit of METL training, training schedules agreed to well in advance by all echelons involved, and the systematic mustering of resources to ensure that training objectives were achieved. As downsizing tapered off, FORSCOM rededicated itself to this proven training

An after-action review following rigorous National Training Center (NTC) training

doctrine. Gates such as Table XII (platoon live-fire qualification), company/team combined-arms live-fire exercises (CALFEXs), and battalion/task force force-on-force external evaluations were ever more consistently and reliably achieved. The renewed emphasis on fundamentals extended into the training base, wherein basic training itself was extended from eight to nine weeks. The Army was concerned that units rotating through peacekeeping in the Balkans would lose their edge with respect to warfighting somewhere else. Happily, operational experience, training, and the use of simulators while deployed kept up individual and small units' skills. Returning units could generally refurbish their training standards at company level and above with rigorous field exercises of a few weeks' duration. These did have to work through General Reimer's DEPTEMPO guidance, discussed above, a requirement that could delay the recovery of full-spectrum readiness in the interest of retaining seasoned personnel for the long haul.[40]

We have already discussed the ever-expanding role of the reserve component participating in and supporting deployments. Of 160,479 soldiers deployed by FORSCOM in 1998, 40,885 were from the reserve component. Across the Department of Defense as a whole, reserve-component man-days of service doubled in five years—to 12.5 million man-days in FY1999. This had implications that played out in training. Over 40,000 National Guardsmen rotated through combat training center rotations. Fifteen enhanced separate brigades had been designated within the National Guard. These combat brigades received priority with respect to equipment and training in the anticipation that they would be ready to deploy as combat brigades in less than 90 days, as opposed to the upwards of 150 expected of other National Guard combat brigades or divisions. One National Training Center and one Joint Readiness Training Center rotation a year were to be given over to the enhanced brigades, in the expectation that they would rotate through on an eight-year cycle. Expectations of units of smaller size and combat support or combat service support missions were even greater. Fifty-two reserve-component units of company size rotated through the Joint Readiness Training Center in 1999, of which a number were expected to be able to deploy in as few as ten days. Combat training center rotations were capstone events, with far more training taking place at home stations or in local exercises. Training affiliations between active-component and reserve-component units deepened in the expectation the reserve-component units would be deploying earlier and more frequently. Teaming paired units from the two components with like-type counterparts for training and training support. Multicomponent units blended contingents from the two components into the same organization. Cases in point included the 32d Air and Missile Defense Command at Fort Bliss, Texas, and the United States Army Civil Affairs and Psychological Operations Command (USACAPOC), a major subordinate command of the Special Operations Command. These blended commands actively controlled a mix of active, National Guard, and Army Reserve units. The newly reactivated 24th Infantry Division (Mechanized) at Fort Riley, Kansas, and 7th Infantry Division at Fort Carson, Colorado, were also multicomponent, each directing the training of enhanced brigades and other units. The Army school system battalions of the Reserve divisions (institutional training) in part offset the damage done by declining TRADOC force structure. These Reservists filled in to provide skill qualification, leadership, and professional development training—as they would in wartime. Reserve initial-entry battalions similarly provided basic combat training and one-station unit training. Unfortunately, manning cuts did adversely affect the availability of full-time personnel within the reserve component. A mix of full-time Guardsmen and Reservists, civil servants, military technicians, and detailed members of the active component provided full-time service to the reserve component. In FY1999 this cadre fell 28 percent short in the National Guard and 38 percent short in the Army Reserve, a considerable constraint on readiness overall. The United States Army had become heavily dependent on the reserve component to succeed in its ongoing missions, but had not yet achieved the resources and processes that would render it more fully prepared for these increased responsibilities.[41]

We have discussed the transformational efforts of Force XXI, with a particular emphasis on tactical maneuver units. We have also discussed the operational and strategic implications of an enhanced expeditionary posture, both in theory and in practice. We should also mention the focus and attention the Army gave to space during this period. In 1997 the United States Army Space and Missile Defense Command stood up. It furthered the traditions of a number of previous commands—the Army had been into missiles and missile defense since the early Cold War—and brought together a potpourri of space-related agencies under one roof. Broadly, the new command oriented on two principal missions: securing space assets and their products to soldiers in the field and providing effective missile defense to the nation and its deployed forces. Of these missions, the first saw explosive growth and the second dramatic technological breakthroughs during the 1990s. Satellite-based GPS rapidly proliferated with respect to numbers and functions after DESERT STORM. By 1999 they were the approved and increasingly irreplaceable solution for navigation, determining position, blue force tracking, and precision strikes in the form of JDAMs. In addition to GPS support, satellites were increasingly essential for communications and provided a vast array of intelligence products drawn from across the entire electromagnetic spectrum. The Space and Missile Defense Command ensured that soldiers had the equipment and training to take advantage of these capabilities, negotiated with joint counterparts to ensure appropriate satellite support for the Army, and contributed to the physical and electromagnetic security of satellites. Physical security shaded into its other mission, missile defense. The ever-improving Patriot Advanced Capability–3 (PAC-3) and the experimental Theater High-Altitude Air Defense (THAAD) both featured hit-to-kill technologies—"hitting a bullet with a bullet," as wags were prone to say. Unlike interceptors fielded during the Cold War, hit-to-kill technologies did not require nuclear warheads to reliably destroy incoming missiles, rendering them enormously more flexible with respect to the circumstances in which they could be used. Engagement times could be dropped by precious seconds through "slew-to-cue" technologies. Air defense missile systems such as the Avenger were upgraded in such a manner that they responded automatically to sensors other than their own electromagnetically networked with them. Thus their armaments were slewing to an incoming target before their own sensors could detect it. When their sensors picked up the target, they were already on it. Such a capability would prove particularly useful in the case of cruise missiles. Cruise missiles are air breathing and fly at low altitudes, leaving them far more fleetingly visible than traditional missiles exposed along the full trajectory of a ballistic arc. During 1999 field tests wedded slew-to-cue technology with the Joint Land Attack Cruise Missile Defense Elevated Netted Sensor System (JLENS), a long name for a blimp or "aerostat," tethered high above the battlefield. The JLENS looked down on cruise missiles with multiple sensors and networked with firing batteries for instant queuing. The tests were successful, with JLENS able to track multiple targets simultaneously and pass them off to both ground-based and sea-based interceptors. True to the Army's continuing commitment to Vuono's six imperatives, the Space and Missile Defense Command never viewed its mandate as technological alone. Its Force Development and Integration Center, also established in 1997, developed guidance with respect to doctrine, training, organization, and personnel management. To guarantee future leadership, the Army established a career functional area for space-related assignments, to which officers first accessed in 1999. Inevitably colleagues referred to these young people as "space cadets," a friendly term of derision often followed by mimicking the theme music from *Twilight Zone*, a popular television series evocative of the bizarre. Whatever the cultural commentary, the Army was in space to stay. The panoply of Force XXI would be dependent on space-based assets and would operate under multiple layers of missile defense.[42]

Conclusions

General Reimer's tenure consolidated the post–Cold War transformational initiatives of the Vuono and Sullivan eras and carried them forward. In 1995 Force XXI was vision and programs more so than proven organization and hardware. By 1999 field experimentation had progressed through the division level. A full brigade sported appliqué versions of the Force XXI panoply and had tested them in the field. Force XXI technologies as envisioned were sufficiently mature to spread them across the force, had funding permitted. Downsizing was complete, and the now smaller Army reestablished the traditional personnel and training regimes that guaranteed readiness. The end of downsizing—and thus stability—was not entirely fortuitous; the Army's performance in the Quadrennial Defense Review persuaded most that further diminishment of ground forces would be dysfunctional. Operational missions to the Middle East, the Balkans, and other overseas locations continued unabated; indeed they increased by half. Capabilities with respect to pre-positioning, airlift, sealift, expeditionary infrastructure, and expeditionary culture within the Army improved as well. Deployments increasingly were a way of life for the active component and also made significant demands on the reserve component. In this challenging environment the roles and missions of active and reserve intermingled as never before. Collaterally, operations in the Balkans and Partnership for Peace advanced the transformations of Warsaw Pact armies as well as our own, consolidating Cold War success. Contractors were ever more present and relied upon throughout the Army, compensating in part for downsizing, multiple prospective venues for deployment, and increased technological complexity. General Reimer had sustained a demonstrably capable full-spectrum force, executed current missions, and significantly advanced Army transformation. The soldiers that had been his credentials stood on the cusp of the twenty-first century considerably better prepared for its challenges because of their actions and preparations during the last four years.

Notes

[1] General Dennis J. Reimer, "Maintaining a Solid Framework While Building for the Future," *Army 1995–1996 Green Book,* October 1995, 21–26; "General Dennis J. Reimer," in William G. Bell, *Commanding Generals and Chiefs of Staff, 1775–2005: Portraits and Biographical Sketches of the Army's Senior Officers* (Washington DC: Center of Military History, 2005), 162; General Dennis J. Reimer, "Where We've Been—Where We're Headed," Address at the Dwight David Eisenhower Luncheon, Annual Meeting of the Association of the United States Army, Washington DC, 17 October 1995, in *Soldiers Are Our Credentials: The Collected Works and Selected Papers of the Thirty-third Chief of Staff, United States Army* (Washington DC: Center of Military History, 2000), iv, 6–11; James L. Yarrison, *The Modern Louisiana Maneuvers* (Washington DC: Center of Military History, 1999), 77–84.

[2] Yarrison, 77–84; *Land Combat in the 21st Century* (Fort Monroe, Virginia: U.S. Army Training and Doctrine Command, 1996); Stuart E. Johnson and Martin C. Libicki, eds., *Dominant Battlespace Knowledge* (Washington DC: National Defense University Press, 1996); John Ferris, A New American Way of War? C4ISR in Operation IRAQI FREEDOM, A Provisional Assessment (Calgary, Canada: Centre for Military and Strategic Studies, 1994); General William M. Hartzog, "TRADOC: Moving the Army into the Future," *Army 1997–1998 Green Book,* October 1997, 49–54.

[3] Robert Middlekauf, *The Glorious Cause: The American Revolution, 1763–1789* (New York: Oxford University Press, 1982), 281–92; W. Glenn Robertson, "First Bull Run, 19 July 1861," in *America's First Battles: 1776–1965,* eds. Charles E. Heller and William A. Stofft (Lawrence, Kansas: University of Kansas Press, 1986), 81–108; John S. Brown, *Draftee Division: The 88th Infantry Division in World War II* (Lexington, Kentucky: University Press of Kentucky, 1986), 105–24; "Pointe du Hoe, 2d Ranger Battalion, 6 June 1943," in *Small Unit Actions* (Washington DC: War Department Historical Division, 1946), 4–68; *Fratricide Risk Assessment for Company Leadership* (Fort Leavenworth, Kansas: Center for Army Lessons Learned, 1992), 1–3; *Fratricide: Reducing Self-Inflicted Losses* (Fort Leavenworth, Kansas: Center for Army Lessons Learned, 1992), 28, 31; Colonel Trevor N. Dupuy, *Understanding War: History and Theory of Conflict* (New York: Paragon House Publishers, 1987); Colonel Trevor N. Dupuy, *Attrition: Forecasting Battle Casualties and Equipment Losses in Modern War* (Fairfax, Virginia: Hero Books, 1990).

[4] Lieutenant Colonel Charles R. Schrader, *Amicicide: The Problem of Friendly Fire in Modern War* (Fort Leavenworth, Kansas: Combat Studies Institute, 1982); Geoffrey Reagan, *Blue on Blue: A History of Friendly Fire* (New York: Avon Books, 1995); General Fred Franks Jr. with Tom Clancy, *Into the Storm: A Study in Command* (New York: G. P. Putnam's Sons, 1997), 488–511; Field Manual 101–5–1, *Operational Terms and Graphics* (Washington DC: Department of the Army, 1997); *Combat Support Systems* (Fort Leavenworth, Kansas: Center for Army Lessons Learned, 1986); *Command and Control System* (Fort Leavenworth, Kansas: Center for Army Lessons Learned, 1987); *Battlefield Logistics* (Fort Leavenworth, Kansas: Center for Army Lessons Learned, 1991); General Dennis J. Reimer, "The Army Is People," *Army 1998–1999 Green Book,* October 1998, 17–26.

[5] Homer, *The Iliad,* trans. Samuel Butler (New York: Barnes and Noble, 1970), 144–57; John Warry, *Warfare in the Classical World* (New York: St. Martin's Press, 1980); *Seven Operating Systems* (Fort Leavenworth, Kansas: Center for Army Lessons Learned, 1986); *Intelligence* (Fort Leavenworth, Kansas: Center for Army Lessons

Learned, 1986); *Deception* (Fort Leavenworth, Kansas: Center for Army Lessons Learned, 1988); Field Manual 2.0, *Intelligence* (Washington DC: Department of the Army, 2004); Lieutenant General Paul E. Menoher Jr., "Tailoring Intelligence to Meet the Needs of Force XXI," *Army 1995–1996 Green Book,* October 1995, 121–26; Lieutenant General Claudia J. Kennedy, "Army Intelligence: Improving Support to Commanders," *Army 1997–1998 Green Book*, October 1997, 129–32.

[6] Yarrison, 119–27; Franks with Clancy, 488–511; George H. Del Carlo, "A Glimpse of the Digitized Battlefield at the National Training Center," *Landpower Essay Series* (Arlington, Virginia: Association of the United States Army, 1993); John C. Johnston, "The Journey to Force XXI's Mounted Component," *Armor* (March-April 1994): 14–16; U.S. Army News Release, Army Selects Experimental Force, 2 December 1994; General William W. Hartzog, "A Time for Transformation: Creating Army XXI," *Army 1996–1997 Green Book,* October 1996, 53–59; General David A. Bramlett, "Forces Command: Combat Ready Soldiers for All Unified Commands," *Army 1997–1998 Green Book,* October 1997, 41–46; Hartzog, "TRADOC: Moving the Army into the Future," 49–54.

[7] Hartzog, "TRADOC: Moving the Army into the Future," 49–54; "Army Weaponry, Equipment and New Technologies," *Army 1997–1998 Green Book,* October 1997, 294–96.

[8] Hartzog, "TRADOC: Moving the Army into the Future," 49–54; "Army Weaponry, Equipment and New Technologies," 294–96; Reimer, "The Army Is People," 17–26.

[9] Lieutenant Colonel H. R. McMaster, Crack in the Foundation: Defense Transformation and the Underlying Assumption of Dominant Knowledge in Future War, Historians Files, CMH; Field Manual 2–0, *Intelligence*; Hartzog, "TRADOC: Moving the Army into the Future," 49–54; *Intelligence*, 1986; *Deception*, 1988; Menoher, 121–26; Kennedy, 129–32.

[10] Information Paper, Tim Muchmore, Precision Guided Munitions: They Cannot Do It Alone, annotated for Army senior leaders, 7 August, 2001, Historians Files, CMH; Army Senior Leader Update, Precision Strike: A Unique American Military Advantage . . . but with Limitations, 14 August 2001, Historians Files, CMH; Peter Grier, "The JDAM Revolution," *Air Force Online: The Journal of the Air Force Association,* September 2006.

[11] Yarrison, 77–95; Briefing, U.S. Army Training and Doctrine Command to the Deputy Chief of Staff for Operations and Plans, "Force XXI WFLA FY99–09 Modernization Recommendations," 31 January 1997, Historians Files, CMH.

[12] Connie L. Reeves, *Department of the Army Historical Summary, Fiscal Year 1996* (Washington DC: Center of Military History, 2002), 72–79, 97: Jeffery A. Charleston, *Department of the Army Historical Summary, Fiscal Year 1999* (Washington DC: Center of Military History, 2006), 8–12, 48–54, 74–76.

[13] Ibid.; Lieutenant General Steven L. Arnold, "Third U.S. Army: Always First," *Army 1996–1997 Green Book,* October 1996, 173–78; Lieutenant General Tommy R. Franks, "Third U.S. Army: Providing Deployable Warfighting Headquarters," *Army 1997–1998 Green Book,* October 1997, 173–77; Lieutenant General Tommy R. Franks, "Third U.S. Army: 'One Team, One Fight, One Future' Is a Reality," *Army 1998–1999 Green Book,* October 1998, 177, 181; Lieutenant General Tommy R. Franks, "Third Army: Ready to Respond and Regionally Engaged," *Army 1999–2000 Green Book,* October 1999, 193–98.

[14] Reeves, 72–79; Charlston, 8–12, 48–54; General Gary E. Luck, "Vigilance on Freedom's Frontier to Counter the 'Face of Uncertainty,'" *Army 1995–1996 Green Book,* October 1995, 77–83; Lieutenant General Robert L. Ord III, "U.S. Army

Pacific: Historic Ties, Dynamic Future," *Army 1995–1996 Green Book,* October 1995, 99–105; General John H. Tilelli Jr., "One of the Cold War's Last Hot Spots, Korea: Deterring War and Defending Freedom," *Army 1996–1997 Green Book,* October 1996, 79–86; Lieutenant General William M. Steele, "America's Army in the Pacific: 'Writing a Glorious Page in the Nation's History,'" *Army 1996–1997 Green Book,* October 1996, 109–14; General John H. Tilelli Jr., "Korea: A Team Defense Against a Renewed Threat," *Army 1997–1998 Green Book*, October 1997, 73–80; Lieutenant General William M. Steele, "A Century of Commitment to the Asia-Pacific," *Army 1997–1998 Green Book*, October 1997, 103–08; General John H. Tilelli Jr., "Our Quality Troops: A Bedrock of Peace and Stability," *Army 1998–1999 Green Book,* October 1998, 87–94; Lieutenant General William M. Steele, "U.S. Army Pacific: Relevant, Responsive and Ready," *Army 1998–1999 Green Book,* October 1998, 113–18; General John H. Tilelli Jr., "Joint/Combined Operations Are Integral to Korea's Defense," *Army 1999–2000 Green Book,* October 1999, 99–104; Lieutenant General Edwin P. Smith, "USARPAC: A Vast Area with Expanding Importance," *Army 1999–2000 Green Book,* October 1999, 123–30.

[15] Reeves, 72–79; Charlston, 8–12, 48–54; Major General Lawson W. Magruder III, "A Total Effort Supporting Regional Democracy," *Army 1995–1996 Green Book,* October 1995, 157–61; Major General William A. Navas Jr., "The Army National Guard: Flexible, Accessible Force," *Army 1996–1997 Green Book,* October, 1996, 89–94; Major General Max Baratz, "Ready and More Relevant Than Ever: A Restructured Army Reserve," *Army 1996–1997 Green Book,* October 1996, 97–107; Major General Lawson W. Magruder III, "U.S. Army South: Fostering Peace in Central and South America," *Army 1996–1997 Green Book,* October 1996, 181–86; Major General Philip R. Kensinger Jr., "U.S. Army South: Expanding to New Horizons," *Army 1997–1998 Green Book,* October 1997, 179–84; Major General Philip R. Kensinger Jr., "U.S. Army South: Peacefully Engaging Our Regional Partners," *Army 1998–1999 Green Book,* October 1998, 183–87; Major General Roger C. Schultz, "Army National Guard: Continuing the Transformation," *Army 1999–2000 Green Book,* October 1999, 107–13; Major General Thomas J. Plewes, "The Indispensable Army Reserve: One Part of a Synchronized Force," *Army 1999–2000 Green Book,* October 1999, 115–22; Major General Philip R. Kensinger Jr., "U.S. Army South: Moving Out and Continuing the Mission," *Army 1999–2000 Green Book,* October 1999, 199–202.

[16] R. Cody Phillips, *Bosnia-Herzegovina: The U.S. Army's Role in Peace Enforcement Operations, 1995–2004* (Washington DC: Center of Military History, 2005); Charles E. Kirkpatrick, *"Ruck It Up!": The Post–Cold War Transformation of V Corps, 1990–2001* (Washington DC: Center of Military History, 2006), 387–458; General William W. Crouch, "U.S. Army Europe: Forward Deployed and Projecting Power," *Army 1996–1997 Green Book,* October 1996, 69–77; General Eric K. Shinseki, "America's Soldiers: Our Ambassadors for Democracy," *Army 1997–1998 Green Book,* October 1997, 65–70; General Eric K. Shinseki, "U.S. Army Europe: Ready Today, Ready in the 21st Century," *Army 1998–1999 Green Book,* October 1998, 79–85; Christopher Bennett, *Yugoslavia's Bloody Collapse: Causes, Course and Consequences* (New York: New York University Press, 1995); Richard Holbrooke, *To End a War* (New York: Random House, 1998).

[17] R. Cody Phillips, *Operation JOINT GUARDIAN: The U.S. Army in Kosovo* (Washington DC: Center of Military History, 2006); Kirkpatrick, 459–534; General Montgomery C. Meigs, "U.S. Army Europe: On Point for the Nation," *Army 1999–2000 Green Book,* October 1999, 89–97; Anthony H. Cordesman, *The Lessons and Non-Lessons of the Air and Missile Campaign in Kosovo* (Westport, Connecticut:

Praeger, 2001); R. Craig Nation, *War in the Balkans, 1992–2002* (Carlisle Barracks, Pennsylvania: Strategic Studies Institute, 2003).

[18] *NATO Handbook* (Brussels: NATO Office of Information and Press, 1995), 50–69; *The Military Balance 1996/1997* (London: Oxford University Press, 1996), 32–103; Kirkpatrick, 110–16; Major A. J. Koenig, Partnership for Peace Exercise Summary, V Corps History Office, July 1997; *Partnership for Peace Framework Document* (Brussels: North Atlantic Council/North Atlantic Cooperation Council, 1994); General Wesley A. Clark, "Transforming NATO's Military for the 21st Century," *SHAPE Officer's Association Newsletter,* no. 109, 5–7; Admiral Guido Venturoni, "NATO—The Search for Peace," *SHAPE Officer's Association Newsletter,* no. 109, 11–16; Jeffrey Simon, "NATO"s Membership Action Plan and Defense Planning: Credibility at Stake," *Problems of Post-Communism* (May-June 2001): 28–36; Shinseki, "America's Soldiers: Our Ambassadors for Democracy," 65–70; Author's personal experience and observations while serving as the Chief of Programs and Requirements, Supreme Headquarters Allied Powers Europe, Mons, Belgium, 1997–1998.

[19] Eric K. Shinseki, *The Army Family: A White Paper* (Washington DC: Center of Military History, 2003), 7–25; Interv with Mary Beth Brown, 15 August 2008, Historians Files, CMH; *Army Families and Soldier Readiness* (Santa Monica, California: Rand Arroyo Center, 1992); *What We Know About Army Families* (Arlington, Virginia: Army Research Institute for the Behavioral and Social Sciences, 1993); *Survey of Army Families, IV* (Arlington, Virginia: Army Research Institute for the Behavioral and Social Sciences, 2001); *TRICARE Prime Handbook* (Washington DC: Department of Defense, 2005).

[20] Charlston, 48–50; Phillips, *Bosnia-Herzegovina*, 16–18; Kirkpatrick, 57–67, 421–25; Crouch, 69–77; Shinseki, "America's Soldiers: Our Ambassadors for Democracy," 65–70; Shinseki, "U.S. Army Europe: Ready Today, Ready in the 21st Century," 79–85; E-mail, Brigadier General John S. Brown (SHAPE) to Major General David D. McKiernan (USAREUR), 21 August 1998, sub: Hungarian IAP and USAREUR Exercise Reduction, Historians Files, CMH.

[21] Reeves, 3–8,72–79, 97–98; Charlston, 48–54, 74–76; Major General John R. D'Araujo Jr., "Army National Guard: A Vision for the Future," *Army 1995–1996 Green Book,* October 1995, 85–89; Major General Max Baratz, "U.S. Army Reserve: More Ready, More Focused and More Capable," *Army 1995–1996 Green Book,* October 1995, 91–97; Major General William A. Navas Jr., "The Army National Guard: Flexible, Accessible Force," *Army 1996–1997 Green Book,* October 1996, 89–94; Major General Max Baratz, "Ready and More Relevant Than Ever: A Restructured Army Reserve," *Army 1996–1997 Green Book,* October 1996, 97–107; Major General William A. Navas Jr., "The Army National Guard: Capable, Cost-Effective and Vital Force," *Army 1997–1998 Green Book,* October 1997, 85–90; Major General Max Baratz, "A Reorganized Army Reserve: Relevant and Ready," *Army 1997–1998 Green Book,* October 1997, 93–100; Major General Roger C. Schultz, "The National Guard's Secret to Success," *Army 1998–1999 Green Book,* October 1998, 95–100; Major General Thomas J. Plewes, "Army Reserve: A True Partner in America's Army," *Army 1998–1999 Green Book,* October 1998, 103–11; Schultz, "Army National Guard: Continuing the Transformation," 107–13; Plewes, "The Indispensable Army Reserve: One Part of a Synchronized Force," 115–22.

[22] Mark D. Sherry, *The Army Command Post and Defense Reshaping, 1987–1997* (Washington DC: Center of Military History, 2008); Briefing, "Project ANTAEUS: Analyzing the Army in Evolving U.S. Strategy," 8 December 1988, Historians Files, CMH; *Project Vanguard Final Report* (Washington DC: Department of the Army,

1990); Lorna S. Jaffe, *The Development of the Base Force, 1989–1992* (Washington DC: Office of the Chairman of the Joint Chiefs of Staff, 1993); Secretary of Defense Les Aspin, *Report on the Bottom-Up Review* (Washington DC: Office of the Secretary of Defense, 1993); Andrew F. Krepinevich Jr., *The Bottom-Up Review: An Assessment* (Washington DC: Defense Budget Project, 1994); *Directions for Defense: Report of the Commission on Roles and Missions of the Armed Forces* (Washington DC: Department of Defense, 1995); Andrew F. Krepinevich Jr., *Missed Opportunities: An Assessment of the Roles and Missions Commission Report* (Washington DC: Defense Budget Project, 1995).

[23] Section 923(a) of H.R. 3230, National Defense Authorization Act of 1996, Public Law 104–201.

[24] Sherry; H.R. 3230, National Defense Authorization Act of 1996, Public Law 104–201; Joint Staff, Charter for the Quadrennial Defense Review, 1996, Historians Files, CMH; Briefing, DAMO-SS Strategy Task Force, 1 November 1996, Historians Files, CMH; Briefing, "Quadrennial Review (QDR): Army Plans and Preparations," October 1996, Historians Files, CMH; President of the United States, *A National Security Strategy of Engagement and Enlargement* (Washington DC: White House, February 1995); Chairman of the Joint Chiefs of Staff, *The National Military Strategy of the United States of America* (Washington DC: Office of the Chairman of the Joint Chiefs of Staff, 1995); Joint Publication 3.0, *Joint Operations* (Washington DC: Office of the Chairman of the Joint Chiefs of Staff, 1995); *Joint Vision 2010* (Washington DC: Office of the Chairman of the Joint Chiefs of Staff, 1995).

[25] Sherry; Briefing, DAMO-SS Strategy Task Force, 1 November 1996; Briefing, "Quadrennial Review (QDR): Army Plans and Preparations," October 1996; Presentation, Congressman Newt Gingrich to the (New) Brigadier General Orientation Course, Fort Leavenworth, Kansas, October 1997; Michael G. Vickers, *Warfare in 2020: A Primer* (Washington DC: Center for Strategic and Budgetary Assessments, 1996); McMaster.

[26] Sherry; Briefing, J8, "Dynamic Commitment: The Transitions Wargames Series in Support of the Quadrennial Defense Review," 23 December 1996, Historians Files, CMH; Briefing, J8 Forces Division, "Baseline Engagement Force Status Report," 23 December 1996, Historians Files, CMH; Briefing, J8, "Multiple LRC Assessment," 23 December 1996, Historians Files, CMH; Briefing, J8, "SECDEF Review Briefing: Smaller-Scale Contingency Force Requirements Study," 25 April 1997, Historians Files, CMH; *Dynamic Commitment 4 Game Book* (Washington DC: Joint Staff, 1997); Briefing, QDR Executive Session, "A Risk Assessment of the POM Force Against the JSR World: J8/SAGD Gaming Input to the Force Assessment Panel," 25 April 1997, Historians Files, CMH; Briefing, CMH, "Evaluation of Army Readiness," Historians Files, CMH; DAMO-SS Slide Series, "Army Units Have Contributed Over 60% of the Engaged Forces on 25% of the Budget," Historians Files, CMH.

[27] Sherry; Briefing, DAMO-FDX, "Deep Attack Weapons Mix Study (DAWMS) and the Close Support End to End Assessment (CSEEA)," November 1996, Historians Files, CMH; John Y. Schrader, Leslie Lewis, and Roger Allen Brown, *Quadrennial Defense Review (QDR) Analysis: A Retrospective Look at Joint Staff Participation* (Santa Monica, California: RAND, 1999); DAMO-SS Fact Sheet, Army Lessons Learned from DAWMS, Historians Files, CMH.

[28] Sherry; William S. Cohen, *Report of the Quadrennial Defense Review* (Washington DC: Department of Defense, 1997); *Defense Planning Guidance, FY 1998–2003* (Washington DC: Office of the Secretary of Defense, 1996); *Transforming Defense: National Security in the 21st Century* (Washington DC: National Defense Panel, 1997); William S. Cohen, *Defense Reform Initiative Report* (Washington DC: Department of

Defense, 1997); Wayne P. Hughes Jr., ed., *Military Modeling for Decision Making* (Alexandria, Virginia: Military Operations and Research Society, 1997); James S. Thomason, ed., *The Quadrennial Defense Review, Lessons Learned from the 1997 Review and Options for the Future* (Washington DC: Institute for Defense Analysis, 1998); Tim Weiner, "Two War Strategy Is Obsolete, Panel of Experts Says," *New York Times*, 2 December 1997; Thomas E. Ricks, "Panel Calls for the Pentagon to Change the Way It Thinks About Future Operations," *Wall Street Journal,* 1 December 1997; George C. Wilson, *This War Really Matters: Inside the Fight for Defense Dollars* (Washington DC: CQ Press, 2000), 25–192.

[29] Wilson, *This War Really Matters*, 25–145; General Dennis J. Reimer, "Address at the Dwight D. Eisenhower Luncheon, Annual Meeting of the Association of the United States Army, Washington, D.C.," 15 October 1996, in *Soldiers Are Our Credentials*, 70–75; Thomas K. Adams, *The Army After Next: The First Postindustrial Army* (Stanford, California: Stanford Security Studies, 2008), 1–101; Note, General Dennis J. Reimer to Brigadier John S. Brown, 16 April 1999, sub: Comparing Interwar German Army Innovation with That of the Post–Cold War U.S. Army, Historians Files, CMH.

[30] Phillips, *Operation JOINT GUARDIAN*; Kirkpatrick, 459–534; Meigs, 89–97; Cordesman; Nation.

[31] Ibid.; Wesley K. Clark, *Waging Modern War* (New York: Public Affairs, 2001); "How Fear of Losses Kept Super-Copters from Kosovo Action," *Herald Tribune,* 30 December 1999; Sean D. Naylor, "Commander Defends Mission That Launched a Thousand Criticisms," *Army Times*, 17 April 2000; General Dennis J. Reimer, "The Strike Force Operational Concept Paper," in *Soldiers Are Our Credentials*, 254–63.

[32] Vincent Demma, Contractors on the Battlefield: An Historical Survey from the Civil War to Bosnia, Historians Files, CMH; Supplementary Report on Army Contracting, Historians Files, CMH.

[33] Ibid.; Sherry; "Constitution of the United States and Amendments," in Mary Beth Norton et al., *A People and a Nation: A History of the United States* (New York: Houghton Mifflin, 2005), A29–A37; Office of Management and Budget Circular A–76, Performance of Commercial Activities, 1999; Interv with Joseph V. Charyk, Chief Scientist, identified in *Defense Acquisition History Project: Oral Finding Aid* (Washington DC: Center of Military History, 2005), 51; Cohen, *Report of the Quadrennial Defense Review*; *Transforming Defense: National Security in the 21st Century*; *The Beauchamp Years: Oral History Interviews with MG Roy E. Beauchamp, TACOM Commanding General 10 July 1997–13 August 1990* (Warren, Michigan: United States Tank–Automotive and Armaments Command, 2002), 1–78; Interv with Mr. Dale G. Adams, Principal Deputy for Acquisition, in *Reflections of Senior AMC Officials, Volume II* (Fort Belvoir, Virginia: U.S. Army Material Command Historical Office, 2006), 167–92; Memo, Deputy Secretary of Defense, 16 January 1998, sub: Department of Defense Reform Initiative Directive #20: Review of Inherently Governmental Functions; E-mail, General Dennis J. Reimer to Brigadier General John S. Brown, 12 January 2009, sub: Book Project, Historians Files, CMH.

[34] Vincent Demma, *Department of the Army Historical Summary, Fiscal Year 1989* (Washington, DC: Center of Military History, 1998), 11–12, 109–10, 133–39, 191–96; Charlston, 3–13, 32–35, 101–03, 108–09; Major General David A. Whaley, "Installations: Linchpin of America's Army," *Army 1997–1998 Green Book*, October 1997, 141–44; Major General David A. Whaley, "Installations: Maintaining Quality Where Soldiers Live," *Army 1998–1999 Green Book*, October 1998, 145–50; Major General Robert L. Van Antwerp Jr., "Readiness, Retention and Quality of Life Depend on Sustaining Army Communities," *Army 1999–2000 Green Book*, October 1999, 165–

70; Wilson, *This War Really Matters*, 146–65; Interv with Mr. George L. Jones, AMC Deputy Chief of Staff for Personnel, in *Reflections of Senior AMC Officials, Volume II*, 195–213; Daniel H. Else, *Military Housing Privatization Initiative: Background and Issues* (Washington DC: Congressional Research Services, 2001).

[35] Demma, *Department of the Army Historical Summary, Fiscal Year 1989*, 3–13, 63–71, 109–10, 137–59; Charlston, 3–13, 25–34, 61–80; Demma, Contractors on the Battlefield: An Historical Survey from the Civil War to Bosnia; Supplementary Report on Army Contracting; Interv with Mr. A. David Mills, Principal Deputy for Logistics, in *Reflections of Senior AMC Officials, Volume II*, 149–66; General Johnnie E. Wilson, "AMC: Changing Today to Sustain and Equip Tomorrow's Soldier," *Army 1998–1999 Green Book,* October 1998, 71–76; Kirkpatrick, 416, 482.

[36] Demma, Contractors on the Battlefield: An Historical Survey from the Civil War to Bosnia; Supplementary Report on Army Contracting; "Army Weaponry and Equipment," *Army 1995–1996 Green Book,* October 1995, 218–320; "Army Weapons and Equipment," *Army 1999–2000 Green Book*, October 1999, 260–334; Reeves, 63–67, 111–19; *Department of Defense Chief Information Officer Desk Reference,* vol. I, *Foundation Documents* (Washington DC: Department of Defense, 2006); Hartzog, "TRADOC: Moving the Army into the Future," 49–54.

[37] Deborah D. Avant, *The Market for Force: The Consequences of Privatizing Security* (New York: Cambridge University Press, 2005); Interv with Lieutenant General James M. Link, in *Reflections of Senior AMC Officials, Volume II*, 81–112; Wilson, "AMC: Changing Today to Sustain and Equip Tomorrow's Soldier," 71–76; Multiple Responses to Secretary of the Army–directed Think Piece on Intellectual Capital, June 2002, Historians Files, CMH.

[38] Ibid.

[39] Charlston, 25–40; Ltr, General Dennis J. Reimer to Army General Officers, 2 June 1998, in *Soldiers Are Our Credentials*, 208–11; Lieutenant General David H. Ohle, "Designing a Holistic System for Human Resource Management," *1999–2000 Army Green Book,* October 1999, 157–64.

[40] Charlston, 41–48; General Dennis J. Reimer, "Training: Our Army's Top Priority, and Don't You Forget It!" in *Soldiers Are Our Credentials*, 51–56; Field Manual 25–100, *Training the Force* (Washington DC: Department of the Army, 1988); Field Manual 25–101, *Battle-Focused Training* (Washington DC: Department of the Army, 1990); General Thomas A. Schwartz, "The Power of FORSCOM Is the Power of People," *1999–2000 Army Green Book*, October 1999, 57–68; General John N. Abrams, "Training and Doctrine Remain the Keystones of Readiness," *1999–2000 Army Green Book*, October 1999, 71–76.

[41] Charlston, 45–48, 61–80; Schultz, "Army National Guard: Continuing the Transformation," 107–13; Plewes, "The Indispensable Army Reserve: One Part of a Synchronized Force," 115–22; Michael D. Doubler, *I Am the Guard: A History of the Army National Guard, 1636–2000* (Washington DC: Department of the Army, 2001), 360–68.

[42] Charlston, 58–60; James Walker and James T. Hooper, *Space Warriors: The Army Space Support Team* (Washington DC: Center of Military History, 2004); James Walker, Lewis Bernstein, and Sharon Lang, *Seize the High Ground: The Army in Space and Missile Defense* (Washington DC: Center of Military History, 2004); Ltrs, General Dennis J. Reimer to Army General Officers, 4 December 1996 and 13 February 1997, in *Soldiers Are Our Credentials*, 93–94, 99–101; Lieutenant General John Costello, "Space and Missile Defense Challenges for the 21st Century," *1999–2000 Army Green Book*, October 1999, 183–88.

The Shinseki Years, 1999–2003

General Eric K. Shinseki became Chief of Staff of the Army on 22 June 1999. He was thoroughly familiar with retiring Chief of Staff General Dennis J. Reimer's vision of the way ahead for the Army and was well prepared to carry it forward. General Reimer brought him out of command of the 1st Cavalry Division in July 1995 to serve as the Assistant Deputy Chief of Staff for Operations and Plans (ADCSOPS), and he was elevated to DCSOPS a year later. In July 1997 he pinned on a fourth star and assumed command of the United States Army, Europe (USAREUR), and the Seventh Army. In this capacity he commanded the Allied forces in Bosnia through sixteen trying months. He returned to serve as Reimer's Vice Chief of Staff from November 1998 through his elevation to Chief of Staff. As ADSCOPS and DCSOPS he was central to the design and implementation of Force XXI. In Bosnia he experienced post–Cold War operational realities firsthand. As Vice Chief of Staff he was, of course, the Chief of Staff's right-hand man. Shinseki's centrality to Army transformation thus far made him an obvious choice for Chief of Staff. It also exposed him to critics grousing about the undramatic recent Quadrennial Defense Review results, or trying to parlay criticisms of Task Force Hawk into a mandate for accelerated transformation—or for Army diminution. Shinseki would be challenged to visibly pick up the pace of transformation while nevertheless maintaining orderliness.

Halfway through his tenure the devastating attacks of 11 September 2001 propelled the nation and the Army into the Global War on Terrorism. From that point the Army would be transforming while at war. Shinseki balanced the design of a full-spectrum force appropriate for an uncertain future with the narrower and more specific demands of immediate operations. Thoughtful, self-effacing, and deliberative by nature, Shinseki maneuvered to satisfactorily address both the future and the present without inciting undue resistance or acrimony. He had worked his way through hard times before. Twice wounded in Vietnam, he had lost much of his right foot and remained in the Army only after securing an exception to policy approved by the Secretary of the Army. Prolonged convalescence steered him into staff and academic assignments for a time. During the course of these he secured a master's degree and taught comparative literature at the United States Military Academy. Upon returning to troop duty he progressed through operational assignments steadily, commanding at every level through division and serving as a division and a

General Shinseki

corps operations officer as well. In the Pentagon he served as a force integration staff officer and as the director of training in the Office of the Deputy Chief of Staff for Operations and Plans (ODCSOPS), valuable experience in what he later characterized as budgetary "short sword fighting."

He and his wife, Patty, whom he married immediately after his graduation from West Point in 1965, shared an iconic affection for turtles. Turtles symbolized the steadiness of effort with which they reconstructed his body and his career. The metaphor reminded them that myriads of small supporting efforts translated into overall success and that in their case such support had included considerable family sacrifice. Shinseki often reintroduced this little picture of collective individual efforts when deliberating with transformational enthusiasts too captured by the big picture of technological leap-aheads. The little picture included the daily welfare of soldiers, attention to families and their morale, and services that could only be rendered by "boots on the ground." Creative tension between the big picture and the little picture would define yet another balance Shinseki would fight to achieve.[1]

Army Transformation

During General Shinseki's tenure, Army Transformation appeared written with a capital *T*. This reflected institutional emphasis and "strategic communications." Shinseki addressed both priorities even before he assumed his new position. Army Chief of Staff designates generally assemble a transition team of specialists and confidants to help them be broadly informed and to "hit the ground running" from their first day in office. Shinseki was familiar with the practice and undertook a particularly elaborate version to gather information and facilitate support for his programs downstream. An assessment group of over a dozen seasoned officers and command sergeants major headed by a brigadier general fanned out to interview over 350 selected general officers, members of the secretariat, congressional representatives and staffers, academics, and pundits. They also conducted sensing sessions with groups of field-grade officers, company-grade officers, warrant officers, noncommissioned officers, junior enlisted men and women, and family members.

This assessment group consolidated its results and fed them to an integration group, charged with developing short- and long-term campaign plans. The integration group authored drafts of the speeches and releases proposed for Shinseki's first two weeks, laid out a detailed program for his first six months, and outlined his entire tenure with respect to such foreseeable programs as Army Transformation. Most of the members of the integration group were senior field-grade officers already identified to serve on the CSA Staff Group (such as on the Army Chief of Staff's personal staff) once Shinseki became Chief, thus ensuring continuity as plans played out. A consulting group of selected senior officers and retirees reviewed the products of the assessment and integration groups as they emerged, and an executive group headed by a brigadier general coordinated the activities of the three other groups and shepherded administrative support. The entire exercise seemed a miniature and compressed version of General Sullivan's modern Louisiana Maneuvers without the field portions, pursued for about the same reasons. Sullivan had envisioned and Reimer had followed through on Force XXI, and now an Army with demonstrably improved expeditionary capabilities featured one brigade and a few headquarters equipped with field-tested appliqué Information Age hardware and software. Continuing on its present course, the Army could infuse the rest of its force with this appliqué over time, deferring more dramatic changes to the still-distant Army After Next. This evolutionary approach, as we have seen, attracted a swarm of critics outside the Army. Inside the Army experiences over the last eight years bubbled up in the form of recommended edits or adjustments. Not the least of these experiences were those of Shinseki himself in Bosnia, where tanks and Bradleys demolished fragile road networks while troops patrolling in much lighter high mobility multipurpose wheeled vehicles (HMMWVs) were horribly exposed. Shinseki's Special Staff Study Group, the name he gave to his four-part transition team, existed for two months, canvassed the most advanced and the most representative thinking within and about the Army, identified areas of concern or recommended effort, and proposed ways ahead that built upon the past while adjusting for the future.[2]

A recurrent theme in the opinions surfaced by Shinseki's Special Staff Study Group had to do with the image of the Army. The Army might have been steadily transforming itself to deal with an uncertain future, but it was not getting credit for it. During the Quadrennial Defense Review and its aftermath Army representatives repeatedly cautioned against an overreliance on technology. To some, they came across as anti-technology. Field experimentation with digitization thus far involved only a small fragment of the Army and could be invisible to outsiders unless they were paying attention. Other than officers actually working with the transformational technologies, few within the Army could persuasively articulate what they were about or where they were going. Recurrent deployments were inevitably of more interest and more visible to the public—and to soldiers. We have already discussed the public relations dilemma provoked by Task Force Hawk. A joke making the rounds asked what the difference was between the Army Staff and *Jurassic Park*. The answer was that one was a zoo full of dinosaurs and the other was a popular motion picture. Shinseki determined to change this image. He did envision substantive changes in the direction transformational efforts had taken thus far, but he also intended to get the entire Army on message with a commonly understood vision of where it was going and how it was going to get there. His somewhat expansive "Thoughts on the Line of Departure" worked their way through a fistful of imperatives before focusing on a final imperative to develop and communicate an Army vision. In addition to audiences within the Army, the vision had to address the American people, Congress, the Department of Defense and Joint Staff, the "CINCdoms" (such as major commands at home and overseas), other services, corporate America, the media, academe, allies, and potential adversaries. Tools included speeches, communiqués, conferences, symposia, meetings, visits, news releases, interviews, films, professional publications, and the Internet. Approaches would be nuanced to audiences. The Office of Congressional Liaison, for example, would ensure that itinerant general officers en route to "the Hill" had a clear understanding of Army Transformation, whereas the Center of Military History would attempt to be similarly helpful to those destined for scholarly forums. In a pithy statement of intent released as he assumed his position, Shinseki acknowledged that most of the business of the Army would roll along under the supervision of leaders subordinate to him, and he foresaw six objectives that would particularly require his personal attention: increasing strategic responsiveness, developing a clear long-term strategy to improve operational jointness, developing leaders for joint war fighting and change, completing the integration of the active and reserve components, manning war-fighting units, and providing for the well-being of soldiers, civilians, and family members. Of these, the first four were clearly transformative. Shinseki came into office with a vision and a campaign plan and allowed himself four months to mature a supportive coalition within the Army for the changes he envisioned. Senior planning groups chaired by the Vice Chief of Staff, General Jack Keane, and others worked on details, drafted implementing strategies, and reinforced a sense of urgency. Shinseki particularly briefed and garnered the support of the Secretary of the Army, the Secretary of Defense, and the Chairman of the Joint Chiefs of Staff. Some of the Army's severest critics resided in the Secretariat and the Joint Staff, and Shinseki wanted "top cover" in those domains when he came forward with fleshed-out plans. Happily, and by design, the four-month mark coincided with the annual meeting of the Association of the United States Army (AUSA). Shinseki and Secretary of the Army Louis Caldera effectively elevated "Strategic Communications" into a principal staff agency transcending traditional public affairs functions alone and reporting directly to the two of them. The annual AUSA meeting provided an ideal forum in which to exercise it.[3]

The Eisenhower Luncheon of the annual meeting of the AUSA is a glittering affair. A grand ballroom in a major Washington, DC, hotel deploys its best tableware across hundreds of tables. Platoons of waiters and waitresses whisk elegantly presented menu courses in and their smeared remnants out with remarkable precision. An elevated head table running much of the length of the room seats the Army's four-star generals, AUSA illuminati (most of whom are retired generals), and selected guests of honor. Intermittent welcoming remarks, invocations, announcements, and inspiring film clips emanate from a podium in the midst of the head table. Seating radiates across the room and into the balconies from this podium, with the most prestigious tables most proximate to it. Tables generally feature a designed mix of corporate leaders, serving military personnel, and invited guests. Most present are in the upper tiers of careers in industry, politics, or the military, but tables often seat a junior officer, noncommissioned officer (NCO), or soldier or two selected by their commands and hosted by the AUSA or its corporate members. Thus each table is a miniature version of what some might call the military-industrial complex, grounded by the presence of soldiers just in from the field. The tables reflect the social composition of the AUSA meeting itself, a five-day extravaganza of luncheons, symposia, presentations, speeches, classes, tutorials, and corporate displays sprawling over acres of floor space. Those seated at tables somewhat removed from the podium at the Eisenhower Luncheon will not miss the show, for massive wall screens project live televised imagery of the speakers and of whatever slides and film clips the speakers or hosts choose to project. Indeed, observers not even in the room can capture the substance of the presentations, if not altogether the atmosphere in which they are presented. Presentations are largely in the background until dessert and coffee are served, and then all attention focuses on the keynote speaker, the Chief of Staff of the United States Army. This is the Army's equivalent of the President's Annual State of the Union message, an opportunity to summarize progress and communicate vision to the audience most immediately instrumental to the success of the Army, while reaching through that audience to transmit the same message to the entire Army "family" and all who care about it. On 12 October 1999, the keynote speaker was General Eric K. Shinseki. Appropriately, and perhaps poignantly, he was introduced by General (Retired) Gordon R. Sullivan, now the president of AUSA. The author of the modern Louisiana Maneuvers would listen as the transformation he had sought took its next steps. Shinseki, waving aside the pedantry of Army historians who counseled that the next millennium actually began on 1 January 2001, started with the premise that the Army was but weeks away from the next century and the next millennium and had huge strides to make to prepare for both. He evoked the memory of Elihu Root and the last turnover of a century, and the gigantic transformation at that time from a frontier army to an army with global responsibilities. In his view the Army was now between wars but was unlikely to have much time before it was tested again. Army transformation would be his highest personal priority as Chief of Staff, a priority that would redefine it as Army Transformation.[4]

Army Transformation, as unveiled at the Eisenhower Luncheon and further promulgated in subsequent forums, artfully repackaged much that had gone before while integrating new initiatives envisioned by Shinseki. The basics could be, and often were, briefed from a single PowerPoint slide. The so-called "Trident" became ubiquitous, an organizing principle for massive multislide briefings, the preeminent slide in slender packets intended for those who could

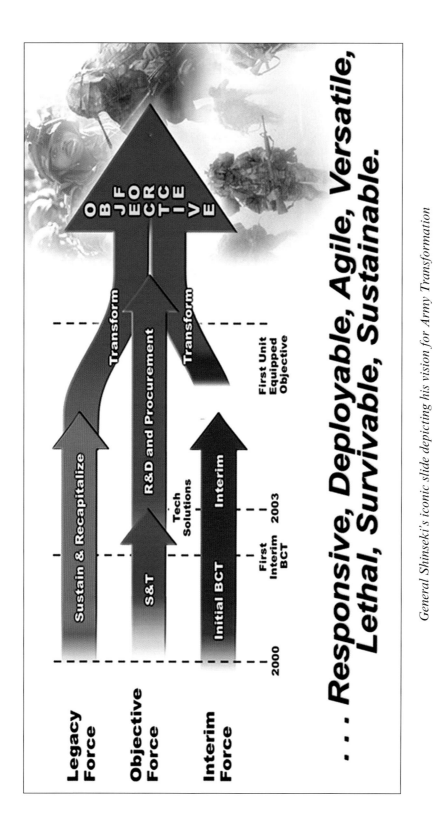

General Shinseki's iconic slide depicting his vision for Army Transformation

give the subject but limited time, and a decorative logo on virtually anything published that had to do with Army Transformation. Junior officers and NCOs in the training base, seasoned leaders throughout the Department of Defense, and key players in government and industry all were talked through this slide by Army Transformation's enthusiastic advocates. The top prong of the Trident was the Legacy Force, in essence the Army XXI that was emerging from Force XXI. The Legacy Force would trundle on in such venerable vehicles as the M1A1 Abrams and M2/M3 Bradley, sporting appliqué versions of Information Age hardware and software. Its massive firepower and formidable armor would outclass prospective adversaries for years to come, and it would fight America's battles until superseded. Deficient with respect to strategic mobility, the Legacy Force would rely on now much-improved sea-lift and Pre-positioning of Materiel Configured to Unit Sets (POMCUS) to deploy. The middle prong of the Trident was labeled the Objective Force, similar to the Army After Next, albeit on a more ambitious timeline. The Objective Force was a vision of future warfare depending upon technologies that did not yet actually exist. Information Age technologies would be intrinsic rather than appliqué, platforms would be lighter yet better protected, weapons would be more precise and more lethal, futuristic capabilities such as robotics and stealth technology would be ubiquitous, and distinctions between light and heavy forces would have blurred. The third prong of the Trident, the Interim Force, was new. Honing in on Shinseki's conviction that contemporary heavy forces were too heavy and light forces too light, it would build and deploy brigade-size units of intermediate weight equipped with the most advanced technologies immediately available. The Interim Force borrowed ideas from both the Experimental Force (EXFOR) and Reimer's Strike Force but was to be neither one of a kind nor experimental. The Interim Force would rapidly deploy sufficient brigades, six, to be operationally significant. By their very nature Interim Brigade Combat Teams would offer opportunities to develop training and doctrine appropriate to the Objective Force, but they were to be deployable fighting units in their own right from the beginning. The three prongs of the Trident would be parallel and complementary but distinct for about a decade. Around 2010 or shortly thereafter the technologies of the Objective Force would be mature, and deployable units featuring them fielded. From that point units would roll over into the new equipment and the three prongs would converge onto a single axis, the Objective Force. Along the bottom of the Trident slide the words "Responsive, Deployable, Agile, Versatile, Lethal, Survivable, and Sustainable" reminded the briefer and those being briefed of the character the Transformed Army would have.[5]

From the beginning Shinseki specified tangible goals for the forces he advocated and programmed actions and assets to achieve them. The Objective Force was to be capable of deploying a combat-ready brigade anywhere in the world within 96 hours, a division within 120 hours, and five divisions within 30 days. Interim Brigade Combat Teams would have similar strategic mobility, albeit not the same depth-of-force structure. Backward planning from these tangible goals drove a proliferation of specifics and details: vehicles that fit into aircraft of contemporary design; load plans such that vehicles, crews, accoutrements, and several days of supply could travel together; scaled-down logistical footprints at the far end; appreciable sustainment from the home station; and so on. Shinseki even set milestones for answering the questions that were at the time unanswerable. Unrelenting and focused research efforts would identify achievable technologies within three or four years' time. These in turn would be harnessed to begin producing fully equipped Objective Force units in eight to ten years' time. The Objective Force would feature a panoply of sensors, communications nodes, unmanned aircraft, robotics, and other advanced hardware but at its core would be the common vehicle platform of the future combat system (FCS). Variants would provide direct fires, indirect fires, and logistical support; serve as troop carriers; and deploy as platforms for advanced communications and sensors. The FCS vehicles would weigh twenty tons or less and displace between three hundred and four hundred cubic feet of internal volume. This would make it about 70 percent lighter and 50 percent smaller than the M1A1 Abrams tank. Stealth technologies and variations of "smart" armor would nevertheless render the FCS vehicles as survivable as the Abrams. Decisions concerning the technologies FCS would incorporate would be made in 2003, while Shinseki was still Chief of Staff. "System Development and Demonstration" would occur in 2006—within three years of the so-called "good idea cutoff line." Five hundred million dollars would go into science and technology (S&T) funding for FCS during Fiscal Year (FY) 2001 alone. Each prong on the Trident slide had resourcing imperatives overprinted on it, from which specifics with respect to funding and timing would flow. For the Legacy Force the imperatives were to sustain and recapitalize, ensuring that the force was in fighting trim until superseded. For the Objective Force, investments in science and technology would flow into more specific research and development that in turn would be followed by procurement. The Interim Force would start with an initial brigade combat team without specialized equipment that would mature into an interim brigade combat team with specialized equipment, once a family of interim armored vehicles (IAVs) had been selected and procured. Concerning the interim brigade combat teams, more later.[6]

Although the Objective Force featured advanced technologies likely to be most effective in high-intensity conflict, Army planners were careful to anticipate the full spectrum of conflict when designing it. This reflected both prudent historical sensibility and mindfulness that yet another Quadrennial Defense Review would report out in 2001. Months before unveiling Army Transformation at the Eisenhower Luncheon General Shinseki and Secretary Caldera pressed Army historians to provide context for the effort and supported contracted historical studies for the same purpose. Much of this work focused on previous "Revolutions in Military Affairs" and sought usable lessons for Army Transformation in such seminal watersheds as the introduction of drilled musketry or the development of *Blitzkrieg.* As helpful as these analyses may have been, Army historians cautioned that most of the Army's historical activity had been operations other than war and that the post–Cold War era seemed to be no exception. The Commandant of the Army War College, Major General Robert H. Scales Jr., picked up on this refrain. The Army War College was tucked under TRADOC and was to host a series of Army

The transformed Army would have to be capable of both high- and low-intensity combat operations.

Transformation war games clustered under the label VIGILANT WARRIORS to test concepts and identify desired capabilities. The series borrowed heavily from the DYNAMIC COMMITMENT series of the first Quadrennial Defense Review and, like DYNAMIC COMMITMENT, featured simultaneous mixes of operations at various points along the combat spectrum. A series beginning in July 2001, for example, featured a conventional invasion of Azerbaijan, Chinese threats to a newly reunified Korea, Iranian operations against the Straits of Hormuz, insurgency in Indonesia, narco-terrorism in Colombia, outsized criminal syndicates in Albania, cyberattacks on the Federal Reserve, and a mix of imaginative terrorist attacks within the United States. The scenarios were set in 2019–2021, when eight of twenty divisions were Objective Force "Air Ground Task Forces." Predictably, the much-transformed Army of 2020 hammered the "Anfarian" invaders of Azerbaijan and arrived in time to face down the garrulous Chinese. Perhaps even more prescient, Red Team opponents playing against the Americans forced challenging transitions in operational tempo upon them. Forces in Sumatra, for example, jumped from humanitarian relief to peace enforcement to combat to post-combat operations to deployments elsewhere. Operations overlapped, forcing near continuous reliance on the reserve component. Terrorist attacks while operations overseas were under way embarrassed civil authorities since so many police, firefighters, and paramedics—"first responders"—were in the reserve component and already activated. The exercise identified pernicious shortages with respect to "high demand/low density" specialties that there never seemed to be enough of: linguists, civil affairs experts, psychological operators, military police, intelligence collectors, explosive ordnance disposal specialists, information operators, and others. The transformed Army's utter dependence on assured communications and access to space assets at every level of the combat spectrum was further underscored. The VIGILANT WARRIOR series did a creditable job of sustaining a broad focus as the Army imagined and sought to develop an Objective Force. It also laid groundwork for the next Quadrennial Defense Review, which ultimately went to Congress on 30 September 2001. Operating on the assumption that no decision made "inside the Beltway" (i.e., within the circumference of Highway 495 and thus within the National Capital Region) is ever permanent, Army planners found it prudent to reemphasize scenarios helpful during the first Quadrennial Defense Review wherein the presence of boots on the ground trumped easy technological solutions. This once again put the Army in the ambivalent position of seeking prudent technological advance while cautioning enthusiasts not to overrate the advantages of technology alone. The VIGILANT WARRIOR series did seek to be inclusive, transparent, and broadly visible. In addition to Army major commands, schools, and training centers, participants included sister services, joint commands, civilian "think tanks," intelligence agencies, allied nations, selected pundits, the National Security Council Staff, and the Departments of State, Defense, and Transportation.[7]

Army Transformation was to be program as well as policy. Each of the prongs on the Trident slide required a multiyear funding stream, generated through the give-and-take of the Planning, Programming, Budgeting, and Execution System (PPBES) and ultimately supported by the administration and Congress. Army Strategic Planning Guidance, a routinely promulgated formal institutional strategy, had to fit within the national strategy, national military strategy, and relevant planning, programming, and budgeting documents promulgated by the Department of Defense. To this end the Army Staff laboriously coordinated and produced a comprehensive Transformation Campaign Plan. The document fell roughly into two halves: a general discussion of philosophy, doctrine, timing, and phasing up front and specific tasks to each of dozens of Army leaders and agencies in the rear. The plan noted security trends drifting away from conventional warfare in the direction of such asymmetric threats as terrorists, insurgents, narco-traffickers, organized criminals, and rogue states armed with weapons of mass destruction. The Department of Defense had stipulated six goals for Transformation: protecting critical bases, projecting and sustaining forces, denying sanctuary, ensuring information systems, enhancing space systems, and leveraging information technology. The "pillars" of Transformation would be strengthened joint operations, wide-ranging science and technology, intelligence advantages, and new approaches to warfare. Operating within this Department of Defense framework, the Army developed twelve "lines of operation" to focus responsibility: Joint and Army strategy (concepts, requirements, and plans); modernization and recapitalization; manning the force and investing in quality people; managing Army readiness and training; training and leader development; Army doctrine; Operational Force design; command, control, communications, computers, intelligence, surveillance, and reconnaissance (C4ISR); deploying and sustaining; developing and acquiring advanced technology; management of force programs; and installations. Each of these lines of operation was explained in the text, and responsibilities toward them were specified in thirty-some pages of tasks to subordinates. The Training and Doctrine Command (TRADOC) commander, for example, was the proponent for training and leader development, Army doctrine, and Operational Force design, whereas the Army Materiel Command (AMC) commander was the proponent for developing and acquiring advanced technology. The Army operations and training officer (G–3) was to serve as "overall integrator and synchronizer," and the director of program analysis and evaluation (PA&E) had the unenviable mission of designing the funding strategy. The Transformation Campaign Plan coordinated myriad efforts across the breadth of the Army and identified the relative timing of key decisions that had to be made. Perhaps the most notable of these decision points was "FCS Milestone B," the point at which the technologies of the future combat system would be settled and concept testing would transition into system development. The plan called for FCS Milestone B in May 2003, the decision to transition from the Interim to the Objective Force in FY2008, and the fielding of the first Objective Force–capable unit in FY2010. Shinseki established a three-star Objective Force Task Force, headed by Lieutenant General John M. Riggs, to serve as "the single overarching integrating activity . . . that provides the direction, means and impetus for the Objective Force. . . ." By the time the Transformation Campaign Plan matured, the Objective Force Task Force was already heavily engaged in deliberations to bring major features of the Army After Next forward to serve in the Objective Force. This was still a somewhat distant target, however. The near target was the Interim Force and its constituent Interim Brigade Combat Teams.[8]

The Interim Brigade Combat Team

Of the three prongs of Shinseki's "Trident," the Interim Force was altogether new, yet Shinseki envisioned the first of its units, an Interim Brigade Combat Team, would be fielded during his watch. A two-brigade Initial Force training with legacy and surrogate equipment was to transition onto newly procured IAVs and be redesignated as the Interim Force in 2002. The first of these brigades was to achieve initial operating capability (IOC) in 2003. Given that the IAV had not yet been selected and most of the specific technological and organizational features of the Interim Brigade Combat Team were not yet agreed on, these objectives imposed an extraordinary timeline. Force development processes that customarily took years were to be compressed into months. The first Interim Brigade Combat Team, the 3d Brigade of the 2d Infantry Division, was in fact certified as ready to deploy in May 2003, after elaborate deployment exercises and back-to-back rotations through the National Training Center at Fort Irwin, California, and the Joint Readiness Training Center at Fort Polk, Louisiana.[9]

Although the Interim Brigade Combat Team was to be deployable more so than experimental, there was to be an experimental aspect to it. The first of the Interim Brigade Combat Teams would have to experiment with new vehicles, equipment, and doctrine to perfect themselves, and they would accumulate experience relevant to the Objective Force as they did so. Insofar as the IAV was a surrogate for the FCS, the Interim Brigade Combat Team would provide a test bed for the tactics, techniques, and procedures of the Objective Force. This could have led to an embarrassing surfeit of quasi-experimental units. When Shinseki assumed office, the 2d Armored Cavalry Regiment at Fort Polk, Louisiana, was already designated as the experimental Strike Force, pursuing the modularity, flexibility, and strategic mobility Shinseki's Interim Force envisioned. The brigades and several headquarters of the 4th Infantry Division at Fort Hood, Texas, were still the EXFOR, pushing along the technological appliqué of Force XXI. This herd of experimental units needed to be thinned. Fortuitously, the Strike Force had not yet advanced to the point of significant organizational or material change. Its conceptual underpinnings were applicable to both the Interim and the Objective Forces, so minimal ground was lost in shifting their initial point of application from Fort Polk to Fort Lewis, Washington. Fort Lewis was a better location for the administrative and logistical overhead and for the intermodal transportation access Shinseki associated with the first of the Interim Brigade Combat Teams. The 3d Brigade of the 2d Infantry Division and the 1st Brigade of the 25th Infantry Division, both at Fort Lewis, would be the first and second Interim Brigade Combat Teams. The 172d Infantry Brigade (Separate) in Alaska would be third, and the 2d Armored Cavalry Regiment shuffled to be the fourth in line. The situation with the 4th Infantry Division was more complex. It had served as EXFOR since 1995 and had accumulated substantial quantities of digital equipment and experience. One of its brigades, as we have seen, had maneuvered through National Training Center Rotation 97–06 in a full-up—albeit often surrogate—Force XXI digital appliqué panoply. Another of its maneuver brigades and its support brigades were substantially equipped with appliqué digital equipment. Most significantly, proof-of-principle exercises for the division as a whole and its interface with corps calendared out over the next two years. Force XXI was now to be Legacy Force, destined to upgrade digitally on already-fielded platforms without throwing off progress toward the Interim Force or the Objective Force. Tight choreography would be necessary to bring its desired capabilities to fruition. Division Capstone Exercise I (DCX I) at the National Training Center in April 2001 and Division Capstone Exercise II (DCX II) sprawling across much of Texas in October 2001 exercised the emergent digital Army Battle Command System over extended distances from the lowest levels through to a corps interface. Although significant issues remained with respect to training, bandwidth, maintenance, and durability, the results were sufficiently encouraging to declare victory. The 4th Infantry Division was declared deployable and assumed the Forces Command Division Ready Brigade (DRB) mission in November 2001. The 1st Cavalry Division was scheduled to convert to the Force XXI hardware and software in 2003, followed by other divisions in turn. Force XXI was now a stipulated posture that units, when funded, would roll over into. It was no longer an experiment—although considerable experimentation and technical development remained to be done. These further improvements were to be incremental and evolutionary. The field was clear for the Interim Brigade Combat Team to serve as the leading edge of Army Transformation.[10]

An organizing principle of the Interim Brigade Combat Team was that its combat vehicles would be on a common chassis. This would radically reduce maintenance, repair parts, and logistical overhead while streamlining procurement. Downsized support requirements would in turn facilitate rapid deployment and reduce the unit's logistical footprint once deployed. Vehicle variants would serve as infantry carriers, reconnaissance vehicles, mortar carriers, antitank guided-missile platforms, engineer vehicles, ambulances, nuclear-biological-chemical surveyors, command posts, fire-support coordination centers, mobile direct-fire gun systems, and artillery platforms. This family of vehicles was to be of medium size, air transportable by the venerable C–130 and all larger cargo aircraft. This implied a weight of nineteen tons or less and not more than 13,000 pounds of axle weight. The integral armor was to be proof against 7.62-mm. armor-piercing ammunition, and add-on armor the crew could mount within two hours of landing was to be proof against 14.5-mm. armor-piercing ammunition and the ubiquitous RPG7 antitank rocket. This stipulation concerning add-on armor led to some confusion as developments progressed, concerning which more later. The IAV also had to be essentially "off-the-shelf" to meet Shinseki's ambitious timelines. Beginning in December 1999, the United States Army Armor Center at Fort Knox, Kentucky, hosted a "platform performance demonstration" to refine operational requirements documents for the IAV, survey the market with respect to near-term industrial possibilities, and anticipate required technology insertions. Thirty-five candidate platforms from eleven major contractors and over a half dozen countries hastily assembled at Fort Knox.[11] Army agencies examined and tested the systems with respect to on- and off-road mobility, day and night live fire, carrying capacity, tactical maneuverability in multiple training scenarios, logistical requirements, C–130 deployability, adaptability to multiple variations and technology insertions, and safety. Shinseki likened the kaleidoscopic mixture of vehicles and activities to the chaotic bar scene from the motion picture *Star Wars*, but there was at least one underlying theme: the recurrent historical competition between wheeled and tracked vehicles as combat platforms of intermediate weight. Wheels once again demonstrated themselves to be superior with respect to speed, gas mileage, noise, comfort, target acquisition on the move, and maintainability. Tracks once again proved themselves to be superior with respect to off-road mobility and turning radius. Traditionally off-road mobility had trumped all other considerations, but Shinseki, mindful of the full range of scenarios contemplated and his own Balkan experiences, made it clear that did not necessarily have to be the case this time. After almost a year of deliberation and evaluation, in November 2000 the Army announced its selection of the wheeled Light Armored Vehicle III (LAV III) competed by General Motors of Canada Ltd. and to be contracted to a partnership between General Motors and General Dynamics Land Systems. This did not sit well with some traditional armor advocates, tracked-vehicle enthusiasts, and the United Defense LP producers of the tracked M113A3. Even as the first brigades' worth of LAV IIIs were being fielded, these opponents mustered congressional support to force on the Army an elaborate side-by-side comparison of the two vehicles. Carefully observed by interested parties, the Army Test and Evaluation Command finally finished further field trials in January 2003, with results understandably similar to those of three years earlier. By that time the horse was pretty far out of the barn, and the M113A3 initiative succumbed—albeit not without further grumbling and criticism. A perhaps less weighty dialogue developed over what to name the newly acquired vehicle. After methodical deliberation, the Army's Center of Military History compiled a list of candidates and recommended the "Buford" in honor of Major General John Buford Jr. of Civil War fame. To the Center, Buford's brilliant performances at Oak Ridge, on the first day at Gettysburg, and elsewhere epitomized the dragoon-like qualities to which the mechanized Interim Brigade Combat Team aspired. Shinseki, when briefed, considered the recommendation thoughtful, but tone deaf. It was hard to imagine grizzled mechanized warriors swaggering around bragging about their "Bufords." He reached somewhat further down on the list and picked "Stryker" in honor of two unrelated Medal of Honor recipients. Private First Class Stuart S. Stryker (World War II) and Specialist Robert F. Stryker (Vietnam) epitomized extraordinary courage and selfless sacrifice, even if they had little to do with mounted or mechanized warfare. The Interim Brigade Combat Teams soon came to be known as the Stryker Brigades.[12]

The Army did not wait upon the selection and receipt of the Stryker to organize and train the first Interim Brigade Combat Team. The vehicle to be chosen was to be but a platform for Information Age technologies and for medium-weight units more adaptable to the full spectrum of combat—particularly at its lower end. On 9 November 1999, Shinseki appointed Major General James M. Dubik as TRADOC Deputy Commanding General for Transformation. Within a month implementing documents had been drafted and a Brigade Coordination Cell established at Fort Lewis to coordinate reorganizing and retraining the 3d Brigade of the 2d Infantry Division. Doctrine and a vision of the future force preceded the actual hardware with which it was to be equipped; Dubik anticipated the

General Dubik
(Photograph taken in late 1997.)

brigade would have its combat vehicles by the time it actually needed them. In the meantime, beginning in February 2000 the brigade made use of thirty-two LAV IIIs borrowed from the Canadian armed forces and other vehicles available locally to serve as surrogates for training. Before reorganizing, the 3d Brigade consisted of two Abrams tank battalions and a Bradley infantry battalion. Notable organizational changes from that point included transitioning to three infantry battalions; adding a reconnaissance, surveillance, and target acquisition (RSTA) squadron; and permanently assigning customary attachments of the supporting arms to the brigade combat team as organic units. A Bradley infantry fighting vehicle customarily has a three-man crew and theoretically can carry up to seven dismounts as well. At full strength a Bradley platoon fields twenty-seven dismounts and a Bradley company eighty-one. The envisioned interim armored vehicle was to have a crew of two and dismount nine. The mathematics would lead to 36 dismounts in a platoon and 108 in a company. Considering that the 3d Brigade was being reorganized to have three infantry battalions (nine companies) rather than one (three companies), the number of dismounts available leaped from 243 to 972—a 400 percent increase. Clearly the interim brigade combat team was as much about putting more "boots on the ground" in the uncertainties of the post–Cold War environment as it was about technological advance. Technological advance did remain central to the vision, however. The swarms of interim armored vehicles filling their various roles—and thus the infantrymen who rode in them—would be seamlessly linked together by a digital network that provided information on demand and continuously updated a common battlefield picture. This

General John N. Abrams observes a technology demonstration.

technological advantage peaked with the RSTA squadron. In addition to three reconnaissance troops mounted on a reconnaissance variant of the interim armored vehicle, the squadron also featured a composite military intelligence company with an unmanned aerial vehicle (UAV) platoon; a nuclear, biological, and chemical (NBC) reconnaissance platoon; and a potpourri of manned and unmanned sensors that grew and changed over time. As the digital network and the ability to detect the enemy progressed, advances were often first visible in the RSTA battalion. The 3d Brigade was further reorganized to have an organic artillery battalion and support battalion and an organic antitank company, engineer company, signal company, military intelligence company, and headquarters company as well. Former customary relationships transitioned into organic constituents at the company level as well; each line company received an antitank platoon and a mortar section. Transformation planners anticipated that a direct-fire mobile gun system and a 155-mm. artillery piece on the common chassis would trail the chosen interim armored vehicle by some years, so they opted for tube-launched, optically tracked, wire-guided (TOW) missile vehicles in the antitank platoons and a mixture of towed 155-mm. artillery and mortars for indirect fire. The reorganization envisioned a requirement for 309 interim armored vehicles overall, and an interim brigade combat team personnel strength of about 3,500. The brigade would displace about 13,000 tons and require the equivalent of 254 C–17 sorties to deploy, as opposed to about 30,000 tons and 480 sorties for the legacy brigade it was replacing. It would have somewhat fewer vehicles and several times the dismounted strength of its predecessors.[13]

Dubik and his Brigade Coordination Cell improvised a training regime for the Interim Brigade Combat Team even as the 3d Brigade of the 2d Infantry Division was reorganizing into its new configuration. The reorganization itself took time, of course, as hundreds of tankers departed, considerably more infantrymen arrived, and supporting arms experienced similar turbulence on a smaller scale. The reconfigured brigade was on the ground beginning in May 2000 but had none of the combat vehicles and relatively little of the digital equipment envisioned. Initial training documents were drafts hastily conjured up by the Brigade Coordination Cell to transform doctrinal vision into materials concrete enough to train troops with. Beginning in April, these were superseded by TRADOC publications that had been more thoroughly staffed. As training progressed lessons learned fed back into nearly continuous revisions of tactics, techniques, and procedures. Training plans and documents understandably had a whiff of the provisional about them, a characteristic that reflected the prototypical nature of the organization being trained and its heavy reliance on surrogate equipment when in the field. The selection of the LAV III as the interim armored vehicle in November certainly helped solidify thinking, but for some time there would not be enough on hand for other than small unit training—which companies rotated through. For all of the improvisation, the Brigade Coordination Cell did have a vision of the direction the brigade was to go in, and TRADOC had had at least a decade of experience electronically simulating training experiences it could not produce in fact. Digital capabilities accumulated more quickly than vehicles or equipment, and simulated operations evolved through increasing levels of scale and complexity. These culminated in a brigade-wide Battle Command Training Program (BCTP) Warfighter exercise (WFX) in September 2001. By this time newly fielded light digital Tactical Operations Centers (TOCs) were on hand for the headquarters and in constituent units. The Warfighter proofed all of this digital connectivity while exercising doctrine and training packages. Technologies not yet on hand were simulated, and the brigade operated in the context of an I Corps scenario. In April 2002 the Army received the first of its newly named and manufactured Strykers. From that point the use of surrogates and simulations decreased as troops increasingly trained with equipment their tables of organization envisioned. Field training at Fort Lewis and Yakima was complemented by rotations through the National Training Center and Joint Readiness Training Center. Joint Forces Command sponsored Exercise MILLENNIUM CHALLENGE 2002, which prominently featured contingents of Strykers strategically delivered by various means of transportation, to include C–130s. As practical experience with the Stryker accumulated, TRADOC committed to finalized field manuals and regulations: those governing the company in January 2003, those governing the brigade in March, and those governing the battalion in April. During the period 4 March through 28 May 2003, the 3d Brigade, 2d Infantry Division—by now often called Stryker Brigade Combat Team One, or SBCT 1—undertook its most exhaustive training yet. Deployment exercises on every conceivable means of transportation, to include tractor trailer, rail, C–5, C–17, C–130, and the fast sealift ship *Bellatrix,* spanned the entire period. Within the period the brigade conducted a full-up fire and maneuver rotation through the National Training Center 1–11 April and through the Joint Readiness Training Center 17–27 May. Every effort was made to replicate the full spectrum of conflict, give the brigade multiple missions at the same time, spread operations across extended distances, and stress digital connectivity. In the aftermath of this rigorous proofing, TRADOC declared SBCT 1 deployable. Less than two months later, the Vice Chief of Staff of the Army then acting as Chief, General Jack Keane, announced that it would soon deploy to Iraq.[14]

When General Shinseki retired in June 2003, he could take considerable pride in the Stryker Brigade Combat Team that had evolved from a mere concept to a practical reality during the four short years of his tenure as Chief of Staff. The organization and its doctrine, training, and equipment were all new. The Army as a whole was not yet altogether certain what it had gained,

The Interim Brigade Combat Team at the National Training Center, April 2003

however. At an Army Staff meeting in 2002 General Keane, a paratrooper by provenance who had commanded the 101st Airborne Division and the XVIII Airborne Corps—and perhaps had seen the motion picture *A Bridge Too Far* yet another time—asked the Chief of Military History for a "think piece" concerning what would have happened if an Interim Brigade Combat Team (IBCT) had been available to the Allies at Arnhem in 1944. Faithfully reconstructing the historical scenario and acquiring assistance from mathematical modelers to represent the weapons systems involved at a common level, the Center came to the not particularly flattering conclusion that with its greater battlefield awareness the IBCT would have had the good sense to flee to the south bank of the Rhine as soon as it detected two panzer divisions lurking in the woods northeast of Arnhem, taking the British 1st Airborne Division with it. Arnhem would still have been a bridge too far, but it would not have cost 7,500 paratroopers to prove it. Some, although certainly not General Keane, considered the Center disloyal for not having had the IBCT dispatch the German opposition with a single stroke. Close quarters combat with heavy armor and massed artillery was precisely the wrong fight for the IBCT, the historians replied. Until the technologies of the Objective Force matured, the Legacy heavy divisions would be responsible for such a fight, with the IBCTs as useful auxiliaries. The IBCTs also had not displaced the Legacy airborne and air assault divisions with respect to early entry. Critics groused that the Stryker did not roll off a C–130 fully combat-loaded and with its guns blazing. Only four of eleven infantrymen could accompany the Stryker on the C–130, it took a few minutes to remount antennas and remote weapons systems upon landing, and it took a few hours to mount the add-on armor required to defeat munitions above 7.62-mm. and rocket-propelled

208

grenades (RPGs). Strykers airlifted by C–130s were feasible for the second wave of an airfield takedown, but not the first. If it was unwise to pit Strykers hull-to-hull against tanks or to drop them onto airfields still under enemy control, it was also flawed logic to perceive them as merely "peacekeepers." A Stryker battalion's firepower dwarfed that of its light or airborne counter-parts, yet the prospects of successfully deploying it to an austere setting were appreciably better than those of a heavy battalion. Given enough space to take full advantage of its tactical mobility and information infrastructure, the Stryker could show its considerable strengths to best effect. Some whiff of this potential came across in the several National Training Center rota-tions of 2002 and 2003. The opposing force (OPFOR) of the 11th Armored Cavalry Regiment came to be wary of the Stryker Brigade's unpredictable tactical dispositions. Familiar with Bradley infantry, they theretofore only had to find the tracked vehicles to ascertain the entirety of a mechanized Blue Force's battle plan. The Strykers carried far more infantry and with their greater mobility were far more prone to deposit them to distant points and to recover them later. Undetectable dismounted ambushes became a huge risk to the OPFOR, as did the hybridization of heavy and light characteristics in the same organization. At the time the "dominant knowledge" Information Age technologies of the Stryker Brigade Combat Team were still not entirely reliable or mature. The questions "where am I" and "where are my buddies" were being answered more reliably than ever, but the question "where is the enemy" remained problematic. Technical delays, equipment malfunctions, processing times, and OPFOR subterfuge combined to continue the fog of war. On the plus side, the Stryker Brigade had the firepower to fight for information if it needed to, could fall back on traditional radio communica-tions to fill holes in the shared operational picture, and recognized that there was a huge capacity for further growth inherent in the digital equipment rattling around in its vehicles. The 3d Brigade of the 2d Infantry Division, now deployable, would experience this further growth on the battlefield.[15]

9-11 and Homeland Defense

At 0846 Eastern Daylight Time on 11 September 2001, American Airlines Flight 11 smashed into the 96th floor of the New York World Trade Center's North Tower. Sixteen minutes later United Airlines Flight 175 slammed into the 80th floor of the South Tower. Thousands of gallons of aviation fuel spewed into the buildings and ignited into firebombs nearing 2,000 degrees Fahrenheit. Hapless survivors caught above the strikes sought rooms free of smoke and debris or made their way to the roofs in the hopes of rescue; those below the strikes fled the buildings in an ever-growing stream. Hundreds of policemen and firemen rushed the other way, striving to clear the buildings and bring out as many alive as possible. Thousands of tons of concrete, steel, and furnishings above the points of impact proved too much for the weak-ened structures to bear. At 0959 the South Tower collapsed, and within thirty minutes the North Tower collapsed as well. Buildings 110 stories high had been reduced to 150 feet of rubble. Shortly before the South Tower collapsed,

The World Trade Center, above, *and the Pentagon,* below, *were attacked on 11 September 2001.*

American Airlines Flight 77 roared into the western face of the Pentagon. Here the resultant firebombs were as severe, but the squat compartmented structure resulted in considerably less destruction. Somewhat later United Airlines Flight 93 crashed into a field near Shanksville, Pennsylvania. It seems the passengers had heard of the fates of the other aircraft by cellular telephones, and Flight 93 went down in the midst of a struggle between passengers and crew and the hijackers to gain control. A total of 2,435 civilians, 343 firemen, and 23 policemen died in the World Trade Center; 125 employees and servicemen died in the Pentagon in addition to those aboard the plane; and 40 passengers and crewmen died aboard Flight 93. The United States had been attacked on its own soil. Americans had a new date that would live in infamy, "9-11."[16]

Within a few days the identity of the attackers was known. Five-man (except in the case of Flight 93, which seems to have been one short) teams of terrorists affiliated with Osama bin Laden's shadowy "World Islamic Front for Jihad Against the Jews and Crusaders" had smuggled plastic weapons aboard each aircraft and overwhelmed the crews. They then substituted one of their own for the pilots and converted each massive jetliner into a suicide bomb. Osama bin Laden was the eleventh child in a family of fourteen children, his family being among the wealthiest in Saudi Arabia. He was a veteran of the Afghan resistance to the Soviet occupation (1979–1989) and reputedly supported by a personal fortune of over $300 million. Over time he had developed the organization al-Qaeda as a personal following dedicated to replacing the pro-Western Saudi government with an anti-Western Islamic state, the withdrawal of American troops from Saudi Arabia, and the recovery of Jerusalem from Israel. The World Islamic Front for Jihad Against the Jews and Crusaders also seems to have included *Al-Gama'a Al-Isamiyya* committed to establishing an Islamist state in Egypt, *Al-Ittihad al-Islami* dedicated to establishing an Islamic state in Somalia and expelling Western influences, *Abu Sayyaf* seeking Islamic autonomy in Mindanao, *Harakut ul-Ansar* seeking to liberate Jammu and Kashmir from India, and a "Movement for Islamic Change" that had seven other aliases and presumptively anti-American goals. The actual relationships and working mechanics among these organizations remained unclear, as did their strengths, capabilities, and resources. It seemed that even smaller splinter groups had broken off from earlier revolutionary organizations and established clusters of ultraradical compartmentalized cells. This secretive cellular structure made detection more difficult, and the compromise of one cell did not necessarily compromise others. "Traditional" Islamic organizations identified as terrorist, such as *al-Fatah*, *Hezbollah*, or *Hamas*, had tended to have a geographical focus and recruited locally from not particularly cosmopolitan sources of manpower. Al-Qaeda, on the other hand, was able to recruit and inspire operatives familiar with air travel, cellular phones, computers, the Internet, the Muslim diaspora residents throughout Europe and the Americas, and languages used on those continents. The World Islamic Front for Jihad Against the Jews and Crusaders may have had diverse objectives, but those within it viewed the United States as a central impediment to achieving them. The Twin Towers were not only a symbol of the wealth and pride of the United States but also a symbol of the secularized, liberal capitalist global economic community that had been an objective of American foreign policy for generations—and of pro-Western regimes within the Islamic World that cooperated with it. Almost five hundred—more than one in five—of the dead at the World Trade Center were from more than eighty nations other than the United States. Contingents from such leading financial institutions as Switzerland's Credit Suisse Group, Germany's Deutsche Bank, and Japan's Dai-Ichi Kangyo Bank perished in the catastrophe. For the United States Army, and for Army Transformation, the 9-11 attacks substantially altered the operational paradigm. Since 1991 the Army had been transforming on the assumption that it was between wars. Now it was at war. Defense planners had dutifully catalogued terrorism along with such other threats as drug traffic, humanitarian crises, and rogue state use of weapons of mass destruction in lists of the challenges for which the nation had to prepare. Now terrorism dwarfed all else on the list and in the national psyche, and a "Global War on Terrorism" commenced. That war, or at least its most recent episode, had begun on American soil. Homeland Defense now numbered among the highest priorities for the transforming Army.[17]

Homeland Defense involves the National Guard, by definition. When not in federal service, the National Guard is heir to the militia tradition of organized forces readily available to state governors under duress. As news of the attack on the World Trade Center spread, New York Guardsmen gathered in their armories, many without notification. This informal mobilization was well under way when New York Governor George Pataki declared a state of emergency, and his Adjutant General ordered 8,000 Guardsmen to state active duty. By the evening of 11 September, 1,500 Guardsmen were already on duty amid the wreckage of the World Trade Center, or at Ground Zero as the site soon came to be called. The balance of the 8,000 was en route to duty stations nearby. The catastrophe pressed the New York City police to the limit with respect to security and traffic control, roles the Guardsmen immediately undertook. Missions expanded to include debris removal and marking, providing and coordinating transportation, medical support, mess support, shelter and lodging, mail delivery, and escort. Individual Guardsmen provided specialized skills with respect to civil engineering, stress management, financial management, and other unique capabilities. Units were also called upon to provide honor guards for memorial services. At the Pentagon, Maryland and Virginia National Guardsmen served in some numbers, but the mix providing military support to civilian authority was different than in New York. The catastrophe at the Pentagon was at least an order of magnitude less than that in New York, and collateral responsibilities to manage the disaster were more in line with the capabilities of local firemen, police, paramedics, and rescue personnel who rushed to the scene. The Pentagon was on federal property and mustered considerable resources of its own from the Military District of Washington. Patches of open ground west of the Pentagon were organized for triage, treatment, and emergency medical response. Casualties were evacuated, personnel accountability established, survival assistance officers appointed, and families notified. About one-tenth of the building was sealed off as unusable and as

National Guardsmen on duty at "Ground Zero" soon after the attacks

a crime scene. The rest of the building returned to duty. Soldiers from the Military District of Washington procured an outsized twenty-by-forty-foot American garrison flag from nearby Fort Myer and draped it over the wound in the building. Passing motorists were cheered by this act of defiance; soon American flags were prominently displayed all over the country in an out-pouring of patriotic solidarity and indignation. On the first day of the Global War on Terrorism the Army stepped into a role somewhat different than its transformative efforts had theretofore focused on. Humanitarian relief and the immediate security of American citizens and vital infrastructure trumped other priorities. Americans and their Army reacted to the catastrophic attack and absorbed what had happened to them.[18]

Attention soon turned from the disaster sites to the larger issue of defending the nation as a whole. The Department of Defense launched Operation NOBLE EAGLE to defend the homeland and facilitate recovery from the attacks. Combat air patrols prowled the skies above New York and other major cities, coordinated by Airborne Warning and Control System (AWACS) aircraft that soon included a North Atlantic Treaty Organization (NATO) contingent in their number. On the ground, Army National Guardsmen fanned out to secure 444 airports considered the most vulnerable to further attacks. Most of these Guardsmen remained under state control, but a further 35,000 were called to federal service to augment security at military bases, ammunition storage sites, and other federal facilities. The Guardsmen were joined by more than 14,000 of their Army Reserve brethren also called to active service. These too provided a ready supply of organized manpower to augment the security of critical sites. They were a reservoir of technical, administrative, and combat service support skills now much in demand. As national and local leaders fathomed the implications of the 9-11 attacks, requirements increased. Guardsmen under state control were dispatched to secure bridges, tunnels, rail stations, dams, power plants, waterways, and harbors. Understandably, nuclear power plants assumed particular prominence among community concerns. The Army Corps of Engineers directly employed over 26,000 military and civilian professionals and routinely contracted the services of 150,000 more. Now it bumped up security, much of it contracted, for its mammoth continent-spanning responsibilities: over 12,000 miles of waterways, over 300 major commercial seaports and 600 lesser harbors, 383 major reservoirs, 276 locks, 75 hydropower plants of its own and 67 nonfederal hydropower plants colocated at its dams, and twelve million acres of forest and watershed. The Canadian border, not high as a defense priority since the early nineteenth century, suddenly was significant again. Cells linked to al-Qaeda reputably operated out of Montreal, and the open border now seemed recklessly vulnerable. About 12,000 cargo trucks a month passed through Vermont's Highgate Springs border crossing along Interstate 89, for example, along with tens of thousands of automobiles. Guardsmen hastily reinforced the U.S. Customs Service at border crossings, relieving agents who were already putting in sixteen-hour shifts. Quaint back roads that routinely had been protected by nothing but a sign now were National Guard outposts. The Mexican border, as we have seen, was already under considerable military-assisted surveillance because of the "War on Drugs." Now Joint Task Force–6 (JTF-6) and related Defense agencies expanded their portfolios to provide increased attention to prospective terrorism. An additional 1,500 soldiers deployed to assist the U.S. Border Patrol, the U.S. Customs Service, and the Immigration and Naturalization Service. As time went on, officials newly mindful of terrorism sought and obtained additional security for highly visible events. The Utah Olympic Public Safety Command, for example, procured an increase from 1,000 to 5,000 in the National Guardsmen serving at the 2002 Winter Olympics. The Army Reserve's 310th Chemical Company, one of the Army's two Biological Integrated Detection System (BIDS) companies, provided biological surveillance at this highly visible event. Throughout the country the Army was called upon to provide both raw, albeit organized, manpower and specialized technical skills in its military support to civilian authority.[19]

The initial infusions of Army manpower and resources into homeland security after the 9-11 attacks were hasty responses to an uncertain situation. As time went on more permanent arrangements were worked out. Operation NOBLE EAGLE continued scouring American skies, albeit with fewer planes in the air and more on ten-minute alert at over two dozen air bases around the country. The massive task of airport security migrated to the newly organized Transportation Security Agency (TSA). It took some time for the fledgling organization to get under way, but as it did the National Guard presence at airports diminished and uniformed TSA agents took over. Within a few years' time some 50,000 of them secured and serviced over 450 airports and coordinated security for related rail and highway transportation as well. Security on federal property or for facilities deemed critical by governors likewise morphed over time to contracted personnel or to civilian agencies. Requirements for military manpower overseas escalated dramatically, as we shall see. In the absence of conscription it was vital to disengage deployable soldiers from routine local security within the United States. In November 2002 Congress passed legislation establishing the Department of Homeland Security. This new mega-agency subsumed the missions of almost two dozen other agencies in the largest reorganization of the federal government since the establishment of the Department of Defense in 1947. In due course the Department of Homeland Security directly employed 210,000 and undertook such monumental tasks as screening two million travelers daily and surveying for radiation more than 97 percent of the cargo inbound through American seaports. TSA worked for the Department of Homeland Security, as did the Coast Guard, Customs Service, Immigration and Naturalization Service, Federal Emergency Management Agency, Nuclear Incident Response Team, and many others. Responsibilities transferred from the Department of Defense portfolio were relatively modest: the National Biological Warfare Defense Analysis Center and the National Communications System. The presence of soldiers actively involved in Homeland Defense thinned, although they remained a ready reserve for surge requirements, natural disasters, or unanticipated contingencies. This reserve posture implied recurrent major commitments. Prior to the 9-11 attacks there was ample precedent for having 30,000 National Guardsmen providing natural disaster relief at one time, and the Global War on Terrorism did not set Mother Nature aside. Demands also surged in such special cases as the Winter Olympics, and the military skills fielded under the auspices of Joint Task Force–6 remained in demand. Local law enforcement agencies and other first responders demonstrated accelerated interest in training related to nuclear, biological, or chemical contamination, weapons of mass destruction, and mass casualty situations. Since the Domestic Preparedness Training Initiative of the Defense Authorization Act of 1997, local commanders had routinely provided such training as directed by and coordinated through the United States Army Forces Command (FORSCOM). With interest at an all-time high, these efforts redoubled. On balance, efforts to routinize Homeland Security for the long-term demands of the Global War on Terrorism tended to free up military manpower for deployments overseas and to commit it to a reserve status for crises at home. This proved timely, as requirements overseas escalated dramatically.[20]

The newly intense interest in Homeland Security transcended the threat of terrorism alone and imparted further momentum to programs already under way with respect to missile defense, securing space assets, and cybersecurity. Secretary of Defense Donald Rumsfeld had been intensely interested in missile defense when he assumed office. One of his first acts was to reorganize the Missile Defense Agency and redirect its focus to achieving a single, layered ballistic missile defense system fully integrating ground, sea, air, and space assets—eliminating redundancy where circumstances required. Eliminations of redundancy could put service programs at risk, of course. For the Army,

Missile defense remained an important priority for Army Transformation.

Rumsfeld's emphasis increased priority accorded to developing the next generation of ground-based midcourse missile interceptors, already one of the most mature of the developing ballistic missile defense technologies. The 9-11 attacks reinforced anxieties concerning potential strategic surprises of many types. The Joint Theater Air and Missile Defense Organization accelerated its efforts to define a concept of operations that melded service, theater, and strategic assets into a seamless joint global architecture. For the Army relevant systems included the emerging Medium Extended Air Defense System (MEADS) and the Patriot Advanced Capability3 (PAC3). The Army was also heavily invested in a suite of capabilities associated with the Joint Land Attack Cruise Missile Defense Elevated Netted Sensor System (JLENS) that used networks of high-level sensors to cue enemy cruise missiles for destruction by the formidable PAC3. Some cost cutters perceived the Army's PAC3 as in competition with the Navy's Aegis and the MEADS as in competition with Air Force alternatives. The post 9-11 environment mellowed cost cutting, however, and reversed whatever willingness there had been to take strategic risks. Now it seemed no service initiative needed be eliminated; multiple systems were complementary, not competitive. Briefing slides, collegially developed by representatives from all services, evolved the terms *integrated* and *layered* to mean valuable assets nested comfortably under elaborate matrices of bubbles, each bubble representing the firing arc of a different air or missile defense weapon—the sum of which came to be all of the weapons under development at the time. Protection that might have been considered gold-plated several months before seemed prudent now. The glue holding this architecture together was reliable communications, much of it space based. The physical protection of space assets emerged as a doctrinal priority, but as a practical matter kinetic attacks in space any time soon seemed unlikely. Only Russia and perhaps China had such capabilities, and little suggested that they were an immediate threat. Cyber-attack seemed more likely, and this threat inspired an even greater interest in cybersecurity. The Department of Defense had recently weathered an expansive cyber-scare in its preparations for "Y2K"—the Year 2000. It seemed that the transition to a year that ended in three zeros, and certain collateral oddities such as the Julian date 90909, might stress out unprepared systems dependent on binary codes. Preventative programs progressed amid public fanfare, to include a made-for-television movie in which computers rendered berserk by undigestable digits destroyed urban civilization amid spectacular special effects. Prospective consequences briefed to Army leaders were somewhat more modest: unlivable buildings without temperature controls, toilets that would not flush, phones that would not work, and a command and control system that collapsed back into messengers and short-range radio communications. The Army spent $600 million proofing over 1,200 sprawling systems in a five-phase remediation process. In the course of this it actually inventoried all of the computers it had accumulated over time and forced commanders into an awareness of where their computers were and why they had them. This tightened the grip of the Army's Chief Information Officer (G–6) in evolving and protecting information management. Information operations (IO) training expanded to include a robust portfolio of courses dealing with computer security, hacking, detecting intrusions, and incident response. The National Guard took the lead for several aspects of military computer defense and stood up computer emergency response teams (CERTs) in every state to defend against intrusions on both state and federal systems. Post 9-11 Homeland Security measures were galvanized by the terrorist acts but went well beyond terrorism in the threats they addressed.[21]

The post 9-11 emphasis on terrorism and Homeland Security affected Army Transformation, but it did not alter it altogether. Before 9-11 Army planners consistently catalogued a long list of challenges in defining capabilities the future Army would need, and these challenges invariably included terrorism and a variety of threats to the continental United States. This broad appreciation of risks was echoed by others. Indeed, the report of the 1998–2001 U.S. Commission on National Security/21st Century, chaired by former Senators Gary Hart and Warren B. Rudman, downplayed conventional threats, presciently recommended a "National Homeland Security Agency," and recommended that Homeland Security become the primary mission of the National Guard—with reorganization, retraining, and reequipping to follow. Army Transformation efforts balked at so radical a realignment, in theory pursued a more balanced full-spectrum force, and in practice continued to develop and field forces that would show best toward the upper levels of the combat spectrum. Immediate post 9-11 deployments thrust the National Guard and Army Reserve into the middle of things with respect to Homeland Security, although over time civilian agencies resumed the lead with Army units in auxiliary, backup, and reserve roles. Certain specialized contributions remained uniquely military, interagency cooperation became more expected and more pervasive than ever, and the thresholds at which local and community leaders called for and expected military support to civilian authority had been permanently lowered. Command relationships altered with the circumstances. The Army had long been the executive agent for Department of Defense relationships with the Federal Emergency Management Agency, and immediately after the 9-11 attacks was appointed Department of Defense executive agent for Homeland Security pending a review of the Unified Command Plan. In due course the review of the Unified Command Plan recommended restructuring and the establishment of the United States Northern Command (USNORTHCOM) to command and control Department of Defense Homeland Defense efforts and coordinate military support to civilian authority nationwide. This command stood up on 1 October 2002. USNORTHCOM would have a three-star National Guard Deputy Commander, recognition of the ever larger and increasingly complex role the National Guard played in its responsibilities. This mirrored further growth in the roles played by the National Guard and Army Reserve overall—at home and abroad. In 2000 the Director of the Army National Guard and Chief of the Army Reserve were both major generals, equivalent in rank to the Assistants to such Deputy Chiefs of Staff as those for Operations and Plans, Logistics, Intelligence, or Personnel. By the end of 2001 they were lieutenant generals, equivalent to the Army Staff principals within each of those venues. Inevitably, momentum developed toward the appointment of a National Guard four-star general, empowered to represent the diverse roles and unique interests of Guardsmen at the highest levels of the Department of Defense. The Guard, Army Reserve, and Army Transformation were in the process of accommodating new expectations with respect to Homeland Security at the same time that they undertook combat requirements overseas unprecedented for an American volunteer army.[22]

Transforming While at War

Osama bin Laden and al-Qaeda bore responsibility for the 9-11 attacks, but their base of operations was nested in Afghanistan under an umbrella of security provided by that country's fanatic Taliban regime. Striking back at al-Qaeda required invading Afghanistan. The Taliban were fierce Islamic fundamentalists who seized power in bloody fighting following the withdrawal of Soviet forces in 1989. They were primarily drawn from the country's Pashtun majority, and active resistance to them broke out along largely ethnic lines. A Northern Alliance of Tajiks, Uzbeks, and Hazaras controlled about 10 percent of the country and fought against Taliban repression. Taliban leaders surrounded themselves with a core of experienced fighters, about 20,000 all told, to which volunteers and conscripts were added to perhaps triple their numbers as the need arose. This capability was considerably reinforced by foreign fighters present as "guests" who shared the regime's ideology. Of these 7,000 Pakistanis were the most numerous and 3,000 multinational al-Qaeda the most formidable. An American air and missile campaign, the opening phase of Operation ENDURING FREEDOM beginning 7 October, had little effect. The Taliban themselves presented few targets worthy of strategic bombing and seemed largely indifferent to hardships that might be visited on the Afghan people. Campaign ineffectiveness changed dramatically beginning 19 October, when twelve-man Special Forces Operational Detachment A teams began arriving by helicopter to assist the Northern Alliance (*Map 3*). About three hundred such soldiers deployed: eighteen A teams, four B teams (company level), and three C teams (battalion level). The Special Forces detachments radically altered tactical circumstances on the ground. The Taliban had some decrepit Soviet heavy equipment that they maintained and used poorly but generally relied on militia infantrymen armed with assault rifles, rocket-propelled grenades, and machine guns speeding around the countryside in pickup trucks. The Northern Alliance was similarly equipped, albeit somewhat more tribal and thus more capable of traditional Afghan long-range sniping. The A teams arrived with global positioning systems (GPSs), laser designators, advanced optics, and satellite communications. When embedded with and assisted by Northern Alliance forces, they could precisely locate Taliban targets and call in air strikes on them. The American inventory of precision-guided munitions now included large numbers of Joint Direct Attack Munitions (JDAMs)—cheap, GPS-guided, and appropriate for pouring out of numerous high-flying B–52 bombers—in addition to more expensive laser-guided missiles generally fired from nimbler fighter-bombers. The unarmored Taliban were horribly exposed to munitions fragmentation when their positions were known, and the combined efforts of Northern Alliance militiamen and Special Forces teams saw to it that their positions were found. In seventy-six days of fighting 6,500 strike missions expended 17,500 munitions, with horrific effects. The Northern Alliance speedily regained the territories traditionally inhabited by Tajiks, Uzbeks, and Hazara and advanced on Kabul. The revolt spread to the Pashtun south with the intervention of expatriates Hamid Karzai and Gul Agha Sharzai, both of whom benefited from Special Forces A teams as they raised and deployed their forces. The Taliban fled, and the various leaders—warlords—who had united against them set about consolidating their collective grip on the country. After considerable negotiation and appreciable United States and United Nations involvement, Hamid Karzai was sworn in as the prime minister of an interim government of Afghanistan on 22 December 2001.[23]

By the time Karzai was sworn in, the easy romp through Afghanistan was over. The tiny Special Forces contingents had been potent auxiliaries, but they exerted no real control on the ground. Afghan domestic warfare included considerable parleying, much of which progressed among the combatants without Americans being particularly aware. Fighting could be vicious and retaliations gruesome, but consanguine consciousness and local deal making

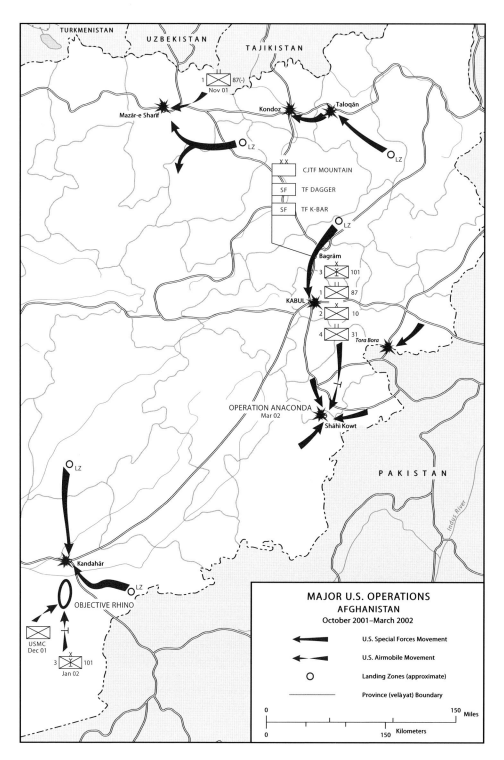

TURKMENISTAN
UZBEKISTAN
TAJIKISTAN

1 ☒ 87(-)
Nov 01

Mazār-e Sharif
Kondoz
Taloqān

○ LZ

○ LZ

XX CJTF MOUNTAIN
SF TF DAGGER
SF TF K-BAR

○ LZ

Bagrām
3 ☒ 101
1 ☒ 87
KABUL
2 ☒ 10
4 ☒ 31
Tora Bora

OPERATION ANACONDA
Mar 02
Shāhī Kowt

PAKISTAN

Indus River

○ LZ

Kandahār

○ LZ

OBJECTIVE RHINO

USMC
Dec 01

3 ☒ 101
Jan 02

MAJOR U.S. OPERATIONS
AFGHANISTAN
October 2001–March 2002

⬅ U.S. Special Forces Movement

← U.S. Airmobile Movement

○ Landing Zones (approximate)

— Province (velàyat) Boundary

0   150 Miles

0   150 Kilometers

Map 3

*Early operations in Afghanistan were dominated by special operations forces.
These were soon heavily reinforced by conventional units.*

softened many blows. As Kandahar fell Taliban leader Mohammed Omar and hundreds of his adherents vanished unmolested into the night, clearing the way for Karzai's and Sharzai's triumphant fighters. American intelligence determined that Osama bin Laden and his adherents had fled into the Tora Bora mountains. Afghan allies picked their way carefully toward them through the rugged terrain. Deep cave complexes and extreme topographical relief limited the effectiveness of precision-guided munitions. Hundreds of al-Qaeda and Taliban do seem to have been killed, but even more—including Osama bin Laden himself—slipped mysteriously through the encirclement into nearby Pakistan. Some deals backfired. Northern Alliance militiamen advancing to secure ostensibly abandoned Konduz were ambushed by diehards, and a dozen *Mullahs* finalizing surrender terms in Mazar-e Sharif were gunned down by Pakistanis not party to the arrangements. Prisoner control was lax. Afghan prisoners often simply wandered away—after some kind of ransom, one suspects. Foreign prisoners took over the Quali Jangi fortress and the Kandahar hospital in spectacular revolts. Concerns for anarchy led to an increasing infusion of American conventional forces. Marines secured an airfield south of Kandahar. The 10th Mountain Division, then based in Uzbekistan, sent troops to assist in the bloody suppression of the Quali Jangi uprising. Units fanned out to secure critical facilities in Kabul, prisoner screening and holding areas, and Bagram Airfield. The headquarters of

221

the 10th Mountain Division moved to Bagram Airfield and assumed control over conventional U.S. ground forces in the country. Beyond securing a few key facilities, the Americans focused on pursuing al-Qaeda and the diehard Taliban who might still be with them. The victorious Afghan warlords were generally agreeable to this modest presence and purpose. The Americans were operating along the sparsely populated Pakistani border distant from Afghan population centers, and the al-Qaeda were, after all, foreigners. In February 2002 allied intelligence identified an enemy concentration estimated at two hundred fighters concentrating in the Shahi Kowt Valley. Major General Franklin "Buster" Hagenbeck, commander of the 10th Mountain Division, resolved to take the battle to the enemy in Operation ANACONDA. Teams of special operators and battalions from the 10th Mountain and 101st Airborne Divisions infiltrated or helicoptered in to surround Shahi Kowt and isolate the battlefield with concentric rings of blocking positions. A largely Afghan main attack was to push in from the west, flushing the enemy into the kill zones of the blocking positions. Intelligence had been flawed. The enemy numbered closer to a thousand, were well dug in and heavily armed, and intended to fight. Overcoming initial surprise and confusion, the allies piled on, eventually bringing 1,200 American soldiers, 2,000 friendly Afghans, and 200 Australian, Canadian, Danish, German, and Norwegian special operators into the fight. They battered their adversaries in fierce fighting, killing about half of them. The other half seems to have escaped into other mountain hideouts or into Pakistan. Combat in Afghanistan became a continuing round of patrolling and raids as the allies sought to grind down the remnant al-Qaeda and Taliban.[24]

Al-Qaeda, although based in Afghanistan, had worldwide connections. The 9-11 attackers had moved fluidly through communities of the Muslim diaspora in Europe and the Americas. The immediate fear was that there were other cells, coordinating with or inspired by al-Qaeda, with further plans. Such fears soon came to fruition in spectacular attacks against Western tourists in Bali, Indonesia, and against housing complexes catering to foreign corporate employees in Saudi Arabia. Intelligence agencies, police forces, and security organizations scrambled to get ahead of this tide. Traditional allies and friends of the United States hastened to assist in an emerging campaign that featured diplomatic, financial, legal, public relations, law enforcement, intelligence sharing, and humanitarian aspects. Muslim nations wary of fundamentalist zealotry assisted as well. Even the Russians and Chinese, perhaps gratified that the United States now seemed less critical concerning their actions against extremists in Chechnya and Central Asia, were cooperative. Much of this worldwide activity was outside of the Army's sphere, but not all of it. Even as fighting in Afghanistan got under way 2,000 additional soldiers from the 1st Cavalry Division reinforced Kuwait, and an upgraded Exercise *Bright Star* was executed in Egypt with contingents from twelve countries. Security at facilities in Saudi Arabia, Qatar, and Oman was quietly reinforced, as were embassy contingents throughout the twenty-five-nation Central Command. Documents and prisoners captured in Afghanistan produced intelligence that enabled preemptive measures elsewhere. Police in Malaysia forestalled a planned attack based on information from Afghanistan, and such information similarly facilitated arrests in Pakistan, Uzbekistan, and Tajikistan. The United States Army, Europe (USAREUR), also played a role in Afghanistan, facilitating the deployment of allied soldiers to expanding NATO and United Nations contingents based in Kabul. Given its resources and geographical proximity, it carried much of the weight for the collateral humanitarian relief effort in Afghanistan. The Deployment Processing Center in Kaiserslautern palletized and shipped more than 2.4 million humanitarian rations, 2.3 million pounds of wheat, and 70,000 blankets in the early days of the campaign. USAREUR also tightened its security in Bosnia and Kosovo. In both cases the Muslim populations generally regarded the Americans as liberators, but extremist elements had accumulated in both communities during the course of the Balkan fighting. By this time the American presence in Bosnia was down to 2,000 soldiers and in Kosovo down to 4,000. A more robust NATO and allied presence remained, and the steadily improving communal police forces proved sufficient to head off whatever attacks might have occurred. On the other side of the world, in the Pacific, Joint Task Force 510 in the Philippines provided logistical, intelligence, and training support to the Philippine Army in its ongoing battle against the Islamic extremists of *Abu Sayyaf.* This conflict had waxed and waned for at least a century, but *Abu Sayyaf* had established demonstrable links to international terrorists recently and were funding operations through piracy, theft, and kidnapping for ransom. Elsewhere in the Pacific commanders implemented expanded force protection plans. Latin America seemed distant from the threat of Islamic terrorism, but even here attacks occurred, and intelligence sources surmised revenue streams connected to drug traffic coursing through the region. Cells associated with or were inspired by al-Qaeda, and the veneer between narco-trafficking and narco-terrorism was thin. The Global War on Terrorism was in fact worldwide, and the Army's involvement with it was worldwide as well.[25]

Lessons drawn or ostensibly drawn from operations in Afghanistan and elsewhere in the Global War on Terrorism would affect Army Transformation. Understandable euphoria pervaded the Department of Defense in the aftermath of the Taliban's speedy overthrow. Some characterized the victory as a new paradigm, witness to the success of small, highly nimble ground forces supported by technologically dominant air forces. Others cautioned that the Taliban militia had been matched by Northern Alliance militia and that American forces had delivered a margin that guaranteed victory rather than by achieving victory themselves. Somewhat less noticed than the tiny American presence on the ground when the Taliban was overthrown was the dramatic growth of American ground forces through the year following. Taliban hostility had threatened to be replaced by warlord anarchy. Geographical fiefdoms emerged: Ismail Khan around Herat, Abdul Rashid Dostum near Mazar-e Sharif, Fahim Khan and Bismullah Khan in the northeast, and so on. To secure vital facilities and maintain pressure on al-Qaeda and remnant Taliban—not of great interest to the warlords once they had regained control of their traditional haunts—U.S. and coalition ground forces in country climbed to 27,000 during 2002. These "boots on the ground" collaterally provided some diplomatic leverage as negotiators nudged the Afghan warlords toward accepting a unity interim government and participating in national elections. Afghanistan provided practical experience with emerging joint doctrine concerning speedily erecting combined and joint headquarters. In theory the Third Army was intrinsically capable of operating as a coalition and joint task force or as a coalition and joint land component command headquarters. In November 2001 Central Command (CENTCOM) designated it the coalition forces and joint land component command headquarters governing Afghanistan. Third Army set up in Camp Doha, Kuwait, and deployed the 10th Mountain Division (Light Infantry) headquarters to Karshi Khanabad, Uzbekistan, and then to Bagram Airfield to serve as its forward headquarters. To its credit, the 10th Mountain Division pulled together a motley assortment of brigades and battalions from other divisions, marines, special operating forces, allied contingents, Afghans, representatives of other services, and others in its planning for ANACONDA and subsequent operations. Execution was successful, albeit flawed, most notably in the case of ANACONDA. The digital communications revolution proved both a blessing and a curse. On the one hand, headquarters as disparate as Bagram (10th Mountain), Doha (Third Army), Miami (CENTCOM), Oman (Special Operating Forces Forward), and elsewhere (e.g., the service contingents other than ground) contributed to the planning and buildup with real-time responsiveness. On the other hand, these same headquarters generated overwhelming volumes of information and guidance—some of it conflicting—when things got hot. Everyone could talk with everyone else, and it seemed they did. Not everyone actually needed to know everything, however. There were too many cooks and too much information. Unforeseen debates concerning priorities and rules of engagement reflected service differences and interrupted operations. The most dramatic event of the battle, fierce fighting for Takur Ghar, particularly exemplified both courage under fire and botched communications. Hagenbeck's 10th Mountain Division headquarters maintained its grip and brought the battle to a successful conclusion, but his baffled staff wondered if it had not experienced a downside to the digital revolution. In the aftermath of the battle there were also recriminations concerning the adequacy of air support, concerning which, more later. Pundits could not help but notice that despite virtually every national intelligence asset having focused for days on the Shahi Kowt Valley, the resultant intelligence proved wrong. More than five times as many enemy as expected were in the battle area. They were dug in along ridgelines and in caves rather than huddled in the villages. They had evaded detection by hugging trees, hiding under dirt-colored blankets, or setting up in the shadows afforded by rugged relief. Their mortars and artillery would be more potent than that of the coalition in the opening phases of the battle. Most notably, their intentions had been misread. They did not flee; they fought. Success ultimately resulted from intelligence Hagenbeck's command fought for rather than downloaded. Shortcomings in the performance of high-tech "unblinking eyes" over the battlefield would give Army—and Defense—Transformers something more to ponder.[26]

Army and Defense Transformers had been pondering the limits of technology well before Shahi Kowt, of course. Contention on that subject, manifested in the Quadrennial Defense Review that reported out in 1997 (QDR1997), remained robust and lively during the Quadrennial Defense Review that reported out in 2001 (QDR2001). The services in general, and the Army in particular, followed up on QDR1997 with postmortems concerning staff and analytic performances and preparations for yet another round. The Army Staff, as we have seen, had ample reason to be proud of the QDR1997 results. The Office of the Secretary of Defense (OSD) had gone into QDR1997 with significant factions arguing that the Army should come down by two divisions to free up funds for modernization, yet the Army itself was to receive less than 10 percent of the modernization funds overall. In a fierce uphill battle the Army persuasively made a case that preserved its force structure, but advocates of shifting funds from personnel to modernization and from ground to air and naval forces remained influential in OSD and the sister services. No one understood these dynamics better than Shinseki, who had served as Deputy Chief of Staff for Operations and Plans (DCSOPS) during QDR1997, and thus been responsible for two-thirds of the functional areas surveyed—including force structure and force modernization. His after-action comments developed proposals in anticipation of QDR2001, advancing the notion that QDR preparations—especially relevant data collection—should be a never-ending process executed by customary staffs rather than quadrennial paroxysms by ad hoc organizations. When asked what the Army's major accomplishments in QDR1997 had been, Shinseki led with the observation that the Army retained the ability to control its destiny. Staff work, analysis, simulations game play, the artful exploitation of contractors, interactions with other services, and educational efforts in Congress and elsewhere had maintained the authoritativeness of the Army's voice within its purview. This in turn allowed the Army to pursue transformation along the lines it thought best. When Shinseki was Vice Chief of Staff he implemented his ideas concerning QDR preparations and this continued when he was Chief. Through the summer of 2000, QDR2001 looked like it was going to be an even better version of QDR1997. Strategic vision translated itself into an impressive mix of joint simulations conducted across the breadth of the combat spectrum, and Army participants persuasively established the importance of the Army each time. Comprehensive studies canvassed historians, defense theorists, conference attendees, and others to develop much the same point. An anticipatory "elevator speech" armed itinerant generals encountering targets of opportunity with materials to succinctly press home the Army's case: the essence of war has not changed, Army units are adaptable across the full spectrum of likely missions, boots on the ground are decisive, one soldier early is worth five soldiers late. Much of this represented repolishing materials worked during QDR1997. Indeed, wags at the Army's Center of Military History commented that it was easy to look like a genius when one kept being asked the same questions.[27]

This happy glide path toward QDR2001 was interrupted by the change of administrations and the arrival of the new Secretary of Defense, Donald H. Rumsfeld. Rumsfeld envisioned a revolution in military affairs that would diminish the role of manpower-intensive ground combat power, particularly that of the Army's heavy forces. His professional and business experiences were strongest with respect to airpower and missile defense. Rumsfeld arrived with a mandate from President George W. Bush to challenge the status quo inside the Pentagon, a mandate he readily embraced. He resolved to review and perhaps rework all that had gone before with respect to QDR2001, empowering OSD's Office of Net Assessment and its director, Andrew W. Marshall, to take a leading role in this review. Marshall had long championed the notion of a revolution in military affairs. His concepts with respect to networked systems, information dominance, remote sensors, and precision-guided munitions were congenial to Army Transformers and had figured in their designs thus far. The suggestions that the Army was overbuilt and that funds to support modernization could be harvested by reducing force structure were unwelcome to the Army, of course. This ground had been covered during QDR1997 and again in QDR2001 thus far, with the Army successfully arguing that the nation needed sufficient force structure to address a mixture of contingencies at all levels of the combat spectrum, that there would be no "timeouts" from the press of ongoing strategic responsibilities, and that no foreseeable technology offered "silver bullets" reliable enough to justify doing away with balanced combinations of arms. To many, Rumsfeld seemed dismissive of these previous analyses and perhaps of the opinions of the uniformed services as well. His personal deliberations proceeded within a narrow circle with considerable secrecy and minimal service participation. Services, particularly the Army, considered themselves in the process of transforming already and became anxious that they might lose control of their destinies. When Rumsfeld and Marshall briefed their findings to the service chiefs and others, they were coolly received even by those who would benefit the most, or suffer the least, from the results. Transformation as they described it seemed less of a program than an ideology: speed, flexibility, precision, "leap ahead" technology, and space-based assets. Ideologies are not necessarily right or wrong, but they are believed rather than proven. Rumsfeld's vision and the services' visions overlapped considerably, but the services had come to their opinions through painstakingly detailed staff collaborative processes and were suspicious of opinions less rigorously derived. Protocols governed service reactions, of course, but debate soon leaked outside the confines of the Pentagon. The Association of the United States Army and individual members of it, for example, openly criticized suggestions that the Army downsize. Someone inspired the majority of the House Armed Services Committee and dozens of other lawmakers to send Rumsfeld a letter decrying proposed reductions in Army force structure. Members of the Army "family" considered it undervalued, misunderstood, unheard, and aggrieved. Then 9-11 happened. Tens of thousands of soldiers were hastily dispatched to security responsibilities throughout the United States. Tens of thousands more were soon drawn into active operations overseas. Hundreds of thousands went to high states of alert, and President Bush declared the United States committed to a global war of unknown duration. Suddenly Army admonitions concerning unpredictable contingencies and full-spectrum requirements seemed prescient. High-tech solutions now seemed insufficient to secure all that was important. In the words of one commentator, the Army was "saved by reality." The immediate contention between the Army and OSD concerning QDR findings fizzled, and the work on it that had preceded the change of administrations was resurrected. QDR2001 results were reported to Congress with little fanfare, modest recommendations for change, and no further manpower cuts envisioned for the Army.[28]

The Army did enjoy one major triumph in advancing the ball from QDR1997 through QDR2001. Throughout QDR1997 the Army had made the case that "support to the nation" (military support to civil authorities) was so critical, recurrent, and consumptive of resources that it should be acknowledged as a component of the national military strategy. At the time the national "strategy" boiled down to maintaining forces sufficient to fight two major regional conflicts—broadly, against Iraq and North Korea—with enough left over for a few minor missions as well. This was not so much a strategy as a force-sizing mechanism, a role no longer being filled by the former Soviet threat. In the aftermath of QDR1997 the prestigious National Defense Panel criticized the two-war strategy as simplistic and as insufficiently mindful of unconventional challenges. The simulations and deliberations of QDR2001 reinforced a more nuanced strategic paradigm, abbreviated as "1-4-2-1." The first "1" was Homeland Defense, securing the United States of America. This was all that the Army had earlier described as support to the nation and more, with a major emphasis on weapons of mass destruction (WMD). Prior to 9-11 the priority accorded Homeland Defense was debatable; after 9-11 it was unquestionable. The "4" in the new strategic paradigm was to deter forward in four regions critical to the United States: Europe, Northeast Asia, the East Asian littoral, and the Middle East/Southwest Asia. Here American forward-deployed forces and forces appearing on a rotating basis would reassure allies and deter adversaries. The "2" in the new strategic paradigm was the capacity to swiftly defeat aggression in two overlapping major conflicts. It broadly carried forward the two major regional conflicts of QDR1997, with further comments and caveats. Of these caveats, the second "1" was the notion that rather than merely turning back both invaders, in one major regional conflict at a time the United States would be capable of inflicting a defeat so decisive it could result in regime change and occupation. In addition, the United States would maintain a rotational base capable of supporting a long-term mix of smaller contingencies, ensuring that specialized units appropriate to them were sufficiently numerous that none were overwhelmed by repetitive deployments. The formula 1-4-2-1 acknowledged complexity and reflected historical experience. The emphasis on Homeland Defense prioritized a wide range of Army programs, those of the National Guard and Army Reserve in particular. The "4" gave due recognition to Army responsibilities in Europe and such engagement programs as Partnership for Peace and to their equivalents in other regions. The concern for repetitive deployments particularly reflected a renewed appreciation of joint wartime executive agency responsibility (WEAR). The Army, for example, was executive agent for the surface movement of all supplies within a theater of operations—whether the supplies were going to air bases, Navy and Marine facilities, special operators, or the Army itself. This gigantic task ran up the probable deployment of Army transportation assets, regardless of the force mix on the ground. The Army was joint executive agent for a fistful of manpower-intensive functions. Reimer's initiative to track deployment personnel tempo (PERSTEMPO), followed up on by Shinseki, made the actual demands on "below the line units" (i.e., units not immediately visible in

227

the stipulated order of battle) apparent. Even before 9-11 such specialties as military police, civil affairs, water purification engineers, and special operators were well above proposed criteria for days deployed in a fiscal year. Pundits who had anticipated Army manpower reductions now hypothesized the Army would increase in size. QDR2001, like QDR1997, marked success for the platoons of staff officers and analysts who had made the Army's case.[29]

The Army may have deflected bureaucratic forays against its manpower, but it had less luck protecting its firepower. For some time the Army had worked toward replacing the aging M109 Paladin howitzer. During DESERT STORM the Paladin struggled to keep the nimbler M1 Abrams tanks and M2 Bradley fighting vehicles in range as they swept across the desert, a problem compounded by dependence upon even more antiquated wheeled transportation to bring ammunition resupplies forward. Beyond the set-piece battle along the international boundaries, tube artillery had little effect on the rest of the fighting. Pundits argued that the eclipse of tube artillery was not a problem, since aircraft armed with precision-guided munitions readily filled its role—not mentioning that DESERT STORM ground commanders generally kept air strikes well clear of their battle space out of a concern for fratricide. Operation ANACONDA rekindled Army anxieties concerning a lack of organic fire support. Manpower caps and the precedent of earlier operations against the Taliban led Hagenbeck's command to deploy with but a few light mortars initially. Airpower proved incapable of redressing this shortcoming, provoking angry recriminations in the heat of the moment: air-to-ground coordination took too long, air coverage was episodic, air strikes were ineffectual, the Air Tasking Order (ATO) was too hard to modify, debates over rules of engagement second-guessed the ground commanders, AC–130 gunships fled the battlefield with daylight, and so on. Embarrassingly, al-Qaeda's indirect fires seemed more effective than those of the Coalition on the first day, breaking up the (Afghan) main attack and delaying Coalition movements elsewhere. American forces were pinned down by a combination of direct and indirect fire. Five Apache helicopters fought bravely to redress the fire support imbalance, themselves being shot up so badly as to be grounded the second day. Initiative, tenacity, and reinforcements eventually turned the battle the Coalition's way. Upon analysis, ground commanders had little for which to blame the Air Force. The ATO was designed for a battle considerably different than the one that was fought. Air Force and Navy planes reconfigured as quickly as time and distance would allow and surged to average sixty combat sorties per day delivering over 2,500 bombs with impressive accuracy. A problem was that to be effective precision-guided munitions require precisely defined targets, a rare phenomenon on the convoluted and intermittently weathered-out ANACONDA battlefield. Al-Qaeda demonstrated the continuing value of "dumb" munitions for suppressive effects. Precision-guided munitions, even JDAMs, are too expensive for suppressing an imprecisely located enemy. Tube artillery and mortar rounds are cheap, ideal for deterring or distracting an unseen enemy one is maneuvering against. In Vietnam, another war fought with an elusive enemy, perhaps two-thirds of American indirect fires had been suppressive.[30]

The Army's twenty-first-century answer to the continuing need for suppressive fires was to be the 155-mm. Crusader self-propelled howitzer. The Crusader could pump up to ten aimed rounds a minute over forty kilometers. This was over twice the rate of fire and range of the venerable Paladin. Amazingly, the Crusader could compute and apply separate firing arcs for each of eight rounds in such a manner that all arrived at the same time. A battery of six Crusaders could put fifteen tons of dumb munitions within a modest circular error probable within five minutes, an incredible potential for suppressive effects. The Crusader presented a thoughtful alternative to the "smart bomb" and featured a digital fire-control system so advanced it precisely delivered cheap dumb munitions at unprecedented rates. The "brains" were in the gun and survived, rather than in the munitions and destroyed. At greater expense one could fire a smart munition from the Crusader and take advantage of such technologies as laser guidance or GPS termination—should a target be precisely enough identified to make this worthwhile. Admittedly the Crusader was a better fit for the shortcomings of DESERT STORM than of ANACONDA. It and a companion armored resupply vehicle were designed to race along at forty miles an hour in support of the advancing M1A2s and M2/3s of the Legacy Force. Since the Legacy Force was programmed to fight the nation's wars for a generation, this seemed a sensible upgrade. Unfortunately, to Rumsfeld and others the Crusader had become a metaphor for an overweight Army trapped in a Cold War mentality. Emboldened by Afghanistan and miffed with the QDR 2001 results, they were determined that the Crusader had to go. Secretary of the Army Thomas E. White, General Shinseki, and their staffs were equally convinced that the Crusader, along with the Comanche helicopter and the Stryker combat vehicle, was critical to advancing Army Transformation during the time it would actually take to develop and field the FCS and the Objective Force. The Crusader carried forward evolving technologies that, when proven, would be critical to the Objective Force. By design, rather than appliqué, it was digitally linked to the Advanced Field Artillery Tactical Data System (AFATDS) and to other battlefield networks. Its three-man crew, down from eight in the case of the Paladin, operated under armor from a computerized cockpit. The advanced metallurgy of the gun tube was integral mid-wall cooled to permit high rates of fire. Frantic to save the contract, designers slimmed the Crusader from sixty to forty tons, rendering it readily deployable by C–17s—and thus making such austere theaters as Afghanistan accessible. Detractors said Crusaders could never have gotten to Takur Ghar. Defenders said it would not have had to; being within forty kilometers would have been enough. Since our Afghan allies had reached the battlefield in gypsy caravans of assorted cars, trucks, and buses, this seemed doable enough. The Army Staff lobbied OSD with the mix of charts, graphs, mathematical models, simulations results, and the like that had worked well in the QDR, demonstrating how Crusader ramped up the capabilities of the Legacy Force, foreshadowed the Objective Force, and could participate in the Objective Force until its own technologies were built into an FCS-mounted non-line-of-sight (NLOS) cannon. The Army's Center of Military History, for example, developed a graph depicting the effects expected of artillery through time. In the Renaissance, when accuracy and rates of fire were low, the destruction of fixed targets—like castle walls—was the dominant effect. Through the nineteenth century, as accuracy and rates of fire improved but troops remained in mass formations, lethality was the dominant effect. In the twentieth century troops dispersed and dug in, and the suppressive effects of artillery were required to maneuver against them. Conventional wisdom in World War II held that it took two tons of artillery to kill a single soldier. This is why masters of the military art like General George S. Patton believed in fire and maneuver, keeping the enemies' heads down with artillery until troops were close enough to kill them with direct-fire weapons. Fortuitously, the Center of Military History's five-hundred-year excursus fed neatly into an argument that the Army needed the Crusader for suppressive fires. Unfortunately for the Army, however, the debate was now ideological more so than empirical. OSD advocates of a revolution in military affairs were willing to "skip a generation" of technical evolution to free up funds for "leap-ahead" technologies. Horrified Army planners wondered how they would explain the consequent blood lost in the meantime. The denouement proved ugly. Rumsfeld's announcement of program termination was abrupt and nonparticipative, although the Army Staff could have seen it coming. The Army Staff circulated "talking points" to Congress favoring the Crusader at about the same time. Congressional supporters of the Crusader assailed OSD with phone calls and missives and demanded an "Army Indirect Fires Report" of Shinseki assessing the consequences. Shinseki, ever one to prioritize integrity over prudence, submitted a report opining that it would ultimately cost between $18 billion and $24 billion to replace the capabilities given up with Crusader. White backed Shinseki. Rumsfeld was reported to have been furious. Rumsfeld saw Shinseki and White as resisting a revolution in military affairs with sauropodian obtuseness. Shinseki and White saw Rumsfeld as dismissive of ground power and as making policy as if the revolution in military affairs had already occurred.[31]

Back to Iraq

On 20 March 2003, an American-led coalition once again invaded Iraq. The immediate cause was Saddam Hussein's refusal to cooperate with the United Nations inspection regime empowered since the Persian Gulf War of 1991 to keep weapons of mass destruction out of his hands. American leaders believed Saddam was stockpiling chemical munitions and pushing ahead with the development of biological and nuclear weapons. They also believed he had established liaisons with international terrorists possibly including al-Qaeda and might selectively arm them with such weapons as well. President Bush had committed himself to preempting attacks on the United States with force if necessary, and circumstances in Iraq were deemed appropriate to enforce this doctrine. Saddam had been fencing with the United States for a dozen years, provoking retaliatory strikes when he fired on aircraft enforcing no-fly zones over northern and southern Iraq. The retaliatory strikes had been conducted in such a manner that over time they dismantled his air defense system, degraded his communications, and crushed what was left of his air force. Army heavy brigades rotated through training exercises in Kuwait on a nearly continuous basis, and pre-positioned equipment and supplies had accumulated in Kuwait, Qatar, and Diego Garcia sufficient to outfit a heavy division. As the crisis built these were tapped to equip the 3d Infantry Division (Mechanized), which rapidly assembled in Kuwait.

230

The 3d Infantry Division was joined by the 1st Marine Division, which also drew heavily upon pre-positioned equipment, and in due course by the 101st Airborne Division, the United Kingdom's 1st Armoured Division, two brigades of the 82d Airborne Division, the 11th Aviation Brigade, and others. The 4th Infantry Division (Mechanized) was programmed to enter the theater through Turkey, and the 1st Cavalry Division was in the queue to reinforce where needed. Commanders in the Gulf had anticipated another round with Saddam Hussein for some time. A state-of-the-art command and control facility suitable for theater requirements had been built in Qatar, for example, and fuel lines extended through Kuwait to establish fuel farms along the Iraqi border. The CENTCOM commander, General Tommy R. Franks, designated the Third Army commanded by Lieutenant General David D. McKiernan as Combined Forces Land Component Command commander, and the Army V Corps and I Marine Expeditionary Force were to be operational headquarters serving underneath him. McKiernan, with General Shinseki's support, handpicked general officers he had confidence in to upgrade the experience of his principal staff sections, to that point headed by colonels. The new team drilled itself through CENTCOM's customary Joint Exercise INTERNAL LOOK and other major simulations to perfect war plans—making changes as they went along. These exercises triggered a pyramid of further simulations as each headquarters in turn drilled its part of the plans, generally assisted by BCTP personnel provided by TRADOC. Thus did the expansive digital training regime envisioned by Generals Sullivan and Franks see its first comprehensive wartime application. Meanwhile units of battalion size and below arriving in Kuwait took to the field and trained toward their responsibilities on their actual equipment and "in the dirt."[32]

Preparations for the operation that would acquire the label IRAQI FREEDOM progressed with admirable teamwork throughout the Department of Defense, but the transformation-related philosophical gap between OSD and the Army nevertheless resurfaced. Buoyed by Afghanistan, Rumsfeld and others resolved IRAQI FREEDOM would be another striking example of the fast-moving, high-technology warfare of the future. The Air Force and Navy were game enough for blows struck from a distance, but Army and Marine planners became anxious about the numbers on two counts. First, even if a knockout blow toppled Saddam's regime with minimal forces committed, what would be the follow-on requirements in an occupied country while the search for weapons of mass destruction went on—and beyond? Second, although the "above the line" forces that would fight the decisive battle had been identified, were the "below the line" forces required to support them going to be on hand? The Joint Staff sought to moderate the emerging debate. The Army's Center of Military History, for example, was tasked to study military occupations of the past to gain an appreciation of what might be required in Iraq. Its canvassing of twenty twentieth-century Army and Marine Corps occupations found wide variations in circumstances, troop strengths, and results but suggested one reliable soldier per hundred occupied people might be a reasonable rule of the thumb. Mathematical modelers employed by the Army Staff did troop-to-task studies and came to broadly similar conclusions. When asked during congressional testimony how many soldiers it would take to secure Iraq, Shinseki forthrightly replied several hundred thousand. He had considerable credibility beyond Army Staff studies, given his personal experiences in Vietnam and the Balkans. A number of Army retirees shared his views and said so. White affirmed Shinseki. With respect to "below the line" forces required to support those in combat, the Army thought it already had the answer in the laboriously constructed time-phased force and deployment list (TPFDL). By this time the TPFDL was a fully automated program that matched combat service support unit requirements to those for combat and combat support, designated specific units, and married them all together into packages that made the best use of available transportation. Thus as combat and combat support units arrived, appropriate mixes of combat service support units would arrive with them. To Rumsfeld and others the numbers for combat service support seemed preposterously large, and the TPFDL seemed far too formulaic and ponderous for the Information Age. The TPFDL was swept aside, and a regime of OSD-vetted Request for Forces (RFF) documents was substituted in its place. Rather than automatically dispatching packages of combat service and support units in accordance with doctrine and experience, a sufficient case would have to be made for each unit. This took time, of course, and distracted key leaders already busy with other things. Many National Guard and Army Reserve units had already been mobilized in accordance with the TPFDL, and these experienced chaos as they waited for the RFF process to catch up—or did not deploy at all. To add to the confusion, the headquarters most involved with force design musings of this type—through the Quadrennial Defense Review and other endeavors—was the Army Staff and their colleagues in TRADOC, yet both were minimally and indirectly involved in the planning for Operation IRAQI FREEDOM. The Theater Commander, General Franks, reported directly to the Chairman of the Joint Chiefs of Staff and Secretary Rumsfeld and consciously limited the leverage of the service staffs within his own CENTCOM staff deliberations. This elevated the most salient issues involved to General Shinseki, who once again bumped heads with Secretary Rumsfeld and the OSD staff. The TPFDL issue was too arcane and too delayed in its effects to evoke much immediate commentary. Its significance would become apparent later, as we shall see. These debates further soured relationships between the Army Staff and OSD. Rumsfeld and his deputy, Dr. Paul Wolfowitz, declared Shinseki wildly off the mark with respect to troop requirements and fumed.[33]

When the ground war started, it moved quickly (*Map 4*). The 3d Infantry Division (Mechanized) raced up the west bank of the Euphrates, sweeping two hundred miles to An Najaf within twenty-four hours. The Marines overran and secured the vital Rumaylah oil fields, then pushed on toward Baghdad over the land between the Euphrates and Tigris Rivers. The British quickly seized Um Qasr and then laid siege to Al Basrah. The Turks had precluded the 4th Infantry Division (Mechanized) from opening a second front through Turkey, so it missed the offensive and had to redeploy through Kuwait. Instead the 173d Airborne Brigade jumped into Kurdistan, linked up with allied Kurdish *Peshmerga,* airlanded reinforcements that included an M1A1 tank company, and opened up a northern front on a shoestring. Special Forces infiltrated into western Iraq, called in air strikes on selected targets, and precluded the area from being a launch site

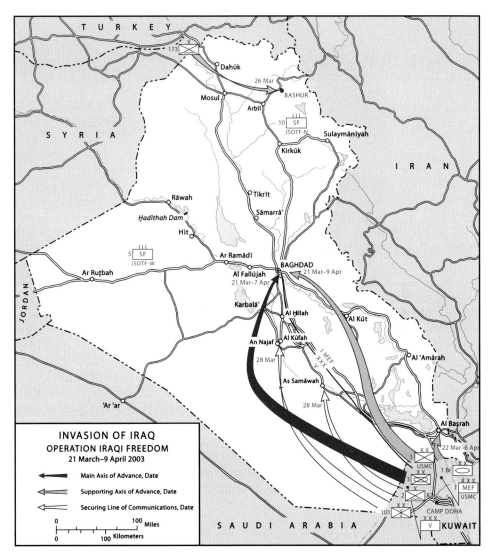

Map 4

for planes and missiles to strike the advancing Coalition forces or Israel. As the converging columns neared Baghdad, a powerful dust storm struck and the elite Iraqi Republican Guard attempted to counterattack under its cover. They were found out and virtually destroyed by aerial bombardment before American ground forces closed with them to finish the job. Although Iraqi conventional forces were destroyed or dispersed with relative ease and few losses, irregular *Fedayeen* and special Republican Guards posed more problems. These dressed in civilian clothes, fought from among civilians, attacked from ambush, and routinely operated out of mosques, schools, and hospitals. They were fanatic and often attacked with suicidal intensity. When they attacked combat units they were blown away

233

The first weeks of IRAQI FREEDOM required high-intensity combat.

by American firepower and gunnery skills. They had more success against the exposed American supply lines, ambushing a disoriented convoy with devastating effects and then forcing an extended battle through the sprawl of An Nasiriyah, for examples. The 101st and 82d Airborne Divisions became committed to rear-area security while their brethren in the heavy divisions forged ahead. Elements of the 11th Attack Helicopter Regiment overflew a massive air defense ambush of machine guns and shoulder-fired rockets coordinated by cellular phone, yet all but one of the redoubtable AH–64 helicopters made it out under their own power. An immediate videoconference described the Iraqi defenses and techniques to other pilots, who then flew their own missions with far less damage. By 4 April the 3d Infantry Division (Mechanized) seized Saddam Hussein International Airport, and by 7 April fought its way into central Baghdad. Jubilant Iraqis took to the streets to tear down posters and statues of Saddam Hussein, and a sense of victory was in the air. To this point the campaign had cost 83 Americans killed and 284 wounded, plus 19 killed and 36 wounded for the British.[34]

The striking victory was not without its warts. Logistical difficulties plagued the final stages of the advance and could have gotten much worse had significant fighting dragged on. TPFDL shortages became visible. For example, of 700 heavy trucks required for line haul only 150 were on hand. Repair parts became increasingly unavailable, prompting units to cannibalize and abandon some vehicles to keep the rest running. Food, fuel, and water were in short supply in places at times. M2/M3 Bradley track became excessively worn, as these vehicles greatly exceeded mileage caps to escort exposed convoys over extended distances. Shortages of manpower precluded securing much that was valuable. An orgy of looting and other crimes shook the country as law and order broke down. Perhaps more ominously, tons of ammunition and hundreds of weapons disappeared from dumps and armories where it had been stored. Iraqi units melted away rather than having been defeated or forced to surrender. Attacks on Americans, although minor at first, continued. Plans for a postcombat phase, such as they were, assumed the Iraqi Army and police would be purged of their criminal elements over time but put back on the streets under new management to assist with law and order. Retired Lieutenant General James "Jay" Garner, the man who had supervised Kurdistan during PROVIDE COMFORT, assumed the role of civil administrator of Iraq with this approach in mind. He was in position less than a month when the Bush administration decided to upscale the reconstruction effort in Iraq and appointed well-connected Ambassador L. Paul Bremer to supersede Garner as civil administrator. Bremer was committed to a more dramatic reconfiguration of Iraq and elected to totally disband the Iraqi Army and ban a far larger percentage of erstwhile Ba'athists from government employment than Garner had considered wise. Whatever the long-term merits of such a drastic approach, the short-term effect was to render tens of thousands of capable people unemployed, alienated, and hostile. This in turn fed a nascent but growing insurgency the thinly spread Americans were not well positioned to contain.[35]

Operation IRAQI FREEDOM provided the first battlefield proofing of many of the constituents of Army Transformation. We will discuss this at some length in Chapter 9. When General Shinseki retired in June 2003, appliqué hardware and software associated with Force XXI—by then the Legacy Force—had seen considerable use. Unfortunately the organization that was most consistently Force XXI–configured, the 4th Infantry Division (Mechanized), was delayed by the Turkish parliamentary decision to block passage, and it began operations in Iraq after Baghdad had fallen. With some haste the Army complemented equipment already in the field with add-ons and surrogates to bring the deployed units into the digital Army Battle Command System. In practice the initiative worked better at the division level and above than at brigade and below, but some of the appliqué systems received strong reviews at all levels. Blue force tracking, for example, radically improved answers to the questions "where am I" and "where are my buddies," and proved popular and useful at all levels. Reach-back capabilities providing access to maps and graphics with variable scale and resolution were also effective and widely used. One battalion commander, for example, reported using traditional paper maps when he started the campaign but being altogether won over to digital mapping before he concluded it. The ability to integrate precision-guided munitions into a scheme of maneuver was better than ever. Concerning all of this, more later. The first Stryker Brigade of the Interim Force was, as we have seen, declared deployable in May and designated for deployment to Iraq in July. Its combat debut would follow Shinseki's departure. The Objective Force was by and large still on the drawing boards. Digital technologies evolving with Force XXI were to be brought into the Objective Force of course, built in rather than appliqué. Some of the unmanned aerial vehicles and robotics near fielding were most properly Objective Force technologies. These too would see service in Iraq after General Shinseki's departure.[36]

The extended contention between Army Transformers and their OSD critics, and more personally between Shinseki and White as compared to Rumsfeld and Wolfowitz, did not end on a high note. The Army was committed to an evolutionary—perhaps accelerated, but nevertheless evolutionary—definition of Transformation. At any given time it intended to be ready to fight at any level of intensity. Technologies would be proven before they were relied upon. This explained the elaborate and extended handoffs over time among the Legacy, Interim, and Objective Forces. The service also believed that technical advance alone was insufficient. Doctrine, training, organization, leadership, and personal skills had to advance with it. What was more, many functions might never be particularly amenable to technological solutions, requiring the steadiness and collective individual efforts of "boots on the ground." It was no accident that Shinseki's most unique contribution to Army transformation, the Stryker Brigade, was also the most manpower-intensive. Rumsfeld and his colleagues pursued a more dramatic revolution in military affairs and were willing to "skip a generation" in development to free up funding for "leap-ahead" technologies. Indeed, they were willing to take risks and force their vision on contemporary battlefields, believing technology was already far enough along to do away with much of the mass the Army considered prudent. Ground forces seemed destined to be bit players in their futuristic vision. Some of the missions most consumptive of boots on the ground were dismissed as "washing windows," best contracted out to lesser allies. This overlooked the historical phenomenon that allies are seldom willing to risk the blood of their soldiers if the United States is not willing to do so as well. The differences in approach and philosophy led to recurrent debates: over the Quadrennial Defense Review results, over the Stryker and the Stryker Brigades, over the Crusader artillery system, over the Comanche helicopter, over the time-phased force and deployment list, and over the forces necessary to secure Iraq. Debate inevitably spilled out of the Pentagon and into public forums. Congress took interest. Shinseki and White understood discipline and deference to civilian authority but also were honor bound to forthrightly answer congressional inquiries when asked. They also considered failure to make their opinions known to their superiors a dereliction of duty. Tension built. When Baghdad fell Rumsfeld and his colleagues considered themselves vindicated. Despite a few misgivings about residual messiness, most commentators saw the campaign as a brilliant victory and perhaps, like Afghanistan, yet another harbinger of the new way of war. Within a few weeks President Bush would pilot a fighter onto an aircraft carrier grandly bearing the banner "Mission Accomplished." Rumsfeld chose not to continue his contention with the Army leadership. He fired White, a political appointee, on 1 May. Shinseki was to retire a little over a month later; Rumsfeld did not attend his 12 June departure ceremony. In his retirement speech Shinseki was complimentary, inclusive, and civil, but he did warn of an Army given too many missions with too few resources. Rumsfeld attempted to replace White with then Secretary of the Air Force James G. Roche and intended to replace Shinseki with a man independent of

Shinseki's mentorship. Shinseki's replacement had not yet been identified, a dramatic departure from having the outgoing and incoming Chiefs of Staff share the podium together. With respect to Roche, Congress—whose members had highly regarded White—balked at so transparent an attempt to put an air-power advocate in charge of the Department of the Army. The Senate declined to move confirmation along and White's former Under Secretary of the Army, Les Brownlee, took over as acting secretary. Shinseki had aspired to design a Transformation program so thoughtful, comprehensive, appropriate, and readily explained that it would acquire "irreversible momentum." Now that design and intent were to be tested by both war and bureaucratic opposition.[37]

Conclusions

General Shinseki consolidated the transformational initiatives of Vuono, Sullivan, and Reimer and integrated them into a comprehensive framework of which he was the architect. The appliqué digital technologies of Force XXI matured during his tenure and achieved their first demonstrable successes in combat. Force XXI morphed into the Legacy Force, and an even more advanced Interim Force went from concept to first units deployable within the mere four years of his tenure. The Interim Force's Stryker Brigade Combat Team was a new organization with new equipment, doctrine, training, and leadership and was poised to advance Shinseki's vision of Army Transformation on the battlefield. The Army of the more distant future, the former Army After Next and now the Objective Force, had been pulled far enough forward to have definitive programs and funding associated with it. Much of its technology remained under development, but its essence already seemed foreshadowed in the emerging Interim Force. The Army had once again made a persuasive case for ground power in a Quadrennial Defense Review and based much of its argument on its flexibility as a full-spectrum force. This proved prescient in the aftermath of 9-11, when a broad array of operational missions nudged the focus of Army Transformation down the combat spectrum. Homeland Defense, unconventional warfare in Afghanistan, a mix of requirements in pursuit of the Global War on Terrorism, and a war in Iraq that started as a conventional war but ended up as something else reinforced the wisdom of nurturing adaptable organizations and leadership. The glide path Shinseki had established for Army Transformation at the outset of his tenure did come under attack in his last year. Under the tenure of Secretary of Defense Donald Rumsfeld the Department of Defense embraced a philosophy of transformation that threatened the breadth of capabilities Shinseki thought appropriate for the Army, and to which he had aspired. The contention became ugly enough that principal subordinates Shinseki had mentored seemed unlikely to succeed him. He had undertaken a comprehensive educational campaign to render the wisdom of Army Transformation as he envisioned it to be self-evident and to impart it with an irreversible momentum. In the absence of a clean handoff to a successor, this particular aspect of his approach would become critical to Army Transformation's future success.

Notes

[1] "Eric K. Shinseki," in William G. Bell, *Commanding Generals and Chiefs of Staff, 1775–2005: Portraits and Biographical Sketches of the Army's Senior Officers* (Washington DC: Center of Military History, 2005), 164; Richard Halloran, *My Name Is Shinseki . . . and I Am a Soldier* (Honolulu: Hawaii Army Museum Society, 2004); General Eric K. Shinseki, "Beginning the Next 100 Years," *Army 1999–2000 Green Book*, October 1999, 21–28; Author's personal experience as General Shinseki's immediate subordinate through six years in three assignments.

[2] Ltr, General Eric K. Shinseki to Brigadier General John S. Brown, 26 April 1999, Historians Files, CMH; Briefing, "CSA-D Guidance," Historians Files, CMH; Briefing, "Leading the Army into the Future," Historians Files, CMH; Briefing, "CSA-D Special Study Group Assessment Team Report, 20 May 99," Historians Files, CMH.

[3] Ibid.; MFR, 17 June 1999, sub: CSA Special Study Group After Action Report, Historians Files, CMH; Assessment Analysis, Historians Files, CMH; America's Army Ready Today, Tomorrow, and into the Next Millennium: CSA Thoughts on the Line of Departure, Historians Files, CMH; Intent of the Chief of Staff, Army, 23 June 1999, Historians Files, CMH; Halloran; Shinseki, "Beginning the Next 100 Years," 41–43.

[4] Author's personal experiences as an attendee at and staff contributor to this and a number of other Association of the United States Army (AUSA) Eisenhower Luncheons. The discussion concerning when the next millennium actually began provoked subsequent good-natured banter between the Center of Military History and the Chief of Staff, Army (CSA), Study Group when no less of an authority than the *Prince Valiant* comic strip came down on the side of the historians.

[5] General Eric K. Shinseki, Address to the Eisenhower Luncheon, Association of the United States Army, 12 October 1999 (Washington DC: Office of the Chief of Staff, United States Army, 1999); Shinseki, "Beginning the Next 100 Years," 21–28.

[6] Army Vision, Headquarters, Department of the Army, Washington DC, 12 October 1999, Historians Files, CMH; *United States Army Transformation Campaign Plan* (Washington DC: Department of the Army, 10 April 2001); White Paper, United States Army, Concepts for the Objective Force, Washington DC, 2001, Historians Files, CMH; General Eric K. Shinseki, "The Army Vision: A Status Report," *Army 2001–2002 Green Book*, October 2001, 23–33; Dennis Steele, "The Army Magazine Hooah Guide to Army Transformation: A 30-Minute Course on the Army's 30-Year Overhaul," *Army* (February 2001): 21–42.

[7] E-mail series, culminating in e-mail, Major General Robert H. Scales Jr. to Lieutenant General Larry R. Ellis, Deputy Chief of Staff for Operations and Plans (DCSOPS), and Brigadier General John S. Brown (CMH), 5 October 1999, sub: Tasker, Historians Files, CMH; Briefing, Dr. James Blackwell, "Transforming the Army: Learning from the Past," Strategic Assessment Center, Science Applications International Corporation (SAIC), Washington DC, Historians Files, CMH; Briefing, Dr. Ralph A. Hallenbeck, "Army QDR CoC: Alternative Strategies—Implications for the Army," Strategy and Policy Analysis Division, SAIC, 15 June 2000; *Army Transformation Wargame 2002* (Carlisle Barracks, Pennsylvania: U.S. Army War College, 2002); *Quadrennial Defense Review 2001* (Washington DC: Office of the Secretary of Defense, 30 September 2001).

[8] The Army Strategic Planning Guidance (Washington DC: Department of the Army, 9 October 2002), Historians Files, CMH; Headquarters, Department of the

Army (HQDA), DCSOPS, Development Instructions: Transformation Campaign Plan, 22 December, 1999; *Army Transformation Campaign Plan*; Memo, Department of the Army G–3, 8 October 2002, sub: Transformation Campaign Plan Revision (TCP)—Final Draft, Historians Files, CMH.

[9] Mark J. Reardon and Jeffery A. Charlston, *From Transformation to Combat: The First Stryker Brigade at War* (Washington DC: Center of Military History, 2007), 1–19; Memo, Chief of Staff, Army, November 1999, sub: Planning Directive 1, in Historians Files, CMH; Memo, Chief of Staff, Army, December 1999, sub: Planning Directive 2, in Historians Files, CMH; *United States Army Transformation Campaign Plan*; Briefing Slide, Army Transformation Office, "The Interim Force—Bridging the Gap," n.d., Historians Files, CMH.

[10] Reardon and Charlston, 1–19; Memo, Department of the Army G–3, 8 October 2008, sub: Transformation Campaign Plan (TCP)—Final Draft, Historians Files, CMH; *Army Strategic Planning Guidance 2005–2020* (Washington DC: Department of the Army, 2002); Kevin J. Dwyer, "4th ID Puts Readiness for Digital War to the Test," *Killeen Daily Herald,* 9 October 2001; Michael Rauhut, "Put Me In, Coach! From Experimental Force to Deployable Unit: The Transition of the 4th Infantry Division (Mechanized)," *Army* (June 2002): 65–70; Briefing Slide, Army Transformation Office, "Resourcing the Interim Force," n.d., Historians Files, CMH.

[11] Candidate platforms included the Dragoon and Pandur from General Dynamics (United States); the Light Armored Vehicle III (LAV III) from General Motors of Canada Ltd.; the Fuchs armored personnel carrier from Henschel (Germany); the LAV III MOWAG from MOWAG (Switzerland); the Bionix infantry fighting vehicle from Singapore Technologies Automotive Ltd.; the VAB armored personnel carrier from Giat Industries (France); the Cobra reconnaissance vehicle from AM General Corporation (United States); the XM1117 reconnaissance vehicle, LAV 300 MK II infantry fighting vehicle, and LAV 600 armored gun system from Cadillac Gage Textron (United States); the FNSS from Turkey; and the armored gun system, medium tactical vehicle light, XM1108 universal carrier, M1064A3 command and control vehicle, M1064A3 mortar carrier, and M113A3 armored personnel carrier from United Defense LP (United States).

[12] Reardon and Charlston, 1–19; Thomas K. Adams, *The Army After Next: The First Postindustrial Army* (Stanford, California: Stanford Security Studies, 2008), 82–86, 123–24, 127–31, 169–72; Briefing Slides, Army Transformation Office, "The Selected IAV Family—Best Value for the Soldier" and "Interim Brigade Combat Team (IBCT) Structure," n.d., Historians Files, CMH; Dennis Steele, "The Army Stages a Kentucky Demo to Define 'the Art of the Possible,'" *Army* (March 2000): 20–26; Scott R. Gourley, "Milestones in Army Transformation," *Army* (March 2000): 27–32; Author's personal experience as Chief of Military History, December 1998–July 2005.

[13] Reardon and Charlston, 1–19; Briefing, Colonel William T. Grisoli, "US Army Transformation Media Roundtable," 20 May 2003, Historians Files, CMH; Briefing Slides, Army Transformation Office, "The Selected IAV Family—Best Value for the Soldier" and "Interim Brigade Combat Team (IBCT) Structure"; *Key Issues Relevant to the U.S. Army's Transformation to the Objective Force* (Arlington, Virginia: Association of the United States Army, 2002); *Key Issues Relevant to the U.S. Army's Strategic Imperatives* (Arlington, Virginia: Association of the United States Army, 2002).

[14] Reardon and Charlston, 1–19; Adams, 82–86, 123–24, 127–31, 169–72; Briefing, Colonel William T. Grisoli, "US Army Transformation Media Roundtable," 20 May 2003; Press Release, Department of the Army, Army Officially Begins Transformation to Brigade Combat Teams, 13 April 2000, Washington DC; "Bin Laden Target of

Urban Warfare Training in Fort Lewis," *Seattle Post Intelligencer*, 10 October 2003; Nick Johnson, "First Stryker Brigade to Achieve IOC This Month, Army Says," *Aerospace Daily*, 21 May 2003; Scott R. Gourley, "IBCT Marks a Digital Milestone," *Army* (December 2001): 55–57; General John N. Abrams, "Training and Doctrine Command: Focusing on the Human Dimension of Army Transformation," *Army 2002–2003 Green Book*, October 2002, 91–98.

[15] Reardon and Charlston, 1–19; Memo, U.S. Army Center of Military History, through Director of Strategy, Plans, and Policy, Office of the G–3/5, for Vice Chief of Staff of the Army, 12 February 2002, sub: IBCT at Arnhem, Historians Files, CMH; Erin Q. Winograd, "Gingrich Tells Top DOD Officials Army's Stryker Shouldn't Be Fielded," *Inside the Army*, 30 September 2002; Neil Baumgardner, "Shinseki Rails Against Stryker Critics," *Defense Daily*, 23 October 2002; Dennis Steele, *The Army Magazine Hooah Guide to Army Transformation: A 30-Minute Course on the Army's 30-Year Overhaul* (Arlington, Virginia: Association of the United States Army, 2001).

[16] Mary Beth Norton et al., *A People and a Nation: A History of the United States* (New York: Houghton Mifflin, 2005), 917–19; Daniel Benjamin and Steven Simon, *The Age of Sacred Terror* (New York: Random House, 2002); Bob Woodward, *Bush at War* (New York: Simon & Schuster, 2002).

[17] Briefing, Joint Staff, "Paradigm Shift: The Devolution of Terrorism, The Coming Challenge for US National Security Forces and the Current Known Threat," n.d., Historians Files, CMH; E-mail, Mr. Avon N. Williams (Office of the General Counsel) to Brigadier General John S. Brown (Chief of Military History), 30 October 2001, sub: Moderate Islam? Historians Files, CMH; George W. Gawrych, *Jihad, War and Terrorism* (Fort Leavenworth, Kansas: U.S. Army Command and General Staff College, 2002); John L. Esposito, *Unholy War: Terror in the Name of Islam* (New York: Oxford University Press, 2002); Peter L. Bergen, *Holy War, Inc.: Inside the Secret World of Osama bin Laden* (New York: Free Press, 2001); *National Military Strategy* (Washington DC: Government Printing Office, 1992); *National Military Strategy of the United States of America* (Washington DC: Government Printing Office, 2004).

[18] Richard W. Stewart, ed., *American Military History*, vol. 2, *The United States Army in a Global Era, 1917–2003* (Washington DC: Center of Military History, 2005), 460–64; Lieutenant General Roger C. Schultz, "Army National Guard: Citizen-Soldiers Protecting and Defending the U.S.A.," *Army 2002–2003 Green Book*, October 2002, 103–10; Dennis Steele, "Recognition of Heroic Deeds at the Pentagon on September 11: Valor, Pain and Tears," *Army* (December 2001): 50–54.

[19] Schultz, "Army National Guard: Citizen-Soldiers Protecting and Defending the U.S.A.," 103–10; Lieutenant General James R. Helmly, "The U.S. Army Reserve: Transforming While at War—Instilling a Culture of Change," *Army 2002–2003 Green Book*, October 2002, 111–20; Major General Hans A. Van Winkle, "Civil Works: This Is the Army Too," *Army* (March 2000): 42–48; Dennis Steele, "Operation NOBLE EAGLE: The Nation's Sentinels," *Army* (August 2002): 15–19; General Larry Ellis, "U.S. Army Forces Command, 1973–2003: Three Decades of Readiness in Peace and War," *Army* (June 2003): 49–54.

[20] "What is TSA?" from http://www.tsa.gov, accessed 16 January 2009; "Department Celebrates Five Years," from http://www.dhs.gov, accessed 16 January 2009; Ellis, 49–54; John Mintz, "Ridges Rise from Adviser to 'Mr. Secretary,'" *Washington Post,* 24 March 2002; Michelle Tan, "The Readiness Shuffle," AUSA Special Report, *Army Times*, 20 February 2006; Michelle Tan, "Guard Aims for 6-Year Cycle, Half Free for U.S. Emergencies," AUSA Special Report, *Army Times*, 20 February 2006.

[21] Lieutenant General Joseph M. Cosumano Jr., "Space, Missile Defense and Information Operations Support the Transforming Army," *Army 2002–2003 Green*

Book, October 2002, 187–94; Major General Stanley E. Green, "Fighting Air and Missile Defense in the Future," *Army* (December 2001): 39–42; Shelba Profitt, "Getting Missile Defense Capabilities into the Hands of the Warfighter," *Army* (December 2001): 47–49; Memo, James L. Yarrison, Center of Military History Pentagon Research Team, for Chief of the Historics Division, 27 October 1999, sub: Meeting with Ms. Browning, ODISC4 Y2K Director, Historians Files, CMH; Dennis Steele, "A Legacy of Being on the Leading Edge," *Army* (August 2002): 17; Brigadier General Richard V. Geraci, "The Critical Battlespace: Computer Network Operations," *Army* (December 2001): 43–46.

[22] Dennis Steele, "National Security Commission Recommends a New Strategic Outlook," *Army* (March 2001): 37–38; U.S. Commission on National Security/21st Century Web site, govinf.library.unt.edu/nssg/Reports/reports.htm-2k, accessed 20 January 2009; Dennis Steele, "Reinforcing Homeland Defense in the Wake of September 11," *Army* (December 2001): 33; U.S. Northern Command Web site, http://www.northcom.mil, accessed 20 January 2009.

[23] Richard W. Stewart, *The United States Army in Afghanistan: Operation ENDURING FREEDOM, October 2001–March 2002* (Washington DC: Center of Military History, 2004); Roger Howard, "Entertaining Osama: Testing the Limits of Taliban Hospitality," *Jane's Intelligence Review* (November 1998): 14–16; Anthony Davis, "Taliban Continue the Killing but Fail to Finish the Crusade," *Jane's Intelligence Review* (November 1998): 17–22; Peter Marsden, *The Taliban: War, Religion and the New Order in Afghanistan* (Karachi: Oxford University Press, 1998); Amin Saikal, "Afghanistan's Ethnic Conflict," *Survival* (Summer 1998); Briefing Slide, Office of the Deputy Chief of Staff for Intelligence (ODCSINT), "Mujahidiin/Taliban," n.d., Historians Files, CMH.

[24] Stewart, *The United States Army in Afghanistan*; Marsden; Saikal; Dennis Steele, "The U.S. Army in Afghanistan," *Army* (April 2002): 19–52; Dennis Steele, "A U.S. Army Line Battalion in the War on Terrorism," *Army* (June 2002): 22–52; E-mail, Brigadier General Mark E. O'Neill to Major General Franklin Hagenbeck, 6 January 2003, sub: Anaconda Lessons Learned—NDU Paper, with notes, Historians Files, CMH.

[25] Bruce Berkowitz, *The New Face of War: How War Will Be Fought in the 21st Century* (New York: Free Press, 2003); Rohan Gunratna, *Inside Al Qaeda: Global Network of Terror* (New York: Berkeley Books, 2003); Dennis Steele, "The Rough Ride to Reaper Estates," *Army* (January 2002): 12–20; Lieutenant General Paul T. Mikolashek, "'Patton's Own' Third U.S. Army: 'Always First': Versatile, Ready Warfighting Command," *Army 2002–2003 Green Book*, October 2002, 201–08; General Montgomery C. Meigs, "U.S. Army Europe: Ready for Deployment on a Moment's Notice," *Army 2002–2003 Green Book*, October 2002, 75–82; Master Sergeant Sue Harper and Staff Sergeant Gregory Jones, "Supporting Afghanistan from Europe: U.S. Army Europe's 21st Theater Support Command," *Army* (August 2002): 41–43; Dennis Steele, "The U.S. Army in the Balkans," *Army* (September 2002): 22–41; Lieutenant James L. Campbell, "U.S. Army Pacific: Providing Indispensable Capabilities to the Army and Pacific Command," *Army 2002–2003 Green Book*, October 2002; Major General Alfred A. Valenzuela, "U.S. Army South: The Component of Choice in U.S. Southern Command's AOR," *Army 2002–2003 Green Book*, October 2002, 209–14.

[26] Stewart, *The United States Army in Afghanistan*; Sean Naylor, "The Lessons of Anaconda," *New York Times,* 2 March 2003; CTNSP/NDU, *Anaconda's Five Lessons for Joint Operations* (Washington DC: National Defense University, 2003), Historians Files, CMH; Handwritten notes entitled "Anaconda" left by Major General Franklin

L. Hagenbeck with the Chief of Military History in the aftermath of a conversation, Historians Files, CMH.

[27] Fax, Office of the Commanding General, U.S. Army, Europe (USAREUR) (General Eric K. Shinseki), to the Chief of Programs and Requirements, Supreme Headquarters Allied Powers Europe (Colonel [P] John S. Brown), 30 June 1998, sub: CMH QDR Questions/Answers, Historians Files, CMH; E-mail and associated correspondence, between the Chief of Programs and Requirements, Supreme Headquarters Allied Powers Europe (Colonel [P] John S. Brown), and the Executive Officer (Colonel John Gingrich) to the Commanding General, USAREUR (General Eric K. Shinseki), 3 Jul 1998, sub: CMH QDR Questions/Answers, Historians Files, CMH; Briefing, "The Army Quadrennial Defense Review: 11 July 2000 Senior Leader Update," Historians Files, CMH.

[28] Ibid.; Speech, George W. Bush, "A Period of Consequences," 23 September 1999, delivered at The Citadel, Charleston, South Carolina; Press Release, Department of Defense, Linda D. Kozaryn and Jim Garamone, "Bush, Rumsfeld Pledge Support to Military," American Forces Press Service, 26 January 2001; Woodward; Timothy Noah, "The Rumsfeld Death Watch," *Slate,* 7 August 2001; John M. Donnelly, "Rumsfeld Makes War," *Chicago Tribune*, 22 August 2001, 1; Bernard Weintraub and Thom Shanker, "Rumsfeld's Design for War Criticized on the Battlefield," *New York Times*, 1 April 2003, 1; Adams, 80–132; *Quadrennial Defense Review 2001*; Elaine M Grossman, "Key Review Offers Scant Guidance," *Inside the Pentagon*, 4 October 2001, 1; David A. Fulghum, "QDR Became Pablum as Decisions Slid," *Aviation Week and Space Technology*, 8 October 2001, 21–22.

[29] Fax, Office of the Commanding General, USAREUR (General Eric K. Shinseki), 30 June 1998, to the Chief of Programs and Requirements, Supreme Headquarters Allied Powers Europe (Colonel [P] John S. Brown), sub: CMH QDR Questions/Answers; E-mail and associated correspondence, between the Chief of Programs and Requirements, Supreme Headquarters Allied Powers Europe (Colonel (P) John S. Brown) and the Executive Officer (Colonel John Gingrich) to the Commanding General, USAREUR (General Eric K. Shinseki), 3 Jul 1998, sub: CMH QDR Questions/Answers; *Quadrennial Defense Review 2001*; Loren B. Thompson, "Saved by Reality: The Army Finds a Future," *Defense Week*, 9 October 2001, 1.

[30] *Conduct of the Persian Gulf War: Final Report to Congress* (Washington DC: Department of Defense, April 1992), 226–96; Stewart, *The United States Army in Afghanistan,* 30–45; E-mail, Brigadier General Mark E. O'Neill to Major General Franklin Hagenbeck, 6 January 2003, sub: Anaconda Lessons Learned—NDU Paper, with notes; CTNSP/NDU, *Anaconda's Five Lessons for Joint Operations*; Handwritten notes entitled "Anaconda" left by Major General Franklin L. Hagenbeck with the Chief of Military History in the aftermath of a conversation; Briefing, Center of Military History, with notes, "The Historical Utility of (Relatively) Dumb Artillery Munitions," Historians Files, CMH.

[31] Crusader 155mm Self Propelled Howitzer, USA, accessed 30 January 2009, http://www.army-technology.com; Secretary of the Army Thomas E. White, "Toward a 21st-Century Army," *Army 2001–2002 Green Book*, October 2001, 17–20; General Eric K. Shinseki, "The Army Vision: A Status Report," *Army 2001–2002 Green Book*, October 2001, 23–33; Vernon Loeb, "Army's New Mobile Artillery System Leads Rumsfeld, Congress to Battle," *Washington Post*, 3 May 2002; "U.S. Needs Crusader Artillery System," *Boston Globe,* 3 June 2002; Speech, George W. Bush, "A Period of Consequences," 23 September 1999, delivered at The Citadel, Charleston, South Carolina; Eric Schmitt, "$11 Billion Artillery System is Dead, Officials Say," *New York Times*, 7 May 2002; Ivan Eland, "Vanquish the Crusader,"

United Press International, 17 May 2002; Briefing, Center of Military History, with notes, "The Historical Utility of (Relatively) Dumb Artillery Munitions."

[32] Colonel Gregory Fontenot, Lieutenant Colonel E. J. Degan and Lieutenant Colonel David Tohn, *On Point: The United States Army in IRAQI FREEDOM* (Fort Leavenworth, Kansas: Combat Studies Institute Press, 2004), 1–85; *Operation IRAQI FREEDOM—"It Was a Prepositioned War"* (Fort Belvoir, Virginia: U.S. Army Material Command, 2003); "Iraq by the Numbers," *Army Times,* 22 March 2004, 28–29; "The Continuing Surprises of Operation Iraqi Freedom" (Fort Leavenworth, Kansas: Combat Studies Institute Press, 2003).

[33] Fontenot, Degan, and Tohn, 1–85; Anthony H. Cordesman, *The Lessons of the Iraq War: Summary Briefing* (Washington DC: Center for Strategic and International Studies, 15 July, 2003); Ltr, Mr. Jay A. Thomson, President and Chief Executive Officer of RAND, to Secretary of Defense Donald H. Rumsfeld, 7 February 2005, Historians Files, CMH; Briefing, Center of Military History, with notes, "Numerical Considerations in Military Occupations Past," Historians Files, CMH; Kim Burger, "Iraq Campaign Raises New Logistics Concerns," *Jane's Defense Weekly,* 10 September 2003; "The Continuing Surprises of Operation IRAQI FREEDOM" (Fort Leavenworth, Kansas: Combat Studies Institute Press, 2003); *Operation IRAQI FREEDOM—"It Was a Prepositioned War."*

[34] Fontenot, Degan, and Tohn, 85–382; Memo, Department of the Army, Office of the Chief of Staff, for Principal Officials of Headquarters, Department of the Army, 1 May 2003, sub: Operation IRAQI FREEDOM Study Group (OIFSG), Historians Files, CMH; Department of the Army, Executive Summary, Attack on the 507th Maintenance Company, 23 March 2003, An Nasiriyah, Iraq, Historians Files, CMH; C. Mark Brinkley, "The Longest Day—of the Iraq War," *Army Times,* 22 March 2004; Leonard Wong, Thomas A. Kolditz, Raymond A. Millen, and Terrence M. Potter, *Why They Fight: Combat Motivation in the Iraq War* (Carlisle Barracks, Pennsylvania: Strategic Studies Institute, 2003).

[35] Fontenot, Degan, and Tohn, 427–35; Dr. Donald P. Wright and Colonel Timothy R. Reese, *On Point II: Transition to the New Campaign, The United States Army in Operation IRAQI FREEDOM May 2003–January 2005* (Fort Leavenworth, Kansas, Combat Studies Institute Press, 2008), 25–33, 87–138; Memo, Department of the Army, Office of the Vice Chief of Staff, for Army Staff, 9 July 2003, sub: Acting CSA Visit to Kuwait and Iraq, 4–6 July 2003, Historians Files, CMH; CSI Roundtable Presentation, On the Ground in Iraq, 16 September 2004, Historians Files, CMH; "Army Refits Force," *AUSA News,* October 2003, 2; Gordon Trowbridge, "Too Many Troops?" *Army Times,* 1 May 2006; Anthony H. Cordesman, *The Lessons of the Iraq War: Summary Briefing* (Washington DC: Center for Strategic and International Studies, 15 July 2003); Kim Burger, "Iraq Campaign Raises New Logistics Concerns," *Jane's Defense Weekly,* 10 September 2003; William H. McMichael, "Unsatisfactory Planning: Swift March to Baghdad Left Ammo Depots Unguarded, GAO Finds," *Army Times,* 2 April 2007, 16; "Iraq: Translating Lessons into Future DoD Policies," RAND, February 2005, Historians Files, CMH.

[36] Fontenot, Degan, and Tohn, 427–35; Wright and Reese; Cordesman; "Iraq: Translating Lessons Into Future DoD Policies," RAND, February 2005.

[37] Shinseki, Address to the Eisenhower Luncheon, Association of the United States Army, 12 October 1999; Shinseki, "Beginning the Next 100 Years," 21–28; *United States Army Transformation Campaign Plan*; United States Army White Paper, Concepts for the Objective Force; Adams, 123–65; Thomas E. Ricks, "Air Force's Roche Picked to Head Army," *Washington Post,* 2 May 2003, 1.

CHAPTER 6

General Peter J. Schoomaker
Redefining Transformation, 2003–2005

General Peter J. Schoomaker became Chief of Staff of the Army on 1 August 2003, more than a month after General Eric K. Shinseki's departure. During this period the choice for Secretary of the Army was in contention as well. These under-laps may not have been altogether accidental. Secretary of Defense Donald H. Rumsfeld had battled the Department of the Army over transformational issues for some time, and circumstances provided an opportunity to break Army leadership continuity that had stabilized its azimuth for change. As we have seen, Sullivan was Vice Chief of Staff to Vuono, Reimer to Sullivan, and Shinseki to Reimer, and a mix of other assignments had furthered the mentorship relationships among the pairs of men. To one looking for an outsider, Schoomaker seemed a good choice. Although he had served as a platoon leader, company and troop commander, battalion operations officer, squadron executive officer, and, most notably, assistant division commander in conventional units, his professional pedigree was dominated by Special Operations. He had served nine years in Special Operations units whose identity remains classified as this is written. He served as Special Operations Officer, J–3, for the Joint Special Operations Command for three years. He served a year in the Pentagon as the Army's Deputy Director for Operations, Readiness and Mobilization, a job with considerable exposure to Special Operations issues, before in succession commanding the Joint Special Operations Command, the Army Special Operations Command, and the United States Special Operations Command. His considerable combat experience—Desert One in Iran, Urgent Fury in Grenada, Just Cause in Panama, Desert Shield and Desert Storm in Southwest Asia, and Uphold Democracy in Haiti—had been Special Operations in nature. After his retirement in 2000 the Office of the Secretary of Defense continued to seek his counsel and brokered meetings including him and General Tommy Franks that substantially affected planning for Afghanistan and Iraq—particularly with respect to Special Operations. Secretary Rumsfeld called Schoomaker back from retirement to serve as Chief of Staff of the Army. If Secretary Rumsfeld and his colleagues thought Schoomaker would bring a fresh pair of eyes to thoroughly reexamine Army Transformation and its premises, they would not be disappointed. If they thought he would embrace a philosophy of war that diminished the

General Schoomaker

size of the Army, shouldered aside conventional ground forces in favor of Special Operators, or prioritized high-tech solutions, they would be less pleased. During Schoomaker's tenure the Army expanded, conventional ground forces reconfigured to play central roles in Afghanistan and Iraq, and the Army became more rather than less measured in its commitment to technical solutions. Army Transformation was in fact redefined during the first two years of Schoomaker's tenure, but not because of Secretarial dictates or philosophical differences with his predecessors. The Army that had been between wars was at war. War imposed challenging demands, and these demands were to be recurrent for years to come. The balance between what could be done for the future and what had to be done for the present necessarily shifted.[1]

Transformation Redefined

Rumsfeld's abrupt dismissal of Secretary of the Army Thomas E. White and selections of Secretary of the Air Force James G. Roche to be Secretary of the Army and General Peter J. Schoomaker to be Chief of Staff caused consternation on the Army Staff and within the Army generally. Department of the Army frictions with Rumsfeld and the Office of the Secretary of Defense (OSD) had been no secret. Indeed, more than a year prior to Shinseki's retirement OSD had leaked the name of General Jack Keane, then the Vice Chief of Staff, as Shinseki's likely replacement. The two men downplayed this affront to work together effectively through the rest of Shinseki's tenure, and Keane ultimately declined Rumsfeld's offer for family reasons. Shinseki and Keane foresaw the upcoming transition would be abnormally challenging and committed the Director of the Army Staff (DAS) to form a "prenomination" transition team to facilitate the arrival and confirmation hearings of whoever was chosen. For decades, as we have seen, the incoming Chief of Staff had been an insider familiar what was going on who selected his own transition team to gather information and polish approaches to areas he particularly wanted to emphasize. The choice of an insider seemed unlikely this time. Beginning 1 March 2003, a generic transition team pulled together briefing materials, laid out tentative timelines and plans, and set aside office space. They did not initially know of Secretary White's imminent departure, which came abruptly on 1 May. Secretaries had invariably transitioned at a time different than that of Chiefs, in part because they were political appointees and the tenures of the Chiefs tended to straddle administrations. When Shinseki departed, Roche's nomination was in trouble with Congress and Schoomaker had not yet been nominated. This decapitation was unprecedented. There had not been an occasion when the Department of the Army was simultaneously without a Secretary and a Chief of Staff in its history, dating back to its establishment during the Truman administration. Secretaries routinely under-lapped, but Chiefs almost never did. Indeed, since the office of Chief of Staff was first established in 1903 there had only been three under-laps. Two Vice Chiefs encountered procedural delays of about a month en route through confirmation to be Chiefs, and Vice Chief of Staff General Bruce Palmer Jr. served as acting Chief for three months in 1972 while General Creighton W. Abrams Jr. closed out his responsibilities in Vietnam. The DAS' surrogate transition team scrambled, now tasked to prepare two senior leaders for Senate confirmation and subsequent service rather than one. The mission came in four phases: "prenomination" until names were known, "preconfirmation" to help the nominees appear before the Senate with sufficient *auctoritas* to be confirmed, "transition" to assist the confirmed candidates in assuming office, and "post-transition" insofar as the new leaders wanted or needed further assistance from the team before it divested itself. Once nominated, Schoomaker pulled officers of his choice into the process, sharpening focus and assisting direction. In time the "presumption of confirmation" for Roche, an assumption of the transition planning, faded. Schoomaker became the subject of intense lobbying. Army Staff principals, major commands, and agencies earnestly sought his time for at least three reasons: to assist in his preparations for confirmation, to inform him with respect to what they were doing, and to convince him that what they were doing was worthy. To most he was an unknown quantity, removed by provenance and time in retirement from the constellation of generals previously considered front-runners for Chief of Staff. The DAS, disciplining the cacophony seeking Schoomaker's attention, issued specific guidance to protect his new-to-the-Pentagon charge: Keep it simple. Put only three points on a briefing slide. If you have more than three points, use another slide. Do not assume he knows the context of what you are briefing. Put things into context. Explain the reasons for what you are doing, and tell him what it means. This sensible effort to downsize complicated briefings and accelerate familiarization provided too great an opportunity for wags to resist. Soon parodies ranging from Grandmother's recipes through Tolstoy's *War and Peace* began circulating on tersely worded three-point slides.[2]

General Schoomaker conducted an introductory session with the Army General Staff Council on 14 August 2003. By this time many Staff principals had been with him one-on-one, but this was his first exposure to the entire assemblage in the same room at the same time. Schoomaker began by making the salient point "this is not about me," encouragement to focus on the problems facing the Army rather than upon who he was and where he came from. He disarmingly noted that he might not have been the first choice for Chief of Staff of anybody in the room and was not Rumsfeld's first choice either, for that matter. He recognized he had much to learn, but having been put in charge he would take charge. He then laid out a way ahead for the Army Staff that was succinct, albeit embellished with homey Wyoming analogies of which he was fond. There would be no introductory grand vision or white paper, nor would there be immediate departures with respect to programs already under way. The Army Staff was programmed for comprehensive feedback on *The Army Plan* (TAP) by 24 September, for example, and he looked forward to reviewing their feedback at that time. Schoomaker handed out and discussed three simple black-and-white PowerPoint slides. The first slide featured two bullets: "Train and Equip Soldiers and Grow Leaders" and "Provide Relevant and Ready Land Power Capability to the Combatant Commander and the Joint Team." Schoomaker explained why he had chosen these particular words to describe the core competencies of the Department of the Army. When doing so he directed all to embrace the current missions, noting, "We can't tell them [OSD and the administration] we don't wash this kind of window." Schoomaker's second slide listed fifteen "focus areas" he particularly wanted to emphasize over the next several months: gathering opinions, promoting debate, assigning responsibilities, and identifying necessary or desirable changes quickly enough to have an impact in the near term. The DAS was to establish a regimen wherein each focus area was drilled by staff principals and relevant agencies, with seminars and briefings to senior leaders en route. Staff principals were offered an "open door" and encouraged to use it. Schoomaker's initial focus areas were: "The Soldier," developing flexible, adaptive, and competent soldiers with a "warrior ethos"; "The Bench," preparing future generations of senior leaders; "The Network," leveraging and enabling network-centric warfare; "Modularity," creating capabilities-based unit designs; "Joint and Expeditionary Mind-Set"; "AC/RC Balance," optimizing the active-component (AC) and reserve-component (RC) mix; "Unit Manning" (later Force Stabilization), providing unit stability, continuity, and predictability to soldiers and their families; "Combat Training Centers/Battle Command Training Program," focused on the current security and joint and expeditionary context; "Leader Development and Education," training and educating Army members of joint teams; "Army Aviation," a holistic review of aviation's role on the joint battlefield; "Installations as Flagships," enhancing the ability to project power and support families; "Current to Future Force," accelerating the fielding of selected capabilities and transforming as constant change; "Resource Processes," redesigned to be flexible, responsive, and timely; "Strategic Communications," telling the Army story; and "Authorities, Responsibilities, and Accountability." Somewhat later "Actionable Intelligence" would be added to this list. Schoomaker's third slide was his most dramatic. It collapsed Shinseki's Trident into a single arrow, the tip of which was labeled "Future Force" and the base "Current Force." Several terms were to disappear from the lexicon. Since the M1A1 Abrams tank was now programmed through 2032 it seemed premature to call it "legacy," and the characterization of a broader "Legacy Force" would go for about the same reasons. Since Stryker Brigades were now in combat and embedded in the Current Force, there was no longer a reason to characterize them as an "Interim Force." Since transformation would be a continuous process, accelerated by urgent wartime needs to deploy proven technologies as soon as possible, there would never really be a singular "Objective Force." The Current Force would evolve into the Future Force in a never-ending process of thoughtfully managed change. Interestingly enough, the change in slides was far more dramatic than changes in funding or programs. The former Legacy Force was to continue receiving appliqué Force XXI technologies as planned, albeit hopefully faster. The Stryker Brigades were to be funded, organized, and fielded as planned, although they were no longer to be characterized as an Interim Force. The characteristics of the former Objective Force remained a long-term goal, albeit with more fluidity from future to present and without as highly structured a timeline as before. Schoomaker espoused a philosophy of transformation more likely to be congenial to OSD staffers while nevertheless preserving his options to follow through on any or all of Shinseki's design. Army Staffers departing the 14 August meeting were heartened for several reasons. Schoomaker was not the Special Operations ideologue some had feared, and he had described an open process involving the Army Staff whereby he would move ahead. Existing programs had not summarily received the axe but would be subject to fair scrutiny before decisions were made. Finally, Schoomaker's approach seemed likely to mute the quarrels with OSD without prematurely surrendering Army equities.[3]

Mention should be made of the Army's senior leadership between the departure of White and the advent of Schoomaker. When White departed, Under Secretary of the Army Les Brownlee assumed responsibilities as Acting Secretary of the Army. Key senators balked at confirming Rumsfeld's proposed move of Roche from Secretary of the Air Force to Secretary of the Army. White and Shinseki were respected in Congress, and their educational efforts on the behalf of Army Transformation had taken root. Proposals to reverse what they had done, or to diminish the Army in favor of high-technology platforms, were met with suspicion. Brownlee was well connected with and highly regarded by Congress. He had retired from active duty as an infantry colonel after more than twenty years of service, including two tours in Vietnam. He had published a thoughtful oral history of General William E. Depuy, a transformational figure associated with the Army's post-Vietnam renaissance. He had served on the staff of the Senate Armed Services Committee for over a decade, most recently as staff director for its chairman, Senator John Warner. Brownlee understood how the "Hill" worked and inspired confidence on it. He proved able to smoothly champion Army interests and equities there while softening the confrontation with OSD. Transformation continued as a process but without its previous publicity or visibility. For example, in their annual state-of-the-Army messages in the Association of the United States Army's (AUSA's) *2003–2004 Green Book*, published in October 2003, neither Brownlee nor Schoomaker used the word "transformation." This contrasted with the previous edition, wherein their predecessors used the word or its derivatives a total of thirty-nine times. Transformation's reduced silhouette was not merely a maneuver to avoid confrontation with OSD. It was also recognition of dramatically altered demands on the Army. As Vice Chief and then Acting Chief of Staff of the Army, General Jack Keane coped with the deteriorating situation in Iraq while running the uniformed Army and facilitating Schoomaker's arrival. By 27 May it was clear the Coalition faced a rising tide of violence in Iraq and that American soldiers would be committed for a longer period in greater numbers than anticipated. At the General Staff Council (GSC) meeting on that date the Army operations and training officer (G–3) spoke to rapidly expanding requirements to reset and rotate units and to escalating demands for up-armored high mobility multipurpose wheeled vehicles (HMMWVs) and body armor. A week later conversation in the GSC turned to the scope and coordination of attacks on Coalition forces and to whether the situation in Iraq should be characterized as an insurgency. Less than a year before, the war in Afghanistan and operations elsewhere were supported by 14,000 soldiers committed to the Central Command (CENTCOM). This was considerably fewer than deployed to Bosnia in 1995–1996, and only somewhat more than deployed to Somalia in 1993. Although fighting in Afghanistan had been more severe and sustained than in these earlier operations, mobilization and deployment requirements were comparable. Now the Army was building rapidly toward 160,000 deployed in Iraq, Afghanistan, and Kuwait and 360,000 deployed or forward stationed overall. Recognition of this huge paradigm shift—from sustaining forces one-twentieth the size of the active component to sustaining forces a third its size in long-term combat operations overseas—sank in during May and June. Keane and Brownlee prepared the Army for its implications. Keane stayed on as Vice Chief long enough to see Schoomaker settled. Brownlee served as Acting Secretary of the Army for eighteen months, longer than any previous Acting Secretary of the Army or Secretary of War ad interim and through more challenging circumstances.[4]

Iraq changed everything. It became the prism through which transformation and all other Army initiatives would be refracted. Schoomaker used the analogy of a rheostat to describe contemporary operations. Earlier wars had been on/off switches, wherein the nation was at peace or at war—and knew it. The Global War on Terrorism was going to last a generation and the "light" would always be on, albeit at varying levels of intensity. This was not altogether new. For a dozen years, as we have seen, the Army had sustained almost a division's worth of active operations overseas almost continuously, with one operation overlapping another in such a manner as to approximate Schoomaker's rheostat. Iraq turned the rheostat up by a factor of ten, and it seemed it would stay there. At the Army General Staff Council meeting on 14 July 2003, General Keane opined that six divisions and four separate brigades would be committed to active operations through March and that with few exceptions their tours would be for twelve months. During Desert Shield/ Desert Storm brigades that deployed as late as January were out of theater by May, and troops had become accustomed to six-month tours in the interval since. Such coming and going had been feasible when the scale was modest, but now planners faced the prospect of moving over half of the deployable Army at the same time to effect a rotation. The somewhat controversial "stop loss" policy immediately emerged as an issue, as did the prospect of committing the reserve component en masse to twelve-month tours overseas—thus requiring further months before and after to mobilize, train, and demobilize them. Deployed Reservists anticipated this requirement. A wag among them returning from Baghdad prominently posted a sign on his truck exclaiming "One

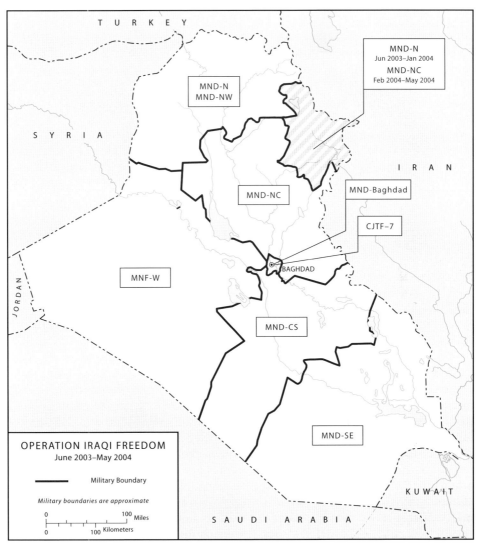

OPERATION IRAQI FREEDOM
June 2003–May 2004

Military Boundary

Military boundaries are approximate

Map 5

Weekend a Month, My Ass!!!" garnering affirmative honks from others he encountered en route. The looming rotation from Operation IRAQI FREEDOM 1 (OIF1) to Operation IRAQI FREEDOM 2 (OIF2) would be the largest unit rotation in American history. During the world wars units deployed for the duration rather than rotating, and Korea and Vietnam were fought with individual replacements rather than unit rotations. More than 244,000 soldiers moved in and out of CENTCOM between March and June 2004 (*Map 5*). Even as this massive rotation was going on, it became clear this was no one-time event. On 26 April 2004, General Schoomaker directed the Army Staff to anticipate that OIF3 and OIF4 would be as large as OIF2 and saw no particular reason

Posting security in urban Iraq

to expect a diminishment soon thereafter. "Focus Area Updates" conducted about the same time reflected the extent to which supporting and improving on operations in Iraq permeated Army thinking. With respect to soldiers, what had to be done to recruit and retain them in sufficient numbers and quality for operations of this complexity on this scale? The United States had never sustained a war of this size with a volunteer army; could it do so now? With respect to the network, how could the Army accelerate blue force tracking and other immediately successful web applications? With respect to jointness, who should control the evermore ubiquitous UAVs and the air space they operated in? With respect to AC/RC balance, what should be done with an apparent surfeit of artillery, air defense, and engineer units for present requirements and, conversely, how could shortages of military policemen, transporters, and civil affairs be made good? With respect to resource processes, how quickly could the Army go from the 500 up-armored HMMWVs it had to the 39,000 it needed in Iraq alone? There also were shortages with respect to dozens of other relatively mundane items, including body armor and M2/M3 Bradley spare parts. With respect to bringing the Future Force into the Current Force, what technology could be mobilized to stem losses to improvised explosive devices (IEDs)? Schoomaker's rheostat had gotten stuck on "high" in wars conducted at the low end of the combat spectrum. This inevitably affected the Army's approach to transforming itself.[5]

From Sullivan through Shinseki Army transformation had evolved with the full combat spectrum in mind, but with a bias toward its upper levels. Scenarios and preparations had trended toward worst (conventional) cases, while collaterally developing technologies and expeditionary capabilities useful for asymmetric circumstances as well. Shinseki's tripartite Transformation paradigm of Legacy, Interim, and Objective Forces neatly summarized broad aspirations for the immediate, interim, and distant futures. The Army had been between wars. Now the Army was at war, and the broad became the specific. The mission of winning the wars it was in trumped other considerations in defining transformation. Schoomaker laid the groundwork for redefinition with the focus areas he identified upon arrival. In the following months staff deliberations and evolving senior leader guidance reinforced a trend toward redefinition. By 2005 redefinition was complete and formally sanctioned in Field Manual 1, *The Army* (FM–1), republished in June of that year. A section titled "Transformation Today" contained the pithy sentence, "Army transformation is not an end in itself; it contributes to accomplishing today's mission as well." The first constituent paragraph within this section was titled "Resetting the Force," and it spoke to all it took to sustain quality while cycling units in and out of combat. A second paragraph titled "Restructuring the Force" committed to a brigade-based structure that was strategically flexible and better able to generate forces for predictable rotations. "Rebalancing the Force" announced a move away from a focus on combat capabilities per se to develop the more diverse capabilities required by contemporary operations. "Stabilizing the Force" described transition to a unit replacement system that would allow soldiers to train, deploy, fight, and redeploy together. Further paragraphs within this section spoke to "Integrating Component Technology of Future Combat Systems," "Developing Networked Information Systems," and "Modernizing Institutional Army Processes." All these had a contemporary more so than a futuristic ring to them. The 2005 edition of FM–1 established eight campaign objectives associated with Army transformation, the first of which was to "support global operations." The other seven were "adapt and improve total Army capabilities," "optimize Reserve Component capabilities," "sustain the right all-volunteer force," "adjust the global footprint," "build the future force," "adapt the institutional Army," and "develop a joint, interdependent logistic structure." Of these, only "build the future force" was oriented on the far horizon. Transformation had been redefined. The new paradigm acknowledged full-spectrum capabilities and the distant future, but focus had understandably shifted to reinforcing capabilities most relevant to success in Afghanistan, Iraq, and the Global War on Terrorism as it evolved.[6]

Recycling Ulysses

Beginning in the summer of 2003 the issue dominating all others for the Department of the Army was the sheer effort of maintaining over a hundred thousand soldiers deployed in Iraq, and over twice that number deployed overall, from an active-duty end strength of 486,000. By September 2003, 144,000 National Guardsmen and Army Reservists were on active duty. When it became clear that tours in Iraq would average twelve months, and that OIF 2 would almost undoubtedly be followed by a similarly sized OIF 3 and OIF 4, a model for sustaining such a force in the field was necessary. Since the early twentieth-century fighting in the Philippines, the model for sustaining American units in combat overseas had been individual replacement. Transoceanic distances made unit rotations impractical, as did heavy losses to combat and disease. Effectiveness proved best maintained when individual replacements fell in upon units and equipment in theater. Generally there were enough "old hands" around to teach newcomers what they needed to know, and generally combat at the unit level was episodic enough to do so. During World War II this system sufficiently outperformed other alternatives so that it was retained in Korea and Vietnam. As Vietnam dragged on, however, the downside of individual replacement became increasingly visible. Unit cohesion eroded as soldiers came and went like so many passengers on a bus. Morale eroded with cohesion as draftees cycled in from a society increasingly opposed to the war, and leadership cracked from the strain of repeated tours. Noncommissioned officers were the hardest hit, and a rule of thumb emerged that the prospect of a third tour highly correlated with separation from the service. In the more benign but nevertheless busy deployment environment of the 1990s, participating in one or two deployments increased retention rates, but a third deployment within six years was more than most soldiers were willing to bear. By the 1990s the Army consisted solely of volunteers, and over half of them had families. Iraq increased deployment burdens by an order of magnitude, and these would be borne by the same volunteers. Schoomaker committed to unit rotations and unit manning upon his arrival. In his view, cohesion, morale, and effectiveness could only be maintained over the long haul by team players confident in each other. He envisioned a force generation cycle wherein units deployed, fought, redeployed, stood down, reorganized, and prepared to deploy again. This would have dramatic implications for organization, command structure, the reserve component, installations, and the very nature of service as a soldier.[7]

Army Staff principals tapped the Army Center of Military History and others for historical and analytic insights relevant to Schoomaker's unit manning proposal. Unit rotation and unit manning had been attempted before. Gyroscope, Overseas Unit Replacement System (OVUREP), Long Thrust, Rotational Plan (ROTAPLAN), Brigade 75, and Cohesion Operational Readiness and Training (COHORT) had all attempted such an approach with varying degrees of un-success. Indeed, the last time something approximating unit manning had been successful for Americans was in the Indian fighting Army of the late nineteenth century. Soldiers in that Army were generally in their regiments for the duration of their service. Units, almost always smaller than the regiments, deployed and redeployed from one outpost, foray, or campaign to another. Service was arduous, but combat was episodic and casualties were relatively few. Soldiers could reasonably anticipate ending a year alongside most of the comrades they had started it with. In this milieu of extended mutual service under tough conditions now legendary cavalry and "foot cavalry" regimental lineages were born. Promotions and schooling were less of an issue then than now, since both happened rarely. Few of the junior enlisted were married. Despite the failures of twentieth-century unit manning initiatives, there were now reasons to believe the Army could return to these nineteenth-century roots. First, post–Cold War combat operations

Unit manning envisioned companies remaining together for an entire tour, to be replaced by a like-type unit.

had been arduous and demanding, but casualties had been few. Huge qualitative overmatches, sensible tactics, and superb medical support kept losses to combat and disease down. The worst days in Iraq saw losses on orders of magnitude less than like-sized forces would have considered routine in World War II, Korea, or Vietnam. Effectiveness in combat did not depend on large recurrent infusions of individual replacements. Second, the Army had gotten into the habit of flying units overseas to marry up with equipment in the field, with minimal turnover times and maximal efficiency. The 3d Infantry Division (Mechanized) had ridden into Baghdad on equipment drawn from Pre-positioning of Materiel Configured to Unit Sets (POMCUS) stocks in Kuwait, and stocks in theater had multiplied since. Indeed, half of the Black Hawk helicopters in the Army were in CENTCOM when Schoomaker committed to unit rotations, and percentages for equipment of other types were high as well. For fifteen years Army units had routinely rehearsed the procedures that rotations into or out of Iraq would require. This included passing along sectors of responsibility in such places as Somalia or the Balkans. The term "right seat" became a verb describing an incoming leader accompanying his predecessor long enough to understand the mission he was undertaking. Third, a dozen years of investment in stateside installations as power projection platforms and the collateral evolution of split-based logistics offered improved sustainment to units operating overseas and to their families remaining at home. Concerning this, more later. Finally, distances that were daunting in 1907 were unimpressive now. Cellular phones, e-mail, and other communications marvels allowed units and individuals to remain connected with their home station and families in an unprecedented manner. An emergency leave to deal with a family crisis or a death in the family did not imply a long-term loss. Global travel by air was routine. The wounded would probably convalesce at a hospital proximate to their families. A soldier fighting in Afghanistan was less removed from his home station than his nineteenth-century predecessor would have been had he been but a two-day ride from Fort Apache. The paradigm of contemporary operations was more akin to those of the Indian-fighting Army than to the bloodbaths of World War I, World War II, Korea, or Vietnam.[8]

If unit manning and unit rotation were to work, there would have to be sufficient units to rotate. The proposed force generation cycle wherein units deployed, fought, redeployed, stood down, reorganized, and prepared to deploy again implied that there would be units at each phase of this cycle at any given point in time. Initial deployments to Operation IRAQI FREEDOM had been on a division basis, as had been the case for major operations since World War I. Reimer's Strike Force and Shinseki's interim brigade combat team had both embodied the concept that brigade combat teams of about thirty-five hundred soldiers would be nimbler as deployment options than divisions of perhaps twenty thousand soldiers. This was even more true because no two divisions seemed to be the same. Schoomaker followed up on this notion, with rotation more so than deployment per se in mind. The term used to describe these smaller contingents was *modular*. Modularity would create standardized expansible units capable of being tailored for any contingency. Tailoring forces by virtue of attachment and cross attachment was a venerable tradition within the Army, but theretofore the vast majority of combat support (e.g., artillery and engineer) and combat service support (e.g., maintenance and medical) assets had been held at the division level or higher and parceled out to combat brigades or battalions on a case-by-case basis. Combat battalions of armor and infantry were organized "pure" and cross-attached at the company and platoon levels to form combined-arms teams (of company size) and task forces (of battalion size). Modular brigades would anticipate customary cross attachments by building them in as organic units. The Training and Doctrine Command (TRADOC) model for a modular heavy brigade combat team, for example, featured two combined-arms maneuver battalions each of which had two tank companies, two mechanized infantry companies, and an engineer company. The brigade had its own organic armed reconnaissance squadron, fires battalion, support battalion, signal company, and military intelligence company as well. Conceptually, it was a miniature division—as divisions to this point had been the lowest level at which all branches were robustly represented. TRADOC designed similarly modular and interchangeable infantry brigade combat teams and aviation, fires, sustainment, maneuver enhancement and reconnaissance, surveillance, and target acquisition brigades. These presented the option of deploying and rotating units of far smaller size than had been the case when the division was the operational "chip on the board."[9]

Schoomaker not only intended to drive operational independence to the brigade level, he also intended to increase the number of brigade combat teams overall. When he arrived the Army had thirty-three maneuver brigades in the active component and fifteen deployable "enhanced brigades" in the National Guard. Of these, almost three-quarters of the active-component brigades and a third of the National Guard brigades were committed at the time. Clearly such proportions were unsustainable. Army planners had long argued that a ratio of one out of five available units deployed was sustainable over the long haul without qualitative erosion. Under duress, one out of three could work for shorter periods: one deployed, one preparing to deploy, and one recovering from deployment. Higher proportions of units deployed would at some point render a rotational model infeasible and force units to remain overseas, sustained by individual replacements. Perhaps conscription would be required as well. Schoomaker aspired to increase the number of maneuver brigades to as many as eighty-two, a 70 percent increase over the forty-eight then available. Such expansion could be achieved by reducing the maneuver battalions in each brigade to two from the customary three (albeit with the addition of a reconnaissance squadron), by bringing all National Guard brigades up to the mobilization expectations of the enhanced brigades, and by transferring personnel from low-demand to high-demand military occupational specialties. By January 2004 restructuring proposals envisioned a redistribution of 100,000 billets, with field artillery, air defense, and engineer specialties losing most heavily. The Department of Defense allowed a temporary increase in manpower of up to 30,000 to allow overhead to facilitate the redistribution. Active-component maneuver brigade combat teams were to increase in number from thirty-three to forty-eight, and National Guard enhanced brigades from fifteen to thirty-four. Once deployed, brigade combat teams were to increase their effectiveness by employing selected units in secondary roles. Artillery, engineers, and tankers, for example, routinely served as infantry in Iraq. In due course many such units fell in on two sets of equipment in Iraq, HMMWVs for routine use and their original table of organization and equipment (TOE) heavy items when tactical circumstances required it. Schoomaker pushed subordinates to achieve modularity quickly, timing reconfigurations into brigade combat teams with rotational returns to Iraq. The 3d Infantry Division seized Baghdad during Operation IRAQI FREEDOM and rotated home in August 2003. Its brigade combat teams were scheduled to return to Iraq in January 2005. That became the milestone to reorganize the division into the new brigade modular format. Short-circuiting traditional force planning procedures, Schoomaker directed the 3d Infantry Division's new commander, Major General William G. Webster, to reorganize his brigade combat teams from three to five while drawing only on manpower and equipment the division already possessed. As subsequent units became due to return overseas, their deployments too became milestones for reorganization. TRADOC caught up with the process, and modular units of TRADOC's design superseded modular units of local design before the 3d Infantry Division actually deployed. The inventory of brigade combat teams steadily expanded, although the notion of creating five from a three-brigade division ultimately was abandoned in favor of creating four. Ambitions for the inventory of brigade combat teams decreased to forty-two in the active component and twenty-eight in the National Guard—still a 46 percent increase. Numbers remained precarious. Through 2005—indeed through 2009, as this author writes—the Army did not achieve the target of only deploying one brigade in three, much less one in five. Brigades routinely rotated back to Iraq with little over a year at the home station, but the principal of unit rotation was nevertheless preserved.[10]

The shift to a brigade-based Army required reexamination of echelons above the brigade. Combat support and combat service support assets formerly held at division and corps levels were harvested to fill out the modular brigade design, providing the brigade unprecedented autonomy and self-sufficiency. This radically diminished the role of division and corps with respect to managing and distributing such assets. A possibility existed that the layers of hierarchy distinguishing division, corps, army, and the army component of a theater might be reduced. At least as early as General Reimer's Army After Next, wargamed simulations experimented with thinning out an echelon of command. In theory, advances with respect to digitization, communications, and situational awareness would allow the Army to "flatten" its hierarchy, as had many civilian corporations. During General Shinseki's tenure this line of thought continued, and analysts coined abstract "unit of purpose" designations to encourage thinking outside of the current organizational framework. The "unit of action" (UA) would be a fixed organization with prescribed tactical missions. The "unit of employment x" (UEx) would coordinate UAs and fight the battle at the higher tactical level. The "unit of employment y" (UEy) would coordinate UEx's and fight the battle at the operational level. Either the UEx or the UEy could serve as a Joint Forces Land Component Commander (JFLCC), depending on the scale of the operations and the theater. Schoomaker continued these deliberations. The UEx emerged as a nimble command with three deployable command posts, a mobile command group, and a special troops battalion providing security, signal, and life support. It could command and control a mix of combat, combat support, and combat service support UAs. The UEy was less nimble and more complex, a regionally focused headquarters with dedicated intelligence, sustainment, civil affairs, and "network" commands with the capacity to command and control some mix of UEx's and combat support and combat service support UEy's. The terms UA, UEx, and UEy facilitated brainstorming but were not intended as actual unit nomenclature. Converting these concepts to field-worthy unit designations brought to the surface practical considerations that altered the neatness of deleting an echelon of command. The Army's Center of Military History had staff responsibility for unit designations. It staffed and briefed alternatives that variously eliminated the terms *brigade, division, corps,* or *army* from the lexicon. The alternatives encountered understandable push-back from individuals with emotional attachments to a particular brigade, division, corps, or army, of course. They also encouraged further precision, since names matter. Most involved in the deliberations had personal memories of unique and complementary roles played by brigades, divisions, corps, and Third Army in Desert Storm and Iraqi Freedom. Continuing operations in Iraq, Afghanistan, and elsewhere in CENTCOM were too challenging, complex, and diverse for Third Army or anyone else to directly control all of the headquarters operating at the tactical level. A single commander could usefully grasp the essentials—that is to say, know enough to be helpful—of but a handful of subordinate operations and battles no matter how much information he or she was provided. Politics often required the presence of a three-star general, but not so many as to justify designating all UEx's as three-star headquarters. Schoomaker sought the counsel of General Sullivan and selected AUSA-connected "grey beards" to review the unit designation alternatives. The supported movement in the direction of nimbler headquarters but counseled that a massive rash of unit redesignations beyond those already made necessary by reorganization might be disruptive and demoralizing. In the midst of war and recurrent rotations, soldiers valued stability. This was, after all, the logic of unit manning. In the end pragmatism trumped neatness. Schoomaker decided the Army needed both two-star and three-star UEx's, to add an echelon or emphasis when necessary. The UA became a brigade combat team, the two-star UEx a division, the three-star UEx a corps, and the UEy a regional headquarters with an army designation. Divisions and corps were now smaller, nimbler, and more flexible as headquarters. They could be constructed into hierarchies and rotated with each other as circumstances required. In due course the entropy of rotations progressed to the point that brigade combat teams routinely served under headquarters wearing patches other than their own.[11]

The implications to the reserve component of post-2003 rotations and reorganization to a brigade-based modular Army were huge. The sheer magnitude of requirements in Iraq and Afghanistan guaranteed they would participate in rotations on an unprecedented scale. Half of the maneuver brigades in the Army were in the National Guard. Of twelve fire brigades envisioned, six would be in the National Guard. Of sixteen maneuver enhancement brigades envisioned, ten would be in the National Guard and three in the Army Reserve. Of five battlefield surveillance brigades envisioned, two would be in the Army Reserve. Of thirty-three sustainment brigades envisioned, eleven would be in the National Guard and eight in the Army Reserve. Of nineteen combat aviation brigades envisioned, eight would be in the National Guard. With these proportions, any sensible rotational scheme would inevitably take reserve-component assets into account. Within two years over 168,000 Guardsmen and 140,000 Reservists were veterans of mobilization and overseas deployment—well over half the total in both cases. Eight National Guard brigade combat teams would be in Iraq and Afghanistan at the same time. The National Guard's 42d Infantry Division would deploy under the new modular design with two active-component and two reserve-component brigade combat teams. The 3d Infantry Division would command and control two brigade combat teams wearing its own patch and also the National Guard's 256th Infantry and 278th Cavalry. The fifteen National Guard enhanced brigades that had been first up for deployment were expanding to twenty-eight modular maneuver brigade combat teams and eight division headquarters of UEx design. Commitment to twelve months on the ground overseas pushed mobilization expectations for deploying reserve-component units to at least fifteen months, to allow time for processing and training. Although reserve-component deployments overseas had risen steadily through the post–Cold War era, with Iraqi Freedom they experienced a further dramatic leap. For individuals deployments had been largely collaborative, with enough slack in the system that they were in effect voluntary. Now the very act of joining the reserve component implied deployment. Recognizing that their citizen-soldiers had multiple careers and that employers demanded a modicum of predictably, the director of the National Guard designed a six-year force generation cycle and the chief of the Army Reserve a five-year cycle. These were analogous to the deploy-reset-retrain-prepare-deploy cycles of the active component, albeit on longer timelines. Individual Guardsmen and Reservists had to be physically and psychologically prepared for the near inevitability of overseas deployment. Headquarters scrubbed their rosters to identify individuals who had not yet deployed. The new rigor was not pleasing to all, and both the National Guard and the Army Reserve experienced perturbations with respect to enlistment and retention. These proved modest in effect, however, and numbers stabilized and improved as the new battle rhythm and revised expectations took hold.[12]

Recurrent rotations altered the rhythm of stateside installations and furthered their transformation into power projection platforms. We have already commented that an institutional bias against "homesteading" eroded in the aftermath of the Cold War. Dramatic reductions in overseas permanent changes of station, quests for family stability amid increasing deployments, and spousal employment combined to diminish personnel managers' expectations that soldiers would progress through diverse posts at home and overseas during the course of their careers. Unit manning specifically embraced the notion that soldiers would have a home station to which they returned between deployments. Given consolidation, and the ever-increasing job options at such mega-posts as Fort Bragg or Fort Hood, it was now possible that most soldiers could spend their entire careers—other than when deployed—at the same post. Their children could grow up in a single school system and their spouses could have geographically stable careers of their own. This approximated the long-standing Navy model that had retained families amid recurrent deployments and marked further evolution from a forward stationed to an expeditionary Army. Divisions in the United States had generally been consolidated at a single post. This tradition continued, and the additional maneuver brigade wearing the division patch that stood up with modularity generally went to the same post as well. By the time of the OIF3 and OIF4 rotations (*Map 6*) to Iraq the manning, equipping, and training demands on installations were so great that brigades had to be offset in their cycles. One or two could be deployed, one in the intense final preparations for deployment and one or two in recovery from deployment. This phenomenon had been foreseen and was built in to the newly designed Army Force Generation (ARFORGEN) model. Each post was its own little hurricane carrying brigades through the cycle in turn, evening out demands on the installation over time because there was such a cycle. The division headquarters rotated overseas as well, but because of the cycle did so with only one or two maneuver brigades wearing its own patch. Combat support and combat service support brigades accompanying it were likely to wear its patch, but even with regard to them the entropy of rotation diminished connections between divisions and brigades. It was not uncommon for a deployed division headquarters to preside over brigades with a half dozen different patches. This practical application of modularity furthered the autonomy of brigades and brigade commanders, perhaps even more than theory and policy would have. If the brigade's connection with the division was diminished, its connection with the installation was reinforced. The ARFORGEN cycle demanded direct liaison between deployable unit and installation, particularly given the recurrent absences of division headquarters. When a brigade deployed, this connection continued. Replacements, convales-

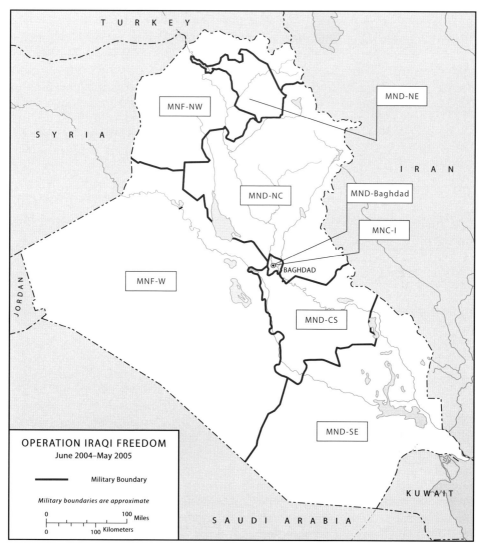

OPERATION IRAQI FREEDOM
June 2004–May 2005

Military Boundary

Military boundaries are approximate

0   100 Miles

0   100 Kilometers

Map 6

cents, unique major end items, and significant inventories of repair parts processed through the installation to and from theater. In accordance with concepts of split-basing, the theater provided consumables and common supply items. As the theater matured, an increasing proportion of the unit equipment required remained in theater for units to fall in upon. This was particularly true when theater usages departed from TOE, such as tankers and artillerymen falling in on up-armored HMMWVs, for example. Equipment that units left behind when deployed was serviced, secured, and stored on the installation. When units returned, the equipment they brought back with them had accumulated enormous maintenance debts. Hard use and a hostile environment

261

wore heavily on it; usage and degradation were up to ten times prewar levels. "Reset" for returning units implied depot overhauls well beyond customary budgets and expenses that dwarfed the so-called "budgets" brigades had previously handled. Congressional supplementals requested for shop work to repair war-related damage climbed from $1.2 billion in 2004 through $2.9 billion in 2005 to $3.2 billion in 2006. Installation logisticians and depots coordinated most of this work through the Army Materiel Command with brigades and below as customers—and with divisions not particularly involved. Units redeployed to the home station, turned in dilapidated equipment, went on block leave, undertook the largely personnel-oriented activities of early recovery, and then drew new or rebuilt equipment before it was time to train again in earnest. The vision of installations as power projection platforms advanced by Generals Sullivan and Franks with the 1993 edition of Field Manual 100–5 had truly arrived.[13]

The rotation of units through Afghanistan and Iraq was complex and demanding, yet the greatest challenges were faced by the individual soldiers within the units—asked to recycle into combat time and again. As we have seen, sustained expeditionary combat on this scale was unprecedented for a volunteer Army. Before 9-11 about one-third of the Army's new accessions did not complete their first tour for one reason or another. Those who were going to wash out disproportionately did so during initial entry training, but a trickle of attrition continued month after month through the lifespan of each cohort. Counterintuitively to most outsiders, deployed units had lower attrition and higher reenlistment rates than the Army at large, a phenomenon explained by those within the Army as the psychological result of doing something important. Enthusiasm did not persist through recurrent deployments, however, with third tours statistically problematic with respect to retention. Schoomaker believed unit manning with attendant home stationing, family stability, and spousal employment options would improve performance in this regard. If casualties were low, first-term attrition stable (and thus predictable), and career soldiers supported by the camaraderie of a "band of brothers" and the indulgence of comfortably established families, perhaps a career of recurrent deployment would be accepted as routine. This depended, of course, on the stress of combat. A mysterious "Gulf War Syndrome" plagued veterans of DESERT STORM. Insofar as symptoms were physical in origin, they seemed linked to varying "cocktails" of pyridostigmine bromide (PB) anti-nerve agent pills, pesticides, chemical agents released from destroyed munitions, toxic fumes from oil well fires, and depleted uranium residue to which troops had been exposed. These potential poisons could be avoided, but posttraumatic stress disorder (PTSD), first defined in 1980 to address diagnoses in Vietnam War veterans, was at play as well. PTSD results from traumatic life-threatening personal experiences that reasonably evoke fear or horror. Symptoms include nightmares, flashbacks, withdrawal, irritability, insomnia, aggression, and poor concentration. Most soldiers involved in significant ground combat are exposed to trauma of the type associated with PTSD. Whether or not they develop the condition depends on a number of factors, perhaps most significantly on a process labeled "recontextualization." During recontextualization an individual comes to grips with the experience, identifies its uniqueness and his or her reaction to it, puts it into the larger context of life experiences and hardships, and eventually "puts it behind him." This process can be enormously advanced by sympathetic and understanding confidants. After World Wars I and II soldiers redeployed from combat, mustered at ports of reembarkation, and steamed home on troopships in the company of others who had shared their experiences. The process took months, and most went through "decompression" wherein they and their comrades mutually worked their way through their experiences before confronting the world outside the Army. Vietnam veterans too often had the surreal experience of desperate combat followed by quick airplane trips into social settings wherein those around them had no idea what they had been through. This lack of decompression was too often repeated after DESERT STORM, with predictable results. Going into IRAQI FREEDOM the Army Medical Command determined not to repeat such mistakes. Decompression after combat was to be a feature of medical discipline as ubiquitous as vaccination, malaria prophylaxis, and tuberculosis testing. Medical personnel were trained to facilitate this task, and primary groups were to collectively discuss potentially traumatic experiences in their presence and outside it. Sharp-eyed unit leaders, medical personnel, and chaplains would observe their flocks carefully, referring those demonstrating signs of PTSD for further evaluation. Execution proved imperfect, with application sporadic in theater and generally too brief upon redeployment. Leaders and key personnel too often excused themselves from participation, arguing other priorities. Career soldiers experiencing symptoms of PTSD too often avoided assistance, embarrassed to demonstrate "weakness." Demobilizing Guardsmen and Reservists were difficult to corral into sessions or to follow up on. Nevertheless the command, medical, and chaplaincy efforts to more directly address PTSD seem to have been of use. A 1990 National Vietnam Veterans Readjustment Survey estimated 31 percent of Vietnam veterans suffered PTSD, of whom subsequent analysts characterized 11 percent as suffering clinically significant impairment. A recent study of veterans of Afghanistan and Iraq suggests about 4 percent developed diagnosis-level symptoms of PTSD. Such figures are subject to interpretation and are inexact, with much that remains to be learned. For the Army, keeping the damages inflicted by PTSD to an absolute minimum was essential if it was to succeed in rotating combat-effective units back and forth from Afghanistan and Iraq.[14]

Stress on soldiers is hugely affected by the care they see given the wounded and the dead. Command comments that 99 percent of soldiers returned "without a scratch on them" may have been true for many or even most units, but it is human nature to contemplate being among that unlucky 1 percent. Medical and medical evacuation assets pushed well forward, minutes away from virtually anywhere troops deployed in Afghanistan or Iraq. Intense training in advanced skills for combat medics, the proliferation of lay "combat lifesavers," aggressive use of forward surgical teams, and skillful use of evacuation assets drove the proportion of soldiers who died of their wounds to less than 10 percent—half of even DESERT STORM's superlative performance. Disease rates were pushed to historical

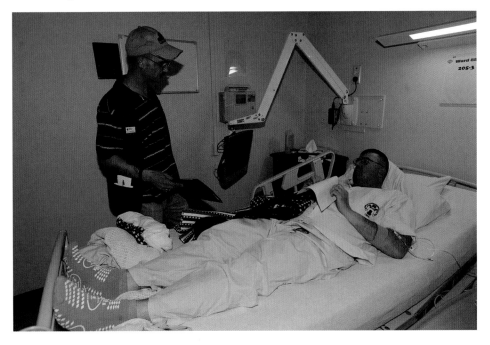

Wounded soldiers remained in the Army, and their recovery became a cooperative effort involving units, medical facilities, families, and volunteers.

lows as well. Ubiquitous and effective Kevlar body armor dramatically reduced mortality rates. Astonished television viewers watched footage of soldiers shot in the chest getting back on their feet and continuing their missions. Ironically, this very success presented a dilemma of another sort. Horrifically wounded soldiers who would have died in earlier wars survived. Body armor protected the core but left limbs exposed, leaving important fractions of the wounded to be amputees or multiple amputees. Blasts from improvised explosive devices caused concussions and traumatic head injuries. The Army family now included thousands of soldiers needing long-term medical care. In an earlier era soldiers permanently disabled by wounds passed to the responsibility of the Veterans Administration and became generally invisible to the Army. This "expeditious, compassionate disposition of the unfit soldier" now proved less satisfactory for several reasons. The "band of brothers" mentality that unit manning was intended to induce encouraged soldiers—both the wounded and their comrades—to be less willing to let go. Families were neighbors, worldwide communications were instantaneous, evacuation pyramided backwards through a discrete number of major hospitals, and hospitals at the mega-posts were capable enough that most convalescence could continue there. Soldiers still in the field telephoned family and friends in the United States to check up on hospitalized comrades. Highly visible examples such as Generals Franks, McCaffrey, and Shinseki inspired severely wounded soldiers to believe they could continue military careers, as did huge advances with respect to prosthetics. Amputees badgered bewildered doctors to return them expeditiously to their units. Brain and other blast-related injuries could be subtle and often required extended observation before a prognosis could be made. Soldiers accumulated in medical hold or medical holdover for prolonged periods of diagnosis or recovery. Fairly or unfairly, many soldiers were suspicious of the treatment they would receive from the Veterans Affairs (VA) department. Mindful of real or imagined problems in the transition from the care of the Army to that of the VA, General Keane directed the Army Medical Command to devise programs of "mentorship." Each soldier considered for medical release or medical retirement was to have a knowledgeable adviser guide him through the process, elaborating options at every turn. The Army Staff and others routinely visited the wounded at nearby Walter Reed Army Medical Center, a pattern mirrored at posts throughout the country. These senior officers in turn became advocates for soldiers they encountered, often soldiers with whom they had served before. Casualties were few enough, the Army small enough, and relationships intimate enough that paradigms governing the severely wounded changed. In due course this expanded sense of responsibility led to the establishment of Warrior Transition Units. The general public became involved. Interest resulted from media attention to such high-profile cases as Jessica Lynch, but also from the patriotic sympathies of public leaders and average citizens. National Guard and Army Reserve casualties brought the issue home to communities all over America. Civic initiatives such as the "Wounded Warrior" program spontaneously emerged. Attention similarly fixed on the fallen and their families. The service vice chiefs collectively drilled death benefits and gratuities and lobbied to bump automatically available life insurance up to $250,000 for deaths out of theater and $400,000 for in theater. The death gratuity was to be $100,000 for all. Survival Assistance Officers were appointed immediately on notification of a fatality, and they established personal relationships with the families of the fallen. A general officer was to be present at each funeral, and uniformed attendance was robust both at funerals stateside and at memorial services overseas. Funerals and memorial services for National Guardsmen and Army Reservists turned out entire communities throughout America. Combat deaths were few enough that these remained unique and memorable events. This attentiveness to the wounded and the dead was visible to serving soldiers. An ironic aspect of war making is that such deference enhances the morale of those still capable of bearing arms. Recurrent rotation into a war with no visible end required soldiers who believed their every need would be met if they were wounded and their family's every need would be met if they were killed.[15]

Adapting to Afghanistan and Iraq

In Chapter 9 we will discuss the performance of Army units in Afghanistan and Iraq, with an emphasis on how Army transformation efforts during the period 1989–2005 played out in that performance. Here we will discuss how events in Afghanistan and Iraq affected technical aspects of Army transformation. The two approaches are related, with one the inverse of the other. We have already described the Army's redefinition of transformation, given the demands of the Global War on Terrorism. We have also described institutional changes to accommodate recurrent rotations. Technologies associated with transformation, and the pace at which they were to be applied, altered as well. Digitization and precision-guided munitions proved valuable, and the deployed Army scrambled to improve on both. Some technologies from the former Objective Force were relevant enough that Army transformers sought to accelerate them, whereas others were deferred or deleted. Research and development morphed in emphasis, and field insights and improvisation fed back into procurement efforts. Several items of erstwhile "legacy" equipment now seemed less obsolescent. The Army still envisioned itself as a transforming force, but the nature and paraphernalia of that transformation changed.

In early 2003 digitization was still nascent for the Army as a whole, although most units had had some exposure to it. Only the 4th Infantry Division, delayed in arriving for Operation IRAQI FREEDOM by the intransigence of the Turks, was truly digitized. The Army scrambled to bolt 1,200 digitizing add-on kits onto vehicles of the 3d Infantry Division and the Marine Expeditionary Force before they attacked into Iraq. The system bore the formidable title "Force XXI Battle Command, Brigade and Below—Blue Force Tracking" (FBCB2-BFT), mercifully shortened to "blue force tracking" (BFT) in the vernacular. BFT featured a rugged, 12-inch laptop-looking computer, a global positioning system (GPS), a satellite terminal and antenna, command and control software, and mapping software. Vehicles thus equipped automatically updated their locations, represented by an icon on the computer screen, throughout the system and thus contributed to a shared picture of the battlefield. BFT also allowed the exchange of electronic text messages and downloaded maps at varying levels of resolution. Although only deployed on key leader vehicles at first, BFT proved immensely popular. Results during IRAQI FREEDOM corroborated the findings of Advanced Warfighter Experiments and other digital exercises over the past ten years. BFT enhanced command and control, reduced fratricide, and facilitated land navigation. British units attacking alongside the Americans were fitted out with forty-seven BFT sets and shared the common operating picture. In April 2003 the 4th Infantry Division arrived in Iraq, multiplying digital capabilities in the theater overnight. Further reinforcing units were equipped with BFT, and the add-on kits were applied more broadly to units already in theater as well. Soon most convoys rolled with BFT in their front and rear vehicles. Dispersed operations day and night—patrolling, security outposts, sweeps for contraband, seizing suspected terrorists, training Iraqi counterparts, and other initiatives—scattered Americans throughout Iraq, increasing the demand for BFT and similar systems. Within five years 55,000 sets had been purchased and applied, and a total of 160,000 were programmed. This is not to mention the new or rebuilt equipment wherein digital capabilities were intrinsic, or the ubiquitous presence of GPS independent of BFT. Digitization was not confined to the tip of the spear. Logisticians used radio identification tags and scanners to inventory arriving containers and equipment into databases and then digitally managed that information as they sped the hardware on its way. Unlike DESERT STORM logisticians they did not build up mountains of supplies but instead smoothed deliveries into something closer to "just-in-time" logistics. During the height of the buildup the 143d Transportation Command downloaded more than a hundred ships through the port of Shuaiba without ever having more than a few hundred containers on the ground at one time. Movement control teams similarly scanned the identification cards of arriving troops into databases to facilitate, among other things, the delivery of up to 600,000 pounds of mail per day. Troops in the field exploited Web connections to share information, reach back into archives for relevant techniques or doctrine, or post inquiries to which specialized agencies responded. Conversations in the Army General Staff Council meeting turned to the particulars of BFT fielding and to competition for satellite bandwidth as an ever more significant Army priority. Digital equipment did need to be improved upon. BFT at the time updated vehicle locations every five minutes. This was helpful, but too slow for fast-moving operations. Digital equipment was too often rendered inoperable by hard use, horrific weather conditions, or inexperienced operators. Operations in Afghanistan and Iraq nevertheless reinforced the Army's determination to digitize itself and further embedded digitization in its definition of transformation. Insofar as there was debate, it was about whether the Army could acquire digital capabilities more quickly and how it could improve them.[16]

It should be noted that eagerness for improved digitization did not particularly translate into interest in accelerating the manned vehicles of future combat systems (FCSs) and much of the other paraphernalia of the Objective Force as a whole. Objective Force technologies perceived as potentially useful in Afghanistan and Iraq were, as we shall see, cherry-picked for greater attention. The 1,200 BFT sets of the pre–IRAQI FREEDOM surge went onto legacy vehicles the 3d Infantry Division and Marines already had on hand. Most of these were venerable M1A1 tanks and M2/3 Bradleys supplied from pre-positioned stocks rather than shipped from a home station. British vehicles were not only venerable, they were foreign in several senses of the term. Hasty digitization created odd combinations. The Army's standard command and administrative vehicle, the HMMWV, was pressed into service patrolling. Given thousands of patrols dispatched each day, it was impractical to mount or support each patrol with tanks or Bradleys. In the face of small-arms fire and IEDs, troops in conventional HMMWVs were horribly exposed. The immediate response in theater was to weld scrap metal onto the exposed sides and undercarriages of the HMMWVs, adding weight but gaining crew protection. The ungainly looking results seemed anything but futuristic, digital capabilities jammed into legacy vehicles resurfaced with debris scavenged from junk yards. Convoy protection generated further throwbacks. Between 800 and 1,300 Coalition supply trucks were on the road at any given time. Logisticians in theater e-mailed Army historians out of theater to get specifications for the fabled gun trucks of Vietnam. Soon up-armored HMMWVs were joined by five-ton trucks fitted with ring mounts, heavy weapons, and slats of improvised armor. HMMWVs and five-tons rolled amid diverse serials of military and commercial vehicles. The miniature fortresses facilitated command and control with appliqué digital equipment

Up-armored HMMWVs with specialized equipment became ever more a requirement in restive Iraq.

while providing security with old guns and even older protective architecture. Wags likened the potpourri of vehicles in a convoy to scenes from the apocalyptic *Mad Max* movies. The Army Materiel Command raced to get ahead of this in-theater improvisation. Within less than a year it designed and developed standardized add-on armor kits and dispatched 7,000 to Iraq. The Army went from 500 up-armored HMMWVs worldwide in the summer of 2003 to 5,000 in Iraq in the fall of 2004. Plans would expand this number to 8,000 in Iraq and 13,000 overall. Thinking beyond up-armored HMMWVs and five-ton trucks, the Army and Marine Corps experimented with hull-shaped (and thus blast-resistant) mine-resistant ambush-protected (MRAP) vehicles. These were available in several designs through domestic and foreign vendors. Although awkward and top-heavy, a design called the Cougar attracted attention when it weathered three hundred IED attacks without a fatality. More immediately available were the Stryker vehicles of the Stryker brigades, first deployed to Iraq in the summer of 2003. They too required improvised add-on armor—bar armor to prematurely detonate shaped munitions—but proved ideal for convoy escort and extended operations. Rolling along on durable tires at impressive speeds, they provided far more heavily armored firepower than HMMWVs and trucks at a fraction of the operating costs of tanks and Bradleys. They were intrinsically digitized and carried ample contingents of heavily armored infantrymen. They soon were recognized as the most singularly capable force for the low- to mid-intensity combat environments they found themselves in. Like other workhorses in Iraq, the Strykers were not particularly futuristic. They represented digitization applied to vehicles of long-existing design. They were Force XXI more so than Objective Force.[17]

Some items in the Objective Force paraphernalia seemed relevant enough to operations in Afghanistan and Iraq that Army transformers sought to accelerate their development and further integrate them into ongoing operations. Cases in point included unmanned aerial vehicles (UAVs), robots, and precision-guided munitions. During the advance on Baghdad V Corps got some useful intelligence from UAVs, but so many manned platforms were deployed on the ground and aloft during the intense operations of that phase that information from UAVs represented a minor fraction of the whole. Information from satellites trumped information from UAVs for deep targets. As operations in Iraq dragged on, however, the daring and persistence with which UAVs could

Unmanned aerial vehicles, varying greatly in size and capabilities, assumed increasing responsibilities for battlefield surveillance.

be used provided an attractive alternative to sustaining pilots aloft and at risk. This was particularly true when trolling supply routes or observing isolated compounds during prolonged periods when the probability of a valuable "catch" was low. During the first year in Iraq "Hunter" UAVs logged about 4,000 hours and "Shadow" UAVs 5,000. This dramatically increased the continuity of overhead surveillance. At times payoffs were dramatic. Suspected "safe havens" were observed for suspicious vehicle traffic, and this was intercepted or engaged by alerted ground forces or aviators when identified. UAVs detected infiltrators attempting to implant IEDs, and these were similarly neutralized by aviators or troops on the ground. Through 2005 the Army did not employ UAVs as lethal platforms from which to launch strikes, although it did note Central Intelligence Agency (CIA) experimentation in that regard. Robotics offered another means to avoid exposing humans. Mounted on miniature tracks or rollers and equipped with cameras and other sensors, these were used to explore caves, tunnels, buildings, and other potential hideouts for explosives, ammunition, and hideaways. They rolled under vehicles to check for signs of munitions or tampering. Although their practical effect was at the time limited, their possibilities seemed promising. What, for example, if they became sophisticated enough to disarm IEDs as well as detect them? What if some fraction of the 800 to 1,300 supply trucks on the road at any one time were driven by robots rather than humans? If UAVs and robots were emerging technologies, precision-guided munitions (PGMs) were proven technology begging for better integration. Such integration required networked sensors, pervasive GPS, and communications that multiplied the number of observers on the ground that could bring Joint Direct Attack Munitions (JDAMs) and other cheap, generally available precision-guided munitions to bear. As operations in Iraq miniaturized and dispersed, Army transformers struggled to push the advantages of PGMs forward to each detached little contingent.[18]

Operations in Afghanistan and Iraq not only sharpened the focus of transformation initiatives already under way, they also deflected research and development into areas theretofore not particularly associated with transformation. The most striking case in point was that of improvised explosive devices. It did not take long for insurgents in Iraq to recognize they were at a huge disadvantage engaging American forces directly. A contingent as small as a Bradley platoon brought awesome firepower to bear that generally dwarfed what the insurgents could field. Elaborate communications brought speedy relief and massive firepower to Americans under attack. Insurgents had at most a few minutes to inflict what damage they could before the odds turned against them. This phenomenon is a timeless feature of guerrilla warfare. The Viet Cong, for example, were heavily outgunned by American forces. They increasingly relied upon mines, grenades, and booby traps to inflict casualties, and these ultimately accounted for over a quarter of the American dead. In Iraq circumstances were even more asymmetric, and Iraqi insurgents fell back upon explosive devices even more quickly. Within a year over half of American casualties resulted from IED attacks. Explosives and munitions were readily available in Iraq, and menus for triggering mechanisms were fairly common knowledge. In October 2003 the Army G–3, Lieutenant General Richard Cody, stood up an IED Task Force to coordinate efforts. Proposed solutions addressed intelligence, training, and technology. Intelligence could help one "get left of boom," a metaphor originating in the fact that times prior to an event appear to the left of it on a chronological chart. Early detection could catch insurgents in the act of planting IEDs or at least allow one to neutralize the IEDs before troops were in danger. Training would improve on such tactics and on other techniques and procedures to mitigate effects. Technology was at play as well. We have already mentioned robots. Electronic remote activation proved useful as well. Insurgents often relied on cellular phones, walkie-talkies, garage door openers, and even remotely controlled toys to detonate munitions. These rely on relatively predictable civilian bandwidths. If these are jammed with sufficient energy, IEDs to be triggered by them can be detonated prematurely or prevented from detonating at all. Soon a number of electronic devices, most notably the "Warlock" but including local improvisations, were turned to this purpose. If denied remote detonation, insurgents would have to run wire, set up mechanical triggers, or bury devices relying on direct ground pressure to achieve detonation. These approaches increased exposure and risk to the insurgents when in relatively open terrain. The IED Task Force evolved into the Army-led Joint IED Defeat Integrated Process Team in 2004 and into the Joint IED Defeat Organization in 2006. In due course its annual budget averaged $4 billion, and it turned research attention to a wide array of promising technologies to detect and defeat IEDs. Within a year of the establishment

Improved individual equipment incorporated advanced technologies and upgraded protection, particularly against improvised explosive devices (IEDs).

of the IED Task Force losses per incident with respect to IEDs fell 30 percent and continued to drop thereafter, but a cat-and-mouse game developed as the adversaries adapted to each other's methods. Other subjects for research and development considerably advanced by technological responses to Afghanistan and Iraq included mortar detection and interception, rocket detection and interception, and prostheses. Were all of the technologies under development to yield their full promise, soldiers of the intermediate future would bat down incoming rounds with speed-of-light lasers and replace lost limbs with equally responsive artificial ones. None of these technologies particularly figured in Army definitions of transformation prior to Operation IRAQI FREEDOM, but now command focus and congressional funding carried them forward in a vision of transformation that altered with operational circumstances.[19]

Not everything the Army needed in Iraq and Afghanistan required technological development, of course. Traditional supply requirements dominated logistical planning without being particularly transformative. Track on tanks and Bradleys, for example, experienced what had been a year's worth of mileage in a month or less. Tank track shoe production went from 15,000 a month to 50,000, and Bradley track shoe production from 28,000 to 70,000. Hard use bumped up the production of supplies of all types. Some hard use did lead to changes that ultimately proved transformative. This was particularly true in the case of equipment borne by individual soldiers. The rocky terrain of Afghanistan beat up the knees and elbows of soldiers frequently going to ground within it. An expedient

271

solution was to buy knee and elbow pads of essentially commercial design. Given that there were no front lines, soldiers throughout Afghanistan and Iraq needed body armor regardless of military occupational specialty (MOS) or assignment. Production soared from 1,200 sets a month to more than 25,000 sets a month. This Kevlar body armor consisted of a helmet and modular front and back plates initially, but exposure to IEDs led to the addition of side plates, shoulder guards, and experimentation with protection for the limbs themselves. Body armor compromised most pockets and limited what could be borne around the waist. Pockets migrated to sleeves and pants legs, and canteens transformed to camel-back tubular hydration systems. Operating in a mix of darkness, ambient light, and artificial illumination, troops took to the Army/Navy Portable Visual Search (AN/PVS) 14 and other monocular night-vision devices so that they were never caught in a single mode of vision if lighting quickly changed. This affected helmet design. Redesigned load-bearing equipment accommodated challenging environments and changing needs. Boots, gloves, socks, underwear, goggles, and myriad other items were adapted to the frigid mountains of Afghanistan, the blazing deserts of Iraq, and circumstances in between. Weight was an issue, particularly in the rugged terrain of Afghanistan, with troop loads pushing past 130 pounds for extended dismounted missions. Designers and procurement officers sought to shave weight with each new version of an item acquired. Much of this new equipment was of commercial design. Beginning in 2002 the Vice Chief of Staff initiated a Rapid Fielding Initiative under the Program Executive Office (PEO)-Soldier to rapidly coordinate, field, and modernize individual equipment, drawing upon off-the-shelf designs when feasible. In due course the Rapid Fielding Initiative directly affected every deploying soldier, and each deploying unit was "hosed down" in its turn with new equipment. Over time the net effect of sustained attention to individual equipment was to move Army transformation from a platform-centric phenomenon toward one considerably more soldier-centric. Along with Kevlar armor, terrain-adapted boots, high wick underwear, and other improvements in safety and comfort, GPS, cellular communications, headsets, microphones, digital displays, and other transformational technologies migrated off of vehicles and onto individual soldiers as well. This progression had long been contemplated, but war funding and unrelenting dependence on dismounts in Afghanistan and Iraq greatly hustled it along.[20]

Two signature programs associated with Army transformation lost traction in the aftermath of Operation Iraqi Freedom: the Comanche helicopter and future combat systems. The RAH–66 Comanche descended from the light helicopter experimental (LHX) program begun in 1982 and had long been touted as essential transformative technology. It featured composite materials, stealth technology, state-of-the-art navigation systems, advanced suites of sensors, and formidable firepower. It was to replace the venerable Kiowa Warrior as an armed scout and light attack helicopter. Although strongly encouraged by OSD, General Schoomaker came to his own conclusions in determining that $14 billion committed to the Comanche could be better spent elsewhere. In his view, two years of warfare and hard use had left Army aviation "busted." Aviation was one of the focus areas Schoomaker identified upon arrival. Deliberations within that focus area soon established that a major fraction of the technologies envisioned for Comanche could be spun forward onto existing platforms. Furthermore, UAVs were becoming increasingly attractive in reconnaissance roles, particularly when missions required prolonged surveillance. The Comanche was designed to infiltrate or breach sophisticated air defenses, fight for information in the face of determined opposition, and pass along targets to massed artillery, attack aviation, and Air Force assets. It was an overmatch for existing requirements in Afghanistan and Iraq, and battles against opponents suitable for its capabilities in the near term seemed unlikely. The aviation actually fighting in Afghanistan and Iraq, on the other hand, was stretched to the limit and could readily and quickly profit from qualitative upgrades. After a bit of haggling within the Army and with OSD, Comanche was terminated in February 2004. The $14 billion saved was diverted to the purchase of eight hundred new helicopters of existing design and to the upgrade of fourteen hundred more. Apache Longbow (AH–64D) modernization, for example, was to progress in blocks, incrementally advancing digital messaging, digital maps, situational awareness, avionics, and sensors. The modernized target acquisition and designation sight/pilot night-vision sensor (M-TADS/PNVS) radically advanced AH–64D target acquisition and night vision and would itself be improved upon by the "Arrowhead" module field retrofit thereafter. The upgraded AH–64D, partnered with contemporary state-of-the-art UAVs and upgraded OH–58D Kiowa Warriors, offered capabilities somewhat shy of those envisioned for the Comanche—but with considerably less cost and considerably more expediency. Future combat systems experienced drift analogous to that experienced by the Comanche, albeit with less dramatic or decisive results. From the beginning FCS had been envisioned as a "system of systems" advancing multiple technologies at once. It had acquired the numerical description "18 +1+1." There were eighteen systems under development to be linked together by one advanced digital network in the support of every single (one) soldier. The eighteen systems included eight manned ground vehicles, four classes of unmanned aerial vehicles, three classes of unmanned ground vehicles, unattended sensors, a non-line-of-sight launch system, and unattended intelligent munitions. The manned ground vehicles were to put infantry, armor, artillery, reconnaissance, and combat service support assets all on the same chassis with common automotives, communications, and computers. The vehicles were to weigh twenty-four tons but be even better protected and more lethal than contemporary vehicles through advanced technologies. For many the futuristic manned ground vehicles defined the term "FCS," with the other systems under development being peripheral and in support. This frame of reference reversed itself as the Army scrambled to harvest technologies from the future force that could be deployed quickly enough to be helpful in Iraq and Afghanistan. We have already noted the accelerated interest in UAVs and robotics (unmanned ground vehicles). Sensors and the advanced digital network seemed feasible for accelerated deployment, albeit on existing platforms, as well. The Army reprogrammed $9 billion for 2005–2011 from FCS programs to technological upgrades for existing ground vehicles. FCS manned ground vehicles had not yet gone the way of the Comanche, but they were to be delayed in favor of incremental upgrades to vehicles and equipment capable of fighting in the near term. Again fighting in Iraq and Afghanistan morphed the Army definition of transformation.[21]

Quadrennial Defense Review 2005

Iraq and Afghanistan dominated Army thinking by 2005 and were the most heavily contemplated subjects for the Department of Defense as well. They were not the only issues, however. The recurrent congressional requirement for a Quadrennial Defense Review proved to be a forcing function encouraging a broader and longer view. Remembering the hard-fought battles of Quadrennial Defense Review 1997 and Quadrennial Defense Review 2001, the Army Staff had maintained a standing Quadrennial Defense Review office to prepare for the next event. Much had changed since 2001. When Quadrennial Defense Review 2001 reported out, troop requirements in Afghanistan were modest and Homeland Defense a dominant concern. By 2005 troop requirements in Afghanistan and Iraq were huge, and manpower requirements routinely associated with Homeland Security were largely civilianized. The Army, active component and reserve component alike, focused on sustained warfare overseas. The Department of Defense adjusted its threat definition. Analysts derived a neat quadripartite chart from perpendicular axes, one running from low to high likelihood and the other from low to high (United States) vulnerability. It populated the low likelihood–low vulnerability quadrant with state-to-state confrontations employing conventional means. As long as the United States maintained its existing advantages, nations were unlikely to seek such a contest. Far more likely, albeit still but a modest risk to the United States if "effectively checked," were irregular challenges such as those the United States already faced in Iraq, Afghanistan, and the Global War on Terrorism. Unlikely, but posing a considerable risk if achieved, was a surprise technological breakthrough that might suddenly put the United States at an unexpected disadvantage. What, for example, if space assets were compromised by laser weapons, digital communications turned against the United States by cyberwarfare, nanotechnology turned into biological weaponry, and so forth? The United States had a wide range of venues wherein security depended on maintaining its technological edge. The high likelihood–high vulnerability quadrant featured weapons of mass destruction slipping into hostile and irresponsible hands. Pundits gave the Department of Defense threat analysis high marks for its insight and departure from tradition. The new threat model combined with ongoing operations to underscore the utility of soldiers and marines. The caveat that irregular warfare had to be effectively checked to remain a modest risk clearly defined a mission area for ground forces. The tens of thousands of troops already actively deployed for that purpose reinforced the point. The philosophical diminishment of traditional challenges, and the actual diminishment of air and maritime forces deployed by feasible traditional opponents, correspondingly diminished the logic of heavily investing in our own air and maritime forces. Research and development to protect against technological breakthroughs was broadly envisioned, not favoring any particular service. Similarly, the imperative of keeping weapons of mass destruction out of the

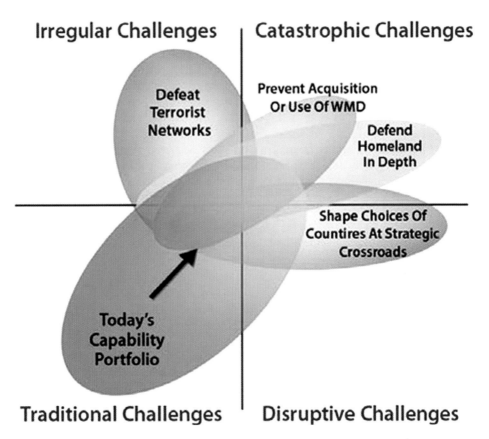

Irregular Challenges | **Catastrophic Challenges**

Defeat Terrorist Networks

Prevent Acquisition Or Use Of WMD

Defend Homeland In Depth

Shape Choices Of Countires At Strategic Crossroads

Today's Capability Portfolio

Traditional Challenges | **Disruptive Challenges**

The Quadrennial Defense Review 2005 quadripartite chart

wrong hands was not service specific. Examining current operations and future prospects, Quadrennial Defense Review–inspired reductions of ground forces were very unlikely. Indeed, the temporary increase of 30,000 to accommodate the shift to modularity now seemed likely to become permanent, and important congressional voices argued for even larger increases. Unlike Quadrennial Defense Review 1997 and Quadrennial Defense Review 2001, Army manpower and force structure were not on the block as potential bill payers. Pundits envisioned reduced procurement of the Air Force's F–22 and other aircraft and the sacrifice of a few planned Navy submarines instead.[22]

In the end Quadrennial Defense Review 2005 did not particularly require bill payers. Reporting out in February 2006, it concluded that overall force structure was about right. The F–22 and some other high-cost Air Force and Navy programs were to be stretched out in time rather than actually reduced. The same was true of the Army's future combat systems. The report did not particularly get into budgets, but subsequent interplay between the Pentagon and Congress did not much alter traditional apportionments among the services or commitments to major programs. Indeed, the Quadrennial Defense Review process now seemed largely detached from the actual allocation of resources. Money was not that great an issue in this time of war, and significant cuts to major programs would require hard battles with congressmen whose constituents and supporters had been gored. Few saw the need or had the stomach for such a battle. Pundits balanced praise of the Quadrennial Defense Review's threat analysis and strategic vision with criticism that significant changes in force structure and funding did not result. They did not have to. The rude fact was that the wars in Iraq and Afghanistan had largely escaped extant planning, programming, and budgeting processes, and funds committed to them could be readily enough adapted to broader purposes. Unlike earlier major wars, Afghanistan and Iraq were not initiated with anticipatory hand-wringing concerning how they were to be paid for. They were to be brief and Iraq, like Kuwait, was to pay for itself through its own intrinsic resources and the largesse of grateful allies. Until this worked out, funding shortfalls were to be handled by congressional supplemental appropriations, as had been the case with Somalia and the Balkans. The Defense budget was the product of long-standing processes, featured huge sunk costs and sweeping existing equities, and was not much given to quick changes. The Defense apportionment envisioned out as far as 2010 was 25 percent for the Army and about 30 percent each for the Navy and Air Force—about what it had been in 1975. Rumsfeld's emphasis on missile defense remained, although the Army Space and Missile Defense Command found itself divided between space services provided to troops on the ground overseas and technological efforts to develop and field advanced missile defense systems at home. Supplemental appropriations overlapped the base budget with respect to expenses addressed, but were separate. The Defense budget paid salaries and procured equipment; supplementals paid the further unprogrammed expenses that operations abroad required. Understandably, supplementals heavily favored the Army and Marine Corps. In Fiscal Year (FY) 2005 the Army "base" budget was almost $100 billion, and supplementals provided almost $60 billion more. In FY2006 the Army base would again be about $100 billion, and supplementals would provide $70 billion more. Army transformational initiatives inevitably drew upon both base and supplemental funding. As we have seen, modernizing technologies were increasingly deployed to fight contemporary Afghan and Iraqi insurgents rather than to prepare for future warfare in the abstract. General Schoomaker was conscious of the congruence between base and supplemental funding, and he determined to push forward with both the Global War on Terrorism and Army transformation relevant to it at the same time. The Department of Defense concurred. In a wartime period of relative congressional largesse, it was easier to modernize by employing supplementals for multiple purposes than to fight tough battles with entrenched interests to alter a funding paradigm that already existed.[23]

Initiatives the Quadrennial Defense Review envisioned for the Army fit readily within the hybrid funding discussed above. Technologies theretofore envisioned for future combat systems were to be spun forward into deploying forces as rapidly as possible. We have already discussed the proliferation of blue force tracking, other digital technologies, UAVs, robotics, and rapidly fielded equipment for the individual soldier in this regard. Procuring, maintaining, and replacing this equipment were arguably wartime expenses. Modular brigades and modularized headquarters at levels above brigade were endorsed by the Quadrennial Defense Review and to proceed as planned. Modularization of such units and headquarters was timed to coincide with their deployments overseas, and much of the expense involved could be characterized as "reset" costs. The reserve component was to continue its decade-plus progression from a force of last resort to an inventory of routinely deployed units, interchangeable with the active component—albeit with longer intervals between deployments. Reserve-component units were to deploy manned and equipped like their active-component counterparts, and additional costs involved achieving that status were wartime expenses. Doctrinal emphasis upon and training preparedness for operations other than war, insurgency, and low-intensity conflict were to increase and improve, complemented by practical experience gained from conducting such operations with a major fraction of the Army overseas at any given time. The intellectual investment associated with such emphasis was not particularly costly, and much of the training expense could again be construed as a reset cost. Special Operations Forces were to increase dramatically in numbers and capability, with Special Forces battalions up by a third and Psychological Operations and Civil Affairs personnel increased by 3,700—again up by a third. Clearly the associated expenses were driven by ongoing operations as well as long-term vision. The Quadrennial Defense Review acknowledged shortcomings with respect to cultural awareness and linguists. Addressing these issues would be hard but not particularly costly. TRADOC readily enough rewrote institutional and unit training regimes to further understanding and sensitivity. Predeployment field training increasingly included encounters with role-playing "natives." Results with respect to cultural obtuseness are not yet determined. Linguists presented a dilemma with respect to recruiting more so than with respect to funding. Although recruiting bonuses would soar as high as $150,000 for some languages within three years, numbers of personnel were not large, and that cost was on par with those associated with a number of other high-demand specialties. By 2008, 14,000 Army linguists would include less than a thousand capable in Arabic, Kurdish, Dari, Pashtu, or Farsi. The Army addressed shortcomings through contracting. In a sense the Army competed against itself, since qualified linguists could choose between being a soldier and being a contractor. Whatever they chose, it was a wartime expense. The Army was to "stabilize" its end strength at 482,400 active component and 533,000 reserve component by FY2011. The subtext was that it was not being asked to give back the 30,000 it had been allowed to accommodate in the modularity initiative and other plus-ups for six years. A lot could happen in six years. Access to the reserve component would be enhanced by extending presidential call-up from 270 to 365 days and granting the Department of Defense authority to have 15 percent of the reserve component on active duty at any one time. Doing the math, this would give the Army a routine active-duty strength of 562,000 in FY2011 and of close to 600,000 until then.[24]

The Quadrennial Defense Review of 2005 was a mixed blessing for the Army. On the one hand, thoughts of reducing ground forces had melted away like a snow cone on summertime Iraqi asphalt. Force structure was secure, as was Army transformation as General Schoomaker and his staff had redefined it. On the other hand, a change in strategic vision had not resulted in a change in budget paradigms. Service apportionments for the base budget went on as before, leaving the Army underfunded within it for ongoing operations, expanding, and transforming. This deficiency was made good by supplemental funding, always a temporary expedient. The danger existed that when supplemental funding one day disappeared, Army transformation would as well.

The Army in 2005

Sergeant Lee Ann Hester was the star of the Association of the United States Army's *Army 2005–2006 Green Book*, published in October 2005. Fully armed and armored, her visage was the front cover. The diminutive "O+" inked on to her helmet band subtly communicated that the hazards she faced might require an immediate blood transfusion. Inside one reads of the incredible courage she and seven other soldiers of the Kentucky Army National Guard's 617th Military Police Company demonstrated on 20 March 2005. Racing to assist an ambushed convoy of tractor trailers, they took on an entrenched force five times their size. Hester, a team leader, outflanked the enemy, positioned her gunner to enfilade a trench line and dispatched a half-dozen insurgents herself with hand grenades and rifle fire. The convoy was saved, the insurgents suffered thirty-four casualties, and Hester was awarded the Silver Star. The recognition accorded her deeds was a considerable departure from earlier practice, wherein Army representatives took great pains to reassure congressional conservatives that the so-called "combat exclusion policy" was workable, and that women could be sensibly distributed throughout the force yet protected from danger. Episodes of females in actual combat had been played down or characterized as aberrations. Just in case one missed the point that times had changed, General Schoomaker's personal article in this *Army 2005–2006 Green Book* issue featured a photograph of him pinning the newly created Combat Action Badge on Sergeant April Pashley, and corporate sponsor Lockheed Martin cooperated with a gritty female "Portrait of a Patriot" on the back cover. IRAQI FREEDOM morphed public attitudes concerning women in combat, in part because of fallout from experiences surrounding another iconic female soldier, Private First Class Jessica Lynch. Lynch had deployed with the 507th Maintenance Company, tasked to support a Patriot Missile battalion. On 23 March 2003, much of the 507th was killed or captured in a string of ambushes around An Nasiriyah, Iraq. Subsequent dramatic rescues of the severely wounded Lynch and other captives, including Specialist Shoshana Johnson, made for gripping real-time television coverage, as did the poignant funeral of Lynch's friend, Private First Class Lori Piestewa. The fate of the 507th remained a subject of concern to the Army, however. General Keane directed a fact-finding review under the direction of the Commanding General of the Training and Doctrine Command, General Kevin P. Byrnes. The review determined that every soldier "performed honorably and each did his or

her duty." There were, nevertheless, critical lapses with respect to
battlefield awareness and an apparent unpreparedness for the
combat that resulted. A troubling
number of weapons malfunctioned,
most notably the only crew-served
weapon—a .50 caliber machine
gun—with the convoy at the time.
In due course the report on the
507th Maintenance Battalion fed
into a larger initiative propelled by
General Schoomaker, the Warrior
Ethos.[25]

The Warrior Ethos was not about
women in combat. It was about
preconceptions that some soldiers
would fight and others would not. It
was also about instilling a personal
commitment "to win" in the heart of
every soldier and rejecting notions
that military service was just "a job."

General Byrnes

In July 2003 the Army's Strategic Studies Institute at Carlisle, Pennsylvania,
produced an interview-based study *Why They Fight: Combat Motivation in the
Iraq War.* Predictably, this study concluded American soldiers fought for each
other, and unit cohesion was a primary combat motivation. It also discovered
that moral and ideological motivators such as liberation, freedom, and democracy were prevalent as well—in a manner more pronounced than had been the
case with draftee armies previously studied. This tracked well with notions
of the Army as a values-centered profession. It also reinforced expectations
concerning personal commitment. Focus on the individual soldier and Army
values was not new. Reimer's "Soldiers Are Our Credentials" and Shinseki's
"Soldiers on Point for the Nation" were cases in point. The doctrinal deliberations of these earlier administrations had favored near-peer opponents and
conventional adversaries, however, trending toward conventional divisions
of labor. The conventional battlefield could be echeloned and combat service
support largely insulated from the consequences of combat. This was, after
all, what had made the combat exclusion policy for women a workable idea—
and thus inversely made the participation of women in combat central to the
concept of a universal Warrior Ethos. Schoomaker's background was heavily
influenced by Special Forces, wherein every soldier was a fighter first and then
had alternate specialties as well. To many this relative lack of specialization
was problematic, rendering Special Forces a logistical burden for someone else
if too many gathered in the same place at the same time. Reducing distinctions between combat, combat support, and combat service support made
sense in Afghanistan and Iraq, however. Artillerymen and engineers deployed,
patrolled, and fought as infantry, and logistical convoys inevitably were a

The Warrior Ethos postulated that there were no rear areas in a combat theater. Soldiers had to be prepared to fight regardless of their occupational specialty or activity.

preferred target for insurgents. The Army adjusted. Initial entry training for soldiers in all specialties featured substantially more physical fitness, hand-to-hand combat, and small-arms marksmanship. Mental and physical toughness were as ardently inculcated as technical competence. Soldiers in all specialties were prepared psychologically and physically to fight "up close and personal." This emphasis continued when soldiers joined their units. A particularly high priority went to innovative live-fire convoy training. Range safety officers struggled with the complexities of dispatching a realistic mix of combat service support vehicles, surprising them with an ambush, and playing through 360 degrees of engagement without unsafe acts or rounds out of the impact area. Multiple integrated laser engagement system (MILES) provided much of the solution, but Schoomaker insisted that each soldier live-fire his or her weapons in the face of realistic scenarios based on Afghan and Iraqi experiences. A training innovator's heaven became a range safety officer's hell. In due course the training, and the message, sank in—fueled by the daily realities of Iraq and Afghanistan. The 2005 version of Field Manual 1, *The Army*, came out on 14 June—the Army birthday. Amid admonitions such as those for combined arms, network-centric warfare, and joint interdependence one would have expected in such a document, there was also considerable development of Army values and the Warrior Ethos. Historical vignettes with pictures illustrated important points. Those depicting combat included a gallant attack by the

369th Infantry Regiment in the Meuse-Argonne, the courageous defense posed by engineer Sergeant First Class Paul R. Smith near the Baghdad airport in 2003, the selfless rescue attempt mounted by Master Sergeant Gary Gordon and Sergeant First Class Randall Shughart in 1993 Mogadishu, the poignant loss of New York World Trade Center firefighter turned National Guardsman Sergeant Christian P. Engeldrum to an IED in Baghdad in 2004, and the exceptional performance of the 724th Transportation Company when caught in a grueling protracted ambush en route to Al Asad, Iraq, in 2004. This mix of examples reinforced the message of the text. Regardless of specialty, all soldiers must be prepared for personal combat.[26]

Returning to Sergeant Hester and the seven soldiers awarded for valor alongside her, the fact that they were National Guardsmen was perhaps as illustrative of the universality of the Warrior Ethos as the fact she was a female. By the end of 2005 the Army sustained 600,000 soldiers on active duty, of whom 72,000 were National Guard and 41,000 Army Reserve. Deployment was becoming an expectation for Guardsmen and Reservists, albeit with five- or six-year intervals as an interval rather than one or two. Once deployed, Guardsmen and Reservists were altogether as likely to see combat as their active-component comrades, generally alongside them. Stark expectations of deployment and combat presented recruiting challenges for the Army, as did the proposed growth of the active component by 30,000. As early as July 2003 the Army General Staff Council mused about a momentary 13 percent dip in recruiting and about the risks that sustained warfare in Iraq and Afghanistan posed to maintaining the Army as all volunteer. The service was already receiving adverse publicity concerning long-standing but now contentious stop-loss policies applied to deploying units. Conversely, other pundits discussed the merits of the draft. By September the recruitment picture brightened, and enlistments were characterized as "OK." The active component exceeded an enlistment goal of 71,000 in 2003 and 77,500 in 2004, but fell 6,400 short of its goal of 80,000 in 2005. Fortuitously, retention remained robust. The active component retained comfortably above 100 percent of target in all categories from FY2003 through 2005, including 103 percent of first-termers and mid-careerists and 129 percent of careerists in FY2005. Hearteningly, the first major unit back from Iraq, the 3d Infantry Division, reenlisted more than 3,700 soldiers by October 2004 and would return to Iraq with over 70 percent combat veterans. Commitment and the Warrior Ethos were certainly at play, as were the facts that the average reenlistment bonus more than doubled from under $5,000 to over $10,000, and the numbers of bonus recipients soared from 7,500 in 2003 through 18,000 in 2004 to 44,500 in 2005. Spouses had much to do with incentives. Surveys suggested that spouses satisfied with family programs, installation support, employment stability, and bonuses enabled their soldiers to reenlist. The reserve component struggled with enlistments and retention through FY2005, generally retaining strength but often "under glide path" for recruitment. In later years the active and reserve components would inch downwards on their previously elevated standards to achieve recruiting goals—until a booming national economy went sour and rendered military service far more attractive to prospects and their parents. Even with an effective bump up to an active-duty strength of 600,000, the Army remained perilously thin for the tasks at hand. The trend toward an ever-greater reliance on contractors that began in the 1990s continued. Estimates held that the United States employed 100,000 contractors in Iraq, representing a wide range of nationalities and specialties. This phenomenon of contracting effectively modifying force structure receives more attention in Chapter 7.[27]

Conclusions

By 2005 General Peter J. Schoomaker had sufficiently redefined Army transformation to mark a departure from its development since 1989. Generals Vuono, Sullivan, Reimer, and Shinseki had been between wars and endeavored to prepare the Army for slates of unknown adversaries at uncertain times and places. Ongoing operations overseas paralleled and somewhat competed with this effort, and Afghanistan proved to be yet another of these through 2003. The most dangerous future adversary was envisioned as near peer, and transformation had had a near-peer focus. It also had had considerable depth, with Army XXI, the Army After Next, and the Objective Force in turn investing in technologies that would be decades in paying off. Iraq changed the paradigm. The war eclipsed all else, and recurrent rotations of units to it dominated all other concerns for the Army. Initiatives with respect to modularity, unit manning, home stationing, infrastructure, and coping with the physical and psychological costs of war proceeded in this light. Transformational programs originating in the period 1989–2003 advanced considerably during 2003–2005 but morphed to prioritize the techniques and technologies most likely to be immediately useful in Iraq and Afghanistan. Appliqué digitization, space-based communications and navigation, unmanned aerial vehicles, robotics, and counter-IED capabilities were substantially funded and moved forward. New platforms proved of less interest. The Comanche was terminated and the manned vehicles associated with FCS slipped to the right. Upgraded legacy vehicles and aircraft, and newly purchased but not newly designed Strykers, filled the gap. Individual soldiers, conversely, carried ever newer and more modern equipment with them. They themselves became platforms for GPS, digital technologies, and ever-improving access to precision-guided munitions. Technology was not enough, however, and a newly reemphasized Warrior Ethos sought to reinforce a fighting spirit in the heart of every soldier regardless of specialty, component, or gender. General Schoomaker himself got high marks for recasting as much of Army transformation as he did into requirements for Afghanistan and Iraq and getting it paid for, albeit with supplemental rather than base budget funds. For fifteen years the Army had been preparing for its next war. Now it had found it.

Notes

[1] General Peter J. Schoomaker, "The Army: A Critical Member of the Joint Team Serving the Nation at War," *Army 2003–2004 Green Book*, October 2003, 23–28; Thomas K. Adams, *The Army After Next: The First Postindustrial Army* (Stanford California: Stanford University Press, 2008), 95–175; Thomas E. Ricks, "Air Force's Roche Picked to Head Army," *Washington Post*, 2 May 2003, 1; Evan Thomas and Daniel Klaidman, "The Battle Within," *Newsweek*, 15 September 2003, 17; Kim Burger, "New Direction for US Army," *Jane's Defense Weekly*, 27 August 2003, 23; Telephone Conversation notes, General (USA, Ret.) Peter J. Schoomaker with Brigadier General (USA, Ret.) John S. Brown, 111330 May 2009, Historians Files, CMH.

[2] Briefing Slides, Army Staff, "Leader Transition Session II: Former Transition Team Members," 30 May 2003, Historians Files, CMH; Army General Staff Council Meeting notes, 9 June 2003, Historians Files, CMH; Army General Staff Council Meeting notes, 16 June 2003, Historians Files, CMH; Briefing Slides, Army Staff, "Leader Transition Azimuth Check, 27 June 2003," Historians Files, CMH; Robert Burns, "Army Shake-Up Has Rumsfeld in Power Position," Associated Press, 26 April 2003; John Barry, "The Army Cleans House," *Newsweek*, 11 August 2003, 8; William G. Bell, *Secretaries of War and Secretaries of the Army: Portraits and Biographical Sketches* (Washington DC: Center of Military History, 2003); William G. Bell, *Commanding Generals and Chiefs of Staff, 1775–2005: Portraits and Biographical Sketches* (Washington DC: Center of Military History, 2003); E-mail, Director of the Army Staff to Army General Staff Council Attendees, 14 August 2003, sub: Observations After Day #1 with the New CSA, forwarded FYI to Army Staff at large, Historians Files, CMH.

[3] Army General Staff Council Meeting notes, 14 August 2003, Historians Files, CMH; Annotated Power Point Slides, briefed by General Peter J. Schoomaker to Army General Staff Council, 14 August 2003, Historians Files, CMH; Author's personal experience as an attendee of the 14 August 2003 Army General Staff Council Meeting; *The Way Ahead: Our Army at War . . . Relevant and Ready, Moving from the Current Force to the Future Force . . . Now* (Washington DC: United States Army, n.d.), Historians Files, CMH; Telephone Conversation notes, General (USA, Ret.) Peter J. Schoomaker with Brigadier General (USA, Ret.) John S. Brown, 111330 May 2009.

[4] Acting Secretary of the Army Les Brownlee, "A Brave and Determined Army Is Destroying Terrorism Worldwide," *Army 2003–2004 Green Book*, October 2003, 13–19; Peter J. Schoomaker, "The Army: A Critical Member of the Joint Team Serving the Nation at War," *Army 2003–2004 Green Book*, October 2003, 23–28; Army General Staff Council Meeting notes, 27 May 2003, Historians Files, CMH; Army General Staff Council Meeting notes, 9 June 2003; Secretary of the Army Thomas E. White, "The Army Is Dedicated to Delivering Victory," *Army 2002–2003 Green Book*, October 2002, 15–22; General Eric K. Shinseki, "'. . . a respectable Army . . . one . . . competent to every contingency,'" *Army 2002–2003 Green Book*, October 2002, 23–33; Bell, *Secretaries of War and Secretaries of the Army*.

[5] General Peter Schoomaker and General Richard Cody, Transcript of the Media Roundtable Conducted at the Association of the United States Army Annual Meeting, 26 October 2004, Historians Files, CMH; Army General Staff Council Meeting notes, 16 June 2003; Army General Staff Council Meeting notes, 14 July 2003, Historians Files, CMH; Army General Staff Council Meeting notes, 21 July 2003, Historians Files, CMH; Army General Staff Council Meeting notes, 11 August 2003, Historians

Files, CMH; Army General Staff Council Meeting notes, 8 September 2003, Historians Files, CMH; Army General Staff Council Offsite notes, 30–31 January 2004, Fort McNair, Washington DC,, Historians Files CMH; Army General Staff Council Meeting notes, 23 February 2004, Historians Files, CMH; Army General Staff Council Meeting notes, 26 April 2004, Historians Files, CMH; Chief of Staff Focus Area Update notes, 16 April 2004, Historians Files, CMH; "Interview: Gen. Peter Schoomaker, U.S. Army Chief of Staff," *Defense News,* 3 October 2005, 118.

[6] Army General Staff Council Meeting notes, 14 August 2003; Army General Staff Council Offsite notes, 30–31 January 2004; Chief of Staff Focus Area Update notes, 16 April 2004; Field Manual 1, *The Army* (Washington DC: Department of the Army, June 2005).

[7] Army General Staff Council Meeting notes, 14 August 2003; General Peter Schoomaker and General Richard Cody, Transcript of the Media Roundtable Conducted at the Association of the United States Army Annual Meeting, 26 October 2004; Office of the Chief of Military History, The Replacement System in the United States Army: An Analytical Study of World War II Experience (Washington DC: Department of the Army, 1950); CMH Information Paper, Robert S. Rush, The Individual Replacement System: Good, Bad or Indifferent? Army Replacement Policy, Cold War and Before (Washington DC: Center of Military History, n.d.); Briefing, Center of Military History to Major General Lawrence Adair, Deputy G1, "What CMH Can Do for You," n.d., Historians Files, CMH.

[8] Rush; Briefing, Center of Military History to Major General Lawrence Adair, Deputy G1, "What CMH Can Do for You," n.d.; Robert M. Utley, *Frontier Regulars: The United States Army and the Indian, 1866–1890* (New York: Macmillan, 1973); The Replacement System in the United States Army: An Analytical Study of World War II Experience; Colonel Gregory Fontenot, Lieutenant Colonel E. J. Degen and Lieutenant Colonel David Tohn, *On Point: The United States Army in Operation IRAQI FREEDOM* (Washington DC: Office of the Chief of Staff, 2004), 1–28; Army General Staff Council Meeting notes, 14 August 2003; Army Regulation 210–20, *Master Planning for Army Installations* (Washington DC: Department of the Army, 1992).

[9] William M. Donnelly, *Transforming an Army at War: Designing the Modular Force, 1991–2005* (Washington DC: Center of Military History, 2007), 3–74; John B. Wilson, *Maneuver and Firepower: The Evolution of Divisions and Separate Brigades* (Washington DC: Center of Military History, 1998); John J. McGrath, *The Brigade: A History, Its Organization and Employment in the US Army* (Fort Leavenworth, Kansas: Combat Studies Institute, 2004); *Army Comprehensive Guide to Modularity* (Fort Monroe, Virginia: U.S. Army Training and Doctrine Command, 2004).

[10] Donnelly, 3–74; *Army Comprehensive Guide to Modularity*; Army General Staff Council Offsite notes, 30–31 January 2004; Briefing Slide, 3d Infantry Division, "COA 5z UA Organization (Current CSA Approved Redesign Concept)," Fort Stewart, Georgia, 12 December 2003, Historians Files, CMH; "Brigade Combat Team Deployments," *Army Times*, 13 October 2008, 15; Telephone Conversation notes, General (USA, Ret.) Peter J. Schoomaker with Brigadier General (USA, Ret.) John S. Brown, 111330 May 2009.

[11] Donnelly, 5–26, 75–78; TRADOC Pamphlet 525–3–91, *Objective Force Tactical Operational and Organizational Concept for Maneuver Units of Action* (Fort Monroe, Virginia: U.S. Army Training and Doctrine Command, 6 November 2001); TRADOC Pamphlet 525–3–92, *Objective Force: Unit of Employment Concept* (Fort Monroe, Virginia: U.S. Army Training and Doctrine Command, 20 May 2003); Briefing, Center of Military History, "Unit Designations in the Army Modular Force," n.d., Historians Files, CMH; Ltr, General Gordon R. Sullivan to General Peter J. Schoomaker, 25

January 2005, Historians Files, CMH; Kelly Kennedy, "Progress Is Being Made: Iraqi Ranks Are Filling Out and 3-Year Cycle Is Almost There, Army Secretary Says," *Army Times,* 20 February 2006, S4.

[12] Lieutenant General Clyde Vaughn, "Army National Guard—Always Ready, Always There," *Army Green Book 2005–2006*, October 2005, 101–04; Lieutenant General James R. Helmly, "Changing to a 21st-Century Army Reserve," *Army Green Book 2005–2006*, October 2005, 107–12; Briefing, Center of Military History, "Unit Designations in the Army Modular Force," n.d.; General Peter Schoomaker and General Richard Cody, Transcript of the Media Roundtable Conducted at the Association of the United States Army Annual Meeting, 26 October 2004; Michelle Tan, "The Readiness Reshuffle: Plan Would Reshuffle Reservists Every 5 Years," *Army Times*, 20 February 2006, S13; Michelle Tan, "Guard Aims for 6-Year Cycle, Half Free for U.S. Emergencies," *Army Times*, 20 February 2006; Michelle Tan, "DOD: Army Exceeds October Recruiting Goals," *Army Times*, 24 November 2004, 12.

[13] General Peter Schoomaker and General Richard Cody, Transcript of the Media Roundtable Conducted at the Association of the United States Army Annual Meeting, 26 October 2004; "Brigade Combat Team Deployments," *Army Times*, 13 October 2008, 14–16; Gina Cavallaro, "Artillerymen Go Back to the Big Guns," *Army Times*, 13 October 2008, 15, 18; Greg Grant, "Army 'Reset Bill' Hits $9 Billion," *Army Times*, 20 February 2006, 16; "Army Refits Force," *AUSA News*, October 2003, 2; "An Army of Change," *AUSA Special Report*, 21 February 2005, S3; General Paul J. Kern, "U.S. Army Materiel Command: Getting Soldiers What They Need When and Where They Need It," *Army 2004–2005 Green Book*, October 2004, 67–74; "Army Brigade, a Symbol of Force Readiness for Decades, Finds Itself Stretched Thin," *New York Times*, 29 March 2007, A8; Matthew Cox, "Iraq War Takes Toll on Readiness," *Army Times,* 27 March 2006; Jim Tice, "Population Explosion Could Stretch Fort Bliss," *AUSA Special Report*, 21 February 2005, S11–S12; Field Manual 100–5, *Operations* (Washington DC: Department of the Army, 1993); Army Regulation 210–20, *Master Planning for Army Installations*.

[14] Army General Staff Council Meeting notes, 23 July 2001, Historians Files, CMH; Army General Staff Council Meeting Notes, 14 January 2002, Historians Files, CMH; Ian Urbina, "Troops Exposure to Nerve Gas Could Have Caused Brain Damage, Scientists Say," *New York Times*, 17 May 2007, A18; "Bittersweet Victory," *AUSA News*, January 2009, 13; Ben Shephard, *A War of Nerves: Soldiers and Psychiatrists in the Twentieth Century* (Boston: Harvard University Press, 2001); David Dobbs, "The Post-Traumatic Stress Trap," *Scientific American* (April 2009): 64–69; Army General Staff Council Meeting notes, 20 October 2003, Historians Files, CMH; Army General Staff Council Meeting notes, 27 May 2003; Todd S. Brown, *Battleground Iraq: Journal of a Company Commander* (Washington DC: Center of Military History, 2007), 59–73, 220–29.

[15] Army General Staff Council Meeting notes, 28 January 2002, Historians Files, CMH; Lieutenant General Kevin C. Kiley, "Preserving Soldier's Life and Health—Anytime, Anywhere," *Army 2005–2006 Green Book*, October 2005, 121–24; Army Principals Staff Call notes, 31 May 2005, Historians Files, CMH; Army General Staff Council Meeting notes, 31 March 2003, Historians Files, CMH; Army General Staff Council Meeting notes, 8 September 2003; "Changing the Concept of Warrior Care," *AUSA News,* January 2009, 11; Chuck Vinch, "They Gave Their Lives," *Army Times*, 25 September 2006, 14–15; AUSA Institute of Land Warfare Defense Report 07–2, *Army Medical Action Plan* (Arlington, Virginia: Association of the United States Army, June 2007); "Focus on the Future: Program Helps Rehabilitating Soldiers Transition Back to Army or Civilian Life," *AUSA News*, January 2009, 14; Lizette

Alvarez, "Obama Offers Plan to Improve Care for Veterans," *New York Times,* 10 April 2009, A12.

[16] Lieutenant General Otto J. Guenther, "Blue Force Tracking," *Army* (April 2004): 13–15; Army General Staff Council Meeting notes, 11 August 2003; Army General Staff Council Offsite notes, 30–31 January 2004; Sergeant Frank N. Pellegrini, "Supporting Gulf War 2.0," *Army* (September 2003): 20–26; Patricia Kime, "Instant Readiness: Lessons Learned in Iraq Available Online and in the Field the Next Day," *AUSA Special Report,* 21 February 2005, S8; Brigadier General Michael A. Vane and Lieutenant Colonel Joseph M. Ozorski, "Transforming the Doctrinal Development Process," *Army* (June 2003): 55–57; Army General Staff Council Meeting notes, 21 July 2003; General Peter Schoomaker and General Richard Cody, Transcript of the Media Roundtable Conducted at the Association of the United States Army Annual Meeting, 26 October 2004.

[17] Lieutenant General Otto J. Guenther, "Blue Force Tracking," *Army* (April 2004): 13–15; Army General Staff Council Meeting notes, 21 April 2003, Historians Files, CMH; Kern, "U.S. Army Materiel Command: Getting Soldiers What They Need When and Where They Need It," 67–74; General Peter Schoomaker and General Richard Cody, Transcript of the Media Roundtable Conducted at the Association of the United States Army Annual Meeting, 26 October 2004; Dennis Steele, "Carrying the Load in Iraq," *Army* (July 2004): 14–22; Pellegrini, 20–26; Army General Staff Council Meeting notes, 21 July 2003; Army General Staff Council Meeting notes, 22 December 2003, Historians Files, CMH; "The Truck the Pentagon Wants and the Firm That Makes It," *USA Today,* 8 January 2007; Mark J. Reardon and Jeffrey A. Charlston, *From Transformation to Combat: The First Stryker Brigade at War* (Washington DC: Center of Military History, 2007), 1–19; Bob Woodward, *The War Within: A Secret White House History 2006–2008* (New York: Simon & Schuster, 2008), 64–67.

[18] General Crosbie E. Saint, Brigadier General E. J. Sinclair, and Major Jonathan O. Gass, "Army Aviation on the Move," *Army* (July 2004): 33–37; Army General Staff Council Meeting notes, 14 August 2003; General Paul J. Kern, "Technology, Transformation and War—A Kaleidoscope of Force," *Army 2003–2004 Green Book,* October 2003, 63–70; Kern, "U.S. Army Materiel Command: Getting Soldiers What They Need When and Where They Need It," 67–74; Army General Staff Council Meeting notes, 23 February 2004; Brown, *Battleground Iraq,* 128–96.

[19] Kern, "Technology, Transformation and War—A Kaleidoscope of Force," 63–70; Richard W. Stewart, ed., *American Military History,* vol. 2, *The United States in a Global Era, 1917–2003* (Washington DC: Center of Military History, 2005), 285–368; Army General Staff Council Meeting notes, 7 April 2003, Historians Files, CMH; Army General Staff Council Meeting notes, 14 April 2003, Historians Files, CMH; Army General Staff Council Meeting notes, 23 February 2003; Lieutenant General James J. Lovelace Jr. and Brigadier General Joseph L. Votel, "The Asymmetric Warfare Group: Closing the Capability Gap," *Army* (March 2005): 29–34.

[20] Kern, "U.S. Army Materiel Command: Getting Soldiers What They Need When and Where They Need It," 67–74; Army General Staff Council Meeting notes, 27 May 2003; Army General Staff Council Meeting notes, 8 December 2003, Historians Files, CMH; Scott R. Gourley, "Equipping Today's Warfighters," *Army* (July 2003): 49–52; Tim Kennedy, "TRADOC Seeks Wartime Solutions from Rapid Equipping Force," *Army* (August 2004): 39–42; Matthew Cox, "Lighter, More Mobile Gear: Army to Battle-Test New Kit," *Army Times,* 23 March 2009, 14–16.

[21] Army General Staff Council Meeting notes, 14 August 2003; General Peter Schoomaker and General Richard Cody, Transcript of the Media Roundtable Conducted at the Association of the United States Army Annual Meeting, 26 October

2004; Saint, Sinclair, and Gass, 33–37; General Frederick J. Kroesen, "From Cheyenne to Comanche," *Army* (May 2005): 11–12; Megan Scully, "The Squeeze on Transformation," *AUSA Special Report*, 21 February 2005, S6; Scott R. Gourley, "Apache Longbow Program Brings New Technology to Army Aviation," *Army* (January 2005): 37–39; Tim Puckett, "FCS Update: FCS Battle Command," *Army* (August 2005): 43–46; Colonel Christopher V. Cardine, "Future Combat Systems and Commonality," *Army* (November 2005): 45–48; Jean-Pierre Lutz, "FCS Update: Command, Control, Communications, Intelligence, Surveillance and Reconnaissance," *Army* (December 2005): 49–50.

[22] Adams, 202–03, 228–33; *Quadrennial Defense Review Report* (Washington DC: Office of the Secretary of Defense, 6 February 2006); Army General Staff Council Offsite notes, 30–31 January 2004; Army General Staff Focus Area Update notes, 10 April 2004, Historians Files, CMH; Army Principals Staff Call notes, 26 April 2004, Historians Files, CMH; Andrew F. Krepinevich, *The Quadrennial Defense Review: Transforming to Meet Tomorrow's Security Challenges* (Washington DC: National Defense University, 17 March 2007); Michele A. Flournoy, "Did the Pentagon Get the Quadrennial Defense Review Right?" *Washington Quarterly* (Spring 2006); Clark Murdock, *An Assessment of the 2006 QDR* (Washington DC: Center for Strategic and International Studies, 4 February 2006).

[23] Ibid.; General Peter J. Schoomaker, "Our Army: Continuity and Change," *Army 2004–2005 Green Book*, October 2004, 25–30; Army General Staff Council Meeting notes, 31 March 2003; Army General Staff Council Meeting notes, 14 April 2003; Army Principals Staff Call notes, 26 April 2004; Robert D. Hormats, *The Price of Liberty: Paying for America's Wars* (New York: Henry Holt, 2007), 251–99; Honorable Francis J. Garvey and General Peter J. Schoomaker, *A Statement on the Posture of the United States Army 2006* (Washington DC: Office of the Chief of Staff, U.S. Army, 10 February 2006).

[24] *Quadrennial Defense Review Report*; Army General Staff Council Offsite notes, 30–31 January 2004; Army General Staff Focus Area Update notes, 10 April 2004; Lovelace and Votel, 29–34; Army General Staff Council Meeting notes, 14 August 2003; Garvey and Schoomaker; *2006 and Beyond: What the Army Is Doing* (Arlington, Virginia: Association of the United States Army, March 2006); Gordon Lubold, "QDR Provides Blueprint for Long War," *Army Times*, 13 February 2006, 9; Elisabeth Bumiller, "Gates Takes His Case for Military Budget on the Road," *New York Times*, 17 April 2009, 9; William H. McMichael, "Gates: Army Budget Must Align with Current, Future Needs," *Army Times*, 27 April 2009, 19.

[25] *Army 2005–2006 Green Book*, October 2005, 4, 23–30; Bernard Rostker, *I Want You: The Evolution of the All-Volunteer Force* (Santa Monica, California: RAND, 2006), 560–71, 674–75; Army General Staff Council Meeting notes, 14 April 2003; Army General Staff Council Meeting notes, 9 June 2003; Army General Staff Council Meeting notes, 14 July 2003; Department of the Army Rpt, Attack on the 507th Maintenance Company, 23 March 2003, An Nasiriyah, Iraq, Historians Files, CMH; Army General Staff Council Meeting notes, 14 August 2003.

[26] Leonard Wong, Thomas Kolditz, Raymond A. Millen, and Terrence M. Potter, *Why They Fight: Combat Motivation in the Iraq War* (Carlisle, Pennsylvania: Strategic Studies Institute, July 2003); Sean D. Naylor, "A Dual for the Enablers of War," *Army Times,* 16 March 2009, 22; Sean D. Naylor, "Report: SF Groups Lack Robust Support Unit," *Army Times*, 30 March 2009, 18; Army General Staff Council Meeting notes, 14 August 2003; Field Manual 1, *The Army*.

[27] *Army 2005–2006 Green Book*, October 2005, 4, 23–30; Army General Staff Council Meeting notes, 27 May 2003; Army General Staff Council Meeting notes, 16 June 2003;

Army General Staff Council Meeting notes, 14 July 2003; Army General Staff Council Meeting notes, 21 July 2003; Army General Staff Council Meeting notes, 14 August 2003; Army General Staff Council Meeting notes, 22 September 2003, Historians Files, CMH; Army General Staff Council Meeting notes, 8 December 2003; Army General Staff Council Meeting notes, 8 March 2004, Historians Files, CMH; Army General Staff Council Offsite notes, 30–31 January 2004; Army Principals Staff Call notes, 31 May 2005, Historians Files, CMH; General Peter Schoomaker and General Richard Cody, Transcript of the Media Roundtable Conducted at the Association of the United States Army Annual Meeting, 26 October 2004; Gordon Lubold, "Troop-level Forecast May Test Patience," *Army Times,* 23 September 2006; Tan, "DoD: Army Exceeds October Recruiting Goals"; Erik Holmes et al., "Retention Pressures," *Army Times*, 8 December 2008, 15; "Recruiting the Best," *New York Times*, 28 December 2008; Army General Staff Council Meeting notes, 11 August 2003; Army General Staff Council Meeting notes, 19 April 2004, Historians Files, CMH; Renae Merle, "Census Counts 100,000 Contractors in Iraq," *Washington Post*, 5 December 2006.

CHAPTER 7

Army Force Structure, 1989–2005

Army Chief of Staff General Carl E. Vuono (1987–1991) recognized that technological modernization alone would not be enough to transform the Army for the challenges it faced. Force mix numbered among five other imperatives he stressed, as did doctrine. His successors followed up on this insight, each making significant adjustments to force structure in his turn. External pundits and critics joined internal debate as the Army sought its way forward. Some of the issues seemed timeless. Centralization reduces overheads, increases efficiency, and simplifies training and maintenance, whereas decentralization increases agility, flexibility, and reaction time in the face of battlefield uncertainties. Mechanization increases firepower and tactical mobility, but it also increases weight and reduces strategic mobility. When at peace the Army has had lots of time but little money; when at war it has had lots of money but little time. Manpower is limited in peace or war. Some parameters under consideration reflected post–Cold War circumstances. Campaigns against peer opponents seemed unlikely in the near term. Likely threats ranged across the spectrum of combat and around the globe, as did actual operations. Operating environments were ever more joint and generally were combined and multi-departmental as well. New technologies introduced parameters of their own. Digital equipment, satellite communications, the Internet, precision-guided munitions, and a panoply of other innovations required due consideration. The Goldwater-Nichols Act rendered Army deliberations less insular than they had been before, so players from outside the Army were increasingly taken into account. Downsizing was the most immediate, and evolution to a "brigade-based" Army the most consequential, of the force structure developments during this period. These in turn forced the redesign of echelons at division level and above. The institutional Army morphed as well, and roles and missions on an unprecedented scale migrated into the purview of contractors, who became a shadow force structure in themselves. The Army of 2005 was a different organization than that which had existed in 1989.

The Critique

The tectonic shift of 1989 inspired thought and fermentation. Much of this was encouraged by Chief of Staff General Gordon R. Sullivan's modern Louisiana Maneuvers. More emerged as bright minds within the Army School

System, student and faculty alike, turned their attentions to the new circumstances in theses and studies. Articles relevant to revised force structure proliferated in professional journals, Training and Doctrine Command (TRADOC) and contracted "think tanks" cranked out polished analyses, and multislide briefings cycled in turn past the Army's senior leadership. Committed to the relative specifics of Force XXI in the near term, Sullivan's successor, General Dennis J. Reimer, valued further debate for the longer term. To facilitate this he directed that the Army Staff and selected others read *Breaking the Phalanx: A New Design for Land Power in the 21st Century* (1997), by Colonel Douglas A. Macgregor. Macgregor emerged as a persistent, prolific, and recurrently visible critic of Army force structure and doctrine—and of much else as well. *Breaking the Phalanx* advanced opinions on the major themes in contention at the time: flattening command hierarchies, reliance on brigade-size combat groups, modularity, unit rotation and replacement, jointness, and nimbler logistics. It was accessible, thought-provoking, and commercially available and brought a sizable body of wide-ranging criticism into a readable whole. Outside the Army the book came to the attention of Speaker of the House Newt Gingrich. He championed Macgregor's ideas in various forums and encouraged their consideration in congressional deliberations. Reimer directed the Center for Army Analysis to war-game Macgregor's operational and doctrinal concepts, and he directed the Army's Center of Military History to provide historical commentary. The Center of Military History cheerfully identified a few historical anomalies, to include alleged misrepresentation of Macedonian tactics at the Battle of Cynoscephalae (197 BC), the source of the phalanx metaphor, before moving on to a broader discussion of general themes. The Army Staff proved not much interested in the battlefield mechanics of Cynoscephalae but was interested in the themes and the background to them. Command hierarchies, brigade-size maneuver units, modularity, unit rotation and replacement, jointness, and logistics would each prove the subject for debate and contention as the Army redesigned itself.[1]

Theorists have long pondered the merits of eliminating one or more rungs in military hierarchies that date back to the Napoleonic Wars, thus "flattening" chains of command. The Pentomic Division of the 1950s sought to reduce vulnerability to atomic weapons by compressing battalion and brigade into a more nimble battle group. Among other flaws, the Pentomic design depended on communications capabilities that did not reliably exist at the time. By the 1990s space-based communications and digital technologies overcame this particular impediment. Widely dispersed forces could communicate without recourse to matrices of ground stations, and huge masses of information passed through cyberspace—and the ether—in high-volume burst transmissions. Innovative businesses gamely flattened organizational hierarchies, anticipating that timely information broadly spread and local initiative could economize on layers of management. Within the Army a number espoused such an idea, including Macgregor. In *Breaking the Phalanx* he proposed compressing army and corps into a joint task force, and division and brigade into a combat maneuver group. He further developed his ideas in subsequent writings, revisiting jointness and the Joint Forces Land Component Command

(JFLCC). Counterarguments to such flattening cited concerns with respect to spans of control. Fighting a battle was different than stocking supermarket shelves, traditionalists argued. To be useful, a commander had to comprehend the battles his subordinates and his neighbors were fighting. This mental picture allowed him to coordinate subordinate combats and to distribute his own assets and those drawn from higher headquarters to best effect. Regardless of the pace and volume of information shared, many believed a single commander could still only command and control three to five subordinate maneuver battles, along with coordinating support and cooperating with neighbors. Beyond such a span of control subordinate commanders would end up essentially unsupervised, doing their "own thing" and inviting chaos. Historically, greater responsiveness and agility has been associated with narrowing spans of control rather than with expanding them. The early nineteenth-century regiment consisted of ten companies, for example, which generally advanced on line with little expectation of maneuver. A brigade when formed, on the other hand, generally consisted of two to five regiments, which the brigade commander was expected to maneuver separately as required. Inspired by theorists like Emory Upton and the World War I success of German *Hutier* tactics, the World War II United States Army narrowed spans of control at lower levels. A mid-twentieth-century regiment typically controlled about three battalions that controlled about three rifle or line companies that controlled about three platoons that controlled about three squads that generally fought as teams or sections of fewer than a half-dozen soldiers each. Downward infusions of leadership and narrower spans of control improved performance on ever more dispersed and dangerous battlefields. Few advocates of flattening military hierarchy advocated flattening it everywhere. Macgregor, for example, would have left battalions and below generally as they were. Joint Task Forces or Joint Force Land Component Commands might be required to control more groups, but companies would not be required to control more platoons. Debate raged about which levels to flatten. Some came to argue for leaving hierarchy intact but leveraging information technologies to reduce manpower and redundancies within headquarters at each level. Such a compromise would preserve traditional spans of control while nevertheless thinning bureaucracy.[2]

A number of Army commentators advocated diminishing the division in favor of the brigade. Increasing effective ranges, lethality, and sensor sophistication gave the brigade a considerably larger geographical footprint than it had had before. The theory that the brigade was but a headquarters to which units were temporarily assigned was trumped by customary associations in garrison and the field. Brigade combat team performance in Operation DESERT STORM demonstrated and reinforced this tendency. Important fragments of the Army were already "brigade-based": armored cavalry regiments, separate brigades, divisions (forward), and the enhanced brigades of the Army National Guard. Post–Cold War downsizing led many of our allies to devolve upon the brigade as their capstone tactical unit. TRADOC's 1989–1991 AirLand Battle Future Concept proposed thinner and more modular divisions, and in 1995 TRADOC introduced a brigade-based alternative as one of three candidates for Force XXI division redesign. Thus Macgregor was in good company when

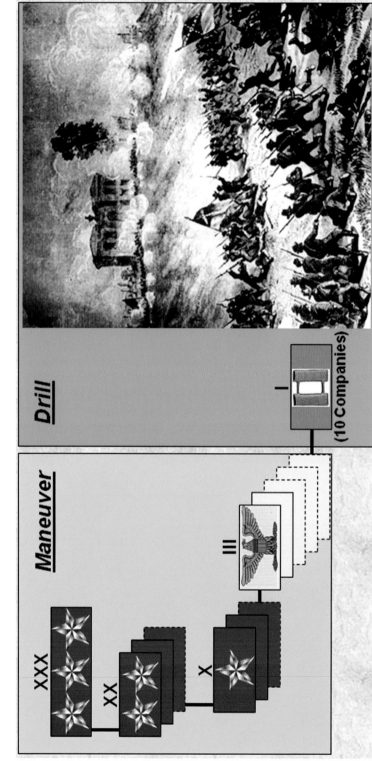

SPAN OF CONTROL: CIVIL WAR

This and facing page, *Center of Military History slides illustrating relationships between number of subordinate elements at an echelon and capacity for coordinated maneuver at that echelon*

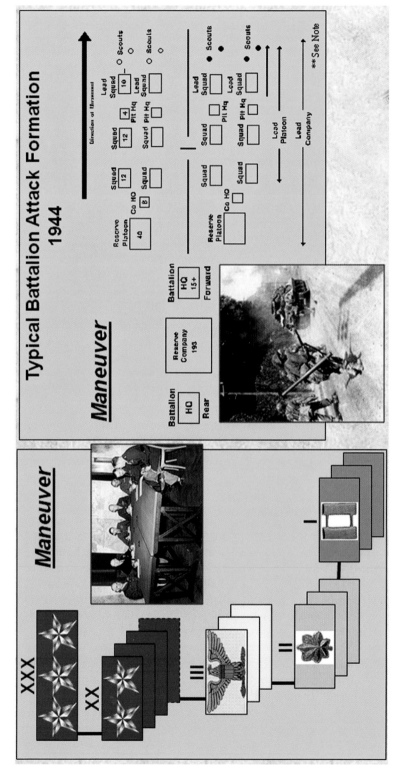

Note: Extracted from Robert S. Rush, "Passchendaele with Treebursts: An Analysis of Cohension, Morale, and Operational Effectiveness of the U.S. and German Organizations in the Hürtgen Forest, Fall 1944" (Master's diss., Ohio State University, 2000).

he argued that the tactical battle was overcentralized at the division level, and he recommended combined-arms combat maneuver groups instead. His variants included heavy combat, airborne–air assault, heavy recon-strike, and light recon-strike and would consist of 4,000 to 5,000 soldiers apiece. This design was beefy in comparison with traditional brigade combat teams and featured enough combat support to render the combat group relatively autonomous. Force structure invested to achieve this autonomy fueled the critics of Macgregor's combat group and of a brigade-based Army. Issues were ability to mass and economies of scale. Lieutenant General Lesley J. McNair famously slimmed down World War II divisions to assets they would almost inevitably use, pooling all else in separate battalions and groups assigned to echelons above division. This allowed the Army to mass such assets, attaching artillery, armor, engineers, and others where they were most needed rather than distributing them across the board. Pooling also encouraged economies of scale and simplified training, maintenance, and logistical support, since like-type units were concentrated organizationally. McNair's approach had notable successes, such as the massing of artillery during the Battle of the Ardennes. As an example of brigade-based thinking, Macgregor's proposed heavy maneuver combat group featured 1,800 soldiers in three combined-arms battalions of two tank companies, two mechanized companies, and a combat engineer company each; 800 soldiers in a reconnaissance squadron with three reconnaissance troops, a tank company, and an attack helicopter-equipped air reconnaissance troop; 750 soldiers in a howitzer and rocket-equipped indirect fires battalion; 550 soldiers in a command, control, communications, computers, and intelligence battalion; and 650 soldiers in a support battalion. With respect to combat and combat support, traditional divisional organization had concentrated infantrymen, tankers, artillerymen, engineers, and aviators in battalions of their own. Divisional artillerymen, engineers, and aviators were supervised in garrison by brigade-level commanders of their provenance. Further artillery, engineer, and aviation brigades and groups reported to the corps headquarters. This organization ensured that branch-qualified field-grade officers and noncommissioned officers (NCOs) of comparable experience supervised individual, crew, and small-unit training. It also ensured that substantial contingents from each branch could be amassed quickly. Armored cavalry squadrons had been exceptions to this general pattern, but they represented relatively small fragments of the overall force structure. Proposals distributing combat and combat support assets across brigades received immediate push back from those who preferred this earlier system.[3]

Advocates of a brigade-based Army proposed organizations that were intended to be modular, readily deployable assets that could be swapped out with like-type units or quickly "plug and play" into a Joint Task Force. Macgregor's proposed combat variants, for example, included heavy combat, airborne–air assault, heavy recon-strike, and light recon-strike. For combat support there would be rocket artillery, aviation, and air defense groups, and combat service support would be provided by sustainment groups. Macgregor further proposed that a three-star Joint Forces Land Component Commander would have three two-star deputies, one to control close combat, one to control deep strike operations, and one to sustain the force. Each could routinely handle from six to nine groups. Much smaller than divisions, yet relatively autonomous and consisting of all arms, the groups would provide blocks with which to rapidly build up a force. Forces could be tailored by increments at the brigade level, avoiding a surfeit of assets not needed in the theater. Critics argued that modularity was not a new thing in the Army and that brigade-based design merely shifted the level at which it occurred. Committing aviation, artillery, engineer, and other units organically into brigades made these less available for distribution outside of them. The brigade or group might be the new building block, but its relative autonomy would make the former practice of swapping battalions around less practical. Autonomous aviation, artillery, air defense, and sustainment groups also would not have had customary relationships with the combat groups with whom they operated. In the division structure the full colonel division artillery (DIVARTY) commander, for example, was the conduit through which external artillery assets funneled. He and his staff were intimately familiar with and to the combat brigade commanders and their brigades, and trained alongside them. The same could be said of division aviation and engineer brigade commanders, the division support command (DISCOM) commander, and the air defense, military intelligence, and signal battalion commanders. Proposed redesign could render customary branch relationships within brigades or groups far more robust, but those across brigades and groups considerably less so. Many in the Army were not yet convinced that brigades, however potent, could succeed without the services that corps and divisions had customarily provided—in garrison or in the field.[4]

Rotational readiness and unit replacement had long appealed to critics of the individual replacement system practiced since the early twentieth century. The combat, combat support, and combat service support units envisioned by advocates of a brigade-based Army were of a size that would make such an approach feasible. Research and commentary concerning the flaws of the individual replacement system, and of Army personnel policies in general, was easy to find. Champions of unit rotation found much to admire in the recurrent generation of Marine Air Ground Task Forces (MAGTF). This thinking was on line with such previous Army initiatives as Gyroscope, Overseas Unit Replacement System (OVUREP), Rotational Plan (ROTAPLAN), and Cohesion Operational Readiness and Training (COHORT). Proposed units would experience cycles of readiness wherein they stood up, absorbed personnel, trained rigorously, and stayed together through deployment, combat, and return. Unit stability would inculcate confidence, esprit, and mutually understood tactics, techniques, and procedures. Macgregor, for example, argued that Chief of Staff Carl E. Vuono suspended the "debilitating" Army personnel system prior to DESERT STORM to knock the Army back into shape for the first Gulf War. Defenders of individual replacement countered that Vuono had actually exercised the system as designed. Rotational readiness would have perhaps a third of Army combat units available for deployment at a given time, as was the case with the Marines. The late Cold War Army's readiness system envisioned sustaining all units in a "band of excellence" wherefrom they could be brought to combat readiness within specified periods of time—days or weeks. The Marines rotated their units through operations in the Pacific at the time, whereas Army units were forward deployed or committed to war plans that required time-phased arrivals. As DESERT SHIELD began Vuono initiated "stop loss" and hosed units down with replacements and resources. With rigorous last-minute training, units selected to deploy quickly bumped up from wherever they were in the "band of excellence" to true combat readiness. The individual replacement system had been justified by brutal demands to keep units up to strength in World Wars I and II. Collaterally, it facilitated schooling, reassignment for professional development, and the remediation of various forms of attrition in peacetime. Historically, unit manning had worked best when casualties were low and combat episodic, as had been the case on the nineteenth-century frontier. Unit rotation per se worked best when the situation was relatively static and there were ample units to rotate, as had been the case through much of World War I. When most or all units were committed, combat sustained, casualties high, and the situation fluid—as in the World War II Huertgen Forest—there had been no real alternative to individual replacement. Cold War planners who championed individual replacement had World War II in mind when they advocated a peacetime personnel system reflecting the wartime realities they envisioned. The system encountered some criticism in Korea and considerable criticism in Vietnam. In its favor, units remained up to strength. Drafted soldiers endured the rigors of combat for a single year, professional soldiers fought for a year at a time, and there were almost always enough seasoned veterans on hand in a unit to bring new arrivals quickly aboard. As Vietnam dragged on, adverse implications for unit cohesion became more apparent. Debates concerning rotational readiness and unit replacement pivoted on the future war envisioned. Would most or all units be simultaneously committed to bloody conflict, or would there be smaller but more recurrent episodes with relatively few casualties involved?[5]

"Jointness" was a desirable attribute the services had actively pursued at least since the Goldwater-Nichols Act of 1986. Emphasis on mutual understanding, cooperation, intervisibility, reduction of redundancy, and integration of combat and sustainment efforts was well placed. The devil was in the details, however, and jointness had important implications for Army force structure. At the grandest level, service representatives debated how much maritime and air supremacy was enough before resources should sensibly be shifted to far less advantaged—and numerically disadvantaged—ground forces. The collapse of the Soviet Union, evaporation of near-peer naval and air rivalry, and disproportionate operational requirements on existing ground forces were grist for Quadrennial Defense Reviews, as we have seen. Expanding Army capabilities for deep battle further complicated relationships with the Air Force and Navy. *Breaking the Phalanx* proposed that a three-star Joint Forces Land Component Commander would have a two-star deputy commanding a robust mix of rocket artillery, aviation, and air defense groups. As the range, precision, capability, and targeting information available to relevant Army forces inevitably increased, they equally inevitably provoked further discussion of roles and missions. "Big sky, little bullet" was ever less practical as a principle for de-conflicting air space. Proliferating cruise missiles and unmanned aerial vehicles complicated the circumstances, as did more capable air defenses for bringing the aircraft and missiles of an enemy down. Some joint enthusiasts argued strike aircraft with precision-guided munitions rendered a robust forward presence of field artillery obsolete. Counterarguments were that precision-guided munitions required precisely defined targets, most artillery fires were used for suppression rather than destruction, and there were still plenty of uses for cheap "dumb" munitions. If seizing and controlling terrain remained important, ground combat remained ultimately decisive. Such an inference was more congenial to the Army and Marines than to the Navy and Air Force, of course. Although the redesign of Army force structure would be broadly supportive of jointness, interservice points of contention would frame and shape its progress.[6]

Logistics were not much developed in most of the writings advocating the dismantlement of divisions, corps, and theater support commands, to include *Breaking the Phalanx*. Some blandly assumed Information Age technologies would inevitably reduce tail-to-tooth ratios, without describing how or why this was to occur. Historically, manpower given over to logistics had increased in an upward parabolic arc from the low-technology (albeit not for the times) Roman legion through the high-technology Army of Excellence division. The Air Force was arguably the most Information Age savvy and highly technical service, and it featured the tiniest percentages of actual combatants. When robust networks of digital equipment were eventually fielded amid phalanxes of robots, swarms of unmanned aerial vehicles (UAVs), fields of sensors, and fleets of future combat vehicles, how was the panoply to be maintained? Logistical force planners lamented that tactical theorists waxed eloquently on the roles and missions of combat and combat support units, and then dispatched logistics with a box or two on a wiring diagram. This was not a new complaint, nor one confined to American theorists. Logisticians surmised a failure to appreciate all that actually goes on in a support battalion and in the echelons supporting it, deficient understanding of "below the line" forces, and capricious neglect of executive agency. With respect to a brigade-support battalion, in a scenario wherein all of the brigades in a theater reported to a single headquarters, the theater communications zone would begin at the brigade rear boundary. Thus each of the many specialties within a field-grade headquarters would draw directly from counterparts at a four-star headquarters without assistance or intervention. If one has never served as a logistician above the brigade level this may seem easy enough, but for most who have the complications seem daunting. "Above-the-line" forces are the "chips" that appear on map boards and figure in schemes of maneuver: divisions, separate brigades, cavalry regiments, and the like. Below-the-line forces are the combat support and combat service support forces traditionally located at the corps echelon and above that enable the above-the-line forces to succeed. Going into DESERT STORM the accepted manpower proportions between below-the-line and above–the-line forces was 1.6 to 1 for an austere theater. In DESERT STORM a proportion of 1.3 to 1 worked, largely because of host-nation offsets. Even if flattening, reorganization, technology, or offsets enabled substantial further reductions, below-the-line forces would still require an attention to detail at least as great as that accorded above-the line-forces. Executive agency defines support the Army is required to provide all services within a theater. Examples include—but certainly are not limited to—Class I (rations) inland, ocean terminals, intermodal container management, transportation engineering, land transportation, military customs inspections, power generation, land-based water resources, overland petroleum, oil, and lubricants (POL), military postal service, prisoner of war (POW) and detainee programs, veterinary support, battlefield medical evacuation, mortuary services, graves registration, and disposal of explosives and munitions. This partial list implies a great deal of additional work. Advocates of dramatic service redesign came to see traditional logisticians as willful "toads in the road" creating obstacles to every proposal they suggested. Logisticians came to perceive the theorists as fanciful dreamers, willing to commit the Army to a force structure it could not support. Creative tension between the two would substantially affect the theoretical and practical course of force redesign.[7]

The Chiefs of Staff, TRADOC, the Army Staff, and feedback from the field were, as we have seen in earlier chapters, principal drivers in transformation as it developed. Deliberations were enriched by voluble internal and external debate. A number of the authors of relevant articles, papers, studies, and briefings stemming from the post–Cold War intellectual ferment played Army "insider" roles as redesign progressed, as the names in our end notes suggest. Subordinates of Generals Reimer and Shinseki sought to position Macgregor in such an inside role as well, but these efforts did not work out. Some in the press depicted Macgregor as a brilliant innovator crushed by the dead weight of bureaucracy. This was caricature, not altogether untrue but certainly overdone. Macgregor's superiors during several unhappy episodes were hardly Neanderthals, possessed advanced degrees themselves, and in some cases were published authors. The interpersonal skills required of a visionary are different than those required to make things happen amid the staff interplay of competing priorities and interests. The military decision-making process (MDMP), imbued in the Army at least since the era of General George C. Marshall, envisioned that all relevant factors would be considered, those empowered to do so would make decisions, and all would then "salute the flag" and move on. Staff work was anonymous, staff officers self-deprecating, and staff decisions revisited, if ever, discretely. Macgregor made his greatest contributions as a gadfly, operating outside of the actual decision-making process, energizing different and diverse audiences, forcing attention upon issues he considered important, and fostering ideas of which respectable proportions proved practical. Emphasis upon brigade-sized maneuver groups, modularity, rotational readiness, unit replacement, revamped command hierarchy, and jointness all did figure in the Army's redesign. Logistics, thinly treated by Macgregor and others but robustly represented in TRADOC and on the Army Staff, figured as well.[8]

The Brigade, 1989–2005

The 1980s vintage Army of Excellence had fixed ideas concerning the role of brigades and how they fit into the larger framework established by divisions and corps. Brigades fought the close battle side by side along a "line of contact." Their direct-fire weapons reliably ranged out to 3,000 meters, which did much to define their "battle space." Maneuver training reinforced an appreciation of how this battle space should lay out. Maneuver umpires were taught such actuarial norms as three M1A1 rounds could be expected to kill a T72 caught in the flank at 2,000 meters, whereas T72s would have to be at 1,000 meters or less to expect comparable results against the M1A1. Happily, a T72 could not expect to penetrate the frontal armor of an M1A1, whereas M1A1s could expect to destroy the T72 by the time they had fired a fourth round at the front slope within 1,500 meters or less. These and related expectations figured into the design of company sectors, "kill zones," and graphical depictions of battlefield plans. Constituent battalions of combat brigades might occupy about ten kilometers of breadth and depth in the defense and about half of that in the attack, although this varied with mission, enemy, terrain, and troops available (METT). A combat brigade traditionally deployed with two battalions forward and one back, and ideally preserved ten kilometers or so of depth for its own brigade rear area. Army of Excellence combat brigades had habitually associated forward support battalions for combat service support. These technically were organic to the DISCOM, but in practice were ever-present with the brigade when it deployed. Brigade combat teams also had habitually associated artillery battalions, but the disposition of these was more variable. The brigade-equivalent division artillery commander deployed artillery to best facilitate the division commander's battle. The same could be said of the battalion level engineer, signal, military intelligence, and air defense commanders within the division that usually detached contingents to the brigade combat teams. The division fought a battle larger than that of its brigades in a temporal as well as a geographic sense. "AirLand Battle" envisioned Soviet attacks arriving in echelons and sought to engage those echelons throughout the depth of the battlefield rather than allowing them to concentrate on the front line of troops (FLOT) unmolested. The brigade was expected to handle enemy first-echelon regiments within about fifteen kilometers of its front, which roughly translated into those likely to bring direct fires to bear within less than twelve hours. The division coordinated and reinforced the brigades, but with its aviation brigade, rocket artillery, and enhanced access to intelligence it focused on engaging second-echelon regiments and divisions extending to 120 kilometers deep, or forty-eight hours out. The corps operated at about the same depth but with more weight, since it had multiple aviation and artillery brigades and greater access to intelligence and air support. If the "sandbox" allotted to the brigade was small in comparison to that of the division and corps, it was diminutive from an Air Force frame of reference. War College students benefited from a "USAF Missions Area Relationships Sideview" graphic (*Diagram*). On this slide "CAS" (close air support) appeared as a small wart over the front line depicted in the middle of the chart. "BAI" (battlefield air interdiction), wherein divisions and corps might play, covered a bit more space, and Air Force purer "AI" (air interdiction) ran deeper still. "DCA" (defensive counter air) and "OCA" (offensive counter air) arched protectively over these smaller domains, and these in turn

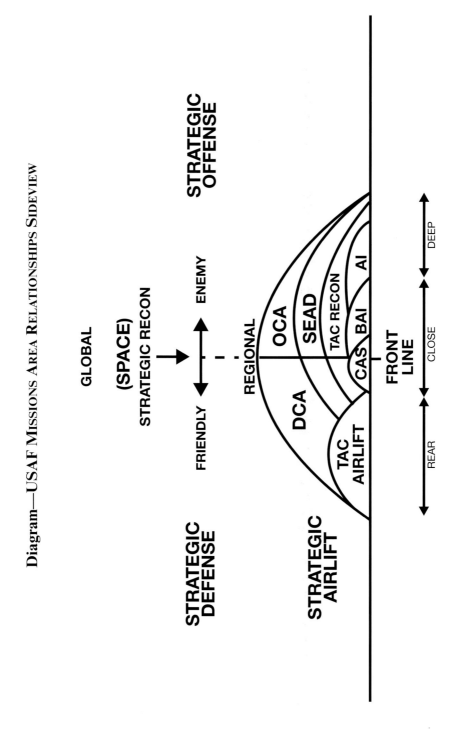

Diagram—USAF Missions Area Relationships Sideview

were dwarfed by "strategic defense" and "strategic offense" extending grandly from one side of the slide to another—and well into an area marked "space." The wart under CAS "belonged" to the Army, defined where the "short sword fighting" of direct combat would occur, and was largely co-terminal with the brigade battle area.[9]

During General Gordon R. Sullivan's tenure as Chief of Staff there was no great interest in departing from the basic Army of Excellence organization he had inherited. As we have seen in Chapter 3, the overwhelming priority was sustaining quality amid traumatic downsizing and geographical relocations. Sullivan believed an organization could only endure so much turmoil at one time without significant degradation, and he well knew how much turmoil the pursuit of the "peace dividend" was already inflicting. The brainstorming of his modern Louisiana Maneuvers ranged broadly through various organizational possibilities but generally came back to the notion with respect to the near term of applying Information Age technologies and other advances to existing force structure. The most dangerous threat was still visualized as a peer or near-peer, and most accepted the logic of TRADOC that "AirLand Battle worked well in the Persian Gulf" and thus pursued a paradigm that "builds upon the strengths of AirLand Battle and evolves it towards the future."[10] Immediate post–Cold War thinking did emphasize improved power projection through greater strategic mobility and advocated greater capabilities to operate across the full operational continuum. The first of these would be achieved in the near term through enhanced sealift, airlift, and pre-positioning. The second would require forces designed with a traditional "war-fighting orientation" to modify methods and organizations when in lesser circumstances. Operations other than war were inherently joint, interagency, and combined. Therefore some civilian agency such as the Department of State would ideally have the lead for the United States in operations short of war, and American forces would deploy to such contingencies in the support of local allies. The Army's primary focus would remain war-fighting against peer or near-peer opponents, and it would organize accordingly. Sullivan and General Fred Franks of TRADOC directed force planners to focus on getting the division right as an echelon of battle command first and then to work up and down the command hierarchy from there. The process implied pruning rather than major surgery insofar as force structure was concerned.[11]

General Dennis J. Reimer shared Sullivan's conviction that near-term upgrades necessarily would be technological appliqué upon existing organizations. Division XXI was by and large a trimmer version of its predecessors, advancing the evolutionary themes of Force XXI. Reimer did, however, preside over at least three steps in the direction of a brigade-based Army. First, looking beyond Force XXI to his Army After Next, TRADOC was open to the possibility of eliminating echelons. As we have seen, Reimer advanced Macgregor's *Breaking the Phalanx* as a basis for discussion and as a model for war-gamed analyses. Several Army After Next war games experimented with abstractly named "echelons of maneuver" and "echelons of concentration" to avoid mind-sets committed to present structure. With time, war-gamed echelons of maneuver began to look a lot like brigade combat teams. Second, the new Army National Guard enhanced brigades developed after DESERT STORM evolved into a prototype emphasizing brigades and diminishing divisions. Enhanced brigades enjoyed priority with respect to resources, training, and mobilization expectations. The newly activated headquarters of the 24th Infantry Division at Fort Riley, Kansas, and the 7th Infantry Division at Fort Carson, Colorado, assumed responsibility for the preparation and training of National Guard enhanced brigades but did not have the support elements theretofore expected of divisions. These instead remained embedded within the enhanced brigades. This independent separate brigade configuration was characteristic of enhanced brigades not committed to the 7th or 24th Divisions as well. Third, Reimer designated the 2d Armored Cavalry as an experimental "Strike Force" and set out to develop it into a strategically mobile force of medium weight capitalizing on the latest technologies. The Strike Force headquarters was to be a highly flexible receptacle into which a broad range of capabilities could plug in. Conceptually, it seemed somewhere between a robust brigade combat team and a division or corps headquarters capable of controlling diverse assets. It also departed from the notion that brigades would deploy on line, responding doctrinally to experiences in Somalia, the Balkans, and elsewhere.[12]

General Eric K. Shinseki continued Reimer's azimuth with the Army National Guard enhanced brigades that became, as we have seen, ever more prone to deploy. He also continued the effort to envision ground warfare abstractly enough to eliminate an echelon of command if it proved desirable. TRADOC analysts developing his objective force took to war-gaming a "Units of Purpose Framework." Fixed organizations designed to accomplish specific "mission essential" tasks were called units of action (UAs). Nimble headquarters that commanded mixes of UAs appropriate for an assigned mission, but which were themselves unencumbered by permanent organic structure beyond that necessary for command and control, were called units of employment (UEs). The battlefields played in most scenarios were nonlinear. Fluid attacks along multiple axes developed via Information Age "dominant knowledge" were keys to success. By 2001 it seemed clear that the best fit for a modernized UA was roughly equivalent to a brigade combat team, with fixed subordinate organizations equivalent to battalions, companies, and platoons. Even as these analyses progressed Shinseki organized, equipped, and trained Stryker Brigade Combat Teams as the battlefield presence of his Interim Force. Stryker Brigades were, as we have seen, robust combined-arms teams including infantry, armor, artillery, engineers, intelligence, and combat service support riding on a common wheeled chassis. It was modernized and digitized insofar as was possible with immediately available technologies or off-the-shelf hardware and software. The Stryker Brigade numbered about 3,500 soldiers and 300 vehicles overall, and the first was ready to deploy before General Shinseki departed as Chief of Staff.[13]

General Peter J. Schoomaker committed to the final steps to a brigade-based Army. The TRADOC design for combat UAs was well along, although support UAs were considerably less developed. The first Stryker Brigade, the 3d Brigade, 2d Infantry Division, had deployed to Iraq and was giving a good account of itself. Actual combat in Iraq was nonlinear after April 2003 and had devolved to the brigade level and below. Schoomaker felt pressed for time for several reasons. First, emerging long-term rotational demands to Iraq and elsewhere threatened to exhaust the Army unless more and nimbler units for rotation could be quickly fielded. Second, evolving force generation processes—manning, equipping, training, deploying, and redeploying—were much more capably supported by installations and others if at the brigade level or below. Finally, the wars in Afghanistan and Iraq generated massive supplemental funding from Congress that could be turned to Army redesign if it benefited these wars in particular. Army transformation ideally could occur before supplementals ceased. Schoomaker decided to tie unit reorganizations to upcoming rotations, starting with the 3d Infantry Division (Mechanized) slated to return to Iraq in 2005. To speed things along he directed the 3d Infantry Division commander to come up with his own redesign without consulting or waiting for TRADOC, multiplying from three line brigades to five modular brigade combat teams drawing entirely upon organic resources. Stung by the slight but inspired by the emphasis, TRADOC narrowed the participants in its own brigade redesign and sped its process along. The two initiatives crossed paths before the 3d Infantry Division actually deployed. Schoomaker accepted a design that extracted four brigade combat teams rather than five from contemporary divisions, a significant increase nevertheless. Under the new plan line brigade combat teams available for rotation—active and reserve—would increase from forty-eight to seventy. As force generation cycles left brigade combat teams wearing the same shoulder patch at different stages, deploying division headquarters became ever more likely to command and control patches other than their own. The division-based Army of the Cold War would evolve into the brigade-based Army of the wars that followed.[14]

Design guidance for Heavy Units of Action, to be drawn from contemporary heavy divisions, included being capable of all contemporary heavy brigade combat team missions and making use of equipment to be available not later than 2005. Schoomaker recognized that despite analyses, exercises, and war-gaming, combat would expose shortcomings and dictate revisions. Revisions would be applied to succeeding overseas rotations as the model was refined. TRADOC analysts tested five distinct proposals before narrowing down to three and then to one. Given the aspiration for seventy brigades overall, numbers made it virtually impossible to field three robust maneuver battalions in each of them. Schoomaker ultimately and grudgingly accepted a two-battalion design. Each of the two battalions was to be a combined-arms battalion with two tank companies, two mechanized infantry companies, and an engineer company. The brigade also featured an armed reconnaissance squadron with three ground troops assisted by a small fleet of UAVs (*Charts 3 and 4*). This considerably improved the brigade's ability to control ground and radically improved its ability to identify enemy locations and call in indirect fires. Such fires would generally come from a two-battery (eight self-propelled 155-mm. guns each) artillery battalion organic to the UA, and the fires of other units coordinated through this battalion. Like the DIVARTY commander of earlier divisions, the commander of the UA's artillery battalion would double

Chart 3—AOE 3D BRIGADE, 2D ARMORED DIVISION, AS TASK ORGANIZED FOR OPERATION DESERT STORM, 1991

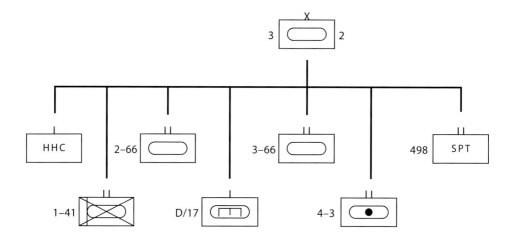

Chart 4—MODULAR 2D BRIGADE COMBAT TEAM, 3D IINFANTRY DIVISION (HEAVY BRIGADE COMBAT TEAM), IN OPERATION IRAQI FREEDOM, 2005

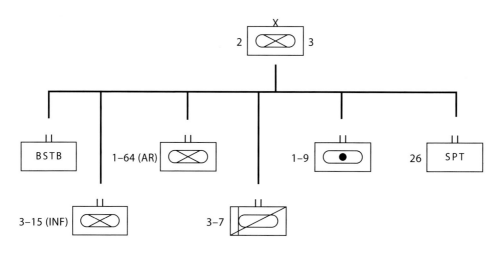

as his commander's senior artillery coordinator. He would have a state-of-the-art target acquisition platoon to help identify targets and ready access to air assets as circumstances required. Combat service support for the UA would be provided by a brigade support battalion including a maintenance company, a distribution company, a medical company, and a forward support company each for the maneuver battalions, reconnaissance squadron, and fires battalion. Initially these forward support companies were envisioned as organic to the battalions they supported, but this ran afoul of the combat exclusion policy for female soldiers—a major fraction of such logistical troops. Instead the companies were assigned to the brigade support battalion, technically not a combat arms unit. A brigade special troops battalion, a somewhat confusing designation resurrected from previous Army experience, included the brigade headquarters company, a signal company, and a military intelligence company. Within the headquarters itself such specialties as psychological operations, civil-military relations, human intelligence, operational law, public affairs, and air defense were represented by assigned personnel. In sum the organization had many attributes of a miniature division, with all relevant branches organic to it and substantial operational autonomy.[15]

The Infantry Unit of Action was to be capable of all contemporary infantry brigade combat team missions and to make use of equipment to be available not later than 2005. Force planners were directed to standardize three theretofore distinct types of units: airborne, air assault, and light. These units had evolved uniquely and differently, primarily because of their divisional settings. Airborne battalions and brigades were constituent to or modeled after the 82d Airborne Division and designed for parachute entry. A separate airborne brigade each existed in Europe and the Pacific. Air assault battalions and brigades were constituent to the 101st Airborne Division (Air Assault) and executed forcible entry via helicopter lift generated from the division's aviation assets. Light infantry brigades were constituent to light infantry divisions and had appreciable organic rolling stock, which made them more mobile on the ground than their airborne or air assault counterparts. They were, however, far better designed to defend difficult terrain than to execute forcible entry. From these differences divergent training, equipment, and ways of doing business had emerged. If Infantry Units of Action were to be modular, all would have to be identically trained and equipped, and capable of both forcible entry and sustained defense. The division as the singular context for training and operations was to drop out of the picture. Combat enablers not organic to the Unit of Action would be provided by separate combat support and combat service support brigades instead. As had been the case with the Heavy Unit of Action, Schoomaker reluctantly accepted a design featuring two maneuver (infantry) battalions and a reconnaissance squadron to achieve the desired number of brigade combat teams for the rotational base (*Charts 5 and 6*). The infantry battalions were to have three rifle companies and a weapons company apiece. The weapons company featured three assault platoons mounted in armored high mobility multipurpose wheeled vehicles (HMMWVs) carrying antitank missiles, grenade launchers, and heavy machine guns. It also had a sniper section, a mortar platoon, and a scout platoon. The reconnaissance

**Chart 5—AOE 2D BRIGADE, 7TH INFANTRY DIVISION,
AS TASK ORGANIZED FOR OPERATION JUST CAUSE, 1989–1990**

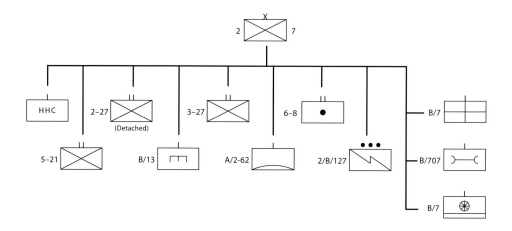

**Chart 6—MODULAR 173D AIRBORNE BRIGADE COMBAT TEAM
(INFANTRY BRIGADE COMBAT TEAM [AIRBORNE])
IN OPERATION ENDURING FREEDOM, 2007–2008**

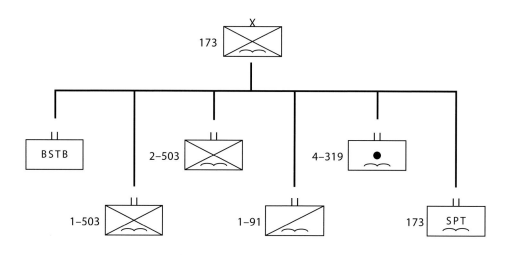

squadron had two motorized reconnaissance troops, a dismounted reconnaissance troop, and an unmanned aerial vehicle platoon. An organic fires battalion had two firing batteries with eight 105-mm. howitzers each and a target acquisition platoon. The brigade special troops battalion included an engineer company, a military intelligence company, and a signal company. The brigade support battalion included a distribution company, a maintenance company, a medical company, and a forward support company each for the infantry battalions, the reconnaissance squadron, and the fires battalion. Force planners again neatly sidestepped the combat exclusion policy for female soldiers by assigning forward support companies to the support battalion rather than to battalions that they would actually support. The model came down about halfway between the relative immobility of paratroopers once they had landed and the effective motorization of the light divisions. Each forward support company had a wheeled transportation platoon capable of lifting a company, and the support battalion could lift two companies more. Thus more than half the brigade could be on organic wheels at the same time. For further wheeled lift, or for any airborne or air assault lift, the Infantry Unit of Action would require outside assets. The overall design had more strategic mobility than light infantry brigades had enjoyed and considerably more staying power—in particular the organic capacity for ammunition resupply—than that of airborne or air assault battalions.[16]

The shift to a brigade-based army implied brigade-based combat support and combat service support beyond that organic to the maneuver brigade combat teams themselves. After considerable deliberation, force planners determined that five types of modular support units of action were required: aviation, fires, maneuver enhancement, battlefield surveillance, and sustainment. Of these, aviation, fires, and sustainment came closest to traditional models and ways of doing business. Maneuver enhancement and battlefield surveillance involved greater novelty and more conceptual difficulties. The Aviation Unit of Action was to provide attack and lift assets, as well as air mobile reconnaissance and security. Paired with an appropriately trained Infantry Unit of Action, it could replicate the air assault capabilities of the 101st Airborne Division (Air Assault) on a brigade scale. It could also serve as a maneuver force in its own right, attaching ground assets as necessary, or untether itself from the ground battle and conduct deep strikes within the range of its aircraft. It would feature two attack helicopter battalions, a utility assault helicopter battalion, an aviation support battalion, an aviation general support battalion, and a signal company as organic units. In addition, it would generally have an unmanned aerial vehicle company assigned. The Fires Unit of Action would provide close support, counterfire, and precision fires on high-value targets. It would include an organic rocket battalion with a forward support company, unmanned aerial vehicles, a target acquisition battery, a brigade support battalion, and a signal company. It would generally have additional rocket battalions, field artillery battalions, and information operations units assigned as well. Like the DIVARTY of yore, it would be able to mass fires under the direction of a full colonel to reinforce the artillery assets already committed to Maneuver Units of Action. With the appreciable reach of its unmanned aerial vehicles and rocket systems, it could also conduct deep battle missions theretofore customarily associated with Corps Artillery. The Sustainment Unit of Action, like the DISCOM it superseded, was to shepherd the combat service support necessary to support up to ten combat or combat service support counterparts. Unlike the DISCOM, forward support battalions (brigade support battalions) serving the maneuver or combat support units of action were not to be organic to it. The Sustainment Unit of Action would have an organic brigade special troops battalion with a signal company, support company, and medical detachment organic to it. Additional support battalions would generally be assigned, most of which featured a mix of ammunition, transportation, maintenance and supply, and services companies. The brigade special troops battalion would generally have finance and personnel detachments assigned, and the Sustainment Unit of Action might attach medical units of up to brigade size. The Sustainment Unit of Action resembled the earlier Corps Support Command (COSCOM) more so than the DISCOM. It would extend its oversight to the forward support battalions organic to the combat and combat support units of action within its purview, but its greater role was to coordinate a mixed array of logistical separate battalions providing services extending to the theater level.[17]

The Maneuver Enhancement Unit of Action and the Battlefield Surveillance Unit of Action both featured functions not readily compartmented at the tactical, or even operational, level. For a time the Maneuver Enhancement Unit of Action was called the Protection Unit of Action since it agglomerated units largely intended to mitigate the effects of hostile action or civil unrest: air defense, chemical, civil affairs, engineer, explosive ordnance disposal, and military police. Several of these functional areas were so critical at the operational and theater levels that brigades purely featuring them as well as units of action incorporating them would be required. Such potentially brigade-pure functions included air defense, civil affairs, engineers, and military police. An air defense brigade might be committed to defend a theater, for example, while air defense battalions assigned to a Maneuver Enhancement Brigade might cover clusters of units of action operating in lesser spaces within it. The Maneuver Enhancement Brigade would have a brigade support battalion and a signal company organic to it, and it would routinely have air defense, chemical, engineer, and military police battalions or companies assigned to it. It would also be likely to have civil affairs, explosive ordnance disposal, and maneuver units attached. The likely attachment of maneuver units recognized the lack of front lines in such places as Afghanistan or Iraq, where commanders at all levels had to be prepared to fight it out on the ground. Battlefield surveillance was another functional area wherein responsibilities quickly escalated from the tactical through the theater level. Major headings included reconnaissance, surveillance, target acquisition, intelligence, and intelligence integration. War-gaming established that the reconnaissance squadrons in the Maneuver Units of Action, and the fleets of unmanned aerial vehicles there and in the Aviation and Fires Units of Action, had vastly increased the intelligence assets available at the tactical level. There was contention as to whether the Battlefield Surveillance Unit of Action also needed ground assets to fight for information, but ultimately it received a cavalry reconnaissance squadron with two ground reconnaissance troops and a long-range surveillance troop. The Battlefield Surveillance Unit of Action would police terrain incidentally or accidentally not covered by Maneuver or Fires Units of Action, but would focus on pulling together the larger intelligence picture and drawing national assets into the local battle. The Battlefield Surveillance Unit of Action would have an organic military intelligence battalion, the cavalry reconnaissance squadron, a signal company, and a support company. It would customarily have special operations forces, unmanned aerial vehicles, aviation battalions, and military intelligence assets under its operational control (OPCON) or attached.[18]

Force structure redesign inevitably trades off advantages and disadvantages, and the move to a brigade-based Army was no exception. On the plus side, the new brigade combat teams were far more modular, numerous, suitable for rotation, robust in their capabilities, and empowered to fight a 360-degree battle without notice than their predecessors. They could operate well beyond the "wart" of the Cold War close battle. The reconfiguration proved timely and appropriate, given realities on the ground in Afghanistan and Iraq. On the debit side, the Army was less capable than it had been of slugging it out with near-peer adversaries, seemed more likely to "orphan" units, and was increasingly dependent on outside help to accomplish its missions. The greatest detriment to dealing with a near-peer was the lack of maneuver reserves within the brigade. Hallowed tradition featured "triangular" units deploying subordinate units "two up and one back." The two forward bore the brunt of initial contact, and the one back defeated enemy penetrations or exploited tactical opportunities as they developed. Since this basic paradigm simultaneously applied at the platoon, company, battalion, brigade, and division levels, commanders had a resilient sponge-like depth when on the defense and waves of potential exploitation forces when on the offense. The new two-battalion brigade combat team could best generate a reserve by pulling companies from its battalions, thus reducing the battalions' capability to generate a reserve, or deflecting its reconnaissance assets into a reserve role. Alternatively, some other brigade could serve as the reserve for a larger array, thus skipping an echelon with respect to reserves. War games revisited the two-battalion versus three-battalion model time and again and found the two-battalion model's thinness of reserves at the brigade level troublesome against a near-peer in a pitched battle. A related issue was the ability to mass such assets as artillery and engineers at the operational level, given the numbers already committed to and organic to brigade combat teams. The disappearance of Corps Artillery and DIVARTY created "who's your daddy?" situations for artillerymen, and these were even more pronounced in the cases of engineers, signal, and military intelligence. In the traditional division battery and company commanders from these branches reported to a field-grade commander who supervised their use and steered their professional development—and that of their subordinates. Now batteries and companies were organic to brigade combat teams, and relationships with superior organizations within their branches were ill defined. The potential for orphanage was also present in the large mix of units customarily assigned, attached, or OPCON to Fires, Maneuver Enhancement, Battlefield Surveillance, and Sustainment Units of Action when on active operations, but presumably independent when not. Efficient branch use outside the brigade, branch competency within the brigade, and professional development of combat support and combat service support officers within and without emerged as potential issues. Bucking the trend, air defense artillery disappeared from the customary constitution of a brigade combat team rather than becoming organic within it. This assumed air supremacy, as did the choice of more air-mobile 105-mm. rather than of more capable 155-mm. artillery for the infantry unit of action. Fleets of UAVs were to fly unmolested under the protective cover of air supremacy as well. The UAVs and virtually every other piece of advanced technology would require contractors to maintain them, and a host of other contractors would backfill holes reorganization had exposed. Concerning such reliance on external support, more later. All the above having been said, the Army faced no near-peer in Iraq or Afghanistan, the unprecedented professional caliber of officers and senior NCOs mitigated orphanage issues, air supremacy was a fact, and ample numbers of capable contractors existed. The brigade-based redesign may not have been the best fit for all circumstances, but it seemed the best fit for the circumstances the Army was actually in.[19]

Headquarters Above Brigade, 1989–2005

The shift to a brigade-based Army implied a radical shift in the composition, roles, and missions of elements above brigade. The overwhelming majority of deployed or deploying soldiers were to be in maneuver units of action, support units of action, or separate functional brigades. Traditionally, divisions, corps, and armies had mustered the lion's share of combat support and combat service support units to support maneuver brigades thinly provided with such assets organically. The Army of Excellence division ultimately had colonels (O-6) commanding an aviation brigade, a DIVARTY, an engineer brigade in the heavy division, and a DISCOM. Each commanded multiple battalions within their purview and advised the division commander on how best to use them. Lieutenant colonels (O-5) in command of division air defense, military intelligence, engineer in the light divisions, and signal battalions provided similar service. Customary formation of brigade combat teams drew off many of these assets, but the division commander retained a robust residue and had the authority and subordinate leadership sufficient to resume control. The "capable" corps similarly controlled a panoply of combat support and combat service support units through constituent corps artillery, corps support command, aviation, engineer, air defense, signal, chemical, military intelligence, civil affairs and military police brigades, and finance and personnel groups. A theater army (the two were the same at the time) commanded personnel; medical; transportation; engineer; air defense; military police; civil affairs; psychological operations; nuclear, biological, and chemical (NBC) and intelligence commands; special ammunition and missile brigades; and special forces and petroleum groups. Numbers were considerable. At wartime strength a theater army medical command numbered about 27,000, a corps engineer brigade about 14,000, and division artillery about 2,600, for examples. A mechanized division numbered about 9,000 soldiers in addition to the 9,000 in its line brigades, a wartime corps about 94,000 in addition to those in its assigned divisions, and a wartime theater army about 196,000 in addition to those in its corps. A mechanized division "slice" theoretically deploying to Southwest Asia would number 47,400, of which 17,500 would be from the division itself, 7,800 would constitute a nondivisional combat increment, and 22,000 would constitute a nondivisional tactical support increment. This robustness of assets at every level was the support and logistical equivalent of guaranteeing "two up and one back" for combat units. Commanders enjoyed a depth of capabilities that readily enabled them to shape the battlefield, react to contingencies, and exploit opportunities. Redundancy seemed prudent if one was to slug it out with a peer adversary.[20]

General Sullivan sought to prune this doctrinal force structure rather than to totally redesign it. His priorities were sustaining quality while radically downsizing and gaining an expeditionary capability through improved pre-positioning, sealift, and airlift. His modern Louisiana Maneuvers looked deeper, but for the near term his Force XXI generally envisioned applying digital technologies to contemporary platforms and force structure. General Reimer followed up with Force XXI but also oversaw experimentation with abstract "echelons of maneuver" and "echelons of concentration" when war-gaming his Army After Next. During General Shinseki's tenure these abstractions matured into the "units of purpose framework" featuring "units of action," "units of employment," and a rigorous effort to redesign the Cold War paradigm from top to bottom. Key questions were whether or not an echelon of command could be eliminated, whether or not headquarters above the unit of action could be rendered smaller and more nimble, and whether or not redundancy could be eliminated given the efficiencies of Information Age technology. With General Schoomaker's shift to a brigade-based Army, the answer seemed to be "yes" to all three questions. The unit of employment would be organized at two levels, a UEx at the higher tactical level and a UEy at the operational level. Between the two of them the traditional functions of theater, army, corps, and division would be divided— eliminating one or two echelons, depending on how one counted. The UEx and UEy would themselves be nimble headquarters, numbering perhaps a thousand soldiers or so each. Manpower that had been committed to them in the Army of Excellence would be siphoned off into support units of action and a discrete number of functional brigades. These modular units would be used to expand or contract the capabilities of UEx's and UEy's without permanently enlarging them. Modular units of action would reduce redundancy as well, since no headquarters would hoard an organic inventory of units "just in case." Units of action would be extractable, removable, and deployable. UEx's and UEy's would provide minimally manned matrices of headquarters above the UA level, with the UA's themselves representing the great mass of the Army's deployable manpower and muscle.[21]

The terms "unit of action" and "unit of employment" were intended to facilitate doctrinal deliberations unencumbered by tradition but were not intended to become permanent nomenclature. Indeed, they could inhibit discussion with those outside the design process, as flabbergasted noninitiates tried to picture what an "SUA" or a "UEy" actually meant. Names matter, and the Army's Center of Military History assumed its institutional responsibility for determining appropriate unit designations once force structure designs were far enough along to justify the effort. Schoomaker directed the Center to choose names that reinforced the intent of his modular initiative, while doing what it could to preserve historical unit lineages and minimize turbulence as secondary priorities. Such terms as platoon, company, troop, battery, squadron, and battalion had been used unmolested in the traditional sense throughout the units of purpose deliberations, so there was no incentive to change nomenclatures applicable at the battalion level and below. The maneuver unit of action seemed to most closely approximate the regimental combat team or brigade combat team of yesteryear. MacGregor's preference for the term "group," in the opinion of the Center, did not seem to offer enough advantages to justify extinguishing beloved and hallowed lineages. Continuous regimental lineages existed from 1636 (in the Army National Guard), continuous divisional lineages from 1879 (also in the Army National Guard), continuous corps lineages from 1918, and continuous numbered army lineages from 1918 as well. Brigades had been reinvented and reintroduced when the Reorganization Objective Army Division (ROAD) replaced the Pentomic Division in the early 1960s. Beginning in 1957 the Combat Arms Regimental System (CARS) perpetuated regimental lineages outside of standing regiments. This system later extended to include whole-branch regiments for selected combat support and combat service support branches. Keeping this tradition in mind, the Center of Military History designed three alternatives that best reconciled with the imperative of reinforcing the modular initiative. In the first the UA carried the lineage of a divisional brigade, the UEx that of a division, and the UEy that of a corps. In the second, the UA carried the lineage of a regiment, the UEx that of a division, and the UEy that of an army. In the third the UA carried the lineage of a division, the UEx that of a corps, and the UEy that of an army. In briefing these alternatives, the Center of Military History developed them sufficiently to identify units, patches, and flags that would disappear in each case. When briefed, General Schoomaker elected to seek the counsel of retired senior officers and asked General Sullivan to head up a "blue ribbon panel" for that purpose. The Chief of Military History carried these distinguished retirees through briefings concerning the Army redesign and the alternative unit nomenclatures and designations that could be associated with it. In the end Sullivan's team commented that all courses of action were feasible, but recommended "Course of Action 1." This alternative involved the least change in the patches soldiers would be wearing and the banners they would be serving under. Sullivan and his colleagues believed tradition enhanced performance. His written response to Schoomaker evoked the book *Band of Brothers* popular, and on the Chief of Staff's Reading List, at the time. Sullivan followed up by noting that most serving soldiers had earned and proudly wore divisional combat patches on their shoulders. For this singular honor to continue to have meaning, divisions would have to continue to have meaning.[22]

The next step was to specifically identify which headquarters were to disappear. The devil was in the details. In accordance with Course of Action 1, the Center of Military History dutifully prepared slides wherein the United States Army, Europe, and Seventh Army and the Eighth United States Army in Korea disappeared, as did the Third Army serving the Central Command and the First and Fifth Armies—the latter two then critical to recruitment, the Army Reserve, and the Army National Guard. Somehow word of these predecisional materials leaked, provoking angry phone calls from the field to the Chief of Military History and concerned phone calls to the Chief of Staff. Sullivan's team of retirees had rightly noted that the average soldier, its highest priority, identified more closely with brigade or division than with corps or army. However, to diminish—or to appear to diminish—four- or three-star headquarters embedded in powerful alliances or political configurations could have significant consequences. The thought that a joint headquarters could replace them was not entirely comforting, since the commander might well not be Army in circumstances that suggested a senior Army leader. A four-star corps was out of the question. An obvious tweak for Course of Action 1 was to swap army and corps, eliminating the corps from the hierarchy and the lexicon. This did not war-game well, since a multitude of two-star headquarters reporting directly to a four-star headquarters could quickly exceed its span of control—particularly if the senior headquarters was joint. Some assumed that if further hierarchy proved necessary, one two-star (division) headquarters could be placed in charge of others. Skeptics tried to imagine division commanders cheerfully submitting to the supervision of their peers. Leaders capable of effectively commanding others are generally more experienced than those they command. Accepting that one should train as one would fight, this proposed subordination would have to occur well prior to actual operations. Schoomaker grudgingly accepted that he was not going to unconditionally eliminate an echelon of command. The UEy would bear a geographical designation and the lineage of a former numbered army. Contingency planners would have two-star "tactical UEx's" and three-star "operational UEx's" to choose from when designing a deployment. Circumstances might suggest the use of one, the other, or both. If the contingency got big enough, the familiar hierarchy of two-star, three-star, and four-star headquarters with sensible spans of control would undoubtedly reemerge. The neat theory of simply eliminating a level of command ran afoul of alliance politics, bureaucratic practicalities, senior leader development, and of spans of control. The headquarters themselves might be smaller than before, but there would not necessarily be fewer of them. Sullivan had anticipated this dilemma, and in his letter to Schoomaker made the comforting comment, "While some would argue that the Army must make dramatic changes [to nomenclature] so that its commitment to Transformation is clear, we do not believe that people who really understand what the Army is doing will be persuaded one way or the other by what the Army calls its units." If the nomenclature for echelons was not to change, the case should be made that their organization and ways of doing business had.[23]

The redesigned division (two-star) and corps (three-star) UEx's were to be very different than before, and the theater/army UEy somewhat less so

313

(*Charts 7 and 8*). Shorn of capabilities that had migrated to support units of action, as of April 2005 the proposed division UEx weighed in at 1,242 personnel. Of these, 292 would be assigned to two nearly identical tactical command posts, each highly mobile and capable of fully controlling the tactical battle from a forward location. Another 277 were to be assigned to the main command post, a somewhat less nimble facility staffed to continuously control support, service support, and administration as well as combat operations per se. Liaison teams adding up to 40 personnel characterized as "joint" and 19 characterized as "digital" enabled the cooperation of other services and also enabled the division to serve as a joint task force headquarters if given the mission. A special troops battalion numbering 592 included 212 in a signal support company (network). The redesigned corps UEx looked much like the division, albeit somewhat beefier to accommodate potentially greater responsibilities—and the greater likelihood it would serve as a joint task force headquarters. With advanced communications and three major nodes apiece, divisions and corps could spread out across vast amounts of space and establish integrated matrices for command and control. Since all nodes were digitally networked, all would simultaneously share identical battlefield pictures. Under this umbrella, maneuver and support units of action would operate with little risk of losing communications with the headquarters assigned to control them. If one link was down, the network could readily replace it with another. Divisions and corps were no longer "chips on the board." They were the superstructure of command within which the chips operated. The UEy, now a regionally focused and named command and control headquarters bearing a numbered army lineage, was a bit more traditional. Planners accepted the need for continuously available intelligence, sustainment, network, and civil-military operations capabilities. Specifics would vary from theater to theater, but each theater would have an assigned core of critical support and combat support assets. Some would be branch-specific traditional brigades such as air defense, engineer, military police, or medical. Whereas corps, divisions, brigades, and below would be deployable assets rotated or rushed into theaters and constructed Lego-like into larger wholes, theater/armies would be continuously committed. Theater/armies, corps, and divisions would all be capable of serving as joint task force headquarters or Joint Forces Land Component Command headquarters if required.[24]

The considerable change envisioned for headquarters brigade and above did not escape criticism, to include critics alleging that it was not actually change at all. Well in the vanguard was Colonel Macgregor, now retired and working with a Washington "think tank." In April 2005 he was invited to make a presentation to members of the House Armed Services Committee. He helpfully entitled it "Transformation and the Illusion of Change: Where Is the Army Really Headed? What Is to Be Done?" thus ensuring that no one missed the point that he was a critic. Macgregor covered a great deal of ground with customary acid and admonition. He characterized the division and corps echelons as "no change." His ideas on command and control had evolved, and he briefed a slide wherein service-pure headquarters above those commanded by

Chart 7—AOE Heavy Corps Design, 1983

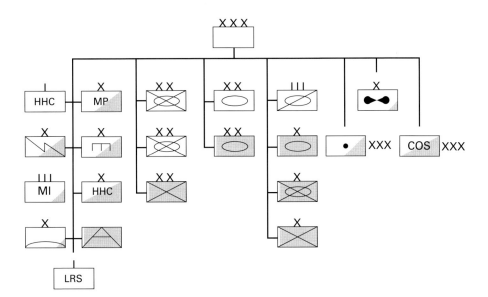

Source: CACDA Chart 83 6505A, Alternative (AOE) Heavy Corps. Shaded Areas indicate Reserve
Component Fill. No Total-Corps TOE was published for the AOE Heavy Corps.

Chart 8—AOE Light Corps Design, 1985

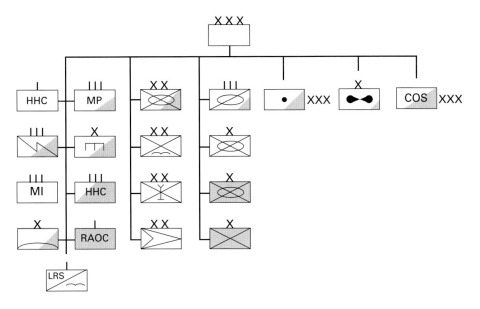

Source: CACDA Chart 84 7262, Proposed XVIII Airborne Corps, Shaded Areas indicate Reserve
Component Fill. No Total-Corps TOE was published for the AOE Light Corps.

a brigadier general (his combat maneuver group) had disappeared, as had any headquarters commanded by a major general. The brigadiers would report to the three-star "purple" commander of a standing joint task force, who in turn reported to a joint four-star combatant commander. If span of control became a problem, more three-star standing joint task forces would be deployed. Fortuitously, the Air Force rather than the Army got to be the "toad in the road" deflecting this particular concept. Since unhappy experiences in World War II North Africa, the Air Force had ferociously advocated consolidating the control of its assets at the theater level—rather than parceling them out to the corps or divisions of the time. The range and reach of aircraft argued against assigning them to geographically constrained headquarters and argued for the centralized economies of scale the theater Air Tasking Order (ATO) was supposed to represent. The Air Force was averse to reporting through multiple layers of non–Air Force commanders; one was enough. The Navy was somewhat less centralized in its thinking and had the precedent of the Marine Air Ground Task Force in its heritage, but it too was wary of subordination to geographically constrained headquarters. If a theater were divided up geographically among a fistful of three-star joint task forces, the units actually assigned to them would overwhelmingly be Army or Marine. This subject was not much debated before the utility of the Army's headquarters redesign was illustrating itself on the ground in Iraq, however. A matrix of division and corps headquarters shorn of former organic assets was sprawled across the country, commanding and controlling diverse mixes of combat, combat support, and combat service support brigades that often did not wear their patches. Reserve-component headquarters and units plunged into the cycle, adding to an overall rotational inventory that allowed a tiny active or activated Army of about 600,000 to maintain about 200,000 deployed for years on end. The military and political requirements of the theaters soon demonstrated ample scope for two-, three-, and four-star headquarters. Schoomaker's final version of redesign did not require him to deploy such a hierarchy, but it did give him the option to do so when necessary.[25]

External Complements to Force Structure

As the Army downsized during the early 1990s and then evolved toward a brigade-based force, some functions it previously accommodated with organic assets migrated outside the service—in all or in part. This reflected the imperative of preserving "core" functions, the downstream consequences of defense reorganizations, the composition of newly designed "units of action" and "units of employment," and efficiencies that could be gained through technological advance. Commanders and staffs of 1989 were thoroughly familiar with a paradigm characterized as the "Battlefield Operating System" (BOS). Walking into a Tactical Operations Center (TOC) at any level, one almost invariably encountered a chart with the headings Intelligence, Maneuver, Fire Support, Mobility/ Survivability, Air Defense, Combat Support, and Command and Control across the top or along one side. Generally the other axis featured time frames, and the chart communicated what each element of the BOS was to contribute during each phase of the battle. Denizens of the TOC, artfully trained by their branch schools, deployed fistfuls of field manuals and training aids to ensure they would wring the most possible out of the BOS for which they were responsible. The more senior among them, hopefully graduates of the Command and General Staff College or its equivalent, deployed further harvestings from their military educations to facilitate bringing the elements of the BOS together, and they trained their subordinates to do so as well. Assets under consideration were almost always Army. A handy packet of school-inspired pocket-sized reference cards issued throughout a brigade based in Germany, for example, spread forty-nine explanatory bullets or sub-bullets across the seven BOS. Of these, only one acknowledged the potential presence of another service. It read "Air Force Air, Plan Targets Early." The second half of the bullet reminded the practitioner of contemporary conventional wisdom that it took a painfully long time to bring the Air Force into play against ground targets. Beneath the division level, commanders and staffs became mindful of assets external to the Army in unusual circumstances, and divisions and corps themselves fought on largely service-pure battlefields. The ever-popular fire support coordination line (FSCL) provided a convenient boundary beyond which to "dump" air strikes that were too hard to figure into existing maneuver schemes. By 2005 much of this insularity had melted away, and the melting was accompanied by a considerable divestiture of force structure. Venues in which this divestiture was most pronounced included air defense, fire support, engineering, and logistics. Conversely, growth occurred in capabilities appropriate to operations other than war. In all these venues, complementary assets to address shortfalls came from outside the service.[26]

Cold War planners intended to achieve air superiority and then air supremacy eventually, but neither could be had without a fight. Until air supremacy was achieved the highest priority for the Air Force would be knocking out Warsaw Pact air forces—offensive counter air. This would collaterally protect Army units from air attack by destroying aircraft likely to attack them, and defensive counter air missions would be mounted as well. However, through the first weeks or months of operations the Army's failsafe would be an umbrella of protection mounted by its own air defense assets. Brigade combat teams customarily deployed with an air defense battery attached, and battalion combat teams with a platoon. The division had an organic air defense battalion, and its commander "double-hatted" as air defense staff executor for the division commander. The same was true of the air defense brigade commander assigned to the capable corps. TOCs at every level built air defenders, whether assigned, attached, or supporting, into their fire support matrices. Crucial considerations included status of weapons and positioning. Status of weapons reflected the permissiveness with which air defenders could fire, constrained by imperatives to properly identify enemy and not shoot down friendly aircraft. "Hold" was very restrictive, "tight" less so, and "free" permissive. The Air Force was understandably paranoid about the proliferation of air defense weapons, even if in friendly hands, and lobbied hard for rigorous controls. Air defenders sought terrain best able to observe aerial avenues of approach, and their favored positions might well conflict with the needs of the ground commander or be outside the envelope of security he could provide. Terrain apportionment, fratricide, and security became issues when small contingents of air defenders scattered across the battlefield to position for their missions. Aircraft and ground-based air defense had played a technological cat-and-mouse game since World War II. Ever more capable air defense weapons forced aircraft to ever higher altitudes for relative safety, but ever more precise guided munitions enabled them to remain effective even at these higher altitudes. The alternative of flying "on the deck" throughout a target run was adrenal but ineffective, and stealth technologies were vulnerable to parallel advances in sensors. This running stalemate between attack and defense was considerably compromised by the proliferation of intermediate-range ballistic missiles and the prospective proliferation of effective cruise missiles. In both cases ever-improving Patriot missiles seemed a promising defense, but not without the advance warning only space-based or top-down, high-altitude sensors could give. These invariably would be in the hands of the Air Force, reinforcing arguments for turning the entire air defense mission over to the Air Force as well. While this was being debated in elevated forums at the Pentagon, facts on the ground in Afghanistan and Iraq diminished Army interest in air defense at the TOC level. In these actual operations the adversaries were incapable of air strikes. Several weeks into the Global War on Terrorism Army observers were bemused by an Air Force claim that their air strikes had achieved air supremacy over Afghanistan. Had they not had air supremacy before the war even started? Whatever the Soviets might have mustered, the enemies the United States was actually fighting had no air capability, and those it seemed likely to fight had relatively little. The Army's core mission of ground combat was manpower-intensive in these unconventional settings, yet required negligible attention to air defense. By January 2004 a sizable fraction of the Army's air defense force structure, with some of the oldest lineages in the Regular Army, was on the chopping block to allow manpower reapportionments elsewhere. Air defense disappeared from all units of action except the maneuver enhancement brigade and was only represented by staff in the much reduced division and corps. As operations overseas matured, perhaps a single maneuver enhancement brigade at a time was assigned to Iraq or Afghanistan. This represented a density of air defenders an order of magnitude less than that of the Cold War. Whatever the doctrine, tactical air defense had migrated to the Air Force as a practical matter. To the TOC denizens of 2005, it was virtually invisible.[27]

Field artillery also experienced material, doctrinal, and practical diminishment during the transition to a brigade-based Army, although less so than air defense. Of seventy-six combat or combat support battalions identified as bill payers in a proposed January 2004 restructuring, almost half were field artillery. We have already discussed the demise of division and corps artillery—and of their commander positions. Within a brigade combat team a field artillery battalion of two batteries (albeit with eight rather than six guns each) replaced the battalion of three batteries that had been customary before. Field artillery not organic to brigade combat teams migrated to the fires brigades. These were formidable mixes of rocket and tube artillery but less numerous than their separate field artillery predecessors. After 2005 the Army sustained about

During IRAQI FREEDOM, combat support and combat service support troops increasingly patrolled as if they were infantry.

two fires brigades in Iraq when more than twenty maneuver brigades were in country, for example. This was perhaps a third of Cold War norms. Fires brigades did not deploy to Afghanistan. Deployed, field artillerymen often assumed missions other than fire support. Indeed, many "mothballed" their guns in secure motor pools and took to patrolling on foot or in HMMWVs fielded as alternate sets of equipment. The visibility of field artillery as artillery dissipated in tactical operations centers. Cold War commanders were used to top-down fire planning that generated elaborate matrices of targets, affectionately referred to as "measles sheets." Each of the numerous targets on a fire support overlay was uniquely numbered, assigned as a priority to one of the artillery battalions or batteries, and figured into one or more schemes of maneuver. In actual operations guns would "register" on their assigned targets, firing on them to refine the precision of their lay. The objective was to rapidly generate huge volumes of fire when called. Most of this fire would be suppressive, meaning one did not exactly know where the enemy was but wanted to "keep his head down"—to degrade his performance. The advent of cheap global positioning system (GPS)-based precision-guided munitions such as Joint Direct Attack Munitions (JDAMs) radically improved aviation's capability to provide fire support, as did technological leaps with respect to attack helicopters. Meanwhile rocket artillery advanced considerably with respect to accuracy and range. The Cold War logic for keeping masses of tube artillery well forward was that it would be ever present to reliably deliver high volumes of fire regardless of the weather. Against a formidable opponent in Europe or Korea this was more important than against lesser opponents in Iraq or Afghanistan. During DESERT STORM tube artillery saw relatively little use after the initial breakthrough, and in Afghanistan and IRAQI FREEDOM it saw little use at all. In conventional direct-fire battles in these theaters the enemy was hopelessly overmatched even without artillery, and unconventional engagements seldom lasted long enough to bring artillery to bear. With a few notable exceptions, to be discussed in Chapter 9, air strikes and attack helicopters were adequate for the modest fire support necessary. The increasing accuracy and range of rocket and even tube artillery further reduced the imperative of keeping artillery well forward, since a given battery could now support a larger number of units at greater ranges. The loss of the Crusader, previously discussed, furthered a sense of malaise among tube artillerymen. Their craft, more than that of most, was associated with the Army's supposedly ubiquitous "Cold War mentality."[28]

Like artillerymen and air defenders, engineers found their roles and force structure altered or diminished with the Army's redesign. The maneuver battalions of the new heavy brigade combat teams did have an organic combat engineer company each, and the infantry brigade combat teams a company. This provided them proportions of engineers comparable to that envisioned by the Army of Excellence. However, divisional engineer battalions and corps engineer brigades and groups disappeared. Outside the maneuver brigades engineers appeared in the maneuver enhancement brigades that were, as we have seen, thinly deployed to Iraq and Afghanistan. Theaters could be, and in practice were, supported by separate engineer brigades. Combat engineers in Iraq and Afghanistan were perhaps half as thick on the ground as they had been in earlier wars and theaters. Combat engineers had a long tradition of fulfilling a secondary role as infantry, and that role came to be well exercised in Southwest Asia. There was not all that much obstacle clearance, demolition, or field fortification for the combat engineers to do, and the bulk of horizontal and vertical construction, demining, and infrastructure refurbishment migrated to civilian contractors. The Cold War pocket-sized reference discussed previously had six bullets under "Mobility/Survivability," only one of which applied to Iraq: "Bulldozer—Who Is in Charge?" It was no longer a corps or division engineer, nor was it one of their subordinates. Notably, the official in Washington, DC, most in the know with respect to engineering issues in Iraq was the commander of the Corps of Engineers. He was responsible for tracking, coordinating, and reporting progress (or lack thereof) with respect to oil infrastructure, the power grid, the road net, irrigation canals, government facilities, base construction, and the disposal of mines and munitions. The Corps of Engineers is an essentially civilian organization led by a small cadre of uniformed officers that relies on contracting to accomplish the bulk of its missions. Through October 2004 perhaps 1,700 of its employees had deployed to Iraq as compared with 86,000 soldiers rotating through conventional engineer units, yet the lion's share of the rebuilding of Iraq was in its hands. This tracked with the revolution in military contracting discussed in Chapter 4, and in particular tracked with the philosophy of the Logistics Civil Augmentation Program (LOGCAP). Such companies as Kellogg, Brown and Root, DynCorps, and Halliburton were ubiquitous in Iraq, and functions filled by uniformed engineers in the Cold War Army of yesteryear migrated to them from its tauter uniformed successor. Mindful of troop ceilings in the theater, Army engineers innovated to make the most of small numbers. A case in point was the forward engineer support team (FEST). It could travel to a bridge or some other structure, transmit measurements and photographs to the Engineer Research and Development Center in Vicksburg, Mississippi, and get advice via interactive tele-engineering concerning the soundness of the structure and remedial actions to take. The FEST served as a metaphor for the redesigned Army engineers: thinner on manpower, high-tech, and heavily integrated with civilian and contracted assets.[29]

In so far as combat service support was concerned, "above-the-line"—formerly division and below—units available to the brigade-based Army were roughly comparable to those of the Cold War Army. Each brigade, whether combat or combat support, had its own organic brigade support battalion tailored to its organization. Maneuver battalions drew a forward support company from this brigade support battalion. Deployed divisions (UEx) or corps (UEx) were additionally assigned or attached sustainment brigades to service their assigned or attached combat and combat support brigades in "tooth-to-tail" ratios roughly proportional to Cold War norms for above-the-line forces. This picture changed with respect to "below-the-line"—formerly corps and above—combat service support forces, however. The Cold War rule of thumb for deployed forces was a 1.6 to 1 ratio of below-the-line to above-the-line forces. Thus if a division of about 18,000 deployed to an austere theater, about 29,000 additional soldiers would be required to support it. Of these additional troops, perhaps half would be in combat service support units. In practice these numbers could be trimmed by host-nation support. In DESERT STORM, for example, the ratio was about 1.3:1 since substantial host-nation and coalition offsets were available in the theater. A major fraction of these offsets were provided by contractors ultimately employed by the Saudis, inspiring much of the momentum toward LOGCAP and related programs in the 1990s. By 2001 operations in the Balkans had firmly established contractors as offsets for erstwhile uniformed force structure, and in Iraq the results proliferated like kudzu. Comparing numbers is tricky because considerable below-the-line combat support force structure migrated into the various UAs and took a slice of combat service support with it, and other below-the-line combat support structure with further slices of combat service support survived as independent brigades serving the theater. The direction of the change is nevertheless clear. Iraq matured as a theater with 100,000 individuals signed to contracts with the United States government serving alongside 160,000 troops also there. The value of such contracts expanded beyond $100 billion annually, as opposed to about $20 billion spent on such contracts annually prior to the invasion of Iraq. This does not include contractors working for the Iraqi government directly or for other clients. It is true that some of the work under contract might not have been undertaken by uniformed soldiers in the Cold War Army, and that both numbers and costs were bumped up by pervasive contractor requirements to provide local security. It nevertheless seems reasonable to assert that the lion's share of formerly below-the-line combat service support for combat units migrated to private contractors. The relative numbers and the nature of the units deployed to Iraq justify such a conclusion. This is not to mention contracted system-specific technicians already embedded in combat and combat support units to service complex or newly fielded equipment. This divestiture of force structure in favor of contractors was not necessarily a problem, as long as contracts were well written, contractors duly diligent, and security adequate. Some areas of contractor endeavor have provoked controversy beyond the scope of this discussion, such as the interrogation of prisoners, the representation of U.S. government policy, or the offensive use of deadly force.[30]

With respect to operations other than war, the Army had in effect already divested itself of its most relevant force structure when the United States Special Operations Command (USSOCOM) stood up in 1987. As discussed in Chapter 2, the Fiscal Year (FY) 1987 Defense Authorization Act (establishing USSOCOM) and denuclearization beginning with the Intermediate Range Nuclear Forces Treaty ratified in 1988 both narrowed the Army materially and psychologically toward a core focus on mid- and high-intensity conventional combat. Technically the Special Forces groups, ranger battalions, civil affairs battalions, psychological operations groups, special operations aviation regiment, and others that migrated to the United States Army Special Operations Command (USASOC, the Army component of USSOCOM) remained part of the Army, but the autonomy of the command in practice was considerable—as if it were another service. USSOCOM had its own budget and was a worldwide joint command independent of the regional commands within which its forces might train or operate. This is not to mention special relationships with the Central Intelligence Agency (CIA), other government agencies, and foreign governments. Coordination between special operators and conventional Army forces was problematic in DESERT STORM, Somalia, Haiti, and the Balkans, and only somewhat improved in Afghanistan prior to 2003. High professional caliber on both sides of the divide and fluidity with respect to personnel assignments across it ameliorated things, but underlying differences were philosophical as well as organizational. Special operators too often considered themselves stepchildren in the conventionally focused Cold War Army and were gratified to see their expertise elevated to equivalent status. The residual Cold War Army, on the other hand, was happy enough to hand off the lead for operations other than war to USSOCOM. If local allies provided most of the manpower and the State Department took the lead for policy, the modest assets of USSOCOM should be adequate for the operations other than war that seemed likely at the time. The rest of the Army could focus on high-end combat and ratchet down to lesser contingencies only if it really had to. Unfortunately, it really had to. Operations other than war were the rule rather than the exception throughout the 1990s. Manpower demands dwarfed anything USSOCOM could sustain, and the State Department effectively surrendered the lead to the Department of Defense in the most troubling cases. Secretary of Defense Donald Rumsfeld heavily emphasized the role and use of Special Operations Forces. He also proved suspicious of the conventional Army's dual-use unit philosophy, particularly with respect to heavy units. Borrowing in part from British precedent supporting operations in Northern Ireland, the Army had taken to deploying tankers, engineers, artillerymen, and other heavy warriors into light infantry roles. Conventional wisdom held that if organization, leadership, and troop quality were of a high standard, units could be readily retrained and equipped for other roles and missions. Balkan operations seemed to prove this. Rumsfeld viewed this approach as a defense of antiquated force structure and pushed for more actual restructuring. By January 2004 plans were in place to convert 100,000 billets from field artillery, engineer, air defense, armor, and ordnance to military police, civil affairs, psychological operations, intelligence, petroleum, water purification, and transportation units. Operations in Iraq and Afghanistan would be pursued by a mix of dual-use conventional units, units that were products of the restructuring of January 2004 and similar restructurings and Special Operations Command assets.[31]

Thinning of ground-based air defense and field artillery recognized circumstances on the ground in Afghanistan and Iraq and also was a concession to jointness. The Air Force could certainly pick up the slack in current operations, and it seemed technologically feasible that it could offset force structure cuts for the longer term as well. If USSOCOM—itself a joint command—could in fact be viewed as a quasi-service, the Army's relationship with it could be viewed as jointness of a different sort. Army communications and intelligence assets were increasingly dependent on joint linkages to be useful or effective. Substantial engineer and combat service support responsibilities had migrated to contractors. Of the erstwhile battlefield operating systems, only "maneuver" remained essentially undivested. There were critics, of course. Some were branch proponents instinctively resisting diminishment within their fields. Others were suspicious of overreliance on agencies and assets not directly under Army control and discipline. Still more were wary of designs that optimized support to operations in Afghanistan and Iraq at the expense of full-spectrum forces. This latter group was joined by the ubiquitous Colonel Doug Macgregor. He took the argument out of the Pentagon and into congressional hearings, where he pointedly noted that the planned two-battalion 3,800-soldier unit of action was far less capable than the three-battalion 5,500-soldier combat maneuver group he had proposed. He flagged up Korean War unpreparedness to illustrate the danger of being too thin on the ground. He particularly commented that "equating near-term need for a pool of units to rotate through Iraq and Afghanistan with transformation is the wrong answer." This was a key philosophical point. Macgregor was still championing an all-encompassing transformation in the abstract. Schoomaker viewed transformation as it had progressed from 1989 through 2003 as a useful base from which to launch into the specific requirements of the Global War on

Terrorism. His first priority was to win the wars we were actually in. The rest of the spectrum could wait.[32]

The Institutional Army

Numbered armies, corps, divisions, brigades, and battalions constitute the operational Army that deploys to engage in the full spectrum of combat around the world. Supporting this is the institutional Army: major commands, bases, and field operating agencies that traditionally do not deploy, and the organizations, agencies, and infrastructure subordinate to them. Like the deployable Army, the institutional Army downsized radically during the early 1990s and restructured to face a changing strategic environment from 1989 through 2005. Downsizing was not, however, accompanied by a proportional reduction in the entries one might find in a phone book, and restructuring was uneven in depth and dimension. In 1989 sixteen headquarters could be characterized as major Army commands (MACOMs), and in 2005 fifteen. Bases in Europe radically decreased in number, as discussed in Chapter 3, but base reductions elsewhere were modest. In 1989 there were thirty-one field operating agencies (FOAs), and in 2005 twenty-nine. Of the fifteen MACOMs extant in 2005, ten had the same names and about the same missions as they had in 1989, and three more had different names but were recognizably successors to previously existing MACOMs. Of the thirty-one FOAs extant in 2005 ten were arguably new, and the rest either carryovers or recognizable successors to previously existing FOAs. Nevertheless, the Army did exploit new technologies, alter its geo-strategic footprint, improve joint efficiencies, and streamline functional alignments as it transformed its institutional sector.[33]

The most obvious institutional adjustments for advancing technologies were the standing up as a MACOM of the Space and Missile Defense Command (SMDC) in 1997 and the reconfiguration of the Army Signal Command into the Network Enterprise Technology Command (NETCOM) in 2002. SMDC assumed two missions of ever-increasing importance: securing space assets and their products for soldiers in the field, and providing effective missile defense to the nation and its deployed forces. Satellite-based GPS had proliferated with respect to numbers and functions and had became an approved solution for navigation, determining position, blue force tracking, and precision strikes with such weapons as JDAMs. Satellites were increasingly essential for communications and provided a vast array of intelligence products drawn from across the electromagnetic spectrum. Missile defense was heavily dependent on space-based assets and was itself an arena wherein huge technological strides took place. The exploitation of space assets and missile defense are inherently joint, so SMDC served as the Army Service Component Command (ASCC) for the United States Strategic Command (USSTRATCOM). Movement to emphasize, consolidate, and rationalize space and missile capabilities resulted in the institution of a career functional area and the absorption of predecessor agencies. The Army Space Command, Army Space Program Office, and Army Strategic Defense Command were FOAs in 1989, but no longer necessary when SMDC achieved MACOM status. NETCOM represented an arena wherein technological advances were perhaps even more radical than those of space and missile defense. In 1989, as we have seen, the Internet did not exist. The Information Systems Command of that year had oversight for six regionally based signal commands and an engineering command. It guaranteed the steady flow of contemporary communications, generally envisioned as point to point. As information technologies exploded in the 1990s, local commanders did what they could to stay abreast with local "off-the-shelf" purchases—uncoordinated with each other and independent of the backbone communications that tied them together. NETCOM assumed the mission of managing the "infostructure" as a comprehensive enterprise and developing a single portal, • Army Knowledge Online, to bring all of the advantages of the Information Age to the Army as a whole. This network was to be seamlessly connected with that of other services, duly secured, uniformly equipped, and featuring classified and unclassified regimes. The era of singular messages trafficking through layers of headquarters had been trumped by the notion that information of all types—tactical, supervisory, or administrative—would be simultaneously available to all who sought it and were authorized access to it. The Army Materiel Command (AMC) and TRADOC, MACOMs with traditional responsibilities for technological development in 1989, remained with those responsibilities within their purviews in 2005. AMC's major subordinate commands shrank from twelve to seven largely by consolidation, in particular by consolidation into such life cycle management commands (LCMCs) as the Aviation and Missile Life Cycle Management Command or the Communications-Electronics Life Cycle Management Command. LCMCs unified research, development, procurement, fielding, sustainment, and disposition into continuous centrally managed streams. AMC's Security Assistance Command was a player in equipment disposition, and its Research, Development, and Engineering Command furthered pure and applied research, lessons learned, and the expedient transfer of technology from development to fielding. TRADOC continued to identify technological requirements via branch centers and schools, the Combined Arms Center at Fort Leavenworth, and the newly established Army Futures Center at Fort Monroe. TRADOC did shed the user-testing responsibilities of the Test and Experimentation Command (TEXCOM). Instead, the Army Test and Evaluation Command (ATEC), Operational Test Command, and Developmental Test Command served as FOAs reporting to the Army Staff. In sum, Army institutional reorganization from 1989 through 2005 was dramatic with respect to space, missile defense, and information technologies, and incremental with respect to technologies of other types.[34]

As the Army's global footprint changed, the structure of MACOMs altered as well. In 1989 geographical responsibilities in the Pacific were divided among the Western Command (WESTCOM), U.S. Army, Japan/IX Corps, and the Eighth United States Army (EUSA). In 2005 EUSA remained autonomous and in defense of South Korea, but the rest of the Pacific folded under the United States Army, Pacific (USARPAC). USARPAC was the Army component command for the Pacific Command (PACOM) and had tactical forces stationed in Hawaii, Alaska, and Fort Lewis, Washington, assigned to it. The diminishment of Japan reflected a broadening from the Cold War focus on

Northeast Asia, as did an expeditionary posture assumed by USARPAC and its subordinate commands. The United States Army, Europe (USAREUR), remained as a MACOM, but its assigned force structure was hugely reduced and it routinely participated in expeditions outside of its traditional area of responsibility. The United States Army, South (USARSO), had been a MACOM headquartered at Fort Clayton, Panama, but was subordinated to United States Army Forces Command (FORSCOM) when the United States returned the Canal Zone to Panama. FORSCOM similarly retained peacetime responsibility for United States Army Central Command (USARCENT), and acquired responsibilities for United States Army, North (USARNORTH), the service component command for operations in North America. This underscored FORSCOM's role as an expeditionary force provider to theater commanders. USAREUR and USARPAC were already forward deployed. FORSCOM would ensure that USARCENT, USARSO, and USARNORTH were effectively deployed and supported as required within their regions and would provide the American tactical units (less those that might come from EUSA, USAREUR, or USARPAC) that would serve under them. The shift to an expeditionary posture was further reflected in the redesign of the Medical Command (MEDCOM) as a MACOM, and of the Installation Management Agency as a FOA. MEDCOM stood up in 1994 and consolidated the former Health Services Command with the Office of the Surgeon General and several smaller agencies. The major subordinate commands of the Health Services Command were largely medical centers (hospitals) presiding over lesser hospitals and clinics within their areas. The draftee Army had been comfortably stocked with medical personnel, and retirees routinely secured treatment at nearby military hospitals and clinics. The reserve component at the time was only visible to the Health Services Command during brief stints of active duty. Downsizing virtually eliminated the services most military hospitals could provide retirees and reduced their services to family members. Meanwhile recurrent lengthy mobilizations of National Guardsmen and Reservists radically increased Army medical responsibilities for them and their families, and uniformed medical personnel participated in cycles of deployment along with other soldiers. The Army became increasingly dependent upon Civilian Health and Medical Program of the Uniformed Services (CHAMPUS), and then TRICARE, programs that subsidized civilian health care providers to serve soldiers, family members, and retirees. Because it was outsourced, this care could be far more geographically dispersed. For example, the Madigan Army Medical Center at Fort Lewis, Washington, a major subordinate command, morphed into the Western Regional Medical Command and Madigan Army Medical Center. Such an approach incorporated civilian medical assets from a multistate area into the Army's overall deployment support apparatus. The Installation Management Agency, established in 2002, also advanced the capability of the continental United States as a power projection platform. During the Cold War the senior tactical commander on a post was generally the installation commander as well—or the installation commander worked directly for him. In a modular Army at war this could disrupt and confuse, since the senior commander and his staff would routinely deploy. It made sense to subordinate installations to a chain of command independent of deployable tactical units, so that they could function uninterrupted regardless of which units deployed through them. The Installation Management Agency, a FOA, facilitated that purpose. In 2006 the Installation Management Command (IMCOM) would consolidate the Installation Management Agency and two other FOAs, the Army Community and Family Support Center and the Army Environmental Center, into an even more potent agency. The institutional Army was better postured for expeditionary combat in 2005 than it had been in 1989, and its geographic footprint was correspondingly altered.[35]

A pursuit of greater joint efficiency was manifest within virtually all MACOMs and FOAs during this period. In part this resulted from provisions of the Goldwater-Nichols Act, previously discussed. In part it resulted from funding strategies to stretch procurement dollars within functional purviews by throwing in with other services and from increasing interdependence as network and precision-guided munitions technologies advanced. In part it was the spirit of the times, as soldiers at all levels were encouraged to be friendly with and respectful to counterparts from other services. With respect to institutional structure, jointness was perhaps most visible in the reconfiguration of army service component commands. A portion of the Army Campaign Plan deliberated in 2005 and adopted in 2006 identified AMC, FORSCOM, and TRADOC as Army Commands. USARCENT, USARNORTH, USARSOUTH, USAREUR, USARPAC, and EUSA were redefined as Army Service Component Commands. Most had served in this function before, but now it defined them. Force structure external to service as an ASCC was pruned out, and what remained was thinned down to discrete units and agencies in two subsets. One subset was regionally focused and consisted of assets uniquely committed to the theater. Another subset was a mix of brigades, groups, and battalions assigned to the theater but, if circumstances required, deployable elsewhere. Briefing slides depicted the first subset in a purple band, indicating that the regionally focused units and agencies had joint interfaces. USASOC, as previously discussed, was the ASCC for the joint and relatively autonomous USSOCOM, and SMDC was the ASCC for the United States Strategic Command. In 1989 the Military Traffic Management Command (MTMC) managed military traffic, land transportation, and common-user ocean terminals and served as the Army component of the United States Transportation Command (USTRANSCOM). An increasing tempo of deployments and the changing nature of supply distribution altered its functions considerably. Cold War emphasis on mass mobilization and deployment in accordance with standing general defense plan (GDP) phased into nearly continuous rotations of soldiers and units to ongoing operations overseas. Meanwhile the "iron mountains" piled up to support the GDP melted away as digital tracking and "just in time" logistics sought to more flexibly and efficiently support smaller contingents of soldiers scattered more widely around the globe. In 2004 MTMC changed its name to the Surface Deployment and Distribution Command (SDDC) to better emphasize the nature of its priorities. The Army Intelligence and Security

Command (INSCOM), although not an ASCC, fulfilled functions that were inherently joint. It conducted intelligence, security, and information operations for "military commanders and national decision makers," and a major fraction of its subordinate commands were brigades or groups in the "purple band" of regionally focused units assigned to the ASCCs. The Army Aeronautical Services Agency, a FOA, was similarly joint and inter-agency. In 2004 the Department of Defense (DoD) stood up the United States Military Observers Group in Washington with the Army as executive agent. It coordinated and approved assignments of DoD military or civilian personnel to serve with United Nations missions, due recognition of increasing incidence and complexity. It could be, and was, argued that the Army and DoD should have done more to evolve their institutional structures toward jointness. On the other hand, considerable and perhaps sufficient movement in that direction did occur from 1989 through 2005.[36]

Functional alignment provided another incentive for changing institutional structure. One function affected was transformation itself, particularly with respect to whether it should be exceptionally handled. General Sullivan perceived a need for radical rethinking, and stood up the modern Louisiana Maneuvers (LAM) Task Force to do this. It was relatively autonomous, particularly after it moved from Fort Monroe to Washington, DC, and reported to the Chief of Staff. General Reimer believed the LAM Task Force had fulfilled its mission and divested it in favor of evolving the particulars of Force XXI—inspired, envisioned, and set in motion by LAM—within the traditional Headquarters, Department of Army (HQDA), and MACOM agencies that advanced such work. General Shinseki was satisfied to further develop Force XXI (his Legacy Force) in such a manner but set up a three-star Objective Force Task Force reporting to him to jump-start the considerably more distant Objective Force (Reimer's Army After Next). General Schoomaker perceived that the Objective Force Task Force had served its purpose and divested it in favor of a Futures Center serving under TRADOC. The institutional exceptionalism accorded transformation swung with perceptions of how revolutionary next steps needed to be. In addition to ultimately shepherding future think, TRADOC also took charge of the Recruiting Command (formerly a FOA), five regionally based recruiting brigades, and the Accessions Support Brigade. Coupled with traditional control of the Cadet Command, Reserve Officers' Training Corps (ROTC) regions, and branch schools, this aligned TRADOC to identify and fulfill the institutional training needs of soldiers from accession through retirement. Radically increased reliance on the reserve component bumped up its institutional status. In 1989 the Chief, Army Reserve, was a two-star general serving in the Pentagon as adviser to the Chief of Staff. In 2005 he was a three-star commanding the United States Army Reserve Command (USARC) and sixty-one subordinate commands from a shiny new headquarters in Fort McPherson, Georgia—while also serving as adviser to the Chief of Staff. The Director of the Army National Guard experienced a similar upgrade in status and responsibility, although Guard units themselves remained under

Interdependence Vignette

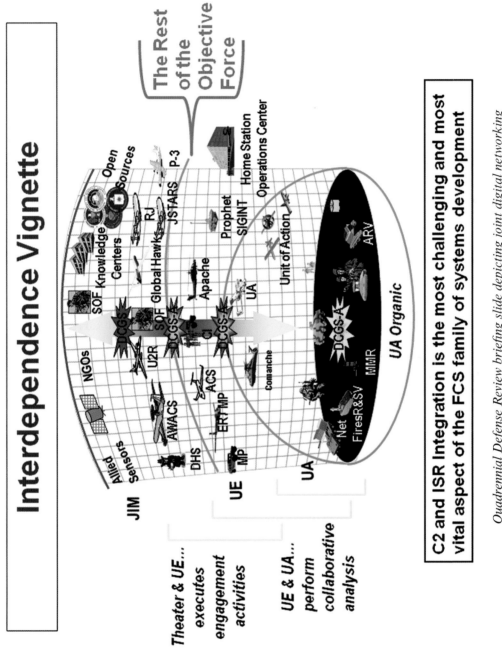

The Rest of the Objective Force

Open Sources

SOF Knowledge Centers

RJ

P-3

JSTARS

Global Hawk

Apache

Prophet SIGINT

Home Station Operations Center

Allied Sensors

NGOs

AWACS

DHS

U2R

SOF

DCGS-

ERT MP

ACS

C1

DCGS-

UA

Comanche

Unit of Action

DCGS-

JIM

UE

MP

UA

Net

FiresR&SV

MMR

DCGS-A

ARV

UA Organic

Theater & UE… executes engagement activities

UE & UA… perform collaborative analysis

C2 and ISR Integration is the most challenging and most vital aspect of the FCS family of systems development

Quadrennial Defense Review briefing slide depicting joint digital networking

state control most of the time. Of the 1989 MACOMs, the United States Army Corps of Engineers (USACE), Criminal Investigation Command (CIDC), and Military District of Washington (MDW) retained their names unchanged and their functions relatively unchanged. With respect to FOAs, the Center of Military History, Civilian Personnel Evaluation Agency, Army Claims Service, Command and Control Support Agency, Judge Advocate General's School, Legal Services Agency, United States Military Academy (USMA), Army Nuclear and Chemical Agency, Army Research Institute, and Army War College demonstrated similar stability. The Concepts Analysis Agency changed its name to the Center of Army Analysis, but since the same individual, Mr. E. B. Vandiver, was in charge in 2005 as he had been in 1989, continuity seems demonstrable. Indeed, Mr. Vandiver quipped that although his agency had changed its name it had not had to change its costly acronym-based signs, since before and after "CAA" still fit. Other FOA name changes represented greater adjustments in breadth and focus, albeit with nevertheless recognizable descent. Thus the Army Equal Employment Opportunity (EEO) and Civil Rights Office inherited responsibilities from the former Army Civilian Appellate Review Agency and the former Army Physical Disability Agency, the Army Force Management Support Agency from the former Army Force Development Support Agency, the Army Logistics Transformation Agency from the former Army Logistics Evaluation Agency, the Army Finance Command from the former Army Finance and Accounting Center, the Army Readiness/ Safety Center from the former Army Safety Center, and the Army Human Resources Command from the former Total Army Personnel Command. The functions of several erstwhile FOAs were divided up among existing or successor agencies: the Development and Employment Agency and the Plans and Operations Information Support Agency between NETCOM and the Chief Information Officer G–6, the Manpower Requirements and Documentation Agency between the Assistant Secretary of the Army (Manpower and Reserve Affairs) and the Human Resources Command, the Army Intelligence Agency between INSCOM and the Deputy Chief of Staff G–2, and the Troop Support Agency among the Army Materiel Command, the Quartermaster Center and School, and the Defense Commissary Agency. The Army Audit Agency, Army Evaluation Center, and Chief Technology Office stood up as new FOAs, and the Office of the Provost Marshal General was reestablished as a FOA.[37]

In 2005 the Chief of Staff committed to an Army Campaign Plan that eventually redefined existing MACOMs as Army Commands, ASCCs, and Direct Reporting Units (DRUs). A few erstwhile FOAs would be bumped up to DRU status. The newly defined Army Commands and ASCCs are identified above. The DRUs included NETCOM, INSCOM, CIDC, USACE, and MDW from among the MACOMs, and the Acquisition Support Center, ATEC, Installation Management Agency, USARC, and USMA from among the FOAs or Major Subordinate Commands (MSCs). This redefinition, when applied, cleaned up lines of authority and pruned force structure, but it did not much alter the roles and missions of the headquarters involved.

Downsizing led to manpower cuts across the institutional Army and a greatly increased reliance on contractors, as discussed in Chapter 4. Critics, especially proponents of thinning and flattening hierarchy, would see Army intransigence in retaining as much institutional overhead as it did. To some, changes that had occurred were merely "moving deck chairs around"—albeit with some of the deck chairs now being contractors. It may be fairer to say that changing strategic, technological, and socioeconomic circumstances did not require as massive a change to the institutional Army as it did to the deployable Army. A major fraction of the institutional overhead remained as germane in 2005 as it had been in 1989. Where change was necessary, the institutional Army did accommodate advances in technology, geostrategic repositioning, greater jointness, and functional alignment.[38]

Conclusions

From 1989 through 2005 Army transformation included dramatic changes to Army force structure. Through the early 1990s downsizing was the dominant theme and the preservation of DESERT STORM–like capabilities while rendering units more capable of full-spectrum and expeditionary combat the priority. As downsizing ebbed, critics and commentators inside and outside the Army argued for further change. With respect to force structure issues, the flattening or thinning of command hierarchy, transition to a brigade-based force, modularity, unit rotation, jointness, logistical support, and institutional structure became the most topical. Hierarchy was not flattened, but it was thinned. The Army converted to a brigade-based force. Modularity and unit rotation were refined in doctrine and heavily exercised in practice. Jointness drove the thinning of air defense and artillery assets, while missions that other services could not do drove increases in force structure most appropriate to operations other than war. Logistics and engineering compensated for downsizing by relying far more heavily on contractors, as did the institutional Army. An underlying tension emerged between transformation in the abstract and transformation oriented on operations the United States was actually in. From 1989 through 2003 the former dominated, with broad preparations and near-peer opponents as worst cases dominating deliberations. Iraq changed that. The rigors of combat, huge demands for unit rotation, and availability of supplemental funds to advance transformation reasonably connected to operations in Iraq and Afghanistan tilted transformation toward the particular, as did the instincts of Chief of Staff General Peter J. Schoomaker. The deployable Army emphasized those aspects of ongoing transformation that optimized for the wars it was in. Other options and potential adversaries received lower priority. The institutional Army adjusted to accommodate technological advance, geostrategic change, joint interdependence, and functional alignments. The overall results with respect to force structure were arguably not the best fit for all circumstances. They seemed, however, the best fit for the circumstances the United States was actually in.

Notes

[1] James L. Yarrison, *The Modern Louisiana Maneuvers* (Washington DC: Center of Military History, 1999); Douglas A. Macgregor, *Breaking the Phalanx: A New Design for Landpower in the 21st Century* (Westport, Connecticut: Praeger, 1997); Army General Staff Council Meeting notes, 30 November 1998, Historians Files, CMH; Army General Staff Council Meeting notes, 29 March 1999, Historians Files, CMH; Memo for Chief of Staff, Army, 16 April 1999, sub: Comparing Interwar German Army Innovation with That of the Post–Cold War U.S. Army–Information Memorandum, Historians Files, CMH; 1999 Division Commanders/TRADOC Commandants Conference notes, Fort Leavenworth, Kansas, 19–21 April 1999, Historians Files, CMH; Briefing, Center of Military History, "The Macgregor Critique," 2000, Historians Files, CMH.

[2] Macgregor, *Breaking the Phalanx*, 59–131; Jonathan M. House, *Combined Arms Warfare in the Twentieth Century* (Lawrence: University Press of Kansas, 2001), 206–13; A. J. Bacevich, *The Pentomic Era* (Washington DC: National Defense University Press, 1986); Brian Nichiporuk and Carl H. Bilder, *Information Technologies and the Future of Land Warfare* (Santa Monica, California: RAND, 1995); Memo, Center of Military History for Deputy Chief of Staff for Programs, United States Army, June 2001, sub: Colonel Douglas A. Macgregor's *Breaking the Phalanx* and Beyond–Information Memorandum, Historians Files, CMH; Douglas A. Macgregor, "Command and Control for Joint Strategic Actions," *Joint Forces Quarterly* (Autumn/Winter 1998–1999): 25–33; Douglas A. Macgregor, "Joint Operational Architecture: The Key to Transformation," *Strategic Review* (Fall 2000): 27–36.

[3] John R. Brinkerhoff, "The Brigade-Based New Army," *Parameters* (August 1997): 60–72; Michael McCormick, *The Brigade Based Division: Saddling the Right Horse* (Fort Leavenworth, Kansas: U.S. Army Command and General Staff College, 1997); John J. McGrath, *The Brigade: A History, Its Organization and Employment in the US Army* (Fort Leavenworth, Kansas: Combat Studies Institute Press, 2004), 77–111; ATLANTIC RESOLVE: USAREUR CINC's Exercise Book, 31 March 1995, Historians Files, CMH; General Wesley K. Clark, "Transforming NATO's for the 21st Century," SOA Newsletter Number 109, Historian's Files, CMH; TRADOC Pamphlet 525–5, *Force XXI Operations* (Fort Monroe, Virginia: U.S. Army Training and Doctrine Command, 1994); TRADOC Pamphlet 525–71, *Force XXI Division Operations Concept* (Fort Monroe, Virginia: U.S. Army Training and Doctrine Command, 1996); Macgregor, *Breaking the Phalanx*, 59–93; Memo, Center of Military History for Deputy Chief of Staff for Programs, United States Army, June 2001, sub: Colonel Douglas A. Macgregor's *Breaking the Phalanx* and Beyond–Information Memorandum.

[4] Macgregor, *Breaking the Phalanx*, 31–93; Douglas A. Macgregor, *Transforming Under Fire: Revolutionizing How America Fights* (Westport, Connecticut: Praeger, 2003); John B. Wilson, *Maneuver and Firepower: The Evolution of Divisions and Separate Brigades* (Washington DC: Center of Military History, 1998); John L. Romjue, *The Army of Excellence: The Development of the 1980s Army* (Washington DC: Center of Military History, 1997); TRADOC Pamphlet 525–5, *Force XXI Operations*, 1994; TRADOC Pamphlet 525–71, *Force XXI Division Operations Concept*, 1996; Memo, Center of Military History for Deputy Chief of Staff for Programs, United States Army, June 2001, sub: Colonel Douglas A. Macgregor's *Breaking the Phalanx* and Beyond–Information Memorandum; E-mail, Lieutenant General Kevin P. Byrnes, Deputy Chief of Staff for Programs, United States Army, to

Brigadier General John S. Brown, Chief of Military History, United States Army, 8 May 2001, sub: Macgregor, Corps and Divisions, etc., Historians Files, CMH; Andrew Feickert, *U.S. Army's Modular Redesign: Issues for Congress* (Washington DC: Congressional Research Service, 19 July 2004).

[5] Macgregor, *Breaking the Phalanx*, 141–223; Macgregor, "Command and Control for Joint Strategic Actions," 25–33; Memo, Colonel Douglas A. Macgregor, Senior Military Research Fellow, National Defense University, for Deputy Chief of Staff for Programs, United States Army, n.d., sub: Response to *Breaking the Phalanx* and Beyond–Information Memorandum, Historians Files, CMH; Briefing, Center of Military History, "Evaluation of Army Readiness," 2000, Historians Files, CMH; Army Regulation 220–1, *Unit Readiness* (Washington DC: Departments of the Army, 16 December 1986); Robert S. Rush, *Hell in Hurtgen Forest: The Ordeal and Triumph of an American Infantry Regiment* (Lawrence, Kansas: University Press of Kansas, 2001); CMH Information Paper, Robert S. Rush, The Individual Replacement System: Good Bad or Indifferent? Army Replacement Policy, Cold War and Before, Historians Files, CMH.

[6] Department of Defense Reorganization Act of 1986 (Public Law 99–143); James L. Lochner III, *Victory on the Potomac: The Goldwater-Nichols Act Unifies the Pentagon* (College Station, Texas: Texas A&M University, 2002); *Joint Publication 3.0* (Washington DC: Office of the Chairman of the Joint Chiefs of Staff, 1995); *Joint Vision 2010* (Washington DC: Office of the Chairman of the Joint Chiefs of Staff, 1995); William S. Cohen, *Defense Reform Initiative Report* (Washington DC: Department of Defense, 1997); Macgregor, *Breaking the Phalanx*, 60–139; Erin Q. Winograd, "Keane: Jointness Must Be Taken Seriously or Services May Lose Control," *Inside the Army*, 17 May 1999, 1–3; Army General Staff Council Meeting notes, 1 November 1999, Historians Files, CMH; Army General Staff Council Meeting notes, 20 November 2000, Historians Files, CMH.

[7] Macgregor, *Breaking the Phalanx*; McCormick; Brinkerhoff; James A. Huston, *The Sinews of War: Army Logistics, 1775–1953* (Washington DC: Center of Military History, 1966); Carter B. Magruder, *Recurring Logistics Problems as I Have Observed Them* (Washington DC: Center of Military History, 1991); Colonel David A. Fastabend, "An Appraisal of the Brigade-Based New Army, *Parameters* (Autumn 1997): 73–81; General Paul J. Kern, *Got It? Some Thoughts on Future Logistics* (Fort Belvoir, Virginia: Army Material Command, 2004); Briefing, Lieutenant General C. V. Christianson to Army Senior Commanders' Conference, "Concept of Support for the Expeditionary Army," 10 February 2004, Historians Files, AMC; Briefing, Army Logistics Transformation Task Force, August 2002, Historians Files, AMC; 1999 Division Commanders/TRADOC Commandants Conference notes, Fort Leavenworth, Kansas, 19–21 April 1999; Briefing, Center of Military History, "The Macgregor Critique," 2000; Memo, Center of Military History for Deputy Chief of Staff for Programs, United States Army, June 2001, sub: Colonel Douglas A. Macgregor's *Breaking the Phalanx* and Beyond–Information Memorandum.

[8] Macgregor, *Breaking the Phalanx*; Army General Staff Council Meeting notes, 30 November 1998; Army General Staff Council Meeting notes, 29 March 1999; 1999 Division Commanders/TRADOC Commandants Conference notes, Fort Leavenworth, Kansas, 19–21 April 1999; Briefing, Center of Military History, The Macgregor Critique, 2000; E-mail, Lieutenant General Kevin P. Byrnes, Deputy Chief of Staff for Programs, United States Army, to Brigadier General John S. Brown, Chief of Military History, United States Army, 8 May 2001, sub: Macgregor, Corps and Divisions, etc.; E-mail, General (USA, Ret.) Dennis J. Reimer to Brigadier General (USA, Ret.) John S. Brown, 28 June 2009, sub: Book Project, Historians Files, CMH;

E-mail, General (USA, Ret.) William W. Hartzog to Brigadier General (USA, Ret.) John S. Brown, sub: Book Project, 26 June 2009, Historians Files, CMH; E-mail, James L. Mowery to Brigadier General (USA, Ret.) John S. Brown, 24 June 2009, sub: Book Project, Historians Files, CMH; E-mail, General (USA, Ret.) Dennis J. Reimer to Brigadier General (USA, Ret.) John S. Brown, 10 October 2009, sub: Follow-Up, Historians Files, CMH; Memo, Center of Military History for Deputy Chief of Staff for Programs, United States Army, June 2001, sub: Colonel Douglas A. Macgregor's *Breaking the Phalanx* and Beyond–Information Memorandum; Frontline Interview: Douglas Macgregor, http://www.pbs.org/wgbh/pages/frontline, posted 26 October 2004, accessed 7 September 2009.

[9] McGrath, 77–102; John L. Romjue, *From Active Defense to AirLand Battle: The Development of Army Doctrine 1973–1982* (Fort Monroe, Virginia: U.S. Army Training and Doctrine Command Historical Office, 1984); Romjue, *The Army of Excellence*; TRADOC Pamphlet 525–5, *AirLand Battle and Corps Operations–1986* (Fort Monroe, Virginia: U.S. Army Training and Doctrine Command, 1981); "Umpires Enforce," card for Return of Forces to Germany (REFORGER) Exercise 1987, Historians Files, CMH; "USAF Missions Area Relationships Sideview," graphical training aid, Historians Files, CMH.

[10] Ltr, TRADOC ATCG, forwarding TRADOC Pamphlet 525–5B, *AirLand Operations: The Evolution of AirLand Battle for a Strategic Army*, 13 June 1991, Historians Files, CMH.

[11] McGrath, 103; McCormick; Ltr, General (USA, Ret.) Gordon R. Sullivan to General Peter J. Schoomaker, 25 January 2005, Historians Files, CMH; MFR, 091300 May 2008, sub: Telephone Conversation with General Gordon R. Sullivan, Historians Files, CMH; TRADOC Pamphlet 525–5B, *AirLand Operations*, 1991; *Force XXI Joint Venture Phase 1 Briefing* (Fort Leavenworth, Kansas: Force Design Directorate, Training and Doctrine Command, 11 December 1995).

[12] William M. Donnelly, *Transforming an Army at War: Designing the Modular Force, 1991–2005* (Washington DC: Center of Military History, 2007), 9–10; Brigadier General Huba Wass de Czega and Major Jacob Biever, "Optimizing Future Battle Command Technologies," *Military Review* (March/April 1998): 15–21; McGrath, 103–04; Michael D. Doubler, *I Am the Guard: A History of the Army National Guard, 1636–2000* (Washington DC: Department of the Army, 2001), 351–52; *Annual Review* (Washington DC: National Guard Bureau, 1996), 35; General Dennis J. Reimer, "The Strike Force Operational Paper," January–February 2009, in *Soldiers Are Our Credentials: The Collected Works and Selected Papers of the Thirty-third Chief of Staff, United States Army* (Washington DC: Center of Military History, 2000), 254–63.

[13] Doubler, 368; Donnelly, 10–14; TRADOC Pamphlet 525–3–91, *Objective Force Tactical Operational and Organizational Concept for Maneuver Units of Action* (Fort Monroe, Virginia: U.S. Army Training and Doctrine Command, 6 November 2001); Mark J. Reardon and Jeffery A. Charlston, *From Transformation to Combat: The First Stryker Brigade at War* (Washington DC: Center of Military History, 2007); Briefing Slides, Army Transformation Office, "The Selected IAV Family–Best Value for the Soldier" and "Interim Brigade Combat Team Structure," n.d., Historians Files, CMH; Nick Johnson, "First Stryker Brigade to Achieve IOC This Month," *Aerospace Daily*, 21 May 2003.

[14] Donnelly, 14–46; McGrath, 131–39; MFR, 111300 June 2009, sub: Telephone Conversation between General (R) Peter J. Schoomaker and BG (R) John S. Brown, Historians Files, CMH; TRADOC Pamphlet 525–3–90 O&O, *The United States Army Objective Force Operational and Organizational Plan Maneuver Unit of Action* (Fort Knox, Kentucky: Unit of Action Maneuver Battle Lab, 2003); "Brigade Combat Team

Deployments," *Army Times*, 13 October 2008; *Army Comprehensive Guide to Modularity* (Fort Monroe, Virginia: U.S. Army Training and Doctrine Command, 8 October 2004); Colonel Jeffrey R. Witsken et al., *Task Force Modularity: The Role of Analysis in the Creation of the Modular Force* (Fort Leavenworth, Kansas: TRADOC Analysis Center, July 2005).

[15] Donnelly, 38–46; McGrath, 131–39; MFR, 111300 June 2009, sub: Telephone Conversation between General (R) Peter J. Schoomaker and BG (R) John S. Brown; TRADOC Pamphlet 525–3–90 O&O, *The United States Army Objective Force Operational and Organizational Plan Maneuver Unit of Action*; Slide, "COA 5z UA Organization (Current CSA Approved Redesign Concept)," 12 December 2003, Historians Files, CMH; Slide, "Heavy Brigade Combat Team Unit of Action Design," Historians Files, CMH; Army General Staff Council Meeting notes, 14 August 2003, Historians Files, CMH; Army General Staff Council Offsite notes, 30–31 January 2004, Historians Files, CMH.

[16] Ibid.; Slide, "Infantry Brigade Combat Team Unit of Action Design," Historians Files, CMH.

[17] Donnelly, 50–63; McGrath, 132–38; Witsken et al.; *Army Comprehensive Guide to Modularity*; Slide, "Support Brigades," Historians Files, CMH; Army General Staff Council Meeting Notes, 21 July 2003, Historians Files, CMH; Army General Staff Council Meeting Notes, 14 August 2003; Army General Staff Council Offsite notes, 30–31 January 2004.

[18] Ibid.; Army General Staff Council Meeting notes, 14 July 2003, Historians Files, CMH; Army General Staff Council Meeting notes, 25 August 2003, Historians Files, CMH; Army General Staff Council Meeting notes, 22 December 2003; Army General Staff Council Meeting notes, 6 February 2004.

[19] Donnelly, 3–81, 83–84; Witsken et al.; *Army Comprehensive Guide to Modularity*; Ltr, General (USA, Ret.) Gordon R. Sullivan to General Peter J. Schoomaker, 25 January 2005; E-mail, General (USA, Ret.) Dennis J. Reimer to Brigadier General (USA, Ret.) John S. Brown, 12 January 2009, sub: Book Project, Historians Files, CMH; E-mail, General (USA, Ret.) Dennis J. Reimer to Brigadier General (USA, Ret.) John S. Brown, 28 June 2009, sub: Book Project; Army General Staff Council Focus Area Update notes, 17 April 2004, Historians Files, CMH; Feickert; MFR, 111330 June 2009, sub: Telephone Conversation with General Peter J. Schoomaker, Historians Files, CMH.

[20] Romjue, *The Army of Excellence*; TOE 87000L300, Armored Division, 1 October 1986; Field Manual 71–5, *Division Operations* (Washington DC: Department of the Army, 1990); Field Manual 100–15, *Corps Operations* (Washington DC: Department of the Army, 1989); Field Manual 100–16, *Support Operations–Echelons Above Corps* (Washington DC: Department of the Army, 1985).

[21] Donnelly, 63–74; MFR, 091300 May 2008, sub: Telephone Conversation with General Gordon R. Sullivan; TRADOC Pamphlet 525–5B, *AirLand Operations*, 1991; *Force XXI Joint Venture Phase 1 Briefing* (Fort Leavenworth, Kansas: Force Design Directorate, Training and Doctrine Command, 11 December 1995); De Czega and Biever, 15–21; Reimer, "The Strike Force Operational Paper," January–February 2009, in *Soldiers Are Our Credentials*, 254–63; TRADOC Pamphlet 525–3–91, *Objective Force Tactical Operational and Organizational Concept for Maneuver Units of Action*, 6 November 2001; MFR, 111300 June 2009, sub: Telephone Conversation between General (R) Peter J. Schoomaker and BG (R) John S. Brown; *Army Comprehensive Guide to Modularity*; Witsken et al.

[22] Donnelly, 63–74; Janice E. McKenney, Reflagging in the Army (Washington DC: Center of Military History, 1997), 3–16; Briefing, Center of Military History, "Unit

Designations in the Army Modular Force"; Ltr, General (USA, Ret.) Gordon R. Sullivan to General Peter J. Schoomaker, 25 January 2005; Memo, DAMH-FPO for Director, U.S. Army Center of Military History, 17 February 2005, sub: CMH Responsibilities while Implementing COA1, Historians Files, CMH; CMH Information Paper, New Army Unit Designations in the Modular Army: Talking Points and Answers to Key Questions, Historians Files, CMH.

[23] Donnelly, 63–74; Briefing, Center of Military History, "Unit Designations in the Army Modular Force"; Ltr, General (USA, Ret.) Gordon R. Sullivan to General Peter J. Schoomaker, 25 January 2005; Memo, DAMH-FPO for Director, U.S. Army Center of Military History, 17 February 2005, sub: CMH Responsibilities while Implementing COA1; CMH Information Paper, "New Army Unit Designations in the Modular Army: Talking Points and Answers to Key Questions"; Author's personal experience as chief of military history, 1999–2005.

[24] Donnelly, 63–74; *Army Comprehensive Guide to Modularity*; Witsken et al.; Briefing, TRADOC, "UE Briefing to the CSA," 27 September 2004, Historians Files, CMH; Briefing Slide, "Unit of Employment X (Division) Headquarters," Historians Files, CMH; Army General Staff Council Meeting notes, 14 July 2003; Army General Staff Council Meeting notes, 8 September 2003, Historians Files, CMH; Army General Staff Council Offsite notes, 30–31 January 2004.

[25] Presentation, Colonel Douglas A. Macgregor to Members of the House Armed Services Committee, "Transformation and the Illusion of Change: Where Is the Army Really Headed? What Is to Be Done?" 21 April 2005, Historians Files, CMH; Memo, Colonel Douglas A. Macgregor for Deputy Chief of Staff for Programs, U.S. Army, sub: Response to *Breaking the Phalanx* and Beyond–Information Memorandum, Historians Files, CMH; Colonel John A. Warden III, *The Air Campaign: Planning for Combat* (Washington DC: National Defense University Press, 1988); Army General Staff Council Offsite notes, 30–31 January 2004; Army General Staff Council Meeting notes, 15 March 2004, Historians Files, CMH.

[26] Field Manual 71–100, *Division Operations* (Washington DC: Department of the Army, 1990); Field Manual 100–15, *Corps Operations*, 1989; TRADOC Pamphlet 525–5, *AirLand Operations: A Concept for the Evolution of Airland Battle for the Strategic Army of the 1990s and Beyond* (Fort Monroe, Virginia: U.S. Army Training and Doctrine Command, 1991); Field Manual 34–8, *Intelligence Battlefield Operating System* (Washington DC: Department of the Army, 1992); SC 25C, *Describe the Synchronization of the Battlefield Operating Systems* (Fort Gordon, Georgia: U.S. Army Signal Center and Fort Gordon, 1992); 2AD(F), *Combat Readiness Check*, Historians Files, CMH; Donnelly, 27–74, 83–86.

[27] Field Manual 44–8, *Combined Arms for Air Defense* (Washington DC: Department of the Army, 1999); Field Manual 44–18–1, *Stinger Team Operations* (Washington DC:, Department of the Army, 1984); Field Manual 44–44, *Avenger Platoon, Section and Squad Operations* (Washington DC: Department of the Army, 1995); Field Manual 44–85, *Patriot Battalion and Battery Operations* (Washington DC: Department of the Army, 1997); Warden; Army General Staff Council Offsite notes, 30–31 January 2004; "The Army as of August 6," *Army Times*, 17 August 2009, 37; Army General Staff Council Meeting notes, 15 March 2004; Army Senior Leader Update, "Precision Strike: A Unique American Military Advantage . . . but with Limitations," 14 August 2001, Historians Files, CMH.

[28] Army General Staff Council Offsite notes, 30–31 January 2004; Army General Staff Council Meeting notes, 15 March 2004; Army Senior Leader Update, "Precision Strike: A Unique American Military Advantage . . . but with Limitations," 14 August 2001; Donnelly, 27–74, 83–86; "The Army as of August 6," 37; Field Manual 71–100,

Division Operations, 1990; Field Manual 100–15, *Corps Operations*, 1989; Briefing for the Honorable Paul D. Wolfowitz, Deputy Secretary of Defense, "Army Indirect Fires Program Review," 19 August 2002, Historians Files, CMH.

[29] Donnelly, 27–74, 83–86; Romjue, *The Army of Excellence*, 134–202; Vince Demma, *Department of the Army Historical Summary, Fiscal Year 1989* (Washington DC: Center of Military History, 1998), 3–13, 63–71, 109–10, 137–59; Jeffery A. Charlston, *Department of the Army Historical Summary, Fiscal Year 1999* (Washington DC: Center of Military History, 2006), 3–13, 25–34, 61–80; Vincent Demma, Contractors on the Battlefield: An Historical Survey from the Civil War to Bosnia, Historians Files, CMH; Supplementary Report on Army Contracting, Historians Files, CMH; "The Army as of August 6," 37; Lieutenant General Robert B. Flowers, "Army Engineers: Supporting the Warfighters and Reconstruction Efforts," *Army 2004–2005 Green Book*, October 2004, 185–90.

[30] Donnelly, 27–74, 83–86; "The Army as of August 6," 37; Fastabend, 73–81; Romjue, *The Army of Excellence*, 204–05; James J. Carafano, *Private Sector, Public Wars: Contractors in Combat–Afghanistan, Iraq and Future Conflicts* (Westport, Connecticut: Praeger Security International, 2008), 1–13; Michelle Tan, "Fraud Gone Wild: CIA Races to Catch Up with Unfit, Greedy Contractors," *Army Times*, 23 February 2003, 10; Dr. Donald P. Wright and Colonel Timothy R. Reese, *On Point II: Transition to the New Campaign, The United States Army in Operation IRAQI FREEDOM, May 2003–January 2005* (Fort Leavenworth, Kansas: Combat Studies Institute Press, 2008), 386–89, 492–97, 506–09; Joseph A. Christoff, GAO Testimony to the Senate Committee on Foreign Relations, "Rebuilding Iraq: Enhancing Security, Measuring Program Results, and Maintaining Infrastructure Are Necessary to Make Significant and Sustainable Progress," 18 October, 2005; Army General Staff Council Meeting notes, 21 July 2003; Army General Staff Council Meeting notes, 25 August 2003; Army General Staff Council Meeting notes, 20 October 2003, Historians Files, CMH.

[31] S2453, *A Bill to Enhance the Capability of the United States to Combat Terrorism and Other Forms of Unconventional Warfare;* H.R. 5109, *A Bill to Establish a National Special Operations Agency Within the Department of Defense to Have Unified Responsibility for All Special Operations Forces Activities Within the Department; National Defense Authorization Act for Fiscal Year 1987;* Charles H. Briscoe, Richard L. Kiper, James A. Schroder, and Kalev I. Sepp, *Weapon of Choice: U.S. Army Special Operations Forces in Afghanistan* (Fort Leavenworth, Kansas: Combat Studies Institute Press, 2003), 38–47; *Conduct of the Persian Gulf War: Final Report to Congress* (Washington DC: Department of Defense, 1992); *United States Forces Somalia After Action Report and Historical Overview: The United States Army in Somalia, 1992–1994* (Washington DC: Center of Military History, 2003); Walter E. Kretchick, Robert F. Bauman, and John T. Fishel, *Invasion, Intervention, "Intervasion": A Concise History of the United States Army in Operation UPHOLD DEMOCRACY* (Fort Leavenworth, Kansas: U.S. Command and General Staff College Press, 1998); Richard W. Stewart, *The United States Army in Afghanistan, Operation ENDURING FREEDOM, October 2001–March 2002* (Washington DC: Center of Military History, 2004); E-mail, Brigadier General Mark E. O'Neil to Major General Franklin Hagenbeck, 6 January 2003, sub: Anaconda Lessons Learned–NDU Paper, with notes, Historians Files, CMH; Charles E. Kirkpatrick, *"Ruck It Up!": The Post–Cold War Transformation of V Corps, 1990–2001* (Washington DC: Center of Military History, 2006), 89–124, 275–320; TRADOC Pamphlet 525–5B, *AirLand Operations*, 1991; Army General Staff Council Offsite notes, 30–31 January 2004.

[32] Army General Staff Council Offsite notes, 30–31 January 2004; Presentation, Colonel Douglas A. Macgregor to Members of the House Armed Services Committee,

"Transformation and the Illusion of Change: Where Is the Army Really Headed? What Is to Be Done?" 21 April 2005.

[33] Briefing, Army Staff, "Adapting the MACOM Structure, Army Campaign Plan Decision Point #58," n.d., Historians Files, CMH; "Command and Staff," *Army 1988–1989 Green Book*, October 1988, 226–40; "U.S. Army Posts and Installations," *Army 1988–1989 Green Book*, October 1988, 252–66; "Command and Staff," *Army 2005–2006 Green Book*, October 2005, 237–62; "U.S. Army Posts and Installations," *Army 2005–2006 Green Book*, October 2005, 271–77; CMH Information Paper, James L. Yarrison, The Responsibilities and Missions of Army Major Commands (MACOMs) and Corps Since World War II, 25 April 2000; "Adapting the Major Army Command (MACOM) Structure," *Stand-To!* 14 March 2006; Army General Staff Council Offsite notes, 30–31 January 2004.

[34] *Space Warriors: The Army Space Support Team* (Washington DC: Center of Military History, 2004); James Walker, Lewis Bernstein, and Sharon Lang, *Seize the High Ground: The Army in Space and Missile Defense* (Washington DC: Center of Military History, 2004); Lieutenant General Larry J. Dodgen, "Space and Integrated Missile Defense: Vital Capabilities for the Nation's Warfighters," *Army 2005–2006 Green Book*, October 2005, 133–36; Janet Abbate, *Inventing the Internet* (Cambridge, Massachusetts: MIT Press, 1999); Gordon Van Vleet, "NETCOM: The Army's Technological Command," *CHIPS,* Fall 2004; General Benjamin S. Griffin, "AMC–Serving Alongside the Warfighter," *Army 2005–2006 Green Book*, October 2005, 73–79; Lieutenant General Anthony R. Jones, "TRADOC, The Army's Foundation: Adapting and Delivering," *Army 2005–2006 Green Book*, October 2005, 95–99.

[35] Briefing, Army Staff, "Adapting the MACOM Structure, Army Campaign Plan Decision Point #58"; "Command and Staff," *Army 1988–1989 Green Book*, October 1988, 226–40; "Command and Staff," *Army 2005–2006 Green Book*, October 2005, 237–62; Yarrison, "The Responsibilities and Missions of Army Major Commands (MACOMs) and Corps Since World War II"; Lieutenant General John M. Brown III, "USARPAC: The Army's Expeditionary Force in the Pacific," *Army 2005–2006 Green Book*, October 2005, 115–18; General B. B. Bell, "U.S. Army Europe and Seventh Army: Leading the Army's Fight for Change," *Army 2005–2006 Green Book*, October 2005, 81–87; Kirkpatrick, 535–49; General Dan K. McNeill, "Army Force Generation: U.S. Army Forces Command Future," *Army 2005–2006 Green Book*, October 2005, 63–70; Lieutenant General Kevin C. Kiley, "Preserving Soldiers' Lives and Health–Anytime, Anywhere," *Army 2005–2006 Green Book*, October 2005, 121–24; *TRICARE Prime Handbook: Your Guide to Program Benefits* (Phoenix, Arizona: TriWest Healthcare Alliance, 2006); Lieutenant General David W. Barno, "Army Installations–the Hometowns of Combat Power," *Army 2005–2006 Green Book*, October 2005, 195–200; About IMCOM, History, http://www.imcom.army.mil, accessed 4 September 2009; 1999 Division Commanders/TRADOC Commandants Conference notes, Fort Leavenworth, Kansas, 19–21 April 1999.

[36] "Adapting the Major Army Command (MACOM) Structure," *Stand-To!* 14 March 2006; Briefing, Army Staff, "Adapting the MACOM Structure, Army Campaign Plan Decision Point #58"; Army General Staff Council Offsite notes, 30–31 January 2004; About SDDC, History, http://www.sddc.army.mil, accessed 5 September 2009; Lieutenant General Claude V. Christianson, "Enhancing Logistical Readiness," *Army 2005–2006 Green Book*, October 2005, 171–76; Major Subordinate Commands, http://www.inscom.army.mil, accessed 5 September 2009; Lieutenant General Keith B. Alexander, Enhancing Army Intelligence in Support of Warfighters," *Army 2005–2006 Green Book*, October 2005, 155–60; "Mission," http://www.usaasa.belvoir.army.mil,

accessed 5 September 2009; Department of Defense Directive 2065.1E, 7 December 2004, sub: Assignment of Personnel to United Nations Missions.

[37] Yarrison, *The Modern Louisiana Maneuvers*, v–viii, 57–71; Lieutenant General John M. Riggs, "Transforming the Army Into the Objective Force," *Army 2001–2002 Green Book*, October 2001, 93–96; Army General Staff Council Meeting notes, 14 August 2003; "Command and Staff," *Army 1988–1989 Green Book*, October 1988, 226–40; "Command and Staff," *Army 2005–2006 Green Book*, October 2005, 237–62; Major General William F. Ward Jr., "Buildup Over; Reserve's Focus Is on Fine-Tuning," *Army 1988–1989 Green Book*, October 1988, 113–21; Lieutenant General James R. Helmly, "Changing to a 21st-Century Army Reserve," *Army 2005–2006 Green Book*, October 2005, 107–12; Major General Major General Donald Burdick, "The Guard: America's Army On Call," *Army 1988–1989 Green Book*, October 1988, 125–32; Lieutenant General Clyde Vaughn, "Army National Guard–Always Ready, Always There," *Army 2005–2006 Green Book*, October 2005, 101–04; Robert Grundborg, *Analysis of ADEA's (Army Development and Employment Agency) Automated Data Processing (ADP) Survey* (Fort Lewis, Washington: Army Development and Employment Agency Operations Research Office, 1987); Army Regulation 690–600, *Equal Opportunity Discrimination Complaints* (Washington DC: Department of the Army, 2004); Army Regulation 10–57, *United States Army Civilian Appellate Review Agency* (Washington DC: Department of the Army, 1979); Army Regulation 10–89, *United States Army Civilian Personnel Evaluation Agency* (Washington DC: Department of the Army, 1989); "Force Structure and Unit History Branch, Using History for a Better Force Structure," accessed 6 September 2009, http://www.history.army.mil/html/forcestructure; Army Regulation 10–25, *United States Army Logistics Integration Agency (USALIA)* (Washington DC: Department of the Army, 2000); Headquarters, Department of the Army, General Orders 21, Establishment of the United States Army Information Management Support Center (IMCEN), 30 September 1994; Briefing Slide, Army Staff, "Chief Information Office/CIO/G–6," 31 August 2009, Historians Files, CMH; Welcome to the United States Army Evaluation Center, accessed 7 September 2009, http://www.atec.army.mil/aec; USACR/Safety Center History, accessed 7 September 2009, https://safety.army.mil; Headquarters, Department of the Army, General Orders 12, United States Army Troop Support Agency, 30 March 1992; United States Army Human Resources Command, accessed 7 September 2009, http://www.hrc.army.mil; Mission and Functions, accessed 7 September 2009, http://www.asmra.army.mil; Ronald Craig, "Evolution of the Provost Marshall General," *Military Police*, April 2004.

[38] Army General Staff Council Meeting notes, 14 August 2003; "Adapting the Major Army Command (MACOM) Structure," *Stand-To!* 14 March 2006; Briefing, Army Staff, "Adapting the MACOM Structure, Army Campaign Plan Decision Point #58."

CHAPTER 8

The Army Family and Army Family Support, 1989–2005

The success of a volunteer army depends heavily on the relative attractiveness of military service. In modern America the well-being of the family, broadly defined, is among the most relevant factors affecting motivations to enlist or reenlist. The equation of Army readiness with family well-being is now so generally accepted as to be a truism. This was not always the case. Family support was ad hoc and local through the 1800s, and until World War II Army regulations generally forbade the enlistment of married men or the reenlistment of junior servicemen with wives and children. The larger standing Army of the Cold War improved upon family support, but most draftees who served were young and unmarried. The all-volunteer Army radically changed service demographics, and unhappy experiences during the Vietnam War made the service mindful of its flaws with respect to families. In 1982 the Army Family Liaison Office stood up to solicit feedback and improve information flow, and in 1983 Chief of Staff General John A. Wickham Jr. published his landmark white paper, *The Army Family. The Army Family* acknowledged that most soldiers were now married, initiated cycles of research and analysis, and launched such powerful programs as the Army Family Action Plan, the Army Community and Family Support Center, and Family Support Groups. As the Cold War ended the Army was making significant advances with respect to family support and accelerating cycles of deployment through the following years, which made even more attention necessary. Cold War programs tended to focus on families with children living at home, and this priority continued. However, more attention was also drawn to spousal issues independent of children, to parents, and to retirees. Families of the reserve component had been largely invisible to the Department of the Army during the Cold War, and soon no longer were. Transition to an expeditionary posture affected the Army family as profoundly as it affected the Army as a whole.[1]

Families with Children

In 1989 the active Army counted 991,035 dependents. Over half of its soldiers were married, and about two-thirds had dependent children. Perhaps one in five of these dependents lived with their sponsor in Europe. To a large extent the fraction of the dependents living in Europe and elsewhere overseas shaped definitions for family support as a whole. Their circumstances, scattered in "penny packets" across foreign lands, were the most challenging, and notions of "command sponsorship" for them drove the Army to define "what right looked like" for dependents everywhere. Since achieving such standards was considerably harder overseas than at home, support to families overseas established the minimum expectations. The underlying premise of command sponsorship was that dependents would be discouraged from arriving unless or until they could be reasonably provided for. In practical terms this generally meant the sponsor arrived unaccompanied, searched for and secured acceptable housing, became familiar with local agencies and facilities supporting families, arranged for transportation, and secured command approval to bring his or her dependents into a benign environment. Government housing in Europe was never sufficient for the numbers involved, particularly after the advent of the volunteer Army, so most dependents lived a year or two "off post" before they could reasonably expect to move "on." Off post their personal finances were whiplashed by fluctuations in the value of the dollar versus the *Deutschmark* and other currencies. A cost-of-living allowance (COLA) was intended to offset imbalances, but it often lagged in implementation and proved too little overall. Posts were generally of brigade size or in brigade-sized clusters, and each endeavored to provide a full suite of services and support to the families in its area. A housing office manned by knowledgeable local nationals helped sponsors find and rent suitable housing off post. A diminutive commissary allowed the purchase of food at stateside prices, and a post exchange was a surrogate department store for other commonly purchased items. One could cash a check, within dollar limits, at the post exchange, and a miniature bank allowed for deposits, withdrawals, and conversion into *Deutschmarks* or some other local currency. Families in financial difficulties could go through Army Community Service (ACS) to secure a loan from Army Emergency Relief (AER). ACS also loaned furniture, kitchenware, and other items to families in transition. Most brigade clusters featured a child care center and an elementary school, thus accommodating children ages 1 through 12—the vast majority of those resident given military demography—for the majority of the workday. Youth services and after-school programs were hit and miss. High school–age dependents often traveled long distances to attend school, and spectacular distances to attend sporting events. The medical establishment serving the soldiers served dependents as well. On post they were screened for minor ailments and preventative care by the same physicians and dentists, and a medical hierarchy pyramided them back through such major facilities as those in Frankfurt, Furth, or Landstuhl. Within units Family Support Groups, generally led by commanders' wives but often led by the wives of other senior personnel, provided standing networks for mutual assistance and communication, which proved particularly useful during prolonged training absences. The most trying periods for families tended to be arrival and departure during permanent change of station (PCS), so formal and informal family support agencies tended to focus on the challenges of this period: acquiring housing, moving and awaiting household goods, resolving PCS expenses, delivering or buying a car, procuring locally usable driver's licenses, figuring out gasoline and other rationing, settling in as a family, entering the children in school, and so forth. The demands of life in Europe, underscored by notions of command sponsorship, came to define the Army's overall obligations toward its families: housing, commissary, post exchange, relief agencies, child care, schools, health care, informal support networks, and PCS assistance. As hard as the Army might try, it was hard to get all this right. United States Army, Europe (USAREUR), Commander General Crosbie E. Saint conspicuously quoted a *Time* magazine comment that his soldiers and their families "live and work in conditions that would cause riots in U.S. prisons." When issues emerged, they could be and were elevated for consideration through the Army Family Action Plan (AFAP). Established in 1984, the AFAP featured hierarchical annual conferences of spouses and support agencies sequentially representing installations, major Army commands, and the Army as a whole. Concerning AFAP, more later.[2]

The framework for family support that serviced isolated outposts in Europe and elsewhere overseas applied within the United States as well, albeit more efficiently and with less effort or perceived need. The mega-posts upon which most soldiers served "stateside" enjoyed economies of scale that dwarfed those of Europe. Local economies took up much of the slack, particularly with respect to housing, high school, and medical care. By the mid-1990s the European archipelago of Army posts, camps, and stations had largely disappeared, and many units that had not simply been inactivated collapsed into the expanding mega-posts of the United States. PCS remained a priority requiring due consideration, but it fell behind the rigors of increasingly recurrent deployments as a focus for family-oriented efforts. The transition from a forward-deployed to an expeditionary Army included changes in attitude as well as physical disposition. The word "dependent" disappeared from the official lexicon, replaced by the less patronizing "family member." Family Support Groups became Family Readiness Groups, for reasons that will be discussed. During the Cold War the family issue that had received the most focused, detailed, and continuous attention in Europe was that of noncombatant evacuation operation (NEO). Families assembled and continuously updated "NEO Packages," which were routinely inspected. Upon appropriate alert, telephone trees would notify families of an impending crisis. Sponsors would speed to motor pools and roll to their general defense plan (GDP) positions, while their dependents streamed in the opposite direction through rendezvous points and holding areas to fly out of Paris or some other as yet relatively unaffected city. In a pinch, they might depart on planes that had flown in units to man Prepositioning of Materiel Configured to Unit Sets (POMCUS) equipment. The NEO Package included maps, instructions, points of contact, food and water for several days of travel, a transistor radio, sturdy clothing, and, thoughtfully, a flashlight. Sponsors were admonished never to let their car have less than half a tank of gas. Dependents who could not drive would be picked up, and a preexisting but temporarily assigned chain of command beginning with the company NEO noncommissioned officer (NCO) would direct the process. With any luck, tens of thousands of dependents would be safely back in the United States before serious fighting began. Dependents were precious cargo to be whisked out of harm's way so that their sponsors could focus on GDP responsibilities. With an expeditionary Army dependents were already out of harm's way, and the Army's tone changed from directive to collaborative. A constellation of studies beginning in the 1980s had established the critical role of family and spousal satisfaction upon retention—and indirectly upon recruitment as well. Families were to be courted, to be convinced that Army life was their most attractive long-term option. Rather than an impediment to be cleared from the battlefield, families were now partners to be positively engaged with an eye toward sustaining the force.[3]

Families need a place to live. For generations the Army's answer to this requirement was to build family housing on its posts, camps, and stations. The number of family units was never actually sufficient, and the proportion of families adequately housed on post plummeted with the heavily married all-volunteer Army. Some new construction occurred during the late Cold War, but the "peace dividend" of the early 1990s reduced funds considerably. Infrastructure diminished dramatically in Europe and sporadically in the United States, but not as rapidly as funding did. By 1994 the housing to be maintained had declined by 17 percent and the funds available to do so by 30 percent. The average family housing unit was sixty-one years old. The combination of limited funds and aging housing created a maintenance backlog on the order of $20 billion, and as many as a third of the funds available annually went to basic maintenance rather than to the revitalization of old quarters or the construction of new ones. Housing ticked up as a source of AFAP issues and general complaints. The Military Housing Privatization Initiative, passed by Congress in 1996, represented a calculated effort to attract private-sector capital to build, manage, and maintain on-post housing. Neighborhoods would be built or refurbished on federal property but privately owned and maintained by investors and developers. Soldiers would use their Basic Allowance for Housing (BAH) to rent such housing and would have exclusive access to it. Troop density and Army policy would ensure high rates of fill. Within a dozen years this Residential Communities Initiative (RCI) would boast more than 83,000 privatized homes spread through thirty-eight locations. Defense spending increased somewhat in the late 1990s and substantially after 9-11. Some portion of this increase went into new construction. Family housing enjoyed a priority behind that of barracks renovation and replacement, however. The Army was shifting from the 1980s vintage standard of two soldiers to a barracks room to one soldier per room, and this imposed huge demands on the only moderately increased funding. Fortuitously, home ownership by soldiers took an increasing proportion of the weight off of military-provided housing. As we have seen, inhibitions against "homesteading" disappeared as overseas stationing diminished. Homesteading became semiofficial policy with Schoomaker's Modular Army. Most enlisted men and many officers through field grade could anticipate recurrent assignments to the same mega-post if they so desired. Families could settle in, and home ownership became more practical. BAH and the Variable Housing Allowance (VHA) could be used for mortgage payments rather than rent, building up a soldier's equity rather than disappearing monthly. This rosy prospect was somewhat limited

Cold War "stairwell" family housing, and, below, *housing generated by the Residential Communities Initiative program.*

by the Army's vision of what BAH and VHA were supposed to pay for, and by local variations in the cost of living. In 1989 BAH (then Basic Allowance for Quarters, BAQ) and VHA taken together were supposed to cover average rents at 80 percent of the cost of living at a standard deemed appropriate for the rank. Junior enlisted with dependents were considered appropriately housed in two-bedroom apartments, sergeants and lieutenants in duplexes, and E-9s and captains and above in single-family homes. By 2005 the BAH inched up to fully cover the average cost of rent and utilities, although the scale of housing deemed appropriate by rank remained. VHA remained problematic and generally delayed with respect to addressing countrywide differences. Soldiers dipped into their base pay or into their spouse's income to live in the housing they preferred rather than in what the Army considered appropriate for their rank. Their money went the furthest around such posts as Fort Polk, Fort Riley, Fort Sill, Fort Campbell, Fort Bliss, and Fort Stewart. Soldiers were comfortably better off than local counterparts around Fort Hood, Fort Knox, Fort Benning, Fort Drum, and Fort Bragg. Fort Carson and Fort Lee teetered around a break-even point, and Fort Lewis, Hawaii, and the National Capital Region were breathtakingly expensive. Given relative assignment stability and the likelihood of family ties in one region or another, it made sense to an increasing number of soldiers to buy their own homes. This change took pressure off the inventory of on-post housing. Oddly, shortfalls in government housing may have reinforced spousal tolerance of the newly expeditionary Army. One survey established that 55 percent of Army spouses in on-post government quarters were satisfied, whereas 92 percent of those who owned their own homes off post were. Each group comprised about a third of the Army's spouses, with most of the remainder renting off post. Motivations to reenlist are complex, but they can include a comfortable lifestyle and a right-sized mortgage.[4]

Family life, in particular raising children, can be expensive. Most families endeavor to keep costs down. For generations Army families have relied upon commissaries (essentially grocery stores) and post exchanges (similar to department stores but with an ancillary responsibility to support morale, welfare, and recreation activities) to assist in this regard. Both originated in the Frontier Army and had a tradition of bringing the products of civilization to isolated outposts. This tradition continued in the Cold War, with commissaries and post exchanges bringing American goods and services to families stationed overseas at prices independent of fluctuations with respect to the value of local currencies. In the United States most major troop concentrations were relatively isolated when the Cold War began. Local municipal development, in part funded by troop and Army family spending, changed this over time. The end of the Cold War was initially traumatic for both the Defense Commissary Agency (DeCA) and the Army and Air Force Exchange Service (AAFES). Downsizing radically reduced their customer base, the constellation of small commissaries and post exchanges scattered across Europe was badly out of position, and flagship major facilities overseas served a fraction of their former customers. AAFES had invested heavily in morale, welfare, and recreation (MWR) activities to support DESERT

STORM, only to have the ax fall as these bills came due. DeCA depended largely and AAFES almost exclusively on nonappropriated funds (NAF) that they themselves generated. Whereas dilemmas posed by downsizing and relocation would be addressed with appropriated funds for most of the Army, this would not be true for DeCA or AAFES. Since towns surrounding most major stateside posts had full suites of grocery stores, supermarkets, department stores, and outlets, some thought was given to letting stateside commissaries and post exchanges go the way of the dinosaur. This sentiment encountered immediate pushback. The 1993 AFAP flagged up the retention of commissaries as its highest priority quality-of-life issue. Surveys repeatedly identified the equivalent pay compensation of shopping at commissaries and post exchanges among the incentives for reenlistment. Broadly averaged, families could save about 30 percent by shopping at commissaries and 20 percent by shopping at post exchanges. Retirees also shopped in commissaries and post exchanges and realized the same savings. Retirees vote locally, and in 1993 they outnumbered serving soldiers for the first time. Whatever local political resistance there might have been to DeCA or AAFES expansion did not appear. Few appropriated funds came their way, but free use of federal land, rent-free status, tax-free status, business models that deemphasized profits, and thoughtful support from the Department of Defense facilitated recovery. DeCA sells at net cost with a 5 percent surcharge. The surcharge is used to maintain and improve existing facilities and to build new ones. After the initial turbulence of closing overseas commissaries and laying off or moving workforces, the DeCA began to plow this money back into stateside posts. In many places they teamed up with AAFES to produce colocated "destination" complexes featuring expansive buildings, food courts with a mix of franchises, and local vendors in addition to the commissary and post exchange per se. For several years a major fraction of spouses surveyed complained of inadequate commissary facilities and services, but this muted as new investment took root in theretofore neglected stateside posts. AAFES operates like a not-for-profit and guarantees a lowest price except with respect to gasoline, alcohol, and cigarettes. It earns enough to pay for maintenance and expansion and to plow from one-half to two-thirds of its earnings back into MWR activities. During the mid-1990s the revenue from AAFES going into MWR suffered. From 1993 to 1994, for example, AAFES sales declined by 14.5 percent and funds passed along to MWR declined from $123.37 million to $110.73 million. Overseas closures and sharp personnel cuts enabled further savings. In concert with DeCA, AAFES invested in and improved upon mall-like shopping facilities. Perhaps as important, AAFES went digital and added online sales to sales in stores or through catalogues. By 1999 DeCA and AAFES had regained traction. New facilities on most major posts brought traditional clients back, along with an ever-increasing number of retirees. Accelerating deployments dramatically increased the numbers from the reserve component on active duty, who could shop with their families. In remote locations, AAFES was often the only option. In 1999 AAFES earned $7.1 billion and was the eighth largest American retailer. Far from going the way of the dinosaur, commissaries and post exchanges were once again central to Army family life, enabling savings of 20 to 30 percent as families stretched their budgets.[5]

Families with children need some form of child care when the parents are not available. When both parents are working outside the home this requirement is more acute, and in the case of sole parents it is particularly demanding. Deployments in effect made temporary single parents of tens of thousands of spouses. In 1990, more than 174,000 Army children required child care services. The Army had not done well initially with the expanded child care requirements of an all-volunteer Army. In the early 1980s over 70 percent of Army child care centers did not meet fire and safety codes, and many were inappropriately reconfigured stables or barracks. Staffs were poorly trained and paid, with annual turnover rates that exceeded 100 percent in some places. Thousands of children were on waiting lists for what some characterized as the "ghettos of child care." Egregious sexual abuse scandals perpetrated by inadequately screened and supervised staff members rocked the system. Improving child care became a recurrent theme of the AFAP and attracted congressional notice. The Military Child Care Act of 1989 stipulated minimums for funding and staffing, higher wages, better training and screening, unannounced inspections, and programs for accreditation. Embarrassed, the Army rushed to clean up its act. Professional cadres were recruited and salaries went up as much as $2 an hour. Training programs, many offering college credit, addressed not only child care centers but also sanctioned caregivers working in their own homes. Turnover plunged. By 2003, 132 child care centers were built or renovated at a cost of $325,470,000. Within two years of the Military Child Care Act, forty Army child development centers had achieved National Academy of Early Childhood Programs accreditation. Within a decade that statistic approached 100 percent. In 1992 the Army Community and Family Support Center implemented a fee schedule based on total family income. This in effect subsidized junior enlisted personnel with several children. The Army also subsidized caregivers in an effort to expand options and employed Web sites to communicate availability. Over time a robust menu evolved on all major posts. Parents could drop their children off for a few hours, for regularly scheduled part days, or for full days. The term "Child Development Center" entered the lexicon to describe activities at revamped or rebuilt former child care centers. Planned curricula promoted learning activities to develop cognitive, motor, social, and emotional skills. "Exploration" occurred as individuals, in small groups, and in large groups organized by age. Child Development Centers accommodated children from six weeks through kindergarten. Family Child Care Homes accommodated children from four weeks to twelve years in smaller numbers in private quarters. These providers were also trained and certified and worked for the Army as private contractors. Family Child Care Homes had the convenience of domestic settings in local neighborhoods, accommodated broader age groups, allowed for nonstandard hours, and permitted siblings to stay together. They featured progressive curricula of activities and were subject to unannounced inspections. Child Development Centers and Family Child Care Homes could surge to provide "24/7" coverage in exceptional circumstances. Here, however, the Army had to be careful not to outdo itself. The system was designed to assist resident parents, not to cover prolonged absences or deployments. All parents were encouraged, and sole parents or dual military parents required, to have notarized family care plans specifying the disposition of their children should they deploy. Elaborate official work sheets smoked out details and were subject to considerable attention during preparations for overseas movement. Generally the children of deploying sole parents or dual military parents stayed with grandparents or extended family members, sometimes with friends or other acquaintances. Concerning this, more later. After an embarrassing start, child care within the Army achieved and exceeded standards appropriate to the demands upon it. Indeed, some knowledgeable commentators flagged up military child care as a model for the nation as a whole.[6]

By 1989 Army deficiencies with respect to preschool child care were well on their way to resolution. The same could not be said of school-age children. Relative inattention stemmed from several sources. In 2001 in a survey of Army families with children, 88 percent had children five years and younger, 68 percent had children six to ten, and 40 percent children sixteen to eighteen. Thus the Army family trended toward younger children. This made sense, given the average ages of soldiers serving and their spouses. Because of funding constraints, program improvements with respect to preschoolers in the early 1990s were often at the expense of their older siblings. MWR programs fall into three categories for funding. Category A is characterized as "Mission Essential" and includes fitness programs, libraries, and recreation centers—with troop use in mind. Category B is characterized as "Community Support" and includes child and youth services, arts and crafts, swimming pools, and outdoor recreation. Category C is characterized as "Business Activities" and includes golf courses, bowling alleys, service clubs, snack bars, and retail activities. MWR programs are funded with a combination of appropriated and nonappropriated funds, using perhaps a third of the former and two-thirds of the latter in an average year. Category A receives the lion's share of appropriated funds, often to the point of full coverage. Category C is expected to generate enough funds to cover its own costs, and then some. Category B is the least able to generate its own revenue, and the most vulnerable to budget shortfalls because of its low priority for appropriated funds. With the "peace dividend" of the early 1990s appropriated funds plummeted. At the same time AAFES and other retailers were crippled in their ability to generate nonappropriated funds, as we have seen. Preschool child care was the most visible and in the highest demand of the Category B MWR issues. It had been propelled toward reform by scandal and garnered the most attention, congressional and otherwise. It tended to sop up the Category B funds that were available. Requirements for school-age children were diverse and diffused by the greater likelihood of off-post venues. Most Army children were not in Department of Defense (DoD) schools, a fact that became more true as redeployment from Europe progressed. In 2003, 106,000 children from all services were in DoD schools, about two-thirds of them overseas. There were 224 of these schools in seven states and fourteen countries. More than five times as many service children were in public or private schools in the United States. Quality varied state by state, and education could be disrupted by changes of station. Students generally got out of school before their parents got off work, creating an after-school dilemma for children not yet old enough to be on their own. Children old enough to be on their own nevertheless benefited from programs supervised by adults, further incentive for a healthy mix of after-school activities. Recognizing that school-age children were underserved, in 1997 the Army combined the theretofore autonomous Child Development Services and Youth Services into a single Child and Youth Services (CYS). From this point the two age groups no longer competed institutionally, but rather became a single continuum for which CYS was responsible. As Family Child Care Homes came on line they helped with a fragment of the after-school dilemma, since they accommodated children up to age twelve. A child going to school in the neighborhood or catching the right bus—not necessarily a small thing—could report in to a caregiver rather than a parent. As AAFES and other nonappropriated moneymakers regained traction, more money was available in the system. Where the Department of Defense operated or could influence local schools (primarily through cost sharing and Department of Education subsidies based on attendance by service family members), after-school programs could be reinforced. Army School Age Services, serving ages six to twelve, expanded this idea to include weekend activities and summer camps and included recreation, sports, arts, life skills, and citizenship in the curriculum. Older children up to age eighteen came under the umbrella of Army Youth Services. Here needs were particularly complex, since the lives of Army teenagers almost inevitably revolved around off-post schools and their activities. The Army Family Action Plan convened teen panels in its annual meetings to come to grips with requirements as teenagers saw them. Army teenagers reported moving from school to school, something they did three times as often as their civilian counterparts, as particularly challenging. American education was intensely local. Transferring credits, reconciling grades, reestablishing schedules, and meeting graduation requirements were all problematic. Beginning in 1996 the Chief of Staff, his wife, and a newly empowered Quality of Life Team began drilling these issues. Their interest fed into a broader initiative that established the Military Child Education Coalition. In 1999 a Secondary Education Transition Study identified the consequences of teenage dependent mobility and recommended remedial measures. Results included memoranda of agreement related to transfers and credits signed with an ever-expanding number of schools, a senior year stabilization option available to sponsors, trained and designated school liaison officers, and guidebooks separately designed for students, parents, and school faculty. The older children were the more practical it was for them to take advantage of such installation facilities as fitness centers, swimming pools, libraries, bowling alleys, arts and craft centers, and so on. Youth Services understood these possibilities and scheduled activities exploiting them. This did increase the likelihood of family member teenagers interacting with soldiers. It seems a time-honored tradition for old soldiers to try to keep their daughters away from young soldiers with admonitions along the lines of "He's too old for you!" That tradition continued. By 2005 the Army had invested considerable time and energy in its school-age children. As home stationing became commonplace and sponsors more likely to deploy than to re-station, family life became more stable for school-age children along with everyone else.[7]

Not all family members require the same services, and services required by some family members are exceptional. The Department of Defense took note of this at least as early as 1975, when Congress passed the Education for All Handicapped Children Act. This legislation stipulated that to receive federal funds states had to ensure a free and appropriate public education for all children with disabilities. Most Army children were in state schools and benefited directly. DoD schools were federally funded, of course, and picked up on this guidance as well. Emphasis was on individualized educational programs that "mainstreamed" students as much as possible. The emphasis on the family surrounding General Wickham's publication of *The Army Family* in 1983 gave due attention to exceptional family members. This included refined tracking and governance of special education and related health issues, training for parents and relevant staff, and publication of a handbook focusing on parents and a handbook focusing on those assisting parents. The purpose was to ensure services, medical and otherwise, were available to accommodate the unique needs of the child. In 1986 the Army initiated mandatory screening to ensure that it was aware of the family member disabilities with which it might have to deal. In 1990 attention to exceptional family members was considerably advanced by the passage of the Americans with Disabilities Act. Mandates broadened and numbers under consideration increased. By June 2003, 59,127 were enrolled in the Exceptional Family Member Program, a number that represented 8.3 percent of active-duty Army family members. Army policy evolved several distinct features. Although medical personnel were always heavily involved, the Exceptional Family Member Program was not a medical lead. Initially it fell under the auspices of the Adjutant General, and later under the Assistant Chief of Staff for Installation Management (ACSIM). At first the top priority was assignment policy, ensuring that disabled family members did not accompany their sponsors into environments that could not support them. This imperative remained important but faded from top priority as overseas assignments diminished in number and stateside mega-posts expanded in capability. Priorities broadened. The Americans with Disabilities Act imposed impressive demands on facilities and programs. ACSIM, with its governance over construction, housing, MWR activities, and such programs as Army Community Service and Child and Youth Services, emerged as a logical lead. Garrison commanders assumed overall responsibility and worked through installation committees wherein a full range of medical, child care, educational, and community agencies were involved. The acronym SNAP (Special Needs Accommodation Process) described recurrent forums where specific issues and cases were addressed. Respite care, providing temporary relief to family caregivers, numbered among the services envisioned. The program was not voluntary. Soldiers on active duty and civilian employees assigned overseas submitted standard forms declaring the status of their family members during PCS. Military medical personnel and educators identified known disabilities, and garrison commanders losing an exceptional family member to PCS notified their counterparts soon to be in receipt. The Individuals with Disabilities Education Act of 1997 broadened definitions to include developmental delays as well as disability per se. Some Army families balked at the emerging extent of disclosure. Privacy could be an issue, as could the prospect of limiting career-enhancing assignments for the sponsor or stigmatizing a family member to his or her disadvantage. Army Regulation 608–75 as it emerged in 2006 leaned toward full disclosure, sanctions for noncompliance, and ensuring there were few surprises when attempting to accommodate exceptional family members. The regulation did call upon the Army Community and Family Support Center to monitor the effects of the program on retention. Retaining families was, after all, a critical institutional imperative to which the Exceptional Family Member Program was intended to contribute.[8]

Families need health care. The traditional model for providing it in the Army had been for family members to show up at the hospitals and clinics that supported their sponsors. Retirees and their families went to these too. Escalating numbers of retirees and radically increased marriage rates in the volunteer Army overwhelmed this system. Beginning in 1966 the Civilian Health and Medical Program of the Uniformed Services (CHAMPUS) contracted with civilian physicians and institutions to support military families stationed distant from military facilities or where particular medical services were not available. Over time this model migrated from the periphery to the center. In 1989 a Government Accountability Office (GAO) study established that 85 percent of the retirees and family members employing CHAMPUS lived within forty miles of military treatment facilities too overloaded to accommodate them. Recruiting uniformed doctors and nurses was consistently problematic, and a focus on treating uniformed service members rendered shortages particularly acute with respect to family medicine, pediatrics, gynecology, and obstetrics. These were, of course, the very specialties young families needed most. Downsizing in the early 1990s rendered these shortages even more acute, while redeployments from Europe brought an ever-larger percentage of Army families within range of American civilian physicians and hospitals. The Army experimented with two approaches to address its family health care dilemma. Catchment area management envisioned major military treatment facilities as regional gateways to care and brought contracted civilian physicians into military facilities. These could be existing facilities or newly established Primary Care to Uniformed Services (PRIMUS) outpatient clinics. Negotiations generally shaved 30 percent or more off a physician's standing fees, in addition to costs avoided by keeping family members out of civilian facilities. An alternative approach deemphasized flagship military medical facilities and instead constructed networks of civilian health care providers with whom services and fees could be negotiated. Beneficiaries would enroll, and a health maintenance organization would manage options. This approach appeared in 1991 as the experimental Tidewater Tri-Service Managed Care Project. As the name implies it was a joint program and addressed 400,000 potential beneficiaries in the Tidewater area of Virginia. The business principles

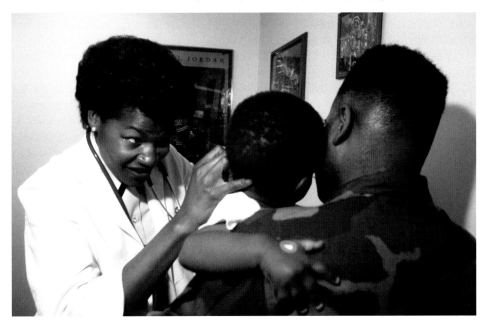

TRICARE provided families flexible off-post alternatives for medical care.

of the project aligned with emerging roles of insurers and health maintenance organizations in contemporary civilian health care, and it multiplied choices available to beneficiaries. The experiment succeeded in providing services and controlling costs and resulted in the nationwide establishment of TRICARE between 1994 and 1998. For a time the idea of working through regional flagship military medical facilities retained traction, and TRICARE was organized into a dozen districts loosely based upon them. In 2004 the number of districts was reduced to three, and the network as a whole dramatically eclipsed its particular nodes in importance. Active-duty service members enrolled in TRICARE Prime. Family members, retirees, and retiree family members chose from options that varied enrollment fees, deductibles, copayments, and limitations. Military treatment facilities and clinics with staffs augmented by contracted civilians remained in the network as important sources of Army health care, particularly for soldiers and family members residing on post. Uniformed medical personnel were increasingly drawn into deployment cycles affecting the rest of the Army, however, diminishing the services they could provide. Retirees and family members residing off post were increasingly drawn to civilian TRICARE providers. For them the gateway to specialized medical care was less likely to be the winnowing process of a military treatment facility and more likely to be decisions made by a civilian primary care manager (PCM) accepting TRICARE. The PCM referred his patients as necessary to specialists also accepting TRICARE. The system evolved to be dispersed, diffuse, and reasonably effective. TRICARE understandably experienced growing pains and was a major source of complaints and recriminations early on. These muted over time. Of eighty-five AFAP issues open in 2003, only eight had to do with TRICARE. These generally reflected a sentiment to expand access to TRICARE—in effect an endorsement—rather than attempts to redress perceived grievances.[9]

Through most of the Cold War the most dramatic and traumatic event Army families recurrently faced was permanent change of station. A family packed up its furniture, moved out of one home, traveled hundreds or thousands of miles, and moved into another—often on short notice. Army Community Service was established in 1965, and installation agencies provided broad menus of family support but particularly homed in on this difficult period. Quarters had to be signed for, rented, or bought. Household goods had to be delivered and claims for damages to them processed. Traditional disparities between household goods' weight allowances for officers, who had been expected to have families and property, and junior enlisted, who had not, became contentious in the volunteer Army. Allowances for E-1 to E-3 ranks increased from 2,000 to 2,500 pounds in 2002 and doubled to 5,000 after 2005—up to about half that authorized a lieutenant. Children moved from one school system to another, too often in the middle of an academic year. ACS "lending closets" helped families during the absence of their household goods, and counselors guided them through the many issues and agencies involved in a move. The good news about the shift to an expeditionary Army was that home stationing reduced the incidence and impact of such moves, and far fewer family moves were to overseas stations. The bad news was that recurrent deployment totally eclipsed PCS as the greatest challenge facing Army families. We will discuss effects on spouses and parents shortly. Children, although resilient, suffered too, and their needs were not well understood. Reactions varied by age group and level of development. About two-thirds of the children of deployed soldiers demonstrated increased levels of fear and anxiety, half had behavior problems or "acted out," and a third experienced increased school and academic difficulty. Younger children were more prone than they otherwise might have been to bed-wetting or separation anxiety, and older children were more prone to hostility, sullenness, withdrawal, or eating disorders. Conversely, about half of these children became closer to family members other than their parents—often grandparents or others with whom they resided—and adolescents generally took on more responsibility than they otherwise might have. Schools, child care centers, and youth services varied wildly in their ability to cope. Schools with large numbers of military family members were more prone to initiate directed programs. Child care centers and youth services on major posts were better endowed and accumulated more relevant experience than smaller posts with intermittent deployments. Periods following deployments presented problems for children too. Children were even more prone than parents to imagine all would be rosy after a loved one's return. "Reintegration" has high points and low points, steps forward and steps back, and children could be readily disappointed if they nurtured overly elevated expectations of post-deployment happiness. Most soldiers deployed after 2001 were exposed to circumstances conducive to posttraumatic stress disorder, and many worked through its actual symptoms after they returned. Recurrent deployments, especially if at brief intervals, exacerbated the problem. Sponsor depression, irritability, anxiety, hypervigilance, flashbacks, or nightmares profoundly affected parent-child relationships, of course. At least one victim could get along only with his dog.[10]

Deployments more than tripled during the 1990s, then increased again by an order of magnitude after 2003. As difficult as the anxiety and pace were for most Army children, they were even harder in the cases of sole or dual-military parents. Sole parents cannot enlist on active duty but can remain if they become sole parents after enlisting. The reserve component is not so restricted. As operations peaked in Iraq, about 12 percent of the women and 4 percent of the men serving on active duty were single parents. Almost 11 percent of Army families were those of dual-military couples. This translated to 6 percent of the uniformed husbands and 42 percent of the uniformed wives. About half of the female soldiers who deployed after 2001 were mothers, and, of these, perhaps a third were sole parents. Assignment officers endeavored not to deploy two uniformed parents at the same time, but even when they succeeded the prospect of one parent being gone and the other likely to leave soon was daunting to children. Sole parents, dual-military parents, and single pregnant soldiers were required to establish a family care plan approved by their commanding officer. Organized around Department of the Army Form 5305, it pulled together proof of counseling, powers of attorney, certifications of acceptance as guardian, provisions for allotments and identification cards, contingency travel arrangements, and other documents and details into a comprehensive package. Soldiers specifically committed to arrange for child care, food, housing, transportation, and emergency needs during their absence and acknowledged fourteen different circumstances that could render them absent—of which the eleventh was deployment. Failure to maintain adequate arrangements could be grounds for disciplinary action or separation. Families in which one spouse was not a service member had to think through the same issues, of course, but the Army assumed the nondeploying spouse—unless an exceptional family member—would handle them. On balance the highly structured and somewhat draconian program did a creditable job of tending to physical needs. Tens of thousands of Army children lived temporarily with grandparents, friends, or extended family members, all the while benefiting from allotments, TRICARE, and identification cards. Popular mythology (not necessarily true or false, but believed rather than provable) holds that "Army brats" are stronger, more adaptable, and more resilient by virtue of facing such challenges. This mythology emerged in an era of traditional nuclear families and PCS as the greatest recurrent hardship. Upticks previously cited with respect to anxiety, behavioral problems, and academic difficulty gave installation commanders responsible for child and youth services, and school faculties, pause. Historians mulled over similar concerns during World War II and Vietnam, substantiating a need for preventative measures. Mental health services through TRICARE and in military facilities were rendered more accessible to adolescents. Relevant training was given to child care providers, military family life consultants augmented mental health care professionals, and school counselors became more mindful of children whose parents were deployed. The subject of children coping with recurrent deployments,

"Living in the New Normal" (also the name selected for a program of the Military Child Education Coalition featuring professional development courses and resources), became a focus for further study and initiatives. The Army Family Action Plan recommended peer support groups, camps, innovations in child care, counseling, and other services to assist in addressing this issue. By 2006, indeed by the time of this writing, the Army's efforts in this regard had not matured and further adjustment seemed necessary. It remains unclear how big of a problem recurrent parental deployments are for otherwise well-cared-for children, or what remedial actions are the most appropriate. It is clear that soldiers are concerned for the welfare of their children and that visible attention to the challenges children face numbers among the prerequisites for retaining families.[11]

Spouses

As the Cold War ended about half of the Army on active duty were married, and of these about 60 percent had children. This meant, of course, that about 40 percent did not—or did not yet—have children. The needs of families without children overlap with but are different than those of families with children, and spouses can and do have concerns that are independent of their children. A longitudinal study of Army officers' wives found expectations of how time away from children was to be spent varied by generation. Wives serving in the Army of the 1930s and 1940s got "out of the house" largely for social purposes. Coffees, teas, bridge clubs, and the like built camaraderie while providing a break from the serious work of maintaining a household. Army wives of the 1950s and 1960s, like their civilian counterparts, had fewer children and more labor-saving appliances and were heavily inclined toward community-building volunteer work as an outlet for talent and energy. Those of the 1970s and 1980s were likely to work outside the home for pay. These threads intermingled. By 1990 about half of all Army wives worked outside the home for pay, more than two-thirds volunteered in one capacity or another, and virtually all sought social contact outside the immediate family. Such statistics underlay the Army issues of 1989–2005 that might best be characterized as spousal: employment, financial security, emotional security, support groups, and volunteer activities. Evolution within each of these progressed in the context of the shift to an expeditionary Army and an accelerating pace of deployment.[12]

The most contentious spousal issue during this period was employment. Traditionally the Army had not taken much interest in spousal employment, assuming a nuclear family where the husband worked outside of the home and the wife worked within it. This model was changing for Americans at large by the 1970s, and the dramatic infusion of married soldiers into the all-volunteer Army brought change with it. By 1989 five out of ten Army spouses were working, and an additional one was seeking a job. The Army itself employed about 22,000. The AAFES employed many, both directly and indirectly, through the MWR activities it subsidized. These generally could be reemployed within AAFES when their sponsors were reassigned, both because

AAFES was ubiquitous and because military spouses employed by AAFES where they were moving to were likely to be reassigned as well. Conventional wisdom held that Army spouses who sought work outside the home should undertake "portable" careers, like nurse or schoolteacher, for examples. Given state and local restrictions and requirements these were not always as portable as hoped for, but the underlying premise remained popular. Military intervention could help. A 1988 Army Research Institute (ARI) study established that an active employment assistance program on post increased spousal employment by 10 percent. With digitization such employment assistance became worldwide. The Military Spouse Career Center now boasts Web-based career assessment tools offering tips on education, training, and employment choices most likely to be compatible with a mobile lifestyle. Spouses are similarly assisted in creating and posting resumés, searching listings, and assessing relative prospects by geographical location. The general advent of home stationing at stateside mega-posts had a large impact on spousal employment. Given geographical stability, spouses enjoyed greater prospects for employment stability. Options broadened from portable careers to realistically include more location-dependent enterprises, such as opening a business or being a realtor. The sponsor could deploy and redeploy as the Army directed; the spouse could continue to work uninterrupted. Permanent changes of station that did occur were overwhelmingly likely to be from one stateside post to another. Accompanied overseas assignments were far less likely than before, unless sought. This offered another spousal employment option. Borrowing on its happy experience with AAFES, in 2003 the Army negotiated the Army Spouse Employment Partnership with ubiquitous employers such as Home Depot, Lowe's, Toys R Us, and Walmart. These employers facilitated the entry of military spouses into their workforce. Once there, they could be reemployed within the system if they moved. Everybody won, and the partnership generated over 42,000 jobs in a half-dozen years. After 9-11 a number of states made military spouses eligible for unemployment compensation if they had to quit their jobs because of a sponsor's permanent change of station. By 2009 two dozen states supported this approach, easing transitions for spouses who remained in pursuit of employment.[13]

Spouses sought employment for a variety of reasons. Surveys established, among other motives, that women wanted to share in achieving family financial security. Army spouses who worked outside the home for pay typically brought in about a third of the family income. This could prove critical in sustaining mortgages and coping with other expenses to which family life was prone. Understandably, spouses wanted to secure their investments and quality of living against the hazards of military life and the uncertainties of their own employment. Servicemembers' Group Life Insurance (SGLI) had long been the approved solution protecting the family in the case of the untimely death of its sponsor. Soldiers were immediately insured for the full amount upon their first day of active duty. Opting out required a conscious act of reduction or cancellation. Grizzled first sergeants saw to it that soldiers understood reduction or cancellation was foolish, tantamount to family abuse, and tempting fate. Virtually all heeded this sensible advice. Small monthly allotments were withdrawn from a

soldier's pay to cover this heavily subsidized term life insurance. Soldiers identified their beneficiaries on the first day and updated this information annually or
prior to each deployment. For much of this period the full amount for SGLI was
$200,000. In 2003 the service vice chiefs addressed massive and prospectively
recurrent deployments to Iraq, and long-term inflation, by lobbying for and
securing an elevation of SGLI to $400,000 at a cost of $26 a month. This was
a good deal and provided considerable peace of mind to sponsors and spouses
alike. Risks were also compensated for with imminent danger pay, commonly
called "combat pay," and a family separation allowance (FSA) for soldiers separated from their dependents for more than thirty days. The former has risen to
$225 a month and the latter to $250 a month at the time of writing. Pay was
excluded for enlisted personnel and partially excluded for officers from taxable
income for every month wherein a soldier served a day in a combat zone. This
also applied to special pay such as flight pay and to bonuses such as reenlistment
bonuses. The Army experienced an uptick in soldiers reenlisting while deployed.
Whatever one's motives for reenlisting, it made financial sense to do so under
circumstances that rendered the bonus tax-exempt. Family finances could go
awry due to fires and floods, family emergencies, and other unexpected circumstances. AER, a private nonprofit organization with semiofficial status, led in
redressing such crises. AER was directed by retired senior officers and NCOs,
replenished its coffers with annual fundraising drives, and in partnership with
ACS benefited somewhat from on-post office space and other amenities. From
August 1990 through January 1991 (the period of Desert Shield), for example,
AER provided $17 million in grants and interest-free loans to 31,000 soldiers.
AER's philanthropic business model overwhelmingly favored interest-free loans
over grants, at a ratio of about nine to one. This reflected the philosophy that
soldiers had steady incomes, financial setbacks could be temporary, and it was
better to assist in developing responsibility than to create dependency. It also
enabled relief funds to go a lot further, since most ultimately recycled. In the
aftermath of 9-11 the greater turbulence of wartime Army life and a national
mood supportive of soldiers—and mindful of the scale of financial relief offered
the families of World Trade Center victims—abridged this traditional model
somewhat. AER continued its emphasis on loans and sponsored financial management training courses, but new nonprofits such as USA Cares and Operation
Homefront rose that heavily emphasized grants. Happily, the two genres did not
much conflict. Indeed, the agencies referred clients to each other depending on
circumstances. USA Cares and Operation Homefront passed money out about
as fast as they took it in, whereas AER also poured money out but sustained
ample reserves via recycling. Most recognized that some Army families would
always be in or near financial crisis, particularly if large numbers were dependent on a single sponsor. From time to time during the Cold War the Army and
the nation had been embarrassed by the incidence of service families qualifying for food stamps. This reinforced steady and relatively successful campaigns
to raise base pay, but these never got altogether ahead of unusual fertility. In
2001 about 14,000 military families were receiving food stamps. An E-1 with
four or more family members solely dependent on him or her would be eligible,
for example, as would an E-5 with seven or more. Congress created the Family

Supplemental Assistance Allowance of up to $500 a month to keep at-risk Army families off of food stamps. Spousal employment affected income in general and food stamp (later Supplemental Nutrition Assistance Program) eligibility in particular. As we have seen, after 9-11 an increasing number of states considered military spouses eligible for unemployment compensation. Instruments facilitating financial security for Army families advanced considerably during the period 1989–2005. This, most thought, would assist in retaining Army families.[14]

As important as spousal employment and financial security are, most couples probably rate their relationships with each other as more central to their happiness. Facilitating romance has never been an Army forte. Senior wives did have a long tradition of attempting to match Army daughters with promising young soldiers, and that continued within the limits of the supply. During the Cold War Officers Clubs and NCO Clubs offered places for singles to meet and mingle on isolated outposts, but these were readily trumped by civilian alternatives in stateside settings. Indeed, by 1996 club systems had walked away from "fine dining" as a moneymaker and focused instead on more casual, quick, and family-friendly alternatives. Primo's Italian Restaurant opened in Fort Hood, Texas, as a representative of this trend, which is not to mention the countless grills and fast food franchises already operating at the time. The Army's Hale Koa Hotel on Waikiki Beach did add the opulent 396-room Maile Tower in 1995, at a cost of 99 million nonappropriated dollars. This offered an exciting romantic getaway that exceeded local occupancy rates, but its traffic nevertheless paled in comparison to more accessible and family-friendly facilities proximate to Disney World in Orlando, Florida. MWR programs as a whole trended toward families with children. If couples found romance, the Army probably had little to do with it. Indeed, it may well have retarded the process with incessant demands on the soldier's time and energy. As weak as the Army was as an aphrodisiac, it did do a reasonable job of assisting relationships once they had formed. Surveys established that Army chaplains ranked third behind family members and close friends as the person one would most likely talk to about a confidential matter. The Army formally embraced Family Life Ministry as the all-volunteer Army was being established in the late 1970s. Selected chaplains attended more than a year of graduate-level instruction on family counseling and then returned to train their peers and chaplain assistants. By 1997 the chaplaincy advanced to a preventative posture. It coordinated Building Strong and Ready Families (BSRF), a brigade-level program targeting first-term married and newly married soldiers. This program cycled contingents of young couples through workshops and overnight retreats focused on communication, conflict management, financial responsibility, Army life, and strategies to strengthen bonds. Most of these couples were not problematic, but chaplains could identify those in need of further assistance. Interestingly enough, post-retreat behavioral surveys noted not only enhanced marital communications, but also increased seatbelt use and decreased tobacco use—a possible indication of what was on the minds of spouses at the time. Independent of BSRF, chaplains conducted workshops and retreats for couples in their congregations. The Army Family Advocacy Program (FAP) was on much the same azimuth as BSRF, albeit with a sterner tone. FAP, coordinated by installation commanders, included general educational and preventative programs, but it also focused on intervention in cases of spouse and child abuse. Remedial measures ranged from counseling through incarceration. In extreme cases family members received up to thirty-six months of transitional compensatory payments to help them start over in the absence of an erstwhile sponsor. FAP was understandably distant to most Army families, but it could be reassuring to know a program existed to assist a friend or neighbor in trouble. It should perhaps be noted that the programs described above were for heterosexual couples. Although attitudes toward homosexuality were softening inside the Army as they were outside it, in 2005 official policy remained that active homosexuality or homosexual marriage was grounds for dismissal.[15]

Army life is challenging. Spouses draw support not only from their sponsors but also from family and friends. Friends become particularly important if the sponsor is deployed and the extended biological family geographically separated. In such circumstances installations, rear detachments, and the variety of agencies headed up by Army Community Service can provide creditable practical assistance but are generally thin on emotional support. One survey, for example, found that 93 percent of spouses experiencing a deployment thought they were doing well caring for their children's health, 89 percent thought they were doing well providing for the other needs of their children at home, 85 percent had access to necessary transportation, and 83 percent of those working were doing well at their jobs. Only 50 percent, on the other hand, thought they were handling personal loneliness well. Anxiety concerning the deployed spouse weighed heavily, leaving the spouse left behind ravenous for timely and accurate information. Rumors of hardship or disaster overseas could be hugely demoralizing. Indeed, in one survey 80 percent of spouses identified "rumor control" as the highest single priority for sustaining spousal morale during a deployment. These phenomena were not new. During the 1980s Family Support Groups stood up in many deployable units to facilitate communications and mutual assistance. These made important contributions to morale and well-being during DESERT STORM but drew important lessons from that conflict as well. Relationships in the group that existed well prior to the deployment, although often just for social purposes, did understandably better than those conjured up on the spot as the deployment progressed. Success was heavily dependent on command and rear-detachment support, particularly with respect to providing timely and accurate information. Spouses selected for leadership because of their sponsor's position did not necessarily make the most effective leaders; true volunteers proved critical. Spouses with children in school tended to stay put, whereas those with toddlers or no children were likely to return to their family for the duration. This exacerbated communications gaps. No Family Support Group member was specifically trained for the role they filled; whether they had acquired appropriate skills through life experiences was a matter of happenstance. On the plus side, over three quarters of the wives surveyed considered their Family Support Group a valuable source of reliable information, and even more found it emotionally comforting. In the aftermath of DESERT STORM sentiment developed for professionalizing at least the top tiers of family support. Borrowing from what they thought they knew about Navy ombudsmen, the British regimental system, and other examples, advocates argued for hiring full-time personnel—and derided the Family Support Groups that did exist as wives' "coffee klatches." The counterargument was that the spontaneity and lack of hierarchy in coffee klatches contributed to success rather than failure. Spouses were not looking for more bureaucracy or yet another personal representative of the commander, nor were the greatest concerns of most how to get a ride to the commissary or fill out official forms. They wanted timely information about their husbands, and the emotional support of others going through the same experience. The singular attribute of virtually all Family Support Groups was a "telephone tree," a communications network whereby each spouse made but a few calls, yet all within the network ended up receiving a call. Calls could last but a few minutes to impart specific information, but most lasted longer as participants shared personal news, thoughts, and feelings. Most meetings started with an agenda, but it was seldom rigorously adhered to and often accounted for but a fraction of the time spent. Sharing and communications were keys to success. Family Support Groups were realms, not kingdoms. Customary rules of military organization did not necessarily apply and indeed were resisted.[16]

Debate concerning the extent to which Family Support Groups should be professionalized related heavily to spousal attitudes toward volunteer work. Conventional wisdom holds that as spousal employment increased, volunteering decreased. Within the Army, the two phenomena have not been directly— or inversely—correlated. The generation of wives who accessed prior to 1945 was unlikely to work outside the home and very unlikely to do so if they had young children. Virtually all of these wives did volunteer work within their communities, although nine out of ten averaged but a couple of hours a week. The generation accessing between 1945 and 1975 doubled their rates of paid employment but more than quadrupled the numbers putting in ten or more hours of volunteer work a week. After 1975 employment skyrocketed, but four out of five wives nevertheless still volunteered in some way. This was about three times the national average. Few in the younger generation believed their volunteer work would advance the careers of their husbands, but instincts to contribute and to "remain part of things" remained robust. Motivations to volunteer were complex. Certainly such venerable publications as the *Army Woman's Handbook* and the *Army Lady Today* encouraged such behavior. Life on frontier or overseas outposts required volunteer work to sustain "normalcy." Career soldiers self-select toward a psychology of team commitment, and it may well be that their spouses do as well. With the advent of the all-volunteer Army and Wickham's *The Army Family,* installation and ACS agencies that had been manned by volunteers began to take on part-time or full-time employed cadres. Volunteer work could be an avenue to employment, perhaps even to a portable government service status. The mix of volunteer work done was at least as complicated as the motives for doing it. Volunteers at Walter Reed Army Medical Center after Iraqi Freedom casualties arrived in large numbers provide an example. Over 1,500 volunteers assisted the medical staff, provided comfort and company to sick or wounded soldiers, ran MWR

Family Readiness Groups supported deployed units and their families.

programs in the hospital, helped visiting family members get around, ran information booths, and so on. A number put in over forty hours a week, but the average was about four. This means, of course, that many were averaging one or two. The nature of the tasks was such that even a little participation was helpful—and welcome. This allowed spouses to both hold down a job and volunteer. Family Support Groups were similarly flexible. Participation ranged from making a few phone calls a week through coordinating elaborate programs at the battalion and brigade levels. After DESERT STORM Army Family Team Building (AFTB) emerged to train volunteers. Early development and implementation had been in the hands of senior leader spouses and volunteers. Modular training, eventually available online, progressed through levels of sophistication and comprehensiveness at a pace that catered to the individual student. All participants came away exposed to practices that strengthened self-reliance, enhanced readiness, and promoted retention. Those advancing through the third level could train others. Skills developed fed directly back into Family Support Groups, now called Family Readiness Groups for reasons to be discussed. The overall capabilities of the Family Readiness Groups sharpened and improved, yet volunteers remained in charge. "Key" volunteers received signed appointment orders from their unit commanders, identifying the Family Readiness Group as a command-sponsored organization rather than a private organization or a nonappropriated fund instrumentality. Commanders were to be held accountable. The *Army Commander's Guide to Family Readiness Group Operations* defined the Family Readiness Group as a "command-sponsored organization of family members, volunteers, Soldiers and civilian employees belonging to a unit that together provide an avenue of mutual support and assistance, and a network of communication. . . ." Insofar as there was a professional element, it was provided by employed or contracted Family Readiness Group Deployment/Support Assistants at the brigade and division levels and Family Readiness Liaisons at the installation level. These assisted the volunteers with navigation as the Army increasingly churned up or interpreted policies with respect to Family Readiness Group (FRG) use of facilities, telephones, computers, copiers, official transportation, fund-raising, reimbursable expenditures, and so on. They were employed as technical experts, not to "impinge on the role and responsibilities of the volunteer FRG leader." Generally they were invited to join the coffee klatch, and often did so. The volunteer tradition remained strong, and its social setting familiar.[17]

Army Family Team Building emerged after DESERT STORM amid the increasingly recurrent deployments of the 1990s. At the time saying goodbye, handling family finances in the absence of the sponsor, and getting timely and reliable information back to families seemed to be the greatest challenges for spouses. In 1994 the Army Community and Family Support Center (CFSC) launched Operation READY (Resources for Educating About Deployment and You). Operation READY exploited a video format and deployed training modules, handbooks, videotapes, and other resources to assist installations, commanders, families, and soldiers preparing for deployment. Spousal training was characterized as a "force multiplier." Saying goodbye was facilitated by elaborate and inclusive predeployment meetings that were in part comprehensive briefings and in part town hall meetings. These were mandatory for service members, and their spouses were strongly encouraged to attend. Preparation for overseas movement included several stations that ensured spouses had appropriate powers of attorney and financial access in their sponsor's absence. English as a Second Language (ESL) instruction, long a requirement for language-challenged soldiers, was extended to wives as well, and Army Community Service focused on particularly challenging cases. Family Support Groups, as we have discussed, were built around telephone trees, peer-to-peer relationships, and the imperative of reliable spousal communications. The term Family Support Group morphed to become Family Readiness Group, in part to emphasize the importance of prior preparations. The name change also marked a shift in philosophy. Post–DESERT STORM reflection suggested that some Family Support Groups exceeded their grasp and their authority. Well-intentioned volunteers sought to be everything to everybody, opening the door for a tiny fraction of spouses who were excessively dependent, overly demanding, or singularly maneuvering for the return of their sponsors. Such spouses took up an overwhelmingly disproportionate amount of the group leaders' time, and they often had practical and psychological problems that exceeded the amateur Family Support Group leader's expertise. Family Readiness Groups expected all boats—that is to say, families—to rise together with respect to preparedness for deployment. Trained volunteers advised and assisted those encountering normal degrees of difficulty and knew who within the command or installation to refer the hard cases to. Selection of rear detachment commanders became more methodical, evolving away from whoever had a physical profile at the time. Within a few years Operation READY added homecoming and reintegration to its areas of focus. Beginning in 2002, Spouse Orientation and Leader Development (SOLD) consciously educated spouses for multiple levels of responsibility: self-reliant participant, direct-level leader, community leader, and strategic leader. DESERT STORM had progressed quickly, decisively, and with few casualties, leaving a modest incidence of posttraumatic stress (other than for Iraqis) in its wake. Insofar as "Gulf War Syndrome" could be diagnosed, its causes seemed to be more chemical than psychological. Recurrent deployments and returns after 1991 introduced long months of anxiety, sometimes jarring returns, and recognition that the cycle could soon repeat itself. With IRAQI FREEDOM this source of stress increased by an order of magnitude, and frequent rotations into a combat zone became common. As casualties mounted spouses became mindful not only of the dead, but also of the larger numbers of wounded requiring long-term care or recuperation. The term *advance medical directive* became the subject of serious discussion, as did wills and beneficiaries. Most deployed soldiers experienced conditions associated with posttraumatic stress disorder (PTSD), and perhaps one in five exhibited symptoms. Spouses were, unfortunately, likely targets if sponsors "acted out" on their depression, irritability, or acute anxiety. Around Fort Hood, Texas, for example, reports of domestic abuse doubled in a few years' time, and violent crimes rose 22 percent. Suicides rose as well. Fortuitously the Family Advocacy Program, previously discussed, had been available since the mid-1990s, and the medical community was newly attentive to PTSD. These were, of course, steps toward resolution rather than resolution itself. At the time of writing PTSD, domestic abuse, and suicide remain high priorities for the Army and its soldiers.[18]

Parents

The parents of soldiers were not traditionally party to programs targeted on Army families. They mattered to soldiers, of course, but were generally invisible to the Army except in narrow circumstances. Parents were formally or informally invited to ceremonies and graduations involving their offspring, but they tended to be restricted by time and geography from attending. An exception was graduation from basic or one station unit training. These programs were often proximate to a soldier's point of entry and a reasonable day trip for families to make. Basic and one station unit training graduations took on the attributes of rites of passage, with families surrendering up their young soldiers to the Army for worldwide deployment. Once in units soldiers might be encouraged by chaplains or thoughtful NCOs to correspond with their parents, but this was not an institutional priority. In the case of unmarried soldiers parents were generally next of kin and beneficiaries with respect to SGLI, wills, and the disposition of personal effects. An iconic and unhappy image of the Army experience is that of a uniformed party knocking on the door of an unfortunate family to notify them that they have lost a son or daughter. Between the departure of a soldier for military service and his ultimate return one way or another, his or her parents and the Army were not much involved with each other—unless the parents were in the Army themselves. Beginning in the 1980s several developments brought parents out of the shadows. Anxious to sustain its numbers, the Army recruited parents in the process of recruiting their children. In an age of digitization, these overtures introduced reciprocity of access. Family Support Groups and Family Readiness Groups, themselves digitized, increasingly brought parents into their orbits, particularly by the

Parents could play a role in enlistment or reenlistment.

means of "virtual" readiness groups. Recurrent deployments, especially when both spouses were working, expanded the soldiers' parents' roles with respect to their grandchildren. In the case of a sole parent in uniform, grandparents often became guardians or in loco parentis. As the Army undertook to retain its wounded soldiers longer, parents were frequently helpmates and, not uncommonly, principal caregivers. All of this progressed in a national social context wherein communications were radically improved, travel appreciably easier, lives longer, and grandparents more involved with their grandchildren than they had been for some time.[19]

With the advent of the all-volunteer Army, recruiters soon recognized the utility of courting parents. After initial floundering, recruiting took off with the slogan "Be All You Can Be" in the early 1980s. This message of personal self-development, the mantra of Army recruiting for twenty years, could be as appealing to parents as it was to their near-adult children. Army leaders opined that the contemporary generation of potential recruits, raised in relative affluence, was inclined to "try life" for a year or so before getting down to the serious business of higher education or employment. Few parents were thrilled with the idea of their offspring meditating, hitchhiking, or lounging around for extended periods before undertaking to support themselves. The Army and parents could be natural allies if young people "found themselves" while purposefully employed, reasonably paid, and acquiring substantial educational and other benefits to help them later on. The Army sought high school graduates, since overall completion of term attrition for them was about a third, whereas it was more than half for high school dropouts. The timing seemed perfect: graduate from high school, spend several years in the Army maturing and learning useful skills, and set off for college or elsewhere with many of the bills already paid. Young people were always the primary target of Army recruiting, but their parents came in as a respectable second. Advertisements frequently flashed to proud parents beaming over their uniformed offspring's newly acquired capabilities and confidence. Messages addressed such practical parental interests as marketable job skills, tuition assistance, "free" medical care, reliable employment, and insurance. Action and adventure were there too, of course, but considerably less so than if the young and testosterone-saturated were the only targets. Through 2003 this formula worked fairly well, allowing for the ebb and flow of the national economy. Virtually every Army Staff meeting in the Pentagon, and most Army staff meetings at lower levels, closely monitored recruitment and reenlistment statistics. Participants proposed new methods when numbers were down and applauded existing methods when they were up. In boom times large civilian enterprises borrowed Army messages and incentives when competing for the young high school graduate labor force. After 2003 recruiting parents proved harder. Most parents want their children to mature and develop; few want them to do so in a war zone. By this time the Army was well into digitization and Web sophistication and applied these strengths in its approach to parents. Army Web sites posted forums encouraging parents to share insights and experiences and to ask questions. Information was ever more accessible, thoughtfully tiered, and attractively packaged. The underlying message of personal self-development remained; the delivery was more interactive. "Be All You Can Be" was replaced by an "Army of One" in 2001 and "Army Strong" in 2006. For parents the message remained consistent. Their children would be better people and get a better start in life by the virtue of military service.[20]

Recruiters were not alone on the Internet, of course. As Internet use exploded during the 1990s and personal computers became commonplace, Family Readiness Groups relied on the Web as well. The personal touch of individual telephone calls remained critically important, but newsletters, announcements, flyers, and the like could easily go out over the Internet. Parents of deployed soldiers were eager for news and soon discovered the Family Readiness Groups. Family Readiness Group newsletters overlapped heavily with unit newsletters, and both provided the type of information parents wanted to obtain. Family Readiness Groups and units were generally happy to pass this information along to parents. It was unclassified, had been cleared for distribution, and seemed likely to dispel rumors. It required but a few additional keystrokes to add new addressees to an electronic message. As parents absorbed information and expressed gratitude for it, the Army's leadership addressed their needs in a more consistent manner. Inclusion of parents within the electronic umbrella of Family Readiness Groups became accepted policy, as did the inclusion of significant others who did not have, or did not yet have, spousal status. Local community leaders and benefactors were often included as well. Vicki Cody, wife of the Vice Chief of Staff of the Army, consolidated information and advice for parents in *Your Soldier, Your Army: A Parent's Guide*, published in 2005 by the Association of the United States Army. Her two sons were soldiers embedded in cycles of recurrent deployment, as had been her husband. *Your Soldier, Your Army* mixed encouragement and empathy with practical details and specific advice. It was the first official or semiofficial publication of its type to target parents of soldiers and was on the Association of the United States Army Web site as well as in hard copy. Advice covered such topics as powers of attorney, documents, files, budgets, key points of contact, emergency notification, and child care plans. It also addressed rumor mongering and scam artists, no small threats in an Internet age.[21]

The publication and sponsorship of *Your Soldier, Your Army* reflected a much-expanded scope of parental involvement with respect to deployment. The foot soldiers of the volunteer Army were not recently drafted teenagers with little money and no property. They were older than Cold War counterparts, and even the unmarried had considerable property to manage. Most owned a car, often an expensive one. Many owned motorcycles. Virtually all owned a fistful of electronic appliances, and many lived off post in rentals they might not want to retain through a prolonged deployment. If they did want to retain the rental, rent was due monthly. If not, their property could move into storage that also involved a monthly rental. A major fraction of this property, particularly expensive cars and motorcycles, went home to Mom and Dad's garage rather than being entrusted to a fenced parking lot on post. Once deployed communications could be intermittent, or in times of crisis cut off, rendering monthly payments problematic. The complexities of property and finance powerfully suggested entrusting someone remaining stateside with specified powers of attorney. This was most often a parent in the case of single soldiers. Financial miscarriages during the deployments of the early 1990s alerted installations to the consequences of inadequate planning, and preparations for overseas movement became increasingly attentive to financial issues. Lawyers at the processing sites, long used to updating wills and SGLI, added powers of attorney to their tasks. Parents found themselves handling rent and other monthly payments, managing bank accounts, and even submitting income taxes. More than a few inherited a beloved pet for the duration. In cases when their soldier offspring was married, these tasks generally fell to the spouse, but he or she generally sought and welcomed assistance. Spouses without children or with toddlers often spent much or all of the deployment with parents, connected to the Family Readiness Group electronically. Those with paid employment or with older children generally stayed put but then were one deep in the case of illness, injury, or some other complication. This again brought forward parental support. Dual military parents and sole parents were required, as we have seen, to produce an official family care plan identifying a guardian for their children in the case of deployment or absence for some other reason. More often than not this was a grandparent. From 2003 on the execution of a family care plan became very likely for soldiers who had one. If their parents were on it, they would probably serve.[22]

Most parents were happy to help out when their children deployed. They were also eager for information. In wars past communications between parents and their deployed children had been largely by letter, supplemented by the rare phone call from mid-century on. In Afghanistan and Iraq soldiers had considerably greater access to telephones and frequently access to unclassified e-mail as well. Improvements with respect to communications and information available were not an unmixed blessing. Around-the-clock news coverage introduced stresses of its own. Parents could become fixated. Each report of casualties sent them into mental calculations concerning where their son or daughter was, and whether he or she could have been involved. If the odds were high that they were, they of course wanted to know more right away, preferably with a comforting message from their offspring that they were all right. Unfortunately, these were the very circumstances wherein commanders were likely to cut off personal communications, both because of operational security and to ensure that the next of kin of the dead were properly notified first. Waiting for a call was in itself stressful. When phone calls did come through, they were rarely at an anticipated time and often awkward. Soldiers did not want to worry their parents and discussed the innocuous more so than the gut-wrenching. Parents did not want to let their worries become their soldier's worries and feigned good cheer as well. Both tiptoed around the grave anxieties they momentarily masked. Soldiers seldom had more than a few minutes to talk, after which both parties agonized over what they should have said or cycled regrets through their minds. Mothers who broke down and cried on the phone, spoiling what was supposed to be an uplifting moment, were prone to feeling guilty—although perhaps less so than those awakened in the middle of the night who yawned into the phone. E-mail allowed more of an opportunity to be expansive, to reflect on comments prior to making them, and to avoid the implications of time zones. Oddly enough, however, letters—often accompanied by "care packages" of treats and consumables from home—remained in many ways the most satisfactory means of communication. Letters were tangible, could be read and re-read, and allowed considered coverage of topics and emotions. They could take weeks to deliver, however, breaking the timely flow of communications. Parents adopted rules of thumb to cope: ration daily exposure to the news cycle; maintain a running list of topics to be discussed and anecdotes to be shared by the phone; don't count on e-mail; have a weekly routine for writing letters and sending care packages—so something is always "in the mail." Of the news being shared, the most eagerly awaited was news of return. Parents counted the days and greeted the return to American soil with joy and relief. There could be debate concerning traveling to be present as the soldier "got off the plane." With unmarried soldiers there seemed to be little problem with adding familiar faces to throngs of well-wishers, but some spouses observed that parents should be elsewhere for about the same reasons they had not attended their offspring's senior prom. Homecoming was celebratory but had its stresses and having in-laws around the house could add further stresses still. Units increasingly took to formal sessions of reintegration counseling to bring soldiers back into their communities and to handle whatever dispositions there might be toward PTSD. Given all that soldiers had been through, it might be best not to overwhelm them with too much family too soon. Let them reconstruct relationships with spouses and children first and then feed in the rest of the loved ones. Traditionally, when transportation was more problematic, parents stayed put and returning soldiers moved along to visit them when ready. Behavioralists had no pat answer as to whether it was better for a returning soldier to cope with all his loved ones en masse, or to do so in a more measured manner. Each family found its own way in this regard.[23]

Not all homecomings were happy. Parents were primary next of kin. If their soldier was killed or missing in action, they were personally notified by a uniformed party. Army provisions to assist them in recovering the body if there was one, arranging burials and memorial services, settling estates, and disposing of personal effects predated the end of the Cold War. If, as was more likely, their soldier was seriously wounded, they received a phone call. Army and parental practices evolved with respect to wounded soldiers following the Cold War. Travel was easier and medical evacuation out of austere combat zones likely. It was practical for parents to fly to their offspring's side in the major hospitals of Germany and the United States. Here they were often greatly assisted by "Fisher Houses" located close to the hospital. Beginning in 1990 the privately financed Fisher House Foundation built and maintained houses featuring multiple suites where the families of wounded soldiers could stay for free, or at very modest expense. By 2003 there were thirty-two such facilities, covering virtually every major hospital to which a soldier wounded overseas was likely to be evacuated. Many of these were proximate to Veterans Affairs hospitals as well, contributing to a continuity of care should the soldier be released from the Army. In addition to the altruism of Arnold, Zachary, and Elizabeth Fisher and their friends, colleagues, and kin, Fisher Houses reflected evolving medical practice. Body armor, speedy evacuation, and medical advances made the casualties of Afghanistan and Iraq even more likely than their predecessors to survive serious injury. Soldiers requiring long-term treatment and rehabilitation who would have died in theater in earlier wars faced prolonged struggles to recover. Many of the maimed would eventually approach full functionality through advanced prosthetics, but the physical and occupational therapy involved was long and hard. A higher proportion of survivors had traumatic brain injuries than before, and these often took months to fully diagnose, much less treat. In Chapter 6 we addressed the Army's growing tendency to retain its wounded soldiers, the interface between the Army and Veterans Affairs, and such programs as Warrior Transition Units and Wounded Warrior programs. Parents, spouses, and other family members, many of them temporarily residing in Fisher Houses, became important players in the recovery. Physical and occupational therapists could give the wounded soldier perhaps an hour a day, and doctors and nurses could be intermittently attentive. Family in residence had much more time to give and did so: accompanying the wounded on walks, assisting with exercises, running errands, monitoring medications, and providing companionship. Wounded soldiers are particularly prone to PTSD, and family members were best positioned to detect its symptoms. Depression, irritability, anxiety, and mood swings are most visible to those who know you best. Having family members around to talk to was therapy in itself, and symptoms detected by the family could be readily shared with doctors in a medical setting. This interplay between uniformed medical personnel and wounded soldier family members was unprecedented. More than 120,000 families stayed at Fisher Houses during their first two decades of operation. This probably represented less than half of the overall family members involved in hospital-based recovery. Soldiers reasonably well along had a voice with respect to where they were evacuated, and the distribution of hospitals around the country made day trips possible for many families. Assuming the role of principal caregiver when a seriously wounded soldier was finally released could be an enormous psychological, physical, and financial drain. In some cases families did not know their options or got lost in the transfer from the Department of the Army to Veterans Affairs. Both agencies endeavored to improve their communications, and both were increasingly aware of the role parents might play.[24]

Retirees

Retirees are also members of the extended Army family. They are here defined as soldiers who have served twenty years or more and thus receive a government pension representing some fraction of their most recent base pay. Retirees are a subset of veterans, with whom they share many interests, although their longer military tenures, professional status, and lifelong pensions set them apart. Army culture is inclined to respect them as elders, and the major fraction of their lives served in the military inclines many toward further involvement and contribution. They are private citizens, but not without organization. Cases in point include The Retired Officers Association (TROA; after 2003 the Military Officers Association of America, MOAA) and the dominance of retirees in such influential organizations as the Association of the United States Army (AUSA) or the United Services Automobile Association (USAA). In 1956 the Cold War Army began publishing the *Retired Army Personnel Bulletin* (later *Army Echoes*), recognition of the value attached to sustaining a relationship. Among other considerations, serving senior leaders anticipated that they too would become retirees, so it made sense to take care of a demographic they soon enough would join. Retiree councils were invited to identify concerns and undertake advisory roles at installations around the country. In 1971 an Army Chief of Staff's Retiree Council representing this emerging nationwide network began meeting semiannually with the Chief of Staff, Sergeant Major of the Army, Deputy Chief of Staff for Personnel, Surgeon General, and other key members of the Army Staff. These meetings addressed retiree concerns and issues as well as potential contributions retirees could continue to make. As the Cold War wound down, the relationship between the Army and its retirees evolved in important ways. The traditional "grey beard" status became even more useful for counsel and communication. Hugely increased reliance on contracting leaned heavily on retiree experience and abilities. Retirees proved instrumental in bringing TRICARE in particular and Army medicine in general on line with new circumstances. Retirees played prominently, directly or indirectly, on the roller coaster of ever-challenging recruiting efforts. Finally, retirees were themselves mindful of end-of-career and end-of-life transitions and helped the Army find its way through a large bulge as the Cold War Army retired and a huge bulge as the World War II Army passed away.[25]

General of the Army Omar Bradley once commented that when generals retired from the Army they should cut out their tongues. By and large senior officers have avoided critiques of their immediate successors, but this has not precluded lively interest in and commentary on professional issues of a broader nature. Some of this became iconic. For example, Major General Aubrey S. Newman, the hero of Leyte famous for his exhortation to "Follow Me," authored "The Forward Edge" in *Army* magazine for over twenty years. "The Forward Edge" offered a rich blend of news, analysis, commemoration, anecdote, insight, historical analogy, and professional advice of the kind respected elders have and should offer to those who come behind them. Retirees took the time to contribute thousands of pieces a year to scores of magazines, journals, newspapers, newsletters, and so on. Some wrote books. Many resisted change, and not all of their contributions were immediately welcome to the Army's senior leadership. Each incremental advance in integrating women, for example, inspired a rant from somebody. By 1989 the "Old Grads" were pretty much over women at West Point, but they still had women piloting attack helicopters, female tactical leadership in combat, and the general erosion of the combat exclusion policy to look forward to. Retiree garrulousness nevertheless proved a positive force in at least one regard. As the implications of the Goldwater-Nichols Act of 1986 played out, the Joint Staff exerted ever more discipline over the activities and public testimony of the services. On balance this was a good thing, reducing rivalry, redundancy, and contention. It also stifled debate. Service "attack dogs" went at each other from time to time during budgetary and Quadrennial Defense Review (QDR) deliberations, but their exchanges were behind closed doors—and a reputation as a service attack dog could limit career options. To the media and the public, uniformed senior leaders were expected to exhibit a mellow "purple" visage and untroubled agreement with administration policy. Some debate nevertheless seemed worth having. How much air and naval overmatch was enough without being too expensive? Who was to cope with the low end of the combat spectrum, and how? What were the limits of precision-guided munitions in particular and technology in general? Should a fifty-year-old funding paradigm favoring the Navy and Air Force be revised when the strategic imperative was "boots on the ground"? Retirees filled in where they sensed their juniors still in uniform had been muzzled. Much of the debate took the traditional forms of articles, letters to the editor, and speeches to self-selected audiences, but under the auspices of AUSA and its embedded Institute of Land Warfare (ILW) it acquired more structure. The largely social AUSA Annual Meeting morphed into a constellation of meetings and seminars revolving around a few grand events. The AUSA Winter Symposium emerged as a second major annual event with a more focused agenda. Separate annual AUSA symposia emerged for Army Aviation, Logistics, Installation Management, Medical, and Space and Missile Defense. Family issues such as education, housing, medical care, and well-being received recurrent attention and were further addressed in AUSA's *Army* magazine and *Torchbearer* circulars. AUSA events mixed retirees and serving soldiers with representatives from more than five hundred "sustaining members"—corporate sponsors who provided goods and services

Association of the United States Army (AUSA) events such as the annual
Eisenhower Luncheon brought together senior military and industrial leaders,
active-duty soldiers, retirees, and interested citizens.

to the Army. An AUSA-hosted discussion of "Armored Fighting Vehicles" could reasonably attract more than forty sustaining members, for example, and "Ammunition and Fuzes" more than twenty. Even "Bearings, Seals, and Couplings" had a following. Collectively considered, sustaining members were broadly informed, robustly funded, and well connected. Their "take" on equipment and force structure debates was consequential, and their interest ensured that arguments would be more widely heard. An Army point of view manifested itself publicly in another way as major news networks increasingly relied on retired Army officers for commentary and analysis. These "talking heads" were not participants in force structure debates while on the air, but their mindfulness of the role and importance of ground forces and their ability to communicate to broad audiences further advanced an Army message.[26]

Army retirees numbered prominently among the sustaining members visiting AUSA symposia. This made sense to the corporations employing them, both from the point of view of business development and from the point of view of having employees who knew their subject matter. In Chapter 4 we discussed the revolution in military contracting that followed the downsizing of the early 1990s and touched upon the role of retirees in that revolution. Recognition that retirees possessed valuable experience, skills, and talents was no new thing. During the Cold War the Army Retiree Recall Program envisioned calling up tens of thousands upon mobilization. In 1987, for example, 232,000 were considered fully qualified, and 122,000 of these had preexisting orders. With post–Cold War downsizing a major fraction of the Army's support structure was swept away. Many units and agencies that were to be heavily reinforced by retirees no longer existed. They were replaced by such major contractors as Brown and Root and Halliburton, who in turn hired retirees and veterans to provide critical skills. As valuable as contingents of retirees proved in shoring up depleted logistics, they proved even more essential to International Military Education and Training (IMET). Between 1994 and 2002 the Department of Defense quadrupled its budget for such training, pursuing stability in the Balkans, Africa, Latin America, and elsewhere. Much of this went to such contractors as Military Professional Resources International (MPRI) and Science Applications International Corporation (SAIC), who in turn relied heavily upon retirees as senior supervisors, administrators, and instructors. This pedagogical role was mirrored within the United States as the Training and Doctrine Command (TRADOC) downsized its uniformed cadre and increasingly relied on contractors to author doctrine and lesson plans and to teach in the classroom. Understandably, the only people particularly qualified for such work were veterans and retirees. Inside "the Beltway" the Army Staff and other agencies, also downsizing, increasingly relied on contracted "think tanks" to support their deliberations. The numbers thus employed burgeoned, and AUSA sustaining membership grew to include firms specializing in consulting, education, recruitment, and training as readily as those specializing in tanks, trucks, and helicopters. This is not to mention sustaining members specializing in such enterprises as banking, insurance, or personal finance who did relatively little government contracting but catered to a military clientele. These too benefited from employing retirees and veterans. In 1990, faced with imminent downsizing, the Chief of Staff launched the Army Career and Alumni Program (ACAP) to prepare departing soldiers for career transitions. Increasingly elaborate transition programs followed, each designed to better match the departee against the market. For retirees the experience could be particularly elaborate, since many had accumulated formidable portfolios but few had interviewed for a job as civilians do or "sold themselves" to an employer. The value of "networking" was bluntly stressed, and this advice often paid off. Seasoned retirees pulled new retirees into corporations behind them, refreshing the organization with sustained currency in military affairs. Demographics shifted. The older industrial model of retiree employment had featured a few senior officers in key positions, largely for business development, and on corporate boards. The new emphasis on training, education, and services considerably broadened the positions to be filled and afforded opportunities to younger men retiring at less senior ranks. "Second careers" could be and often were numbered in decades rather than years.[27]

As the Army of the 1990s dramatically downsized, the greatest single concern for retirees was the quality of their medical care. Traditionally the Army medical structure had been robust enough and retirees few enough that their medical needs had been accommodated alongside those of serving soldiers. When the Army slashed its medical force structure along with the rest of its force structure and began deploying its uniformed medical personnel overseas in large numbers, this was no longer possible. Like the numbers of active-duty family members, the numbers of retirees had grown dramatically with time. At the beginning of World War II there were but 15,000 Army retirees and in 1955 only 99,000, but in 1993 their numbers surpassed those of active-duty soldiers and by 2005 720,000 retirees considerably outnumbered the 501,000 soldiers on active duty. Clearly a medical establishment designed to accommodate active-duty soldiers alone could not collaterally handle such numbers, and passing them along to Veterans Affairs would not work without significant additional resources either. Given that "cradle to grave" medical care had always numbered among the advertised incentives promoting an Army career, many began to refer to the erosion of medical care as a "broken promise." As we have seen, active-duty family members also cited access to medical care as a principal concern during this period, and the ultimate solution was the geographically dispersed and civilian-based TRICARE network. TRICARE in theory should have been even more attractive to retirees than to active-duty family members, since they were more dispersed geographically and more complicated in their medical needs. TRICARE in practice proved problematic initially, needing considerable legislative support and policy tinkering to work effectively. Issues included negotiating reimbursement fees high enough to attract physicians into the network, reducing copayments and catastrophic caps low enough to out-compete alternatives, accommodating pharmaceutical needs, and maturing the bureaucracy to tolerable levels of impedance. Here the numbers and organization of the retirees proved helpful, both to themselves and to active-duty family members and the Army as a whole. As the Cold War wound down, representatives of the Navy, Marine Corps, Coast Guard, and Air Force equivalents to the Chief of Staff, Army (CSA), Retiree Council began attending its meetings, and vice versa. Whatever their differences with respect to equipment and force structure, they shared a common vision of how service members and their families should be treated—both before and after retirement. Together they represented over two million retirees and with spouses were perhaps double that number. They overlapped heavily with veterans' organizations and were, as we have seen, connected to the influential in other ways. Private organizations took up issues retiree councils raised. The Resolutions Committee of the Association of the United States Army, for example, took information briefings from the Retiree Council and the Army Staff before its own interventions with congressional leaders and committees. Appropriately informed yet private, AUSA and similar organizations from sister services could push for reforms beyond boundaries the administration might have preferred. Old people vote; political leaders know it. Systematic and focused attention, year after year, yielded results. Each session of Congress reported some incremental improvement to TRICARE, most notably with the National Defense Act of Fiscal Year 2001. TRICARE for Life and the TRICARE Senior Pharmacy emerged as viable programs attracting favorable customer comment. A workable retiree dental program emerged as well. Physicians accepted TRICARE in increasing numbers, identifying it as reliable and accommodating, albeit parsimonious. Copayments remained modest, and catastrophic caps were more than halved from an initial $7,500 a year. Pharmaceuticals offered a number of inexpensive options, including drugs by mail. TRICARE as a bureaucracy matured, gaining in efficiency while reducing overhead and relying heavily on the Internet and other digital technologies. Within a decade of its experimental origins in Tidewater Virginia, TRICARE evolved into a viable medical system for an expeditionary Army. It would not have progressed as quickly as it did without the sustained attention of Army retirees and their peers from sister services.[28]

Army retirees protected and improved upon their lot through organization and sustained focus. In doing so they sought not only fairness to themselves, but also to make military service more attractive to potential recruits. This was on the mind of the Army's senior leaders as well. Retirement benefits always numbered among incentives to enlist or reenlist, and sustaining high-quality manpower always numbered among arguments for protecting retirement benefits. Beyond providing examples of comfortable retirement, retirees were encouraged to participate more directly in recruitment. During a dip in accessions, Chief of Staff General Eric K. Shinseki bluntly stated that recruiting was the mission and that everyone was a recruiter. Sustaining communications with retirees became a priority, to lend them currency when helping out. Web sites and digital communications helped immensely, in particular when Army Knowledge Online (AKO) matured as a cyber-universe available to retirees. Exchanges were not always rosy. A few retirees commented to Shinseki that the shift from "Be All You Can Be" to "An Army of One" as a recruiting slogan did not appeal to them. Shinseki retorted that he was not trying to recruit sixty-year-olds, and that "An Army of One" tested well with the youth demographic. His key imperative was to provide enough of a teaser to get interested "youngsters" onto an Army Web site, where well-packaged information capably presented could interest them further. Getting the interested onto a Web site was something retirees could and did do, sometimes having more success with parents than with the prospects themselves. Attributes retirees embodied, such as job security, secure pensions, and reliable health care, tended to impress those with life experience more so than the young. Supportive—or at least nonoppositional—parents could be helpful. Retirees were directly credited with hundreds of accessions and undoubtedly contributed to thousands more. They became eligible for the Recruiting Referral Bonus, although this probably represented their formal acceptance into the recruiting program more so than any particular interest they had in the cash flow. Incremental legislative and policy advances with respect to subjects of retiree interest further strengthened the hands of recruiters. Cases in point included pay raises tied to those of serving soldiers, the working mechanics of the survivor benefits program (SBP), concurrent receipt of retirement and disability pay, combat-related special compensation, transition assistance, and the staffing and training of retirement services offices. Even in death retirees and veterans continued to serve. A military funeral is an impressive event, and military participation in a funeral can lend a sense of purpose and dignity to a life well lived. Army retiree deaths averaged ten thousand a year, and the deaths of veterans

Military funerals honor the dead and inspire the living.

were at least an order of magnitude higher. The Army Staff went to great lengths to cover these funerals and related special requests, leaning heavily on the reserve component as it did so. More than a few wakes and memorial services featured memorabilia from long-ago campaigns. Men who had lived a lifetime doing something else wanted to also be remembered for the valor and service of their youth. Campaign histories and maps provided by the Center of Military History found a place amid family photographs and personal effects. The final departure from a lifetime of service can be both poignant and inspiring.[29]

Families of the Reserve Component

As the Army adapted to post–Cold War circumstances, families of the reserve component shared the concerns of their active-component counterparts, albeit with differences of nuance. Having lived most of their lives outside of an Army framework, they by and large resolved issues with respect to housing and spousal employment independently of anything the Army could or would do for them. Issues with respect to financial security, health care, and child care, on the other hand, tended to morph with mobilization and presented concerns the Army was called upon to address. Information and emotional support proved no less important to families of the reserve component than to those of the active component and demanded initiatives as well. Families of the reserve component faced unique challenges while addressing such issues. Most obviously, they were geographically dispersed. In 1988, for example, the soldiers of an average National Guard battalion lived scattered across a 150-mile radius. Fewer than 150 reported to the average armory, and 4,600 facilities in 2,858 locations sprawled across the country. The situation was much the same for Army Reserve units, and the Individual Ready Reserve, independent of units as an organizing principal, was even more widely scattered. Guardsmen were subject to state as well as federal mobilization and could be called up to deal with a crisis while their families were at risk from the same crisis. Natural disasters could be personal disasters as well as military missions. Years of tiering in the anticipation of national mobilization had relegated the reserve component to something of a "second string" status. Reserve-component families were not much visible to the senior leaders of the Army during the course of the Cold War. Indeed, during that period they were not much visible to the senior leaders of the reserve component either. The shift that transformed the reserve component from strategic reserves in depth to routinely deployed operational forces profoundly affected family life. Let us examine component unique aspects with respect to how the Army handled the financial security, health and child care, information dissemination, and emotional support concerns of reserve-component families in the face of these challenges.[30]

The pursuit of financial security presented complexities. Guardsmen and Reservists with families by and large had civilian careers. For those who were employed, sustaining a relationship with their employer was critical. The deploying spouse wanted to know he or she could again pick up job and career upon returning, and the nondeploying spouse needed that confidence as well. When the issue was two weeks of summer training and reserve-component units were unlikely to deploy short of the "Big One," this was rarely a problem. DESERT STORM and accelerating deployments in its wake raised sufficient resistance from employers for Congress to pass the United Services Employment and Reemployment Act of 1994. In theory this guaranteed a return to previous employment, but ways could be found to evade it if the employer truly lost confidence in the reliability of the employee. The Department of the Army courted major employers nationwide, and the National Guard focused on local employers within states. VIP tours, employer days, symposia, letters, and other outreach efforts proliferated as the service emphasized patriotism, community spirit, government contracting, and the value added to an employee by virtue of military service. Employers were mindful of the law and generally inclined to be supportive but chafed at unpredictability. By the mid-1990s unforeseen deployments often took out employees for nine months, and after 9-11 this number rose to eighteen—twelve months actually deployed and six preparing or returning. With increasing diligence and some success the reserve component committed to programmatic rotation, aspiring to give units five to six years at home for every nine to twelve months deployed. The Army Reserve, for example, reorganized most of its units into ten Army Reserve Expeditionary Packages (AREPs) and then cycled these through levels of readiness. Demands overseas, although high,

Reserve-component soldiers filled a wide range of responsibilities when called on to serve.

stabilized, allowing greater predictability to soldiers and their employers. Given predictability, corporations and large businesses could accommodate five- and six-year cycles into routine personnel turbulence, as could most federal, state, and local government agencies. This was much harder for small businesses and the self-employed. Coworkers and family members could cover in some, but not all, cases. Dentists and physicians running small practices, for example, were likely to lose those practices if deployed for a year. In due course self-selection tilted membership in the Guard and Reserve away from those who could not afford to routinely deploy. This made it even harder to acquire certain specialties, such as medical and dental, but not necessarily harder to acquire manpower overall. By 2000 60 percent of National Guard accessions were first-time, rather than the fifty-fifty split between first-time and prior service previously considered ideal. Presumably the first-timers were younger, with fewer family obligations. Many would be students, to whom educational benefits would appeal and from whom a single deployment could be expected before they left the military for other things. Soldiers would not serve if they could not afford to.[31]

A key consideration with respect to whether reserve-component soldiers with families could afford to serve was how much they were paid. Steady campaigning by the Department of Defense and its supporters had kept military salaries roughly comparable with those of civilian counterparts with equivalent responsibility, education, and experience. This was less true while Army downsizing progressed and the national economy prospered through the mid-1990s, and more true when deployments accelerated and the economy faltered thereafter. After 9-11 Congress was generally receptive to annual pay raises, and deploying soldiers could count on separation pay and hazardous duty pay as well. In addition, enlisted were relieved and officers partially relieved from taxes while deployed, and selective reenlistment bonuses could be handsome. Many found themselves making more money while serving on active duty than they had as civilians, and some much more. Teachers, for example, generally earned more when serving as active-duty soldiers, and certainly the recently unemployed did. Families found themselves measuring risks versus rewards. Some reserve-component soldiers engineered multiple tours by volunteering as individual replacements. As average active-duty stints stretched beyond twelve months, such cost-cutters as the post exchange and commissary became more important to reserve-component families. Even in the Cold War spousal possession of a military identification card had been a bit of a perk. When the sponsor was on active duty and geography permitted, post facilities could be scoured for good deals—perhaps a favorable price on a television or some other major appliance, for example. When active-duty stints stretched to months and years rather than days and weeks, commissary and AAFES benefits could be exploited more systematically. Families living close to major installations could cut some costs as much as 20 to 30 percent, as their active-component counterparts did. Soldiers and families chafed at restrictions that did remain and lobbied for ever greater access to the benefits of military life. In 2003, for example, the law was amended to allow reserve-component soldiers, family members, and retirees with identification cards unlimited access to commissary stores. Robust pay and benefits were of little help if soldiers were not actually paid, of course. There were considerable growing pains in this regard. Automation designed in the 1970s to handle pay for drills and summer camp was overwhelmed by the much larger and more complex demands of mobilization. Special pay had to be entered by hand, as did the transition to an active status. Finance clerks were often themselves recently mobilized and not much more current than the automation that served them. Employers generally cut off pay immediately, whereas it often took several pay cycles—months—to get pay properly flowing to mobilized soldiers. Pay complaints and transactions often required laborious workarounds to bypass the system as originally designed. Fortuitously, reserve-component finance personnel gained increasing experience with and training in these workarounds through the accelerating deployments of the 1990s before being faced with massive deployments after 9-11. Surveys from 2001 through 2004 established that base pay was generally handled satisfactorily but entitlements, particularly those emerging after 9-11, were not. Ironically, overpayments became a significant problem too. Finance personnel worked hard to manually kick in benefits and entitlements for deployed soldiers but were often delayed in terminating them when a soldier returned. Without knowing it, Reservists and Guardsmen could accumulate considerable debt to the government. Forestalling this required careful scrutiny of leave and earnings statements by soldiers and their supervisors. The long-term fix was to replace manual workarounds applied by transient personnel with an overhauled pay system. The Forward Compatible Payroll (FCP) went online in March 2005, comprehensively automating pay and entitlements and eliminating previous workarounds. In 2006 the Defense Integrated Military Human Resources System (DIMHRS) would integrate pay and personnel systems. This meant, for example, that the pay system would automatically take note of such relevant personnel actions as promotion, assignment to an overseas theater, or reassignment from one.[32]

Health care and child care were as big an issue to the families of the reserve component as they were to those of the active component, but these were not much visible to the Cold War Army. When active-duty training averaged two weeks, it made little sense to involve the families in government programs. Whatever arrangements they already had at home or through employers would have to do. The soldiers themselves benefited from annual medical attention when mobilized, although those in the Individual Ready Reserve often went long periods without seeing a military doctor. During DESERT SHIELD/DESERT STORM predeployment screening picked up a sizable catalog of medical issues, especially dental. From that point medical screening became less cursory as a feature of the annual cycle. With respect to families, the ever-increasing frequency and duration of mobilizations made a military connection with respect to health care more feasible. In addition, the maturation of TRICARE offered an alternative that fit in well with the geographical dispersion of Army Reserve and National Guard families. Beginning in 1992 the Army emphasized preenrollment in the Defense Enrollment Eligibility Reporting System (DEERS). This positioned families to apply for entitlements and benefits as their circumstances suggested. Eligibility for TRICARE and its related dental program evolved through complexities, depending on whether the sponsor was not activated, preactivated, activated, or recently inactivated. As TRICARE matured, an activated sponsor and his dependents were eligible for TRICARE without premiums. During preactivation and inactivation coverage could be continued with modest costs. Since preactivation eventually spread to 90 days and postactivation to 180, totals could come to two years of coverage. In due course TRICARE Reserve Select (TRS) emerged, allowing eligible soldiers to buy into programs extending coverage for themselves and their families through periods of preactivation and postactivation as well. This compared favorably with alternatives in many cases and further eroded distinctions that had separated the active and reserve components. Insofar as health care involved child care, the evolution described above benefited adult and child alike. Army child and youth services also evolved to be more accommodating to the reserve component. Families were eligible upon activation, and utilization could make sense if the geography was right or the spouse was visiting the AAFES, commissary, or some other facility. Reserve-component sole parents grew to depend on Army child and youth services as well. In many cases Reservists or Guardsmen backfilled active-component soldiers who had in turn deployed. In these cases the mobilized soldiers benefited from the facilities on the installation that they now manned.[33]

As entitlements and benefits available to the reserve component accumulated, they needed to be communicated to soldiers and their families. Announcements and handouts at drill did not necessarily get back to spouses. By 1988 the National Guard and Army Reserve had formed Family Support

Groups, for about the same reasons that units in the active component had them. During DESERT SHIELD/ DESERT STORM family support liaison officers were deployed to mobilization sites for the first time. These undertook not only to keep soldiers informed, but also to counsel spouses with respect to services and benefits. The link was considered crucial since the soldier could be largely out of communication once deployed, and the spouse would be running the household. Feedback with respect to Family Support Groups from DESERT SHIELD/DESERT STORM within the reserve component paralleled that within the active component. This resulted in reform, renewed emphasis, increased involvement in such training programs as AFTB and later SOLD, and the change in philosophy discussed previously that redesignated Family Support Groups as Family Readiness Groups. Family Readiness Groups

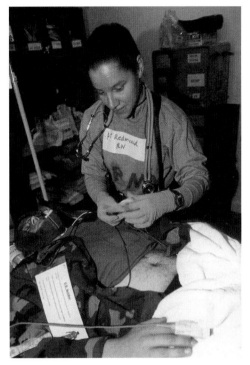

Reserve-component soldiers with special skills could deploy as individuals to join units.

within the reserve component faced additional challenges, however. We have already discussed geographical dispersal. In addition, there was the greater likelihood that soldiers of the reserve component would deploy to headquarters and units they had not previously trained in. This meant the spouse would be as unfamiliar with the Family Readiness Group as the sponsor was with the unit. This phenomenon resulted in part from the improvisation that went into designing each unique major headquarters overseas and in part from turbulence when bringing understrength units up to strength and compensating for the nondeployable. Deployment as an individual was intrinsic in service as an Individual Ready Reserve (IRR), Individual Mobilization Augmentee (IMA), or in a United States Army Reserve Command (USARC) Augmentation Unit (UAU). Family Readiness Groups, already struggling with geographical separation, scrambled to take such new arrivals into the fold. Leadership proved critical. Diligent work through telephone trees and e-mail got news and information out, and increased attention at mobilization sites and in other venues ensured that counseling with respect to benefits and other assets was available. Difficulty getting people together degraded some of the social purposes served by Family Readiness Groups. The informal coffee klatch atmosphere of most Family Readiness Group get-togethers, and the frequency with which they occurred, proved important to spousal team

381

building. Given geographical dispersal to start with, and the likelihood of fillers from even further afield, physically bringing Family Readiness Groups together was more challenging to the Reserve than to the active component. The National Guard and Army Reserve leaned heavily on the Web to get their messages out, establishing "virtual" Family Readiness Groups to reach all of the eligible and provide at least some correspondence and interaction. Topics broadened to include child and youth services, volunteer options, and training opportunities—typically not constituent to Family Readiness Groups, although certainly among Army family programs. In 2002 the Army Reserve stood up the IRR/IMA/UAU Family Program Office. This specifically addressed the needs of those who customarily mobilized as individuals. The reserve component evolved methods to disseminate information to families and to provide physical and emotional support that was understandably different than that of the active component.[34]

Conclusions

From 1989 through 2005 the Army as an institution advanced considerably with respect to family support appropriate to its new expeditionary posture. While doing so, it broadened in focus from families with children to address spouses, parents, and retirees as well. The families of the reserve component became actively involved. The first step was to close out most overseas stations and to convert stateside mega-posts into ever-ready deployment platforms. Family housing became increasingly privatized, and assignment and pay policies encouraged families to buy their own homes. After a period of turbulence AAFES and the commissary system regained their footing, saving Army families considerable money and plowing funds back into morale, welfare, and recreation services. These services included child care and youth services, of which the former became a national standard and the latter a useful supplement to indigenous school and community activities. Consciousness of and attention to exceptional family members became routine and systematic. Health care morphed from a post-centric model to a diffuse network of military and civilian care providers suitable for geographically dispersed populations. TRICARE ultimately proved suitable for active-component, reserve-component, and retiree families alike. Spousal employment emerged as an issue to which the Army gave serious attention, with some success. Other mechanisms to ensure family financial security evolved as well. Family Support Groups evolved into Family Readiness Groups and reinforced physical and emotional well-being while furthering a long-standing volunteer spirit. Parents were drawn in as never before, drawing support and information from Family Readiness Groups and directly assisting their deployed offspring. Retirees, who now outnumbered those actively serving, continued to serve as counselors, contractors, and advocates and provided persuasive examples of fruitful military careers to those who might consider one. Families of the reserve component worked out their own unique solutions with respect to financial security, health care, child care, information dissemination, and emotional support in the face of geographical dispersal, elongated force generation cycles, and civilian careers.

Home stationing with respect to the active component and having a home with respect to the reserve component lent domestic stability to the platforms from which the expeditionary Army was launched. This evolution took place in the context of accelerating deployments, and then sustained combat. Families faced and dealt with all the rigors of deployment, separation, combat, and reintegration. Some faced wounds, and some faced death. Sustaining the force in the face of hardship and challenge drew upon the collaboration of the Army, Army families, parents, and retirees, as well as of the soldiers actually deployed. An underlying premise was to keep the soldier serving because of confidence that his or her family—as well as country—was better off for his or her having done so.

Notes

[1] General Eric K. Shinseki, *The Army Family: A White Paper* (Washington DC: Center of Military History, 2003), 1–19; General John A. Wickham Jr., *The Army Family* (Washington DC: Department of the Army, 1983).

[2] Vincent H. Demma, *Department of the Army Historical Summary, Fiscal Year 1989* (Washington DC: Center of Military History, 1998), 109–36, 161–81; Shinseki; Wickham; General Crosbie E. Saint, "Changes Pose Challenges for Army Forces, Europe," *Army 1988–1989 Green Book: The Year of Training*, October 1989, 56–70; Author's personal experience from twelve years' military service in Europe.

[3] Shinseki; Army Regulation 210–20, *Master Planning for Army Installations* (Washington DC: Department of the Army, 1992); *Families and Mission: A Review of the Effects of Family Factors on Army Attrition, Retention and Readiness* (Washington DC: Rand Arroyo, 1987); *The Reciprocal Nature of Work and Family: Spouse's Perception of the Army/Family Interface and Its Impact on Soldier Retention* (Washington DC: Walter Reed Army Institute of Research, 1989); *Survey of Army Families I* (Washington DC: Army Research Institute, 1987).

[4] Shinseki, 1–19, 33–57; Demma, 109–36, 161–81; William Joe Webb et al., *Department of the Army Historical Summary, Fiscal Years 1990–1991* (Washington DC: Center of Military History, 1997), 45–47; L. Martin Kaplan, *Department of the Army Historical Summary, Fiscal Year 1994* (Washington DC: Center of Military History, 2000), 118–19; Connie L. Reeves, *Department of the Army Historical Summary, Fiscal Year 1996* (Washington DC: Center of Military History, 2002), 125–27; Jeffery A. Charlston, *Department of the Army Historical Summary, Fiscal Year 1999* (Washington DC: Center of Military History, 2006), 108–09; *MWR Annual Report: Fiscal Year 1994* (Arlington, Virginia: Policy and Plans Directorate, U.S. Army Community and Family Support Center, 1995); *MWR Annual Report: Fiscal Year 1995* (Arlington, Virginia: Policy and Plans Directorate, U.S. Army Community and Family Support Center, 1996); *MWR Annual Report: Fiscal Year 1996* (Arlington, Virginia: Strategic Planning and Policy Directorate, U.S. Army Community and Family Support Center, 1997); *MWR Fiscal Year 1999 Annual Report* (Arlington, Virginia: U.S. Army Community and Family Support Center, 2000); Bradford Booth, Mady W. Segal, and D. Bruce Bell, *What We Know About Army Families: 2007 Update* (Washington DC: Caliber, 2007); Public Law 104–106, *The National Defense Authorization Act for Fiscal Year 1996* (Washington DC: 104th Congress, 1996); Lieutenant General Robert Wilson, "Installations and Families: Restoring the Balance, *Army* (April 2008): 19–27; Rick Maze, "Congress' Unfinished Business: 6 Benefits Lawmakers Need to Fix Right Now," *Army Times*, 1 June 2009, 14–15; Brendan McGarry, "Pay Atlas: Where Your Paycheck Goes Furthest–and Where It Comes Up Short," *Army Times*, 7 September 2009, 20–22; Rick Maze, "Path to Better BAH," *Army Times*, 6 July 2009, 8.

[5] Roberto Salas, *An Analysis of AAFES and Its Relevance to the Future of the Army and Air Force* (Fort Leavenworth, Kansas: Command and General Staff College Master of Military Arts and Science, 2009), 11–48; Webb et al., *Department of the Army Historical Summary, Fiscal Years 1990–1991*, 47–49, 59–60; Stephen E. Everett and L. Martin Kaplan, *Department of the Army Historical Summary, Fiscal Year 1993* (Washington DC: Center of Military History, 2002), 99, 110; Kaplan, 111–13, 120–21; Stephen L. Y. Gammons and William M. Donnelly, *Department of the Army Historical Summary, Fiscal Year 1995* (Washington DC: Center of Military History, 2004), 81, 89;

MWR Annual Report: Fiscal Year 1994; *MWR Fiscal Year Annual Report: Fiscal Year 1995*; Charlston, 101–02, 111.

[6] Shinseki, 1–19; Lizette Alvarez, "Wartime Soldier, Conflicted Mom: Overseas and Back Home, Torn Between Service and Family," *New York Times,* 27 September 2009, 1, 22; Demma, 109–36, 161–81; Webb et al., *Department of the Army Historical Summary, Fiscal Years 1990–1991,* 45–47; Gail L. Zellman and Anne Johansen, *Examining the Implementation and Outcomes of the Military Child Care Act of 1989* (Santa Monica, California: RAND National Security Research Division, 1998); Dwight D. Oland and David W. Hogan Jr., *Department of the Army Historical Summary, Fiscal Year 1992* (Washington DC: Center of Military History, 2001), 165–67; Reeves, 125–27; *MWR Annual Report: Fiscal Year 1996*; Army Regulation 600–20, *Army Command Policy* (Washington DC: Department of the Army, 2008); "Army MWR: Child, Youth and School Services," http://www.armymwr.com/portal/family/childandyouth, accessed 8 October 2009; *Be All That We Can Be: Lessons from the Military for Improving Our Nation's Child Care System* (Washington DC: National Women's Law Center, 2004).

[7] Shinseki, 8, 17, 27–32; Department of Defense Instruction 1015.10, *Programs for Military Morale Recreation and Welfare (MWR)* (Washington DC: Government Printing Office, 2007); Demma, 109, 136, 161–81; Webb et al., *Department of the Army Historical Summary, Fiscal Years 1990–1991,* 45–47; Zellman and Johansen; Everett and Kaplan, 99, 110; Gammons and Donnelly, 81–83; Reeves, 125–27; *MWR Annual Report: Fiscal Year 1994*; *MWR Annual Report: Fiscal Year 1995*; Charlston, 101–02, 111; Karen Jowers, "DoDEA Students Score High in Academic Assessment," *Army Times*, 28 September 2009, 13; Karen Jowers and Rick Maze, "Gates Agrees to Study Opening More DoD Schools," *Army Times*, 21 September 2009, 16; "Army MWR: CYS System of Care," http://www.armymwr.com/portal/family/childandyouth, accessed 12 October 2009; E-mail, Ms. Mary Jo Reimer to Brigadier General (USA, Ret.) John S. Brown, sub: John–Some Things on the Army Teen Panel, 27 November 2009, Historians Files, CMH; Notes, Ms. Patty Shinseki to Brigadier General (USA, Ret.) John S. Brown, on draft Chapter 8 Manuscript, 21 April 2010, Historians Files, CMH.

[8] Public Law 94–142, *Education for All Handicapped Children Act* (Washington DC: United States Congress, 1975); Mary Ellen Condon-Rall, *Department of the Army Historical Summary, Fiscal Year 1983* (Washington DC: Center of Military History, 1990), 75–76; Terrence J. Gough, *Department of the Army Historical Summary, Fiscal Year 1986* (Washington DC: Department of the Army, 1995), 21–25; *Performance Report . . . Community and Family Programs Surging Ahead* (Arlington, Virginia: U.S. Army Community and Family Support Center, 1987); Demma, 171–78; Shinseki, 18; Army Regulation 608–75, *Exceptional Family Member Program* (Washington DC: Department of the Army, 2006).

[9] Shinseki, 3–32; Demma, 166–71; Webb et al., *Department of the Army Historical Summary, Fiscal Years 1990–1991,* 52–53; Oland and Hogan, 170–75; Kaplan, 114–17; Charlston, 103–06; *MWR Fiscal Year 1999 Annual Report*; Lieutenant General Ronald R. Blanck, "Healthy Soldiers Are the Army's Best Credentials," *Army 1997–1998 Green Book*, October 1997, 145–49; Lieutenant General Ronald R. Blanck, "The Army Medical Department: On Call for the 21st Century," *Army 1999–2000 Green Book*, October 1999, 171–75; Lieutenant General James B. Peake, "We Will Always Be There—Caring Beyond the Call of Duty," *Army 2001–2002 Green Book*, October 2001, 151–56; Lieutenant General James B. Peake, "Delivering Quality Health Care to Soldiers and Their Families," *Army 2002–2003 Green Book*, October 2002, 175–80; Major General Kevin C. Kiley, "Caring for Soldiers in War and Peace," *Army 2004–*

2005 Green Book, October 2004, 163–68; Lieutenant General Kevin C. Kiley, "Preserving Soldier's Lives and Health—Anytime, Anywhere," *Army 2005–2006 Green Book*, October 2005, 121–24; *Survey of Army Families 1991* (Arlington, Virginia: United States Army Research Institute for the Behavioral and Social Sciences, 1991); *Survey of Army Families 2001* (Arlington, Virginia: United States Army Research Institute for the Behavioral and Social Sciences, 2001); *TRICARE Prime Handbook* (Phoenix, Arizona: TriWest Healthcare Alliance, 2005); "History of TRICARE," http://www.tricare.mil, accessed 26 October 2009.

[10] Shinseki, 3–32; Demma, 166–71; Webb et al., *Department of the Army Historical Summary, Fiscal Years 1990–1991,* 52–53; Oland and Hogan, 170–75; Kaplan, 114–17; *MWR Annual Report: Fiscal Year 1994*; Charlston, 103–06; *MWR Fiscal Year 1999 Annual Report*; Maze, "Congress' Unfinished Business," 14–15; "Strong Families Critical for Army," *AUSA News,* November 2008, 18; Karen Jowers, "Study Shows Deployments Take Toll on Children," *Army Times*, 20 July 2009, 8; Alvarez, 1, 22; Kelly Kennedy, "Daddy ? Are You OK? Post-Traumatic Stress Disorder Wrenches a Service Member's Heart and Home," *Army Times,* 21 September 2009, 10–11; Dr. Steven J. Cozza, *Children and Families of Combat Veterans,* Center for the Study of Traumatic Stress (http://www.centerforthestudyoftraumaticstress.org), accessed 18 October 2010; Author's personal experience as an Army dependent and then Army officer, 1949–2005.

[11] Army Regulation 600–20, *Army Command Policy*, 2008; Shinseki, 7–32, app. 1; Alvarez, 1, 22; Rick Maze, "Stretched and Stressed, Leaders' Spouses: Families Need Help Now," *Army Times,* 15 June 2009, 52; Department of the Army Form 5305, *Family Care Plan* (Washington DC: Department of the Army, 2005); "Helping Spouses, Children Cope in Wartime," *AUSA News,* January 2008, 22; Gina Cavallaro, "Program Helps Troops, Families Prepare for Possible Casualties," *Army Times*, 23 February 2009, 18–19; Jowers, "Study Shows Deployments Take Toll on Children," 8; Karen Jowers, "Program Aims to Help Kids Adapt to Service Members' Return," *Army Times,* 14 September 2009, 10; Notes, Ms. Patty Shinseki to Brigadier General (USA, Ret.) John S. Brown, on draft Chapter 8 Manuscript, 21 April 2010.

[12] Demma, 166–71; Shinseki, 7–25; Deirdre E. Painter, "The Distaff Factor: Attitudinal Change and Continuity Through Four Generations of Army Wives," Student thesis, United States Military Academy, 3 May 1984, 1–25.

[13] Shinseki, 7–25; William J. Webb, *Department of the Army Historical Summary, Fiscal Year 1988* (Washington DC: Center of Military History, 1993), 28–33; Demma, 166–71; Webb et al., *Department of the Army Historical Summary, Fiscal Years 1990–1991,* 52–53; Charlston, 103–06; *MWR Fiscal Year 1999 Annual Report; What We Know About Army Families* (Arlington, Virginia: Army Research Institute for the Behavioral and Social Sciences, 1993); *What We Know About Army Families: 2007 Update*; *The Reciprocal Nature of Work and Family*; *Survey of Army Families 1995* (Arlington, Virginia: Army Research Institute for the Behavioral and Social Sciences, 1995); *Survey of Army Families 2000* (Arlington, Virginia: Army Research Institute for the Behavioral and Social Sciences, 2000); Sylvia E. J. Kidd, "Staying on Top of Army Family Issues," *AUSA News*, June 2009, 28–29; Military Spouse Career Center Home Page, http://www.military.com/spouse, accessed 2 November 2009; Army One Source: Army Spouse Employment Partnership, http://www.myarmyonesource.com, accessed 2 November 2009; Karen Jowers, "Spouses Find Rules for Unemployment Cash a Puzzle," *Army Times*, 20 April 2009, 25.

[14] Shinseki, 7–25; Webb, *Department of the Army Historical Summary, Fiscal Year 1988,* 28–33; *How to Support Army Families During Overseas Deployments: A Sourcebook for Service Providers* (Arlington, Virginia: Army Research Institute for the

Behavioral and Social Sciences, 1996); *SGLI/VGLI Handbook* (Washington DC: Veterans Benefits Association, 2002); "SGLI" on Department of Veterans Affairs Web site, http://www.insurance.va.gov, accessed 3 November 2009; *Department of Defense Financial Management Regulation* (Washington DC: Department of the Army, 2009), vol. 7A, ch.10; "Combat Pay (Imminent Danger Pay)," in http://www.usmilitaryabout. com, accessed 3 November 2009; Rick Maze, "The Changing Face of Special Pay," *Army Times,* 30 April 2007, 14–15; Jim Tice, "BEAR Program Options Decrease," *Army Times,* 9 March 2009, 20; Karen Jowers, "Emergency Aid: Services' Relief Societies Mostly Offer No-Interest Loans," *Army Times*, 9 March 2009, 10–12; Rick Maze, "Family Food Aid Would Rise Under Senate Plan," *Army Times*, 20 July 2009, 9; Jowers, "Spouses Find Rules for Unemployment Cash a Puzzle," 25.

[15] Painter, 1–25; Shinseki, 7–32; Reeves, 119–23; *MWR Annual Report: Fiscal Year 1996*; "Building Strong and Ready Army Families," http://www.army.mil, accessed 4 November 2009; Victoria Niederhauser, Jay Maddock, Francine Ledoux, and Martin Arnold, "Building Strong and Ready Army Families: A Multi-Risk Health Reduction Pilot Survey," *Military Medicine* 170 (2005): 227–33; *Spring 2000 Sample Survey of Army Families* (Arlington, Virginia: Army Research Institute of the Behavioral and Social Sciences, 2005); *What We Know About Army Families: 2007 Update*; Army Regulation 608–18, *The Army Family Advocacy Program* (Washington DC: Department of the Army, 2006); Demma, 175–76; *Defense Force Management: Department of Defense Policy on Homosexuality* (Washington DC: Government Accounting Office, 1992); Kyle Dropp and Jon Cohen, "Acceptance of Gay People in Military Grows Dramatically," *Washington Post,* 19 July 2009, 1.

[16] Shinseki, 7–25; Reeves, 122; *MWR Annual Report: Fiscal Year 1996;* Charlston, 101–03; *MWR Fiscal Year 1999 Annual Report*; Brian F. Waters, *Family Support Groups: Making the Most of a Combat Multiplier* (Fort Leavenworth, Kansas: Command and General Staff College Master of Military Arts and Science, 1994), 1–47; Mandy W. Segal and Jesse J. Harris, *What We Know About Army Families* (Alexandria, Virginia: United States Army Research Institute of the Behavioral and Social Sciences, 1993); *What We Know About Army Families: 2007 Update*; Audrey M. Burnam et al., *Army Families and Soldier Readiness* (Santa Monica, California: RAND, 1992); *Survey of Army Families, 2001* (Alexandria, Virginia: United States Army Research Institute of the Behavioral and Social Sciences, 2001); United States Army, *Looking Back: Family Support Group Lessons Learned During DESERT SHIELD/ DESERT STORM* (Carlisle Barracks, Pennsylvania: United States Army War College, 1993); Department of the Army Pamphlet 608–47, *A Guide to the Establishment of Family Support Groups* (Washington DC: Department of the Army, 1993); Comments of Ms. Traci Cook and Ms. Rose Smyth, in "Commander-FRG Team Leaders," *Army* (November 2007): 68, 70.

[17] Shinseki, 7–27; Gammons and Donnelly, 81–82; Waters, 1–47; Painter, 1–25; Sheila Gibbons, "Commanders Wives," *Ladycom,* June 1984, 51–58, 63–65, 70; Clella R. Robbins, *Army Woman's Handbook* (New York: McGraw Book Company, 1942); Helen Westpheling, *Army Lady Today* (Charlotte, North Carolina: Heritage House, 1959); *The Reciprocal Nature of Work and Family*; *Evaluation of Army Family Team Building (AFTB)* (Fairfax, Virginia: Caliber Associates, 2002); Comments of Ms. Barbie Peppie, in "Commander-FRG Team Leaders," *Army* (November 2007): 67–68; *Army Commander's Guide to Family Readiness Group Operations* (Washington DC: United States Army Community and Family Support Center, 2005).

[18] Florence R. Rosenberg, *Survey of Army Families 1991: A Summary of Results* (Washington DC: Walter Reed Army Institute of Research, 1991); *What We Know*

About Army Families: 2007 Update; Waters, 1–47: Shinseki, 7–25; Joel M. Teitelbaum, *Army Supports to Prevent and Mitigate Family Dysfunction During Military Combat Operations* (Washington DC: American Psychological Association–National Institute for Occupational Safety and Health Conference, 1992); Rick Maze, "Volunteer Help Favored by Families During War," *Air Force Times,* 4 November 1991, 5; "Operation Ready Smart Book," from http://www.armyfrg.org, accessed 11 November 2009; Gina Cavallaro, "Program Helps Troops, Families Prepare for Possible Casualties," *Army Times*, 23 February 2009, 18–19: Kelly Kennedy, "Daddy? Are You OK?" *Army Times*, 21 September 2009, 10–12; Notes, Ms. Patty Shinseki to Brigadier General (USA, Ret.) John S. Brown, on draft Chapter 8 Manuscript, 21 April 2010; Briefing, Department of the Army, "ARMY SOLD XXI: Spouse Orientation and Development for the 21st Century," August 2002, Historians Files, CMH; Michael Moss and Ray Rivera, "At Fort Hood, Some Violence is Too Familiar," *New York Times*, 10 November 2009, 1, 22.

[19] Shinseki, 1–12, 27–60; TRADOC Regulation 350–6, *Enlisted Initial Entry Training (IET) Policies and Administration* (Fort Monroe, Virginia: United States Army Training and Doctrine Command, 2005); *VA Life Insurance Programs for Veterans and Servicemembers* (Philadelphia, Pennsylvania: Department of Veterans Affairs, 2009); A. O. Scott, "Delivering Bad News and Truths About War," *New York Times,* 12 November 2009, 1, 11; Mike Link and Kate Crowley, *Grandparents Colorado Style: Places to Go and Wisdom to Share* (Cambridge, Minnesota: Adventure Publications, Inc., 2009), 6–11.

[20] Daniel Vandergriff, *Manning the Future Legions of the United States* (London, Praeger Security International, 2008); "Ask Sergeant Star," http://www.goarmy.com, accessed 21 November, 2009; "Army Career Training," http://www.goarmyparents.com, accessed 21 November 2009; Army Senior Staff Council Meeting notes, 7 July 1999, Historian's Files, CMH; Army General Staff Council Meeting notes 21 July 1999, Historians Files, CMH; Army General Staff Council Meeting notes, 23 August 1999, Historians Files, CMH; Army General Staff Council Meeting notes, 13 September 1999, Historians Files, CMH; Army General Staff Council Meeting notes, 16 March 2000, Historians Files, CMH; Army General Staff Council Meeting notes, 2 August 2000, Historians Files, CMH; Army General Staff Council Meeting notes, 8 January 2001, Historians Files, CMH; Army General Staff Council Meeting notes, 5 March 2001, Historians Files, CMH; Army General Staff Council Meeting notes, 9 July 2001, Historians Files, CMH; "Retention Pressures," *Army Times,* 8 December 2008, 15.

[21] Shinseki, 7–25; Charlston, 101–03; *MWR Fiscal Year 1999 Annual Report*; Waters, 1–47; Segal and Harris; *What We Know About Army Families: 2007 Update*; *Army Commander's Guide to Family Readiness Group Operations*; Teitelbaum; Vicki Cody, *Your Soldier, Your Army: A Parent's Guide* (Arlington, Virginia: Association of the United States Army, 2005).

[22] Shinseki, 7–22; Cody, 1–28; *Legal Assistance Handbook* (Fort Gordon, Georgia: U.S. Army Signal Center and Fort Gordon, 2009); Title 10, United States Code, Section 1044a; Army Regulation 220–10, *Preparation for Overseas Movement of Units* (Washington DC: Department of the Army, 2004); Army Regulation 350–9, *Overseas Deployment Training* (Washington DC: Department of the Army, 2004); Army General Staff Council Meeting notes, 9 July 2001, Historians Files, CMH; Army General Staff Council Meeting notes, 25 November 2002, Historians Files, CMH; Army Regulation 600–20, *Army Command Policy*, 2008; Alvarez, 1, 22; Maze, "Stretched and Stressed, Leaders' Spouses," 52; Department of the Army Form 5305, *Family Care Plan.*

[23] Shinseki, 7–22; Cody, 6–51; Todd S. Brown, *Battleground Iraq: Journal of a Company Commander* (Washington DC: Center of Military History, 2007), 59–73, 220–29; Ben Shepherd, *A War of Nerves: Soldiers and Psychiatrists in the Twentieth Century* (Boston: Harvard University Press, 2001); Alvarez, 1, 22; "Army Families: Strength Behind the Soldier," *AUSA News*, November 2009, 20; Alex Witchel, "Confessions of a Military Wife," *New York Times Magazine,* 6 November 2005, 62–67; Trista Talton, "What Means the Most," *Army Times*, 14 September 2009, 31; Kidd, 28; Author's personal experience, both as a deployed soldier with parents and as the parent of a deployed soldier.

[24] Army Regulation 600–8–1, *United States Army Casualty Program* (Washington DC: Department of the Army, 2007); *Casualty Notification Guide for the Casualty Notification Officer* (Fort Gordon, Georgia: Military Personnel Services Division, U.S. Army Signal Center and Fort Gordon, 2002); Cody, 14–51; "Fisher House CEO to Receive Marshall Medal," *AUSA News,* October 2009, 2; Kiley, "Preserving Soldiers' Life and Health—Anytime, Anywhere," 121–24; Army Vice Chief of Staff of the Army Council Meeting notes, 13 April 2000, Historians Files, CMH; Army General Staff Council Meeting notes, 9 July 2001; Army General Staff Council Meeting notes, 28 January 2002, Historians Files, CMH; Rick Maze, "No Help for Wounded Soldier's Mom, She Says," *Army Times,* 28 September 2009, 10; William H. McMichael, "Obama: Changing VA's Mission Could Take Years," *Army Times*, 17 August 2009, 4.

[25] Demma, 131–32; Army General Staff Council Meeting notes, 9 November 1999, Historians Files, CMH; "About Us," Military Officers Association of America, http://www.moaa.org, accessed 25 November 2009; "Association of the United States Army Officers and Council of Trustees," *Army 1994–1995 Green Book*, October 1994, 320; "Army Echoes," http://www.armyg1.army.mil/rso/echoes, accessed 25 November 2009; Lieutenant General Ellis D. Parker and Sergeant Major of the Army Richard A. Kidd, "A Vital Network to Champion Retiree Issues," *Army 1998–1999 Green Book*, October 1998, 189–92.

[26] "A Continuing Inspiration," *Army 1994–1995 Green Book*, October 1994, 5; Everett and Kaplan, 31–38; Gammons and Donnelly, 33–36; Army General Staff Council Meeting notes, 21 July 2003, Historians Files, CMH; Army General Staff Council Meeting notes, 1 April 2002, Historians Files, CMH; Public Law 99–143, *The Department of Defense Reorganization Act of 1986*; James R. Lochner III, *Victory on the Potomac: The Goldwater-Nichols Act Unifies the Pentagon* (College Station, Texas: Texas A&M University Press, 2002); Mark D. Sherry, *The Army Command Post and Defense Reshaping, 1987–1997* (Washington DC: Center of Military History, 2009); Army Senior Leader Update Briefing, "Precision Strike: A Unique American Military Advantage . . . but with Limitations," 14 August 2001, Historians Files, CMH; Army Senior Leader Update Briefing, "The Army Quadrennial Defense Review," 11 July 2000, Historians Files, CMH; General Gordon R. Sullivan, "Relevant and Ready: AUSA Supports Soldiers and Families," *Army 2006–2007 Green Book*, October 2006, 9; "AUSA Sustaining Membership Program," http://www.ausa.org, accessed 25 November 2009; Briefing, Army General Staff, "Army Strategic Communications, America's Army: One Team, One Fight, One Future," 14 January 1999, Historians Files, CMH; David Barstow, "One Man's Military-Industrial-Media Complex," *New York Times*, 30 November 2008, 1, 26–27.

[27] "Advertisers in this Issue," *Army 2005–2006 Green Book*, October 2005, 369; Mary L. Haynes, *Department of the Army Historical Summary, Fiscal Year 1987* (Washington DC: Center of Military History, 1995), 57–58; Charlston, 3–13, 32–35, 101–03, 108–09; Interv with A. David Mills, Principal Deputy for Logistics, in *Reflections of Senior Army Material Command Officials, Volume II* (Fort Belvoir,

Virginia: U.S. Army Material Command Historical Office, 2006), 147–66; Army General Staff Council Meeting notes, 10 April 2000, Historians Files, CMH; Army General Staff Council Meeting notes, 5 March 2001; Army General Staff Council Meeting notes, 1 April 2002; Deborah D. Avant, *The Market for Force: The Consequences of Privatizing Security* (New York: Cambridge University Press, 2005); Briefing, "The Role of BAL in Global Industry," Bethesda, Maryland, Burdeshaw Associates Ltd, 1999; "AUSA Sustaining Membership Program"; Kaplan, 120; "Defense Military Pay Office–National Capital Region, Retirement Information Guide" (Fort Myer, Virginia: Defense Military Pay Office, 2004); Author's notes from his own retirement transition workshop, June 2004, Historians Files, CMH.

[28] Shinseki, 3–32; Peake, "Delivering Quality Health Care to Soldiers and Their Families," 175–80; Lieutenant General John A. Dubia and Sergeant Major of the Army Robert E. Hall, "Top Retiree Issues: Health Care, Communications and Education," *Army 2005–2006 Green Book*, October 2005, 219–22; Army General Staff Council Meeting notes, 19 July 1999, Historians Files, CMH; McMichael, 10; *TRICARE Prime Handbook*; "History of TRICARE"; Parker and Kidd, "A Vital Network to Champion Retiree Issues," 189–92; Lieutenant General Ellis D. Parker and Sergeant Major of the Army Richard A. Kidd, "Tackling the Tough Issues That Retired Soldiers Face," *Army 1999–2000 Green Book*, October 1999, 203–05; Army General Staff Council Meeting notes, 16 March 2000; Army General Staff Council Meeting notes, 6 August 2002, Historians Files, CMH; Lieutenant General John A. Dubia and Sergeant Major of the Army Richard A. Kidd, "Retired but Still Serving and Focused on Health Care Issues," *Army 2001–2002 Green Book*, October 2001, 185–88; Lieutenant General John A. Dubia and Sergeant Major of the Army Robert E. Hall, "CSA Retiree Council Focuses on Health Care and Communication," *Army 2003–2004 Green Book*, October 2003, 213–16.

[29] Army General Staff Council Meeting notes, 17 April 2000, Historians Files, CMH; Army General Staff Council Meeting notes, 7 May 2001, Historians Files, CMH; Army General Staff Council Meeting notes, 23 July 2001, Historians Files, CMH; Army General Staff Council Meeting notes, 27 August 2001, Historians Files, CMH; "Careers and Jobs," http://www.goarmy.com, accessed 1 December 2009; Parker and Kidd, "A Vital Network to Champion Retiree Issues," 189–92; Lieutenant General John A. Dubia and Sergeant Major of the Army Richard A. Kidd, "The Chief's Retiree Council: Still Serving" *Army 2000–2001 Green Book*, October 2000, 199–202; Army General Staff Council Meeting notes, 17 April 2000; Army General Staff Council Meeting notes, 30 July 2001, Historians Files, CMH; Army General Staff Council Meeting notes, 15 October 2002, Historians Files, CMH; Lieutenant General John A. Dubia and Sergeant Major of the Army Robert E. Hall, "Once a Soldier Always a Soldier," *Army 2004–2005 Green Book*, October 2004, 205–08; Lieutenant General Frederick E. Vollrath and Sergeant Major of the Army Jack L. Tilley, "CSA Retiree Council Promotes Strategic Communication, Health Care," *Army 2007–2008 Green Book*, October 2007, 249–51; Army General Staff Council Meeting notes, 9 November 1999; Army General Staff Council Meeting notes, 30 July 2001; Army General Staff Council Meeting notes, 3 January 2000, Historians Files, CMH; Army General Staff Council Meeting notes,10 July 2000, Historians Files, CMH; Army General Staff Council Meeting notes, 28 October 2002, Historians Files, CMH; Army Regulation 600–8–7, *Retirement Services Program* (Washington DC: Department of the Army, 2008); Department of Defense Directive 1300.15, Military Funeral Support, 2007.

[30] Shinseki, 7–25, 34–55; Major General Donald Burdick, "The Guard: America's Army on Call," *Army 1988–1989 Green Book*, October 1988, 124–32; Michael D.

Doubler, *I Am the Guard: A History of the Army National Guard 1636–2000* (Washington DC: Department of the Army, 2001), 301–68; James T. Currie and Richard B. Crossland, *Twice the Citizen: A History of the United States Army Reserve 1908–1995* (Washington DC: Department of the Army, 1997), 343–82, 475–580.

[31] Ibid.; *United Services Employment and Reemployment Rights Act*, Title 38, United States Code, Sections 4301–4333; Army General Staff Council Meeting notes, 24 April 2000, Historians Files, CMH; Army General Staff Council Meeting notes, 3 May 2000, Historians Files, CMH; Major General Roger C. Schultz, "The National Guard's Secret to Success," *Army 1998–1999 Green Book*, October 1998, 95–100; Army General Staff Council Meeting notes, 2 January 2002, Historians Files, CMH; Army General Staff Council Meeting notes, 28 January 2002; Lieutenant James R. Helmly, "Profound Change While Fighting the War," *Army 2004–2005 Green Book*, October 2004, 103–14.

[32] Doubler, 301–68; Currie and Crossland, 475–580; Burdick, 124–32; Major General Max Baratz, "A Restructured Army Reserve," *Army 1996–1997 Green Book*, October 1996, 97–107; Army General Staff Council Meeting notes, 3 January 2000; Army General Staff Council Meeting notes, 3 May 2000; Helmly, 103–14; Army General Staff Council Meeting notes, 28 January 2002; Joe Burlas, "More Fixes to Reserve Pay Issues on the Way for Mobilized Soldiers," *Armywide News,* 22 October 2004; "Reserve Pay and Benefits," http://www.army.com, accessed 22 December 2009.

[33] Doubler, 301–68; Currie and Crossland, 475–580; Major General William F. Ward Jr., "Top-Notch Training and Equipment Raise Reserve Readiness Levels," *Army 1989–1990 Green Book*, October 1989, 100–107; Major General Roger W. Sandler, "Reserve: Finding Steel as It Slims, Reshapes," *Army 1992–1993 Green Book*, October 1992, 122–29; Army General Staff Council Meeting notes, 16 March 2000; Army General Staff Council Meeting notes, 6 August 2002; Lieutenant General Roger C. Schultz, "The Army National Guard: Ready to Serve Our Nation," *Army 2003–2004 Green Book*, October 2004, 97–102; "TRICARE: Choices for the National Guard and Reserve," http://www.tricare.mil, accessed 21 December 2009.

[34] Shinseki, 7–32; Burdick, 124–32; Major General William F. Ward Jr., "Performance in Panama Underscores Readiness," *Army 1990–1991 Green Book*, October 1990, 104–13; Major General Robert W. Sandler, "When the Call Came Reserve Was Ready," *Army 1991 Green Book*, October 1991, 100–106; Sandler, "Reserve: Finding Steel as It Slims, Reshapes," 122–29; Schultz, 107–13; Army General Staff Council Meeting notes, 23 October 2001, Historians Files, CMH; Army General Staff Council Meeting notes, 25 October 2002, Historians Files, CMH.

CHAPTER 9

The "Transformed" Army in Action

Generals Vuono, Sullivan, Reimer, and Shinseki, as we have seen, envisioned Army transformation as an extended project. A driving force was money; there was only so much to invest in the indeterminate intermediate and distant futures. With General Schoomaker the future war became the present one, money flowed, and the focus of transformation narrowed while its pace increased. The Army that fought in Iraq, Afghanistan, and elsewhere during the Global War on Terrorism was appreciably different than that of the Cold War and became more so with each month that passed after March 2003. If the Army of DESERT STORM and RESTORE HOPE can generally be thought of as "before" transformation and that of the Global War on Terrorism as "after," comparisons can be made—with caveats and qualifications, of course. Had considerable attention to and investment in expeditionary capabilities resulted in forces that deployed more quickly and effectively? Did the Army dominate the conventional battlefield, overmatching opponents who sought to seize or contest critical terrain? Was the Army the flexible, adaptable force transformers aspired to, transitioning smoothly to various points on the combat spectrum? Did investments in high technology pay off on low-intensity battlefields? Was the "transformed" Army sustainable? Answers to these questions should permit a critique of fifteen years of institutional endeavor.

An Expeditionary Army: Getting There

Deployments are difficult to compare. Factors such as diplomacy, politics, timing, and perceived need radically affect the working mechanics of force flow. Deployments associated with DESERT STORM, for example, progressed in two impulses: an initial rush to put in forces sufficient to defend Saudi Arabia (DESERT SHIELD), and a somewhat larger effort after the decision to eject Saddam Hussein from Kuwait by force had been made. The first of these impulses dispatched the 82d Airborne Division, the 101st Airborne Division (Air Assault), the 24th Infantry Division (Mechanized), the 1st Cavalry Division, and the 3d Armored Cavalry Regiment, primarily deploying from Forts Bragg, Campbell, Stewart, Benning, Hood, and Carson. A dozen years later the forces initially committed to IRAQI FREEDOM included the 82d Airborne Division, the 101st Airborne Division (Air Assault), the 3d Infantry Division (Mechanized), the 4th Infantry Division (Mechanized), and the 3d Armored Cavalry Regiment,

Pre-positioned equipment and supplies greatly facilitated preparations for Operation IRAQI FREEDOM.

again primarily deploying from Forts Bragg, Campbell, Stewart, Benning, Hood, and Carson. Parallels with respect to size, force structure, and geography were striking. The buildup for DESERT SHIELD progressed with all possible haste, as Saudi oil fields were exposed and vulnerable. The buildup for IRAQI FREEDOM featured less urgency, since the Iraqis were not postured to attack and no one really knew where the volatile diplomacy of the moment was leading. Nevertheless, the buildup of ground combat power in theater prior to IRAQI FREEDOM progressed significantly more quickly and efficiently than during DESERT SHIELD. In the dozen years that separated the two operations, as we have seen, the Army sought to improve upon its expeditionary posture by pre-positioning, increased sealift and airlift, and lightening the weight of deploying units. The first two of these initiatives yielded immediate benefits during IRAQI FREEDOM. The third did so in due course.[1]

Chapter 3 discussed dramatic changes with respect to pre-positioning after DESERT STORM. Subsequent chapters described the further growth and exercise of pre-positioned stocks. INTRINSIC ACTION emerged as a recurrent deployment operation sustaining a heavy battalion combat team in Kuwait on a nearly continuous basis. In 2002, as post 9-11 tensions with Iraq mounted, this continuous presence expanded to a brigade combat team. Contingents flew in from the United States and drew equipment from Camp Doha, north of Kuwait City. In December the 2d Brigade, 3d Infantry Division, was on hand and had drawn equipment in Kuwait when the National Command Authority decided to expand to a full division. On 6 January 2003, the remaining 3d Infantry Division (Mechanized) troops from Forts Stewart and Benning began streaming by air into Kuwait. Here they married up with equipment, much of it speedily relocated from other pre-position sites, at Camp Doha and at newly reconfigured Camp Arifjan. Long-rehearsed pro-

394

cedures progressed smoothly, and the troops rolled on to desert assembly areas. Time elapsed between landing at the airport and being fully established in the desert was measured in hours, with twelve hours being respectable for a company. The formidable pre-positioned panoply and drilled procedures resulted in a reinforced heavy division on the ground in a fraction of the time it had taken the 24th Infantry Division (Mechanized), also deploying from Forts Stewart and Benning, to arrive for DESERT SHIELD. The Marines were similarly well prepared, and within sixteen days off-loaded a division equivalent force boasting 120 M1A1 tanks, 276 amphibious assault and light-armored vehicles, and 63 howitzers. During DESERT SHIELD anxious paratroopers waited almost a month for tanks to arrive, stoically characterizing themselves as "speed bumps" in the meantime. Prior to IRAQI FREEDOM two heavy divisions (one Army and one Marine) beat the paratroopers—and the Iraqis—into the battle space. The dramatic success of pre-positioning was not just a matter of guessing right about having stockpiles in Kuwait. Flexibly packaged pre-positioned stocks moved efficiently across hundreds or thousands of miles of ocean to meet the timelines of troops arriving by air. Carefully rehearsed teams of soldiers, civilians, and contractors managed by the Army Materiel Command sped equally rehearsed units of pre-positioned savvy soldiers on their way to confront the enemy.[2]

In addition to pre-positioning, the Army relied on improved sealift and airlift to enhance its strategic mobility. In this it was dependent on the United States Transportation Command (USTRANSCOM) and the Navy and Air Force. The sister services may not have embraced transporting the Army as their highest priority, but substantial progress was nevertheless made. Sealift capabilities, as we have seen, ramped up, with the inventory of highly efficient roll-on/roll-off ships (RO/ROs), for example, climbing from seventeen in 1990 to thirty-six in 1996. Relevant infrastructure at home stations and in selected ports dramatically improved as well. The digitized 4th Infantry Division (Mechanized) was chosen to be the first heavy division to deploy to IRAQI FREEDOM with its own equipment from home station. Equipment and supplies moved smoothly by road and rail from Forts Hood and Carson to Beaumont, Texas, and other ports. Here it loaded quickly into more than forty ships and then steamed into the eastern Mediterranean. Troops continued to train at the home station, earmarked to fly in and join their equipment when it debarked in Turkey pursuant to opening a northern front in Iraq. Unfortunately, the efficiency of the sealift was compromised by the intransigence of diplomacy. At the eleventh hour the Turkish Parliament refused to support the American plan and denied the 4th Infantry Division permission to debark in and operate from Turkey. The 101st Airborne Division had better luck. Destined for Kuwait, it deployed as planned through upgraded infrastructure from Fort Campbell to Jacksonville, Florida, by road, rail, and air. More than 250 helicopters flew to Florida, then were reconfigured and stowed for the 9,000-mile voyage to Kuwait. The 101st had made much the same trip with about the same equipment en route to DESERT SHIELD in 1990. In 1990 the division took almost three months to close; in 2003 it took a little more than one. The much greater speed can be largely attributed to greater deployment efficiencies and effectiveness developed during the intervening dozen years. Meanwhile ships bearing the 4th Infantry Division gave up on the Turkish option, sped through the Suez Canal to Kuwait, and off-loaded there. They caught up with the Central Command (CENTCOM) *Blitzkrieg* just as conventional operations were sputtering to a close. Not counting time lost waiting off the coast of Turkey the overseas movement of the 4th Infantry Division was efficient, albeit ill-starred. The 1st Cavalry Division and 1st Armored Division were moving in the queue behind the 4th Infantry Division but were delayed rather than rushed forward as the "running start" to the campaign got off to an auspicious beginning.[3]

The diplomatic imbroglio that delayed the 4th Infantry Division's deployment by sea did position the Army to demonstrate post–Cold War enhancements in its ability to deploy by air. Perhaps the most notable postwar development in that regard was the C–17 Globemaster III. The C–17 can routinely carry payloads of 160,000 pounds 4,400 kilometers and can land on unimproved runways only 3,500 feet long and 90 feet wide. It can drop 102 paratroopers and deliver the mammoth seventy-ton M1A1 Abrams heavy common tank. It has four 40,400-pound thrust F117-PW-100 turbofan engines and avionics that facilitate control in dramatic descents. The first C–17 flew in 1991, and the first Air Force squadron so equipped became operational in January 1995. The 4th Infantry Division had been intended to open a northern front in Iraq, drawing off Iraqi forces from the main attack, covering the friendly Kurds, and tightening the squeeze on Baghdad. Even while bobbing off the Turkish coast it accomplished some of that purpose, but American commanders still wanted a more direct effort. Special Operations Forces were already on the ground with the Kurdish *Peshmerga*, and the 173d Airborne Brigade from Vicenza, Italy, was directed to parachute in to reinforce them. Entering Iraq at 30,000 feet to avoid air defenses, the C–17s screamed down to 1,000 feet to drop the paratroopers onto Bashur Airfield in Kurdistan, then roared back aloft to high altitude. The paratroopers linked up with the *Peshmerga* and quickly secured the airfield for follow-on traffic. A stream of C–17s soon flowed across the airfield, most notably twenty-seven that delivered the M1 tanks, Bradleys, and M113s of Task Force 1-63 Armor. Suddenly the Special Operating Forces were powerfully reinforced with a brigade combat team sporting heavy armor. The Vice Chief of Staff of the Army quipped that it was like reinforcing a Navy SEAL team with a carrier battle group. The small contingent posed the Iraqis a large dilemma. If they massed to fight it, they were horribly exposed to American airpower delivering precision-guided munitions. If they dispersed, they would be defeated in detail or swamped by the *Peshmerga*. Unnerved by these threats and mindful of developments in the south, Iraqi forces began to disintegrate. The Kurds and Americans seized the initiative. Bashur would not have been technically feasible in 1989. For a time supplies of all types flowed through Bashur in the wake of the combatants, until the Turks ruled that traffic and commerce in nonlethal supplies across their border were permissible. Elsewhere American airlift also showed well, although not as dramatically as at Bashur. Veteran workhorses such the C–5 and C–130 continued to move freight and personnel. Soldiers deploying to join their equipment or draw from

The HMMWV-mounted 2d Armored Cavalry Regiment represented greater deployability through lighter "platforms" with appliqué digital technology.

pre-positioned stocks generally flew in by commercial air. These techniques had worked well during DESERT STORM and continued to work well during IRAQI FREEDOM. The difference was that soldiers and units had been deploying like this for a dozen years, and most "learning curves" had long since been surmounted. Aerial ports of embarkation (APOE) and aerial ports of debarkation (APOD) were well-rehearsed drills, generally amid facilities that had been designed and built to accommodate them.[4]

The third post–Cold War initiative to improve strategic mobility, lightening the units to be deployed, played less directly in the initial deployment to IRAQI FREEDOM. The units that advanced on Baghdad were not much lighter than their predecessors of DESERT STORM, although there were fewer of them. Only the 2d Armored Cavalry Regiment was custom-built for lightness and also participated in the conventional phase of the campaign. The 2d Armored Cavalry Regiment had been redesigned as General Reimer's experimental Strike Force and rode in up-armored high mobility multipurpose wheeled vehicles (HMMWVs) with a panoply of modernized equipment. Its capabilities proved ideal when the battle for lines of communication trailing the 3d Infantry Division (Mechanized) developed in earnest. A particularly attractive feature of the 2d Armored Cavalry Regiment was that it could be readily shuttled about within the theater by air. However, the poster child for custom-designed lightness was the Stryker Brigade, introduced and brought to fruition by General Shinseki. The first of these was declared deployable in May 2003, too late for the opening shots of IRAQI FREEDOM. Its lightness and mobility would influence the campaign subsequently, concerning which, more later. A development related

397

to custom-designed lightness was the attempt to render units already light more lethal. We have already discussed the introduction of the Javelin antitank missile, which was useful against bunkers as well as vehicles. The Javelin showed well in the several IRAQI FREEDOM engagements wherein it was used. Light units benefited heavily from advances with respect to aviation and air support, concerning which, more later. Light units had also gotten into the habit of working small contingents of tanks and Bradleys into their operations. The introduction of the C–17, as we have seen, considerably enhanced the ability to get armor into a light scenario early on. Joint Readiness Training Center (JRTC) rotations picked up on this prospect, and by the mid-1990s they almost inevitably featured light brigades operating with a heavy company team attached. Infantrymen and paratroopers learned to make a little bit of armor go a long way in difficult terrain or a fluid situation, offsetting their own relative lack of firepower once on the ground. The M551 Sheridan and the aborted armored gun system had been intended to fill such a role, but there was no real substitute for actual tanks if you could get them. The deployment to IRAQI FREEDOM seeded light units with contingents of armor. The 173d Airborne Brigade got Task Force 1-63 Armor, the 82d Airborne Division got Task Force 1-41 Infantry (Mechanized), and the 101st Airborne Division got Task Force 2-70 Armor. Pre-positioned stocks offered a further means to enhance capability while keeping weight down. The 82d Airborne Division motorized itself overnight with pickings left over in Kuwait after the 3d Infantry Division passed through. Some paratroopers drove off to battle in pre-positioned engineer dump trucks. Wags observed that it was better than stealing cars from the locals. The 101st Airborne Division benefited from large inventories of pre-positioned helicopter Class IX, reducing the tonnage it had to bring by itself. Although only the 2d Armored Cavalry Regiment actually came as a lighter unit, a number of other 1990s' developments nevertheless economized on strategic lift.[5]

Deployment to IRAQI FREEDOM demonstrated impressive advances, but it was not flawless. Indeed, in one sense it regressed as leaders and planners eager for speed, flexibility, and minimal force structure walked away from the established time-phased force and deployment list (TPFDL) process without providing an alternate means to ensure adequate combat service support. The TPFDL was a somewhat mechanical Cold War legacy whereby the Joint Operations Planning and Execution System (JOPES) employed computer databases and recurrent conferences to ensure adequate "below-the-line" logistical forces were always associated with the "above-the-line" tactical forces intended to fight the battle. It fit in well with the operations plan for Iraq (OPLAN 1003) as it existed in 2002, which in turn represented an inheritance from the general defense plans (GDP) of the Cold War and from DESERT STORM. As planners dialed up or dialed down the tactical forces associated with a given course of action, the TPFDL would automatically dial up or dial down forces to support them. Since a major fraction of these forces were in the reserve component, the TPFDL played a critical role in initiating mobilizations. Since deployments are joint, the JOPES followed up on the TPFDL to guarantee appropriate sealift and airlift. The heft of below-the-line forces can appear daunting, since customary proportions had been 1.6 below the line to 1 above it. From time to time commentators opine that all of that support is not really necessary, or that branches and specialties have inflated particular requirements for parochial purposes. Under the lash to design a plan that could be executed quickly and with minimal force structure, CENTCOM planners thrashed through six TPFDL conferences before abandoning the TPFDL in favor of a call-forward system. In their favor, one could cite pre-positioning and considerable improvements to Kuwaiti logistical infrastructure, as well as expectations that contracting would reduce the load. Fuel lines now flowed directly into staging areas on the Iraqi border, for example, and even in DESERT STORM contracting had reduced requirements for below-the-line forces by 20 percent. A mantra of the time was "speed kills"; the campaign would progress so quickly and decisively that all the TPFDL logistical baggage would not really be necessary. The mantra was correct enough in the case of IRAQI FREEDOM that logistical thinness proved an embarrassment rather than a disaster. The advance outran the advantages of Kuwaiti infrastructure within a few days. By and large contractors, other than embedded technicians, performed unreliably amid high-intensity conflict. Only 150 heavy trucks were available for transportation, whereas the TPFDL called for 700. Orphaned supplies accumulated in vast "dumps" in Kuwait. Forward troops were consistently close to the margin with respect to food and water, somewhat less so with respect to fuel and ammunition. Repair parts, lubricants, and oil simply did not move; cannibalization and foraging became common practice to sustain the offensive. The medical supply system "failed to work." Fortuitously, Iraq collapsed before the Third Army reached a Clausewitzian "culminating point." The call-forward system did allow more control than the mechanical TPFDL, but it introduced petrifaction of a different sort. Pressure to minimize numbers elevated the level at which decisions to deploy were made. Harried, fatigued, and otherwise preoccupied senior leaders had to be persuaded concerning the details of each force package. Bias emerged; combat forces slid forward and logisticians back. Activated Reservists and Guardsmen accumulated at mobilization sites, away from their civilian lives but not yet called forward. As much as it had accomplished in becoming more expeditionary, the Army fell between two stools with respect to the initial logistics of IRAQI FREEDOM. The institutional Army had not yet gotten around to transforming the Cold War TPFDL into a more responsive system. CENTCOM planners acted as if they had.[6]

If DESERT SHIELD offers a reasonable parallel to IRAQI FREEDOM with respect to deployment, there is no real parallel for ENDURING FREEDOM, the liberation of Afghanistan. Afghanistan, like Siberia and Timbuktu, had long been a metaphor for the distant and inaccessible. In 2001 there were no existing plans for ground intervention in Afghanistan, and actions against hostile elements there had been largely confined to ineffectual long-distance strikes with precision-guided munitions. The 9-11 attacks precipitated a frenzy of planning to go where American forces had not gone before. In this endeavor a few 1990s vintage developments facilitated success: the maturation of United States Special Operations Command (USSOCOM) and in particular the 160th Special Operations Aviation Regiment (SOAR), interest in a force projection doctrine and in particular the concept of an intermediate staging base (ISB), the introduction of the C–17, and the logistical concept of split-basing. The endeavor was also facilitated by Afghan factionalism and an ongoing civil war against the Taliban. The CENTCOM commander, General Tommy Franks, determined to reinforce the Afghan resistance with Special Operating Forces capable of accessing American airpower and then to build up a mix of conventional and Special Operating Forces sufficient to pursue American interests after the Taliban regime collapsed. In the face of enormous strategic distances, he needed intermediate staging bases close enough to support operations in Afghanistan, yet shielded from counterattack. Such secure platforms would allow him to prepare and stage units for combat and to accumulate logistical assets without exposing them. Doctrine suggests 500 miles is an upper limit to the distance from which an ISB will be useful. Since Afghanistan is more than 500 miles across in all directions and deep in the heart of Asia, this provoked intense diplomacy with several neighbors. The former Soviet air base of Karshi Kanabad in Uzbekistan proved the best approach from the north. Teams of soldiers, airmen, and contractors soon put it into shape to handle a growing stream of C–17s. From the south Pakistan gave overflight and qualified support, short of allowing combat elements to openly base there. Instead such elements were based on the aircraft carrier USS *Kitty Hawk.* In a logistical pinch American forces had so employed an aircraft carrier off of Haiti in 1994 and experimented with the possibility thereafter. By 2003 the role of a floating ISB was generally accepted as a possibility for the mammoth ships, albeit one not much loved by the Navy. Further afield bases in the Persian Gulf and Indian Ocean adequately supported aircraft with longer "legs." The forces Franks hastily gathered to initiate hostilities against the Taliban numbered over forty thousand. At the tip of the spear were a few hundred Special Operations Forces inserted by breathtaking airlifts to embed within the Afghan resistance. More than thirty ships and about four hundred aircraft also supported the operation, as did a growing logistical footprint at Karshi Kanabad and Central Intelligence Agency (CIA) operatives already in Afghanistan. As the fighting progressed more conventional forces moved in, first to secure key facilities and then to conduct operations directly. The force structure was always a potpourri of different assets and initially impossible for the theater to sustain. Split-basing came into play, as home stations fulfilled many requirements. Installations within Afghanistan, such as Bagram Air Base in the north and Camp Rhino in the south, stood up to further sustain the campaign effort. Stockpiles built up there reduced reliance on split-basing without ever eliminating it—particularly with respect to Classes VII and IX. Within months troop strength had climbed to ten thousand in country but was kept low to avoid mission creep or the appearance of an occupation. As a deployment ENDURING FREEDOM displayed both improvisation in unique circumstances and the exercise of force projection capabilities developed over time.[7]

Initial entries into Afghanistan and Iraq were impressive displays of expeditionary force projection. Less noticed but also impressive were recurrent rotations of units into and out of theater. In earlier wars units were deployed for the duration, and individuals rotated into and out of them—if rotation

The Sadr uprising provoked widespread street fighting throughout Iraq.

occurred at all. Units did rotate as units into and out of the Balkans and Afghanistan, as we have seen. In the spring of 2004 a massive unit rotation replaced units that had been in Iraq a year or more with an entirely fresh set. The scale of this troop movement was so vast it may be better thought of as a demonstration of force projection rather than of force sustainment. Within a three-month period more than 260,000 troops and 50,000 pieces of equipment moved. Brigades and divisions came and left, by and large through ports and airports in Kuwait. Ironically, this massive movement was punctuated by the largest and most dangerous uprising of the Iraq war. Shi'a militants inspired by Moqtada al-Sadr suddenly threw themselves into the fighting, forcing combat well beyond the Sunni areas wherein it had previously concentrated. Vital logistical routes from Kuwait were contested and compromised, with bridges, culverts, and roadways seized or blown. The 1st Armored Division and 2d Armored Cavalry Regiment, at the time rotating out, pivoted abruptly and returned to the fight. Logisticians scrambled to make good the repair parts, ammunition, and other supplies these units had already turned over to the units that had replaced them. Improvised airlifts sustained isolated units while ground main supply routes were hastily restored. Troop flows continued into Iraq while the newly refurbished 1st Armored Division and 2d Armored Cavalry Regiment reinforced the units already on the ground. Back off their haunches, Coalition forces delivered crushing blows to Shi'a insurgents at

401

Al Kut, An Najaf, and Karbala. Several months later soldiers and marines similarly bludgeoned Sunni militants in Al Fallujah. Events of this period paved the way for the transfer of sovereignty and national elections. They also marked the last time Iraqi insurgents seriously attempted to forcibly seize and hold ground from the Coalition. Taken as a whole, the unit rotations between Operation IRAQI FREEDOM I (OIF I) and Operation IRAQI FREEDOM II (OIF II) offer yet another impressive display of American expeditionary capabilities. Airlift and sealift enabled a massive transfer of troops and equipment, while logisticians were flexible enough to reverse the tide of withdrawal, improvise quick fixes for broken links, and support an impromptu counteroffensive. It should be noted that the rotations and the battles involved the troops of thirty-two nations other than the United States, few of whom were self-sufficient with respect to transportation, logistics, or command and control.[8]

War at the High End

Army transformation, as we have seen, aspired to full-spectrum capabilities but tilted toward high-end conventional combat. If revolutionary developments were to occur, one might have most expected them within this range. The first several weeks of IRAQI FREEDOM offer an example of warfare at this level, and thus an opportunity to make comparisons with DESERT STORM—also fought at this level. In the dozen years that separated the two campaigns, the Army labored to harness Information Age digital technologies to the demands of the battlefield, creating a posture of "dominant knowledge." It also sought to radically improve technologies that had existed during DESERT STORM, and to render "jointness" a reality more than just a platitude. Although there was some triumphalism after Baghdad fell and before Iraqi liberation soured into Iraqi insurgency, claims of a revolution in military affairs seem notably absent from most eyewitness accounts. Indeed the aspirations for "shock and awe" many associated with defense transformation were widely derided, and pundits discovered the Information Age battlefield was still chaotic, bloody, and confusing. Some noted that the poster child for Army transformation, the 4th Infantry Division, had not made it into the conventional fray, suggesting that transformation essentially remained untested. This was only partially true. Advances with respect to command and control, navigation, friendly situation awareness, battlefield surveillance, precision-guided munitions, and joint operations significantly affected the course of the combat. Some aspects of this advance had already become so commonplace that they hardly inspired comment. Others were appliqué. Taken as a whole, they seemed potent enough to convince General Tommy Franks, the CENTCOM commander, that he could achieve a lopsided victory on par with DESERT STORM while deploying far less force. Insofar as the conventional phase of the campaign was concerned, he proved correct. If not quite yet a revolution in military affairs, IRAQI FREEDOM certainly heralded one.[9]

Command and control was most notably affected by advances with respect to communications between DESERT STORM and IRAQI FREEDOM. Satellite-facilitated communications and networked computers were ubiquitous in 2003, whereas these were still in their infancy in 1991. One is struck, for example, by the extent to which senior leaders coordinated via video teleconferences (VTCs). During the 1990s video teleconferencing rapidly evolved from highly expensive yet unreliable proprietary assets to readily available standards-based technology. The Kosovo campaign was coordinated by VTC at the highest levels and IRAQI FREEDOM at several levels below that. Commanders and staff officers scattered from the Persian Gulf through other overseas stations and the United States routinely talked to each other face-to-face. E-mail exchanges were even more continuous and largely overcame the correspondence difficulties of operating in different time zones since one could reply when ready. VTC was not available at the tactical level, but satellite phones and blue force tracking (which included a satellite-enabled messaging capability) were. Commanders well forward could stay in reliable communications with their own command and control nodes and higher headquarters. This encouraged up-front leadership and enabled units to operate across daunting frontages and in multiple directions. A few cases in point include the 2d Armored Cavalry Regiment sprawling out to secure over two hundred kilometers along the lines of communications, the five simultaneous V Corps attacks of 310300Z March on an arc stretching from As Samawah to Karbala, and the Thunder Run of 5 April wherein the brigade commander of 2d Brigade Combat Team, 3d Infantry Division, accompanied the attacking column while maintaining control of two other battalions attacking in an opposite direction. During DESERT STORM communications were severely degraded while Tactical Operations Centers (TOCs) and Tactical Actions Centers (TACs) were moving, and commanders relied on awkward patchworks of radio relays to stay in touch. Fragile communications contributed to methodical tactics, as loss of control could have led to catastrophic results. During IRAQI FREEDOM brigade combat teams pirouetted nimbly across much vaster distances, not infrequently shifting axes of advance and passing objectives from one to another like so many bus tokens. Such freewheeling tactics would not have been feasible without the communications to support them. The most stunning single demonstration of advanced communications occurred in the aftermath of an imbroglio. For a catalog of reasons the deep attack of the 11th Attack Helicopter Regiment on 23 March did not go well. Enemy innovations, mismatched tactics, operational overreach, the fog of war, and Murphy's Law conspired to render the regiment combat ineffective. Within hours veterans of the disaster were linked up by satellite phone in a conference call with aviators from the 101st Airborne Division and other units. This after-action review ranged back and forth as pilots of the 11th recounted their harrowing experiences and all parties involved shared opinions concerning appropriate responses and countermeasures. Attack helicopter tactics, techniques, and procedures throughout the theater changed overnight. Within days the 101st conducted a very different—and successful—deep attack building upon lessons learned by and exchanged with their less fortunate predecessors. Other successful operations followed. In World War II veterans of combat were shipped back to the United States to impart battlefield wisdom to those who would follow. In IRAQI FREEDOM the turnaround time for such mentorship was measured in minutes rather than months. This paralleled a broader "reach-back" capability that gave combatants instant access to anything that had been posted on defense networks or throughout the Internet itself. As advanced as communications were, however, the revolution with respect to them was not quite complete. Leaders spoke of a "digital divide" separating those with ready access to satellite phones and blue force tracking from those without it. Radio remained dominant at the tactical level, and most long-range electronic communications moved through venerable mobile subscriber equipment (MSE) employing line-of-sight antenna nodes that had to be stationary when used. Ambitious signal planning rapidly constructed a robust network of these nodes in the wake of the advance, but not quite fast enough to reliably support leading or outlying units. Near the bottom rung of the ladder one still found that recurrent nightmare for mechanized commanders, a support platoon rolling with a convoy of trucks through the middle of a firefight with a radio in the lead vehicle and one in the rear, but none in between.[10]

Land navigation immeasurably advanced with the general availability of satellite-based global positioning systems (GPSs). These had made their battlefield debut during DESERT STORM but were then too unfamiliar and too thinly distributed to achieve their full potential. Perhaps a vehicle or two in a company had had one and could reliably navigate with it. Sweeping across the featureless desert in formation, the rest of the vehicles lined up on the relative few who actually knew where they were. This worked out reasonably well given the openness of the terrain, the size of the forces involved, and the minimal maneuver required at company level. Accounts of IRAQI FREEDOM describe considerably greater complexities with respect to tactics, terrain, and maneuver and considerably more incidence of companies, platoons, and even sections operating independently. They also report leaders at every level moving out with a "Plugger" or some other GPS device in one hand and a map in the other. The map was more often than not reinforced by satellite photographs and imagery derived from such software programs as "TopScene" or "FalconView." Those who had blue force tracking aboard could draw on it to assist in navigation as well. At least one commander who weathered the blinding sandstorms of the last week in March set his maps aside and relied on GPS and blue force tracking from that point. Despite the pace and intricacy of the tactics, one reads little about lost or disoriented units. Virtually all knew where they were with elegant precision, and those momentarily disoriented quickly recovered. During the first Thunder Run into Baghdad on 5 April the lead tank, embroiled in combat and engulfed in smoke, took the wrong ramp out of the appropriately nicknamed "Spaghetti Junction" at the intersection of Highway 8 with the Qadisiyah Highway. Equipped with a "Plugger," the tank commander quickly regained his bearings, executed a horseshoe turn, smashed down a guardrail, and resumed his march to the Baghdad International Airport. The rest of the armored column dutifully followed, some wondering why they were executing a corkscrew in the middle of an intersection under fire. In Chapter 4 we discussed the historical ubiquity of units lost on the battlefield and the elaborate control measures commanders habitually imposed to maintain orientation. With IRAQI FREEDOM much of

Iraqi cities presented huge problems to traditional land navigation.

that disappeared. The prospect of units becoming lost was at least an order of magnitude less. Control measures thinned out, and most were communicated electronically. Elaborate collections of hand-drawn map overlays, phase lines a kilometer or so apart, company boundaries, and "measles sheets" of reference points were out. Orders were often simply to go some place and do something, and command radio nets were free of units trying to figure out where they were or where they should be. Indeed, the most studied and consequential incident of battlefield misdirection during IRAQI FREEDOM makes the point in an inverse sort of way. On 23 March the 507th Maintenance Company had six global positioning systems (including Garmin and ETREX VISTA) and received a CD-ROM disc containing orders and directions. The captain commanding misinterpreted his course to be Route Blue through the outskirts of An Nasiriyah, whereas it was actually to detour onto Route Jackson well clear of An Nasiriyah. The convoy initially followed GPS waypoints without incident, but in the darkness and confusion momentarily departed from Route Blue and crossed a bridge into An Nasiriyah itself, then drove through it. Referring to his GPS, the commander recognized his mistake. He knew exactly where he was, but he was in the wrong place. He also knew where he needed to be and a way to get there. At that point he made the fateful decision to drive back through An Nasiriyah. It is noteworthy that there were so few incidents of this type, given the distances being moved, the relative autonomy of traveling serials, and the thinness of security and traffic control en route. Land navigation was not yet zero defects, but it was vastly improved.[11]

Awareness of the friendly situation was considerably advanced by improved communications and the fidelity of GPS coordinates, but true revolution in that regard was presaged by appliqué blue force tracking (BFT). The Army hastily bolted 1200 Force XXI Battle Command Brigade and Below–Blue Force Tracking (FBCB2-BFT) kits onto selected Army, Marine, and British vehicles. This put at least one in each maneuver company. Each kit featured a laptop computer, a global positioning system, a satellite terminal and antenna, command and control software, mapping software, and a transponder. The transponder automatically updated all other vehicles within the system concerning its location via satellite communications. One finds, for example, the commanding general of the 3d Infantry Division monitoring the progress of the Thunder Runs into Baghdad on the screen of his blue force tracker. This swept the requirements for situational updates off of the division command radio net, freeing it up for actual decision making. An iconic anecdote from DESERT STORM relates to an incident at Safwan. The theater commander ordered the crossroads at Safwan secured on the last day of the war and subsequently decided it would be a great place to conduct cease-fire talks. Two hundred kilometers to the rear, his headquarters was beyond tactical communications and getting orders and information back and forth proved problematic. The Corps commander believed he had been instructed to interdict the crossroads at Safwan, and did so with attack helicopters. No one at theater or army headquarters realized that there were no American ground units at Safwan, and that the nearby airfield was occupied by Iraqis. Only a bit of post–cease-fire bullying allowed the talks to go forward as envisioned. A parallel iconic anecdote from IRAQI FREEDOM relates to the lightning movements of the 3-7 Cavalry after the breakthrough at the Karbala Gap. The theater commander, over a thousand kilometers from Baghdad and updating himself via BFT, noted a blue icon well to the north of Karbala. Concerned that it represented an isolated unit, he called the Army commander on a satellite hotline. The Army commander chuckled and told him to open up his Tracker screen a notch or two. When he did so, a stream of icons representing the rest of a major armored thrust appeared in the wake of the advancing cavalrymen. The two generals then talked face-to-face via VTC, contemplating current circumstances and next steps. They consciously did not interfere with the ongoing battlefield leadership of the corps, division, and brigade commanders. All instantaneously shared the same picture of the battlefield, and senior leaders could concentrate on decisions appropriate to their level without pestering their subordinates for updates. BFT not only facilitated command and control, it also greatly reduced the risk of fratricide. During DESERT STORM a large percentage of the casualties that did occur were due to fratricide, and virtually every brigade-size unit had some incidence of blue-on-blue engagements. The lethal and precise M1A1 tank could capably engage targets at ranges considerably in excess of those wherein they could be confidently identified, particularly in limited visibility or at night. Other advanced weapons systems experienced similar dilemmas. Commanders responded with elaborate protocols for clearing fires and with increasingly cautious or lock-step maneuvers. By the last day of the ground war these precautions approached paralysis in some cases. During IRAQI FREEDOM the friendly situation was better and more broadly known, although through-sight identification had not much improved and only a fraction of the vehicles on the battlefield had BFT. Proximity to vehicles with BFT and the general availability of GPS radically reduced the likelihood of one unit wandering into another unit's line of fire. Tactics remained fluid. Indeed, some of the most daring departures from linear tactics appeared toward the end of the conventional combat. Units attacked on converging axes in the open desert, bobbed along separate trails in vegetated terrain, and fought amid the confusion of urban sprawl, all the while confident they knew where other friendly units were. The situation was imperfect and blue-on-blue engagements did occur, but circumstances had radically improved since DESERT STORM.[12]

Awareness of the enemy situation was the third leg of the triad "where am I, where are my buddies, and where is the enemy" discussed at some length in Chapter 4. Whereas coping with the first two questions proved to have been enormously advanced between DESERT STORM and IRAQI FREEDOM, coping with the third was less so. Dominant knowledge enthusiasts envisioned an "unblinking eye" provided by satellites, manned aircraft, and unmanned aerial vehicles hovering over the battlefield and precisely identifying enemy locations. DESERT STORM had presaged such a capability, particularly with respect to the detailed imagery gathered prior to the breeches in the first days of the ground war. When the fighting became fluid, such information could not be gathered, interpreted, and distributed quickly enough to be useful. Ground commanders had to fight for immediately pertinent tactical intelligence, as they had always done. During IRAQI FREEDOM improved technical means of surveillance, newly available unmanned aerial vehicles, and a nascent network to automatically disseminate their findings in real time improved this situation to a point. That point seemed to be fixed facilities and large concentrations of tactical vehicles mustered in combat array. The unhappy fate of the *Adnan, Hammurabi,* and *Nebuchadnezzer Divisions* when they moved to reinforce the *Medina Division* south of Baghdad offers an example of American detection and destruction capabilities, as does the fate of the *Medina Division* itself. The Iraqis mistakenly believed a gigantic sandstorm would provide them sufficient cover, only to be obliterated by GPS-enabled munitions relying on thermal and infrared detection. Attempts to maneuver major units in the face of American surveillance and joint attack capabilities proved suicidal. The digital divide discussed earlier and Iraqi camouflage and countermeasures combined to erode intelligence on levels less grand, however. Vehicles that were dispersed, hidden amid vegetation or urban sprawl, and mindful of their thermal signatures tended to escape the unblinking eye. These had to be discovered and knocked out in the old way. Even more vexing were unconventional attacks such as those launched by the *Fedayeen.* These combatants generally wore civilian clothes, employed human shields, fought from converted civilian pickup trucks, employed automobiles as car bombs, feigned surrender to close in for attacks, misused mosques and other protected sites as bases, and pressed attacks regardless of casualties. They seemed to take their cues from lessons learned in Somalia, Chechnya, and Palestine. Given that the *Fedayeen* generally bubbled up out of urban sprawl, technical intelligence was very limited in its ability to detect the group's presence and even more limited in its ability to ascertain the group's intentions. The mix of intelligence available to columns embarking on the Thunder Runs into Baghdad on 5 and 7 April illustrate the point. Unmanned aerial vehicles (UAVs) correctly identified a fistful of mortar positions, a few tactical vehicles, barriers across the road, and probable ambush sites. Scouts defined opposition along the line of departure. Commanders rolled with up-to-date street maps and satellite imagery in their turrets. They knew the kinds of opposition they were likely to encounter, but not where or for how long. Dismounted ambushes were recurrent. By and large units gathered tactical intelligence by drawing fire and relied upon their wits, superb gunnery, and robust armor to get them through. Information was too fleeting and the "network" too immature to dump the intelligence they were gathering into some kind of joint database all operations centers could see and all platforms in range could act on simultaneously. Spot reports and calls for fire were discrete events, as they had previously been, and much of the fighting was at close range with little notice. The ability to see the enemy had advanced considerably since DESERT STORM, but not nearly as quickly as the ability to identify one's own location or the locations of friendly units.[13]

Once the enemy was identified, the next imperative was to render him ineffective in combat. DESERT STORM witnessed an effective use of precision-guided munitions (PGMs) that fueled discussion of a revolution in military affairs. As impressive as the DESERT STORM performance was in this regard, its use of PGMs paled in comparison to that of IRAQI FREEDOM. In the intervening dozen years PGMs improved somewhat in quality and radically in availability. Whereas less than 10 percent of the tonnage dropped on the Iraqis in 1991 had been precision guided, over two-thirds of bombs dropped in 2003 were. Munitions were far more plentiful because they were far cheaper. The air-launched cruise missiles, Tomahawk missiles, and laser-guided bombs of the first Gulf War easily ran to hundreds of thousands if not millions of dollars each, and inventories were quickly exhausted. Successors to these models continued to perform well against high-value targets but, as discussed in Chapter 4, much cheaper Joint Direct Attack Munitions (JDAMs) became the weapon of choice when the GPS coordinates of the target could be reliably identified. Given the pervasiveness of GPS systems among ground forces, this was commonly the case. Unlike missiles guided by laser designation or requiring other electromagnetic feeds, JDAMs were little degraded by dust or limited visibility. A radical increase in the numbers of precision-guided munitions radically altered the nature of the fighting. Cases in point included putting "G-Day" before "A-Day," daring thrusts through restrictive terrain, refined urban operations, and the demolition of four Republican Guard divisions in the middle of a fierce sandstorm. "A-Day" is the point at which air bombardment commences, historically a preparatory phase to soften up an enemy for ground assault. In DESERT STORM the air war lasted thirty-nine days before "G-Day," the launching of the ground assault. The Iraqis anticipated a repeat of this pattern in IRAQI FREEDOM, allowing them ample time to sabotage their oil fields after hostilities began.

The Americans attacked on the ground and in the air nearly simultaneously, achieving surprise and overrunning the southern oil fields before they were set on fire. Iraqi preparations for such destruction were picked up by UAV shortly prior to the ground attack. The Americans were confident that the incredible accuracy of their munitions against conventional targets, coupled with their destruction of enemy air defenses during a decade of SOUTHERN WATCH and the disposition of the strongest enemy forces away from the border, justified a surprise assault without preliminary bombardment. They demonstrated similar daring in subsequent operations. The term Karbala Gap, for example, is relative. It is not much of a gap: not very wide and not very open. Ground traffic is confined to constricted routes readily brought under fire from several directions, including Karbala itself. Nevertheless the 3d Infantry Division bulled its way through at the first opportunity, counting on precision-guided munitions and accurate direct fires to immediately suppress any who might contest its advance. The division drove into other tight spots with similar aggressiveness, confident it could blow its way out of what would have been "kill sacks" in earlier wars. Urban sprawl had long been considered a severe impediment to mechanized operations. Urban terrain was cluttered, the enemy was likely to be dug in, and the prospect for collateral damage and civilian casualties was high. Precision-guided munitions greatly reduced these risks. Even the most stubbornly dug-in enemy could be precisely targeted with powerful penetrating munitions while nearby buildings remained unscathed. When the 101st Airborne Division was securing An Najaf, for example, it routinely dropped 500-pound bombs on the verge of mosques, schools, and hospitals without damaging them. Buildings known to be occupied by insurgents were demolished with elegant efficiency, whereas nearby buildings went unharmed. This selectivity was most notable during the attack on Baghdad itself. Armored columns roared through the city after two weeks of air attacks, blazing away with devastating direct fires and supported by JDAMs and other precision-guided munitions. The casualties they inflicted on the enemy were horrific, yet this was no Stalingrad, Hue, or Groznyy. Damage and disruption experienced by the vast majority of Baghdad's five million people were minimal. There was no great stampede of refugees and no resultant humanitarian crisis. Most citizens stayed put and out of the way, relying on their own stockpiles of food and water until transportation of these items into the city resumed. Identifiable combatants were not so lucky, as the demolition of the Republican Guard in the middle of a raging sandstorm attested. This discussion is not intended to imply PGMs rendered warfare antiseptic. There were errors, misplaced strikes, and occasional difficulties marrying munitions up with targets. The fog of war had not yet disappeared, surprises occurred, and fighting could be fierce. The *Fedayeen* in particular employed tactics and ruses that got it close too quickly to make PGM strikes practical. It was swept away by close-in American firepower instead. It was Iraqi conventional units conventionally deployed and fixed defenses that proved the most vulnerable to American PGMs. Here the mismatch was arguably an order of magnitude greater than it had been a mere dozen years before.[14]

American firepower proved more lethal than ever.

Extensive use of precision-guided munitions during IRAQI FREEDOM was inherently joint. Calls for fire originated with forward observers from all four services and from the maneuvering commanders themselves. Platforms launching precision-guided munitions included B–52 bombers, F/A–18 Hornets, AH–64D Longbow Apache helicopters, Multiple Launch Rocket System (MLRS) field artillery, and Navy ships offshore, to name but a few. The marching array of sensors and the network that tied all this together, although imperfect, put a potent joint panoply at the service of embattled commanders. As recently as DESERT STORM ground commanders deconflicted air strikes more so than they integrated them, and the fire support coordination line (FSCL) offered a convenient control measure to dump missiles and bombs well clear of maneuvering troops. A few horrific fratricides reinforced the tendency of ground commanders to keep air support at arm's length. GPS and JDAMs changed that. IRAQI FREEDOM ground commanders routinely wove air and missile strikes tightly into their own maneuvers, bringing them as close to their vehicles as they did to mosques, schools, and hospitals. Dramatically enhanced jointness was apparent throughout the theater, nowhere more so than in the desert vastness stretching westwards from the Euphrates River to the Jordanian border. During DESERT STORM swarms of Iraqi "Scud" missile launchers had hidden themselves in this wilderness, bedeviling Israel with recurrent missile strikes. Israeli intervention could have derailed the Coalition fighting the first Gulf War. A difficult and only partially successful campaign to contain this effort sucked off a major fraction of the American sorties available in theater. In IRAQI FREEDOM a joint special operations task force for western Iraq (JSOTF-West) stood up to preclude a repeat performance and also to deny free use of the western desert to the Iraqis. Special Operations Forces (SOF) had, as we have seen, evolved into virtually a separate service, so a joint special operations task force was particularly ecumenical. Racing across the desert in light vehicles or inserted by helicopter, SOF hammered enemy forces with airpower and long-range artillery, wrested airfields from Iraqi control, deployed fleets of UAVs, seized the critical Hadithah Dam, and compromised Iraqi use of the desert vastness. Operating in the region was inherently a strain on Iraqi logistics. If they massed to hunt down the SOF they would be hammered by airpower; if they dispersed they could be defeated by SOF qualitative superiority. At the height of the fighting the Air Force lifted a tank-heavy combat team into newly captured Tallil Air Base by C–17. This multiplied the ground-based firepower and protected mobility of the SOF severalfold, and it further underscored the jointness of the campaign. The tightening web of SOF, UAVs, manned aircraft, and satellite surveillance rendered Iraqi rocketry exposed indeed. American airmen believed the message communicated had been "you launch, you die." Those Iraqi missiles that did launch were rendered ineffectual by Coalition joint theater air and missile defense. The first to launch, an Ababil–100, was detected within two seconds by the USS *Higgins*, an Aegis destroyer afloat in the Gulf. It automatically flashed a warning to the theater air defense operations center, which alerted the Patriot (PAC3) batteries. Battery radars picked the incoming missile up, computers dictated a firing solution within fourteen seconds, and two Patriots destroyed the missile well short of its target. The pattern repeated itself, slapping down Iraqi missiles and sparing American casualties such as the twenty-eight killed and almost a hundred wounded when a Scud hit a barracks in Dhahran during DESERT STORM. The 32d Army Air and Missile Defense Command coordinated the effort, and its commander served as deputy to the Coalition Force Air Component Command for theater air and missile defense (TAMD). TAMD illustrated jointness at the most sophisticated level: advanced technologies, robust and redundant networks, integrated and automated information sharing and resolution, and decisive responses from whichever platforms or assets made sense. DESERT STORM was a joint campaign. IRAQI FREEDOM was even more so.[15]

The Army had not yet committed to a brigade-based posture in the spring of 2003, but the conduct of operations through the fall of Baghdad certainly demonstrated further movement in that direction. During DESERT STORM brigade combat teams had occupied the geography and exceeded the firepower of World War II divisions. Improved communications and professionalized leadership had given them considerable autonomy even then, a factor that played in the advocacy of a brigade-based Army discussed in Chapter 7. During IRAQI FREEDOM the maneuver confidence enabled by GPS, blue force tracking, satellite communications, air supremacy, and ready access to precision-guided munitions considerably furthered this trend. Rather than the great wheel of brigades' on line characteristic of DESERT STORM, IRAQI FREEDOM featured brigades maneuvering independently, each on its own axis. The V Corps' five simultaneous attacks of 31 March, for example, were each conducted by a brigade combat team. In the approach to An Najaf, one brigade circled to the north and another to the south. Throughout the battles for Baghdad the staple for operational maneuver was the brigade combat team, securing one major objective after another, then bringing on a climax when the 2d Brigade of the 3d Infantry Division thundered into the heart of Baghdad and spent the night in Saddam Hussein's presidential palace. Throughout the conventional phase of IRAQI FREEDOM, brigade combat teams assumed the operational roles occupied by divisions in earlier wars, whereas divisions performed as if corps, corps as if armies, and Third Army as if an army group. This bump-up in capability and responsibility in part accounts for so few soldiers achieving such striking results. The brigade combat teams of IRAQI FREEDOM did not look much different than those of DESERT STORM, however. Old dogs like the M1 tank, M2/3 Bradley, AH–64 attack helicopter, and M113 personnel carrier were still there and performing capably—incrementally upgraded but demonstrably the same pieces of equipment. Wheeled vehicle fleets also looked pretty much the same as they had in 1991. Infantrymen did have the newly developed Javelin missile, and its innovative top-attack capability proved useful in urban combat—particularly when clearing rooftops or engaging targets in defilade. The M109A6 Paladin was an arguably new artillery piece, but it featured a 1950s vintage chassis and justifiably retained the venerable M109 nomenclature. Appliqué advances with respect to command and control, navigation, friendly situation awareness, battlefield surveillance, precision-guided munitions, and joint operations combined to make the brigade combat team considerably more potent than it had been before. It looked the same but was different.[16]

During DESERT STORM a Coalition of almost a million uniformed personnel, of whom over two-thirds were Americans, decisively defeated 540,000 Iraqis in the Kuwaiti theater of operations and drove them from it. To do so the Coalition suffered an estimated 379 fatalities, of whom about half were Americans. The campaign took forty-three days and overran about 24,000 square miles of territory, most of which was unpopulated. In the same period of time during IRAQI FREEDOM, a Coalition of about a half million uniformed personnel, of whom about nine in ten were Americans, destroyed Iraqi armed forces numbering 540,000 backed by reserves estimated at 650,000. Coalition forces overran 170,000 square miles of territory encompassing thirty million people. They suffered 172 fatalities, of whom 139 were Americans. The first campaign liberated a small friendly country; the second destroyed a large hostile regime. In both cases American forces were at a peak with respect to state of training and professional caliber. In both cases Iraqi regular forces were equipped with formidable panoplies of modern weapons. During IRAQI FREEDOM Iraqi irregulars fighting amid urban sprawl brought a new dimension to the conflict. The metrics are hardly rigorous and only arguably comparable, but they do suggest the Army of IRAQI FREEDOM prior to 1 May produced several times the result soldier for soldier and fatality for fatality as the rightly celebrated Army of DESERT STORM. In the intervening dozen years the Iraqis had stood still or slipped backwards; the Americans had further improved themselves—considerably. Coming out of DESERT STORM the United States Army qualitatively overmatched any potential opponent who might presume to seize or contest critical terrain on a conventional battlefield. Coming out of the first weeks of IRAQI FREEDOM, this was even more true.[17]

Adaptability: The Pivot to Unconventional Warfare

As IRAQI FREEDOM soured from liberation into insurgency, pundits found fault with the Army and its leadership. Transformation had overstressed conventional warfare, their thinking went, and the Army had merely increased its capabilities for a type of warfare within which it already had no peer. Meanwhile capabilities at the low end of the combat spectrum had been neglected, and IRAQI FREEDOM unmasked dramatic qualitative weaknesses with respect to that low end. If these accusations were true, a major fraction of the deliberations steering Army transformation and Quadrennial Defense Reviews would have been for naught. Low-intensity scenarios, as we have seen, consistently figured into the analytic mix, even if conventional scenarios always seemed the most dangerous and consequential. Units were supposed to be able to transition nimbly from one point on the combat spectrum to another, fighting what the Commandant of the Marine Corps famously characterized as the "three block war." A body of relevant doctrine did exist. Most soldiers and virtually all combat units had served in stability operations since DESERT STORM, although only in Somalia and Afghanistan did these become as "kinetic" as they would in Iraq. Advocates for the Army, with considerable justification, pointed out that shortcomings in Iraq were quantitative far more so than they were qualitative. If the Army and Marines had been dealt a fair hand with respect to numbers, they opined, problems would have been far less acute. Greater numbers would have made a significant difference, but they also might have masked rather than remedied qualitative flaws that did exist. These fell under the broad headings of intelligence, command and control, and the approach to the Iraqis. Similar problems manifested themselves in Afghanistan as well, but less visibly so since ambitions with respect to Afghanistan were much more modest during this period.[18]

During the Vietnam War designers of Army doctrine took an understandable interest in counterinsurgency and stability operations. The writings of Mao Zedong figured heavily in their assessments of the threat, and the successful British campaign in Malaya from 1948 through 1956 figured heavily in their assessments of appropriate responses. These responses clustered under the headings counterguerrilla, population, and resources control and nation building. Within each of these venues the United States Army developed considerable sophistication by 1970, and this manifested itself in a body of doctrine available to operators and students alike. Cases in point included Field Manual 100–20, *Field Service Regulations—Counterinsurgency*, published in 1964 and Field Manual 31–23, *Stability Operations*, and Field Manual 31–73, *Advisor Handbook for Stability Operations*, published in 1967. In 1962 the Army's capstone doctrinal manual, Field Manual 100–5, *Operations*, also gave considerable attention to counterinsurgency and stability operations. Interest waned in the aftermath of Vietnam, and Army doctrine as a whole shifted back to an overwhelming emphasis upon high-end conventional combat in a European-like setting. Special Operations Forces were an exception to this trend, and sustained their own doctrinal interest in low-intensity conflict. As we have seen, the Special Operations Command evolved into a largely autonomous quasi-service and took appreciable doctrinal responsibility with it, following the Fiscal Year (FY) 1987 National Defense Authorization Act. The doctrinal emphasis upon high-end conventional combat seemed justified by DESERT STORM itself, but with the aftermath came a queasy feeling that low-intensity conflict could not simply be left to the SOF. What occupation there was of Iraq in 1991 seemed clumsy, and Kurdistan and Somalia soon bubbled up as crises beyond the capabilities of SOF alone to contain. The 1993 version of Field Manual 100–5, *Operations*, reintroduced an emphasis on low-intensity conflict under the heading of "operations other than war." Field Manual 100–23, *Peace Operations*, soon followed. By this time the Center for Army Lessons Learned (CALL), established at Fort Leavenworth in 1985, was quickly turning insights captured from the field into recommended tactics, techniques, and procedures for the Army at large. These fed into the development of further doctrine and increasingly were distributed electronically. Veterans of Somalia, Haiti, and the Balkans joined the dialogue, adding their inputs in the forms of student papers, studies, and, eventually, doctrine. Analysts shaping Army transformation and Quadrennial Defense Reviews were, as we have seen, dutifully mindful of the lower end of the combat spectrum. Were one to sample an array of Fort Leavenworth student papers, *Army* magazine articles, or blogs popular with company commanders dating from the period 1998 through 2003, one would encounter a respectable appreciation of the working mechanics of stability operations. Certainly the paramount importance of gaining popular support was understood, as was the necessity of achieving balance among counterguerrilla, population, and resources control and nation building. The cliché "winning hearts and minds" was not much used, but the underlying principle seems to have been grasped by most. Shortly before IRAQI FREEDOM kicked off, these musings came together in the new and intellectually respectable Field Manual 3–07, *Stability Operations and Support Operations*.[19]

Doctrine is of little use unless it is applied, of course. When IRAQI FREEDOM launched, the United States Army had already been heavily involved in stability operations for over a dozen years, and the number of soldiers involved at any given time had often been in the tens of thousands. Earlier chapters have described deployments to Kurdistan, Somalia, Haiti, Bosnia, Kosovo, Afghanistan, and other places. In each case operational plans gave deference to existing doctrine, in part because of the nearly universal presence of School of Advanced Military Studies graduates on staffs at the division level or above. Problems and shortcoming were addressed in after-action reviews (AARs) and in the musings of veterans in various official and unofficial publications. These in turn found their way through the Center for Army Lessons Learned and other routes into evolving tactics, techniques, and procedures (TTP) and, ultimately, doctrine. Not everyone paid sufficient attention to AARs, lessons learned, TTP, and doctrine, of course—a perennial issue in a very busy Army with its share of anti-intellectual bias. The recurrent experience of stability operations year after year did much to ameliorate such inattention as did occur. By 2003 virtually every combat brigade in the active component had deployed somewhere in the past dozen years. Most active-component soldiers had as well.

Training center rotations included role players acting the part of local nationals.

Senior officers and noncommissioned officers (NCOs) were not uncommonly veterans of several such deployments. Experience and expectation leavened Army training programs. Predeployment training for the Balkans consciously and conscientiously leaned toward requirements at the low end of the combat spectrum. National Training Center scenarios from the mid-1990s inevitably included some mix of guerrillas, hostile civilians, and innocent bystanders. The Joint Readiness Training Center, oriented on nonmechanized units, was even more sophisticated in this regard. Here scenarios featured a robust mix of low-end and high-end combat. Participants encountered civilians, refugees, guerrillas, terrorists, third-country NGOs, and the ever-present media. When a unit was on the cusp of deploying, a number of the actors participating in their training might well be drawn from the country to which they intended to deploy. Practice in training reflected itself in performance in the field. The presence of patrols, population engagement, checkpoints, raids, and security missions at the training centers became actual responsibilities in the field.[20]

Doctrine, training, and practical experience all suggested that stability operations were manpower intensive. One could not police the streets, secure key infrastructure, or gain the confidence of the people with firepower alone. Without coming to precise figures, soldiers of all ranks were aware that numbers mattered and that there were appropriate ratios between populations to be secured and the troops committed to do so. The successful British counterinsurgency in Malaya from 1948 through 1956 considerably influenced American doctrine of the Vietnam era and thus played indirectly into the rekindled interest in stability operations during the 1990s. The British effort

415

arguably fielded about twenty-five soldiers per thousand in the population, or about one for forty. North Atlantic Treaty Organization (NATO) and NATO-aligned forces in Bosnia and Kosovo were only somewhat shy of this ratio initially and enjoyed considerable success. The United States and its allies fielded fewer than five soldiers per thousand in Haiti and Somalia, achieving modest results in the first case and ultimately losing control in the second. As intervention in Iraq loomed imminent, the Joint Staff's director of strategic plans and policy (J–5) and the Army operations and training officer (G–3) separately canvassed the Army's Center of Military History and others for insights into potential occupational requirements. The Center of Military History reviewed twenty United States Army occupations during the twentieth century, with force ratios that ranged from a low of one to five hundred in postwar Japan to a high of one to ten in Vietnam. Ironically, the lowest ratio ended in great success because the Japanese emperor accepted defeat and mandated cooperation, whereas the highest ratio ended in defeat because of sanctuaries available to the insurgents and recurrent conventional attacks by the North Vietnamese Army. Occupations are complex and can feature collateral requirements for external defense, humanitarian relief, peacekeeping, law and order, and nation building. Noting the uniqueness of each situation, the Center opined that one soldier or more to a hundred inhabitants seemed to have been a reasonable rule of thumb. Coming at the problem from a different angle, CENTCOM Combined Forces Land Component Command (CFLCC) planners arrived at much the same result. Envisioning constabulary responsibilities throughout Iraq, CFLCC troop-to-task analysis determined twenty combat brigades with their supporting units would be required, satellited on sixteen major cities or provinces. This came to about one soldier for a hundred Iraqis. General Eric K. Shinseki was mindful of these and other assessments when he famously responded to congressional inquiry that several hundred thousand troops would be required to secure Iraq, although his own personal experiences in Vietnam and Bosnia may have influenced him more. For reasons discussed elsewhere the Coalition attempted to occupy Iraq with force-to-population ratios roughly equivalent to those in Somalia. The assertion that Iraqis would welcome them as liberators proved a fantasy in all but Kurdistan. In May 2003 Ambassador L. Paul Bremer III swept away plans for employing the former Iraqi Army for security when he disbanded it, and he further alienated many citizens of consequence with a severe "de-Ba'athification" policy. Whatever the long-term purposes of these initiatives, they immediately aggravated the Coalition's difficulties with respect to numbers. Law and order had broken down even as American units in Iraq were still engaged in intense conventional fighting. Looting, revenge killings, and crimes of all description swept the country. Soldiers recovering from the rigors of combat were diverted to secure porous borders with Syria and Iran and to search for weapons of mass destruction. The remainder had to pick and choose the facilities they could secure, leaving the rest to the natives. When initial unrest subsided, Coalition numbers remained too few to gain a secure grip. A journal kept by a Bradley company commander illustrates the point. Initially assigned to secure the environs of Camp Anaconda near Balad, he was soon familiar with the terrain and people in it. He was effectively mayor pro tempore of a number of villages, spoke a little Arabic himself, and had access to interpreters. In due course he had sustained a continuous presence with foot patrols, delivered hard knocks to Iraqi "outsiders" attempting to mortar the base, established working relations with the locals, and been invited to more than one dinner and offered the hand of more than one bride. This progress was recurrently interrupted by taskings to go elsewhere: a raid on an insurgent concentration in the deep desert, a relief expedition to Samarra, participation in search-and-clear operations elsewhere, and yet another extended battle for Samarra. Since there were no actual reserves, these operations featured pickup teams hastily assembled from multiple parent units. Each time the captain returned with his company to Balad, their grip had slipped further. Cooperating locals had been killed or intimidated, indigenous security had folded or deserted, insurgents had become more organized and daring, and other Americans had unwittingly compromised modus vivendi on his turf. He lost traction, and his own soldiers became increasingly impatient with mercurial locals. Abuses occurred. His company could, in his opinion, have overcome its imperfections had it remained in place, but it was too often someplace else. Across Iraq the campaign acquired a certain "whack the mole" aspect to it. Identifiable insurgents—an immediate threat—attracted hastily assembled contingents wielding overwhelming force. Population and resources control and military security to nation-building projects were a lesser priority and intermittently resourced in most places. In theory the newly redesigned Iraqi Army and police forces were to fill this void. In practice these took time to become effective. Stability operations are manpower intensive, and the Army of 2003 knew this. More than any other factor, the dearth of numbers best explains outcomes in Iraq. Troop shortages magnified the effects of qualitative shortcomings with respect to intelligence, command and control, and the approach to the Iraqis, since there was no depth of reserves to make up for "slack."[21]

The United States Army rolled into Baghdad with an intelligence structure well suited to the high-end warfare it was engaged in at the time. Satellite, airborne, and ground sensors picked up enemy movements and positions, drawing hurricanes of direct and indirect fires on to them. Signals intelligence reinforced the technical mix. Intelligence was top driven, with the most elaborate staffs and sophisticated equipment concentrated at the upper echelons. These developed intelligence products to feed down the chain. Units at lower echelons had responsibilities to report what they encountered, information that fed up the chain to be sorted, sifted, and analyzed by those with the breadth of vision to do so. The fog of war and enemy countermeasures resulted in imperfect information and a few surprises, to be sure, but the invading Army had a clearer picture of enemy physical capabilities than had ever been the case before. The prolonged struggle against *Fedayeen* along the lines of communications introduced an opponent against which centralized and technical intelligence means proved less useful. This phenomenon expanded with the insurgency through the summer and fall of 2003. Insurgents blended in with the civilian population, hid their weapons, attacked via ruse or remote device, embraced suicide bombing, and presented fleeting targets. Countering such threats required human intelligence (HUMINT) drawn from the local population, which in turn meant the population needed to be secured against intimidation. In the absence of reliable native troops, American soldiers assumed responsibility for policing the streets, securing local populations, drawing intelligence from them, and striking down terrorists or insurgents before they themselves could strike. This stood the intelligence paradigm on its head. Only local commanders familiar with the streets and the populations they secured could extract the intelligence circumstances required. Battalion commanders hastily beefed up their intelligence (S–2) staffs to provide better direction. Lack of linguists proved a huge impediment. Squads, platoons, and even companies were dispatched to search buildings or pick up suspects with nary an Arabic speaker among them. Perplexed junior leaders came across weapons or contraband and hauled off for questioning all proximate adult or near-adult males, amid crying children and wailing women. When identities could not be determined, all who remotely fit a description were snatched up. Informants often proved to be unreliable or, worse, to be settling personal scores. Since they usually were off site or hidden incognito behind a mask inside a vehicle while a raid took place, they did not moderate the tendency toward enlarged catchments. Detainee numbers soared, and with them resentment. Companies had no, and battalions limited and improvised, means to accommodate detainees. They also had guidance to pass them along quickly since their means to interrogate were so limited and intelligence might be lost. Detainees accumulated in huge holding areas, distant from where they were apprehended and unlikely to be interrogated in a timely manner. In the early months a major fraction of the linguists that were available were committed to the search for weapons of mass destruction or to the contracting necessary to establish an emerging constellation of base camps and other facilities. The common soldier and intelligence specialist alike soon recognized existing methods of gathering intelligence were dysfunctional. Tactical HUMINT teams (THTs), of which there were only ten organic to a division, were deployed in larger numbers from the reserve component and pushed down to local commanders. Linguists were recruited and deployed as a top priority. Intelligence staff officers, recognizing the need for immediate tactical intelligence, relaxed restrictions on who could interrogate and how long they could do so at the point of capture. The intelligence apparatus was virtually redesigned from the bottom up to prioritize the timely acquisition and use of HUMINT. By late 2003 the improvements had gained traction, as the capture of those who mortared the Al Rasheed Hotel while Deputy Secretary of Defense Paul Wolfowitz was in it, and then the capture of Saddam Hussein himself, would attest. Nevertheless, shortcomings with respect to HUMINT in Iraq and Afghanistan lingered for years as a critical weakness of the transformed Army. These shortcomings were the greatest and the most consequential in the six months that followed the fall of Baghdad.[22]

Shortcomings with respect to command and control were also at their greatest and most consequential in the six months that followed the fall of Baghdad. The chain of command that ran from CENTCOM down through tank crews and rifle squads was ideally poised to smash the Republican Guards—or any other conventional adversary, for that matter. From the lowest echelons through V Corps organizations were standing, well prepared for their specified mission-essential tasks and stable with respect to personnel and equipment. Third Army had required augmentation and improvisation to stand up as Combined Forces Land Component Command, but all of that had taken place well ahead of IRAQI FREEDOM. Indeed, the Army and others had gone to great lengths to ensure that CFLCC was a "dream team" with respect to rank, fill, and quality, and this team had refined itself with training and experience real and simulated. CENTCOM, a standing organization, was similarly favored with respect to fill, quality, and extent of preparation. Within two months of the fall of Baghdad CENTCOM and CFLCC summarily departed the theater, turning operational control over to a Combined Joint Task Force–7 (CJTF-7) hastily assembled around the V Corps headquarters. For some time the United States and its allies had considered fielding standing joint task forces capable of immediately taking over during such circumstances, but preparations remained largely theoretical. NATO's Allied Rapid Reaction Corps was in fact a capable (British-led) standing headquarters that deployed to Bosnia in 1995 and Kosovo in 1999. NATO was not in Iraq, however, and the more usual practice was to hastily cobble together headquarters with laundry lists of individual taskings to augment whatever was on the ground at the time. This approach applied to V Corps in the spring of 2003, along with a change of command and the rotation out of many seasoned players. The V Corps was, as we have seen, exceptionally potent as a ground tactical headquarters. It was thin with respect to jointness, however, even thinner with respect to allied representation, too underranked in its staff to run a theater, and altogether lacking in the combat service support overhead necessary to support a theater. All of this had to be improvised. Services were understandably reluctant to move personnel from documented billets elsewhere to fill an emerging yet still ad hoc joint manning document in V Corps, so many positions were filled 120, 60, or even 30 days at a time—often by activated Reservists or faculty borrowed from schools. Officer and NCO manpower requirements within the headquarters soared from under 300 to about 1,000, but actual fill in many staff sections hovered under 50 percent for months. Where one general officer served in the command post in June, nineteen ultimately served eight months later. The force structure and manning issues of CJTF-7 did not finally stabilize until the spring of 2004. Beneath CJTF-7 the divisions were standing organizations enjoying high levels of talent and fill, but their structure was not particularly suited to the circumstances they found themselves in. Sprawled in penny packets across the vastness of Iraq to secure it, their mobility was impaired by the weight of their combat vehicles and the expense of maintaining them. Coverage rather than concentration was the new priority, and major constituent organizations—notably artillery, air defense, and combat engineers—found their conventional roles considerably less relevant. Operations were increasingly dominated by HMMWV and foot patrols, and organizations had to adjust. In Chapter 7 we discussed the modular redesign of Joint Task Force (JTF)–capable corps and division headquarters, modular brigade combat teams, and the shift to a brigade-based army. In due course these adjustments fielded a force better suited to circumstances in Iraq, as

Detainee operations proved problematic as their scale increased.

did reapportionment of billets among the branches and ever-expanding numbers of up-armored wheeled vehicles, but these changes had not yet occurred in 2003 and early 2004, the period wherein resistance in Iraq morphed into insurgency.[23]

Paucity of numbers, underdeveloped capabilities with respect to human intelligence, and an ad hoc command structure all complicated the Army's approach to the Iraqis. Perturbations on the civil side, including a flawed hand-off from the Office of Reconstruction and Humanitarian Assistance (ORHA) to the Coalition Provisional Authority (CPA), severe de-Ba'athification, and the estrangement of the capitulated Iraqi Army made things worse. Army transformers had little to do with the most serious mistakes made in Iraq, but as circumstances plunged downhill further design shortcomings manifested themselves. Beyond those previously discussed with respect to intelligence, linguists, and command structure, these included detainee operations, rules of engagement, and partnering. We have described the escalating numbers of detainees swept up "just in case" during the course of operations by soldiers who did not speak the language or much understand the culture. These accumulated in large holding areas such as Camp Bucca and Abu Ghurayb, while too few interrogators struggled to cope with them. Their numbers invited the use of contractors to supplement military interrogators and the watering down of traditional distinctions between military police securing the prisoners and military interrogators drawing information from them. Commanders of the facilities had multiple priorities and distractions, personnel were inexperienced and in cases undisciplined, the pressure to secure actionable intelligence was high, and widely infamous abuses occurred. The Army had anticipated capturing far more prisoners of war than it actually did during the conventional phase, and one might have anticipated adequate preparations. Prisoners of war under conventional circumstances are different than potential insurgents, however. They generally have an internal chain of command capable of facilitating life support, are of limited intelligence value, and can be secured en masse at a remote site with relatively few people. At Abu Ghurayb potential but perishable intelligence value and the imperative of separating the guilty from the innocent placed additional demands on the captors. In due course manning, training, and policies improved at major holding areas. Perhaps more important, input to them thinned as battalions and brigades refined detention practices and acquired a capability to hold detainees long enough to sort them out, and Iraqi institutions stood as backup to carry some of the load. The inadvertent heavy-handedness that overstocked Abu Ghurayb manifested itself in rules of engagement as well. Soldiers are expected to fire when fired upon, and there is no such thing as having too much firepower in a conventional engagement. Insurgents consciously provoked overreactions from the forces they engaged, firing from positions likely to result in civilian casualties. Troops conditioned to the violence of conventional combat were likely to respond to potshots with disproportionate force. Artillery and air strikes on fleeting mortar or rocket positions became particularly problematic. It takes time for units to acquire a feel for the appropriate level of response. One wants to decisively outgun an adversary while keeping collateral damage at a minimum. Results in Iraq understandably varied by unit and circumstance, and each rotation of units periodically required yet another reconditioning. Long experience in NATO, the Balkans, and other peacekeeping operations had conditioned American soldiers to anticipate like-type local or third-country counterparts. A battalion commander, for example, could reasonably expect to talk matters over with a battalion commander from another nation—even if an adversary—and have a lot in common. This paradigm was attempted in Iraq, with concerted efforts to stand up and train Iraqi battalions that would partner with Americans in a traditional manner. Constraints concerning a "proper" military sphere were self-defined. Local militia were treated with suspicion, given their proneness to factional, religious, and clan loyalties at cross-purposes with the national state the Coalition aspired to erect. Civilian leaders and agencies were often kept at a distance, hopefully to be someone else's counterpart—and problem. This approach did not work out neatly. Leadership and individuals within newly raised Iraqi battalions often owed factional, religious, or clan loyalties. Militias were the de facto security in much of the country. Most local civilian leaders and agencies would have had no Coalition counterpart unless a soldier assumed the role; security was too problematic. Over time the Army in Iraq took a broader approach, most notably with the "Anbar Awakening" somewhat after the period of this study. It began moving in that direction much earlier than that. In 2003 company commanders were already de facto security advisers to mayors of villages and towns. The 1st Cavalry Division prepared for its rotation in Iraq with a curriculum as heavy on urban management as it was on counterguerrilla tactics, techniques, and procedures. Its "lines of operation" included services, governance, economic intervention, and the training and employment of Iraqi security forces along with combat operations.[24]

Afghanistan offers a rather different model of the transformed Army's capability to transition to unconventional operations. IRAQI FREEDOM started out as a major conventional battle that morphed into a counterinsurgency. Insofar as there was a conventional phase in Afghanistan, it was fought by Afghans with technical assistance and fire support from the Americans. Through 2005 and some years beyond the United States Army never attempted anything that remotely resembled an occupation in Afghanistan, nor did it assume meaningful responsibilities for population and resources control. With respect to boots on the ground in comparison to the Afghan population, its numbers gradually rose from miniscule to tiny during this period. Effective control resided with victorious anti-Taliban warlords at first, and then with a United Nations–brokered representative national government perched atop an alliance of former warlords, arguably elected officials and the newly influential. The United States Army was broadly supportive of United Nations negotiations and programs for nation building, but it focused on hunting down residual al-Qaeda and those Taliban still disposed to fight. Concurrently an also small NATO-led International Security and Assistance Force (ISAF) stood up to secure Kabul and its environs while the nascent Afghan government got under way. Special Operating Forces dominated initial operations and significantly influenced them thereafter, lending their long-sustained emphasis upon low-intensity conflict to the course of events. Structural and practical weaknesses with respect to HUMINT, while clearly present, proved less severe than in Iraq. In part this was because of the long tenure of the Central Intelligence Agency in the theater and contacts they had sustained over time with local warlords. In part it was also because of the severity of the Taliban's defeat and the long time it took them to reestablish a presence sufficiently threatening to intimidate local cooperation. The Taliban and al-Qaeda were immeasurably assisted by sanctuaries in the remote tribal areas of Pakistan, at the time beyond the effective reach of the Americans. Those who escaped, most notably Osama bin Laden himself, reorganized there. Allied command and control at the upper levels was about as improvised and ad hoc in Afghanistan as in Iraq, although there was never a vacuum induced by wholesale leadership departures such as that preceding CJTF-7. After an initial phase wherein major players reported through CENTCOM and USSOCOM separately, Combined Joint Task Force Mountain, based on the 10th Mountain Division, assumed responsibility for Operation ANACONDA on 15 February 2002. In June 2002 CJTF-180, based on Headquarters, XVIII Airborne Corps, took over. In November 2003 CJTF-180 restructured to subordinate itself to Combined Forces Command–Afghanistan (CFC-A). CJTF-76 (based on the 25th Infantry Division and then the Southern European Task Force) and CJTF-82 based on the 82d Airborne Division followed in due course. CFC-A would be inactivated in 2006, introducing further restructuring and turbulence. As had been the case in Iraq, each of these redesigns was accompanied by newly emergent joint-manning documents, plaintive requests to services and allies to provide personnel, intermittent levels of fill, and occasional lapses of grip. When IRAQI FREEDOM launched, Afghanistan became a clearly secondary theater, with further consequences for the manning of its senior headquarters. A standing CJTF would have helped, as would have a policy of replenishing senior headquarters by individual rather than "unit" rotation. Given the amount of augmentation necessary to render a division or corps into a CJTF, the results were ad hoc anyway, reducing the logic of labeling them as unit rotations. Detainee operations in Afghanistan avoided the overwhelming numbers of Iraq—unless one counts those accommodated by the tender mercies of the warlords—but critical issues with respect to the status of detainees, responsibilities for securing and interrogating them, and ultimate disposition did emerge. During this period civilian casualties were not yet excessive, so rules of engagement with respect to air strikes and the use of firepower did not come under the scrutiny they would later on. Efforts to stand up a truly counterpart Afghan National Army were plagued by ethnic and tribal loyalties, competition with local militias, and mismatched professional ethics—as was the case in Iraq. Afghanistan echoed without mirroring Iraq with respect to the Army's adaptability to unconventional warfare. In both cases the Army seems to have been reasonably served by doctrine and experience, but far too few in numbers to adequately apply either in the face of the missions ultimately assumed. There nevertheless were qualitative shortcomings, aggravating the paucity of numbers, that became manifest as operations progressed. Outstanding among these were lack of linguists, inadequate capabilities for HUMINT, recurrently ad hoc senior headquarters, unpreparedness for detainee operations, conventionally biased rules of engagement, and unrealistic expectations concerning the roles and nature of requisite counterparts.[25]

Goodness of Fit: Army Transformation on the Unconventional Battlefield

Given the bias of Army transformation toward high-end combat and shortcomings with respect to unconventional warfare discussed above, how much did the technological innovations from 1989 through 2003 contribute to war at the low end? More than is often supposed. A brief example may make the point. In Chapter 3 we discussed Somalia and mentioned the fighting in Mogadishu on 3–4 October 1993—famously recaptured in the book and then the motion picture *Black Hawk Down*. These re-creations and official accounts provide ample testimony to the courage, tenacity, and initiative of the American soldier in trying circumstances. They also describe columns lost in a rabbit warren of streets, unknown friendly locations, unknowable enemy locations, huge difficulties bringing firepower effectively to bear, and vehicles overmatched by ubiquitous enemy firepower. Soldiers of the Stryker-borne 5-20th Infantry Battalion had their own so-called Mogadishu moment on 4 September 2004, when an OH–58D helicopter went down hard in the urban sprawl of Tall' Afar. The pilots, although injured, escaped the wreckage and crawled to the relative safety of a nearby rock wall. The insurgents seem to have been familiar with Mogadishu precedents, and a race developed between Americans trying to prevent another *Black Hawk Down* and Iraqis trying to reproduce one. The first combatants on the scene were the 5-20th's Scout Platoon. The OH–58D's icon had remained visible on their Force XXI Battle

Command, Brigade and Below (FBCB2), so they knew where it was. Scalable electronic downloadable maps gave them an exact appreciation of the geography, global positioning systems gave an exact appreciation of their own positions, and blue force tracking showed the locations of friendly vehicles. As they raced through the streets, a potpourri of light munitions ricocheted harmlessly off the armor of the wheel-borne Strykers. They knew where they were going and how to get there, and they got there first. They had not won the race by much, however, as increasing volumes of fire into their hasty positions around the helicopter amply attested. More troubling, UAVs flying above the fray downloaded imagery of an accelerating enemy buildup, including insurgents unloading rocket-propelled grenades (RPGs) and machine guns from civilian vehicles. A relief column, Company B of the 5-20th Infantry, was churning its way through the dusty streets of Tall' Afar toward them. Ever more numerous insurgents divided their attention between attempts to crush the isolated platoon and blocking positions to delay the relieving company. The blocking positions soon disappeared in dirt plumes raised by GBU31 bombs precisely laid by F–16 fighter-bombers that had scrambled overhead. Company B ignored residual small arms pinging off their vehicles and rolled on to the helicopter crash site. The half-score soldiers who clattered out of the back of each Stryker bore a formidable panoply: Kevlar body armor, laser designators, Single Channel Ground and Airborne Radio System (SINCGARS) radios, Rapid Fielding Initiative (RFI) accoutrements, a mix of automatic weapons, and lots of ammunition. The insurgents again tried to overwhelm the now reinforced position. This was a mistake. Hurricanes of well-aimed fire swept them off the rooftops, out of the streets, and ultimately from surrounding buildings room by room. Americans were hit, but their body armor minimized the damage done. With the coolness of troops who completely dominate their battlefield, the Americans brought forward a heavy expanded mobility tactical truck (HEMTT) wrecker and a Palletized Load System (PLS) flatbed truck. The recovery team sawed off the helicopter blades and loaded all the wreckage on the flatbed, and the entire contingent then disengaged by stages and drove away. There would be no pictures of jubilant insurgents dancing on a helicopter, no American bodies dragged through the streets, no captured materials, and no hostages. There also would be no book and no movie. The episode illustrated transformational advances with respect to combat per se, but also illustrated advances relevant at the low end of the combat spectrum with respect to land navigation, blue force tracking, battlefield surveillance, command and control, and information operations.[26]

Some fraction of low-intensity conflict involves actual combat, people trying to kill each other with simultaneous exchanges of fire. When combat erupts, nuances that separate high-intensity conflict from low-intensity conflict fade or disappear for the soldiers involved. It all seems intense to them. The difference is often in the prelude. Insurgents, lurking in difficult (in the case of Iraq, urban) terrain and hiding among the local population or in sanctuaries, generally determine the time and place of engagements. Suffering an overall deficit with respect to firepower and equipment, they seek a momentary surprise advantage to strike a lethal blow. With enough such blows, the gnat will bring down the elephant. Counterinsurgents in such cases must survive the initial blow and then escalate their own combat power rapidly enough to render the insurgents net losers in the engagement. Several aspects of Army transformation favored the Americans with respect to this timeless asymmetry. Their venerable M1 tanks and M2/3 Bradleys were already highly survivable against virtually all munitions the Iraqi insurgents deployed. Advanced body armor significantly improved the survivability of individual soldiers as well. Indeed, footage exists of soldiers knocked to the ground by shots to their chests, only to get back on their feet to continue the mission. The Stryker combat vehicle offered a potent combination of mobility and survivability, and increasing proportions of up-armored HMMWVs enhanced the survivability of the average mounted patrol. Perhaps most important, American contingents traveled within an envelope of all-around surveillance networked with similarly distributed firepower. The System Enhancement Package (SEP) of the M1A2 tank, with independent thermal sights for tank commander and gunner and automatic weapons for each, was the ultimate expression of survivability, surveillance, and firepower. "Boxes" of American vehicles, be they tanks, Bradleys, Strykers, or HMMWVs, traveled down avenues wide enough to accommodate them ready for a fight, or overwatched infantry similarly deployed for all-around protection in narrower quarters. When fired upon, contingents as small as a platoon immediately generated withering counterfires. These could be quickly reinforced by incredibly precise GPS or laser-guided munitions, delivered from planes or helicopters loitering overhead or hastily scrambled. Precision served the dual purpose of speedily inflicting casualties on identified enemy while avoiding collateral damage to unintended targets. Once located, the enemy seldom survived long if he remained in place. Direct-fire ambushes on American combat units, even small ones, became increasingly unpopular as an insurgent technique. Over time, direct-fire ambushes on American logistical convoys became costly as well. On several occasions, most notably during the April 2004 uprisings and at An Najaf, Samarra, and Al Fallujah several months later, insurgents chose to dig in, hold ground, and fight. The results were lopsided blood baths. At Al Fallujah, for example, two Marine regimental combat teams reinforced by two Army battalions and supported by 350 close air support (CAS) strikes and 7,000 rounds of artillery routed a dug-in force of 4,500 that had had months to prepare, killing 1,200 in the process. The Army battalions suffered one and five dead, respectively, and the attacking force as a whole sixty-three. Incidents of open force-on-force combat dropped off from that point. If the insurgents intended to attrite Coalition forces, they would have to find another way.[27]

Counterinsurgents should not wait passively to be ambushed, of course. They deploy networks of surveillance in the hopes of identifying their assailants before they themselves become a target. The boxes of vehicles described above featured robust arrays of thermal sights, night-vision goggles, daylight sights, and trained eyeballs. Infantrymen deployed with suites of sensors as well. Ideally these arrays were but the core of a surveillance network much broader with respect to space and time. UAVs were a prime aspect of Army transformation, and they matured rapidly in Iraq and Afghanistan. Smaller craft could

425

be overhead in minutes, and larger ones could loiter for hours. The absence of pilots rendered them less time-constrained and more daring. Beyond nosing around in front of a moving column to detect an ambush, they could canvass broadly for unusual or suspicious activity. As Iraqi insurgents increasingly abandoned direct-fire engagements in favor of improvised explosive devices (IEDs), UAVs often were able to detect their activity. Sometimes intelligence was so timely IED installation parties could be taken under fire. Other times disturbances in the ground or thermal variations clued alert observers. In this effort time-stamped film footage enabled comparisons over time, rendering what had changed that much more visible. The ubiquity of global positioning systems significantly enhanced surveillance. Film footage had a precise location. Spot reports from patrols, over-flying aircraft, and even casual passersby acquired elegant precision as well. Cooperating Iraqis could be issued cellular phones and GPS to improve the timeliness and sharpen the precision of their reports. Gone were the days of agonizing over where a patrol actually was in the dark in order to confidently locate whatever they had seen. In some locations continuously running cameras provided permanent surveillance, not unlike in an American shopping mall. All of this imagery generated vast amounts of data. Fortuitously most of it was digital, and computers could be mustered to catalogue and keep track of it—and to monitor it with respect to specific parameters. Such computer-assisted monitoring was even more common with respect to signals intelligence than it was with respect to image intelligence. As insurgents increasingly backed away from direct confrontation, surveillance took on an aspect that often seemed more forensic than tactical. This was perhaps appropriate since crime and insurgency seemed so intertwined. Detainees were screened for biometrics such as fingerprints and iris scans, as were others coming under military supervision. Entered into databases, these could be drawn on later to identify personnel or perpetrators. Official accounts of engagements and incidents acquired the feel of police reports more so than spot reports. Persons apprehended in the vicinity of an incident were checked for gunshot residue and blood spatter and handled accordingly. Human intelligence fed into the data pool as well: tracked, cataloged, and analyzed. Much of the surveillance conducted in Iraq and Afghanistan would have been familiar to counterinsurgents from earlier wars, but much was new with Army transformation as well. Unmanned platforms and sensors, digital technologies, and computer-assisted analyses took surveillance to a new level.[28]

We have mentioned that the ubiquity of GPS considerably facilitated battlefield surveillance. It greatly advanced land navigation as well, of course. Not getting lost is as important in low-intensity as in high-intensity conflict. Indeed, it may be even more so since smaller units move across vaster spaces. Targets are fleeting, and counterinsurgents are often called upon to mass quickly in isolated or obscure locations. In Iraq the imperative of following up on intelligence tips to snatch individual insurgents or police up contraband weapons sent small contingents of Americans hurrying through the darkened streets of cluttered urban sprawl. In this they were immeasurably assisted not only by GPS, but also by electronically downloadable maps and overhead graphics that enabled them to "zoom in" and "zoom out" to varying levels of

Armored Operations in Urban Terrain

New Reality...

- Crude Enemy Weapon Choice
- Engagement Compression
- Multiple/360 Enemy Avenues
- Enemy Terrain Advantage

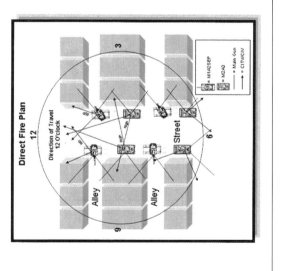

New Realizations...

- Forces New Tactics/Methods
- Confidence in Armor Package
- Dual Sight Capability Critical
- Combined Arms Maneuver

A 1st Cavalry Division slide used to brief standard operating procedures, 2004.

resolution. American patrols already enjoyed huge advantages with respect to night-vision equipment, and these further navigational technologies enabled them to take full advantage of it in an urban setting. They could find their way efficiently in totally unfamiliar terrain, and with a few days to familiarize themselves, they could master whatever terrain they were in. Indeed, more than one battlefield account stands a traditional paradigm on its head and finds the counterinsurgent better able to exploit the terrain than the insurgent. From time immemorial insurgents have struck from hiding places and faded away into trackless terrain that baffled pursuit. The working mechanics of urban combat in Iraq often brought insurgents into neighborhoods other than their own, relying on local guides or finding their own way. Mechanized Americans sped through the streets confident of their own locations and that of their brethren, and with a little time on the ground knew where to lay down "spider-webs" of interlocking positions to intercept, isolate, and bring to ground their adversaries. Engagements could acquire the tenor of a "cops and robbers" television drama, with desperate insurgents fleeing on foot through unfamiliar streets or careening along in cars while counterinsurgents pursued or raced laterally to position for a few clear shots. Given American marksmanship and gunnery, a few clear shots could be decisive. Insurgents proved particularly vulnerable when "puddling," gathering briefly to figure out where they were or what they wanted to do—often unmindful that they were being observed because of high-power sights and asymmetries in night-vision capability. For spiderwebs to work, each participant must know the location of the others. In cops and robbers dramas the good guys have an amazing facility to track street corners and each other's radio chatter, ultimately swamping the bad guys in a sea of blinking lights. In Iraq blue force tracking (BFT) facilitated similar fidelity in coordinating movements, if not necessarily with the same colorful quips and timely dramatic results. In the Tall' Afar incident discussed above, for example, the downed OH–58D's icon remained visible on the screens of its rescuers, and the rescuers' icons were visible on the screens of each other. Such electronic assists to command and control were exploited time and again. American forces converged in the dark on one target after another with a minimum risk of fratricide. Small units and even individual vehicles safely crossed each other's line of fire at a pace and with a frequency that would have been unthinkable a dozen years earlier. As is often the case, the value of this capability may be best illustrated by performance in its absence. More than one operation foundered when someone's BFT icon disappeared from the screen, provoking anxious tiptoeing as all parties involved attempted to reestablish contact. The most egregious fratricides of the war occurred in the absence of BFT. A case in point was a spectacular shoot-out in Al Fallujah in September 2003, when Americans, Iraqi police, and Jordanian security forces all shot into each other as a small contingent of insurgents passed somewhere between them. It should perhaps be noted that the concluding events in a GPS-facilitated take-down of a house or a BFT-facilitated interception of a moving vehicle were rarely high tech. Final encounters in a dingy apartment or on a darkened street were generally "up close and personal," testing training, reaction time, and resolve rather than technology.[29]

Army transformation focused heavily upon command and control. We have already discussed the utility of blue force tracking and a shared operational picture. In conventional combat prior to the fall of Baghdad we found widely scattered units coordinating effectively via satellite-facilitated communications. This remained true during unconventional combat. The explosive events of April 2004 provide ample evidence. Suddenly and unexpectedly Moqtada al-Sadr's Mahdi Army rose in revolt, and further vast stretches of Iraq came to be contested with insurgents. Ground communications and landlines were cut. Areas populated by Shi'a, theretofore quiescent and with a minimal American presence, became battlegrounds. Tiny allied garrisons and even armed contractors clung to isolated outposts. The 1st Armored Division, en route to rotate home and with units already in Kuwait, was extended, and its so-called "Extension Campaign" offers a metaphor for advances in command and control during the previous dozen years. Within days the division reinforced Al Hillah and An Najaf, and it counterattacked from Baghdad and Kuwait to oust insurgents from Al Kut. On 18 April the division was given tactical control of all Coalition units in four hastily designed Joint Operating Areas (JOAs) covering much of southern Iraq. Since fighting in Al Fallujah was ongoing and Sunni areas of Iraq were still contested, forces available for fighting in the south consisted of units of the 1st Armored Division racing in from wherever they had been in the process of redeployment, and contingents cobbled together from whatever other units could momentarily be spared elsewhere. The force that relieved An Najaf, for example, was notably eclectic. It included the headquarters of the 3d Brigade Combat Team, 1st Infantry Division, its constituent Task Force 2-2 Infantry, the light 1-14 Infantry dispatched from the separate brigade in Mosul, and a Stryker company each from the 5-20 Infantry, 2-3 Infantry, and 1-23 Infantry, plus supporting units. These bits and pieces came together across hundreds of miles on the fly, downloading electronically generated orders and graphics that were readily tweaked or adjusted as circumstances changed. Electronic reach back gave them access to relevant maps, overhead graphics, and local information. The Strykers in particular had embedded rather than appliqué FBCB2, and they used it to great advantage while shepherding swarms of logistical vehicles from all across Iraq around blown bridges and through threatened areas to reconfigure the theater logistical posture. With logistics reset, American forces in the south overmatched the insurgents and then ground them down in a series of lopsided engagements. A chastened al-Sadr sought and obtained negotiated political egress from his military debacle and shifted to politics rather than force when confronting the Coalition. A robust network of ground-based antennae nodes sustained radio communications across most of Iraq throughout the crisis, and satellite communications filled in where these proved inadequate. The Mahdi uprising may have been envisioned as an Iraqi version of the Tet offensive, but deft American movements rendered it far less costly or consequential. Digital and satellite-facilitated mechanisms for command and control exploited during it had not existed a dozen years before, and these allowed the Americans far more daring movements at far less risk. This capability proved of value regardless of the scale of ongoing operations.[30]

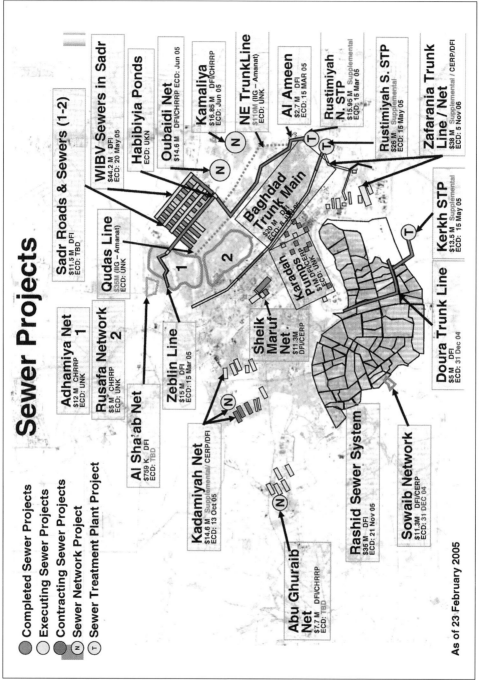

A 1st Cavalry Division slide illustrating a nontraditional aspect of Army operations in IRAQI FREEDOM

The technologies that enabled command and control advanced information operations (IO) as well. Information operations matured as a concept during the 1990s and encompassed efforts to protect friendly information systems, attack or exploit enemy information systems, and use information and information systems to further one's goals. By doctrine it included electronic warfare (EW), computer network operations (CNO), psychological operations (PSYOPS), military deception (MILDEC), and operations security (OPSEC). Underlying principles were not new, but Space and Information Age technologies greatly altered the manner in which they were applied. American leaders in Iraq and Afghanistan understood that long-term solutions were ultimately political and that success depended on the support of the indigenous population—and thus upon visibly demonstrating that cooperation with the Coalition was in its best interest. Information management within Task Force Baghdad during the tenure of the 1st Cavalry Division offers an example. "Full Spectrum Information Operations" were mobilized to lend legitimacy to Coalition combat operations, the training and employment of Iraqi security forces, support to essential services, the promotion of sound governance, and various economic initiatives. Rather than merely tracking engagements, casualties, and suspects, task force databases also monitored water, sewage, electricity, and garbage throughout Baghdad in elaborate detail. One could find, for example, that the 3d Brigade Combat Team at one point supervised unfinanced requirements for twenty water projects totaling $8.8 million, fourteen sewer projects totaling $10.5 million, eighteen electricity projects totaling $12 million, and four solid waste projects totaling $1.1 million. Pictures promulgated of the situation "before" included standing ponds of contaminated water blocking off streets, power lines dangling dangerously across roads or underfoot, darkened apartments without electricity, and mountains of garbage. Photographs of the situation "after" could include a small child happily drinking clean water from a tap in a lighted apartment. Relevant projects were numerous, heavily contracted, and often small scale and required detailed management. Beyond the information necessary to monitor progress, there was also the requirement to make this progress visible to the Iraqis with a "drumbeat" of local coverage. The Coalition sought to "put an Iraqi face" on both the nation building and collateral security. Whenever possible, local contractors using local labor were employed. Commander's Emergency Response Program (CERP) funds proved particularly useful in this regard. With respect to security, Iraqi forces were showcased after the several months of eddying that followed Ambassador Bremer's dissolution of the Iraqi Army in May 2003. Task Force Baghdad, for example, married three Iraqi National Guard brigades to twelve American brigade-size units, and fifty-eight Iraqi National Guard companies to 322 American companies. On joint patrols these helped overcome language and cultural barriers and proved particularly useful dealing with sensitive sites such as mosques. The Coalition did not pursue information operations in a vacuum, of course. Insurgents proved adept at connecting through the Internet with each other and with sympathizers, getting their own version of a given story out early, and muddying the Coalition's message of progress. Arab media could be suspicious of Coalition motives and actions and receptive to insurgent accounts of both. Video posted on the Web of Coalition casualties inflicted by insurgents and of civilian casualties ostensibly inflicted by the Coalition proved particularly vexing. Americans recognized the limitations of both the media and insurgent photography at night and sought to stay beneath the "IO threshold"—the point of uncomfortable or negative visibility in the international press—by doing the fighting they initiated at night. This minimized the risks of adverse graphic imagery getting into circulation while taking advantage of Coalition night-vision superiority. The approach influenced ever larger operations. The III Corps planners, for example, believed the April 2004 uprising had spiked well above the IO threshold, whereas the clearings of An Najaf in August and Samarra in September had stayed beneath it. Over time the Coalition developed considerable sophistication exploiting or blocking insurgent communications. The battle for "hearts and minds" remained intense, however, and seldom offered a clear sense of success. In a digital age information operations contended with bias and suspicion dating back centuries. Worldwide communications offered everyone access to conflicting imagery and commentary instantly. All knew that ultimate resolutions were political, not military.[31]

In the case of Iraq's number one killer of Coalition troops, improvised explosive devices, Army transformation from 1989 through 2003 offered pieces relevant to a solution without yet having actually pulled them together. For much of the 1990s professional interest in landmine warfare was in eclipse as the United States came under pressure from its European allies and others to join the Convention on the Prohibition of the Use, Stockpiling, Production, and Transfer of Anti-Personnel Mines and on Their Destruction (1997 Mine Ban Treaty). Landmine hazards in Bosnia dampened the rosy view that unattended explosives were a thing of the past, as did the fact Russia and China refused to sign the treaty. Mine clearance in the Balkans evolved into a major enterprise, promoting interest in explosive ordnance detachments (EODs) and relevant robotics. The conventional phase of Operation IRAQI FREEDOM did not particularly feature landmine warfare. Certainly nothing approached the vast mine belts of DESERT STORM. As American columns converged on Baghdad, however, there were insufficient forces to secure huge ammunition dumps when the Iraqi Army melted away. Some estimate that as many as three million tons of munitions remained outside of Coalition control. These began showing up as IEDs. Triggering mechanisms included trip wires, pressure sensors, electrical lines, remote devices, and suicide bombers. As battles large and small demonstrated the undesirability of direct-fire engagements with the Americans, IEDs became the weapon of choice for the insurgents, inflicting over half of all casualties month after month. Remote devices such as cell phones and garage door openers came to be preferred for triggering. Trip wires and pressure sensors required victims to make actual contact, and electrical lines could be readily traced to their point of origin. The Army had experimented with jamming as a constituent of electronic warfare and soon developed a capability to jam some Iraqi remote IED-triggering devices as well. Meanwhile experience and selective training made troops more conscious of IEDs and countermeasures to them, and the Army rushed to up-armor HMMWVs and other vehicles. These measures did reduce vulnerability. IED attacks on Coalition forces went up, but casualties from them did not. In September 2004, for example, of about 700 IED incidents about 150 produced casualties. A year later the number of IED incidents had doubled, whereas the number producing casualties remained about the same. In another year the number of IED incidents doubled again, but the number producing casualties again remained about the same. The balance of IED incidents without casualties was about evenly split between IEDs discovered and cleared, and those detonated without producing casualties—often by virtue of a friendly device. The relative success of electronic countermeasures forced insurgents back into the use of electrical lines or detonation cords, again bringing them closer and making them easier to find. Effective surveillance increased the likelihood IEDs would be discovered before they were detonated, as came to be the case more often than not. Knowing what to look for and good scouting were part of the solution, as were newly introduced advanced sensors and UAVs. UAVs, as we have seen, could loiter for hours without endangering pilots. They could pick up suspicious roadside activity, and advanced sensors could detect disturbances the naked eye could not. Robots such as "Talon" and "PackBot" came into play, allowing closeup inspections without putting humans at risk. In time robots would be able to handle and even disarm IEDs. Surveillance fed into intelligence, and intelligence sought to campaign against IEDs at their source. As HUMINT improved, cells deploying IEDs and factories producing them could be compromised or destroyed. Such preemption was particularly important in the case of VBIEDs, vehicle-borne IEDs. About two-thirds of these were to be guided to detonation by suicide bombers, and foot-borne suicide bombers bearing explosive vests joined the battle as well. Suicide bombers may have represented foreign influences, and they considerably increased in number as direct-fire engagements with Coalition forces proved too costly. In February 2005 there were sixty-five car bombings for example, whereas there had only been ten in February 2004. Insurgents did experiment with complex attacks, integrating suicide bombers into larger forces attacking with direct and indirect fires. In due course the Coalition worked out tactics for these, intercepting suicide bombers through traffic control and heightened vigilance, employing advanced technologies and trained dogs to detect the presence of explosives, and preempting suicide bombers with attacks on the cells and facilities that supported them. Countermeasures were never perfect, but they did keep casualties down. If IEDs continued to inflict casualties at the rate per attack of the summer of 2004, American casualties from IEDs would have more than quadrupled—and casualties for the war as a whole more than doubled. In Chapter 6 we discussed the eventual systemization and funding of the counter-IED campaign under the auspices of the Joint IED Defeat Organization, JIEDDO. Even before JIEDDO stood up, bits and pieces of transformational technologies were already being redirected against IEDs.[32]

Sustaining a Transformed Army

Operations overseas inevitably created sustainment demands. Many of these would have been comparable whether Army transformation during

1989–2003 had been attempted or not, but within a few venues Army transformation initiatives were directly tested. Computer-facilitated distribution-based combat service support experienced the rigors of combat. Recurrent rotations meant recurrent recycling. Dependence on contracting amply illustrated strengths and weaknesses. The transformed or transforming Army shared the load with untransformed allies. Specific equipment acquired during the course of transformation introduced specific logistical demands. Manpower was ever an issue. Recognizing that this study is not the place to describe or assess logistical efforts from 2003 to 2005 as a whole, let us focus on these particular areas wherein transformation and logistics particularly overlapped.

Chapters 3 through 6 described an accelerating commitment to computer-facilitated distribution-based logistics. Chapter 7 described force structure redesign wherein table of organization and equipment (TOE) logistical units became modular and brigade-based. Transformers intended to radically increase the efficiency of Army logisticians while reducing their "footprint" on the battlefield. Information Age technologies would enable "total asset visibility"; logisticians would always know in detail where everything was and who needed what. The fabled "iron mountains" and ponderous unit trains of yesteryear would be gone, and trimmed down arrays of logisticians in theater would deliver all that units required "just in time." Like Walmart, Amazon.com, or FTD Florists, the Army would manage assets and diminish overhead with elegant precision. This revolution in military affairs worked to a point in Afghanistan and Iraq. Combat service support digital automation was ubiquitous, and logistical information was in fact universally shared once communicated. Radio frequency identification (RFID) tags speedily identified the contents of containers and allowed them to be accurately tracked. Ports of debarkation became considerably more efficient, with nowhere near the numbers of lost containers or "frustrated cargo" of DESERT SHIELD/DESERT STORM. Aspirations to track beans, bullets, and all else from the "factory to the foxhole" did not quite surmount the digital divide discussed above, however. Combat service support units at lower levels, many of which were from the reserve component, were by and large last in line for upgrades to radios, satellite communication sets, and other advanced communications. When logistical units exceeded the range of venerable ground-based mobile subscriber equipment (MSE), they generally fell back on fragile radio relays to communicate complex information. Few had the direct satellite communications—or bandwidth—necessary to move large volumes of data quickly. Understandably, this affected relatively unpredictable commodities such as Class IX (repair parts) far more than it did relatively predictable ones such as fuel or water. Mechanized units fell back on cannibalization for many of their maintenance needs. MSE service improved in Iraq as units settled into the occupation and nodes stabilized, but the country never did get full coverage—and coverage in Afghanistan was far worse. The digital divide, as earlier discussed, was largely the result of Army transformation having been caught in mid-stride. As supplementals increased and money flowed, more and better satellite communications, expanded bandwidth, and access to commercial alternatives pushed transformational technologies down the logistical chain.

434

Daily convoys supplied units deployed throughout Iraq.

Improved electronic communications could not fully compensate for at-risk ground communications, however. We have discussed the fierce battles for the lines of communication that preceded the fall of Baghdad. Logistical convoys, true to historical precedent, became a favored target for the insurgents. Once the occupation settled in, at any given time of day somewhere between 800 and 1,300 trucks were on the road ferrying supplies from Kuwait into Iraq. Others made local runs or brought supplies in from Turkey. Attempts to interrupt Coalition logistics were often a prelude to insurgent attacks or an effort to spoil Coalition initiatives. The widespread attacks of April 2004 gave considerable attention to interrupting Coalition lines of communication. Anticipating such interruptions and distractions, Coalition forces got in the habit of stockpiling supplies prior to major initiatives of their own. A case in point was the buildup prior to the second battle of Al Fallujah. "Just in case" logistics partially recovered from their eclipse behind "just in time." Iron mountains like those of DESERT STORM may have been a thing of the past, but iron foothills were not.[33]

Chapters 6 and 7 discussed the accelerated move toward a brigade-based Army coincident with recycling units through Iraq and Afghanistan, and Chapter 6 discussed coming to grips with the human demands of that recycling. In both cases initiatives associated with Army transformation occurred sooner and perhaps more comprehensively because of wartime demands. Wartime unit recycling also forced a modest increase in active-duty manpower, pressed ever greater operational requirements upon the reserve component, and eroded restrictions upon the role of women in combat. Again these results, previously discussed, picked up the pace in a direction that Army transformation was already moving. Army transformation did not particularly forecast the multiple roles individual units would assume in Iraq and the logistical implications of those multiple roles. After the fall of Baghdad artillery battalions had relatively few calls for fire, combat engineers had relatively

Mine-resistant ambush-protected (MRAP) vehicles

few obstacles to breach, and air defenders continued with negligible threats from above. Tankers employed armored firepower with good effect from time to time but as often patrolled in HMMWVs or on foot. Light infantrymen, conversely, found they patrolled more effectively when motorized. Heliborne delivery was not consistently practical, nor could it achieve the desired interface with the local population. Only the Stryker brigades seemed appropriately designed for the mix of missions at hand. Other units drew supplemental or even alternate sets of equipment, often leaving some fraction of their TOE equipment at their home station. HMMWV-mounted patrols, customarily several vehicles in convoy, became a signature of the war. Theater requirements for HMMWVs soared, then soared again when the IED threat forced a general shift to up-armored HMMWVs. Eventually demands for mine-resistant ambush-protected (MRAP) vehicles would spike as well. Vehicle requirements in theater and the dual (or multiple) roles assumed by most units drove prepositioned stocks to new highs. Logisticians in Iraq found themselves responsible for more than 50,000 vehicles supported by 90,000 twenty- or forty-foot containers full of supplies and equipment. Estimates for the total items of equipment in the inventory ran as high as 2.8 million. Components included crew-served weapons, night-vision systems, blue force tracker identification terminals, and improvised explosive device counter systems. Individual equipment was available for issue as well, particularly the advanced body armor that saved so many lives. Kevlar armor with ceramic plates had originally been envisioned for combat units only, but its proven effectiveness and the all-around dangers of the Iraqi battlefield drove demand up. Whereas the Army requirement for constituent plates stood at 10,000 in December 2002, it rose to 110,000 in March 2003 and 475,000 in December 2003. Overall coordination

436

of logistical support for Coalition forces fell to the 377th Theater Support Command (TSC), designed as the Army's only deployable TSC and consisting largely of Reservists. Interestingly enough, the 377th TSC did not rotate as did other headquarters and units. Instead the headquarters sustained itself by individual replacements, although subordinate logistical units did rotate. In this particular case the value of continuity trumped other considerations to sustain combat units as they cycled into and out of Iraq.[34]

Chapter 4 explored a revolution in military contracting beginning in the 1990s, and subsequent chapters have revisited that topic. By 2003 contractors were an integral, if not always intentional, aspect of Army transformation. They provided flexibility, mustered unique skills, partially offset downsizing, and became an indispensable shadow workforce. Estimates of their numbers in Iraq vary wildly, depending in part on definitions. At the core would be such altogether embedded personnel as the logistical assistance representatives (LARs) servicing new or specialized equipment, or the Logistics Civil Augmentation Program (LOGCAP) personnel managing forward operating bases and other Coalition facilities. Looking more broadly, one finds such personnel as the lower-level staffs of LOGCAP facilities or the commercial truck drivers who dominated most logistical convoys. Most projects and many sites were physically secured by contracted personnel. Hundreds of thousands more contractors were temporarily employed on specific projects, often under the auspices of CERP and other programs in part designed to keep local manpower gainfully employed—and out of the insurgency. In the case of commodities being managed "from the factory to the foxhole," the front end of the equation was almost entirely in the hands of contractors. Best estimates suggest that more than 100,000 in Iraq were directly signed on to contracts with the United States government, and several times that number were temporarily employed on projects or by friendly agencies and individuals at any given time. Some American logistical nimbleness would have been impossible without contracted support. In a matter of months most soldiers went from sleeping on the backs of vehicles or "in the dirt" to living in prefabricated buildings or converted Iraqi facilities. Logistics Support Area (LSA) Anaconda alone had two hundred buildings surrounded by thirteen miles of fence. Even soldiers living in Saddam Hussein's former palaces relied upon contractors for such base operations support (BASOPS) functions as utilities, maintenance, and mess support. When the insurgency bubbled up and IEDs became a major threat, Third Army hastily converted thousands of wheeled vehicles to an up-armored posture. By December 2004 six thousand had intrinsic built-in armored protection, ten thousand had custom-manufactured protective add-on kits, and almost five thousand had improvised ad hoc armor. All of the built-in armor and add-on kits came via contract, and virtually all of the add-on kits were mounted by contractors. When it became apparent IRAQI FREEDOM would require recurrent rotations and that vehicles in Iraq grossly exceeded traditional monthly mileages, contractors stood up the programs and infrastructure to refurbish hundreds of vehicles a month as part of the "reset" process. Arab-speaking linguists proved essential as the occupation lengthened and deepened, and most came under contract. Many of these uniquely qualified personnel were not eligible for service in the United States Army, and others found that service as a contractor paid better. In addition to circumstances wherein only contractors could have gotten the job done, there were many others wherein it was more practical and convenient to pass the job along to them. A case in point was the destruction of ubiquitous unexploded ordnance. The Corps of Engineers signed on five civilian firms and 2,600 contractors to a program that ultimately destroyed 450,000 tons of munitions. Contractors proved essential to the success of IRAQI FREEDOM, but there was a down side. A stated goal of the Army in Iraq was to "maximize contracted CSS [combat service support] capabilities to minimize CSS force deployments." Prior to April 2004 transportation, field services, bulk fuel, retail fuel, food service operations, and BASOPS functions were heavily dominated by contractors. The system seemed to be working well, other than the usual grousing about time lags separating statements of work from actual execution and the relative inflexibility of contracts once signed. The April 2004 conflagration shook the premise that uniformed and contracted CSS were interchangeable. Contractors took significant casualties, encountering risks considerably beyond those they had signed up for. The first battle of Al Fallujah was precipitated by the murder and mutilation of contractors. Five times as many contractors as soldiers were killed in the spectacular Good Friday ambush of the 724th Transportation Company. Contractors were killed, endangered, or kidnapped across the country. Many fought for their lives alongside the soldiers they were supporting. Most performed ably and well, but more than a few did not show up for work or refused to assume further risks. The logistical paradigm changed. Higher proportions of combat troops were diverted to securing installations and convoys. Outposts were consolidated, rationalized, and reduced in number—reducing "presence" in many Iraqi communities. Troops were diverted to theretofore contracted functions, and the force structure altered as more CSS formations were brought in. Contractors expanded their own security, hiring more guards, deploying more weapons, and charging accordingly. The goal of contracting as much CSS as possible remained, with the hedge that the Army always be postured to operate under "nonpermissive conditions" anywhere in Iraq. This changed force structure somewhat, but the underlying logic of Army transformation's revolution in military contracting remained. The Army was too small and too combat oriented not to contract for functions it had always considered "below the line."[35]

Cooperation with Allies had been problematic for Army transformation since its origins in the 1990s. Most Allies operated within a framework of American communications and logistical support when deployed, and the United States in turn was dependent on them to offset its paucity of manpower. In Iraq only the British were remotely on par with the technologies Army transformation involved, yet American Patriot missiles nevertheless shot down one of their planes in the first few days of IRAQI FREEDOM. British vehicles were fitted out with appliqué BFT in numbers sufficient to render their units intervisible with American counterparts, and by and large fit in capably with American communications. Other Coalition forces were not so well tucked in, and problems were hugely aggravated when the Coalition integrated Iraqi units into the effort. Part

American and Iraqi soldiers on a combined operation

of the problem stemmed from initial differences of opinion concerning the roles Iraqi soldiers were to play. Ambassador Bremer and the Coalition Provisional Authority, mindful of Saddam Hussein's excesses, envisioned a small Iraqi Army oriented on the borders with a minimal domestic role. American commanders, facing an emerging insurgency, wanted Iraqi auxiliaries that would become partners as the struggle progressed. Two militaries began to emerge: the CPA endorsed Iraqi Armed Forces (IAF) and a paramilitary Iraqi Civil Defense Corps (ICDC) parented locally throughout Iraq by various divisions and brigades. On 22 April 2004, the initiatives came together when the ICDC became the Iraqi National Guard (ING) of the IAF, and the CPA accepted a substantial and growing domestic role for the Iraqi Army. The Iraqi Army and the Iraqi National Guard both originated as garrison-based troops with little sustainment capability and virtually no deployable combat service support. They imposed a considerable burden on the Coalition CSS structure that was mitigated over time by a heavy reliance upon contracting. Contracting could in fact deal with such basics as food, water, fuel, transportation, and the maintenance of venerable equipment—whether of U.S. or Soviet design. It could not bring the Iraqis within the envelope of Army transformation, however. Shortages of equipment, maintenance issues, and concerns for security compromises argued against plugging the Iraqis directly into blue force tracking, networked battlefield surveillance, or the entirety of the American digital command and control system. GPS and unencrypted radios could be and were issued to Iraqis with no particular degradation or risk. By and large Iraqi units operated within an American framework during this period, and American headquarters or liaison teams gave them indirect access to precision-guided munitions, networked battlefield surveillance, GPS-facilitated friendly situation awareness, and other military technologies of the Information Age. For some time the United States had struggled with multitiered national technical capabilities within NATO. In Iraq it encountered an extreme case. The good news was that Iraqi companies and battalions performed increasingly capably within the American framework. The bad news was that they could only go so far with respect to modernization or scale of operations without a change of approach.[36]

Afghanistan and Iraq imposed, as we have seen, huge maintenance demands upon the Army's legacy vehicles and aircraft. Mileages and hours greatly exceeded customary usages. Such mundane items as road wheels and track shoes were consumed at unprecedented rates, creating major shortages and multiplying production several-fold. In a matter of months thousands of HMMWVs went from being unarmored to up-armored, in most cases by virtue of factory-made or locally improvised add-on kits. This added hundreds of pounds to the weight borne by suspension systems, with predictable maintenance implications. Beyond this wear on traditional fleets, there were maintenance demands associated with the new equipment brought in by Army transformation. Stryker vehicles and the potpourri of MRAPs introduced later were new, but traditional enough in their design to maintain routinely. More challenging were the tens of thousands of appliqué electronic components that increasingly digitized the force. Appliqué BFT kits, as we have seen, ballooned from 1,200 to 55,000 in a few years' time. Each consisted of multiple components, as did the hardware that enabled FBCB2. The most critical or sensitive items of this equipment operated in temperature-controlled environments, but most were routinely exposed to horrific heat, suffocating dust, and the tender mercies of inexperienced operators. At the unit level the technical sophistication to repair these electronic components did not exist, and units were only marginally capable of debugging the software as well. Dependence on embedded contractors was nearly absolute for all but the simplest of interventions. The simplest intervention of all, of course, was simply to remove a "black box" and replace it with another, evacuating the original back through channels until it ultimately reached a facility capable of repairing it—generally a depot or factory. This reinforced a maintenance trend that had been under way for some time, rendering the maintenance of Army vehicles ever more akin to the maintenance of high-technology aircraft—and requiring a corresponding depth of spares. It also further added to the significance of lines of communication, as the bits and pieces that made for a transformed Army moved along them. Fortuitously electronic components could be and often were moved by helicopter. Other similarly proliferating high technologies in Afghanistan and Iraq included UAVs, robotics, and the various jammers and sensors introduced to combat IEDs. Each of these required substantial debugging, and each came with a maintenance trail highly oriented toward evacuating constituent components. Much the same could be said of upgrades to such common missiles as the Army Tactical Missile System (ATACMS), Patriots, and Hellfire, and of advances in avionics as well. Of the technologies associated with Army transformation, only JDAMs and other joint munitions did not imply a substantial overhaul to the Army maintenance system. These were maintained by others in bases far away, but with modular replacement systems and industrial links analogous to those in the direction Army maintenance was traveling.[37]

Perhaps the most demanding sustainment challenge the Army faced, manpower, was not particularly related to Army transformation per se—although it was tightly interwoven with the smaller and leaner Army some futurists believed transformation made possible. Previous chapters have described an ever-increasing reliance on the reserve component and steady improvements in family programs and other initiatives to encourage soldiers to reenlist. Chapter 6 described the move to a brigade-based Army, military occupational specialty (MOS) reallocations, and increases in manpower ceilings in the context of rotational demands for Afghanistan and Iraq. By the end of 2005 the Army sustained 600,000 soldiers on active duty, of whom 72,000 were National Guard and 41,000 Army Reserve. The active component exceeded an enlistment goal of 71,000 in 2003 and 77,500 in 2004, but fell 6,400 short of its goal of 80,000 in 2005. Fortuitously, active-component retention remained robust. The average reenlistment bonus more than doubled from under $5,000 to over $10,000, and the numbers of bonus recipients soared from 7,500 in 2003 through 18,000 in 2004 to 44,500 in 2005. The reserve component struggled with enlistments and retention through FY2005, generally retaining strength overall but often "under glide path" for recruitment. Some called for a return to the draft, although this was never seriously considered. Somewhat after the period of this study a souring national economy and declining casualties in Iraq contributed to bringing recruitment back on track, as did extraordinary efforts by the Army Recruiting Command and those assisting it. Until that time, manpower was tight and the wars in Iraq and Afghanistan depended on repeated rotations from a military manpower base that was perilously thin.[38]

Conclusions

Army planners often speak of an "80 percent solution," an unperfected plan that nevertheless accomplishes the mission with available time and resources. This seems a useful metaphor for the performance of the transforming Army in Afghanistan and Iraq. Prior to 2003 Army transformers had ample time but little money. After 2003 they had ample money but little time. The Army nevertheless showed well in diverse and challenging circumstances. Certainly it demonstrated its newly expeditionary posture by deploying more quickly and capably than ever before. When faced with opponents in conventional array, it dominated them by margins even greater than those of DESERT STORM. Relative casualties were more akin to nineteenth-century colonial wars than to twentieth-century conventional battles. The pivot from conventional to unconventional operations proved problematic, largely because of a dearth of manpower to cope with recognizably manpower-intense requirements. Reasonably served by doctrine and experience, the Army did demonstrate qualitative shortcomings with respect to human intelligence, linguists, the con-

441

figuration of its command and control, rules of engagement, detainee operations, and its overall approach to the locals outside of self-defined constraints for a "proper" military sphere. Much of the technology associated with Army transformation did prove useful in unconventional operations. Cases in point included satellite-facilitated command and control, blue force tracking and related measures for friendly situation awareness, unmanned aerial vehicles and other enhancements to battlefield surveillance, GPS navigation, digital information management and reach back, ubiquitous precision-guided munitions, and an increased capacity for joint operations. Digitally facilitated "just in time" logistics worked out imperfectly; perilous ground communications dictated a partial return to "just in case" stockpiling. Vehicle fleets did have to be reconfigured for stability operations, providing alternate sets that emphasized up-armored wheels over armored tracks. Contractors proved indispensable in the light of technical sophistication and manpower constraints, but relative divisions of labor had to be reworked in the light of battlefield experience. Maintenance did continue to move in the direction of "black box" exchange more so than onsite repair. The greatest tactical challenge of the war, improvised explosive devices, emerged to inflict over half the American casualties in both wars. In the face of this threat the Army devised countermeasures that kept casualties down despite an order of magnitude increase in attacks. This capacity to muster tactics, technique, and technology to minimize casualties was a hallmark of both campaigns. Absent Army transformation, casualties undoubtedly would have been multiplied many-fold to achieve the same results. Russian experiences in Afghanistan and Chechnya suggest a probable fate had the Army failed to advance. Transformation enabled the United States to dispatch conventional foes handily and to sustain prolonged major counterinsurgencies with relatively few casualties and a small volunteer Army.

Notes

[1] *Conduct of the Persian Gulf War: Final Report to Congress* (Washington DC: Department of Defense, 1992), 371–449; Gregory Fontenot, E. J. Degen, and David Tohn, *On Point: The United States Army in Operation IRAQI FREEDOM* (Fort Leavenworth, Kansas: Combat Studies Institute Press, 2004), 29–84.

[2] *Operation IRAQI FREEDOM–"It Was a Prepositioned War"* (Fort Belvoir, Virginia: Historical Office, U.S. Army Material Command, 2003); E-mail, Major William Story (CFLCC/3d Army Forward Historian) to Mr. William W. Epley, CMH, 22 July 2003, sub: CSI Paper, Historians Files, CMH; General Paul J. Kern, "Technology, Transformation and War–A Kaleidoscope of Force," *Army 2003–2004 Green Book*, October 2003, 63–70; Army General Staff Council Meeting notes, 7 January 2003, Historians Files, CMH; Army General Staff Council Meeting notes, 14 July 2003, Historians Files, CMH; MFR of Telephone Conversation, Brigadier General (USA, Ret.) John S. Brown with General (USA, Ret.) Gordon R. Sullivan, 091300 August 2008, Historians Files, CMH; "Speed Bumps: 82nd Airborne's Shaky Line in the Sand," *Army Times*, 21 October 1991; Birger Bergesen and John McDonald, *Assessment of Contingency and Expeditionary Force Capabilities* (McClean, Virginia: Science Applications International Corporation, 1994); After Action Review, 2d Brigade, 1st Cavalry Division, Intrinsic Action 95–3, 17 October 1995, Historians Files, CMH.

[3] U.S. Transportation Command: A Short History (Scott Air Force Base, Illinois: U.S. Transportation Command Office of Public Affairs, 2005); Lieutenant General Johnnie E. Wilson, "Power Projection Logistics Now . . . and in the 21st Century," *Army 1994–1995 Green Book*, October 1994, 137–43; Army Regulation 210–20, *Master Planning for Army Installations* (Washington DC: Department of the Army, 1992); Army General Staff Council Meeting notes, 14 August 2003, Historians Files, CMH; *Lessons Learned: Executive Summary* (Fort Hood, Texas: 4th Infantry Division, 17 June 2004); Rick Atkinson, *In the Company of Soldiers: A Chronicle of Combat* (New York: Henry Holt, 2004), 11–42; *Conduct of the Persian Gulf War: Final Report to Congress*, 371–449; Fontenot, Degen, and Tohn, 29–84; General Tommy Franks, *American Soldier* (New York: Reagan Books, 2004), 321–431.

[4] Betty R. Kennedy, *Globemaster III: Acquiring the C–17* (Scott Air Force Base, Illinois: Air Mobility Command Office of History, 2004); Fontenot, Degan, and Tohn, 222–30; Lieutenant Colonel Thomas W. Collins, "173rd Airborne Brigade in Iraq," *Army* (June 2003): 42–46; E-mail, Major William Story (CFLCC/3d Army Forward Historian) to Mr. William W. Epley, CMH, 22 July 2003, sub: CSI Paper; Kern, 63–70; Army General Staff Council Meeting notes, 7 January 2003; Army General Staff Council Meeting notes, 14 July 2003; Franks, *American Soldier*, 432–536; Atkinson, 11–42; *Conduct of the Persian Gulf War: Final Report to Congress*, 371–449.

[5] *Conduct of the Persian Gulf War: Final Report to Congress*, 371–449; Fontenot, Degen, and Tohn, 94, 178, 219–20, 441–95; General Dennis J. Reimer, "The Strike Force Operational Concept Paper," in *Soldiers Are Our Credentials: The Collected Papers and Selected Works of the Thirty-third Chief of Staff, United States Army* (Washington DC: Center of Military History, 2000), 254–63; History—2nd Stryker Cavalry Regiment (Heidelberg, Germany: Seventh Army Public Affairs, 2009); 82d Airborne Division, *Campaign Plan Overview Briefing* (Fort Bragg, North Carolina: 82d Airborne Division, 2004); Army General Staff Council Meeting notes, 1 April 2002, Historians Files, CMH; Army General Staff Council Meeting notes, 21 July

2003, Historians Files, CMH; Major Wayne Eyre, "Heavy-Light Integration: Why Reinvent the Wheel?" *Army Doctrine and Training Bulletin,* May 1999.

[6] Fontenot, Degen, and Tohn, 73–84, 408–11; Franks, *American Soldier*, 321–432; Army General Staff Council Meeting notes, 25 November 2002, Historians Files, CMH; Army General Staff Council Meeting notes, 14 July 2003; Memo, Department of the Army, 9 July 2003, sub: Acting CSA Visit to Kuwait and Iraq, 4–6 July 2003, Historians Files, CMH; Kim Burger, "Iraq Campaign Raises New Logistics Concerns," *Jane's Defense Weekly*, 10 September 2003; Gordon Trowbridge, "Too Many Troops," *Army Times*, 1 May 2006, 8–9; Briefing, Multi-National Corps–Iraq, "What Did We Learn That Illuminated the Future of This Fight?" 3 April 2005, Historians Files, CMH; Office Call notes, Project and Contracting Office, Iraq, with Chief of Military History, 7 July 2005, Historians Files, CMH; Michelle Tan, "No Easy Exit," *Army Times*, 24 August 2009; Army General Staff Council Meeting notes, 21 July 2003; Army General Staff Council Meeting notes, 12 January 2004, Historians Files, CMH; Army General Staff Council Meeting notes, 26 April 2004, Historians Files, CMH.

[7] Franks, *American Soldier*, 238–320; Charles H. Briscoe, Richard L. Kiper, James A. Schroder, and Kalev I. Sepp, *Weapon of Choice: U.S. Army Special Operations Forces in Afghanistan* (Fort Leavenworth, Kansas: Combat Studies Institute, 2003), 33–92; Richard Stewart, *The United States Army in Afghanistan: Operation ENDURING FREEDOM, October 2001–March 2002* (Washington DC: Center of Military History, 2003), 3–30; Army General Staff Council Meeting notes, 4 February 2002, Historians Files, CMH; Army General Staff Council Meeting notes, 25 November 2002; Sean D. Naylor, "Alliances Bolster Taliban Strength," *Army Times,* 5 January 2010, 16; Ruhullah Khapalwak and David Rohde, "A Look at America's New Hope: The Afghan Tribes," *New York Times*, 31 January 2010; Master Sergeant Sue Harper and Staff Sergeant Gregory Jones, "Supporting Afghanistan from Europe: U.S. Army Europe's 21st Theater Support Command," *Army* (August 2002): 41–43; E-mail, Brigadier General Mark E. O'Neill to Major General Franklin Hagenbeck, 6 January 2003, sub: Anaconda Lessons Learned–NDU Paper, Historians Files, CMH.

[8] CMH Information Paper, Robert S. Rush, The Individual Replacement System: Good, Bad or Indifferent? Army Replacement Policy, Cold War and Before (Washington DC: Center of Military History, n.d.); General Peter Schoomaker and General Richard Cody, Transcript of Media Roundtable Conducted at the Association of the United States Army Annual Meeting, 26 October 2004, Historians Files, CMH; Army General Staff Council Meeting notes, 14 August 2003; Army General Staff Council Meeting notes, 8 September 2003, Historians Files, CMH; Army General Staff Council Meeting notes, 20 October 2003, Historians Files, CMH; Army General Staff Council Meeting notes, 26 April 2004; Dr. Donald P. Wright and Colonel Timothy R. Reese, *On Point II: Transition to the New Campaign, The United States Army in Operation IRAQI FREEDOM, May 2003–January 2005* (Fort Leavenworth, Kansas: Combat Studies Institute Press, 2008), 322–58, 489–525; Peter R. Mansoor, *Baghdad at Sunrise: A Brigade Commander's War in Iraq* (New Haven, Connecticut: Yale University Press, 2008), 242–340.

[9] Fontenot, Degen, and Tohn, 1–26, 383–426; Robert H. Scales Jr., *Certain Victory: The United States Army in the Gulf War* (Washington DC: Office of the Chief of Staff, United States Army, 1993); Thomas K. Adams, *The Army After Next: The First Postindustrial Army* (Stanford; California University Press, 2008); James R. Blaker, *Transforming Military Force: The Legacy of Arthur Cebrowski and Network Centric Warfare* (London: Praeger Security International, 2007); Eric L. Haney with Brian Thomsen, *Beyond Shock and Awe: Warfare in the 21st Century* (New York: Berkley Publishing Group, 2006); D. Robert Worley, *Shaping Military Force: Revolution or*

Relevance in a Post–Cold War World (Westport, Connecticut: Praeger Security International, 2006); Franks, *American Soldier*, 321–81.

[10] Fontenot, Degen and Tohn, 1–26, 42–44, 174–76, 209–21, 258–82, 340–47, 383–426; Franks, *American Soldier*, 321–431; Atkinson, 103–296; David Zucchino, *Thunder Run: The Armored Strike to Capture Baghdad* (New York: Atlantic Monthly Press, 2004), 1–66; Scales, 213–320, 370–76; *Conduct of the Persian Gulf War: Final Report to Congress*, 543–76; Todd S. Brown, *Battleground Iraq: Journal of a Company Commander* (Washington DC: Center of Military History, 2007), 231–36; Army General Staff Council Meeting notes, 5 August 2002, Historians Files, CMH; Army General Staff Council Meeting notes, 14 July 2003; Army General Staff Council Meeting notes, 11 August 2003, Historians Files, CMH.

[11] *Conduct of the Persian Gulf War: Final Report to Congress*, 543–76, 806–07; Scales, 151, 186, 203, 254, 305, 362; Fontenot, Degen, and Tohn, 85–382; Atkinson, 103–298; Zuccino, 1–308; John S. Brown, "The Battle for Norfolk," in Frederick W. Kagan and Chris Kubik, *Leaders in War: West Point Remembers the 1991 Gulf War* (New York: Frank Cass, 2005), 11–24; Army General Staff Council Meeting notes, 5 August 2002; Army General Staff Council Meeting notes, 14 July 2003; Army General Staff Council Meeting notes, 11 August 2003; E-mail, Major William Story (CFLCC/3d Army Forward Historian) to Mr. William W. Epley, CMH, 22 July 2003, sub: CSI Paper; TRADOC Case Study for the Chief of Staff, Attack on the 507th Maintenance Company, 23 March 2003, An Nasiriyah, Iraq, Historians Files, CMH.

[12] Lieutenant Otto J. Guenther, "Blue Force Tracking," *Army* (April 2004): 13–15; Zucchino, 67–69; Fontenot, Degan, and Tohn, 329–82; General Fred Franks Jr. with Tom Clancy, *Into the Storm: A Study in Command* (New York: G. P. Putnam's Sons, 1997), 433–87; Franks, *American Soldier*, 515–19; Briefing, Department of the Army, "Friendly Fire Determination," 9 August 1991, Historians Files, CMH; Briefing, Army Combat Identification Task Force, "Combat Identification," 22 November 1991, Historians Files, CMH; Sean D. Naylor, "Friendly Fire: The Reckoning," *Army Times*, 21 August 1991; Army General Staff Council Meeting notes, 14 July 2003; Army General Staff Council Meeting notes, 11 August 2003.

[13] Scales, 370–73; H. R. McMaster, Crack in the Foundation: Defense Transformation and the Underlying Assumption of Dominant Knowledge in Future War, Historians Files, CMH; Eric T. Olson, "Attacking the Republican Guard," in Kagan and Kubik, 25–43; H. R. McMaster, "The Battle of 73 Easting," in Kagan and Kubik, 105–17; Fontenot, Degan, and Tohn, 241–328; Franks, *American Soldier*, 501–30; Ltr, James A. Thomson, CEO, RAND, to Donald A. Rumsfeld, SecDef, 7 February 2005, sub: Iraq: Translating Lessons Into Future Defense Policies, Historians Files, CMH; Anthony H. Cordesman, Center for Strategic and International Studies, "The Lessons of the Iraq War: Summary Briefing," 15 July 2003, Historians Files, CMH; Major David J. Rude and Lieutenant Colonel Daniel E. Williams, "The Warfighter Mindset and the War in Iraq," *Army* (July 2003): 35–40; Zucchino, 1–66, 86–308; Atkinson, 103–277; Army General Staff Council Meeting notes, 14 July 2003; Army General Staff Council Meeting notes, 11 August 2003.

[14] *Conduct of the Persian Gulf War: Final Report to Congress*, 657–808; Scales, 364–73; Fontenot, Degan, and Tohn, 195–208, 258–81, 329–82, 400–406, 414–26; Army Senior Leader Update, "Precision Strike: A Unique American Military Advantage . . . but with Limitations," 14 August 2001, Historians Files, CMH; Peter Grier, "The JDAM Revolution," *Air Force On Line: The Journal of the Air Force Association*, September 2006; Ltr, James A. Thomson, CEO, RAND, to Donald A. Rumsfeld, SecDef, 7 February 2005, sub: Iraq: Translating Lessons Into Future Defense Policies; Anthony H. Cordesman, Center for Strategic and International Studies, "The Lessons

of the Iraq War: Summary Briefing," 15 July 2003; Franks, *American Soldier*, 382–477; Dennis Steele, "Baghdad: The Crossroads," *Army* (June 2003): 30–34; E-mail, Major William Story (CFLCC/3d Army Forward Historian) to Mr. William W. Epley, CMH, 22 July 2003, sub: CSI Paper; Zucchino, 102–16, 261–308; Atkinson, 103–24, 215–56; Army General Staff Council Meeting notes, 26 August 2002, Historians Files, CMH; Army General Staff Council Meeting notes, 14 July 2003; Army General Staff Council Meeting notes, 11 August 2003.

[15] Fontenot, Degan, and Tohn, 15–22, 329–82, 383–424; Field Manual 100–5, *Operations* (Washington DC: Department of the Army, 1986); *Conduct of the Persian Gulf War: Final Report to Congress*, 88–179, 234–40, 589–98; Scales, 157–212, 355–84; Franks, *American Soldier*, 432–536; Atkinson, 103–296; Zucchino, 261–308; Anthony H. Cordesman, Center for Strategic and International Studies, "The Lessons of the Iraq War: Summary Briefing," 15 July 2003; General Crosbie E. Saint, Brigadier General E. J. Sinclair, and Major Jonathan O. Gass, "Army Aviation: On the Move," *Army* (July 2004): 33–37; Lieutenant General Larry J. Dodgen, "Integrating Global Missile Defense," *Army* (December 2005): 29–32; Major General Robert P. Lennox, "Air and Missile Defense Goes Global," *Army* (December 2006): 36–44; Army General Staff Council Meeting notes, 14 July 2003; Army General Staff Council Meeting notes, 11 August 2003.

[16] John J. McGrath, *The Brigade: A History* (Fort Leavenworth, Kansas: Combat Studies Institute Press, 2004), 77–140; Scales, 364–73; Fontenot, Degan, and Tohn, 195–208, 258–81, 329–82, 400–406, 414–26; Ltr, James A. Thomson, CEO, RAND, to Donald A. Rumsfeld, SecDef, 7 February 2005, sub: Iraq: Translating Lessons Into Future Defense Policies; Anthony H. Cordesman, Center for Strategic and International Studies, "The Lessons of the Iraq War: Summary Briefing," 15 July 2003; Franks, *American Soldier*, 382–477; Steele, "Baghdad: The Crossroads," 30–34; E-mail, Major William Story (CFLCC/3d Army Forward Historian) to Mr. William W. Epley, CMH, 22 July 2003, sub: CSI Paper; Zucchino, 102–16, 261–308; Atkinson, 103–24, 215–56; Army General Staff Council Meeting notes, 14 July 2003; Army General Staff Council Meeting notes, 11 August 2003; "Operation IRAQI FREEDOM: A Chronology," *Army* (May 2003): 47–52.

[17] *Conduct of the Persian Gulf War: Final Report to Congress*, 2–16, 292–97, 313–17, 333–46; Scales, 65–69, 355–84; Fontenot, Degan, and Tohn, 99–102, 329–82, 427–36; Franks, *American Soldier*, 321–536.

[18] Thomas E. Ricks, *Fiasco: The American Military Adventure in Iraq* (London: Penguin Books, 2006), 85–148; Bob Woodward, *The War Within: A Secret White House History, 2006–2008* (New York: Simon & Schuster, 2008), 1–41; Douglas Macgregor, "Fire the Generals!" *Defense and the National Interest,* 30 April 2007; Greg Jaffe, "Critiques of Iraq War Reveal Rifts Among Army Officers," *Wall Street Journal,* 29 June 2007, 1, 11; Lieutenant Colonel Paul Yingling, "A Failure in Generalship," *Armed Forces Journal* (May 2007); Eric Herring and Glen Rangwala, *Iraq in Fragments: The Occupation and Its Legacy* (Ithaca, New York: Cornell University Press, 2006), 161–209; William Terdoslavich, "From Shock and Awe to Aw Shucks," in Haney with Thomsen, *Beyond Shock and Awe*, 11–63; Andrew J. Bacevich, *The New American Militarism: How Americans Are Seduced by War* (New York: Oxford University Press, 2005), 175–204; Wright and Reese, 49–85.

[19] Wright and Reese, 49–85; Jeffrey J. Clarke, *Advice and Support: The Final Years, 1965–1973* (Washington DC: Center of Military History, 1988); James L. Collins Jr., *The Development and Training of the South Vietnamese Army, 1950–1972* (Washington DC: Center of Military History, 1975); Lewis Sorley, *A Better War: The Unexamined Victories and Final Tragedy of America's Last Years in Vietnam* (New York: Harcourt

Brace, 1999); Field Manual 100–20, *Counterinsurgency* (Washington DC: Department of the Army, 1964); Field Manual 31–23, *Stability Operations* (Washington DC; Department of the Army, 1967); Field Manual 31–73, *Advisor Handbook for Stability Operations* (Washington DC: Department of the Army, 1967); Field Manual 100–5, *Operations*, 1962; *The National Defense Authorization Act for Fiscal Year 1987*; Scales, 355–90; Richard W. Stewart, *The United States Army in Somalia, 1992–1994* (Washington DC: Center of Military History, 2003); Field Manual 100–5, *Operations*, 1993; Field Manual 100–23, *Peace Operations* (Washington DC: Department of the Army, 1994).

[20] Wright and Reese, 55–65; Lawrence A. Yates, *The US Military's Experience in Stability Operations, 1789–2005* (Fort Leavenworth, Kansas: Combat Studies Institute Press, 2006); Gordon W. Rudd, *Humanitarian Intervention: Assisting the Iraqi Kurds in Operation PROVIDE COMFORT, 1991* (Washington DC: Center of Military History, 2004); Walter E. Kretchik, Robert F. Baumann, and John T. Fishel, *Invasion, Intervention, "Intervasion": A Concise History of the U.S. Army in Operation UPHOLD DEMOCRACY* (Fort Leavenworth, Kansas: Combat Studies Institute Press, 1998); Stewart, *The United States Army in Somalia*; R. Cody Phillips, *Bosnia-Herzegovina: The U.S. Army's Role in Peace Enforcement Operations, 1995–2004* (Washington DC: Center of Military History, 2005); R. Cody Phillips, *Operation JOINT GUARDIAN: The U.S. Army in Kosovo* (Washington DC: Center of Military History, 2006); Stewart, *The United States Army in Afghanistan*; Responses to E-mail, John S. Brown, 21 May 2002, sub: SA Directed "Think Piece," Historians Files, CMH; Briefing, Center for Army Lessons Learned for the Chief of Military History, 20 January 2000, Historians Files, CMH.

[21] John J. McGrath, *Boots on the Ground: Troop Density in Contingency Operations* (Fort Leavenworth, Kansas: Combat Studies Institute Press, 2006); Andrew J. Birtle, *U.S. Army Counterinsurgency and Contingency Operations Doctrine, 1860–1941* (Washington DC: Center of Military History, 1998); Richard Clutterbuck, *The Long, Long War: Counterinsurgency in Malaya and Vietnam* (Westport, Connecticut: Praeger, 1966); Robert Thompson, *Defeating Communist Insurgency: Experiences from Malaya and Vietnam* (London: Chatto and Windus, 1972); Kretchik, Baumann, and Fishel; Stewart, *The United States Army in Somalia*; Briefing, Center of Military History, "Numerical Considerations in Army Occupations Past," Historians Files, CMH; Wright and Reese, 25–129; Kevin C. M. Benson, "PH IV CFLCC Stability Operations Planning," in Brian M. De Toy, ed., *Turning Victory into Success: Military Operations After the Campaign* (Fort Leavenworth, Kansas: Combat Studies Institute Press, 2004); Brown, *Battleground Iraq*.

[22] Wright and Reese, 191–272; Field Manual 34–1, *Intelligence and Electronic Warfare* (Washington DC: Department of the Army, 1994); Fontenot, Degan, and Tohn, 195–208, 258–81, 329–82, 400–406, 414–26; Army Senior Leader Update, "Precision Strike: A Unique American Military Advantage . . . but with Limitations," 14 August 2001; Ltr, James A. Thomson, CEO, RAND, to Donald A. Rumsfeld, SecDef, 7 February 2005, sub: Iraq: Translating Lessons Into Future Defense Policies; Anthony H. Cordesman, Center for Strategic and International Studies, "The Lessons of the Iraq War: Summary Briefing," 15 July 2003; Franks, *American Soldier*, 382–477; Field Manual 34–52, *Intelligence Interrogation* (Washington DC: Department of the Army, 1992); Atkinson, 159–256; Brown, *Battleground Iraq*, 74–219; Mansoor, 33–85, 114–24; Briefing, Multi-National Corps–Iraq, "What Did We Learn That Illuminated the Future of This Fight?" 3 April 2005; Army General Staff Council Meeting notes, 26 August 2002; Army General Staff Council Meeting notes, 14 July 2003; Army General Staff Council Meeting notes, 11 August 2003.

[23] Fontenot, Degan, and Tohn, 29–84; Franks, *American Soldier*, 382–477; Wright and Reese, 139–83; Briefing, V Corps, "V Corps and CJTF-7 Transitions and Challenges," 30 September 2004, Historians Files, CMH; E-mail, Major William Story, CFLCC/3d Army Forward Historian to Mr. William W. Epley, CMH, 22 July 2003, sub: CSI Paper; ATLANTIC RESOLVE CINC's Exercise Book, 31 March 1995, Historians Files, CMH; Briefing, General Wesley K. Clark to the NATO Norfolk Conference, "The 21st Century Force: Defining Requirements," 12 November 1998, Historians Files, CMH; Brown, *Battleground Iraq*, 74–219; Mansoor, 1–154; William M. Donnelly, *Transforming an Army at War: Designing the Modular Force 1991–2005* (Washington DC: Center of Military History, 2007); *Army Comprehensive Guide to Modularity* (Fort Monroe, Virginia: U.S. Army Training and Doctrine Command, 2004); Telephone Conversation notes, Brigadier General (USA, Ret.) John S. Brown with General (USA, Ret.) Peter J. Schoomaker, 111330 May 2009, Historians Files, CMH; Army General Staff Council Meeting notes, 26 August 2002; Army General Staff Council Meeting notes, 14 July 2003; Army General Staff Council Meeting notes, 11 August 2003.

[24] Wright and Reese, 139–83, 241–67, 427–77; Benson; Major General Antonio M. Taguba, *Article 15–6 Investigation of the 800th Military Police Brigade (The Taguba Report),* 15 February 2004, Historians Files, CMH; Lieutenant General Anthony R. Jones, *AR 15–6 Investigation of the Abu Ghraib Prison and 205th Military Intelligence Brigade*, 24 August 2004, Historians Files, CMH; Brown, *Battleground Iraq*, 74–219; John A. Nagl, *Learning to Eat Soup with a Knife: Counterinsurgency Lessons from Malaya and Vietnam* (Chicago: University of Chicago Press, 2005), ix–xvi; Clarke; Collins, *The Development and Training of the South Vietnamese Army, 1950–1972*; Briefing, Multi-National Corps–Iraq, "What Did We Learn That Illuminated the Future of This Fight," 4 March 2005; Briefing, Major General Peter Chiarelli, Commanding General, 1st Cavalry Division, to the Joint Staff, "Task Force Baghdad: Operation IRAQI FREEDOM II," 16 March 2005, Historians Files, CMH.

[25] Briscoe, Kiper, Schroder, and Sepp; Stewart, *The United States Army in Afghanistan*; Doug Stanton, *Horse Soldiers: The Extraordinary Story of a Band of U.S. Soldiers Who Rode to Victory in Afghanistan* (New York: Scribner, 2009); Anthony H. Cordesman, *The Lessons of Afghanistan: War Fighting, Intelligence and Force Transformation* (Washington DC: Center for Strategic and International Studies, 2002); Sean D. Naylor, *Not a Good Day to Die: The Untold Story of Operation ANACONDA* (New York: Penguin Group [USA], 2005); "U.S. Military Command in Afghanistan Is Redesigned," *Stars and Stripes,* 9 March 2007; Chris Stump, "New CJTF Commander Promises Continued Success," American Forces Press Service, 28 March 2005; Douglas DeMaio, "10th Mountain Division Takes Afghanistan Task Force Command," American Forces Press Service, 21 February 2006; CMH Information Paper, 30 November 2001, sub: Military Commissions, Historians Files, CMH; Dexter Filkins, "4 Afghan Soldiers are Killed by a Mistaken Airstrike," *New York Times*, 31 January 2010, 11; Sean D. Naylor, "McChrystal Pushes to Grow Afghan Army," *Army Times*, 12 October 2009, 26.

[26] Mark Bowden, *Black Hawk Down: A Story of Modern War* (New York: Penguin Books, 1999); *United States Forces, Somalia, After Action Report and Historical Overview: The United States Army in Somalia, 1992–1994* (Washington DC: Center of Military History, 2003); Mark J. Reardon and Jeffery A. Charlston, *From Transition to Combat: The Initial Stryker Brigade Deployment to Iraq* (Washington DC: Center of Military History, 2006); Army General Staff Council Meeting notes, 23 February 2004, Historians Files, CMH.

[27] Wright and Reese, 313–59; Brown, *Battleground Iraq*, 237–65; Mark J. Reardon, "Hell in a Very Small Marketplace: Abu Ghraib—April 2004," in John T. Hoffman,

gen. ed., *Tip of the Spear: U.S. Army Small-Unit Action in Iraq, 2004–2007* (Washington DC: Center of Military History, 2009), 13–36; Zucchino, 1–17, 67–85; Kris Osborn, "Abrams to Get High-Tech Upgrade," *Army Times*, 6 July 2009, 25; Matthew Cox, "Flexibility Key to Future GCVs," *Army Times*, 21 September 2009, 22; Dennis Steele, "The Siege of Raider Base," *Army* (August 2004): 26–34; Lieutenant General Richard Leahy, "The Medium-Weight Force: Lessons Learned and Future Contributions to Coalition Operations," *Army* (September 2004): 49–56; Mansoor, 277–333; Dick Camp, *Operation PHANTOM FURY: The Assault and Capture of Fallujah, Iraq* (Minneapolis, Minnesota: Zenith Press, 2009), 123–295; Briefing, Multi-National Corps–Iraq, "What Did We Learn That Illuminated the Future of This Fight?" 3 April 2005; Army General Staff Council Meeting notes, 11 August 2003; Army General Staff Council Meeting notes, 23 February 2004.

[28] Wright and Reese, 221–32, 313–59; Zuccino, 102–32; Mansoor, 85–154, 304–33; Camp, 97–107; 157–78; Mark D. Sherry, "Fighting in the Valley of Peace: Najaf—August 2004," in Hoffman, *Tip of the Spear*, 65–84; Christopher Drew, "For U.S., Drones Are Weapons of Choice," *New York Times*, 17 March 2009, 1; Briefing, Major General Peter Chiarelli, Commanding General, 1st Cavalry Division, to the Joint Staff, "Task Force Baghdad: Operation IRAQI FREEDOM II," 16 March 2005; Dennis Steele, "UAV: The Buddy Overhead," *Army* (May 2005): 44–45; Dennis Steele, "Commanders in Iraq: Some Lessons Learned," *Army* (June 2005): 24–30; Kris Osborn and Michael Hoffman, "Services Hammer Out Rules for UAV Operations," *Army Times*, 22 September 2008, 18; P. W. Singer, "Humans and Hardware," *Army Times*, 23 March 2009, 38; Dennis Steele, "Growing Pains: Getting UAV Aviation off the Ground in Iraq," *Army* (January 2006): 20–26; Kris Osborn and William Matthews, "Scans of Eyes, Fingerprints Help Army Find Insurgents," *AUSA Special Report*, Historians Files, CMH; Colonel Robert P. Walters Jr. and Lieutenant Colonel Daniel E. Soler, "The Battlefield Surveillance Brigade in Iraq," *Army* (December 2009): 40–45; Colonel Christopher B. Carlile, "Leading the Army's UAS Synchronization Efforts," *Army* (January 2010): 35–38; Army General Staff Council Meeting notes, 15 October 2001, Historians Files, CMH; Army General Staff Council Meeting notes, 5 September 2002, Historians Files, CMH; Army Vice Chief of Staff Council Meeting notes, 21 March 2002, Historians Files, CMH.

[29] Wright and Reese, 196–201, 313–59; Zucchino, 67–85; Mansoor, 1–32, 114–54; Brown, *Battleground Iraq*, 237–71; Kelly Kennedy, *They Fought for Each Other: The Triumph and Tragedy of the Hardest Hits Unit in Iraq* (New York: St. Martin's Press, 2010); Charles W. Sasser, *None Left Behind: The 10th Mountain Division and the Triangle of Death* (New York: St. Martin's Press, 2009); Camp, 11–30; Richard E. Killblane, "Good Friday Ambush: Abu Ghraib—9 April 2004, in Hoffman, *Tip of the Spear*, 37–64; Scott Pace et al., *The Global Positioning System: Assessing National Policies* (Santa Monica, California: RAND, 2004); Army General Staff Council Meeting notes, 20 May 2002, Historians Files, CMH; Army General Staff Council Meeting notes, 11 August 2003; Army General Staff Council Meeting notes, 14 August 2003.

[30] Franks, *American Soldier*, 432–564; Zucchino, 67–85, 117–32; Atkinson, 61–78, 277–303; Wright and Reese, 139–83, 322–59; Brown, *Battleground Iraq*, 231–36; Mansoor, 114–54, 277–333; Camp, 63–78, 123–40; Kennedy, *They Fought for Each Other*, 66–72, 162–67, 180–88; Sasser, 15–30, 281–95; Dennis Steele, "Back with the 3-15," *Army* (September 2005): 38–41; Reardon, "Hell in a Very Small Marketplace: Abu Ghraib—April 2004," 13–36; Sherry, 65–84; Dennis Steele, "The New Battle for Baghdad: Persistent Presence," *Army* (March 2007): 26–56; Scott R. Gourley, "JTRS JPEO Update: From On the Rocks to On the Air," *Army* (May 2008): 65–70; "Air-Ground Integration in Company

Command; Building Combat Ready Teams," *Army* (April 2006): 71–74; Captain Christopher L. Budihas, "So, You're Going to Iraq," *Army* (January 2005): 24–31; Briefing, Multi-National Corps–Iraq, "What Did We Learn That Illuminated the Future of This Fight?" 3 April 2005; Briefing, Major General Peter Chiarelli to the Joint Staff, "Task Force Baghdad: Operation IRAQI FREEDOM II," 16 March 2005; Army General Staff Council Meeting notes, 11 August 2003, Historians Files, CMH; Army General Staff Council Meeting notes, 23 February 2004.

[31] Wright and Reese, 273–307, 519–22; Field Manual 100–6, *Information Operations* (Washington DC: Department of the Army, 1996); Field Manual 3–13, *Information Operations: Tactics, Techniques and Procedures* (Washington DC: Department of the Army, 2003); Briefing, Major General Peter Chiarelli to the Joint Staff, "Task Force Baghdad: Operation IRAQI FREEDOM II," 16 March 2005; Mansoor, 33–84, 334–57; Camp, 123–53, 289–95; Dennis Steele, "Helping Iraq: A Block-by-Block Battle," *Army* (September 2004): 42–44; Thomas E. Ricks, "A Light in Ramadi," *Army* (March 2009): 54–68; Martin G. Clemis, "The Cultural Turn in U.S. Counterinsurgency Operations," *Army History* (Winter 2010): 21–27; James R. Crider, "Operation CLOSE ENCOUNTERS: One Unit's Strategy to Build an Alliance with the Iraqi People," *Army History* (Fall 2009): 22–36; Captain Bill Putnam, "Winning Iraqi Hearts and Minds," *Army* (January 2005): 7–8; Stanley T. Grip Jr., "The Avghani Model, *Army* (May 2008): 47–54; Lieutenant Colonel Craig T. Trebilcock, "The Modern Seven Pillars of Iraq," *Army* (February 2007): 25–33; Captain Aaron T. Render, "Saba Al Bor—A City Reborn," *Army* (January 2007): 34–36; Colonel Norvell B. De Atkine, "Islam, Islamism and Terrorism," *Army* (January 2006): 55–62; Memo for Army Staff, 9 July 2003, sub: Acting CSA Visit to Kuwait and Iraq, 4–6 July 2003; Briefing, Multi-National Corps–Iraq, "What Did We Learn That Illuminated the Future of This Fight?" 3 April 2005; Army General Staff Council Meeting notes, 2 January 2002, Historians Files, CMH; Army General Staff Council Meeting notes, 14 April 2003, Historians Files, CMH; Army General Staff Council Meeting notes, 23 December 2003, Historians Files, CMH.

[32] Memo, Chief of the Histories Division for Chief of Military History, sub: Recent Landmine Treaty Developments, 14 April 2000, Historians Files, CMH; Fontenot, Degan, and Tohn, 85–140; Wright and Reese, 313–17; Brown, *Battleground Iraq*, 74–159, 255–60; Sasser, 163–86; Kennedy, *They Fought for Each Other*, 42–65, 142–61; William H. McMichael, "Unsatisfactory Planning: Swift March to Baghdad Left Ammo Depots Unguarded, GAO Finds," *Army Times*, 2 April 2007, 16; Joint IED Defeat Organization, "IED Trends," as reproduced in *Army Times*, 27 October 2008; John T. Bennett, "Turning Point in Fight Against IEDs," *Army Times*, 1 October 2007, 34–35; Blake Morrison and Peter Eisler, "IED Numbers Drop as Troops Attack Bombs' Source," *Army Times*, 26 November, 2007, 10; "The Struggle for Iraq," *New York Times*, 18 March 2007, 12; William H. McMichael, "Head of Anti-IED Agency Says It's Been Effective," *Army Times*, 8 May 2007, 16; Greg Grant, "An Evolving Enemy," *Army Times*, 6 March 2006, 14; Greg Grant, "Savvy Attacks: Three Years of Fighting Have Produced Capable and Sophisticated Insurgents," *Army Times*, 13 February 2006, 14–15; Nina Kamp, Michael O'Hanlon, and Amy Unikewicz, "The State of Iraq: An Update," *New York Times*, 19 March 2006, 12; Clay Wilson, *Improvised Explosive Devices in Iraq: Effects and Countermeasures* (Washington DC: Congressional Research Service, 2005); Army General Staff Council Meeting notes, 2 January 2002; Army General Staff Council Meeting notes, 14 April 2003; Army General Staff Council Meeting notes, 23 December 2003.

[33] Wright and Reese, 489–558; Field Manual 4–0, *Combat Service Support* (Washington DC: Department of the Army, 2003); *Operation IRAQI FREEDOM: "It Was*

a Prepositioned War"; Burger; Matthew Cox, "Iraq War Takes Toll on Readiness," *Army Times*, 27 March, 2006, 17; Harper and Jones, 41–42; Scott R. Gourley, "The Arsenal of the Ground War," *Army* (May 2003): 37–44; Sergeant Frank N. Pellegrini, "Supporting Gulf War 2.0," *Army* (September 2003): 20–26; Dennis Steele, "Carrying the Load in Iraq," *Army* (July 2004): 14–22; Lieutenant Colonel Peter B. Everitt, "The Mobility Officer—Master of Deployment," *Army* (April 2005): 33–36; Charles W. Fick Jr., "Army Field Support Brigades Move Out in Europe and Iraq," *Army* (December 2005): 23–28; Matthew Cox, "What They Need, When They Need It," *Army Times,* 22 October 2006, 16; "Army Prepositioned Stocks: Indispensable to America's Force-projection Capability," Association of the United States Army, December 2008; Army General Staff Council Meeting notes, 2 September 2002, Historians Files, CMH; Army General Staff Council Meeting notes, 14 July 2003; Army General Staff Council Meeting notes, 11 August 2003.

[34] Wright and Reese, 489–527; Eric Peltz et al., *Sustainment of Army Forces in Operation Iraqi Freedom: Major Findings and Recommendations* (Santa Monica, California: RAND, 2005); *Actions Needed to Improve the Availability of Critical Items During Current and Future Operations* (Washington DC: Government Accountability Office, 2005); William H. McMichael, Gina Cavallaro, and Rick Maze, "Help Is on the Way," *Army Times*, 3 August 2009, 16–17; William McMichael, "Paying for More Troops," *Army Times*, 31 August 2009, 8; Gordon Lubold, "QDR Provides Blueprint for a Long War," *Army Times*, 13 February 2006, 9; *The Rebalance of the Army National Guard*, Association of the United States Army, January 2008; Michelle Tan, "Guard, Reserve Chiefs Laud Components' Evolution, *Army Times,* 15 October 2007, 28–29; Lizette Alvarez, "G.I. Jane Stealthily Breaks the Combat Barrier," *New York Times,* 16 August 2009, 1, 20–21; "Dwell Time Key to Resolving Out-of-Balance Issues, Casey Says," *AUSA News*, September 2009, 2; Ltr, John G. Montgomery, Civilian Aide to the Secretary of the Army, to General Eric K. Shinseki, 5 August 1999, Historians Files, CMH; Gina Cavallaro, "Casey's To-do-now List," *Army Times*, 18 January 2010, 20–21; Michelle Tan, "OEF, OIF Deployments Total Nearly 3 Million," *Army Times*, 4 May 2009, 26–27; Dennis Steele, "Gen. Petraeus' Second Iraq Report," *Army* (June 2008): 40–51; Gourley, "The Arsenal of the Ground War," 36–44; Dennis Steele, "Third Army: Directing Traffic at the Crossroads of Two Wars," *Army* (February 2010): 18–35; "Army Prepositioned Stocks: Indispensable to America's Global Force-Projection Capability," Association of the United States Army, December 2008; Matthew Cox, "Iraq War Takes Toll on Readiness," *Army Times*, 27 March 2006; Tan, "No Easy Exit," 18–19; Major General David E. Kratzer, "The Role of the 377th Theater Support Command," *Army Reserve Magazine* (Spring 2003): 28–35; Army General Staff Council Meeting notes, 2 January 2002; Army General Staff Council Meeting notes, 14 July 2003; Army General Staff Council Meeting notes, 11 August 2003.

[35] Wright and Reese, 489–527; Field Manual 100–10–2, *Contracting Support on the Battlefield* (Washington DC: Department of the Army, 1999); Charles Devarics, *Contractors Fill Key Role Through the Logistics Civil Augmentation Program* (Fort Belvoir, Virginia: US Army Material Command, 2005); Christopher Drew, "High Costs Weigh on Troop Debate for Afghan War," *New York Times*, 15 November 2009, 1, 14; Cox, "Iraq War Takes Toll on Readiness"; Killblane, 37–64; Bill Loper, "Majority of Funding Targets Iraq, Afghanistan Operations," *AUSA News*, August 2009, 22; "DOD Makes Changes to Civilian Job Management," *AUSA News*, November 2009, 15–17; Scott R. Gourley, "Equipping Today's Warfighters," *Army* (July 2003): 49–52; Steele, "Carrying the Load in Iraq," 14–22; Fick, 23–28; Army General Staff Council Meeting notes, 2 January 2002; Army General Staff Council

Meeting notes, 14 July 2003; Army General Staff Council Meeting notes, 11 August 2003; E-mail, General (USA, Ret.) Dennis Reimer to Brigadier General (USA, Ret.) John S. Brown, 10 October 2009, sub: Follow-Up, Historians Files, CMH; Briefing, Multi-National Corps–Iraq, "What Did We Learn That Illuminated the Future of This Fight?" 3 April 2005.

[36] Briefing, General Wesley K. Clark to the NATO Norfolk Conference, "The 21st Century Force: Defining Requirements," 12 November 1998; Jeffrey Simon, "NATO's Membership Action Plan and Defense Planning: Credibility at Stake," *Problems of Post-Communism*, May/June 2001, 28–36; Wright and Reese, 427–77; Aaron D. Boal, "On the Ground: Training Indigenous Forces in Iraq," in De Toy, *Turning Victory into Success*; *Rebuilding Iraq: Preliminary Observations on the Challenges in Transferring Security Responsibilities to Iraqi Military and Police* (Washington DC: US Government Accountability Office, 2005); Briefing, Multi-National Corps–Iraq, "What Did We Learn That Illuminated the Future of This Fight?" 3 April 2005; Briefing, Major General Peter Chiarelli to the Joint Staff, "Task Force Baghdad: Operation Iraqi Freedom II," 16 March 2005; Army General Staff Council Meeting notes, 21 July 2003.

[37] Fontenot, Degen, and Tohn, 383–426; Wright and Reese, 489–527; Briefing, Multi-National Corps–Iraq, "What Did We Learn That Illuminated the Future of This Fight?" 3 April 2005; Scott R. Gourley, "Tomorrow's Technology," *Army* (February 2010): 38–48; Fick, 23–32; Gourley, "The Arsenal of the Ground War," 36–44; Matthew Cox, "Flexibility Is Key to Future of GCVs," *AUSA Special Report,* 12 October 2009, 16–17; Staff Sergeant Tanya L. Trebes, "Agile Robotics," *Army* (March 2010): 99–104; Matthew Cox, "Small Unmanned Vehicles Provide New Capabilities," *AUSA Special Report*, 12 October 2009, 3; Army General Staff Council Meeting notes, 2 January 2002; Army General Staff Council Meeting notes, 14 July 2003; Army General Staff Council meeting notes, 11 August 2003; E-mail, General (USA, Ret.) Dennis Reimer to Brigadier General (USA, Ret.) John S. Brown, 10 October 2009, sub: Follow-Up.

[38] Army General Staff Council Meeting notes, 27 May 2003, Historians Files, CMH; Army General Staff Council Meeting notes, 16 June 2003, Historians Files, CMH; Army General Staff Council Meeting notes, 14 July 2003; General Peter Schoomaker and General Richard Cody, Transcript of Media Roundtable Conducted at the Association of the United States Army Annual Meeting, Washington DC, 26 October 2004; Gordon Lubold, "Troop-level Forecast May Test Patience," *Army Times*, 23 September 2006; Michelle Tan, "DoD: Army Exceeds October Recruiting Goals," *Army Times,* 24 November 2008; Erik Holmes et al., "Retention Pressures," *Army Times*, 8 December 2008, 15; Army General Staff Council Meeting notes, 11 August 2003; Army General Staff Council Meeting notes, 19 April 2004, Historians Files, CMH.

CHAPTER 10

Concluding Thoughts

From 1989 through 2005 the United States Army attempted a centrally directed and institutionally driven revolution in military affairs relevant to ground warfare that exploited Information Age technology, adapted to post–Cold War strategic circumstances, and integrated into parallel Joint and Department of Defense efforts. This transformation, if successful, would be comparable to the shifts to an Army for Empire around the turn of the last century, to the mobilization-based Army that fought World Wars I and II, to the atomic-armed early Cold War Army, and to the all-volunteer late Cold War Army. These earlier transformations adapted to radically altered strategic, socioeconomic, and technological circumstances of their times. Beginning in 1989 the end of the Cold War again radically altered the strategic circumstances, the arrival of the Internet and the Information Age altered the socioeconomic, and such products of the microchip as advanced sensors and precision-guided munitions changed the technological circumstances in which the Army found itself. Earlier transformations were not about technology alone; they were also about doctrine, organization, training, administrative practices, and service culture. This was true from 1989 through 2005 as well. Earlier transformations provoked debate, engaged multiple actors, drew mixed responses from Congress and others, and extended across indistinct temporal boundaries. This also was true from 1989 through 2005. Let us review the results of Army transformation from 1989 through 2005. Then let us flag the compromises and trade-offs accepted during its course. Finally, let us comment on what this study may contribute to further finding our way ahead.

Army Transformation, 1989–2005

Chief of Staff General Carl E. Vuono and others recognized that the Army was approaching a historical watershed at least as early as 1989. Under Vuono's auspices the study projects QUICKSILVER, VANGUARD, and ANTAEUS anticipated an end to the Cold War and massive funding cuts while attempting to fathom a way ahead for the Army. Departing from several generations of historical precedent, Vuono and his successors committed to maintain a small Army at the highest possible levels of readiness and modernization, rather than a larger Army as a skeletal framework for national mobilization. Several presidential administrations and Offices of the Secretary of Defense and Joint Staffs were of a like mind, leaving how much to cut the Army rather than whether to cut it the subject of continuing debate. JUST CAUSE, DESERT STORM, and deployments to Northern Iraq, Kuwait, Somalia, Haiti, the Balkans, Afghanistan, and elsewhere provided recurrent reminders that the end of the Cold War brought no end to violence and strife. The redesigned Army had to be expeditionary to remain relevant, dispatching potent forces on short notice throughout the globe. Conversely, the United States seemed unlikely to fight a peer or near-peer adversary any time soon, so large forward deployed forces and mammoth mobilization plans were out. Chief of Staff General Gordon R. Sullivan and his colleagues recognized the revolution-ary implications of the Information Age. Modernization and technological dominance had long been tenets of the American way of war. Now these took a new twist as Sullivan and his successors added digitization to downsizing and deployability as Army imperatives. Army exploitation of digitization and other advanced technologies hopefully would lead to a revolution in military affairs, although Army spokespeople were generally too cautious to embrace that term. Such revolutionary transformation would require radical changes to doctrine, organization, training, administration, and service culture. These occurred, albeit not as thoroughly as some proposed. There were more cooks than ever stirring the broth. These proved to be both a blessing and a curse.[1]

With respect to Information Age technologies, the Army exploited along three overlapping avenues. First, digital networks hugely improved communi-cations and the shared battlefield picture. At higher levels and in administra-tive circumstances the Secure Internet Protocol Router Network (SIPRNET), the Nonsecure Internet Protocol Router Network (NIPRNET), and general use of the Internet evolved to revolutionize military communications just as the Internet was revolutionizing commercial communications. Digital burst transmission, expanding bandwidth, improved durability, microwave, and sat-ellite access drove such communications down to the tactical level, steadily expanding the network as they did so. This, in turn, enabled global positioning systems (GPSs) and blue force tracking to reliably answer such perennial ques-tions as "where am I?" or "where are my buddies?" Logistical variants revo-lutionized capabilities to track and manage cargo, inventories, and supplies. Second, networked communications and global positioning systems improved the effectiveness of precision-guided munitions by at least an order of mag-nitude. Most notably the GPS-guided Joint Direct Attack Munition (JDAM) provided a cheap all-weather precision-guided munition. Because it was cheap it became ubiquitous, with profound effects for the conduct of operations on the ground. Third, networked communications wedded to advanced sensors appreciably improved capabilities to detect the enemy and to do something about them. Unmanned aerial vehicles (UAVs) were most notable in this regard but hardly alone in the arrays of sensors and cameras that populated the battlefield and the space above it. What was known of the enemy could be immediately shared with all on the same network. Beyond digitization and other fruits of the microchip, technology advanced in other venues as well. Cases in point included body armor, prostheses, and fuel standardization. Technological exploitation was not just serendipitous. From Sullivan on, Army leaders experimented in networked battle labs and other simulations to identify promising technical mixes. Advanced Warfighting Experiment (AWE) took this experimentation into the "dirt" of major training centers and other field circumstances. Spiral development batted equipment back and forth between producer and consumer as evolution and scale of application progressed. Three generations of exploratory or experimental enterprises came and went: the modern Louisiana Maneuvers, the Experimental Force (EXFOR), and Strike Force. Each moved technologies along within its purview. Blue force tracking, for one example, went from a potpourri of black boxes on a tank platoon to a combat theater-wide network of intervisible transponders in less than a decade. Within the limits of its funding, the Army pushed itself into the Information Age.[2]

Changing technologies drove changes in doctrine. The facts that small contingents in motion instantly and almost invariably knew where they were and where their buddies were had large implications. During DESERT STORM and earlier periods more than two-thirds of the transmissions on an average command net were given over to trying to determine such basic information, leaving less than a third for actual command and control. Given the ranges and lethality of modern weapons, this led to heavily choreographed and tightly controlled tactics. Late Cold War general defense plan (GDP) "Battle Books" were awash with detailed control measures: terrain-referenced unit boundaries, phase lines every couple of kilometers, battle positions thickly arrayed like paisley, measles sheets of coordination points and target reference points, and so on. The best Battle Books even had photographs, so crews would know exactly where their vehicles were supposed to go during each phase of the action. The featureless desert of DESERT STORM worked hardships on such battlefield controls, prompting the ponderous movement of vast armored phalanxes as fratricide-wary commanders struggled to stay on line. Even so, incidental fratricides constituted a major fraction of the casualties. A dozen years later, GDP Battle Books seemed a quaint anachronism. Control measures, such as they were, arrived electronically and were more likely to appear on a computer screen than a map overlay. Many abandoned paper maps altogether in favor of "zoom in, zoom out" electronic versions. Friendly units were represented by electronic icons, and the momentary absence of such an icon prompted a flurry of radio transmissions to find out why it was not visible. Command net proportions reversed themselves, with more than two-thirds of transmissions committed to fighting the battle and less than a third to ascertaining the status of units. Tactics loosened up, and armored columns sped merrily along on separate axes confident that they knew where their buddies were and that long-range gunnery and precision-guided munitions could pick off enemies that exposed themselves in intervening ground. Commanders worried less about keeping under the protective umbrella of artillery. Field artillery, particularly Multiple Launch Rocket Systems (MLRSs), had improved considerably in range and accuracy. More important, relatively cheap GPS-guided JDAMs provided ready access to potent air-delivered precision-guided munitions. Gone were the days when an incoming friendly air strike prompted concerns for fratricide approaching paranoia, and prudent ground commanders dumped air strikes on the far side of the fire support coordination line (FSCL). Companies and even platoons routinely integrated JDAM strikes into maneuver schemes as they picked their way through contested ground. During DESERT STORM few battalions actually called in an air strike, and only the highly trained Air Force Tactical Air Control Party (TACP) could be relied upon to bring one in. In Afghanistan and Iraq Army lieutenants and sergeants routinely had JDAMs at their beck and call. As discussed in Chapter 7, Colonel Douglas Macgregor titled his influential book *Breaking the Phalanx*. The phalanx the United States Army actually broke up was its own. With respect to operations other than war, Army doctrine gave respectable and increasing attention to the lower end of the combat spectrum throughout the period. This attention increased considerably after 9-11. There was not a similar resurgence of doctrinal interest in the upper level of the combat spectrum, nuclear warfare.[3]

Nimbler doctrine requires nimbler organization. In DESERT STORM the newly greater lethality and larger geographical footprint of brigade combat teams suggested that they were assuming the operational role formerly held by divisions. Force XXI was by and large technical appliqué on existing divisional structure, but Chief of Staff General Dennis J. Reimer's Strike Force was a definitive attempt at brigade-based organization. It improved upon the brigade-size "Division Forwards," National Guard Enhanced Brigades, and separate brigades of the time as a harbinger of things to come. Chief of Staff General Eric K. Shinseki's Interim Brigade Combat Team, later the Stryker Brigade Combat Team, furthered the trend. Shinseki's Legacy Force was the appliqué Force XXI, his Interim Force was brigade-based, and his Objective Force was to draw heavily upon the lessons learned from his Interim Force. Chief of Staff General Peter L. Schoomaker finalized commitment to a brigade-based Army and phased the transition division by division into deployments overseas. Schoomaker agreed with operational doctrine advocating a shift to brigades, but he also had the responsibility to efficiently rotate units in and out of Iraq and Afghanistan. Interchangeable modular brigades were more practical than divisions in this regard and soon were organized as heavy, infantry, aviation, fires, maneuver enhancement, sustainment and reconnaissance, surveillance, and target acquisition brigades. Headquarters above brigade were divested of their huge inventories of combat support and combat service support units. Most of these were invested into the modular brigades, with a few kept as specialized separates at the theater level. Corps and divisions became slimmed down headquarters focused exclusively on command and control. These were to be constructed into command hierarchies as circumstances required. Modular brigades plugged Lego-like into this command structure, building up the forces necessary without much overhead above the brigade. The reserve component was subsumed into this structure, both in theory and in fact. Recurrent rotations into Afghanistan and Iraq would have been impossible to sustain without converting reserve-component units into full operational participants, albeit cycling on different timelines. This was in part because of the sheer numbers required and in part because a large

A Stryker Brigade Combat Team in action

disproportion of combat support and combat service support specialties—the "enablers"—resided in the reserve component. Even tapping the reserve component was insufficient to address some shortages, so significant numbers of Air Defense, Field Artillery, and Engineer billets were reprogrammed into combat service support. Further shortages were offset by contracting, as a shadow workforce of civilian contractors became essential to Army operations and force structure both at home and overseas. In Afghanistan and Iraq they offset huge requirements for force structure, as discussed in Chapter 9.[4]

Doctrine and organization are of little use unless the latter trains in accordance with the former. During the early 1990s Army leadership was preoccupied with maintaining quality control amid plummeting budgets and radical downsizing. The mantra was "no more Task Force Smiths" and the imperative was to hold the fewer remaining units to standards at least as high as those of their late Cold War counterparts. This in itself was ambitious, given funding, but Army trainers soon introduced other imperatives as well. The entire Army began training toward expeditionary capabilities that had once been those of light forces alone. Rotations to the National Training Center and elsewhere prominently featured reception, staging, onward movement, and integration (RSOI). Heavy units flew in, drew pre-positioned equipment, settled into it, and raced to the field. What they did in training was replicated in operations, as deployments increased and much of the Army rotated through "commuter containment" in Kuwait and elsewhere. Heavy divisions got into the habit of designating Division-Ready Brigades, held to peaks of readiness and deployability. Emergency Deployment Readiness Exercises (EDREs) and

457

Sea Emergency Deployment Readiness Exercises (SEDREs) tested the ability of units to react on short notice. After the invasion of Iraq huge rotational demands solidified the Army Force Generation (ARFORGEN) model as brigade-based cyclical training, premised upon routine deployments. Units trained, deployed, returned to home station, stood down, reorganized, and then started the cycle all over again. Units trained more broadly on the combat spectrum than had been the case for most during the Cold War. Major training exercises almost invariably featured vignettes drawn from low-intensity conflict. This emphasis meshed with ever-increasing deployments: Northern Iraq, Somalia, Haiti, the Balkans, and elsewhere. Training packages to specifically prepare units for these deployments emerged, deepening an appreciation for operations other than war. Prior to DESERT STORM the Army made considerable use of electronic simulators, the unit conduct-of-fire trainer (UCOFT) being a case in point. With the digital revolution these were networked in ever larger arrays, overcoming geographical separation as desired. This allowed widely dispersed individuals, units, and headquarters to participate in training and mission rehearsal exercises. Electronic "reach back" prolonged and deepened the experience. Constituent elements of the training could be recovered for review—as could virtually any policy, guidance, doctrine, tactic, technique, or procedure. Frequent use of digital training aids enhanced familiarity with digital equipment as it became ever more pervasive throughout the Army. In 1991 "digital warriors" were anomalous; in 2005 they were ubiquitous. Distributed training proved particularly useful in the reserve component, to whom geographical dispersion had always been a considerable impediment. This improvement was timely, as the National Guard and Army Reserve were increasingly drawn into overseas deployments. They sought to achieve training standards comparable to those of their active-component counterparts before deploying. With IRAQI FREEDOM active- and reserve-component units became virtually interchangeable, although coursing through Army Force Generation cycles on different timelines.[5]

Administrative and logistical policies changed with doctrine, organization, and training. Most notably, the ARFORGEN cycles of the brigade-based Army depended on unit manning to succeed. Since the early twentieth century the Army had relied on individual replacements to keep up unit strengths overseas. Now combat-ready units replaced each other, often flying in and drawing equipment that was already in theater. Provided casualties remained low, the advantages to training, cohesion, and esprit seemed obvious. Bringing units up to strength for ARFORGEN cycles and providing overstrengths for deployments forced a new paradigm on personnel managers. The easy fungibility of individual replacement was considerably circumscribed, and timing with respect to schools and other professional self-development opportunities had to be reworked to accommodate ARFORGEN. Accelerating deployments, particularly after IRAQI FREEDOM began, put major installations into nearly continuous preparations for overseas movement (POM). Almost every month some unit was shipping out and another returning, prompting the full slate of medical examinations, inoculations, legal counsel, property disposition, powers of attorney, equipment and barracks turn-ins, ammunition and equipment draws, and all else that went with the process. "Stop loss," the retention policy that kept soldiers in deploying units beyond their anticipated separation dates, became contentious as it became commonplace; it no longer seemed reserved for the "Big One." Installations came into their own as power projection platforms, shouldering aside tactical units that had once considered themselves capable of managing such processes. Since divisions and corps were now just headquarters and themselves deploying, this installation assumption of mission was timely. Once deployed, units remained connected to the installation that had launched them via split-basing. Advanced digital communications, reliable air transportation, and a determination not to create unnecessary logistical "iron mountains" overseas came together to migrate some support from overseas theaters back to American installations. Calculable supplies such as food, water, and fuel came from the theater. Less predictable items, such as repair parts, featured limited inventories forward and "just in time" policies for replenishment. Information Age accounting, tracking, and requisition allowed far greater efficiency, although the vagaries of combat did force some stockpiling as a precaution. Most of these "just in time" assets came from the industrial base, but unique items and items requiring the intervention of depots could track back to the installation. The briefer the unit deployment, the more likely this was. People—emergency leaves, exceptional individual replacements, rest and recreation beneficiaries, short-term medical issues, and others with stateside business—trekked back and forth from "down range" to the installation in a volume unprecedented in earlier wars. The reserve component was drawn into this vortex and experienced administrative adjustments even greater than those of the active component. A driving force was the near certainty of deployment, sooner or later. This forced out those who could not afford to or who were not inclined to deploy, for a period perturbing both recruitment and retention. The reserve component became an operational force. Inefficiencies that had accumulated over time with respect to pay, promotion, professional development, personnel administration, and training were necessarily addressed. What had worked when soldiers showed up one weekend a month and two weeks in the summer did not work when they routinely deployed for as much as a year into a combat theater.[6]

Army culture evolved with the shift to an expeditionary Army, most notably with respect to family life. "Homesteading" in the vicinity of the new mega-posts became a new norm. Soldiers rotated through repeated tours overseas while their families remained established at a single location. Stability encouraged spousal employment and careers, home ownership, and the education of children within a single school system. Post exchanges, commissaries, child care centers, and other on-post facilities remained attractive, but families increasingly availed themselves of these while nevertheless investing their housing allowances in homes of their own off post. TRICARE evolved as practical medical care for geographically dispersed families increasingly unable to rely on military medical facilities. Downsizing and deployments hit the uniformed medical establishment as severely as the rest of the Army, so this transition to subsidized civilian medicine proved timely. TRICARE proved even more useful to retirees and reserve-component families, given their greater geographical dispersal. The Army actively courted

An Army family reunites.

families, both because it seemed the right thing to do and because of favorable effects on recruitment and retention. Family Readiness Groups and constellations of related programs deepened communications and cooperation between families and their units and across the families themselves. These tapped into a growing array of helpful agencies ranging from such venerable stalwarts as Army Emergency Relief and Army Community Service through such relatively recent initiatives as the Exceptional Family Member Program or the Family Advocacy Program. Family Readiness Groups, increasingly drawn to digital communications, extended their reach to include parents and significant others as well as Army families per se. Administrative and emotional support for and by families became increasingly important as deployments escalated during the 1990s and escalated again in significance with IRAQI FREEDOM. Permanent change of station (PCS), long the largest disruption in Army family life, paled in comparison to the rigors of recurrent deployments to a combat theater. Ulysses recycled overseas again and again, forcing whole new rhythms of personal and family adjustment—especially if illness or injury were involved. Posttraumatic stress disorder (PTSD) became a widely recognized household term, as most deployed soldiers were exposed to its potential causes at one time or another. Watchful spouses and families endured processes of decompression along with soldiers and their units. This is not to mention the emotional pressure already on the spouses and families themselves, or the exceptional circumstances of sole parents and those who filled in for them. No deployed soldier was immune from danger. Iraq and Afghanistan were wars without boundaries, forcing constant vigilance in 360-degree fights. This prompted Chief of Staff General Peter J. Schoomaker to ardently pursue a Warrior Ethos, psychologically committing every soldier to the demands of combat regardless of specialty or component. This further committed the reserve component and its families to the rigors endured by the active component. In some ways the lot of reserve-component families was harder, given their geographical dispersal and relative isolation from military facilities. Fortuitously Information Age technology provided partial redress, connecting them with their soldier when he or she was deployed, and with supportive groups and agencies whether he or she was or not.[7]

Like earlier Army transformations, the period from 1989 through 2005 witnessed changes to doctrine, organization, training, administration, and service culture as well as to technology. It also, as had been the case in earlier transformations, provoked considerable debate among diverse actors. More players than ever before were now involved. During World War II Chief of Staff General George C. Marshall and Secretary of War Henry L. Stimson by and large designed transformation within the Army Staff and then made overtures for funding directly to Congress. The early Cold War added the Department of Defense to shepherd service rivalries. The late Cold War diffused deliberations within the Army from the Army Staff per se. The Training and Doctrine Command (TRADOC) and Army Materiel Command (AMC) assumed important high-level institutional responsibilities toward the future—beyond the casual contributions individual officers in such assignments had always made. Army transformation 1989–2005 occurred in the wake of the Goldwater-Nichols Act, which again changed the matrix of players. Goldwater-Nichols tightened the grip of the Department of Defense and the Joint Staff upon the services and increased the autonomy of theater commanders within their spheres. It also pushed Secretarial political appointees deeper into the bowels of the service staffs than they had been before. A former model, not always adhered to, had been that the Army Staff conducted deliberations internally without much thought to politics, and then the Secretary of the Army and his administration colleagues edited and ran political interference. Now deliberations with respect to most administrative and logistical topics involved the Secretariat—and their attendant political considerations—from the outset. This facilitated like-mindedness between services and the administration but also added more cooks, considerations, and complexity. Goldwater-Nichols sanctioned a "purple" mind-set as a tonic to service parochialism. Much of its approach was within service educational systems, but the greater grip of the administration, Department of Defense, and Joint Staff did stifle externally visible debate. Services were supposed to get along harmoniously rather than bickering, as had been their tradition. Some believed debate was still worth having, however, and retirees found ways to move it along. The Association of the United States Army (AUSA) provides an example of a retiree-facilitated service voice. Its annual conventions morphed from being primarily social to providing active forums engaging key players in the Army, industry, and politics. Specialized conventions multiplied in numbers and focal areas. AUSA's Institute of Land Warfare (ILW) emerged as a clearinghouse for Army-oriented publications and arguments. General Omar N. Bradley once famously advised

461

cutting out the tongues of retired generals. By 2005 this approach would have been too late, as AUSA and others sustained prominent "green" voices in an increasingly "purple" world. Contractors figured prominently among AUSA members and attendees, and they grew in importance in service deliberations as well. Downsizing gutted much of the Army's capability to anticipate the future. Civilian (heavily populated by military retirees) "think tanks" expanded or proliferated to fill the void. Vital Quadrennial Defense Review instruments such as Dynamic Commitment or the Deep Attack Weapons Mix Study (DAWMS) were heavily dependent on contracted support. Contractors often provided continuity that used to be the province of Department of the Army civilians, thus giving them a voice of their own. Congressional staffers could hire the same contractors the Army did, in effect watering down the uniqueness of service advice and counsel. This progressed amid a culture-wide diffusion of knowledge management. Internet Web sites proliferated wildly, and niche "bloggers" came into their own as alternatives to more heavily edited traditional media. Debate, information, and disinformation coursed along the Internet with more diversity than ever before.[8]

Given the discussion to this point, did the Army achieve a centrally directed and institutionally driven revolution in military affairs relevant to ground warfare that exploited Information Age technology, adapted to post–Cold War strategic circumstances, and integrated into parallel Joint and Department of Defense efforts? With respect to centrally directed and institutionally driven, Chiefs of Staff by and large retained control of transformation initiatives and had the support of the Army Secretariat while doing so. Recognizing the inevitability of Department of Defense, Joint, and congressional initiatives, they sought to stay out in front of them with studies and proposals of their own. Vuono's QUICKSILVER and ANTAEUS were cases in point, working out sensible programs for downsizing before being forced into them. When Quadrennial Defense Reviews emerged as congressionally sanctioned mechanisms for change, Chiefs of Staff invested heavily to ensure that Army positions were persuasively made. Platoons of contemplative colonels, iron majors, war gamers, analysts, computer geeks, and "PowerPoint rangers" mustered to engage in twenty-first-century decision making. Even beyond the bonds of collegiality, Chiefs actively courted Army near-peers to ensure that such consequential fiefdoms as TRADOC and AMC remained synchronized with the Army Staff. Four-star conferences were meaty, restricted with respect to observers, and freewheeling. Sullivan went so far as to entrust transformation to a four-star General Officer Steering Committee (GOSC), and all went to considerable lengths to sustain cohesion at the highest level. Chairmen and vice chairmen of the Joint Chiefs of Staff were trying to accomplish much the same thing across the services, again relying on recurrent targeted meetings to do so. Army senior leaders worked within this larger system. For most of this period Army aspirations and Defense aspirations for transformation were broadly compatible, and relationships collegial. When a contrarian rant from a service "attack dog" seemed desirable, someone associated with AUSA could provide it unbidden. The principal leverage enjoyed by the Chiefs of Staff with respect to transformation was influence over the Army budget. Far from simply going to Congress and asking for money, the uniformed Army Staff worked first with the Army Secretariat and major commands to establish requirements, and then the Department of the Army competed within the Department of Defense before Congress was approached—officially. Politically appointed assistant secretaries of the Army for Research, Development, and Acquisition; Manpower and Reserve Affairs; Installations, Logistics, and Environment; Financial Management; and Civil Works occupied critical positions with respect to funding or overseeing aspects of Army transformation. Generally these paired off with uniformed Army Staff three-star generals within their purview, and the two formed relationships and worked together—often colocating and sharing office staff and other assets. The Director of the Army Staff emerged as a key player, coordinating the activities and agendas of Army Staff and Secretariat alike. Army Staff and Army Secretariat served alongside each other in Quadrennial Defense Review panels, promoting like-mindedness as approaches to the future developed. Although they had considerably different backgrounds and somewhat different priorities, the Army Staff and Army Secretariat grew through the changes of Goldwater-Nichols to work well together. Their relationships were particularly responsive to good relationships between the Chief of Staff and the Secretary of the Army. Each Chief worked hard to keep these agreeable and to keep Secretaries enthusiastic about next steps with respect to transformation as they emerged. To operationalize transformation initiatives, Chiefs shifted to exceptional organization to get across what they perceived as major hurdles, and they then reverted back to traditional organization when the time seemed right. Sullivan's modern Louisiana Maneuvers (LAM) and LAM Task Force and Shinseki's Objective Force Task Force were examples of exceptional organization. Reimer migrated the LAM Task Force back to traditional TRADOC and Deputy Chief of Staff for Operations and Plans (DCSOPS) responsibilities once Force XXI was well under way, and Schoomaker similarly redefined the Objective Force as the Future Force under TRADOC auspices while he was focusing on the wars at hand. Beyond immediate decision makers, transformation needed the knowledgeable support of hundreds of thousands inside the Army and out if it were to succeed. To this purpose, Chiefs employed mechanisms for "strategic communications" to reach out to the Army rank and file and the interested public. The interested public, of course, could influence Congress. The most formal and evolved strategic communications programs were those of General Shinseki in pursuit of Army Transformation, but all Chiefs and Secretaries understood the imperative to achieve consensus and mobilize support. Given all the players and influences, at least one light-hearted observer likened a Chief of Staff pursuing transformation to a surfer. With skill and daring the Chief could substantially determine the Army's course, but he did have to ride the wave—and if he momentarily lost balance he would plunge into the unfeeling mercies of crosscurrents and contrary forces.[9]

If we accept that Army transformation in 1989–2005 was by and large centrally directed and institutionally driven, was it a revolution in military affairs? Was there anything exponential about it? One can reasonably argue that small digitized contingents were ten times less likely to become lost or disoriented, ten times more likely to know where their comrades were, and ten times less likely to commit fratricide than their counterparts of a dozen years before. Although data are not rigorous, comparisons of Desert Storm with Iraqi Freedom support such conclusions. In both cases the soldiers who fought were superb human material at a peak of training and professionalism, so differences in performance seem best explained by transformative efforts in the interim. Certainly precision-guided munitions were ten times less expensive in 2003 than they had been a decade before, and the tendency to use them correspondingly an order of magnitude higher. This integrated airpower into ground maneuver far more tightly, and radically increased the numbers of troops on the ground sufficiently equipped and confident to bring it into play. Less measurable but surely as consequential, Information Age–networked communications profoundly altered command and control. Satellite-based communications tied units together across vast distances and linked them seamlessly to joint counterparts and other agencies. Commanders and staffs deliberated face-to-face from different continents. The disjunction of time zones largely disappeared with e-mail; one's message was immediately available to act upon when one's antipodal counterpart was awake and ready to read it. A small point to some, but important to those who work there, headquarters and tactical operations centers quieted as phones rang less and mouses clicked more. What was known to one could be immediately known to all, a shared battlefield picture. Commanders and staffs at all levels spent far less time trying to determine the locations and status of their own forces, leaving them far more time to determine what to do with them. Blue force tracking was instrumental in this, as were various digital means to manage logistics and administration. The picture of the enemy remained understandably less clear than that of friendlies, but advanced sensors and UAVs did improve it. Again, what was known by one could be immediately known by all, further enriching the shared battlefield picture. Information Operations assumed a digital dimension, and rivals competed for information and ideation in cyberspace as surely as they did on the ground. None of the phenomenon described above was complete by 2005, and virtually all soldiers then serving recall some incident when transformational technologies failed to work as designed. Participants rightly spoke of a "digital divide" separating echelons and portions of the Army with the most modern hardware and software from those without it. Nevertheless, the revolution was at least far enough along that Generals Tommy Franks and Dave McKiernan believed they could stand traditional technique on its head and attack with a small force without preliminary bombardment into the operational depth of Iraq. From a "rolling start" they accrued reinforcements on the move, staying several steps ahead of the enemy because they knew more faster—and could act on their knowledge. In Chapter 1 we established that revolutions in military affairs do not occur overnight. Mechanized warfare we characterize as *Blitzkrieg*, for example, originated in World War I but did not mature until the battles for France and Central Europe in 1944–1945. With respect to achieving the equivalent in Information Age warfare, the United States Army of 2003–2005 may still have been to the "left" of General George S. Patton's Third Army, but it was considerably to the "right" of the British at Cambrai.[10]

Much of Army transformation in 1989–2005 represented adaptation to post–Cold War circumstances more so than entry into the Information Age.

The shift to an expeditionary footing offers the most striking case in point. Plus-ups with respect to sealift and airlift featured technological advances in the newer ships and planes, but in essence they were about increasing capacity rather than about advancing technology. Pre-positioned stockpiles that accumulated around the world consisted almost entirely of vintage equipment. Infrastructure initiatives to improve deployability were old-fashioned construction projects mindful of providing additional power sources and electrical outlets. Initial attempts to make heavy forces lighter and light forces more lethal, such as the Stryker combat vehicle or the Javelin missile, were not particularly dependent on Information Age technologies. Digitization undoubtedly improved the effectiveness of expeditionary forces, but technology was not the underlying premise of an expeditionary posture. The shift to a brigade-based Army was a hybrid, in part inspired by the possibility of doing more with less when digitized, but in part inspired by the efficiencies of transporting and rotating brigade-sized units without the encumbrance of division and corps overheads. The final design of brigade combat teams was determined by rotational demands in Iraq at least as much as by potential combat with a near-peer adversary. Unit manning similarly fit best with current circumstances: frequent deployments, rigorous tactical demands, and few casualties. Post–Cold War circumstances ramped up the Army's involvement in operations other than war, and then Iraq after May 2003 multiplied that involvement tenfold. Low-intensity conflict had long been recognized as manpower-intensive and had long been considered unresponsive to technological advance. In Chapter 9 we found the Army's transformational technologies to be more useful than many suppose in Afghanistan and Iraq, although not altogether able to offset the mismatch between national ambitions and the manpower deployed to achieve them. One initiative, the campaign against improvised explosive devices (IEDs), wedded advancing technology and timeless tactics, techniques, and procedures in innovative ways. This kept casualties stable despite manyfold increases in attacks. Acquiring, processing, and corroborating human intelligence was another largely nontechnical venue wherein the Army came up short initially and improved itself over time with a combination of traditional and innovative means. The post–Cold War world was a very different environment for the Army than the one that had gone before, and not only because it corresponded in time to the Information Age. Army transformation in 1989–2005 took both Information Age technologies and post–Cold War circumstances into account.[11]

Trade-offs: Transformation and Vulnerability

An Army's equipment, force structure, doctrine, and training are never perfect. They cannot equivalently meet all conceivable challenges and certainly are not timeless. At best they are appropriate for an Army's present circumstances or for specific operations for which they have been designed. Trade-offs inevitably emerge to comport with priorities and resources available. Beginning in the late 1980s, as we have seen, the United States' Cold War Army transformed. It embraced Information Age technologies, adapted to post–Cold War circumstances, and integrated into parallel Joint and Defense transformation efforts. The Cold War Army was built upon paradigms that had worked well in the global wars of the twentieth century and that served well in facing down a mammoth near-peer adversary. In transforming, the Army leadership stepped away from decisions made by earlier leaders in earlier times. The leaders shifted from a philosophy of national mobilization to one favoring a small but ready standing Army. They abandoned the top, and arguably for a period the bottom, of the combat spectrum in favor of conventional forces of general utility. The Army became expeditionary. It digitized. It reorganized to become brigade-based and unit-manned. These changes served the nation well, but they present risks should circumstances change. As is often the case, today's adaptations create potential future vulnerabilities. Let us address these potential vulnerabilities in historical context, reviewing the relevant decisions made and weighing the advantages and disadvantages of each.

The post–Cold War Army was standing more so than mobilization-based. America's founding fathers were generally adverse to a standing Army, viewing one as an invitation to tyranny and oppression. After a few hard knocks they accepted the wisdom of such an Army on the frontiers, but they kept it small and underresourced. This presented dilemmas with respect to expansion when wars did occur. Two schools of thought emerged. One, championed by Secretary of War John C. Calhoun, envisioned an "expansible" Army. Existing units were skeletons to which further flesh could be added. A peacetime regiment could prepare for war by doubling its privates. Such an approach worked fairly well in the Mexican War, but it was overwhelmed by the manpower demands of the Civil War. The Civil War inspired an alternate vision, that of small cadres of professionals organizing and training divisions of recruits and draftees. In World Wars I and II the United States employed a hybrid. Understrength Regular and National Guard divisions filled out with volunteers and draftees, then they bore the brunt of early combat. Meanwhile, tiny cadres created new divisions out of a mass of draftees. Mobilization from the Cold War to World War III would have started from a higher plane. The active Army was several times larger than it had ever been in peacetime, and mobilization plans were more thoroughly rehearsed. America's allies were similarly committed to programs of mass mobilization supported by the conversion of formidable industrial bases. As discussed in Chapter 2, Chief of Staff General Carl E. Vuono (1987–1991) initiated studies to anticipate inevitable post–Cold War budget cuts and downsizing. QUICKSILVER examined table of organization (TOE) and VANGUARD table of distribution and allowances (TDA) structure. More secretively ANTAEUS, named after the mythical titan who remained powerful as long as he touched the ground, explored inactivations in Europe. Army planners boiled the basic force structure options down to two. They could sustain an active Army of five corps, twenty divisions, and constituent units at reduced strength, training, and readiness, while maintaining a mobilization apparatus sufficient to bring them up to strength in a crisis—and to add new divisions in due course. Alternatively, they could slash force structure and maintain fewer units at high levels of manning, training, modernization, and readiness. Given lead time, the first option, America's traditional one, would generate mass more efficiently. The second option would provide forces more readily available to immediately respond to crises. Mindful of the "Hollow Army" embarrassment of the 1970s, the newly perceived lack of peer competitors, the speed with which JUST CAUSE and DESERT SHIELD/DESERT STORM came upon them, and the volatility of the post–Cold War world, the Army Staff recommended and Vuono accepted the second option. The Department of Defense, working through studies of its own, readily concurred. The active Army would be smaller, but immediately deployable. Readiness trumped mobilization potential. When Vuono committed to this smaller but still potent active Army, the reserve component remained as a hedge against unforeseen requirements for expansion. Their eight divisions, twenty-three separate brigades, and scores of supporting units, while not exactly skeletal, offered an organizational framework as mobilization progressed. Beyond these a robust training base featuring active and

The United States mobilized on an unprecedented scale for World War II.

reserve assets made raising new divisions en masse feasible. Some thought had gone into finding the cadre for such units. In 1987, for example, the Army Retiree Recall Program had 232,000 qualified retirees on its books and had issued preexisting orders to 122,000 of them. The working mechanics of the draft, although rusty, were still within the memory of administrators capable of implementing them. The Center of Military History had a point system for bringing back the divisions of World War II and flags on hand to do so. However, accelerating deployments during the 1990s, followed by huge rotational demands in Iraq and Afghanistan, changed the nature of the increasingly downsized reserve component. Several years into IRAQI FREEDOM the Chief of the Army Reserve rightly, and with some pride, observed that the reserve component was now an indispensable operational force rather than a strategic reserve. Far from waiting around for the "Big One," Reserve and National Guard units routinely deployed in the aftermath of 9-11, albeit with timelines for their force generation cycles different than those of the active component. The training base was much smaller than in 1987, heavily dependent on contractors in lieu of soldiers, and not particularly focused on mass mobilization. The draft was now alien to the Army as an institution, as it was to the nation at large. The potential for national mobilization was in eclipse. During World War II the United States was a nation of 132 million people that put 15 million in uniform. In 2007 it was a nation of 300 million that characterized 30,000 additional troops as a "surge."[12]

The Cold War Army was a nuclear power. Within a few years of the Intermediate-Range Nuclear Forces (INF) Treaty of 1988, this was no longer true. The INF Treaty eliminated nuclear missiles with ranges between 500 and 5,500 kilometers, such as the Pershing II. A series of presidential nuclear initiatives soon swept away the rest of the Army's nuclear munitions, such as the venerable Lance missile and artillery-fired atomic projectiles. Eliminating the Army's tactical nuclear weapons made sense at the time. Mammoth Warsaw Pact forces that had been their original logic were dissipating. The elimination of American tactical nuclear weapons accompanied a corresponding elimination of Soviet tactical nuclear weapons and thus facilitated further engagement in the interests of peace. America's European allies, striving to put Cold War dangers behind them, were eager to be rid of weapons that made them logical nuclear targets. Nonnuclear precision-guided munitions (PGMs) seemed capable of many roles envisioned for tactical nuclear weapons, offsetting lesser yields with greater accuracy. The Goldwater-Nichols Act of 1986, emphasizing jointness and hostile to redundancy, reinforced a notion that nuclear munitions were best left to the Air Force and Navy. The Army would be nimbler and more capable as a conventional force if unencumbered by nuclear weapons and their attendant logistics and security. Tactical nuclear weapons had driven an Army subculture and a way of life. Generations of artillerymen grew up in the zero defects mentality of the nuclear surety program. Excruciating regimes of training, exercise, and inspection ensured that soldiers were up to their tasks, nuclear materials were never in inappropriate hands, and units had the skills necessary to survive in a nuclear environment. With a penumbra effect, nonnuclear units were affected by such preparations. Operational readiness tests and field exercises generally featured at least one nuclear scenario. The code word YORKTOWN, for example, designated a friendly nuclear strike at a specified location and triggered a rehearsed sequence of drilled responses. Crews and squads were familiar with dosimeters and detection kits, understood downwind diagrams and vehicle protective factors, and rehearsed the various hazards of an imagined nuclear battlefield. In 1989 the Army had 141 nuclear-weapons-certified units. In 1992 it had one. Over time interest and training diminished, and practical knowledge of nuclear warfare at the unit level precipitously declined. Few Cold Warriors thought the Army would conduct business as usual amid nuclear holocaust. They did expect much of it to survive, however, and believed it could continue major operations in the face of a few nuclear strikes. The intellectual underpinnings of the Army's approach to nuclear warfare were laid in an era when its adversaries could count on delivering relatively few nuclear weapons to their targets. The Army's intent at the time was not to be held hostage to such a threat. By 2005 India, Pakistan, North Korea, and Iran seemed destined to join those who could reliably deliver at least a few nuclear weapons to their targets. Army units were less well prepared for such attacks than they had been thirty years earlier.[13]

At about the same time that the Army abandoned the top end of the combat spectrum, it became partially divorced from the lower end as well. A provision of the Fiscal Year (FY) 1987 National Defense Authorization Act split off the United States Special Operations Command (USSOCOM) to be a joint command in its own right, with a budget independent of the services. Such "special operators" as Army Green Berets, Navy SEALs (sea-air-land teams), and aviators in various classified programs migrated there. The failed 1980 hostage rescue mission in Iran illustrated the stakes involved when services cooperated ineffectively, as did features of the Grenada intervention in 1983. The Special Operations Command became analogous to a theater with respect to command and control, and it was relatively autonomous once forces had been committed to it. Unlike a theater command, however, its area of operations was worldwide. The overwhelming majority of Special Operations Command manpower came from the Army. The redesign effectively removed the Army—and Marines—from primacy with respect to envisioning and executing low-intensity conflict. USSOCOM became responsible for operations, resource planning, and, increasingly, doctrine and training. This evolution was not entirely unwelcome to the rest of the Army. Low-intensity conflict hardly fired the service's imagination, and the Army as an institution had happily returned its attention to conventional warfare in Europe in the course of its post-Vietnam "Renaissance." Given dramatically dwindling resources following 1989, one less priority was comforting. TRADOC studies opined that low-intensity conflict would involve a State Department lead, local allies would provide the vast majority of the manpower required, and the small special operations community would be generally sufficient to tip the balance in the favor of the United States and its allies. If the rest of the Army were to become involved, it would do so with conventional forces temporarily departing from core missions. To be fair, recurrent Quadrennial Defense Reviews and the Army's own doctrine and transformational efforts did address the full combat spectrum. Insurgencies, terrorism, drug violence, refugee crises, natural disasters, and humanitarian relief inevitably numbered among the crises with which analysts and scenario writers were to deal. Far more of the "boots on the ground" during accelerating deployments to operations other than war during the 1990s were from conventional units rather than from special operations forces, a fact duly noted by Army planners. The Army never fully embraced such missions as core, however. Transformation addressed the full combat spectrum but emphasized the conventional. The most riveting analytic scenarios were against regional near-peers, and the transforming Army seemed most capable of dealing with these as well. "Phase IV," the aftermath of major operations, achieved little focused attention in either doctrine or operational planning. Chapter 9 discusses the Army's pivot to unconventional operations after 2003. The energy Lieutenant General David H. Petraeus applied to deliver and promote effective counterinsurgency doctrine when he was Combined Arms Center commander has become the stuff of legend. He and his colleagues were not deriving new knowledge, however. They were organizing and reemphasizing knowledge and experience that had long been within the organization and rendering it accessible to soldiers who needed it at the time.[14]

The post–Cold War Army became expeditionary. America was a world power rather than a continental power following the Spanish-American War of 1898. From that point it crossed vast oceans to fight its principal adversar-

For an expeditionary Army, deployability is essential.

ies. During World Wars I and II the United States Army entered most theaters benefiting from a glacis provided by embattled allies already there. During the Cold War American soldiers joined their allies on the glacis, forward deploying in Europe and Asia. When the Cold War disintegrated these forces seemed out of place, other than in Korea. JUST CAUSE and DESERT SHIELD/DESERT STORM underscored the unexpectedness with which contingencies could emerge. Chief of Staff General Gordon R. Sullivan (1991–1995) explored Army redesign with his modern Louisiana Maneuvers and committed to an expeditionary rather than a forward-deployed posture. This decision allowed him to take the great majority of the vast manpower (and thus budget) cuts imposed out of Europe, collaterally divesting the Army of considerable European infrastructure as well. The "stateside" active Army remained largely intact, albeit often reflagged, and turned its attention to how it could best get to the different places it might need to go. Solutions were to improve sealift and airlift, to pre-position equipment, and to lighten the weight of deploying units. The Ready Reserve Fleet went from seventeen roll-on/roll-off (RO/RO) ships in 1990 to thirty-six in 1996. These included Fast Sealift Ships (FSS) that sped along at twenty-seven knots carrying brigade sets of seven hundred vehicles—the lift equivalent of 116 World War II Liberty ships. Airlift in general and the Civilian Reserve Air Fleet (CRAF) in particular showed well during DESERT SHIELD/DESERT STORM and further improved in its aftermath. The Cold War Army had relied upon pre-positioned unit sets of equipment to facilitate the Return of Forces to Germany (REFORGER). Now it relocated brigade sets to Southwest Asia, Korea, Italy, afloat (in the Indian Ocean), and in reserve in the United States. During DESERT SHIELD/DESERT STORM 99 percent of the troops deployed by air and married up with equipment moving by sea. With pre-positioning, much of the equipment might already be there, as was the case with the 3d Infantry Division (Mechanized) in IRAQI FREEDOM. Efforts to make deployable units lighter had mixed results, as discussed in Chapter 9. The assumption of an expeditionary posture further required upgrading the infrastructure of stateside posts to be "power projection platforms," logistics initiatives such as dual basing, improved asset and inventory controls to diminish Cold War "iron mountains," training programs that routinely deployed troops under realistic circumstances, and such support to families as Family Readiness Groups and TRICARE. The shift to an expeditionary posture was necessary, but not without its consequences. Post–Cold War soldiers deploying from the continental United States were almost invariably unfamiliar with the lands and cultures into which they deployed. During JUST CAUSE in Panama American soldiers had already trained proximate to many of the objectives they seized. GDP exercises rendered potential German and Korean Cold War battlefields equally familiar. Within platoons a few soldiers or more knew the local language. This easy familiarity disappeared with forward deployment.[15]

The Army became digitized and embraced the Information Age about as quickly as it arrived. The Army's room-sized World War II Electronic Numerical Integrator and Computer (ENIAC) was arguably the world's first computer, and Signal and Artillery branches kept pace as technology progressed from the vacuum tube through the transistor, integrated circuit, and microprocessor. Hypertext markup language (HTML), hypertext transfer protocol (HTTP), and a practical browser came out separately around 1990. Taken together, they were for digital communications what movable type was for printing. Networking on a vast scale through multiple sites and addresses became practical. Sullivan's Louisiana Maneuvers featured linked "Battle Labs" increasingly dependent on digital technology. Other Army agencies followed. Soon "off-the-shelf" digital equipment proliferated throughout the Army, and in 1994 the Army Digitization Office stood up with considerable powers to discipline the process. Leaders at every level got into the habit of tapping away at personal computers, and digital technologies became integral to administration, logistics, and communications. The digital revolution Army transformers sought most fervently was tactical. DESERT STORM exposed huge problems with respect to fratricide, battle command, and battle space management largely because capabilities to move and shoot had considerably outpaced capabilities to command and control. TRADOC boiled the issues involved down to three questions: Where am I? Where are my buddies? Where is the enemy? General Sullivan initiated and Chief of Staff General Dennis J. Reimer (1995–1999) matured digital solutions. The general proliferation of satellite-based GPS rendered it an order of magnitude less likely that soldiers would become lost, although some still managed. Networks that automatically self-reported GPS locations, such as the Enhanced Position Location Reporting System (EPLRS) and the Inter-Vehicular Information System (IVIS), matured into what we now call blue force tracking (BFT). Reliably finding the enemy proved harder, but once enemy information was known to anybody it could immediately be made available to everybody, simultaneously broadcasting a shared battlefield picture. Digitization seemed most promising wedded to other advanced technologies, particularly sensors and "shooters." Robotics and ever-improving UAVs provided breakthroughs as "eyes on target"—sensors. The development and mass deployment of JDAMs in the late 1990s radically increased access to precision-guided munitions—shooters. In the institutional blink of an eye the effective cost of precision-guided munitions dropped by an order of magnitude. They were available for all targets, not just high-value targets. An Army that was never lost, always knew where its own people were, quickly found the enemy, and inevitably destroyed them when it did would be truly revolutionary. Digitized warfare as the Army waged it was highly dependent on space assets, air supremacy, and adequate electromagnetic bandwidth. Were any of these to be compromised, thirty years of technological progress would be compromised as well.[16]

The Army of 2005 was well on its way to being brigade-based and unit-manned. Chief of Staff General Peter J. Schoomaker (2003–2007) faced the enormous challenge of establishing a rotational base large enough to sustain operations in Afghanistan and Iraq without breaking the Army. He was mindful of the downside of individual replacement in World War II, Korea, and Vietnam, and he determined that units would rotate into Iraq as stable, trained, mutually confident "bands of brothers." For some time theorists had opined that existing army, corps, and division structure presented too much overhead and that technology had rendered the brigade combat team most viable as an operational "chip on the board." Reimer's Strike Force and Shinseki's Stryker Brigade anticipated such a development, as had a considerable body of TRADOC analysis and interpretation. Brigade combat teams were small enough to make unit manning feasible. They could rotate through force generation cycles, absorbing replacements en masse before their training phases. Brigade combat teams could be modular, constructed only of units they would customarily employ. This allowed thinning out such "big war" specialties as air defense, artillery, and engineers that had been concentrated at the division and levels above it. Manpower saved allowed more brigade combat teams and other critical units, thus expanding the rotational base. Schoomaker aspired to raise active-component brigade combat teams from thirty-three to forty-two and those in the National Guard from fifteen to twenty-eight. For a time he contemplated eliminating an echelon of command—army, corps, or division—to further economize and "flatten" the command hierarchy. In the end it seemed spans of control would become too large, so divisions and corps instead slimmed down to modular headquarters without the combat support and service support units formerly assigned to them. These assets went into brigade combat teams or other modular "units of action," became theater assets, or were inactivated. The connection between division and brigade diminished, and deployed division headquarters routinely controlled brigades not wearing their patch. The brigade-based Army as it existed by 2010 forfeited former abilities to mass air defense, artillery, engineer, and other assets. Many of these were tied into the brigade combat teams, and others no longer existed. What if such massing were once again needed? Unit manning works if casualties are few and combat episodic. Should the United States Army again face a foe capable of inflicting significant casualties, it would have to reconsider individual replacement. Being brigade-based and unit-manned is appropriate for present circumstances, not for all circumstances.[17]

Thoughts on the Way Ahead

Someday the Army will undoubtedly seek to transform again. When it does, it will look back on its ongoing transformation to a Digitized Expeditionary Army, just as it now looks back on its earlier transformations to the All-Volunteer Late Cold War Army, the Draftee Early Cold War Army, the Mobilization-Based Armies of World Wars I and II, and the Army for Empire that preceded them. If past is precedent, some mix of technological advance, socioeconomic change, and changing strategic circumstances will indicate that thorough transformation rather than modest adaptation has become necessary. Until that point the Digitized Expeditionary Army will continue to mature, further evolving away from the Late Cold War Army in which it is rooted. Perhaps new vehicular platforms, revived shades of the future combat systems (FCSs), will replace such venerable stalwarts as the M1 Abrams and M2/3 Bradley. Perhaps not. This will not be crucial, as the essence of the Digitized Expeditionary Army will have been networked digital communications, Information Age sensors and munitions, and speedy deployability. This Army has already been tested by war and contingency, and it undoubtedly will be tested again. Accepting the considerable risk of imagining the future rather than examining the past, let us project material previously discussed in this chapter—and thus in this study—forward. Are there thoughts worth sharing with those who would lead the Digitized Expeditionary Army into near-term contingencies? Are there thoughts worth sharing with those who might seek to again transform the Army in the more distant future?

On balance, the trade-offs accepted to transform to the Digitized Expeditionary Army have worked out. Combat-ready units have frequently been in demand on short notice since 1989, whereas circumstances requiring mass mobilization have not occurred. Nuclear attack has never seemed imminent. Despite some difficulties, general purpose forces have adapted well to low-intensity conflict in Iraq, Afghanistan, and elsewhere. There seems to be little to complain about with respect to quality in that regard, since American soldiers have "kept the lid on" in two volatile countries with a fraction of the force structure customarily required given the sizes of their restive populations. The expeditionary Army has deployed quickly to hot spots around the globe and has capably sustained itself once there. American soldiers are seldom lost, almost invariably know where their comrades are, and share a common picture of the battlefield. Their sensors and shooters network with devastating effect. Unit-manned brigade combat teams filled with veterans routinely rotate past each other overseas, maintaining their qualitative edges as they do so. All of this having been said, what if circumstances change? American vulnerabilities are no particular secret. Most know the United States has a smallish Army that as now committed has no actual strategic reserve and that capabilities to expand this force are largely eroded. Many consider the United States casualty averse and believe it will fold if drawn into a fight more deadly than it has the stomach for. Nuclear weapons proliferation presents a particular danger in this regard, especially if these can be detonated without presenting suitable targets for retaliation. The United States Army is, quite simply, unprepared for nuclear attack. The low end of the combat spectrum, however, seems the most likely venue wherein American arms will continue to be challenged. Iraq and Afghanistan offer ample testimony to the manpower intensiveness of such conflicts, which does not match up well against a small Army with a moribund mobilization base. The world's most dangerous trouble spots reside in areas with which American soldiers are least culturally familiar, hugely complicating deployments into them. Potential adversaries work diligently to develop the means to compromise American bandwidth and aerospace supremacy, both vital to digitized warfare as Americans wage it. Future adversaries are likely to play to the Digitized Expeditionary Army's weaknesses and avoid its strengths. The Army and the nation cannot afford to simultaneously overmatch all potential threats at once, hence the trade-offs that have created the vulnerabilities. Given this dilemma, a sports metaphor may be helpful. Football teams cannot be equally adept at all their plays at once. Each week they rehearse the menu that best fits their upcoming adversary. There are huge differences between knowing what is supposed to happen, having the ability to make it happen, and actually making it happen. Rehearsal focused on the imminent contest primes performance in it. General Frederick M. Franks Jr., former TRADOC commander and beloved mentor to many, spoke of fighting "from the neck up." To him the "art of war" was to be broadly prepared, prescient enough to identify the next challenge, and timely enough to specifically prepare for it. An Army, like a football team, needs plays to transition from one adversary to the next. It cannot be physically ready, but it can be conceptually ready, for all of the contingencies it can foresee. In a sense the battlefield debut of the Digitized Expeditionary Army offers an illustration of this point. The tactical units poised to invade Iraq were initially Legacy Force with respect to digitization, less those of the 4th Infantry Division (Mechanized) so long at sea. However, the conceptual underpinnings of digitization had been worked out, and requisite hardware and software was on hand—albeit in limited quantities. Within weeks Legacy units became digitized by appliqué, hurriedly trained with their new equipment, and performed quite well in their newly digitized posture. Units rotating into theater were "hosed down" with equipment and training in turn, each arriving more digitized and better prepared than the one before. Thought came first; hardware followed. Those destined to lead the Digitized Expeditionary Army in future contingencies might do well to keep this precedent in mind. Hopefully they will prepare diligently, think broadly, remain flexible, and tweak a generally prepared Army for the specifics of each next mission at hand.[18]

How will the Army's leadership know that the time for yet another transformation is upon them? If past is precedent, they won't be altogether sure. The prospect of change will inspire resistance and ignite debate. Some galvanizing event, like Pearl Harbor, may guarantee focus and garner resources, but by then it may well be too late to conjure up a transformational game plan. The mobilization for World War II, as we have seen, was rehearsed in World War I. Similarly, the Digitized Expeditionary Army that deployed after 9-11 was a half generation in the making. Digitization and the use of cyberspace will continue to evolve through generations more. The starting point for the next transformation will be more apparent after the fact than it will be as it begins. Leaders will anticipate the future as best they can, adapting rather than transforming until they believe a watershed—technological, socioeconomic, and strategic—justifying radical change has been reached. With respect to technology, the next major leap ahead seems likely to be propelled by robotics. Other promising candidates include directed energy weapons, cyberelectronic warfare, nanotechnology, and genetic engineering, but robotics are already pervasive enough and far enough along that one can envision near-term breakthroughs equivalent to the HTML, HTTP, and practical browsers that transformed isolated computers into a planetary Internet. Already unmanned aerial vehicles piloted from Nevada attack targets in Pakistan, "PackBots" hunt for roadside bombs and scout out buildings in war zones, Modular Advanced Armed Robotic Systems (MAARSs) carry machine guns and grenade launchers athwart

Future technologies must integrate with doctrine, organization, training, administrative practices, and service culture.

miniature tracks, and autonomous trucks negotiate courses scores of miles in length. Sixth-graders compete in statewide contests to design Lego robots that best clear away debris, negotiate obstacle courses, or fight each other. If contemporary robots are metaphorically equivalent to the biplanes of 1917 and today's sixth-graders are the military-age manpower of the 2020s, where will robotics be in twenty years? With respect to prospective socioeconomic change, one obvious candidate among several is the graying of America. In twenty years the proportion of senior citizens in the United States seems likely to double, the proportion of Americans gainfully employed to stagnate because of automation, and the proportion of youths of traditional military ages to decline because of lower birth rates. Surely these dramatic demographics will have military as well as socioeconomic consequences. With respect to changing strategic circumstances, a popular candidate for concern has been the rise of China. This development is certainly worthy of note with respect to its military implications, but nothing makes confrontation inevitable and much argues against it. China, like Europe, Japan, India, Australia, South Africa, and even Russia and most of South America, has benefited mightily from the interdependent, Internet-connected, increasingly globalized world economy. Far from hunkering down in Soviet-style self-isolation, the Chinese are gamely playing the international economic system within its rules and have much to lose should it be disrupted. They are also aging, as are Americans and virtually everyone else most prospering within the global economic system. Societies not aging are by and large have-nots, with the highest growth rates in such garden spots as Zaire, Yemen, and Oman. Most of Africa and much of the Middle East share in this trend, with medical advances and fertility not yet balanced by family planning or the emancipation of women. Youth cohorts accumulate in large numbers, far beyond the capability of local economies to absorb them. Emigration is ever less of an answer, as increasingly automated advanced countries need less and less unskilled labor. These fertile but disadvantaged nations are prone to strongman rule and account for a major fraction of the world's armed quarrels. They have access to modern weapons. Some have fielded large, and a few formidable, armies. Historically, armed have-nots with a youth bulge have often been threats to more prosperous and less fecund neighbors. There is no reason to believe this pattern will not continue. Whatever the specifics of the next technological, socioeconomic, and strategic watersheds, worthy candidates are already brewing.[19]

For the purpose of conjecture, imagine that the next leap in military technology sufficient to be transformative is associated with robotics. Army transformers will not find it sufficient to issue contingents of robots to existing organizations and consider their mission complete. Like their predecessors, they will have to manage profound doctrinal, organizational, training, administrative, and cultural changes in addition to technological modernization per se. With respect to doctrine, for example, what battlefield role do the robots play? Are they bionic exoskeletons, radically enhancing the capabilities of individual warriors who advance arrayed like the corporate mercenaries in *Avatar*? Are they remotes, individually piloted by soldiers at a safe distance from danger—like UAVs and PackBots today? Are they automated teammates, cruising along to execute the mandates of humans sprinkled among them? Are they autonomous, executing precoded missions with lethal effects? Are they some mix of the above? Robots would be ill-used if not set within a conceptual framework. Doctrine can drive technology. If doctrine writers determine that what they really want are bionic exoskeletons, industry is that much more likely to develop them. Robotic units will be differently organized than all-human ones. One could perhaps envision a platoon of bionic exoskeletal warriors, but it would have to come with its own robust maintenance section. If a support platoon consists of one human and twenty automated trucks, does a truck company consist of three people? Do UAVs piloted from Nevada come under the tactical control of humans further forward? When a mechanized robotic platoon clears a wood line, does the human platoon leader dismount? Robotics will introduce huge training implications. Human mastery of the associated hardware and software will demand a prodigious honing of intellectual, neuromuscular, and physical skills. Teenagers invest days into perfecting their skills with a single Internet avatar. How much more difficult will it be to manage multiple robotic avatars simultaneously? How much of a defile drill can be automated, and how much requires human deci-

Nontraditional and noncombat missions will continue.

sion making? Beyond maintenance and logistics for robots, a robotic Army has profound administrative implications for humans as well. How does the Army recruit the talent it needs, particularly if the youth demographic with the requisite skill is an ever-smaller proportion of the population—and heavily competed for by industry as well? What do promotion pyramids look like when entry-level soldiers assume battlefield responsibilities equivalent to those of sergeants today? One presumes, for example, that conflating a four-man tank crew into one would end up with a human tank commander, not a loader. With respect to culture, the implications are breathtaking. Who exactly constitutes the "band of brothers" that inspires soldiers above and beyond the call of duty? What establishes prestige when rank, age, physical vigor, and gender have so much less to do with battlefield outcomes than "geek" insight and selected neuromuscular skills? To what extent can decisions to kill be delegated to automatons? Can robots take meetings where assassination—or paralyzing boredom—seems likely? What are the new proportions between fighters and sustainers? In the Air Force, according to common belief, only a tiny fraction of the whole actually flies planes and constitutes a "gene pool" for senior leadership. Would that be true in a robotic Army? Will units be awarded campaign streamers based on the percentage of humans that deploy, or will robots count too? Admitting that we are on a slippery slope from analysis to fantasy, we can return to our original point. Whatever the technological advances are that are deemed transformative, exploiting them will require due attention to doctrine, organization, training, administration, and service culture. It will also require adaptation to socioeconomic and strategic circumstances. If the United States, for example, deploys fewer older soldiers and robots to hold off hordes of young men armed with Industrial Age weapons and a few "nukes," it faces challenges well beyond those of technology alone.[20]

Can the Army conduct a centrally directed and institutionally driven transformation in the future? As we have seen, maintaining substantial control over its own destiny was difficult during the period 1989 through 2005, and there seems no reason to believe this will get any easier. The Department of Defense and Joint Staff will have legal preeminence and seem likely to at least in part differ with service priorities. Squabbling with sister services will flag up issues to the Joint Staff that may or may not be resolved in the Army's favor. With robotics in mind, for example, the flying altitudes and levels of supervision of unmanned aerial vehicles are already points of contention among the Army, Navy, and Air Force. At what level of aircraft sophistication should seasoned licensed pilots serve instead of young uniformed reprogrammed computer buffs? The Secretariat will continue to extend deep within the bowels of Army decision making, particularly with respect to research, development, financial management, and human resources. This means that the tipping point for including political as well as "purely military" considerations will come sooner rather than later. TRADOC, AMC, and United States Army Forces Command (FORSCOM) will continue as four-star behemoths with critical transformational responsibilities, inspiring further creative tensions between themselves and the Army Staff. Contractors will have their own priorities and the connections and leverage to pursue them. The most robust will have the ears of Congress and the administration, who themselves will have a lot on their minds other than Defense transformation. If there are new players, they may be newly empowered scions of the "blogosphere" and the "24/7" news cycle. Less subject to editing and constraint than traditional media, they have a demonstrated ability to capture public attention and to hyper-reinforce the passions of niche audiences. One Chief of Staff considered assigning Army Staff members to surreptitiously get the Army view across on selected blogs, and another considered the opposite tactic of banning soldiers from blogs altogether to avoid compromising sensitive information. Both proposals appalled legal counsel, and neither got beyond casual contemplation. They do, however, underscore the importance accorded "strategic communications" by Chiefs and the Army Staff. At the time of writing, the emerging Army Enterprise System offers considerable promise as a means to sustain coherent shared pictures. Several techniques served the Army well from 1989 through 2005 with respect to maintaining a grip on its future. The first was to get out in front of other participants with respect to serious staff work and specific proposals. Since being bested by the British at Casablanca and earlier World War II conferences, the Army Staff has lived in fear of confronting plans and proposals more thoroughly thought through than its own. Vuono's ANTAEUS, Sullivan's LAM Task Force, Reimer's Army XXI, and Shinseki's Army Transformation all represented determined efforts to establish "going-in positions" persuasive enough that others would rather edit them than compete with them. By and large the approach worked, with the partial exception of Army Transformation's clashes with Office of the Secretary of Defense alternatives. A second and related approach has been to stock Quadrennial Defense Review (QDR) and similar Defense-wide deliberations with "top drawer" talent, ensuring mastery of such analytic enterprises as Dynamic Commitment or DAWMS. Time and again rigorous analysis pointed to a need for more rather than fewer ground forces, staving off potential cuts. A third imperative was to ensure consensus within the Army when negotiating outside it, no sure thing amid legitimate debate, branch concerns, potent fiefdoms like TRADOC and AMC, and the enlarged role of the Secretariat. Sullivan's GOSC and the four-star board of directors associated with the modern Louisiana Maneuvers are best appreciated in this light, as are similar initiatives by his successors and the elaboration of Shinseki's transition survey and interview process. The Director of the Army Staff shepherded elaborate protocols to align the Army Staff and the Army Secretariat, a process that could be and generally was much advanced by good personal relations between the Secretary of the Army and the Chief of Staff, and between assistant secretaries of the Army and their Army Staff counterparts. A fourth approach was to sustain the support of retirees, contractors, and others of the interested public, as these directly or indirectly assisted the Army with Congress and others. It is no accident that AUSA conventions played such a prominent role in the general promulgation of Army messages. Finally, exceptional organizations such as the LAM Task Force, the Experimental Force, and the Objective Force Task Force stood up, served for a period, and then divested. These had valuable roles to play but could have become dysfunctional had they survived too long. Timing was everything to ensure that they improved rather than degraded the grip on the future. An earlier paragraph likened a Chief of Staff attempting to keep a grip on transformation to a surfer tracking his course while keeping his balance. That metaphor for both possibility and challenge seems likely to remain valid.[21]

An Army pursuing transformation can reasonably anticipate significant distractions from that purpose. These can come under at least three headings: contemporary contingencies, making up for mismatches, and "political" distractions. The current contingency will almost inevitably trump hypothetical future missions with respect to attention and resources, particularly if lives are at risk and casualties involved. General Sullivan when arriving, as we have seen, opined that there would be "no time out from readiness" regardless of the challenges of downsizing and transformation. He proved correct. Northern Iraq, Somalia, Haiti, Kuwait, the Balkans, Afghanistan, and Iraq involved the Army in near-continuous cycles of deployment, as did hosts of lesser contingencies, operations, and exercises. Each of these legitimately was the priority of its time. Soldiers were in danger; they needed to be optimally led and well supported. As operations progressed, mismatches appeared between preparations previously made and threats actually encountered. Sensible enemies develop or strike at weaknesses, perhaps in unanticipated ways. This produces distraction of a different sort, that of rushing to resolve the immediate threat while postponing initiatives not relevant to it. The efficiencies of systematic evolution are abandoned for the effectiveness of quick, if costly, solutions. The campaign against IEDs offers an example of this phenomenon. Perfect foresight might have rendered IEDs simply one more target of prolonged transformational efforts. Instead billions of dollars and significant supervisory efforts were thrown into spasms of up-armoring, proliferating electronic countermeasures, revamping tactics, and acquiring relevant new equipment. Results were creditably successful but underscored the fact that the unanticipated threat can quickly become the priority, brushing other transformational initiatives aside. Another genre of distraction encountered by Army transformers might best be described as "political." Raised through their adult lives in a unique environment, uniformed Army senior leaders can be caught off-balance by the emphases of their political leaders. A case in point might be the "Aberdeen Sex Scandal" of 1996. A number of officers and noncommissioned officers stood accused of heinously abusing their positions to solicit sex from female trainees. One might have thought the Uniformed Code of Military Justice, with severe sanctions against such behavior, might have ground along on its own to mete out punishment. However, Army leaders who refused to comment on cases still under investigation appeared obtuse to the public—perhaps even insufficiently interested. Efforts by the Secretary of the Army and others to rectify this backfired, as defense attorneys accused them of prejudging the case and exerting undue command influence and sought a gag order on the Secretary himself. The media picked up on the theme and connected the dots to other cases at other times in other places. Sexual abuse and gender inequality already were, understandably, "hot button" political issues. The Army leaped to set right its image. Congressional hearings, hot lines, admonitions of "zero tolerance" policies, sexual harassment training, gender sensitivity classes, and uniformed presentations to civilian audiences proliferated. The effort siphoned off an enormous amount of supervisory time addressing an issue few if any had anticipated—and attempted to prove the essentially unprovable. On a lighter note, General Shinseki provoked a different time-consumptive flap when he appropriated the black beret for the Army at large from the ever-popular but somewhat tribal Rangers and then bought berets from China to procure enough of them. Other examples abound, diverting Army senior leaders at least a couple of times each year from whatever they thought they were going to be doing. To question the root cause would be to question the constitutional principle of civilian control over the military. Fortuitously, aspects of the Goldwater-Nichols Act assist in controlling distraction. The sharpened division of labor between theater commanders as force employers and services as force providers theoretically reduces the focus of the Army Staff on events overseas, ideally providing more time to focus on forces yet to deploy. Sustained effort in that regard should make it easier to fathom adversaries in advance, reducing the distraction of reconciling capability mismatches. For all of the complexities involved in bringing the Secretariat deeper into the traditional purview of the Army Staff, this renders an earlier appreciation of politically charged issues likely. Hopefully fewer such flaps will escape the Department of the Army. Like priests, Army officers often find that their distractions are their vocation. No Secretary of the Army or Chief of Staff will ever be able to focus exclusively on Army transformation. Divisions of labor should reflect this, empowering some leaders and agencies to

THE ARMY BUDGET, 1905–2005
(ANNUAL PERCENT CHANGE)

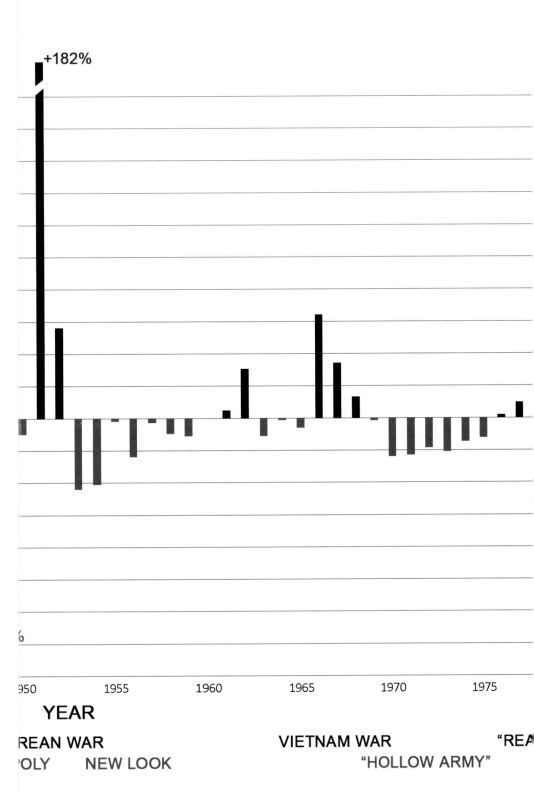

+182%

YEAR

1950   1955   1960   1965   1970   1975

REAN WAR   VIETNAM WAR   "REA

OLY   NEW LOOK   "HOLLOW ARMY"

| 1980 | 1985 | 1990 | 1995 | 2000 | 2005 |

GAN BUILD-UP"   DESERT STORM   GWOT
                        "PEACE DIVIDEND"

sustain momentum with respect to transformation regardless of the other issues at hand.[22]

The most significant single impediment to Army transformation in 1989–2005 was, as we have seen, funding. Congress must approve and appropriate the money the Army spends, passing along the costs to the American people who vote for them (*Chart 9*). The tectonic shifts centered on 1989 that rendered transformation necessary also inspired an understandable desire for a "peace dividend" throughout the electorate. From 1989 through 1993 the Army lost over a third of its effective budget. Much of this was absorbed by shedding force structure and European infrastructure, but austerity pervaded modernization, research and development, and other activities as well. The Army's percentage of the overall Defense budget declined slightly, hovering around 26 percent of the whole through most of the 1990s. By comparison, the Navy and Air Force averaged a third of the budget each during this period. Their expensive high-tech platforms were arguably more popular with Congress, whereas the Army budget remained dominated by mundane personnel costs. In this fiscal environment the Army could and did experiment with prototypes and over time stood up and trained with experimental units. General Fred Franks' digital epiphany occurred, for example, while observing an IVIS-equipped tank platoon. In due course this was followed by a company team, a battalion task force, and, with National Training Center (NTC) 97–06, a brigade combat team. It took ten years to progress from a digitally seasoned platoon to a digitally seasoned division, and this division was a brigade combat team short with respect to digital equipment. It is worth noting that this digital equipment was by and large appliqué on venerable existing platforms. The proposed future combat systems initiated by General Shinseki "slipped to the right" with respect to fielding. Prior to IRAQI FREEDOM plans for Army digitization extended decades into the future, with a few units at a time becoming so equipped. With IRAQI FREEDOM, as is generally the case in American wars, money previously doled out sparingly flowed freely. Much of this took the form of supplementals rather than base budget. The Army's base budget in 2005 and 2006 was $100 billion each year, for example, but the Army received supplementals of $60 billion in 2005 and $70 billion in 2006. Transformation narrowed in focus to the exigencies of Iraq and Afghanistan, but exponentially picked up its pace. Blue force tracking mounted on vehicles exploded from 1,200 to 55,000 sets during General Schoomaker's tenure, and fieldings with respect to advanced avionics, UAVs, satellite communications, precision-guided munitions, and other relevant technologies kept pace. The Rapid Fielding Initiative (RFI) hosed down units with off-the-shelf equipment as they prepared to deploy. Within the course of a few unit rotations, the Army in Iraq and Afghanistan had transformed. Future Army transformers might profit from examining this pattern. When the Army substantially redeploys from Iraq and Afghanistan, budgets are likely to plummet. In particular, supplementals will dry up. Transformers must gather what money they can and invest in prototypes and small prototypical units. If robots are the next big thing, there will not be very many of them in "peacetime." Perhaps residual operations overseas will allow them to be tested in the field, as will

481

the successors to AWEs and NTC 97–06. Transformation will be gradual, prototypical, evolutionary, and sparsely funded unless or until a new crisis is reached. Then money will flow. Successful transformation will depend upon being well positioned to spend a lot of money quickly and efficiently, deflecting it into the new war or emergency at hand. Veterans of fiscal year closeouts understand the basics: prioritized "want" or decrements lists, contracts poised for immediate obligation, understandings with service and industrial providers, tiered spending plans, and personnel trained to execute them. Woe be unto the division comptroller who receives year-end money he or she cannot spend by midnight on 30 September. The phenomenon of dramatic infusions of money propelling a theretofore nascent transformation has ample precedent. The Philippine "Insurrection" enabled the transformation to an Army for Empire, Pearl Harbor the conclusive transformation to a mobilization-based Army, the Berlin crisis and Korean War the transformation to the Early Cold War Army, the embarrassment of the Iranian hostage crisis and the "Reagan buildup" the transformation to the Late Cold War Army, and IRAQI FREEDOM the transformation to the Digitized Expeditionary Army. In each case years of thought, debate, experimentation, and even rehearsal preceded the crisis, but the crisis freed up the funding to actually transform the Army as a whole. Theoretically it is possible to transform an Army in peacetime; the United States has never actually done so. From 1989 through 2003 Army transformers positioned the Army to effectively throw money quickly into a Digitized Expeditionary Army when money came available. This was a creditable, if more modest than hoped for, accomplishment. It may well be the peacetime achievement future transformers should reasonably aspire to.[23]

Conclusions

From 1989 through 2005 the United States Army attempted, and largely achieved, a centrally directed and institutionally driven revolution in military affairs relevant to ground warfare that exploited Information Age technology, adapted to post–Cold War strategic circumstances, and integrated into parallel Joint and Department of Defense efforts. To thus transform it not only modernized equipment, it also substantially altered doctrine, organization, training, administrative and logistical practices, and service culture. The transformed Army has withstood the test of combat, performing superbly with respect to deployment and high-end conventional combat and capably with respect to low-intensity conflict. For all of its impressive strengths, however, the Digitized Expeditionary Army accepted trade-offs to best fit contemporary circumstances with the funds available. It now lacks a mobilization base for expedient expansion, is unprepared for nuclear warfare, is unlikely to be familiar at the unit level with countries into which it will be deployed, would have difficulty massing selected combat support and combat service support assets, and is vulnerable to compromises of bandwidth or aerospace supremacy. These vulnerabilities result from decisions sensible at the times they were made, but plans should exist to redress each on short notice—should it become necessary. The Army will continue to digitize and modernize into the foreseeable future. At some point a new juxtaposition of strategic, socioeconomic, and technological watersheds will become so great another transformation will become necessary. That transformation, like its predecessors, will have to address doctrine, organization, training, administration and logistics, and service culture to become complete. If it is to be centrally directed and institutionally driven, Army leaders will have to take positive steps to remain in control. Techniques that proved useful in that regard from 1989 through 2005 included anticipatory up-front planning, drilled teams of articulate analysts, mechanisms to achieve and sustain consensus, strategic communications, and the occasional use of exceptional organizations. There will be distractions in the future as there have been in the past. Legacy contingency missions will follow one another, capability mismatches will emerge demanding speedy resolution, and politically contentious issues will absorb supervisory time. Army leadership must organize itself to accommodate these while sustaining the momentum of transformation. There will not be enough money most of the time. Future transformative efforts will most likely roll on for years as patchworks of research initiatives, prototypes, and experimental units. Hopefully these will provide blueprints applicable to the organization as a whole, when crisis erupts and money again flows. The quality of the next transformation will reflect the quality of these blueprints. Five Chiefs of Staff and innumerable soldiers and civilians served their country well transforming the Army from 1989 through 2005 and operating with that transforming Army in the field. Much is instructive in their experience. Hopefully it will prove useful to those who "pick up their rucksacks" to follow behind them.

Notes

[1] See Richard W. Stewart, ed., *American Military History*, vol. 2, *The United States in a Global Era, 1917–2003* (Washington DC: Center of Military History, 2005), 369–497; D. Robert Worley, *Shaping U.S. Military Forces: Revolution or Relevance in a Post–Cold War World* (Westport, Connecticut: Praeger Security International, 2006).

[2] See James F. Dunnigan, *Digital Soldiers: The Evolution of High-Tech Weaponry and Tomorrow's Brave New Battlefield* (New York: St. Martin's Press, 1996); James R. Blaker, *Transforming Military Force: The Legacy of Arthur Cebrowski and Network Centric Warfare* (Westport, Connecticut: Praeger Security International, 2007); Max Boot, *War Made New: Technology, Warfare and the Course of History 1500 to Today* (New York: Gotham Books, 2006), 307–436.

[3] See John L. Romjue, *American Army Doctrine for the Post–Cold War* (Fort Monroe, Virginia: Military History Office, U.S. Army Training and Doctrine Command, 1996); Thomas K. Adams, *The Army After Next: The First Postindustrial Army* (Stanford: Stanford Security Studies, 2008); Field Manual 71–1, *The Tank and Mechanized Infantry Company Team* (Washington DC: Department of the Army, 1988); Field Manual 71–1, *The Tank and Mechanized Infantry Company Team*, 2005; Field Manual 100–5, *Operations* (Washington DC: Department of the Army, 1986); Field Manual 3–0, *Operations* (Washington DC: Department of the Army, 2008); Douglas A. Macgregor, *Breaking the Phalanx: A New Design for Landpower in the 21st Century* (Westport, Connecticut: Praeger, 1997).

[4] See John L. Romjue, *The Army of Excellence: The Development of the 1980s Army* (Fort Monroe, Virginia: Office of the Command Historian, U.S. Army Training and Doctrine Command, 1993); John J. McGrath, *The Brigade: A History* (Fort Leavenworth, Kansas: Combat Studies Institute Press, 2004); William M. Donnelly, *Transforming an Army at War: Designing the Modular Force, 1991–2005* (Washington DC: Center of Military History, 2007).

[5] See Anne W. Chapman, *The Army's Training Revolution, 1973–1990: An Overview* (Fort Monroe, Virginia: Office of the Command Historian, U.S. Army Training and Doctrine Command, 1994); Benjamin King, *Victory Starts Here: A 35-year History of the US Army Training and Doctrine Command* (Fort Leavenworth, Kansas: Combat Studies Institute Press, 2008); General Peter Schoomaker and General Richard Cody, Transcript of Media Roundtable Conducted at the Association of the United States Army Annual Meeting, Washington DC, 26 October 2004, Historians files, CMH.

[6] See Donnelly; Randy Talbot, *Forging the Steel Hammer: TACOM LCMC Support to the Global War on Terrorism, 2001–2005* (Warren, Michigan: U.S. Army TACOM Life Cycle Management Command, 2006); Philip A. Shiman, "Defense Acquisition in an Uncertain World: The Post–Cold War Era, 1990–2000," in Shannon A. Brown, gen. ed., *Providing the Means of War: Historical Perspectives on Defense Acquisition, 1945–2000* (Washington DC: Center of Military History and Industrial College of the Armed Forces, 2005), 283–309.

[7] See Eric K. Shinseki, *The Army Family: A White Paper* (Washington DC: Center of Military History, 2003); Ben Shepherd, *A War of Nerves: Soldiers and Psychiatrists in the Twentieth Century* (Boston: Harvard University Press, 2001); David Dobbs, "The Post Traumatic Stress Trap," *Scientific American* (April 2009): 64–69; Michael D. Doubler, *I Am the Guard: A History of the Army National Guard, 1636–2000* (Washington DC: Department of the Army, 2001).

[8] See James R. Lochner III, *Victory on the Potomac: The Goldwater Nichols Act Unifies the Pentagon* (College Station, Texas: Texas A&M University Press, 2002);

George C. Wilson, *This War Really Matters: Inside the Fight for Defense Dollars* (Washington DC: CQ Press, 2000); Deborah D. Avant, *The Market for Force: The Consequences of Privatizing Security* (New York: Cambridge University Press, 2005).

[9] See Mark Sherry, *The Army Command Post and Defense Reshaping, 1987–1997* (Washington DC: Center of Military History, 2009); James L. Yarrison, *The Modern Louisiana Maneuvers* (Washington DC: Center of Military History, 1999); Joint Pub 3–0, *Doctrine for Joint Operations* (Washington DC: Department of Defense, 1995); Edward N. Luttwak, *The Pentagon and the Art of War: The Question of Military Reform* (New York: Simon & Schuster, 1985); Lochner.

[10] See MacGregor Knox and Williamson Murray, *The Dynamics of Military Revolution, 1300–2050* (New York: Cambridge University Press, 2001); Gregory Fontenot, E. J. Degen, and David Tohn, *On Point: The United States Army in Operation IRAQI FREEDOM* (Fort Leavenworth, Kansas: Combat Studies Institute Press, 2004); Donald P. Wright and Timothy R. Reese, *On Point II: Transition to the New Campaign, The United States Army in Operation IRAQI FREEDOM, May 2003–January 2005* (Fort Leavenworth, Kansas: Combat Studies Institute Press, 2008).

[11] See Stewart, *American Military History,* vol. 2, 369–497; Worley; Wright and Reese.

[12] See Marvin A. Kriedberg and Merton G. Henry, *History of Military Mobilization in the United States Army, 1775–1945* (Washington DC: Department of the Army, 1955); Robert R. Palmer, Bell I. Wiley, and William R. Keast, *The Procurement and Training of Ground Combat Troops* (Washington DC: Office of the Chief of Military History, 1948); R. Elberton Smith, *The Army and Economic Mobilization* (Washington DC: Office of the Chief of Military History, 1959); John S. Brown, *Draftee Division: The 88th Infantry Division in World War II* (Lexington, Kentucky: University of Kentucky Press, 1986); Sherry; Mary L. Haynes, *Department of the Army Historical Summary, Fiscal Year 1987* (Washington DC: Center of Military History, 1995), 32–35, 57–68; Lieutenant General Jack C. Stultz Jr., "The Army Reserve: A Positive Investment for America," *Army 2009–2010 Green Book*, October 2009, 131–34.

[13] See *Treaty Between the United States and the Union of Soviet Socialist Republics on the Elimination of Theater Intermediate Range and Shorter Range Missiles*, entered into force 1 June 1988, United States Department of State, http://www.state.gov; Robert A. Doughty, *The Evolution of U.S. Army Tactical Doctrine, 1946–1976* (Washington DC: Center of Military History, 2001); Romjue, *American Army Doctrine for the Post–Cold War World*; Brian Alexander and Alistair Miller, *Tactical Nuclear Weapons in an Evolving Security Environment* (Washington DC: Brassey's, 2003); Vincent H. Demma, *Department of the Army Historical Summary, Fiscal Year 1989* (Washington DC: Center of Military History, 1998); John S. Brown, "Historically Speaking: The Denuclearization of the United States Army," *Army* (May 2008): 102–03.

[14] See S. 2453, *A Bill to Enhance the Capability of the United States to Combat Terrorism and Other Forms of Unconventional Warfare;* HR 5109, *A Bill to Establish a National Special Operations Agency Within the Department of Defense to Have Unified Responsibility for All Special Operations Forces and Activities*; *The National Defense Authorization Act for Fiscal Year 1987*; Demma, 35, 76–78; Sherry, 36; *AirLand Operations: The Evolution of AirLand Battle for a Strategic Army* (Fort Monroe, Virginia: U.S. Army Training and Doctrine Command, 1991); *The National Defense Panel Assessment of the 1997 Quadrennial Defense Review* (Arlington, Virginia: National Defense Panel, 1997); *The Army Quadrennial Defense Review: Senior Leader Update* (Washington DC: Department of the Army, 11 July 2001); David Cloud and Greg Jaffe, *The Fourth Star: Four Generals and the Epic Struggle for the Future of the*

United States Army (New York: Crown Publishers, 2009); Andrew J. Birtle, *U.S. Army Counterinsurgency and Contingency Operations Doctrine, 1860–1941* (Washington DC: Center of Military History, 1998).

[15] See Stewart, *American Military History*, vol. 2; Yarrison; *The Conduct of the Persian Gulf War: Final Report to Congress* (Washington DC: Department of Defense, 1992), 30–47, 358–59, 365, 371–450; Birger Bergesen and John McDonald, *Assessment of Contingency and Expeditionary Force Capabilities* (McClean, Virginia: Science Applications International, 1994); Lieutenant General Johnnie E. Wilson, "Power Projection Now . . . and in the 21st Century," *Army 1994–1995 Green Book*, October 1995, 137–43; Army Regulation 210–20, *Master Planning for Army Installations* (Washington DC: Department of the Army, 1992); General Peter J. Schoomaker and General Richard Cody, Transcript of the Media Roundtable Conducted at the Association of the United States Army Annual Meeting, Washington DC, 26 October 2004.

[16] See Ms, Clayton R. Newell, Digitizing the Army (Arlington, Virginia: Association of the United States Army); Janet Abbate, *Inventing the Internet* (Cambridge, Massachusetts: MIT Press, 1999); Yarrison, 1–51, 87–95; Adams; *Report to Congress on Army Digitization* (Washington DC: Army Digitization Office, 1995); Romjue, *American Army Doctrine for the Post–Cold War World*; "Combat Identification Technology Demonstration Presentation to Senior Officers Review Group," Combat Identification Systems Program Office, 14 February 1992, Historians Files, CMH; General William M. Hartzog, "TRADOC: Moving the Army into the Future," *Army 1997–1998 Green Book*, October 1997, 49–54; Army Senior Leader Update, "Precision Strike: A Unique American Military Advantage . . . but with Limits," 14 August 2001, Historians Files, CMH; Peter Grier, "The JDAM Revolution," *Air Force Online: The Journal of the Air Force Association* (September 2006).

[17] See Donnelly; McGrath; Mark J. Reardon and Jeffery A. Charlston, *From Transformation to Combat: The First Stryker Brigade at War* (Washington DC: Center of Military History, 2007); *Objective Force Tactical, Operational and Organizational Concept for Maneuver Units of Action* (Fort Monroe, Virginia: U.S. Army Training and Doctrine Command, 2001); *Objective Force Unit of Employment Concept* (Fort Monroe, Virginia: U.S. Army Training and Doctrine Command, 2003).

[18] See Stewart, *American Military History*, vol. 2; Fontenot, Degen, and Tohn; Wright and Reese; Birtle; John S. Brown, "Numerical Considerations in Military Occupations," *Army* (April 2006): 125–26; Colonel Qiao Liang and Colonel Wang Xiangsui, *Unrestricted Warfare: China's Master Plan to Destroy America* (Panama City, Panama: Pan American Publishing Company, 2002); Eric L. Haney and Brian M. Thompson, eds., *Beyond Shock and Awe: Warfare in the 21st Century* (New York: Berkley Caliber, 2006).

[19] See P. W. Singer, *Wired for War: The Robotics Revolution and Conflict in the 21st Century* (New York: Penguin, 2009); Boot; P. W. Singer, "War of the Machines," *Scientific American* (July 2010): 56–63; Jaclyn Schiff, "The Graying of America: Census Shows Americans Are Living Longer, Retiring Earlier," CBS/AP, 9 March 2006; Liang and Xiangsui; Richard Bernstein and Ross H. Munro, *The Coming Conflict with China* (New York: Random House, 1998); Thomas P. M. Barnett, *The Pentagon's New Map: War and Peace in the Twenty-First Century* (New York: Putnam Publishing Group, 2004); *CIA World Factbook* (Washington DC: Government Printing Office, 2008); Lewis F. Richardson, *The Statistics of Deadly Quarrels* (Pittsburg: Boxwood Press, 1960).

[20] See Singer, *Wired for War*, for an accessible discussion of robotics. Much of this paragraph is, admittedly, inspired by science fiction. This does not mean that it is

flawed for its purpose, only that it is conjectural. Movies, such as the *Star Wars* series, *Battlestar Galactica*, and *Avatar*, and the corpus of literature associated with them might prove helpful in that regard.

[21] See Sherry; Yarrison; Maurice Matloff, *Strategic Planning for Coalition Warfare, 1943–1944* (Washington DC: Center of Military History, 1959); Wilson, *This War Really Matters*; Farhad Manjoo, *True Enough: Learning to Live in a Post-Fact Society* (New York: Wiley, 2008); Blaker; Worley.

[22] See Stewart, *American Military History,* vol. 2; Gordon W. Rudd, *Humanitarian Intervention: Assisting the Iraqi Kurds in Operation PROVIDE COMFORT, 1991* (Washington DC: Center of Military History, 1991); Richard W. Stewart, *The United States Army in Somalia, 1992–1994* (Washington DC: Center of Military History, 2002); Charles E. Kirkpatrick, *"Ruck It Up!" The Post–Cold War Transformation of V Corps, 1990–2001* (Washington DC: Center of Military History, 2007); Clay Wilson, *Improvised Explosive Devices in Iraq: Effects and Countermeasures* (Washington DC: Congressional Research Service, 2005); "House Members to Visit Aberdeen Proving Ground," CNN Interactive, 21 November 1996; "Military-Civilian Panel to Probe Army Sex Scandal," CNN Interactive, 22 November 1996; "Three Soldiers Arraigned in U.S. Army Sex Scandal," CNN Interactive, 6 December 1996; Army General Staff Council Meeting notes, 2 January 2002, Historians Files, CMH; Army General Staff Council Meeting notes, 14 April 2003, Historians Files, CMH; Army General Staff Council Meeting notes, 23 December 2003, Historians Files, CMH.

[23] See Demma, 38–42: William Joe Webb et al., *Department of the Army Historical Summary, Fiscal Years 1990 and 1991* (Washington DC: Center of Military History, 1997), 129–33; Dwight D. Oland and David W. Hogan Jr., *Department of the Army Historical Summary, Fiscal Year 1992* (Washington DC: Center of Military History, 2001), 104–07; Stephen E. Everett and L. Martin Kaplan, *Department of the Army Historical Summary, Fiscal Year 1993* (Washington DC: Center of Military History, 2002), 18–22; L. Martin Kaplan, *Department of the Army Historical Summary, Fiscal Year 1994* (Washington DC: Center of Military History, 2000), 27–34; Stephen L. Y. Gammons and William M. Donnelly, *Department of the Army Historical Summary, Fiscal Year 1995* (Washington DC: Center of Military History, 2004), 11–22; Connie L. Reeves, *Department of the Army Historical Summary, Fiscal Year 1996* (Washington DC: Center of Military History, 2002), 39–46; Jeffery A. Charlston, *Department of the Army Historical Summary, Fiscal Year 1999* (Washington DC: Center of Military History, 2006), 19–24; Briefing, U.S. Army Training and Doctrine Command to the Deputy Chief of Staff for Operations, "WFLA FY99–09 Modernization Recommendations," 31 January 1997, Historians Files, CMH; Robert D. Hormats, *The Price of Liberty: Paying for America's Wars* (New York: Henry Holt, 2007); Army General Staff Council Meeting notes, 31 March 2003, Historians Files, CMH; Army General Staff Council Meeting notes, 14 April 2003; Army Staff Principals Staff Call Meeting notes, 26 April 2004, Historians Files, CMH; Honorable Francis J. Harvey and General Peter J. Schoomaker, *A Statement on the Posture of the United States Army 2006* (Washington DC: Office of the Chief of Staff, United States Army, 10 February 2006).

Selected Key Civilian and Military Participants in Army Transformation, 1989–2005

Secretaries of the Army (Twelve Months or More)

Michael P. W. Stone, 14 August 1989–20 January 1993
Togo D. West Jr., 22 November 1993–4 May 1997
Louis Caldera, 2 July 1998–20 January 2001
Thomas E. White, 31 May 2001–9 May 2003
Romie L. "Les" Brownlee (Acting), 10 May 2003–18 November 2004
Francis J. Harvey, 19 November 2004–9 March 2007

Chiefs of Staff of the Army

General Carl E. Vuono, 23 June 1987–21 June 1991
General Gordon R. Sullivan, 21 June 1991–20 June 1995
General Dennis J. Reimer, 20 June 1995–21 June 1999
General Eric K. Shinseki, 21 June 1999–11 June 2003
General Peter J. Schoomaker, 1 August 2003–10 April 2007

Training and Doctrine Command Commanders (Twelve Months or More)

General John W. Foss, August 1989–August 1991
General Frederick M. Franks Jr., August 1991–October 1994
General William W. Hartzog, October 1994–September 1998
General John N. Abrams, September 1998–November 2002
General Kevin P. Byrnes, November 2002–July 2005
General Anthony R. Jones (Acting), August 2005–September 2005
General William S. Wallace, September 2005–December 2008

Army Materiel Command Commanders

General William G. T. Tuttle Jr., September 1989–January 1992
General Jimmy D. Ross, January 1992–February 1994
General Leon E. Salomon, February 1994–March 1996
General Johnnie E. Wilson, March 1996–May 1999
General John G. Coburn, May 1999–October 2001
General Paul J. Kern, October 2001–November 2004
General Benjamin S. Griffin, November 2004–November 2008

Forces Command Commanders

General Edwin H. Burba, September 1989–April 1993
General Dennis J. Reimer, April 1993–June 1995
General John H. Tilelli Jr., June 1995–July 1996
General David A. Bramlett, July 1996–August 1998
General Thomas A. Schwartz, August 1998–December 1999
General John W. Hendrix, December 1999–November 2001
General Larry R. Ellis, November 2001–May 2004
General Dan K. McNeill, May 2004–January 2007

Assistant Secretaries of the Army, Research, Development and Acquisition/Acquisition, Logistics and Technology (Twelve Months or More)

Steven K. Conver, March 1990–September 1993
Gilbert F. Decker, April 1994–May 1997
Kenneth J. Oscar (Acting), May 1997–May 1998
Paul J. Hoeper, May 1998–January 2001
Kenneth J. Oscar (Acting), January 2001–January 2002
Claude M. Bolton, January 2002–January 2008

Deputy Chiefs of Staff for Operations and Plans/G–3

Lt. Gen. Gordon R. Sullivan, July 1989–May 1990
Lt. Gen. Dennis J. Reimer, May 1990–June 1991
Lt. Gen. J. H. Binford Peay III, June 1991–March 1993
Lt. Gen. John H. Tilelli Jr., March 1993–July 1994
Lt. Gen. Paul E. Blackwell, July 1994–August 1996
Lt. Gen. Eric K. Shinseki, August 1996–June 1997
Lt. Gen. Thomas N. Burnette Jr., July 1997–August 1999
Lt. Gen. Larry R. Ellis, August 1999–November 2001
Lt. Gen. David D. McKiernan, November 2001–August 2002
Lt. Gen. Richard A. Cody, August 2002–June 2004
Lt. Gen. Buford C. Blount (Acting), June 2004–October 2004
Lt. Gen. James L. Lovelace, October 2004–December 2007

Deputy Chiefs of Staff for Programs/G–8

Lt. Gen. Kevin P. Byrnes, December 2000–November 2001
Lt. Gen. Benjamin S. Griffin, November 2001–October 2004
Lt. Gen. David F. Melcher, October 2004–December 2006

Director of the Objective Force Task Force

Lt. Gen. Johnny M. Riggs, June 2001–November 2003

Executive Directors of the Louisiana Maneuvers Task Force

Brig. Gen. Tommy R. Franks, May 1992–June 1994
Brig. Gen. David Ohle, June 1994–June 1995
Col. Richard A. Cowell, June 1995–February 1996
Col. Wayne W. Boy, May 1996–July 1996

BIBLIOGRAPHICAL NOTE

Kevlar Legions: The Transformation of the U.S. Army, 1989–2005, is based on official documents, briefings, meeting notes, oral and e-mail testimony, professional publications, studies, and the commentary of veterans. It has also been enabled and enriched by secondary sources, official and unofficial. The project has extended for over ten years, and my access to each genre of primary source material has benefited immeasurably from subject matter experts in the agencies, holdings, and archives where they work.

Documents and briefings supporting the text have not, by and large, been retired to the National Archives and Records Administration. When they have been, most will probably reside in the Records of the Army Staff, Record Group (RG) 319, while other documents are in record groups responsible for the major Army commands (MACOMs) and Department of Defense agencies. In two years' service as the executive officer of the Army Deputy Chief of Staff for Operations and Plans (1995–1997) and seven years' service as the Army Chief of Military History (1998–2005), I personally gathered a considerable body of these documents and briefings in anticipation of a project of this type. These are characterized as in Historians Files, U.S. Army Center of Military History (CMH), in the endnotes and were turned over to CMH's Historical Resources Branch, Field Programs and Historical Services Division. They are located in the branch's archives as documents supporting *Kevlar Legions.* That branch also holds the supporting materials for the annual Department of the Army historical summaries (DAHSUMs). The DAHSUMs are invaluable sources in themselves, and their supporting materials even more so. Each year CMH's Historical Support Branch, Histories Division, dutifully vacuums up significant documents, records, briefings, and self-summations from Department of the Army and Army Staff constituents and agencies. Once these have been gathered and organized, a historian is given the mission of distilling them into a manuscript of reasonable length, such as the *Department of the Army Historical Summary, Fiscal Year 1989*. In due course, DAHSUMs are published and accessible on the Internet through http://www.history.army.mil, at which point the documents from which they derive migrate to the Historical Resources Branch. Until that point, they remain in the custody of the Historical Support Branch and the assigned authors working with them. Over time these holdings have become, understandably, vast. In the endnotes, I have cited DAHSUMs as the sources of statistics and agreed upon facts because the DAHSUMs are so readily accessible. When dealing with decisions or points of contention, I have instead cited the relevant original documents or briefings.

Documents and briefings originating outside of the Department of the Army and the Army Staff travel different routes and thus become accessible at different nodes. Major Army commands have their own historians and historical offices. These also canvas their staff agencies and subordinate commands for significant documents, records, briefings, and self-summations; consolidate these on an annual basis; and produce annual summaries analogous to the DAHSUM. The process is overseen and periodically inspected by CMH's Field and International Branch, Field Programs and Historical Services Division, and the annual summaries come into the Center via that branch. The documents, records, briefings, and self-summaries remain in the MACOM historical offices, each of which has its own archives. In the endnotes, I do not cite the MACOM annual summaries but instead cite the original materials in such a manner as to identify the headquarters of origin. The reader will note a considerable reliance on the U.S. Army Forces Command, Army Materiel Command (AMC), Space and Missile Defense Command, and Training and Doctrine Command (TRADOC) documents, records, and briefings. At the time of research and writing, the historical archives for Forces Command were located in Fort McPherson, Georgia; for the Army Materiel Command in Fort Belvoir, Virginia; for the Space and Missile Defense Command at Redstone Arsenal in Huntsville, Alabama; and for the Training and Doctrine Command in Fort Monroe, Virginia. The reader will also observe documents and briefings drawn from operational and tactical headquarters and units deployed overseas. Other than those collected personally, these largely became available through deployed military history detachments. Military history detachments are three-man Army National Guard and Army Reserve units mobilized and deployed to support operational headquarters under the staff supervision of CMH's Field and International Branch. Among other responsibilities, they collect and organize significant documents, records, and briefings and forward copies to the Field and International Branch. I had access to such materials when they were still in the hands of that branch, but these have now been moved to the U.S. Army Heritage and Education Center (AHEC) at Carlisle, Pennsylvania.

Meeting notes reinforce my citations in numerous places. The meetings most frequently cited are those of the Army General Staff Council (GSC). One will also find references to Army Staff meetings chaired by the Vice Chief of Staff of the Army (VCSA), selected Army Staff offsites and four-star conferences, and planning sessions associated with the Quadrennial Defense Review (QDR). In each case, a field-grade representative of the Director of the Army Staff (DAS), affectionately referred to as a "dwarf," sat in on the meeting and consolidated notes, which were stored and promulgated electronically. When I was Chief of Military History, seven such officers under the supervision of a full colonel shared this responsibility. Inevitably the colonel became "Snow White" and the office "Snow White and the Seven Dwarves." The dwarves' notes consolidated material actually covered at meetings with submissions by each attendee reflecting what he or she would have shared had there been time. The DAS remains the proponent for these records, which are vast and have only incidentally achieved printed form. In my endnotes, when I cited Army General Staff Council Meeting notes, date, Historians Files, CMH, I am referring to my own handwritten notes taken during the meeting, which were turned over to CMH's Historical Resources Branch. The notes are bulleted and reflect what was actually said or exchanged. They can be reinforced by the dwarves' electronic records as necessary, should one have appropriate access. The Chief of Military History routinely attended meetings at this level to further the historical record, as well as to participate as a member of the Army Staff.

Oral histories and correspondence considerably improve the account, particularly with respect to nuance, eyewitness testimony, and exchanges that may not have made it into the official record. CMH's Oral History Activity, Histories Division, routinely interviews departing principals of the Army Staff and the Department of the Army. Most of these interviews are not yet transcribed, but all are recorded and cataloged. MACOM historians have the same responsibility, and similarly interview their principals. Army and MACOM historians also conduct interviews on major developments, to advance projects and studies, and as directed. The Oral History Activity, strongly encouraged by the Department of the Army Historical Advisory Committee (DAHAC), has undertaken a project to identify the interviews that have been conducted across subordinate headquarters and to draw them all into a single electronic database. Transcripts can be immediately available electronically, and knowledge of audio versions and where they are stored readily found out. Happily for historians, the junior officers who help their Army Staff principals prepare for interviews (or testimony) also help them write their entries for the annual *Army Green Book* of the Association of the United States Army. For at least a generation the *Army Green Book* has been the unofficial forum through which senior Army leaders have communicated the accomplishments and aspirations of their commands and agencies to the Army at large. Understandably, there is a huge overlap between what a principal might choose to share with a historian and what he or she reports in these annual self-assessments. In my endnotes, when a point has been made in both an interview and an *Army Green Book* article, I have cited the *Army Green Book*. For most, the *Army Green Book* is far more accessible and does commit key individuals to certain comments at specific points in time. In this study, the use of personal accounts has a third leg beyond interviews and articles. Once a chapter was written in draft, I circulated it to senior leaders particularly involved. They often came back to me with comments and clarifications, some of them extensive. Most responded by e-mail, some by telephone. Copies of the e-mails and memorandums for the record of the telephone conversations were turned over to CMH's Historical Resources Branch, there to be found along with other primary materials supporting *Kevlar Legions*. The Center of Military History publishes selected speeches, messages, and papers of each Army Chief of Staff sometime after the end of his tenure. Of these, I have particularly relied on the collected works of Generals Gordon R. Sullivan, Dennis J. Reimer, and (unpublished at the time of use) Eric K. Shinseki.

The subject of Army transformation during 1989–2005 understandably attracted considerable professional interest beyond that manifested in official documents and briefings. I have already discussed the value of the *Army Green Book* and also drew on and cited professional writings from *Army* magazine. Other professional journals that figured prominently in my endnotes include *Armed Forces Journal, Armor, Army History, Army Logistician, Infantry, Joint Forces Quarterly, Military Review, Parameters,* and *Strategic Review. Army Times* caters to a somewhat different audience in a considerably different format but also provided many articles relevant to my subject. A particularly rich vein with respect to professional writing has been student papers and, within them, theses supporting the master of military arts and science (MMAS) program. Candidates for the MMAS are seasoned officers who often speak with authority on projects and events they have participated in at the field-grade level. They are mentored by the accomplished faculty of the Command and General Staff College and the School of Advanced Military Studies, who ensure that students achieve appropriate levels of clarity, scholarship, and documentation. The result is often a thoughtful primary source and through its documentation a window into others. Helpfully, MMAS theses, and much else, are available through the Combined Arms Research Library (CARL) or online through http://www.cgsc.edu. The Army War College and other Army and Department of Defense schools also produce and catalog student papers, which furnish reasoned insights from officers with firsthand knowledge of their subjects. It is often said that the Pentagon is run by its "iron majors." There is no reason that their writings should not be useful.

Veteran commentary is embedded in each type of primary source discussed above but also comes through the military history detachments and through recurring assessments and surveys such as those by the Center for Army Lessons Learned (CALL) or the Army Research Institute (ARI) for the Behavioral and Social Sciences. A primary responsibility of the military history detachments, previously discussed, is to conduct, transcribe, and catalog interviews within their commands or purview. Subjects include those in key positions, those who have had striking experiences, and those selected to achieve a mix representative of a given unit's composition. Copies are deposited with the command, with the historical offices of the Army Reserve or Army National Guard as appropriate, and with CMH's Field and International Branch. I had access to interviews that were still in the hands of the Field and International Branch, but these have now been forwarded to the U.S. Army Heritage and Education Center. The choice of AHEC for storage makes great sense, as it has evolved into the repository for all such "unofficial" materials as interviews and private papers. CALL is also an ideal source for veteran commentary, as it has assessed tactics, techniques, and procedures since 1973, and has built up a considerable inventory of historical materials while doing so. Its publications are widely available and individually cited in my endnotes. Most are accessible online through http://www.usacac.army.mil/cac2/call. ARI is even more venerable and has been assessing and surveying soldiers for generations. In my endnotes, I cited its studies individually. Many are available online through http://www.hqda.army.mil/ari.

A subject as complex and as institutionally significant as Army transformation inevitably generated studies and assessments. Those developed within the Army Staff, TRADOC, AMC, and other Army agencies became visible and are accessible as described above. I have mentioned the role of the Center for Army Lessons Learned and the Army Research Institute for the Behavioral and Social Sciences in engendering and consolidating veteran commentary. They conduct studies relevant to my topic as a matter of course as well. Other government agencies conducting studies that appear in my endnotes include the Congressional Research Service, U.S. Army Community and Family Support Center, and Walter Reed Army Institute of Research. The Army is heavily dependent on contractors to sustain its intellectual endeavors, and these organizations produce studies that become central to deliberations. Contractors of this type that appear in my endnotes include Burdeshaw Associates, Caliber Associates, the Center for Military and Strategic Studies, the Center for Strategic and International Studies, RAND, and Science Applications International Corporation (SAIC). Independent of both the Department of the Army and contracting, the Association of the United States Army's Institute of Land Warfare is prolific, relevant, and visible in my notes.

I have depended on some primary sources to relate the activities of the Joint Staff, Department of Defense, Congress, and the George H. W. Bush, William J. Clinton, and George W. Bush administrations to Army transformation. Beyond those available through Army archives, these have not been the products of comprehensive archival research meriting discussion here. Some documents were personally collected over the ten years I was involved in Army transformation deliberations and appear in the endnotes in Historians Files, CMH. More records were offered by colleagues from the Joint Staff, Department of Defense, Navy, Air Force, and Marine Corps familiar with and supportive of the project. These materials were turned over to CMH's Historical Resources Branch. Beyond this gathered material, I relied on secondary sources when dealing with agencies outside the Army. Fortunately, the Office of the Secretary of Defense, Office of the Chairman of the Joint Chiefs of Staff, Office of the Secretary of the Navy, Office of the Secretary of the Air Force, and the Congressional Research Service have produced much that proved useful and that appears in my endnotes. The *Congressional Record*, of course, is available online at http://www.gpoaccess.gov/crecord.

Secondary sources have considerably improved the reach and grasp of this volume. To my knowledge, this is the first attempt at a comprehensive study of the subject throughout the period, but important patches of ground have already been plowed. The Center of Military History has published superb studies that illuminate important aspects of my topic. Cases in point include Shannon A. Brown's *Providing the Means of War: Historical Perspectives on Defense Acquisition, 1945–2000*; Anne W. Chapman's *The Army Training Revolution, 1973–1990: An Overview* (the reprint of a TRADOC volume); William M. Donnelly's *Transforming an Army at War: Designing the Modular Force, 1991–2005*; Robert A. Doughty's *The Evolution of U.S. Army Tactical Doctrine, 1946–76* (a reprint of a Leavenworth Paper); Robert K. Griffith Jr.'s *The U.S. Army's Transition to the All-Volunteer Force, 1968–1974;* Francis T.

Julia's *Army Staff Reorganization 1903–1985*; Charles E. Kirkpatrick's *"Ruck It Up!" The Post–Cold War Transformation of V Corps, 1990–2001*; Marvin A. Kreidberg and Merton G. Henry's *History of Military Mobilization in the United States Army, 1775–1945*; Edgar F. Raines Jr.'s *The Army and the Joint Chiefs of Staff: Evolution of Army Ideas on the Command, Control, and Coordination of the U.S. Armed Forces, 1942–1985*; Mark J. Reardon and Jeffery A. Charlston's *From Transformation to Combat: The First Stryker Brigade at War*; John L. Romjue's *American Army Doctrine for the Post–Cold War* (the reprint of a TRADOC work); John L. Romjue's *The Army of Excellence: The Development of the 1980s Army* (the reprint of a TRADOC book); Mark D. Sherry's *The Army Command Post and Defense Reshaping, 1987–1997;* Richard W. Stewart's *The U.S. Army in Afghanistan: Operation ENDURING FREEDOM, October 2001–March 2002*; and *United States Forces, Somalia, After Action Report and Historical Overview: The United States Army in Somalia, 1992–1994*; James Walker's *Seize the High Ground: The Army in Space and Missile Defense* and *Space Warriors: The Army Space Support Team* (both reprints of Space and Missile Defense Command publications); John B. Wilson's *Maneuver and Firepower: The Evolution of Divisions and Separate Brigades;* and James L. Yarrison's *The Modern Louisiana Maneuvers.* Beyond these studies that particularly address transformational issues, my endnotes also cited an even broader array of Center of Military History products that describe specific campaigns, operations, or developments.

Army MACOMs publish secondary sources too. Some addressing transformational subjects that recurred in my endnotes include *Army Comprehensive Guide to Modularity* (Fort Monroe, Virginia: U.S. Army Training and Doctrine Command, 2004); Charles H. Briscoe, Richard L. Kiper, James A. Schroder, and Kalev I. Sepp, *Weapon of Choice: U.S. Army Special Operations Forces in Afghanistan* (Fort Leavenworth, Kansas: Combat Studies Institute Press, 2003); James T. Currie, *Twice the Citizen: A History of the United States Army Reserve, 1908–1995* (Washington DC: Office of the Chief, Army Reserve, 1997); Michael D. Doubler, *I Am the Guard: A History of the Army National Guard, 1636–2000* (Washington DC: Department of the Army, 2001); John J. McGrath, *The Brigade: A History, Its Organization and Employment in the US Army* (Fort Leavenworth, Kansas: Combat Studies Institute Press, 2004); John L. Romjue, *From Active Defense to AirLand Battle: The Development of Army Doctrine, 1973–1982* (Fort Monroe, Virginia: U.S. Army Training and Doctrine Command Historical Office, 1984); TRADOC Pamphlet 525–3–91, *Objective Force Tactical Operational and Organizational Concept for Maneuver Units of Action* (Fort Monroe, Virginia: U.S. Army Training and Doctrine Command, 6 November 2001); and TRADOC Pamphlet 525–3–92, *Objective Force: Unit of Employment Concept* (Fort Monroe, Virginia: U.S. Army Training and Doctrine Command, 20 May 2003). Beyond these, my endnotes also cited an even broader array of publications that describe specific campaigns, operations, and developments. Those of the Strategic Studies Institute (Army War College) and Combat Studies Institute (Command and General Staff College) are particularly visible and are accessible online.

Sadly, not every worthy manuscript makes it to publication—at least not right away. The Historical Resources Branch of the Field Programs and

Historical Services Division of the Center of Military History is a treasure trove of thoughtful and well documented not yet published manuscripts. Those that recurred in my endnotes include Lieutenant Colonel H. R. McMaster's Crack in the Foundation: Defense Transformation and the Underlying Assumption of Dominant Knowledge in Future War; Clayton R. Newell's Digitizing the Army; Deirdre E. Painter's The Distaff Factor: Attitudinal Change and Continuity Through Four Generations of Army Wives; and Robert S. Rush's The Individual Replacement System: Good, Bad or Indifferent? Army Replacement Policy, Cold War and Before. In due course, hopefully, these and other worthy manuscripts, or successor documents, will be published.

Unofficial secondary sources that are commercially available also have given appreciable attention to Army transformational issues. Roughly in the order that they appeared in my endnotes, these include MacGregor Knox and Williamson Murray, *The Dynamics of Military Revolution, 1300–2050* (Cambridge, United Kingdom: Cambridge University Press, 2001); Michael Roberts, *The Military Revolution, 1560–1660* (Belfast: M. Boyd, 1956); Geoffrey Parker, *The Military Revolution: Military Innovation and the Rise of the West, 1500–1800* (Cambridge, United Kingdom: Cambridge University Press, 2001); George and Meredith Friedman, *The Future of War: Power, Technology and American World Dominance in the 21st Century* (New York: Crown Publishers, 1996); Martin Van Creveld, *The Transformation of War* (New York: Free Press, 1991); Major General Robert H. Scales Jr., *Yellow Smoke: The Future of Land Warfare for America's Military* (New York: Rowman and Littlefield, 2003); D. Robert Worley, *Shaping U.S. Military Forces: Revolution or Relevance in a Post–Cold War World* (Westport, Connecticut: Praeger Security International, 2006); Mark D. Mandeles, *Military Transformation Past and Present: Historic Lessons for the 21st Century* (Westport, Connecticut: Praeger Security International, 2007); Max Boot, *War Made New: Technology, Warfare and the Course of History, 1500 to Today* (New York: Gotham Books, 2006); Admiral William Owens and Ed Offley, *Lifting the Fog of War* (New York: Farrar, Straus and Giroux, 2000); Brad C. Hayes with others, *Transforming the Navy* (Newport, Rhode Island: U.S. Naval War College, 2000); John S. Brown, *Draftee Division: The 88th Infantry Division in World War II* (Lexington: University Press of Kentucky, 1986); Brian M. Linn, *The Echo of Battle: The Army's Way of War* (Cambridge, Massachusetts: Harvard University Press, 2007); Robert M. Citino, *Blitzkrieg to DESERT STORM: The Evolution of Operational Warfare* (Lawrence, Kansas: University Press of Kansas, 2004); Bernard Rostker, *I Want You! The Evolution of the All-Volunteer Force* (Santa Monica, California: RAND, 2006); George C. Wilson, *This War Really Matters: Inside the Fight for Defense Dollars* (Washington DC: CQ Press, 2000); Jonathan M. House, *Combined Arms Warfare in the Twentieth Century* (Lawrence, Kansas: University Press of Kansas, 2001); Brian Alexander and Alistair Millar, *Tactical Nuclear Weapons in an Evolving Security Environment* (Washington DC: Brassey's, 2003); Thomas P. M. Barnett, *The Pentagon's New Map: War and Peace in the Twenty-First Century* (New York: Barnes and Noble, 2004); Janet Abbate, *Inventing the Internet* (Cambridge, Massachusetts: MIT Press, 1999); Katie Hafner and Matthew Lyon, *Where Wizards Stay Up Late: The*

Origins of the Internet (New York: Touchstone, 1998); James F. Dunnigan, *Digital Soldiers: The Evolution of High-Tech Weaponry and Tomorrow's Brave New Battlefields* (New York: St. Martin's Press, 1996); James R. Blaker, *Transforming Military Force: The Legacy of Arthur Cebrowski and Network Centric Warfare* (Westport, Connecticut: Praeger Security International, 2007); Thomas K. Adams, *The Army After Next: The First Postindustrial Army* (Stanford, California: Stanford Security Studies, 2008); Colonel Trevor N. Dupuy, *Understanding War: History and Theory of Conflict* (New York: Paragon House Publishers, 1987); Colonel Trevor N. Dupuy, *Attrition: Forecasting Battle Casualties and Equipment Losses in Modern War* (Fairfax, Virginia: Hero Books, 1990); Wesley K. Clark, *Waging Modern War* (New York: Public Affairs, 2001); Bruce Berkowitz, *The New Face of War: How War Will Be Fought in the 21st Century* (New York: Free Press, 2003); Robert D. Hormats, *The Price of Liberty: Paying for America's Wars* (New York: Henry Holt, 2007); Douglas A. Macgregor, *Breaking the Phalanx: A New Design for Landpower in the 21st Century* (Westport, Connecticut: Praeger, 1997); Douglas A. Macgregor, *Transforming Under Fire: Revolutionizing How America Fights* (Westport, Connecticut: Praeger, 2003); Eric L. Haney with Brian Thomsen, *Beyond Shock and Awe: Warfare in the 21st Century* (New York: Berkley Publishing Group, 2006); and P. W. Singer, *Wired for War: The Robotics Revolution and Conflict in the 21st Century* (New York: Penguin, 2009).

ABBREVIATIONS

AAE	Army Acquisition Executive
AAFES	Army and Air Force Exchange Service
AAR	after-action review
AC	active component
ACAP	Army Career and Alumni Program
ACS	Army Community Service
ACSIM	Assistant Chief of Staff for Installation Management
ACTD	Advanced Concept Technology Demonstration
ADCSOPS	Assistant Deputy Chief of Staff for Operations and Plans
ADO	Army Digitization Office
AEF	American Expeditionary Forces (World War I)
AER	Army Emergency Relief
AFAP	Army Family Action Plan
AFATDS	Advanced Field Artillery Tactical Data System
AFTB	Army Family Team Building
AI	air interdiction
AMC	Army Materiel Command
AN/PVS	Army/Navy Portable Visual Search
AOE	Army of Excellence
APOD	aerial ports of debarkation
APOE	aerial ports of embarkation
AREP	Army Reserve Expeditionary Package
ARFORGEN	Army Force Generation
ARI	Army Research Institute
ARNG	Army National Guard
ARPA	Advanced Research Projects Agency
ARTADS	Army Tactical Data System
ARTBASS	Army Training Battle Simulation System
ARV	armed robotic vehicle
ASA (RDA)	Assistant Secretary of the Army for Research, Development, and Acquisition
ASAS	All Source Analysis System
ASCC	Army Service Component Command
ASD SO/LIC	Assistant Secretary of Defense for Special Operations and Low Intensity Conflict

ATACMS	Army Tactical Missile System
ATC	associate transportation company
ATD	Advanced Technology Demonstration
ATEC	Army Test and Evaluation Command
ATO	Air Tasking Order
AUS	Army of the United States
AUSA	Association of the United States Army
AWACS	Airborne Warning and Control System
AWD	Advanced Warfighting Demonstration
AWE	Advanced Warfighting Experiment
AWR	Army War Reserve
BAH	Basic Allowance for Housing
BAI	battlefield air interdiction
BAQ	Basic Allowance for Quarters
BASOPS	base operations support
BAT	Brilliant Anti-armor Technology
BCIS	Battlefield Combat Identification System
BCT	brigade combat team
BCTP	Battle Command Training Program
BFT	blue force tracking
BIDS	Biological Integrated Detection System
BOS	Battlefield Operating System
BRAC	base realignment and closures
BSFV-E	Bradley Stinger Fighting Vehicle–Enhanced
BSRF	Building Strong and Ready Families
BSTB	brigade special troops battalion
BUR	Bottom-Up Review
C2	command and control
C4ISR	command, control, communications, computers, intelligence, surveillance, and reconnaissance
CAA	Center of Army Analysis
CACDA	Combined Arms Combat Developments Activity
CALFE	combined-arms live-fire exercise
CALL	Center for Army Lessons Learned
CARS	Combat Arms Regimental System
CAS	close air support
CAS3	Combined Arms Service Staff School
CBAS	Company/Battalion Administrative System
CBRS	Concepts-Based Requirements System
CBS	Corps Battle Simulation System
CCIR	commander's critical intelligence requirements
CENTCOM	Central Command
CEO	Chief Executive Officer
CEP	circular error probable
CERP	Commander's Emergency Response Program

CERT	computer emergency response team
CFC-A	Combined Forces Command–Afghanistan
CFLCC	Combined Forces Land Component Command
CFSC	Community and Family Support Center
CHAMPUS	Civilian Health and Medical Program of the Uniformed Services
CI	counterintelligence
CIA	Central Intelligence Agency
CIDC	Criminal Investigation Command
CINC	commander in chief
CIS	Commonwealth of Independent States
CJTF	Combined Joint Task Force
CMH	U.S. Army Center of Military History
CMTC	Combat Maneuver Training Center
CNO	computer network operations
COHORT	Cohesion Operational Readiness and Training
COLA	cost-of-living allowance
CONUS	continental United States
CORM	Commission on Roles and Missions
COS	Chief of Staff
COSCOM	Corps Support Command
CPA	Coalition Provisional Authority
CPX	command post exercise
CRAF	Civilian Reserve Airlift Fleet
CSA	Chief of Staff, Army
CSI	Combat Studies Institute
CSS	combat service support
CYS	Child and Youth Services
DA	Department of the Army
DAS	Director of the Army Staff
DAWMS	Deep Attack Weapons Mix Study
DCA	defensive counter air
DCGS	Distributed Common Ground System
DCGS-A	Distributed Common Ground System–Army
DCSLOG	Deputy Chief of Staff for Logistics
DCSOPS	Deputy Chief of Staff for Operations and Plans
DCX	Division Capstone Exercise
DeCA	Defense Commissary Agency
DEERS	Defense Enrollment Eligibility Reporting System
DEPTEMPO	deployment tempo
DHS	Department of Homeland Security
DIA	Defense Intelligence Agency
DIMHRS	Defense Integrated Military Human Resources System
DIS	distributed interactive simulations
DISCOM	division support command

DIVARTY	division artillery
DMR	Defense Management Review
DoD	Department of Defense
DOPMA	Defense Officer Personnel Management Act
DRB	Division Ready Brigade
DRF	division ready force
DRID	Defense Reform Initiative Directive
DRU	Direct Reporting Unit
EDRE	Emergency Deployment Readiness Exercise
EEO	Equal Employment Opportunity
EFMB	Expert Field Medical Badge
EGRU	EPLRS Grid Reference Unit
EIB	Expert Infantryman's Badge
ENIAC	Electronic Numerical Integrator and Computer
EOD	explosive ordnance detachment
EPLRS	Enhanced Position Location Reporting System
ER/MP	extended range/multipurpose
ERP	Early Retirement Program
ESL	English as a Second Language
EU	European Union
EUSA	Eighth United States Army
EW	electronic warfare
EXFOR	Experimental Force
FAADC2	Forward Area Air Defense Command and Control
FAP	Family Advocacy Program
FARA	Federal Acquisition Reform Act
FBCB2	Force XXI Battle Command, Brigade and Below
FBCB2-BFT	Force XXI Battle Command Brigade and Below—Blue Force Tracking
FCP	Forward Compatible Payroll
FCS	future combat system
FEST	forward engineer support team
Fires R&SV	fires reconnaissance and surveillance vehicle
FIST	fire support team
FLOT	front line of troops
FM	Field Manual
FOA	field operating agency
FORSCOM	United States Army Forces Command
FRG	Family Readiness Group
FSA	family separation allowance
FSCL	fire support coordination line
FSCS	Future Scout and Cavalry System
FSS	Fast Sealift Ships
FY	Fiscal Year

504

G–3	operations and training officer
GAO	Government Accountability Office
GATT	General Agreement on Tariffs and Trade
GDP	general defense plan
GHQx	General Headquarters Exercises
GOSC	General Officer Steering Committee
GOWG	General Officer Working Group
GPS	global positioning system
GSC	General Staff Council
GSU	Garrison Support Unit
HEMTT	heavy expanded mobility tactical truck
HHC	headquarters and headquarters company
HMMWV	high mobility multipurpose wheeled vehicle
HQDA	Headquarters, Department of Army
HTI	Horizontal Technical Integration
HTML	hypertext markup language
HTTP	hypertext transfer protocol
HUMINT	human intelligence
IAF	Iraqi Armed Forces
IAV	interim armored vehicle
IBCT	Interim Brigade Combat Team
ICDC	Iraqi Civil Defense Corps
IDA	Institute for Defense Analyses
IED	improvised explosive device
IFF	identification friend or foe
IFOR	Implementation Force
ILW	Institute of Land Warfare
IMA	Individual Mobilization Augmentee
IMAP	Installation Management Action Plan
IMCOM	Installation Management Command
IMET	International Military Education and Training
IMETS	integrated meteorological system
INF Treaty	Intermediate-Range Nuclear Forces Treaty
ING	Iraqi National Guard
INSCOM	Army Intelligence and Security Command
IO	information operations
IOC	initial operating capability
IRR	Individual Ready Reserve
ISAF	International Security and Assistance Force
ISB	intermediate staging base
ISR	intelligence surveillance and reconnaissance
ITMRA	Information Technology Management Reform Act
IVIS	Inter-Vehicular Information System

J–5	Joint Staff's director of strategic plans and policy
J-STARS	Joint Surveillance Attack Radar System
JASSM	Joint Air to Surface Standoff Missile
JDAM	Joint Direct Attack Munition
JFLCC	Joint Forces Land Component Command(er)
JIEDDO	Joint IED Defeat Organization
JIM	joint interagency multi-national
JLENS	Joint Land Attack Cruise Missile Defense Elevated Netted Sensor System
JOA	Joint Operating Area
JOPES	Joint Operations Planning and Execution System
JRTC	Joint Readiness Training Center
JSOTF	Joint Special Operations Task Force
JTF	Joint Task Force
JTIDS	Joint Tactical Information Distribution System
KDP	Kurdistan Democratic Party
KLA	Kosovo Liberation Army
KTO	Kuwaiti Theater of Operations
LAM	Louisiana Maneuvers
LAN	local area network
LAR	logistical assistance representative
LAV	Light Armored Vehicle
LCMC	life cycle management command
LHX	light helicopter experimental
LOGCAP	Logistics Civil Augmentation Program
LRS	long-range surveillance
LRU	line replaceable unit
LSA	Logistics Support Area
M-TADS/PNVS	modernized target acquisition and designation sight/pilot night-vision sensor
MAARS	Modular Advanced Armed Robotic System
MACOM	major Army command
MAGTF	Marine Air Ground Task Forces
MDMP	military decision-making process
MDW	Military District of Washington
MEADS	Medium Extended Air Defense System
MEB	Marine Expeditionary Brigade
MEDCOM	Medical Command
METL	mission essential task list
METT	mission, enemy, terrain, and troops available
MFO	Multinational Forces of Observers
MHPI	Military Housing Privatization Initiative
MI	military intelligence
MILDEC	military deception

MILES	Multiple Integrated Laser Engagement System
MILPERCEN	United States Army Military Personnel Center
MILSPEC	military specification
MLRS	Multiple Launch Rocket System
MMAS	Master of Military Arts and Sciences
MMR	multi-mission radar
MOAA	Military Officers Association of America
MOS	military occupational specialty
MP	military police
MPRI	Military Professional Resources International
MPS	Maritime Pre-positioning Squadron
MRAP	mine-resistant ambush-protected vehicle
MRC	major regional contingency
MRE	meal ready to eat
MSC	Major Subordinate Command
MSE	mobile subscriber equipment
MTOE	modified table of organization and equipment
MWR	morale, welfare, and recreation
NAF	nonappropriated funds
NATO	North Atlantic Treaty Organization
NBC	nuclear, biological, and chemical
NCO	noncommissioned officer
NCOES	Noncommissioned Officer Education System
NCOPD	noncommissioned officer professional development
NDU	National Defense University
NEO	noncombatant evacuation operation
NETCOM	Network Enterprise Technology Command
NGO	nongovernmental organization
NIPRNET	Nonsecure Internet Protocol Router Network
NLOS	non-line-of-sight
NSA	National Security Agency
NTC	National Training Center
OC	Observer Controller
OCA	offensive counter air
ODCSOPS	Office of the Deputy Chief of Staff for Operations and Plans
ODT	overseas deployment training
OER	officer evaluation report
OIF	Operation IRAQI FREEDOM
OOTW	operations other than war
OPCON	operational control
OPD	officer professional development
OPFOR	opposing force
OPLAN	operations plan
OPMS	Officer Personnel Management System

OPSEC	operations security
OPTEMPO	operational tempo
ORHA	Office of Reconstruction and Humanitarian Assistance
OSACOM	Operational Support Airlift Command
OSD	Office of the Secretary of Defense
OVUREP	Overseas Unit Replacement System
PAC	Patriot Advanced Capability
PACOM	Pacific Command
PA&E	program analysis and evaluation
PARP	(PfP) Planning and Review Process
PB	pyridostigmine bromide
PC	personal computer
PCM	primary care manager
PCS	permanent change of station
PEO	Program Executive Office
PERSTEMPO	personnel tempo
PfP	Partnership for Peace
PGM	precision-guided munition
PIP	product improvement
PLGR	precision lightweight GPS receiver
PLL	prescribed load list
PLS	Palletized Load System
POL	petroleum, oil, and lubricants
POM	preparations for overseas movement
POMCUS	Pre-positioning of Materiel Configured to Unit Sets
POW	prisoner of war
PPBES	Planning, Programming, Budgeting, and Execution System
PPBS	Planning, Programming, and Budgeting System
PRIMUS	Primary Care to Uniformed Services
PSYOPS	psychological operations
PTSD	posttraumatic stress disorder
QDR	Quadrennial Defense Review
QTB	quarterly training brief
RAID	United States Reconnaissance and Interdiction Detachment
RAOC	Rear Area Operations Center
RC	reserve component
RCI	Residential Communities Initiative
R&D	research and development
READY (Operation)	Resources for Educating About Deployment and You
REDCON	readiness condition

508

REFORGER	Return of Forces to Germany
REMBASS	Remote Battlefield Sensor System
RFF	Request for Forces
RFI	Rapid Fielding Initiative
RFID	radio frequency identification
RIF	reduction in force
RJ	Rivet Joint
RMA	revolution in military affairs
ROAD	Reorganization Objective Army Division
RO/RO	roll-on/roll-off
ROTAPLAN	Rotational Plan
ROTC	Reserve Officers' Training Corps
RPG	rocket-propelled grenade
RSO&I	reception, staging, onward movement, and integration (exercises)
RSTA	reconnaissance, surveillance, and target acquisition
S–2	battalion intelligence officer and staff
SAIC	Science Applications International Corporation
SAMS	Standard Army Maintenance System
SBCT	Stryker Brigade Combat Team
SBP	survivor benefits program
SDDC	Surface Deployment and Distribution Command
SEAD	suppression of enemy air defense
SEAL	sea-air-land team (Navy)
SEDRE	Sea Emergency Deployment Readiness Exercise
SEP	System Enhancement Package
SERB	Selective Early Retirement Board
SETAF	Southern European Task Force
SFOR	Stabilization Force
SGLI	Servicemembers' Group Life Insurance
SHAPE	Supreme Headquarters Allied Powers Europe
SIDPERS	Standard Installation/Division Personnel Reporting System
SIGINT	signal intelligence
SIMITAR	Simulation in Training for Advanced Readiness
SINCGARS	Single Channel Ground and Airborne Radio System
SINCGARS-SIP	Single Channel Ground and Airborne Radio System–System Improvement Program
SIPRNET	Secure Internet Protocol Router Network
SMDC	Space and Missile Defense Command
SNAP	Special Needs Accommodation Process
SOAR	Special Operations Aviation Regiment
SOF	Special Operations Forces
SOLD	Spouse Orientation and Leader Development
SPBS-R	standard property book system–redesignated

SPT	support
SQT	skill qualification test
SSG	Senior Steering Group
S&T	science and technology
STANAG	standardization agreement
TAB	target acquisition battery
TAC	Tactical Actions Center
TACCS	Tactical Army Combat Service Support Computer System
TACFIRE	Tactical Fire Direction System (Army)
TACP	Tactical Air Control Party (Air Force)
TACWAR	Tactical Warfare model
TAMD	theater air and missile defense
TAP	*The Army Plan*
TDA	table of distribution and allowances
TEXCOM	Test and Experimentation Command
THAAD	Theater High-Altitude Air Defense
THT	tactical HUMINT team
TOC	Tactical Operations Center
TOE	table of organization and equipment
TOW	tube-launched, optically tracked, wire-guided
TPFDL	time-phased force and deployment list
TRADOC	Training and Doctrine Command
TROA	The Retired Officers Association
TRS	TRICARE Reserve Select
TSA	Transportation Security Agency
TSC	Theater Support Command
TTP	tactics, techniques, and procedures
TUAV	tactical unmanned aerial vehicle
U2R	U2 reconnaissance aircraft
UA	unit of action
UAU	USARC Augmentation Unit
UAV	unmanned aerial vehicle
UCMJ	Uniformed Code of Military Justice
UCOFT	unit conduct-of-fire trainer
UE	unit of employment
UNITAF	Unified Task Force
UNMIH	United Nations Mission in Haiti
UNOSOM	United Nations Operations in Somalia
UNPROFOR	United Nations Protection Force
URL	uniform resource locator
USAA	United Services Automobile Association
USACAPOC	United States Army Civil Affairs and Psychological Operations Command
USACE	United States Army Corps of Engineers

USAF	United States Air Force
USAR	United States Army Reserve
USARC	United States Army Reserve Command
USARCENT	United States Army Central Command
USAREUR	United States Army, Europe
USARNORTH	United States Army, North
USARPAC	United States Army, Pacific
USARSO	United States Army, South
USASOC	United States Army Special Operations Command
USMA	United States Military Academy
USNORTHCOM	United States Northern Command
USSOCOM	United States Special Operations Command
USSTRATCOM	United States Strategic Command
USTRANSCOM	United States Transportation Command
VA	Veterans Affairs
VBIED	vehicle-borne improvised explosive device
VERRP	Voluntary Early Release/Retirement Program
VHA	Variable Housing Allowance
VSIP	Voluntary Selective Incentive Program
VTC	video teleconference
WAC	Women's Army Corps
WEAR	wartime executive agency responsibility
WESTCOM	Western Command
WFX	Warfighter exercise
WMD	weapons of mass destruction
WORRM	Weapon Optimization and Resource Requirements Model

MAP SYMBOLS AND TERMS

Military Units

Function

Armor

Cavalry (Armored)

Infantry

Infantry (Airborne)

Infantry (Air Assault)

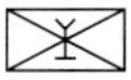

Infantry (Mechanized)

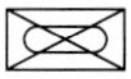

Marine Corps

Size Symbols

Platoon   ●●●

Battery, Company, or Cavalry Troop   I

Battalion or Cavalry Squadron   II

Regiment or Group   III

Brigade   X

Division   X X

Corps   X X X

513

Examples

V Corps

1st Cavalry Division

7th Infantry Division

3d Brigade, 101st Airborne Division (Air Assault)

5th Special Forces Group (Airborne)

3d Armored Cavalry Regiment

1st Battalion, 504th Infantry (Airborne)

Company A, 4th Battalion, 6th Infantry (Mechanized)

1st Platoon, Company C, 3d Battalion, 504th Infantry (Airborne)

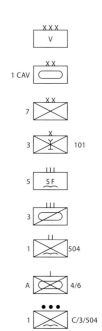

Abbreviations

Br	British
CJTF	Combined Joint Task Force
Eg	Egypt
Fr	France
JSOTF-N	Joint Special Operations Task Force–North
JSOTF-W	Joint Special Operations Task Force–West
Ku	Kuwait
MEF	Marine Expeditionary Force
MNC-I	Multi-National Corps–Iraq
MND-Baghdad	Multi-National Division–Baghdad
MND-CS	Multi-National Division–Center-South
MND-N	Multi-National Division–North
MND-NC	Multi-National Division–North Central
MND-NE	Multi-National Division–Northeast
MND-NW	Multi-National Division–Northwest
MND-SE	Multi-National Division–Southeast
MNF-NW	Multi-National Force–Northwest
MNF-W	Multi-National Force–West
NG	National Guard
Rn	Ranger
SA	Saudi Arabia
SOF	Special Operations Forces
Sy	Syria
TF	Task Force

515

516